TRAVELER'S TOOL KIT

MEXICO AND CENTRAL AMERICA

TRAVELER'S TOOL KIT

MEXICO AND CENTRAL AMERICA

Everything you need to know to eat well, stay healthy, travel safely, save money, and have a ball!

Rob Sangster and Tim Leffel

MENASHA RIDGE PRESS
BIRMINGHAM, ALABAMA

Published by Menasha Ridge Press
Printed in the United States of America
Distributed by Publishers Group West
First edition, first printing

Library of Congress Cataloging-in-Publication Data

Sangster, Rob.
    Traveler's tool kit: Mexico and Central America: everything you need to know to eat
well, stay healthy, travel safely, save money, and have a ball!/Rob Sangster and Tim
Leffel. —1st ed.
    p. cm.
    Includes index.
    ISBN-13: 978-0-89732-984-2
    ISBN-10: 0-89732-984-8
    1. Mexico—Handbooks, manuals, etc.   2. Central America—Handbooks, manuals,
etc.   3. Travel—Mexico—Handbooks, manuals, etc.   4. Travel—Central America—
Handbooks, manuals, etc.   I. Sangster, Robert Powell.   II. Leffel, Tim.

    F1209.T7194 2008
    917.28045'4—dc22
            2007046129

Text design by Barbara Williams
Cover design by Travis Bryant and Barbara Williams
Cover photograph © Tim Leffel
Interior photographs © Rob Sangster and Tim Leffel except as follows:
    Creative Commons—pages 52, 74, 86, 88, 90, 118, 156
    Paola Gianturco—pages 120, 124, 159, 281, 490; mural in color section
    Ann Holmes—pages 207, 235, 268, 365
    iStockPhoto.com—pages 119, 123, 126
Cartography by Steve Jones and Tim Leffel
Indexing by Ann Cassar/Cassar Technical Services

Menasha Ridge Press
P.O. Box 43673
Birmingham, Alabama 35243
www.menasharidge.com

CONTENTS

v

Dedications

I'm deeply grateful to all those who provided personal and professional support. My warmest thanks go to Lisa C. Turner, a brilliant editor, gifted writer, and traveler of the mind, for her loving inspiration. And to my son, Scott Sangster, explorer of the present and future. And Jo Frances Powell Sangster and Robert Francis Sangster, my parents, who showed by example that experiencing the world should be a priority. And Kathy Sangster, my sister, who made everything easier through her friendship.

The book benefited, as always, from Bob Sehlinger's enthusiasm and counsel.

I've never collaborated on a writing project before. Tim's good nature and depth of knowledge about the subject matter of this book made the experience a real pleasure.

—*Rob Sangster*

I have gained inspiration (and occasional kicks in the rear) from Rob, our publisher, and my family. But I would like to dedicate this book to the memory of my father-in-law, Stuart Marcus, who smartly decided not to wait too long to discover what's outside our borders.

—*Tim Leffel*

We both salute all the kindred spirits with whom we've shared the wonders of the road. May the wind be ever at your backs.

ACKNOWLEDGMENTS

Sincere thanks from Rob and Tim to:

Joshua Berman, author and expert on Belize and Nicaragua

Darrin DuFord, author and expert on Panama

Dr. Emily McClure, family-medicine practitioner and travel-medicine specialist

Steve Millburg, a superb editor who added greatly to the value of this book

Nancy Natilson, world-traveling businesswoman

Carol Pinnell, owner, adventure-travel agency

Dr. M. G. Threlkeld, travel-medicine specialist

WHAT THIS BOOK IS ABOUT

> Whatever you can do, or dream you can do, begin it;
> boldness has genius, power and magic in it.
> —Johann Wolfgang von Goethe
> *Faust*

You sit with your back against the sun-warmed stones of the temple on top of Pyramid IV in Tikal, Guatemala, the largest city of a Maya empire that flourished for more than a thousand years. Two hundred feet below you, gigantic cedar, ceiba, and mahogany trees shelter the howler monkeys, toucans, and stealthy jaguars that inhabit the endless rain forest.

Having made the steep climb to the top of Pyramid IV, you're in the mood to meditate on what happened to the great civilization about which you knew so little before your trip began. Now you've learned how remarkable the Maya were: phenomenal builders, fine artists, glyphic writers, and such excellent astronomers that they produced an incredibly accurate calendar and tracked the planets and stars.

As the setting sun floods the sky with layers of orange and gold, you realize that Tikal is a metaphor for the world. Archaeologists have freed six towering step pyramids and several acropolises and great plazas in Tikal, but hundreds of significant structures are still jungle-clad and inaccessible. There is so much yet to learn about the culture of the Maya. So it is with the world. We have so much to learn about our fellows in other cultures, and about ourselves.

We were born to be travelers, in time as well as space. In fact, every one of us is already a traveler—in a big way. After all, we're passengers aboard a giant rock speeding through space at more than 66,000 miles an hour. Because we are explorers of the universe, it makes sense to get to know our home planet better.

HERE'S WHAT IT'S ABOUT

Traveler's Tool Kit shows you how to find delicious, affordable meals anywhere in Mexico and Central America, not just where to eat in Cuernavaca. Instead of rating Panama City's "best" hotels (usually meaning the most expensive), this book shows you how to locate comfortable, affordable lodging anywhere. You'll learn how to travel happily by air, bus, and all sorts of local transport, negotiate successfully with cab drivers and merchants, and cut the costs of travel dramatically. You will be convinced that you can afford to travel—and that you can't afford not to.

Traveler's Took Kit: Mexico and Central America has four goals:

First is to inspire you to travel by revealing the rich rewards that can change your life forever.

Second is to address, one by one, all the obstacles and inhibitions that some people use to persuade themselves they can't travel, at least not until "later."

Third is to empower you. This is a practical, "how to" book that provides information and resources that build the skills to enable you to visit the places of your dreams.

Fourth is to guide you through one of the most accessible, fascinating, and affordable regions of the world: Mexico and Central America. *Traveler's Tool Kit* gives you the feel of each country, the pluses and minuses, and the things that are fun and instructive. We help you decide where, when, and how you really want to travel.

$AVE Money Assuming that money is an issue, as it is for many, *Traveler's Tool Kit* shows you dozens of ways to save money without detracting from the quality of your trip. As a bonus for avoiding high-priced tourist circuits, you'll meet more local people and learn about their hopes and values. You'll learn how to connect with a network of travelers who will help you find the most enjoyable things to do and provide guidance on how much to pay for them. You may even discover ways to earn money from your travels after returning home or decide that you could live a better life if "home" were somewhere else.

Common sense tells you a lot about what kind of travel clothing and equipment you'll need—but not everything. You can learn the rest the hard way on the road or the easy way right here in *Traveler's Tool Kit.*

Hundreds of books recount daring adventures at altitudes or depths most travelers will never reach. Vicarious thrills are fine—but *Traveler's Tool Kit* shows you how to plan your own real-life adventures.

Planning a trip is like running a whitewater rapid: preparation determines success. You scout the rapid carefully, evaluate alternative routes, and then plot your course. As you begin your run through the whitewater, you know what to expect and are in the right state of mind. After that, it's mostly a matter of hanging on for an exciting ride. If, on the other hand, you enter a rapid without a good plan, you may get a chilly surprise. In the same way, planning a trip to a foreign destination can initially seem mystifying, but learning a simple process will enable you to avoid costly, frustrating, and possibly dangerous mistakes.

Traveler's Tool Kit prepares you for travel experiences that far surpass those of a mere vacation. Too many vacations consist of lying down, dressing up, and paying someone else a lot of money. Too often, destinations are accumulated as trophies to be displayed during dinner-party conversations by collectors who have no idea how much they missed.

Travel provides an opportunity to think of beginnings and endings, to spend time alone, to challenge fears and inhibitions, to experience freedom and joy. The traveler becomes a treasure-house filled with images of Lake Atitlán surrounded by volcanoes in the Guatemalan highlands, and of Chichén Itzá, Calakmul, Uxmal, and other haunting Maya sites in Mexico's Yucatán Peninsula, and of the cloud forests, monkeys, surf, and leatherback turtles of Costa Rica.

International travel may seem overwhelming to someone who's never tried it. Before traveling abroad, most people have little reason to know the difference between a passport and a visa. Add issues of language, currency, customs, transportation, food, and lodging, and there's a lot to think about. No one says you have to fling yourself into the water as if you're an Olympic swimmer. If you're more comfortable testing the water with a toe, do it that way. Build confidence by limiting challenges, keeping the number of unknowns manageable.

ABOUT MEXICO AND CENTRAL AMERICA

Part of the beauty of traveling to Mexico and Central America is that there are no visas to worry about. Border crossings are easy. No jet lag. English is commonly spoken. In fact, the so-called language barrier is really made of papier-mâché. The people are friendly, and the delicious food may be unfamiliar—but not very. You have the opportunity to engage gently in the virtually worldwide practice of bargaining. You'll be in a culture that is used to dealing with those who are beginning their careers in international travel.

Organizing a trip is one of the ways to take charge of your life. Shakespeare's Cassius said it well: "Men at some time are masters of their fates: The fault, dear Brutus, is not with our stars, but in ourselves, that we are underlings." On the same subject, Tom Robbins said in *Jitterbug Perfume*, "If you insist on leaving your fate to the gods, then the gods will repay your weakness by having a grin or two at your expense." If you believe that travel is essential to a fulfilling life, you

---

Some aspects of the world are changing at a ferocious pace. That's why we give special attention to topics of critical interest to travelers.

- **$AVE Money** *Internet resources:* a list of the most powerful Web sites that constitute a vast travel-related resource (including essential information about how to save money)
- *Lodging:* how to find great, affordable lodging anywhere
- *Health:* how to stay healthy and protect yourself against diseases
- *Safety:* how to make choices that avoid trouble and enable you to relax
- *Insiders' tips:* how to have the best experiences in each country you visit

can make it happen. The starting bell rang for each of us at birth, and there's all too little time to get through the gate and down the track.

CARPE DIEM!

Above all else, you must make the decision to overcome inertia. Here's a parable to illustrate that. Two couples in their 20s, the Browns and the Greens, were neighbors. The Greens moved away but stayed in touch. One day, Mrs. Green called Mrs. Brown to say the Greens were planning a trip to Costa Rica. She invited the Browns to come along. Well, Mr. Brown said he was just too busy, couldn't get away from his job right then. That evening he told his wife he didn't much like the idea of going someplace where most people didn't speak English. The Greens made that trip and invited the Browns on a couple of others, but the answer was always about the same. After all, said Mr. Brown, "We'll have plenty of time to travel after I retire." The Greens kept traveling. The Browns couldn't figure out how the Greens could afford it, much less where they got the courage to go to such exotic places. After Mrs. Green started an importing business and Mr. Green joined the board of directors of the World Wildlife Fund, the couples fell out of touch.

Mr. Brown finally did retire, but by then he didn't feel much like traveling; in fact, those foreign places seemed even more intimidating. Before long, Mr. Brown died—and Mrs. Brown just didn't have the energy to go anywhere.

One sunny afternoon, years later, Mrs. Green thought, "I wonder whatever happened to the Browns?" Glancing up, she waved at her husband as he jogged toward her on the beach in Acapulco.

ABOUT THE AUTHORS

When reading a book, especially one offering advice, most readers want to know a little about the author. So here are sketches of the people behind these words.

ROB SANGSTER

As I grew up in Boston, my parents often used nice weekends to visit New England's historic nooks and crannies, New Hampshire's apple orchards, and the deep, cool woods of Maine. Later, living in Houston, the family traveled from the eerie bayous of Louisiana to the bone-dry canyons of Big Bend National Park in Texas. In other words, travel, even of limited scope, was established as a value in my mind.

After attending Stanford Law School and practicing corporate law for a few years, I decided that wasn't how I wanted to spend my life. I switched to the public sector in finance and housing policy in Washington, D.C. Then I returned to the private sector as a developer of housing for low-income people and, on the side, owned a natural-foods restaurant and an importing company, and started a foundation that donates equipment for disinfecting contaminated water in less developed countries.

Fairly early on, I had an opportunity to join a group running 277 miles of Colorado River whitewater in the Grand Canyon in 14-foot wooden dories. The three-week trip came at a time when I thought I was too busy to get away. Wrestling my left brain to the ground, I went anyway.

The length of the trip gave me enough time to separate myself from home and business and to synchronize completely with where I was. That taught me how important it is to be on the road long enough at a stretch for a magic "click" to occur in my psyche. Returning to find my business running smoothly, I gave up the fantasy of being indispensable. That first glimpse of the potential rewards of travel was a turning point.

Living fully is infinitely more important to me than earning the last dollar. Besides, learning about people and experiencing the physical majesty of our planet are better than money in the bank. I think of the priest who reportedly said, "In all my years, I've never once heard a man on his deathbed declare, 'My only regret is that I didn't spend more time in the office.' " I'll never say that either.

I've traveled in more than 100 countries, including Mexico and Central American countries, Australia, New Zealand, Bhutan, Myanmar, China, India, various other Asian countries, about half of the countries in Africa and South America, a fair number of the Pacific Islands, most of Western and Eastern Europe, the former Soviet Union, and the Antarctic continent. I've visited favorite places more than once. India, New Zealand, Chile, Botswana, Peru, Namibia, and Guatemala are at the top of that list. I now live, write, and sail for six months of each year on the coast of Nova Scotia.

My first book, *Traveler's Tool Kit: How to Travel Absolutely Anywhere* was a Book-of-the-Month Club selection and is now in its third edition. I've written a weekly newspaper column, "On the Road Again," and for two years wrote and delivered weekly travel-related essays on public radio.

I write regularly for various national publications, contributing frequent feature articles to *International Travel News,* and am Contributing Editor for *Transitions Abroad.* I was International Travel Expert for, and published more than 50 articles on, Gorp.com, a major travel site. I've written for or been quoted in the *Los Angeles Times, Washington Post, Seattle Times, Responsible Travel Handbook,* and *Insideout* Magazine, and at Journeywoman.com, Planeta.com, and EscapeArtist.com, among others. My first novel, a legal–political thriller, is in final revision.

TIM LEFFEL

I grew up in the Shenandoah Valley of Virginia, in an area filled with family farms, national forests, and Mennonites riding horse-drawn buggies along the back roads. I am the son of two teachers, so all my early travels were languid U.S. road trips in the summer—camping, swimming in lakes, and visiting relatives between New York State and Texas.

My foreign travel didn't begin in earnest until I was well out of college and running hard on a work treadmill as a marketing executive at RCA Records, first in Nashville and then in New York City. When my now-wife and I both lost our jobs within a six-month period, we took it as a fateful sign and set off to see the world. One trip circling the globe turned into two, then into three. Our friends and relatives thought we'd gone off the deep end, but we came back fine, eventually. Along the way, we taught English in Istanbul and Seoul—living in the latter for 14 months. I started to get travel features published in magazines on a

regular basis and began reviewing hotels around the world for a travel trade publication. I've since written for more than 50 publications spanning the high end (*Robb Report*) to the low end (*Arthur Frommer's Budget Travel*). Like Rob, I am a regular columnist for *Transitions Abroad* magazine.

I've dispatched articles from five continents and have published two other travel books: *The World's Cheapest Destinations: 21 Countries Where Your Money Is Worth a Fortune* (now in its second edition) and *Make Your Travel Dollars Worth a Fortune: The Contrarian Traveler's Guide to Getting More for Less*. I also edit the award-winning online travel magazine *Perceptive Travel* (**www .perceptivetravel.com**) and rant on an almost daily basis on the Cheapest Destinations blog (**travel.booklocker.com**) I write about stuff you need to pack for the Practical Travel Gear blog (**practicaltravelgear.blogspot.com**).

I live in Nashville, Tennessee, with my wife and daughter and have a small beach house on the Gulf Coast of Mexico, in the Yucatán (so my daughter is a lucky girl who got her first passport at age 3). Many of my travels are now to Latin America, where I am slowly but surely improving my Spanish.

LITERARY HOUSEKEEPING

This is a good place for a little literary housekeeping. It's difficult to find pronouns that automatically include both genders, and it's tedious to use the phrase "he and she" repeatedly. Because grammar and common usage haven't caught up with social consciousness, we try to alternate, as appropriate, male and female references.

The two authors collaborated on some chapters and wrote others independently, so we've dispensed with the group-think "we" and use "I" for opinions and travel stories throughout.

CHAPTER 1

How Travel Will Change Your Life

The world is a book, and those who
do not travel read only a page.
—St. Augustine
The City of God

Shall we live life—or watch it pass? Will we be participants—or spectators? It takes a lot more effort to travel than it does to sit in front of the tube. Let's look at what makes that effort so worthwhile.

Perspective. A small article reporting that a volcanic eruption has devastated a village in Nicaragua will escape the scanning eye of most readers, but if you've met those villagers and listened to their music, that article leaps off the page. You read it, and your heart aches. Freed from the cocoon of familiar places, the traveler learns how people elsewhere live and what they care about. After you've been there, you own a bit of the place, know something of the people, and begin to understand their emotions. When expressions of artists in a dozen cultures have enriched your mind, you develop true appreciation for the immense breadth of human creativity.

Travelers develop an understanding of the strivings of billions of humans, of lives filled from dawn to dusk with hard work, disease, and hopelessness. Learning about the politics, customs, and attitudes of very different cultures helps us understand our own culture better. Surely if the faithful of various religions are ever to coexist peacefully, they must learn more about one another.

> He who never leaves his country is full of prejudices.
> —Carlo Goldoni,
> *Pamela Nubile* (1757)

We come to realize that much of what we have accepted as true actually reflects the values of the country, even the neighborhood, in which each of us grew up.

Do you remember the fable of the blind men and the elephant? One blind man put his arms around the elephant's sturdy front leg and said the animal resembled a tree. Another grasped the trunk and insisted the elephant was like a snake. A third ran his hand along the great flank and declared that an elephant is very like a wall. In other words, it's hard to have an accurate perspective on humankind when your experience is limited to a single culture—and what you see on the 24-hour news channels.

A mariachi band in the town of Tequila, Mexico

Firsthand information. Traveling frees you from relying on what's reported by the media. You become able to interpret and respond to international events on your own. Relations among nations are affected by how well people in different cultures know one another as individuals rather than as stereotypes. Surely, aspirants to national political leadership ought to have traveled the world before being entrusted with our future.

Beauty. The greatest beauty devised by nature and humankind awaits, from the breathtaking majesty of alpine landscapes and coral reefs to the architectural brilliance of Spanish cathedrals and ancient pyramids.

Special places. You may be beckoned by the lure of a specific place, a vision with a mysterious resonance. It may be a Maya temple, a waterfall, a carnival, a beach, or an entire culture—any image reinforced until it becomes a command.

Special interests. Visit Panama to identify rare birds. Stroll through Guatemalan markets to purchase the world's most colorful textiles. Dive among exotic tropical fish on the famous reef off Belize. Visit Antigua, Guatemala, to polish your Spanish. Whether you like art, wine, food, architecture, or just better weather, travel can gratify your special interests.

Personal growth. A person would have to be brain-dead to wander about the world for weeks or months without growing from the experience. There's plenty of time for contemplation, even solitude. Personal growth may take years to be recognized, or it may become evident with dramatic suddenness.

Planning a complicated trip is no easy task. When you return, having successfully solved every problem that came up along the way, your feelings of competence and confidence are strengthened. For example, after riding a bicycle solo from Ireland to India, the writer Dervla Murphy said she felt little need to conform to the conventional Irish view of a "woman's role."

Travel provides the opportunity to set new priorities and decide how to reallocate your time. If you record your insights as you travel, they won't be swept away by the familiar routines of home.

Personal challenges. Trekking, diving, and climbing stretch physical capabilities and awaken what someone called the "adrenaline angel." Other activities challenge the mind. Surely, some of the finest moments of our lives are those that stretch us the most. We think we can't do it—and then we do.

Renewed energy. After the exercise, daily mental stimulation, constant variety, and excitement of travel, you return home full of plans, eager to reenergize your life and get into action.

Escape. Some people travel not to get to some place as much as to get away from some place. From beaches to bar stools, people talk about travel as an escape—from a weak economy, a lost job, an unhappy relationship, or the daily treadmill. Some, looking ahead to careers and family, feel it might be now or never for travel. Others, tired of responsibility or newly retired, hope that travel will stimulate changes in their lives.

Curiosity. Travel satisfies, at least in part, our curiosity about the other side of the mountain and the land beyond the horizon. In the big picture, the earth is no more than a tiny dot, not the center of anything. At the very least, we should learn as much about it as we can.

> Most of us abandoned the idea of a life full of adventure and travel sometime between puberty and our first job. Our dreams die under the dark weight of responsibility. Occasionally the old urge surfaces, and we label it with names that suggest psychological aberrations: the big chill, a mid-life crisis.
> —Tim Cahill, *Jaguars Ripped My Flesh* (1987)

Awakened emotions. Travel evokes positive emotions such as excitement and awe, but other emotions as well. You'll sometimes be in the midst of people whose living conditions are not quaint or merely lower than those of your own society. They are wretched. In some countries, many people can't afford education or even nutritious food. They're chronically ill with diseases that could be prevented or cured in the more developed world. Some can't earn a living because there's no longer a market for the products of their labor. After having seen people as individual human beings

> Memories of travel experiences are a treasure.

rather than electronic images on a screen, you may find yourself emotionally kidnapped, compelled by compassion to do something to improve their conditions. It doesn't happen to all travelers, but it might just happen to you.

Appreciation. Seeing that many people in the world don't have expensive cars, a huge house, or even running water helps travelers develop deep appreciation for their own good fortune. We also observe that the fruits of consumerism can be outweighed by the values of community and strong family relations.

Friendship. Memories of people last the longest. As we travel, we trade life stories, speak honestly, and break free from familiar roles. Friendships made on the road, with local people as well as other travelers, are one of life's deepest pleasures.

Reward. Plain and simple, a trip is a reward for hard work.

Freedom. Travel means freedom from the weight of possessions and from ruts: freedom to be the person you think of yourself as being.

Memories. Hemingway said it best: "If you are lucky enough to have lived in Paris as a young man, then wherever you go for the rest of your life, it stays with you, for Paris is a moveable feast."

If you understand the reasons for your desire to travel, that's good. If not, that's fine too. Someone suggested, perhaps with tongue in cheek, that the desire to travel may be genetically programmed into some people. If so, I have that gene. I can't *not* travel.

HOW WE TALK OURSELVES OUT OF TRAVELING

Because the reasons to travel are so compelling, why do so many people stay at home? They have different reasons, and, for them, the reasons are valid. But the objections can be overcome by knowledge and motivation. That's what this book is about.

Not enough money. Prices listed in glossy tour brochures persuaded Ted that he couldn't afford to travel abroad. The photographs were beautiful and the

> Actual costs of travel are far lower than you think.

hotels glamorous, but the prices seemed out of reach. He didn't suspect that the actual costs of travel can be far lower than in the brochures, especially if he learned to deal directly with local tour operators—or travel independently. He didn't know how to find great deals on airfare. He didn't realize that good food and lodging are available for far less than he routinely pays at home. Naturally, he had no idea how to calculate how much a trip would cost.

> And don't let the feeble excuse of work keep you back; remember the Haitian proverb: If work is such a good thing, how come the rich haven't grabbed it all for themselves?
> —John Hatt,
> *The Tropical Traveler,*
> (1982)

Too little time. Erik said, "I just can't get away." He feels harried every day and thinks he's indispensable at work. The idea that he could organize things so that everything would carry on successfully in his absence has never occurred to him. Because he secretly feels more important when his nose is jammed to the grindstone, he can't conceive of taking a two-month sabbatical. He'll die sooner than he should—or maybe he'll read this book!

Leslie, on the other hand, said, "*They* won't let me get away." Her employer's manual says she's entitled to only one week of paid vacation a year—and she's never questioned it. She doesn't realize how many options she has that could free more of her time for living a full life.

Language. The only foreign words Sandra knows came from menus in Mexican restaurants. That never bothered her until she began thinking about taking a trip overseas. She doesn't know that English has spread throughout large parts of the world and that she can learn how to communicate easily even where no English is spoken.

Inertia. For Larry, the primary obstacle is plain old inertia: the TV-and-a-six-pack barrier. His homebound rut is too comfortable. If he's forced out of the house for a vacation, he doesn't see any reason not to return to the same old places. To him, "remote" means the instrument he uses to click from channel to channel. If he stumbles onto an exciting National Geographic program, he's satisfied with the pale electronic image of life he can control with his index finger.

Control. Andy sees himself as being in control of his world, and that's the way he likes it. When he thinks of traveling abroad, he feels uneasy. He's afraid he wouldn't know what's going on and couldn't be in charge. Besides, at home everyone knows who he is. Over there, he'd be just another guy. He wouldn't like that at all.

Safety. Lydia heard of a woman who went to Ambergris Caye and had her purse stolen "right there on the beach the very first night." So she decided to stay at home. She'll never find out how mistaken she is about safety abroad and how easily she could protect herself.

I never aspired to being a great traveller. I was simply a young man, typical of my age; we traveled as a matter of course. I rejoice that I went when the going was good.
—Evelyn Waugh, When the Going Was Good (1934)

Health. Bonnie heard that some people get upset stomachs in Mexico, so why go there? She'll never bother to learn how to keep herself healthy on the road.

These reasons for staying home are understandable. Travel can be expensive if you don't learn how to spend money wisely. Health and safety are issues unless you recognize the risks and guard against them. You need knowledge to make the right choices.

By the time you reach the end of *Traveler's Tool Kit,* you'll find that every reason not to travel was written on the wind.

CHAPTER 2

Why Mexico and Central America Are Today's Smart Destinations

Most people follow. Smart people lead.

Many people yearn to travel. Europe would be nice, but—wow!—those prices. And Africa? Too big a leap for the first international trip. Asia and the Middle East? Well, maybe in a few years. So, they sigh and rent a condo at the same beach where they've gone for the past five years.

Then there are the really smart people who say, "Let's go to Latin America."

Starting with Mexico and Central America, those are today's smart destinations.

FORGET ABOUT JET LAG

Reaching destinations such as China, Thailand, Australia, and South Africa from the United States requires up to 22 hours in transit. When you finally wobble off the plane, you're in a time zone so different that the hands on your internal clock are spinning in opposite directions. Then you walk around like a zombie, trying to overcome the dreaded jet lag. On a monthlong trip you'll get your footing. For a short trip, it's a heavy price to pay.

While the trip to Europe is easier, it's still going to cost you seven to eleven hours, depending on your departure point, to cross many punishing time zones.

In contrast, getting to Mexico or Central America from the 48 contiguous states is a snap. Travel times are short. At most, you'll breeze through two time zones and hit the ground full of energy.

You don't need even one visa, and crossing borders is almost painless. English is common enough that, with a little preparation, you can get by without being a whiz in Spanish. And the food is . . . hearty. (Yes, that means not many of the cooks were trained in Paris.)

HISTORY, LANDSCAPE, AND CULTURE

Long before Columbus dropped in on North America at the end of the 1400s, the Maya had developed a sophisticated society that had ruled its region for a thousand years. The Aztecs were already a powerhouse in what is now Mexico (until the Spanish destroyed them at Tenochtitlán in 1521). Architecture and artifacts from the era of Spanish colonization have mostly disappeared from the United States, but they're still common in Mexico and Central America. For perspective, most of the church buildings in town squares are far older than their counterparts in Boston.

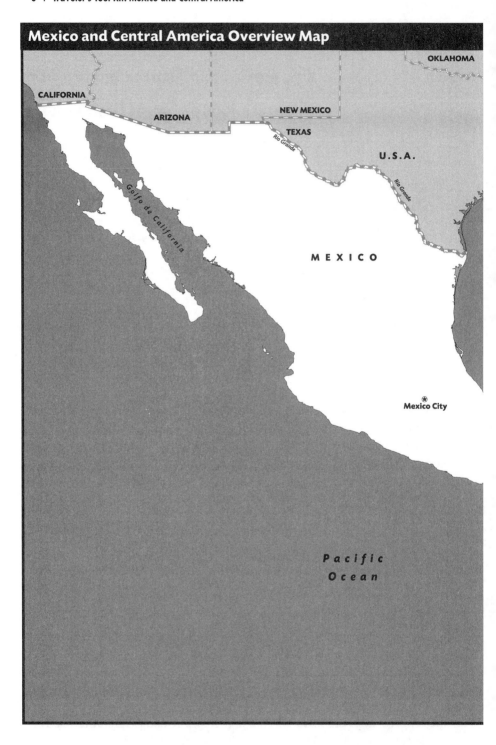

Mexico and Central America Overview Map

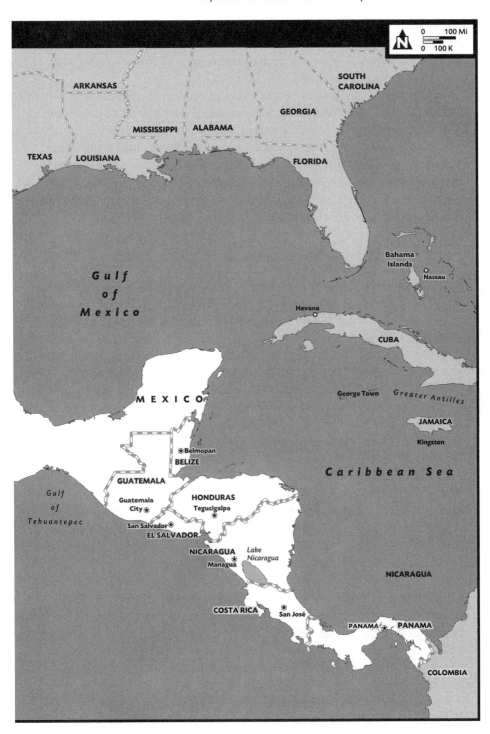

However, more separates us from those countries than just a few national borders. We have different histories and traditions. The smoldering volcanoes, brightly colored coral reefs, and dense jungles don't remind us at all of Kansas—any more than a toucan makes us think of a crow.

And the tens of millions of people who live between the Rio Grande and the Panama Canal are certainly not homogenous. Even residents of Belize and Guatemala, next-door neighbors, are very different from one another.

As a bonus, people in Mexico and Central America are friendly and hospitable, and take great joy in living. This region is not like some European cities where some people may feel too busy to talk with you or lend a hand or offer advice. Not everyone appreciates American foreign policy at the moment, but if the subject is brought up, chances are it will be done politely.

EASY ON THE BUDGET

Mexico and Central America are very affordable. While prices are high at some tourist hot spots, those are the exceptions. Elsewhere, count on some of the best values in the world. When you stay in family-owned inns and eat at nontourist restaurants, you'll be amazed at how far your money will stretch.

Expect higher costs in tourist areas.

Many travelers who visit Mexico or Central America like the region so much they decide to spend more time there, perhaps in a vacation home or something suitable for retirement. Some of the countries dangle multiple incentives to entice you to put down roots. Real estate is a bargain, the cost of living is low, and life is far less hectic than at home.

SAFER THAN HOME

Most conflicts that existed in Mexico and Central America are in the past. In Mexico, political disturbances in Oaxaca and Chiapas were short term and not directed at travelers. Guatemala signed a peace accord between the parties more than a decade ago. Nicaragua is now building beach condos and courting ecotourists like crazy. El Salvador has drifted back into tropical slumber. And Panama has become a booming economic center and haven for retirees. Can you believe a 100-story retirement tower has been planned for Panama City?

The terrorist threat discussed endlessly in the United States, and very troubling in certain other parts of the world, is not a matter of consequence in Mexico and Central America. There are few certainties in the world, but travelers have little reason to fear being targets of terrorism or car bombs in any of the countries visited in this book.

What about crime? Americans know they live in a violent country, but just ask them to speculate about crime rates somewhere else. They'll think America is safer, but are they correct?

Let's look at some data from the United Nations. The United States is at the *top* of the world list in terms of adults prosecuted per capita. Canada is 8th. Mexico is 31st, and no country in Central America is even on the list. As far as physical assault is concerned, the United States is 6th, Canada is 9th, Mexico is 20th, and Costa Rica is 50th. In burglaries, Canada has the 9th-highest rate, and the United States is 17th-highest—both far worse rankings than those of our neighbors to the south.

Not all the statistics are rosy. Mexico, especially because of drug wars along the border, and Guatemala have serious problems with gun homicides. These crimes aren't about tourists, but they are a signal not to hang out in questionable places.

In some spots around the world, anti-Americanism runs high. But America, despite its sometimes-disliked foreign policies, is not seen as the enemy in most of Latin America (Hugo Chavez's efforts to stir the pot notwithstanding). Besides being a major buyer of Latin American exports, the United States also supplies most of the tourists who bolster every economy. And, of course, many in Latin America have cousins in Brooklyn or Denver or LA.

EASY ON YOUR HEALTH

In terms of a traveler's health, Mexico and Central America are not nearly as risky as central Africa or the Amazon—but they're not Milwaukee, either. In other words, there are relatively few challenges to good health, but there are some. The main foes are those pesky mosquitoes that carry malaria or dengue fever. Then there are the occasional assaults on your system from contaminated food or water. It's all manageable as long as you know what to expect and you prepare yourself. *Traveler's Tool Kit* deals in depth with eating and drinking safely and how to maintain good health (please see Chapter 12, Keeping Healthy, and Chapter 16, Eating and Drinking).

> Age need not be a deterrent to travel.

ADVENTURES GALORE

Few international destinations offer a greater variety of outdoor fun than Mexico and Central America (okay, snow sports aren't so great there). Take your pick: white-water rafting and kayaking, tough treks and easy walks, mountain biking and pedaling along shady lanes. Snorkel the afternoon away, or dive down a vertical wall known as "The Devil's Drop." Photograph waterfalls and volcanic landscapes, or bask in the sun on a pristine beach. What about days of world-class birding followed by margaritas in a sidewalk cafe?

Maybe you prefer ziplining among orchids, butterflies, and scarlet macaws in the cloud forest. Would you

> The word "American" is usually spoken by outsiders with strange anticipation, as if, at some moment, they expect me to do something unusual or entertaining.
> —Randy Wayne White,
> *The Sharks in Lake Nicaragua* (1999)

rather search for ocelots, jaguars, giant anteaters, and white-lipped peccaries—or go after tarpon, groupers, and snappers? You can spend the morning in the botanical heaven of a virgin rain forest, then stroll through a museum and listen to a symphony in the evening.

That should be enough to whet your imagination. Now it's time to get serious about choosing where to go. Read on.

PART ONE: Destinations

CHAPTER 3

The Best of Mexico and Central America

MEXICO

Tangy as a fresh margarita, spicier than a habanero pepper, and as complex as a well-made mole sauce, Mexico is full of personality. The Mayas, the Aztecs, the Toltecs, and the Spanish all left the imprints of their rich cultures on Mexico—and so did Texas. It takes more than one taste of the resulting soup to get the full flavor.

Mexico has a cuisine all its own and a long list of attractions that make it one of the most popular countries on Earth for tourists. With a number of the world's finest beaches, most of the great Maya ruins, and some of the prettiest colonial cities in Latin America, the country has enough going for it to keep travelers entranced for visit after visit.

Mexico has always had a big influence on the United States—and vice versa. Even someone who doesn't speak Spanish can probably recollect a few dozen words learned from Mexican friends, music, and restaurants.

Mexico is a big country, the 15th-largest in the world by area and the most populous Spanish-speaking nation. This is not Belize or Panama, where you can cross the country in an afternoon. In fact, all of Central America would fit in the southern half of Mexico. Within this vast area, Mexico has a lot in common with its neighbor to the north in terms of geographic variety—but with a balmier climate and almost no snow. It also has far more history, with impressive cities that date back more than 1,000 years and Spanish colonial towns and cities that make Boston look like a youngster.

The country welcomes more than 20 million visitors each year from the United States. Unfortunately, 75 percent of all foreign tourists go to five resort areas: Puerto Vallarta, Los Cabos, Mazatlán, Acapulco, and the Cancún–Riviera Maya coast. In many ways, these resort areas have as little to do with the real Mexico as do Fort Lauderdale or Myrtle Beach with the real United States. Because there are so many tourists in the Cancún hotel zone, the percentage of Mexicans there is probably lower than it is in Miami Beach. Since everything in these fantasylands is priced for foreign tourists, a visit can cost almost as much as a vacation at home.

In general, the beach resorts advertised in your Sunday paper are designed and priced for package tourists looking for sun, sand, and nightlife. Not a bad

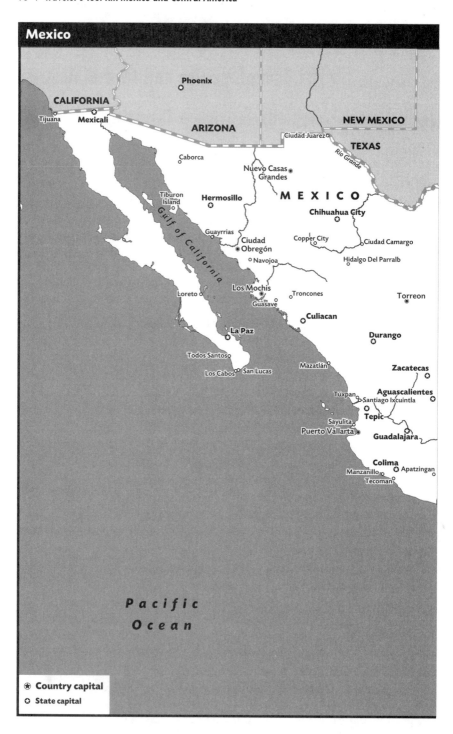

Mexico

Phoenix

CALIFORNIA

Tijuana   Mexicali

ARIZONA

NEW MEXICO

Ciudad Juarez

TEXAS

Rio Grande

Caborca

Nuevo Casas Grandes

M E X I C O

Tiburon Island   Hermosillo

Chihuahua City

Guayrrias

Ciudad Obregón

Copper City

Ciudad Camargo

Navojoa

Hidalgo Del Parralb

Gulf of California

Loreto

Los Mochis

Guasave

Troncones

Torreon

Culiacan

Durango

La Paz

Todos Santos

Zacatecas

Los Cabos   San Lucas

Mazatlán

Aguascalientes

Túxpan

Santiago Ixcuintla

Sayulita

Tepic

Puerto Vallarta

Guadalajara

Colima

Manzanillo

Apatzingan

Tecoman

Pacific
Ocean

⊛ Country capital
○ State capital

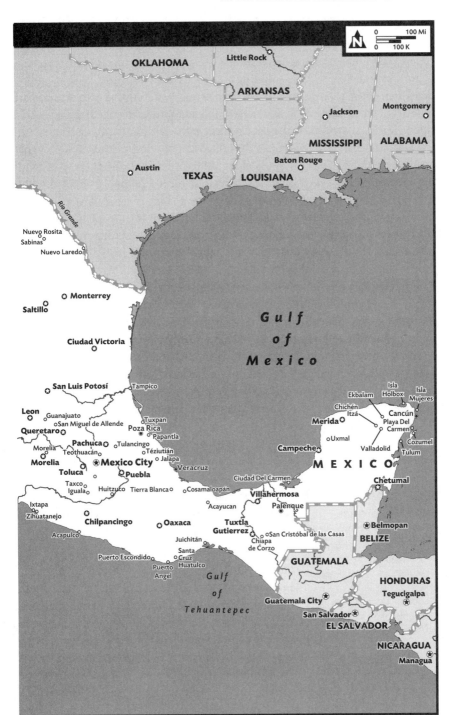

OKLAHOMA

Little Rock

ARKANSAS

Jackson

Montgomery

MISSISSIPPI

ALABAMA

Baton Rouge

Austin

TEXAS

LOUISIANA

Rio Grande

Nuevo Rosita
Sabinas
Nuevo Laredo

Monterrey
Saltillo

Ciudad Victoria

Gulf
of
Mexico

San Luis Potosí

Tampico

Isla
Holbox

Isla
Mujeres

Ekbalam

Chichén
Itzá

Cancún

Leon
Guanajuato
Queretaro
San Miguel de Allende
Tuxpan
Poza Rica
Papantla

Merida

Playa Del
Carmen

Pachuca
Tulancingo
Teziutián

Uxmal

Cozumel

Morelia
Teothuacán
Campeche

Valladolid

Tulum

Morelia

Mexico City

Jalapa

MEXICO

Toluca
Puebla

Veracruz

Taxco
Iguala
Huitzuco
Tierra Blanca

Ciudad Del Carmen

Chetumal

Cosamaloapán

Villahermosa

Ixtapa
Zihuatanejo

Acayucan

Palenque

Belmopan

Chilpancingo

Oaxaca

Tuxtla
Gutierrez

San Cristóbal de las Casas

BELIZE

Acapulco

Juichitán

Chiapa
de Corzo

Puerto Escondido

Santa
Cruz
Huatulco

GUATEMALA

Puerto
Angel

Gulf
of
Tehuantepec

Guatemala City

HONDURAS

Tegucigalpa

San Salvador

EL SALVADOR

NICARAGUA

Managua

0   100 Mi
0   100 K

package, but they'll quickly deplete your budget and may make you wish you'd experienced more of authentic Mexico. On the plus side, if this is your first time out of your home country, these resorts are a good way to ease into a foreign culture, especially if you are traveling as a family with little ones. Just be sure to break free of the all-inclusive cocoon and venture out on your own at least part of the time. And take a look at our recommendations under the Highlights section to learn about some laid-back towns near the resorts.

Mexico is a bargain! Away from the gringo zones, prices in Mexico are roughly one third to one half what they are in the United States or Canada for food, lodging, entertainment, and ground transportation. Travel on public transportation is reasonably comfortable, and in general the roads are good. The people are friendly, the towns are colorful, and there are hundreds of miles of good beaches. What makes Mexico even more attractive from a budget standpoint is that the cost of an international flight from the United States or Canada is only slightly more than you'd pay for a domestic flight.

Between Baja California on the west coast and the Yucatán Peninsula on the east coast are countless things to see and do. Some of the highlights include the massive Copper Canyon, Spanish colonial architecture, amazing ruins, and as many mountains and volcanoes as you have energy to explore.

Mexico has 27 UNESCO World Heritage sites. That's the greatest concentration of these cultural treasures of any country in the Americas. Ranging from historic colonial squares to Maya ruins to nature preserves, the "must see" attractions here are so numerous that experiencing them all would require three or four trips to the country.

You can spend a fortune in Mexico at $750-per-night hotels, or you can get by on a frugal budget of $30 per day. Between these extremes, a couple looking for a reasonable level of comfort can travel here for far less than at home, getting good value and enjoying a unique culture. Because it's so close, there's not a lot of time lost in air travel—and no jet lag.

Mexico has the third-highest mountain in North America, at 18,490 feet. Pico de Orizaba is an inactive volcano near the village of Tlachichuca, in Puebla State on the border with Veracruz. It attracts serious mountain climbers who carry ropes and attach crampons to reach the snow-covered summit at sunrise.

Mexico's People

The image of a sleeping Mexican leaning against a wall in the sun under a huge sombrero is a degrading and inaccurate stereotype. Mexico's people are a multicultural blend of indigenous (who probably started arriving at least 12,000 years ago) and European (obviously lots of Spanish influence), with great diversity from region to region. They've built a complex society with democratic elections and a relatively stable economy based on agriculture, minerals, and oil. In addition to having a huge influence on the U.S. economy, Mexico has a long history of peaceful relationships with its neighbors. The total population is about 109 million, with the three largest cities being Mexico City, Guadalajara, and Monterrey. The per-capita gross domestic product of about $11,000 may seem low compared to that of the United States, but it's far above most other Latin American countries. Of the countries in this book, only small Costa Rica has a higher standard of living.

As in many countries, there is a defined stratification based on skin color and heritage, with most of the people in power being those who look the most European. The country's poorest are often the indigenous descendants of the Maya and Aztecs. Even though Mexico's poor suffered greatly under the rule of the Spaniards, this former domination still influences the language, customs, and traditions.

Overall, it's the people of Mexico who captivate many visitors and keep them coming back. They are traditionally friendly, gregarious, and willing to lend a hand when needed. They have also earned a reputation as industrious workers who take their jobs seriously. At the same time, the pace is slower than it is up north. Siesta time is a reality, and relationships guide business decisions more than hard numbers do. You'll find it's a relief to adjust to their pace.

> Mexico has the second-largest population of Catholics in the world (after Brazil). Almost half of the Mexican population goes to church weekly.

Highlights

Some fat guidebooks might try to include everything worth seeing in Mexico, but that does the reader no favor. "Seeing Mexico" on one trip is just as hard as trying to cover all of the United States. When you are planning an itinerary for your first trip or two, see the highlights below and the sample regional itineraries that follow.

- A meteorite crashed to Earth in the **Yucatán** region of Mexico 65 million years ago. It is thought that the consequences of that massive impact wiped out the dinosaurs. There's a huge crater in this unique geographic zone, with not one river on the surface but plenty of underground streams and lakes. After the crash, cracks and fissures filled with water, and eventually some 3,000 of them became *cenotes*—sinkhole pools, some of which are now popular scuba-diving sites featuring swims through long, sunken tunnels.
- The Yucatán is also famous for the largest concentration of **Maya ruins** anywhere. The most visited are Tulum, Chichén Itzá, and Uxmal, but dozens of others are open to the public in the states of Yucatán, Quintana Roo, and Campeche. Amazingly, new sites are still being discovered. Ek Balaam, north of Valladolid, just opened to the public a few years ago.

Girl and pigeons playing in a park in Mérida, Mexico

- Mexico's **colonial cities** are a delight, and a lot of money has been spent on restoring central plazas and converting mansions into boutique hotels. The most popular large colonial cites are Mérida, Guanajuato, San Miguel de Allende, Puebla, and Oaxaca.
- **Guadalajara** is the original home of mariachi music, Mexican cowboys, and **tequila**, which make it, and the state of Jalisco, good places to experience Old Mexico. The tourism office can supply maps of dozens of tequila distilleries and help arrange a tour or driver. Most distilleries are open to the public and offer samples of their *blanco* (white), *reposado* (slightly aged), and *añejo* (aged) versions. For about $75, you can ride the Tequila Express train (**www.tequilaexpress.com .mx**) through the countryside from Guadalajara to the Herradura distillery for a tour, a big lunch, and plenty of tequila along the way. A mariachi band entertains riders on the train. Buy tickets in advance, as it often sells out.

> Mexico City's legislative assembly passed a law in late 2006 allowing gay couples to register their union legally, giving partners inheritance and pension rights.

- **Taxco** is known as Mexico's Silver City because it was once a prime silver-mining area. Hundreds of jewelry shops sell high-quality silver pieces—and souvenir trinkets—to visitors. Spend the night so you can visit the 18th-century Baroque church and walk the town's streets when they're not full of day-trippers. The hilly lanes remind many of a European town. Or visit during Easter week or the November silver fair to see Taxco at its busiest.

- The **Teotihuacán ruins**, 31 miles northeast of Mexico City, are the remains of one of the oldest and largest ancient settlements in the Americas, most active from roughly 100 BC to AD 500. At its peak, this was the largest city in the Americas, with a population of more than 150,000, larger than Rome's in AD 500. Its stepped pyramids influenced later Maya and Aztec architecture. The scale is awe-inspiring: the enormous Pyramid of the Sun has 243 steps to the top. The ruin of Tula, the capital of the Toltecs, is only 5 miles away and is not nearly as crowded.

Parícutin Mountain, in southern Mexico, is one of the planet's youngest peaks. The area was once flat farm land, but a volcano that erupted for nine years, starting in 1943, became a cone almost 1,400 feet high. Lava flows buried two villages except for a church steeple that sticks out of the solidified black lava.

- **Mexico's beaches** attract throngs of U.S. and Canadian vacationers, especially when it's cold up north. The most popular beaches include the stretch from Cancún south, the west coast north and south of Puerto Vallarta, and parts of the Baja Peninsula. In a country with 6,000 miles of coastline, it's easy to leave the major resort zones behind and find a quiet place to play in the surf. Here are some alternatives as little as 10 miles out of the resort zones. Try Isla Holbox, Tulum, or Isla Mujeres instead of Cancún or Cozumel. Visit Loreto or Todos Santos instead of Los Cabos. Stop at Sayulita instead of Puerto Vallarta or Troncones instead of Ixtapa.

Itineraries

If You Have a Week in Mexico

There's no way you can "do" Mexico in a week. It's better to pick one region for a weeklong trip, then come back another time. The following areas can each be covered in one week without spending too much time en route.

1. The Yucatán region is the most visited in Mexico because of the popularity of the Cancún and Riviera Maya beaches. There's far more to it than that, however, with cenotes to explore, dozens of Maya sites, and the beautiful colonial city of Mérida. There's also a long string of beaches on the Gulf of Mexico side of the peninsula that are deserted most of the year—good spots to rent a beach house for a reasonable price to serve as a base for exploration. One popular route is to head south from Cancún to see the ruins at Tulum and Copa, then venture to Valladolid and Chichén Itzá. Move on to Mérida with a trip to the Uxmal ruins (and smaller ones nearby) and a stay in a hacienda hotel. Spend a couple of nights at a beach on the Caribbean coast, where you can swim, snorkel, scuba dive, or even dive in a cenote. (See "Activities" on page 25.)

The Great Pyramid at Uxmal, in Yucatán state

The best time to visit the Yucatán is December through April, when there's little rain and the temperatures are not scorching. Between mid-July and November, rain is more frequent. And keep an eye out during hurricane season (June through November).

2. The colonial center of the country holds a collection of towns and cities that earn the cliché description of "charming." Guanajuato and San Miguel de

Allende are the best known and serve as good starting or ending points. In between are worthwhile visits to Querétaro (a sophisticated city of 1.25 million), Morelia (whose historic mansions earned it a UNESCO World Heritage designation), and Zacatecas (a great strolling city with a famous cable car ride). Many companies offer organized tours of this region, but it's easy to do on your own. Bus connections are straightforward, and none of the distances is greater than five hours. Guanajuato was founded in the 16th century as a silver-mining center and is now a well-preserved UNESCO World Heritage site. San Miguel de Allende is a beautifully kept colonial town with fine lodging, food, and entertainment to serve visitors. From there, it's also an easy trip to the Puebla pottery center.

Most of these towns have an "eternal spring" climate, so while summers are a bit hotter, there's no bad time of the year to avoid.

3. Chiapas and Palenque are good places if you'd rather not be surrounded by other tourists. After years of being considered out of bounds for tourists because of political conflict, Chiapas is now calm, and travelers are trickling back in to see San Cristóbal de las Casas, an enchanting highland colonial city with a major Saturday market, and Chiapa de Corzo, a jumping-off point to mountain hikes and the Sumidero Canyon. In this area, visitors experience some of the most authentic indigenous culture in the country.

Because they are a little off the beaten track, the Maya ruins in Palenque are far less crowded than the Yucatán ruins. However, many rate this site in the dense jungle as one of the most impressive the Maya produced. Since many other ruins and market towns in this area are tough to reach on your own, it's worthwhile joining a guided tour that can be booked locally.

Because of the higher altitude, the Chiapas region is cooler, but it can also be quite wet. It's best to avoid the rainy season, August through October. Palenque can reach close to 90 degrees in May and June.

4. Mexico City and the surrounding areas offer a lot to see in one region. Mexico City will meet any city-loving traveler's appetite for shopping, museums, and dining. On the other hand, if you don't love big (population of 20 million) cities, you may find the smog and traffic congestion overwhelming. Easy day trips or overnight trips from the capital include the Teotihuacán ruins, the pottery center of Puebla, the colonial silver center of Taxco, and the popular tourist town of Cuernavaca.

At an altitude of 7,349 feet, Mexico City stays surprisingly cool year-round, and a jacket is needed in December and January. Because these months are also the smoggiest, avoid coming then if you have respiratory problems. As noted in the section about safety later in this chapter, a bit of extra precaution is needed here.

5. Spend a week on a west coast beach for sun, surf, and whale-watching. The glitzy resort areas can be fun for a few days, but get away to more-secluded spots where you meet ordinary people who don't work in the tourism industry. From Los Cabos, head north for an hour and enter a different world. From Puerto Vallarta, Mazatlán, or Ixtapa, head in either direction for an hour, and you'll find mellower spots with pristine beaches.

Temperatures in the southern Baja Peninsula can hit 100°F in summer and drop to 50°F at night in December and January. June through October is the rainy season on the mainland west coast, with the rest of the year consistently warm and sunny.

6. Ride the rails through the Copper Canyon. Many travelers board the Chihuahua al Pacifico train at Chihuahua City and get off in the fishing village and beach town of Los Mochis (or vice versa), but this journey can easily be broken up into a series of stops. This has been called the most dramatic train ride in North America, with views of canyons carved more than 6,000 feet into the earth's surface. Passengers may visit Cuauhtémoc, a community of German-speaking Mennonite ranchers, and get off at Divisadero or Bahuichivo to hike down into the Copper Canyon. If you have a few extra days, experience the unusual culture of the Tarahumara people, renowned as long-distance runners.

The best time to take the trip is September through November, when temperatures in both the highlands and the canyon bottom are mild and there's little rain. December through February can get cold and even snowy. May, June, and July can get too hot for hikes down into the canyon.

7. Oaxaca and beaches. Gastronomic delights, colonial architecture, and high-quality crafts draw many visitors to Oaxaca and its environs. Oaxaca City is acknowledged as having the best food in the country. It is, of course, the home of *mole poblano* sauce, a complex concoction that combines chocolate, a variety of dried chili peppers, nuts, charred avocado leaves, and a mixture of spices. South of the city are the relatively undiscovered beaches of Puerto Escondido, Puerto Angel, and Santa Cruz Huatulco.

July through October is the rainy season, so these are the least desirable months to visit, with September

> Mexico City is generally listed as the second-largest city in the world in terms of population (behind Tokyo), and some estimates put it first. Despite Mexico City's many slums, its residents are the wealthiest of any city in Latin America, with an annual gross domestic product per capita of $17,696. The city reportedly has the most museums of any city in the world: 135.

> Parasailing—holding onto a parachute and going up in the air while a motorboat pulls you along—got its start on the west coast of Mexico.

being the worst. Although temperatures are mild all year in most of the state, the beaches are hot and tropical.

If You Have Two Weeks or More in Mexico

If you have more time, combine several of the preceding options, and just strike out and discover more. Because of the comfortable bus system and good highways, it is easy to combine different regions of Mexico. Nearly any of them will offer plenty to keep you occupied for a couple of weeks.

To explore farther, venture west from the Yucatán to Campeche and Palenque. Travel from Ixtapa on the Pacific through Mexico City to Veracruz, the area where the Americas' oldest civilization—the Olmecs—was based. Explore the whole Baja Peninsula or a long stretch of the mainland coast. Combine a trip to Oaxaca with a trip to San Cristóbal de las Casas in Chiapas.

Better yet, just make a loose itinerary and slow down to a Mexican pace. Take it easy and spend more time socializing. Just because you have more than a week doesn't mean you need to spend it all on the move!

Activities

- There are plenty of whales to watch on the west coast and Baja coast of Mexico. You can see California gray whales from your hotel balcony in much of Cabo San Lucas from January through March, when the whales arrive to give birth. Get up close with a short boat ride. In several places on the mainland coast, including Puerto Vallarta, visitors spot a variety of other whale species from mid-December through March.
- One of the world's prime rock-climbing spots is El Potrero Chico Canyon, about one and a half hours north of Monterrey. It has more

Mexico's Sweet Gifts to Our Palate

Where would the world of desserts be without vanilla and chocolate? We have Mexico to thank for both. Derived from an orchid, vanilla originally grew near today's Veracruz. It was used by the Totonacs, a rival to the Aztecs, as a flavoring for tobacco. The Spanish named it *vainilla*, meaning "little pod." The extract is a popular souvenir or gift to bring back from Mexico and is one of the great shopping bargains.

Chocolate was also carried to Europe by the Spanish conquistadors, after they discovered the Aztec rulers sipping from a cup containing a drink made from cacao beans. Mexican hot chocolate is still a special treat served throughout the country, though not in the bitter original form the Aztecs preferred.

than 600 climbing routes that please beginners to hard-core enthusiasts who spend the night halfway up, sleeping on a small scaffold hooked to the rocks with ropes.

In terms of biodiversity, Mexico has more species of reptiles than any other country, at 717. It's second in the number of mammals, with 502, and fourth in amphibians, with 290 species. There are more than 50 species of hummingbirds.

- The west coast of Mexico is a surfer's paradise, with huge waves and much warmer water than in California. Some of the best breakers pound the Baja Peninsula, especially at Todos Santos. The coastal areas on the mainland west coast offer dozens of other spots that attract plenty of people toting boards, including Puerto Escondido, east of Acapulco.

- Tiburon Island in the Gulf of California is a thriving wildlife refuge. There are only about 650 human residents but millions of birds. Hire a boat and cross a channel to get there, then hike to the top of the island for a panoramic view over the cacti.

- Mexico has dozens of scuba-diving areas, including the extensive Caribbean reef shared with Belize and Honduras. Hidden Worlds Cenote Park (**www.hiddenworlds.com**) includes many cenotes that are part of Nohach Nah Chich, one of the largest underwater cave systems in the world. The most impressive is an eerie wonderland called Cenote Dos Ojos (near Tulum). The water is clearest from November through March.

Cost Comparisons

There are really two Mexicos when it comes to costs: package tour Mexico and the real Mexico. Expect the following prices anywhere in the interior and on beaches that aren't lined with resorts full of foreign tourists. In those areas, Mexico can be a better value than Costa Rica or Belize. At deluxe hotels and fine-dining establishments in coastal areas, though, all bets are off. At some luxury resorts in Los Cabos and Puerto Vallarta, the restaurant and bar menus may make you think you're in Manhattan or London.

- Liter of water in a convenience store: 40–80 cents
- Bottle of beer in a bar or restaurant: $1.25–$2.50
- Bottle of beer in a store: 50–80 cents
- Half kilo of oranges, in season: 40–50 cents
- Half kilo of mangos, in season: 50–80 cents
- Half kilo of tortillas: 60–90 cents
- Cup of coffee, juice, or soda in a restaurant: 70 cents–$1.60
- A *paleta* (similar to a Popsicle) or ice-cream cone: 40–80 cents
- 10-minute taxi ride across town: $2.50–$8
- Taxi from airport to hotel: $6–$20 most areas, $25–$60 in resort areas
- 3-star or equivalent hotel: $40–$80, but $75–$125 at beach resorts

Accommodations

Hotels in Mexico run from $10 cheapies with fans and no hot water to $1,000-a-night palaces that seduce visitors with seclusion and pampering. In most cases, however, what you get for your money is quite good when compared to lodging in Canada or the United States. Prices may not be as cheap as they are in many Central American countries, but quality and service are more consistent in all budget ranges.

The best thing Mexico has going for it is the plethora of interesting inns with a strong sense of place. In nearly every sizable town or city with tourist traffic, there are a number of historic colonial buildings that have been converted into stunning hotels. Some are upscale boutique hotels going for $200-plus per night, but just as many are simpler affairs that cost $40 to $100 per night. These inns offer a great way to enjoy Mexican architecture, especially in historic cities such as Mérida, San Miguel de Allende, and Guanajuato. A great resource for finding well-run ones at the middle and upper end of the scale is the Mexico Boutique Hotels site (**www.mexicoboutiquehotels.com**).

Except at the popular beach resorts, shoestring travelers can generally find a clean, fan-cooled room for less than $20. For an air-conditioned budget room with a private bath, expect to pay $20 to $35. Midrange rooms with more amenities, such as room service and a pool, range from $30 to $80. Above $80, outside the beach resorts, you should easily find a three-star or four-star hotel or a nice inn with lots of historic character. Beachfront resort hotels in popular areas such as Cancún, Ixtapa, Puerto Vallarta, and Los Cabos fetch rates that are starting to rival those in the Caribbean: expect to pay $120 to $400 per night for an average resort (without meals), and the sky is the limit for the exclusive retreats that are used to hosting celebrities and millionaires.

> The cliff divers of Acapulco execute "the world's highest regularly performed headfirst dive," according to the *Guinness Book of World Records.* The 115-foot plunge is equivalent to diving off a 12-story building.

At the most popular hotels and during key holidays (see the "Holidays and Festivals" section on the next page), plan ahead and have reservations. Many other times, you can just look around and stay at a place that catches your fancy.

User-review Web sites (such as **www.tripadvisor.com** and **www.virtual tourist.com**) are good places to look for lesser-known hotels, but you'll find a more thorough listing at regional Web sites focused on a specific area. These include sites such as **www.yucatantoday.com** for the Mérida region, **www.san miguelguide.com** for the San Miguel de Allende area, **www.loreto.com** for that Baja town, and **www.playadelcarmen.com** for the Riviera Maya center. For the coastal resort areas, consult *The Unofficial Guide to Mexico's Best Beach Resorts.*

High-end hotels show up on most international "best of" lists, such as those published annually by *Travel + Leisure* and *Condé Nast Traveler.* Most of them are on the west coast, in Los Cabos, and in Mexico City. Check **www .luxurylatinamerica.com** for reviews of the top hotels in the country.

Food and Drink

What is called "Mexican" food in the United States and Canada doesn't begin to match the variety of the cuisine that is actually served in Mexico. And you're not likely to find sour cream, cheddar cheese, mango salsa, vegetarian burritos, or flour tortillas.

Holidays and Festivals

Sunday is still church-and-family day in much of Mexico. A lot of places are closed, and many excursions don't run that day. The country loves its fiestas, too. Individual ones in certain towns or states join the national ones that go on every month or so. The times when hotel rooms are the scarcest are Semana Santa (the week before Easter), Christmas, and El Día de los Reyes (The Day of the Kings, January 6).

Consult a guidebook for individual cities, but here are the primary holidays to remember:

- January 1: New Year's Day
- January 6: Day of the Three Kings
- February 5: Constitution Day
- February 24: Flag Day
- February or March: Carnival, before the beginning of Lent
- March 21: Birthday of Benito Juárez, a revered revolutionary and national leader
- March or April: *Semana Santa,* the week before Easter
- May 1: Labor Day
- May 5: Cinco de Mayo. Most people mistakenly believe this is Mexico's independence day, but it actually commemorates a battle victory against the French. (The real Independence Day is September 16.)
- June 1: Navy Day
- September 16: Independence Day
- September 29: Festival de San Miguel in San Miguel de Allende, which includes the Pamplonada, a miniversion of Spain's running of the bulls.
- October: Cervantes Arts Festival in Guanajuato, a celebration of Don Quixote.
- October 12: Columbus Day
- November 1–2: Día de los Muertos (Day of the Dead). The epicenter is the city of Oaxaca.
- November 20: Anniversary of the 1910 revolution
- December 12: Feast day of Mexico's patron saint, the Virgin of Guadalupe. Not a national holiday, but a major festival occasion.
- December 24: Christmas Eve
- December 25: Christmas

There's also a lot of regional variation with Sonoran cuisine being very different from what is common in the Yucatán or Mexico City. Common meals in Oaxaca are very different from what is served in Veracruz or Puerto Vallarta.

The easiest way to try typical local cuisine is to get the meal of the day (*comida corrida* or *menú del día*) for lunch at a nontourist restaurant. This is usually served between noon and 4 p.m. Eateries typically have three or four main courses, with perhaps a soup and a side of rice and beans or other vegetable, plus tortillas. With a drink, the price will rarely top $6; at market stalls it can be as little as $2.50 for a filling meal. Snack places, such as *taquerías* (taco stands) or *torta* (sandwich) counters, are good for a quick bite on the run and can serve delicious food.

Mexicans supposedly eat 1.2 billion tortillas per day, so no matter what you're eating, there are liable to be fresh corn tortillas on the table. You can buy them by weight very cheaply from little stores or *molinas* (mills) in every Mexican town. Most Mexican cuisine is not all that spicy when served; condiments placed on the table are used to spice food to taste. There are exceptions (including a lot of breakfast items), so ask about spiciness if you are sensitive.

Fish and seafood are prevalent on the coasts, of course, and there are a lot of coasts in Mexico. Serving style can range from simple fried whole fish and ceviche to intricate dishes in Puerto Vallarta that wouldn't look out of place in a gourmet restaurant in Miami or New York.

Lunch is the main meal for Mexicans. Dinner is usually a lighter affair. Seafood places serving locals usually close by 5 or 6 p.m. In tourist centers there are plenty of big dinners on offer. To get the most out of your Mexican dining experiences, pick up a book called *Eat Smart in Mexico*. It's a terrific guide to regional cuisines from all over the country and slim enough to carry as you travel.

Mexico's big draws in its early years of tourism development were simple: beautiful beaches and cheap booze. The beaches are more crowded now, and the booze isn't quite so cheap. Still, Mexico is blessed with fine beer, and tequila standards have gone up so much that the best stuff can now fetch more than $100 a bottle. Having a beer with a meal costs barely more than having a soda, and what you get is certainly better than mass-market American beer. Most Mexican beers are light lagers, but Bohemia is a big step up. There are several dark beers, including the well-known Negra Modelo.

While tequila has gotten too expensive for many Mexicans to drink regularly, it's still far cheaper to order a tequila drink in Mexico than in the United States, and what you get will generally be better quality: 100 percent agave instead of the cheap *mixto* Jose Cuervo and Sauza brands that are the most popular exports. The liquor with a worm in the bottom is not tequila but mezcal, a rougher, less refined spirit from a similar agave plant. There are some high-end artisanal versions, but they're definitely an acquired taste.

There's never been much of a wine industry in Mexico, but lately some decent wines are coming out of the northern Baja Peninsula. If you order wine in a

Rob Sangster climbs the Pyramid of Kukulkán, in the Maya center of Chichén Itzá.

restaurant, you're more likely to get a passable brand from Chile or Argentina. Rum is almost as popular as tequila these days, with plenty of it coming from nearby Cuba, Puerto Rico, and Guatemala.

Delicious fresh-squeezed juices are universally available, for about the same price as a soda. The sodas are mostly American brands (but made with sugar, not high-fructose corn syrup) and the iconic Jarritos brand. The latter can be fun to try, as you have 11 flavors to pick from, including tamarind and guava. There's not much of a coffee culture in Mexico, despite some great beans grown in Chiapas. When you find a coffee shop run by ex-Cubans, it will serve good stuff. Note that milk is seldom fresh: it's the Parmalat-style (ultrapasteurized) boxed milk, which has a long shelf life and doesn't need refrigeration before opening.

Mexicans love their ice cream and *paletas*—the delicious Popsicle-like treats that are so refreshing on a hot day. Flavors include tamarind, mango, and cucumber chili. Except in rare cases, the ice cream is made from long-life pasteurized milk and the *paletas* are made with purified water, so you shouldn't face any risk of sickness from either at a busy shop.

Transportation

Most of Mexico's population gets around by **bus**, and the bus system overall is probably the best in Latin America. For one thing, on most city-to-city routes there is at least a first-class bus and often an even higher "executive-class" option. First class is comfortable enough, but the highest class will often come with impressive legroom, only three seats across, and complimentary snacks and drinks. Some executive-class buses have only 24 seats. First and executive classes are express buses, so they'll get you there in a hurry. Specific prices are noted in the chart below, but on any route it's roughly $5 to $7 per hour traveled in first class and about $8 to $10 per hour in executive.

Second-class buses are best avoided, but they may be the only choice in some areas. These are less comfortable, may not be air-conditioned, and will stop for anyone waving an arm beside the road. (Of course, if you are that person waving your arm, that's a good thing!) These are generally half the price or less of first class.

Sample bus routes and costs (highest class available):

City 1	City 2	Travel Time	Cost
Monterrey	Mexico City	12 hours	$74
Cancún	Mérida	4 hours	$35
Oaxaca	Mexico City	6 hours	$55
Mexico City	Puebla	2 hours	$12
Acapulco	Ixtapa	1.5 hours	$11
Guadalajara	Puerto Vallarta	5.5 hours	$32
San Miguel de Allende	Guanajuato	1 hour	$10

The Guachimontones ruins in Jalisco state

For links to all the bus sites in Mexico, see **www.differentworld.com/mexico/common/pages/bus_info.htm.**

If you're young, or at least young enough at heart for travel by **12-person van**, Bamba Experience (**www.backpackingmexico.com**) offers a hop-on, hop-off service that covers a circuit between Mexico City and Cancún, with touring stops at the most interesting places and attractions in between. Prices are in the range of $115 for up to 8 days and $170 for up to 15 days.

Mexico's **airline** industry is amazingly far behind those of Asia, Europe, and the United States when it comes to domestic flight options. A few carriers offer budget flights, but none of them have made a real national go at it yet. So expect to pay as much or more for a short, monopoly-controlled flight in Mexico as you would pay for a longer flight in the United States. Unless you are in a big hurry, an executive-class bus is generally a far better value.

Train service is so limited in Mexico that most guidebooks don't even have the word "train" or "railroad" in their index. The only regularly running train trips currently open to travelers are the sightseeing ones outlined earlier in this chapter: the Tequila Express in Guadalajara and the Copper Canyon trip through the Sierra Madre mountains. There's also an interesting train line called Expreso Maya that runs various tours between Villahermosa in the state of Tabasco, and Cancún (in the state of Yucatán), with stops in Palenque, Campeche, Mérida, Chichén Itzá, and other spots. It runs only certain times of year, however, and is mostly booked by group tour operators. For more information, go to **www.expresomaya.com.mx.**

Subways operate in Mexico City, Guadalajara, and Monterrey. In Mexico City, this can be the best way to avoid the horrendous traffic—just keep your valuables tucked under your clothing. A ride one way will run about 20 cents. Figuring out the local city bus routes can be daunting. Fortunately, **taxis** are cheap enough to use regularly: figure on $2 to $8 for the typical short-to-long ride across town. The main exceptions are in Cancún, where predatory drivers stick it to the tourists, and Mexico City, where it is safer to pay a bit more for a radio taxi or a driver for the day. In much of the country, you can hire a driver for $8 to $12 per hour or $50 to $150 a day, depending on the car model, the distance, and the driver's English skills.

Few **boat connections** are necessary in Mexico, the main exception being the car ferries between the Baja Peninsula and the mainland. There are three routes between the two land masses, with the longest being an 18-hour trip from La Paz (north of Los Cabos) to Mazatlán. This site lists all the phone numbers: **www.loscabosguide.com/bajaferries.** You need to make reservations well in advance for cabins, but there is no way to do so on the Web. The best bet is to call direct or enlist the help of a travel agent.

Renting a car is relatively straightforward in Mexico, as competition is strong and many of the familiar international rental companies operate there.

In most tourist spots you can reserve through the company's Web site. Just be advised that the cheapest rates will probably be for a manual-transmission car with no air-conditioning, and that what would be called a compact in the United States will be a midsize or larger in Mexico. In theory, your own car insurance and credit card should be sufficient to cover you for damages (check the fine print), but probably not for liability. It is risky to decline liability insurance anyway unless you are very fluent in Spanish. If you cause an accident and don't have obvious proof of insurance, you can get holed up in the local jail while the authorities sort it out. In a rural town, that could be a while.

Activity Costs

Activity and excursion costs vary so drastically across Mexico that it is very hard to generalize about prices. Most tourists who stay at package resorts spend double or triple what they would if they arranged the trip on their own directly. Guests who book through their hotel routinely pay $100 and up for a day trip to visit Chichén Itzá from Cancún, to go whale watching in Puerto Vallarta or Cabo San Lucas, or to visit Puebla from Mexico City.

You can shave off a significant sum—and have a more interesting day as well—if you arrange an excursion on your own or book it through an independent agency outside the hotels. The bus system, described previously, is comfortable and comprehensive. You can also hire a car and driver for the day for less than a tour-bus excursion, and go at your own pace.

Here are some sample costs for excursions you can set up on your own through a local agency. These are meant to be representative examples only. Actual costs at the source can vary.

- Chichén Itzá tour from Mérida: $40
- 6-hour deep-sea fishing trip from Puerto Vallarta or Cabo San Lucas: $80–$140 per person
- Guided jungle cenote snorkeling trip: $40
- Cenote diving trip, 1 tank and gear rental: $65
- Cozumel scuba-diving trip, 1 tank: $50
- Horseback-riding or bird-watching trip in the ecological reserve near Santa Cruz Huatulco: $30–$80, depending on length and lunch
- All-day "booze cruise" from Puerto Vallarta: $30–$50
- 1-day tour of anywhere with a hired car and driver: $50–$150

Tour Companies

At least a hundred tour companies lead trips to Mexico from the United States and Canada, and another few dozen arrange simple beach packages. To find high-quality tour companies that cover the region you are interested in, use magazines such as *International Travel News*, *Specialty Travel Index*, and *National Geographic Adventure*.

Some of the large international agencies that get good marks for responsible tourism practices include Intrepid Travel (**www.intrepidtravel.com**), G.A.P Adventures (**www.gapadventures.com**), Djoser (**www.djoserusa.com**), Elderhostel (**www.elderhostel.org**), and Culture Xplorers (**www.culturexplorers .com**). Many smaller agencies that specialize in a particular region also follow sustainable tourism practices and try to encourage cultural interaction.

In addition, every Mexican town with tourists has lots of local outfitters, some of them running the actual tours that are booked with an agency in your home country. Check your guidebook and ask around to find a good match where you are staying.

Useful Details

Getting there and away: The major airlines from the United States and Canada fly into different parts of Mexico, with Continental offering the most choices. Also serving Mexico are Frontier, Spirit, the Mexican airlines, and loads of charter planes taking package tourists on vacations. Fees and a hefty departure tax push the cost of a round-trip ticket up nearly $100. Fares to the beach resorts are highest from December through March.

Two dozen overland crossing points are strung out along the extensive border, so getting into Mexico from California, Arizona, New Mexico, or Texas is not difficult, either in your own vehicle or by public transportation.

If you are driving your own vehicle across, have your paperwork in order: registration, driver's license, proof of insurance, title or a note from your bank if the car is not paid for, and your passport. A credit card is necessary too for a bond or you'll have to leave a large cash deposit. You should purchase liability insurance for Mexico before you leave the United States or add Mexico to your current policy. As a last resort, you can buy a policy from an agency on the U.S. side of the border.

Because of the large number of Mexicans living in the United States, you can actually get from almost any U.S. city to Mexico on a bus if you have far more time than money. Look for postings in Hispanic neighborhoods.

Amtrak train service is available to El Paso and Del Rio in Texas and San Diego, California. At these points you can cross the border on foot and then catch a Mexican bus onward.

Visas: Americans, Canadians, and Europeans receive an automatic visa for Mexico upon arrival and can in most cases stay for 180 days without an extension. Australians can stay for 90 days. Everyone receives a tourist visa card upon entry and must hold on to it until leaving the country. The fee for this is folded into the airline ticket for anyone who arrives by plane. Those who arrive by cruise ship or by land and are staying for less than three days do not pay a fee.

Border crossings: Mexico shares borders with Guatemala and Belize, and it's possible to travel to either one overland. The Belize crossing is in Quintana Roo

State, near Chetumal. There are several crossings into Guatemala in Chiapas and Campeche states.

Currency: The Mexican currency is the peso. It generally trades at between 10 and 11 to the U.S. dollar. Confusingly, prices are marked with the "$" sign, so ask which currency is meant if you are not sure. Otherwise, you could pay $80 for something that is supposed to be $8! Only hotels, tourist excursions, and real estate are routinely priced in dollars.

Currency exchange booths are common in any areas with tourists, and banks change money for similar rates. As in most countries, the worst rates are at the airport, so only exchange a day's worth upon arrival to get you on your way. Taxi drivers will often accept dollars because Mexicans can freely exchange currency. There is no real black market and no advantage to taking the risk of making exchanges outside the official channels. Many Mexican ATMs will allow withdrawals in pesos or dollars.

Departure tax: It varies by airport from $18 to $38 per person, which is included in the air-ticket price.

Weather and when to go: Because of all the different elevations and microclimates in Mexico, it is hard to make generalizations about the country's weather—except that, overall, it's hotter than most of the United States, Europe, and Canada. Summer is the rainy season in most areas.

Some areas are blessed with springtime weather year-round while others routinely top 100°F two or three months a year. In most spots, however, the ideal time to visit is December through March or April, when humidity and temperature are likely to be at their lowest. Just keep in mind that storms from the north can bring down temperatures in a hurry. Cancún tourists may find 80-degree beach weather one day turns into 60 degrees and windy the next. Some weather is not what you'd expect: while the Pacific coast is generally hottest in July and August, May is the hottest month in most other parts of the country.

Hurricanes generally develop from August through November, so keep an eye on weather forecasts. This period carries the greatest risks on the coasts. It can pay to purchase trip-cancellation insurance if going then.

The most moderate temperatures are where the most expatriates have settled: Guadalajara, Morelia, San Miguel de Allende, Lake Chapala and Ajijic, and Oaxaca. See the itinerary sections for specific weather advice, and check local weather reports through the resources listed in Chapter 4, How to Plan Your Trip.

Electricity: Current and outlet shapes are the same as in the United States.

Internet access and telephones: Internet cafes are abundant and cheap. Going online usually costs less than a dollar an hour. Hotels charge far more, of course, though Internet access is often free in locally run boutique hotels and guesthouses, where Wi-Fi may be available. Wi-Fi is not yet very common in bars and coffee shops, however. These are seen as places to socialize, not work.

The telephone system is a state monopoly, so the best option is to buy a Ladatel phone card that can be inserted into card-reading pay phones. The cost to phone the United States is roughly 40 cents per minute. Phone kiosks charge about the same rate. Most Internet cafes offer headsets and have Skype Internet calling installed, so this is your cheapest option if you have a Skype account or are calling another Skype user.

Most U.S. cell phones will work in populated areas, but call your carrier first to make sure and to switch on your roaming capability. Roaming costs can be more than $1 a minute.

Language: Spanish is the primary language in Mexico, spoken by 94 percent of the population. Various dialects descended from the Maya and Aztec languages survive in rural areas. English is taught in schools and is commonly spoken by tourism-industry workers and business executives. Outside tourist areas, however, a Latin American Spanish phrase book will be quite helpful. Those who want to learn a lot of Spanish in a hurry can immerse themselves in a language school for one or two weeks. Programs are available in nearly every city. Please see Chapter 24, Communications.

Safety: In most of Mexico, visitors will feel as safe as or safer than they do at home. In most states, crime is not much of an issue, and physical risks are almost unheard of. Overall, Mexico's crime rates are better than those of the United States in many aspects. According to UN figures, the United States has a higher incidence (per 100,000 people) of murder with a firearm, aggravated assault, rape, and theft.

There are exceptions. Mexico City has a well-deserved reputation for heavy crime. This, combined with terrible pollution, make it a place best visited in moderation for great dining and shopping. Things have improved markedly in recent years, but it's still a place to be extra careful. Its crime statistics are on par with those of Washington, D.C. Pick a hotel in a well-patrolled area (such as Zona Rosa, Paseo de la Reforma, and Polanco). See the Teotihuacán ruins, visit a few museums, and do a bit of shopping and eating—then head elsewhere if you are concerned.

Of the tourist areas, Acapulco has the worst crime problem, chiefly because it's on a major coastal smuggling route for drugs, which has resulted in clashes between authorities and gangs. Only a few incidents have affected tourists, but dozens of police and military personnel have been killed.

The other major hot spots are all along the U.S. border, where drug smuggling and people smuggling attract gang activity and violence. If you plan on driving into Mexico, get through the border zone as quickly as possible, and don't cross at night.

Keep an eye on the news coming out of Mexico while you are making plans. As the 2006 disturbances in Oaxaca and demonstrations in Mexico City showed us, however, political tensions can flare up in a hurry. The key is to be aware of the risks so you can take the proper precautions and then enjoy yourself.

The Pacific coast of Mexico

On a different kind of safety issue, note that wave action on the eastern and Gulf beaches is usually quite calm, but this is not true at some places on the west coast. Both the Baja Peninsula and the west coast of the mainland have many beaches where crushing waves and strong rip currents make them better for surfing than swimming. Check the local situation before diving into the water, especially with children.

Health care: Mexico has some of the best health-care facilities in Latin America. Hospitals and dentists do a booming business in "health tourism," in which U.S. or Canadian residents travel south for elective surgery or dental work for a fraction of what it would cost at home. Many Mexican doctors and dentists were trained in the United States. Prescription prices lure many seniors on shopping trips. In rural areas, clinics can be rudimentary and understaffed, so it pays to have evacuation insurance if you will be in remote areas for an extended time.

In areas where there are a great number of American and Canadian retirees, health-care facilities are above average because demand for good-quality services is high.

Things to buy: Mexico is a shopping paradise, with a wide range of regional handicrafts and a well-developed jewelry industry. It is also one of the kitsch capitals of the world, with enough poorly made junk on sale to fill a few cargo ships. So the real challenge is to separate the high-quality items from the shoddy ones and to ask yourself, "Would I buy this at home? Will I still be happy I bought it a year or two from now?"

Some of the most notable items are specific to a certain region. These include Huichol bead items from natives of the Sierra Madre mountains, Maya masks and carvings from the Yucatán, Day of the Dead items and black pottery from Oaxaca State, items incorporating talavera tile from Puebla, and a wide variety of textiles and crafts from Michoacán state.

We're not sure whether the Museo de las Momias (Museum of the Mummies) in Guanajuato has more mummies than any other museum in the world, but with more than 100 mummified corpses on display, it probably has the record.

Most ethnic clothing from Mexico doesn't wear well at home, but the guayabera shirts made in the Yucatán are an exception.

Shipping items home from Mexico is not easy, fast, or reasonably priced. The postal system is so unreliable that a letter routinely takes a month to arrive, and packages are slower. For anything of value, use a shipping service such as DHL. The best bet is to buy only what you can carry home, but shops are happy to arrange shipping if you fall in love with something large.

Please see Chapter 25, Shopping and Shipping.

Resources

Guidebooks and other references: There's no shortage of guidebook choices for Mexico. Almost every travel publisher offers at least one guide, and most put out three or four regional editions. Here are a few notable books that are not part of a regular guidebook series.

- *The People's Guide to Mexico* is one of my favorite guidebooks ever, covering any region. It's a joy to read and a breath of fresh air.
- *Eat Smart in Mexico* is worth carrying along for every trip to a restaurant or market stall. Lonely Planet also puts out a useful *World Food Mexico* guide.
- *The Treasures and Pleasures of Mexico* is probably the best guide for serious shopping advice.
- Espadaña Press publishes colonial architecture guides to specific locations. See **www.colonial-mexico.com** for a listing.
- *Mexico: Health and Safety Travel Guide* is a thorough resource listing 60 hospitals and 220 physicians in 50 of Mexico's tourism locations. It also contains health advice and pharmaceutical translations.
- *The Unofficial Guide to Mexico's Best Beach Resorts* is the best resource for researching beach hotels.

There are specialized Mexico guides to traveling by RV, hiking, diving, kayaking, and many other activities: search **www.amazon.com**.

More than a dozen guides address moving to or retiring in Mexico. These include *Head for Mexico, The Plain Truth about Living in Mexico, Choose Mexico*

City Hall in Mérida, Mexico

for Retirement, Live Better South of the Border in Mexico, and *Living Abroad in Mexico.* The best for figuring out the culture and the importance of certain language elements is *There's a Word for It in Mexico.*

The People's Guide to Mexico and *The Rough Guide to Mexico* contain extensive lists of novels and historical-fiction books set in Mexico. Some popular favorites include Graham Greene's *The Power and the Glory,* Malcolm Lowry's *Under the Volcano,* James Michener's *Mexico,* B. Traven's *The Treasure of the Sierra Madre,* Juan Rulfo's *Pedro Páramo,* and Carlos Fuentes's *The Death of Artemio Cruz.* Good anthologies include *Travelers' Tales Mexico* and *Mexico: A Traveler's Literary Companion.*

Web sites: The official Mexico tourism site is **www.visitmexico.com** (with links to official sites for state and city tourism organizations).

- The People's Guide to Mexico (**www.peoples guide.com**) is an extension of the irreverent and highly recommended book of the same name.
- Mexico Connect (**www.mexconnect.com**) is a subscription-based site ($30 per year) that has been online since 1996. It is probably the most thorough resource on the Internet for info about traveling or living in Mexico.

The birth-control pill got its start in a lab in Mexico City: the steroid was synthesized from Mexican yams.

- MEXonline (**www.mexonline.com**) is one of the most popular and comprehensive guides to the country.
- Moving to Mexico? See **www.mexpatriate.net**.
- Our Mexico (**www.ourmexico.com**) has lots of stories, news, and links.
- Travelers Guide to Mexico is an online guidebook: **www.travelguidemexico.com**.
- Gay Mexico (**www.gaymexico.com.mx**) covers the scene in different locales.
- Mexico Boutique Hotels (**www.mexicoboutiquehotels.com**) and Luxury Latin America (**www.luxurylatinamerica.com**) are the best sites for detailed information on upscale lodging.

Retirement Opportunities

Depending on who is doing the estimating, between 150,000 and 400,000 Americans, some 25 percent of all U.S. expatriates, live full time in Mexico. It's possible that the exodus of retirees to Mexico in coming years will rival earlier migrations to Florida and Arizona. Retirees are lured by an attractive climate, a lower cost of living, a less stressful life, and less expensive medical care.

Foreigners can buy property free and clear in Mexico, though near the coasts there is a land trust arrangement that effectively turns the purchase into something more akin to a lifelong lease that can be sold or passed on to heirs.

Mexico has never offered incentives to get retirees to move there because it doesn't need to. However, in a recent move the government extended to foreigners all the benefits it offers to Mexican senior citizens. That's a big deal.

Some of the most popular areas for retirees are San Miguel de Allende (where there are as many as 40,000), Lake Chapala in Jalisco, Guanajuato, Puerto Vallarta, Guadalajara, Mérida, and several spots on the Baja Peninsula. There are plenty of other possibilities, however, for anyone looking for a less expensive place in the sun.

Helping Out

Just about every aid and charity organization has a presence in Mexico, so anyone wishing to lend a hand or donate to a good cause won't have to look far. Groups organized and funded locally in a specific location in Mexico are likely to have lower overhead than large international operations. Use Charity Navigator (**www.charitynavigator.org**) to see how much of an organization's funds go to field work rather than administration and fund-raising.

If interested in volunteering, check the "Volunteer Work Abroad" section of the *Transitions Abroad* Web site (**www.transitionsabroad.com**) or get downloadable listings of who operates in Mexico at the Directory of Development Organizations (**www.devdir.org**). Opportunities include rural building and ecology projects, positions teaching English, medical and dental aid programs, and ocean conservation projects.

BELIZE

Belize is defined by the Caribbean Sea, inland jungles, and an incredibly laid-back atmosphere. The coral reef offshore, second in length only to Australia's Great Barrier Reef, is a magnet for scuba divers and snorkelers. Add to that a string of unspoiled atolls plus two islands whose small towns are ideal for relaxation, and you have a Caribbean paradise.

The country's wild and rugged interior will please the most intrepid hiker, especially as elevation rises toward the borders of Guatemala and the Yucatán Peninsula. Whether traveling independently or with a group, you'll find hundreds of bird species along with tapirs, howler monkeys, and even the elusive jaguar.

What you won't find are strings of high-rise resorts or the all-inclusive enclaves that exist like self-contained spaceships at far too many destinations. Instead, there's human-scale lodging and a leisurely pace that offers time to observe and enjoy. Topography and history make Belize more attuned to the Caribbean lifestyle than any other country in Central America.

You might hear eight different languages if you travel around the country, but English rules. That's because Belize was once a British colony—British Honduras—until it gained independence in 1981. Belize is the only country in Central America where you needn't know a single word of Spanish.

Combine easy access, friendly people, and good food and music, and it's no wonder visitors leave saying, "What a great place. Let's come back here."

Belize, a favorite of diving pioneer Jacques Cousteau, has grown into a major diving and snorkeling destination. The long coral reef, stretching all the way down to Honduras, has hundreds of good diving spots, but many visitors come specifically to dive the Blue Hole, a giant collapsed cavern that drops more than 400 feet into the sea bed. This spot doesn't have the teeming underwater life of the reef and atolls, but it is popular for its spooky rock and coral formations.

In addition to almost 350 miles of reefs to explore, there are some 200 islands scattered along the coast (plus a few more that are barely large enough to stand on). The two that have a wide range of tourist facilities are Ambergris Caye and Caye Caulker, though others offer a single dive lodge, sometimes even an upscale hotel.

Belize has done a much better job than most Caribbean islands in preserving its marine assets and keeping dive tourism from becoming destructive, though it is treading a delicate line as the number of visitors rises. All the reef areas are designated as protected marine reserves.

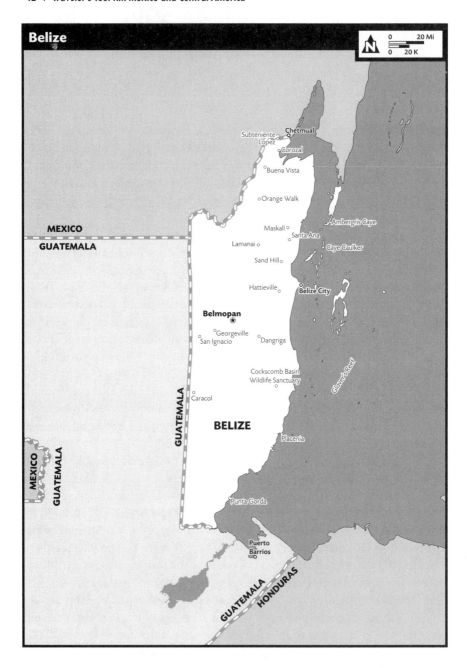

This is also a prime sportfishing destination. Fishermen and -women from around the world seek tarpon, barracuda, sailfish, and marlin, and hang out in remote, rustic hotels set up as fishing lodges long before the popularity of scuba diving. Two very different types of fishing experiences are offered: over and around the reefs, and farther out in the deep sea. Everyone, novice to expert, is thrilled by the number and variety of the fish.

Sparsely populated Belize, the size of Massachusetts, has fewer than 300,000 permanent residents. It welcomes close to 1 million tourists a year, most of them cruise-ship passengers who disembark at Belize City for the day and then move on. It is still quite easy to avoid the crowds, though, because more than half of the other tourists go to either Ambergris Caye or Caye Caulker.

> Ambergris Caye is named after a substance produced in a sperm whale's intestines. Pirates harvested it after it washed up on shore, selling the waxy, flammable substance in Europe, where it was used to make perfume.

Many travelers visit Belize as part of a multicountry overland tour. It's only a few hours south of Cancún and Tulum in Mexico. You can leave Belize City in the morning and be in Guatemala or Honduras in time for dinner. It's a popular stop on "Ruta Maya" tours that visit the string of Maya ruins from Mexico through Central America.

There are two drawbacks to Belize. First, it's no great bargain in terms of prices. For a variety of reasons, including stiff trade barriers, Belize is more than twice as expensive as Guatemala and costlier than Mexico next door. This is especially noticeable at the middle of the budget range, where finding memorable mid-range hotels can be a challenge. Second, this is not the best destination for beach bumming or golfing. Most of Belize's beaches are underwhelming, and there's only one (isolated and expensive) full 18-hole golf course. Come here instead to explore the reefs, take in nature, see some ruins, and leave feeling mellow.

Belize's People

The people of Belize are a mix of cultures and have far more diversity than those of any other Central American country. The population has always been so diverse that there's little racial intolerance. One of the most distinctive cultures is that of the Garifuna people, descendents of Africans who arrived from elsewhere in the Caribbean beginning more than 200 years ago. Some also were brought as slaves by the British. Then there are the descendants of the Maya, and descendants of the original British settlers. There's even a large contingent of Mennonites from Canada.

Basic education is compulsory, and there's a solid university system. The government is relatively democratic and stable, but because distribution of wealth is as lopsided as in the rest of Central America, there's a deep-seated cynicism about politicians (but not the kind of anger that leads to protests).

Most of the people of Belize are Christian, with the Catholic Church holding almost as much sway as in the Spanish colonial countries. There are many Protestants, however, including several thousand Mennonites. (See "The Mennonites of Belize" later in this chapter.)

Industry is limited, so much of the population has historically made its living from farming, fishing, or providing services. With tourism growing a bit each year, hotels, restaurants, and tour companies have become major employers.

Highlights

- The main attraction is the huge **barrier reef** running along the country's whole shoreline. It's a UNESCO World Heritage site and a big draw for divers from around the world. Snorkelers have a fine time without the need for training and diving gear. The water is amazingly clear, and with some 600 species of fish, shellfish, and other marine life, there's plenty to see.
- By the laid-back standards in Belize, **Ambergris Caye** is close to touristy but still pretty mellow. To get around the island, most people walk, use a one-gear bike, or ride a golf cart. Even the more upscale hotels are low-rise with plenty of elbow room, and there are dozens of unpretentious inns along the shore. The closest any establishment comes to a dress code is a meek request to "please wear shoes." The typical day is spent swimming, diving, snorkeling, or lying in a hammock resting up for enjoying a fine meal and dancing the night away.
- When Ambergris Caye got a little pricey for backpackers, they moved to the smaller **Caye Caulker,** where prices are lower and the pace is even slower. Visitors tend to stay longer, get to know local folk, find a favorite beer (maybe Belikin) and band, and hang out. A zillion books have been read and more than a few written on its shores. For trading stories about Central America, this is the place.

> Belize and the United States are among the handful of countries that never switched to the metric system. Distances are measured in miles, gasoline is dispensed in gallons, and produce is weighed by the pound.

- The interior **jungle and highlands** are home to hundreds of native and migratory bird species, from waterfowl in the marshes to colorful macaws and toucans in the trees. Based in a well-run jungle lodge or riverside cabin, travelers enjoy guided hikes, canoe trips, bird-watching excursions, horseback riding, tubing, kayaking, visits to Maya ruins—and more.
- The Cockscomb Basin Wildlife Sanctuary is the world's only **jaguar preserve.** Hikes range from a few hours to a circuit that takes four days. Even if you don't see one of the elusive jaguars, there are plenty of other creatures about, many near the park headquarters.
- Belize musicians crank out some of the best **music** between Mexico and Brazil. Catch Garifuna shows and jam sessions on the coast to hear some lilting, percussive music that's a mix of influences from the Caribbean

and West Africa. To get a taste in advance, listen to Andy Palacio's album *Wátina*. Palacio and most other notable musicians are known for the native "punta rock" music, which is a steamy dance-hall mix of traditional Garifuna percussion and modern electronic gadgetry.

- While the **Maya ruins** don't get the same attention as their spectacular counterparts in neighboring countries, they are interesting in their own right and have the extra benefit of being less crowded. Lamanai ("submerged crocodile") is an impressive site that can be reached by riverboat through the jungle. A well-done visitor center and special exhibits dedicated to the most intact excavations help piece it all together. The Lamanai Field Research Center (**www.lamanai.org**) works with many universities to continue conservation, archaeology and other scientific study in the area. Caracol was the largest Maya city in Belize, covering 70 square miles at its peak in the middle seventh century. This vast site had a population of more than 140,000—about half that of the whole country of Belize today. For a while, it was the major challenger to Tikal for supremacy in the Maya empire. Its 138-foot tall "sky house" is still the tallest structure in the country. The thick jungle surrounding it makes for great bird-watching.

- Both **river and sea kayaking** are available. River-kayaking trips are generally along the Mopan River, with Class I to III rapids and a tour of the Xunantunich Maya ruins or waterfalls and jungle. Sea-kayaking trips explore islands, reefs, and mangrove coasts. Several North American outfitters offer comprehensive trips you can book from home, either based in one spot or going island to island and stringing up hammocks or camping. We can't endorse a particular outfitter but have heard good things about several: G.A.P Adventures (**www.gapadventures.com/tour/BKS**), Island Expeditions (**www.islandexpeditions.com**), Toadal Adventure (**www .toadaladventure.com**), Adventure Life (**www.adventure-life.com**), and Slickrock Adventures (**www.slickrock.com**). Adventure Life, based in Placencia, offers a six-day package. Island Expeditions also offers rentals for independent paddlers.

- For those who want to explore a waterway without paddling, Belize offers a great solution: **river tubing.** Sit in an inner tube, float down a river, and watch the scenery roll by. There are plenty of places to tube in Belize, but the most interesting is the Caves Branch River near Belmopan. As the river goes through caves, the scenery switches between indoor and outdoor. The best time to do this, and many other inland activities, is February through April, when the weather is dry. (See the "Weather and When to Go" section on page 55 for details.) See the Web sites listed in the "Resources" section of this chapter for more on tubing and spelunking (cave exploration).

Casual dining in Caye Caulker, Belize

- If you're up for a sweaty hike and a swim through a lake in a cave, you'll get to see 14 skeletons from sacrifices to the Maya gods at **Actun Tunichil Muknal** (often shortened to "ATM") cave. Oh, and there are hundreds of shards lying around, where a lot of pottery was placed in the ninth century in an appeal to the rain god to end a long drought.
- **Sailing trips** for anything from an afternoon to two weeks can be arranged through captains in Belize City, Placencia, or Caye Caulker. Ask at the marina or your hotel, or book through a tour or travel company with good contacts. For advance arrangements, consider Belize Charters (**www .belizecharters.com**), Belize Sailing Charters (**www.belize-sailing-charters .com**), or Under the Sun (**www.underthesunbelize.com**).
- For divers, **Glover's Reef** offers drop-offs as dramatic as those at the Blue Hole, but without any closed-in feeling. The reef sits on top of an underwater mountain range and quickly drops to depths of as much as 2,600 feet. Six islands in the area have basic lodges for divers and snorkelers.
- While Ambergris Caye and Caye Caulker are popular island vacation areas, they're better suited for diving and snorkeling than enjoying a beach. For a real **beach experience,** head to Placencia, farther south. It's close to atolls but also has the best stretches of sand and some great live-music venues.
- A trip to **Honduras** or neighboring **Guatemala** is easy to arrange from Belize. The Tikal Maya ruins in Guatemala are only a few hours from the Cayo jungle of western Belize. From the south of the country, a ferry

takes you to Livingston, Guatemala. From there, you can take a river trip up the Río Dulce and eventually on to another great Maya site, Copán, in Honduras. Several companies run chartered boat trips between Dangriga Belize and Puerto Cortes, Honduras.

Itineraries

If You Have a Week in Belize

Option 1: Base yourself on Ambergris Caye or Caye Caulker for a few days, then stay in a jungle or river lodge. Hike the rain forests, go tubing, or take a riverboat excursion. Take a side trip to one of the Maya sites.

Option 2: Stay on the coast, splitting your time among Ambergris Caye, Caye Caulker, and Placencia. A few hours' rides or quick prop-plane hops separate the three. Snorkel or dive the nearby reefs and check out the manatees. Spend an afternoon exploring Belize City—with a population of 65,000, it's more like a town—exploring the harbor and taking a side trip to the excellent zoo. For a splurge, visit a more remote island with a single lodge, such as Lighthouse Reef (Lighthouse Reef Resort, **www.scubabelize.com**) or Caye Chapel Island (Caye Chapel Island Resort, **www.cayechapel.com**).

If You Have Two Weeks or More in Belize

In two weeks, you can cover much of the country without rushing. The classic two-week vacation involves a week of diving or snorkeling with island hopping, combined with a week experiencing the interior—jungles, rivers, and ruins.

You can easily fit in a trip by bus or plane to the great Maya ruins of Tikal (in Guatemala), either from one of the northern cities or from one of the jungle lodges. From the latter, Tikal is less than four hours by bus. Spend a couple of nights at or near Tikal to fully experience the area. A trip by boat to the Garifuna town of Livingston (in Guatemala) or parts of Honduras is also easy to fit into a two-week itinerary. You take a boat for three hours from Punta Gorda in Belize to Livingston, where the Río Dulce flows over a sandbar into the sea. From there, it is easy to arrange trips by boat up the river into the jungle or by bus to other points in Guatemala. For Honduras, you take a boat to Puerto Barrios, Guatemala, go by bus or taxi to the Honduran border, and then proceed to Copán or elsewhere.

Cost Comparisons

The following are representative costs across Belize and do not include places where prices are inflated, such as deluxe hotels and fine-dining establishments. In general, expect to pay more—even double—on Ambergris Caye, especially for meals.

The Mennonites of Belize

The conservative Mennonites of Belize, originally from the Netherlands, settled in and moved out of several countries before being welcomed by Belize in the mid–20th century. The country badly needed skilled farmers, and the settlers from this religious group now supply nearly all of the country's eggs, cheese, and chicken, some of its produce, and quite a bit of its furniture. The settlers have split into several sects, partly defined by how they view the use of technology. Some communities are open to visitors: try the Spanish Lookout Village area near San Ignacio or Blue Creek near Orange Walk, both in the northern half of the country. Ask before snapping any photos, because many strict Mennonites object to photographs.

- Liter of water in a convenience store: 30–60 cents
- Bottle of beer in a bar or restaurant: $1.50–$2.50
- Bottle of beer in a store: 65 cents–$1
- Meal of the day in a locals' restaurant: $3 (rice and beans)–$8 (meal with meat or fish)
- Half kilo of oranges, in season: $1.25
- 1 hour of Internet access in a cafe: $3–$4
- Cup of coffee, juice, or soda in a restaurant: 40–80 cents
- 10-minute taxi ride across town: $3–$5
- Taxi from airport to hotel: $5 (Municipal Airport)–$20 (International Airport)
- 3-star or equivalent hotel: $60–$150.

Accommodations

Anyone expecting the bare-bones, cheapie hotels common in Guatemala and Honduras will be disappointed in Belize. Lodging can also seem overpriced compared to Mexico's offerings. The quality is consistently good, though, featuring clapboard inns rather than standard concrete-block construction. As long as you go with the flow and don't expect ultraefficient service, your stay will probably be memorable.

Most accommodations in Belize are rustic wood structures designed to take advantage of sea or mountain breezes. Even in the cheaper hotels, you'll usually have a private bath. Try the Toucan Trail Web site (**www.toucantrail.com**) for a listing of more than 100 simple hotels that cost $60 or less per night. Finding one for less than $30 can be trying. Midrange hotels with more amenities run from $65 to $150. The largest concentration of lower-priced hotels is on Caye Caulker, where nothing tops $150 per night (yet), and many are still less than $50 per night.

Special Hotels in Belize

Belize has some of the top hotels and resorts between Mexico and Costa Rica, including two owned by legendary movie producer, director and wine-maker Francis Ford Coppola. For a special splurge, check into these options: Blancaneaux Lodge (one of Coppola's; **www.blancaneaux.com**), Caye Chapel Island Resort (**www.belizegolf.cc**), Cayo Espanto (**www.aprivateisland.com**), Chan Chich Lodge (**www.chanchich.com**), the Inn at Robert's Grove (**www.robertsgrove.com**), the Lodge at Chaa Creek (**www.chaacreek.com**), Turtle Inn (Coppola's other inn; **www.turtleinn.com**), or Victoria House (**www.victoria-house.com**). For detailed reviews on these and others, see Luxury Latin America (**www.luxurylatinamerica.com**).

You have to spend more than $200 a night to get impressive service and facilities: the equivalent of a four- or five-star hotel. It is not uncommon to see hotels on Ambergris Caye listed at $300 or more (room only) in high season. At this level, it can make sense to book an air-and-hotel package, which typically runs $1,400 to $2,500 per person for a week, including transfers between Belize City and Ambergris Caye and transportation to a jungle lodge, if applicable.

The top-end hotels do go all out, however, and can be worth a splurge. Just realize that a splurge will cost more than one in neighboring countries: Cayo Espanto, on its own island (**www.aprivateisland.com**), lists regular rates starting at $1,695 per night—though that does include meals and drinks.

At jungle lodges such as Blancaneaux (**www.blancaneaux.com**) and Chan Chich (**www.chanchich.com**), you have miles of protected wilderness to explore: an amazing 192,000 acres of protected parkland at the former and 130,000 acres at the latter. All of them, including less pricey options, offer a wide range of guided tours and excursions, including canoeing, jungle hikes, horseback riding, and trips to Maya ruins. These are an especially good bet for families. Rates start at about $150 double in high season for a midrange jungle lodge and can reach four digits with an excursion package and a family-size villa at Blancaneaux or Chan Chich. The busiest tourist seasons in Belize are around Christmas and Easter. During these times, expect to pay the top of the rate scale. Otherwise, most hotels charge a high-season price from December through April or May, then a low-season price the rest of the year. Some hotels, especially in the interior, may close for part of the year.

Besides the Toucan Trail site, other Web sites in the "Resources" section of this chapter can connect you to hotels.

Scuba divers catch sight of the largest fish in the world—the whale shark—in waters off Belize from March through late May. Reaching 55 feet long, they're hard to miss but are no threat to swimmers.

Food and Drink

Belizean cuisine has not had much of an identity. Most everything was borrowed from somewhere else, such as jerk chicken, conch fritters, empanadas, and tamales. The positive side is that you are pretty much assured of finding food you like. Immigrants from Hong Kong have set up Chinese restaurants, Mexican dishes are common, and there's no shortage of pizza places. English or American breakfasts are served wherever travelers roam.

For locals, the most popular dish is beans and rice. The second most popular is rice and beans. Yes, they're different: in the latter, the beans are cooked separately, sometimes in a stew with meat, and then spooned onto the rice. Fortunately, an ample supply of coconuts, cashews, and seafood means it doesn't take much effort to get beyond the monotony.

If you like seafood, you'll have plenty to choose from. Try Creole-style fish with peppers, onions, and tomatoes. Conch and lobster are very popular. Meat dishes range from standard chicken fare to entrées featuring deer or guinea pig. Most dishes are not spicy, but hot sauce is always on the table to liven things up.

Restaurants range from simple hole-in-the-wall places where you can get a filling lunch for $5 to $8 to gourmet outposts that can top $100 per person. A typical restaurant dinner will run $15 to $25 per person on Ambergris Caye, a bit less on Caye Caulker. Imported ingredients are expensive, so if you are camping or staying in a place with a kitchen, buy locally produced goods. Tortillas, rice, beans, and local vegetables in season are less than $1 a pound.

Vegetarians have an easy time in tourist areas but need to make their preferences known elsewhere, as meat is often used as a flavoring even when it's not

---

Holidays and Festivals

- December 31–Jan. 1: New Year holiday
- January 6: Day of the Three Kings (family celebrations)
- March or April: *Semana Santa* (Holy Week, Easter)
- May 1: Labor Day
- May 2–3: Day of the Cross at Lake Atitlán
- June 30: Army Day
- July 25: Town fair in Antigua
- July 27: *Rabin Ajau* beauty pageant festival in Cobán
- August 15: Assumption Day
- September 15: Independence Day (largest fair is in Quetzaltenango)
- October 12: Discovery of America Day
- October 20: Revolution Day
- November 1 and 2: All Saints' Day and All Souls' Day
- December 14–21: Town fair in Chichicastenango
- December 25: Christmas

listed. Safe choices include spinach and cheese tamales and the wonderful varieties of bread, including coconut, pumpkin, and banana.

Cashews are native to Belize and are a key part of the economy, but they aren't always easy to find. Fried plantain chips are an inexpensive snack.

Dining hours are more American than European: lunch is commonly served between noon and 1 p.m., and dinner starts about 6 to 6:30.

The local beer, Belikin, won't win any awards, but it does the trick on a hot day. There's a stout version if you're looking for more body. Belize has four rum distilleries, so rum cocktails are popular and reasonably priced. With high import duties, wine is a luxury. Interesting local alcoholic drinks include the fruit liqueur Nance and cashew wine—made from the fruit of the cashew tree rather than the nut.

> Each March, a few foreigners enter La Ruta Maya Belize River Challenge, a four-day, 170-mile canoe race along the Macal and Belize rivers from San Ignacio to Belize City. See **www .larutamaya belize.com.**

Belize has a wonderful variety of fruit, so mango, lime, and watermelon juices are a good option. The coffee is disappointing outside the tourist zones.

Transportation

An ever-changing cast of **bus companies** plies the roads of Belize. This is how most of the population gets around. The lowest fare class uses converted school buses that make lots and lots of stops. Pay a few dollars more for an express bus that's less crowded and will get you there faster.

Sample bus routes and costs (highest class available):

City 1	City 2	Travel Time	Cost
Belize City	Punta Gorda	7 hours	$14
Belize City	San Ignacio	2.5 hours	$5.50
Belize City	Corozal	3 hours	$6
Belize City	Belmopan	1.25 hours	$4
Belize City	Flores (Guatemala)	5 hours	$22
Belize City	Chetumal (Mexico)	3 hours	$10
Placencia	Dangriga	2 hour	$5

Some private **shuttle services** are cheaper than a taxi but faster than buses. For instance, the San Ignacio Shuttle makes three trips every day between San Ignacio (in the Cayo District) and the Belize City International Airport. This two-and-a-half-hour drive costs $32.50 U.S. per person and can be booked in advance.

Internal flights save a lot of time and are reasonably priced. A flight from Belize City to Placencia costs in the neighborhood of $70. A flight to Caye

Caulker is only $30 from Belize City. Flying to Flores, Guatemala, is about $105 before taxes. Contact Tropic Air (**www.tropicair.com**) and Maya Island Air (**www.mayaislandair.com**) for schedules and current prices.

Belize has no passenger **train service.**

Taxis in Belize do not have meters, so you must work out the fare before starting off. Prices are relatively standardized, so ask around to find out how much a trip should cost.

> The Community Baboon Center west of Belize City has not one baboon. It's a howler monkey conservation center.

To reach Ambergris Caye without flying, you take a **water taxi.** The fare from Belize City to San Pedro on Ambergris Caye is $10. Other water taxis head to Caye Caulker ($7.50) and farther afield.

Renting a car in Belize is expensive, even by Central American standards. Expect to pay at least $70 a day with insurance for a basic vehicle without air-conditioning. To get a solid vehicle that will seat four comfortably, $100 a day is not uncommon. In most cases, you're better off using public transportation. The main exception would be for a day of sightseeing around Belize City. In one day, it would be relatively easy to visit the Belize Zoo, the ruins of Xunantunich and Cahal Pech, and another stop or two in the San Ignacio region. With four or even two people sharing, this would cost less money (with more control) than an organized excursion tour.

Most rental-car companies in Belize will not allow you to take a car into another country, so if you're planning a multicountry trip by rental car, it's best to start in Mexico or to ask around to find a local shop with liberal policies. Be prepared to leave a hefty deposit.

Visitors can **drive** into Belize from Guatemala or Mexico with the following on hand:

- Travel documents and identification
- Proof of ownership (vehicle registration)
- Proof of insurance (Belize insurance available from any of the companies at the borders)
- Rental documents (for rental vehicles)

> The jabiru stork, the largest flying bird in the Americas, stands five feet tall and has a wingspan of 12 feet. The best place to catch sight of them is in Crooked Tree Wildlife Sanctuary in April or May.

Activity Costs

All prices are per person.

- Day-long trip to Lamanai ruins, with lunch, from Ambergris Caye: $150
- Snorkeling boat trip from Ambergris Caye to Bacalar Chico National Park and Marine Reserve: $80–$100, including lunch
- Chartering a fishing boat and captain for the day: $200–$400, depending on size and distance
- Organized half-day fishing tour: $450–$800 for a group
- Renting snorkel mask and fins: $5–$15
- PADI open-water scuba certification course: $350 (plus lodging)
- Diving trip with gear rental: $90–$200 per day
- 1-day whitewater kayaking trip on the Mopan River: $95 from Belize City
- Half-day sailing tour: $60–$100 self-piloted, $120–$200 with a captain. Expect to pay thousands of dollars for a weeklong sailing trip with a captain and cook.
- Day-long jungle tour trip from Belize City to Crooked Tree Wildlife Sanctuary: $100–$140, including short flights. Guided local tour from a lodge: $20–$50
- Self-guided kayaks: free (at some hotels)–$10 an hour. Guided all-day trips with an itinerary: $40–$100, usually including lunch
- Tubing trip on Caves Branch River: $150–$200 on an organized tour booked from Ambergris Caye, less than $40 if you arrange it on your own and take public transportation
- Cave tubing trip to Actun Tunichil Muknal: about $100 from operators in Cayo
- Day trip to Tikal: more than $300 by plane from Ambergris Caye or less than $50 by bus from western Belize. A better bet is to take a bus to Flores, Guatemala, and spend a night or two there, exploring Tikal at a more leisurely pace.

Tour Companies

What you plan to do in Belize has a lot to do with the kind of tour company you choose. This is not a "go see the sights" destination: most visitors come for diving

---

Live-aboard Dive Boats

The best way to get to a wide variety of underwater sites in Belize is on a dive boat. Because the barrier reef is so long, it can be quite a trip getting to various locations from a hotel. To avoid transit time, many divers choose live-aboard boats, sleeping and eating on the vessel. That allows time for more dives, including night dives. Trips run from two to five days, and beginners can arrange certification trips.

Companies offering live-aboard Boats in Belize include:

- Nekton Diving Cruises (**www.nektoncruises.com**)
- Aggressor Fleet (**www.aggressor.com**)
- Peter Hughes Diving (**www.peterhughes.com**)

---

trips, jungle trips, or a combination of the two. If you're a diver and you've used a certain dive company elsewhere, odds are it is active here as well. See "Live-aboard Dive Boats" above for info on these options.

Some of the operators we list in Chapter 6, The Organized Tour, run trips to Belize. For tour operators based in Belize, with links, start with these listings: **www.belizenet.com/touropix.shtml.**

Mayawalk Tours (**www.mayawalk.com**) is one of the few companies authorized to take visitors into the Actun Tunichil Muknal cave.

Island Expeditions (**www.islandexpeditions.com**) has been running Belize adventure trips since the 1980s and offers multiday kayaking trips.

Action Belize (**www.actionbelize.com**) is known for its fishing trips and yacht charters.

Discovery Expeditions (**www.discoverybelize.com**) has an office in San Pedro on Ambergris Caye and sets up a lot of custom tours.

All the jungle lodges, including Chaa Creek (**www.chaacreek.com**) and Maya Mountain Lodge (**www.mayamountain.com**), offer a long list of soft and hard-core outdoor adventures.

Useful Details

Getting there and away: Daily air connections go through Houston (on Continental) and Miami (on American). Other flights arrive via Delta, US Airways, and TACA. Many travelers combine Belize with a trip to the Yucatán in Mexico—flying into Cancún—or arrive overland from Tikal and Flores in Guatemala.

Visas: Most nationalities arriving in Belize receive automatic approval to stay for up to 30 days, which can be extended six months for $25.

Border crossings: It is simple to cross to or from Mexico near Chetumal, Mexico, or to or from Guatemala on the road from Flores and Tikal. In the far south, another road connects with Modesto Méndez, Guatemala. Ferries from Punta Gorda run scheduled trips to Livingston and Puerto Barrios in Guatemala.

Currency: The Belize dollar is generally stable at a rate of two to the U.S. dollar. Because ATMs are not common in many parts of Belize, carry more cash or traveler's checks than usual. Buying with a credit card will often result in a 5 percent premium. Pickpockets prowl Belize City and elsewhere, so use a money belt, and be generally cautious. (See Chapter 17, Safety and Security.)

Departure tax: It's $35 when flying out (often included in your ticket), $18.75 when departing by land, and $3.75 when departing by boat. Part of this is a conservation fee, so at least some of it goes into protecting the environment.

Weather and when to go: The prime time is January through May, when the weather is dry and it's not oppressively hot. Although it's a subtropical area, temperatures can dip to 50°F at night in December and January on the coast and below that in the mountains. Daytime highs vary by only about 10 degrees throughout the year, from the high 70s to high 80s.

There's not a clear "shoulder season," but the best value is probably April through June along the coast. The winter escapees from up north have stopped coming, and summer vacationers haven't gone into high gear. Also, this is the time when underwater visibility is at its best. On the flip side, it's a dry and dusty time to visit the interior. If that's your main destination, you're better off visiting December through March, when everything is lush and green after the rainy season.

Temperatures stay in the 80s on the coast in most of the summer and humidity is at its highest, but many people still visit then, and all facilities are open. Peak hurricane season is considered to be August through November, so keep an eye on forecasts if planning a trip then. Rain and insects are at their peak September through November. Jungle trips at that time can be difficult, and roads can get washed out.

Electricity: Voltage and outlet shapes are the same as in the United States and Canada.

Internet access and telephones: Broadband access is available most places where tourists congregate, usually at $3–$4 per hour. Wi-Fi is just starting to show up, even in high-end hotels.

The phone system has gone from terrible to decent in recent years. Pay phones use a PIN-style calling card that is available in most shops. International calls will run 40 cents or more per minute, so stay in touch with e-mail or Internet

Nature under Threat

Belize took a dramatic drop in the last *National Geographic Traveler* steward-ship survey, in late 2006. The survey is meant to measure the perceived health of UNESCO World Heritage sites. The survey found deteriorating conditions at the reef and along the coasts, partly because of the government's temptation to embrace mass tourism. Larger resorts, increased building, and more frequent cruise-ship visits are all taking their toll. To do your part to lessen the impact, follow the advice outlined in *Traveler's Tool Kit* and help show local people that sustainable, low-impact tourism pays off.

phones when you find them. Sending a postcard home to the United States or Canada costs a very reasonable 20 cents.

Language: English is the language.

Safety: Belize has a reputation as one of the safest countries in Central America, and Belmopan is by far the safest capital city in the region. Most of the crime occurs in Belize City. Exercise normal caution with your valuables, of course, but attacks on tourists are rare. Most people feel safer in Belize than in the United States.

Health care: There are no serious epidemic diseases in Belize and no unusual health threats, but antimalaria tablets may be needed for an extended stay in the jungle.

You can drink the water safely in much of Belize, though drinking purified water is still a good idea. It's widely available in shops, hotels and restaurants.

The only major hospitals are in Belize City, Belmopan, and San Ignacio. Having evacuation insurance isn't a bad idea, as it could get you airlifted to better facilities in Mexico or the United States. Prescription medicines are no bargain in Belize, so bring what you need. Routine medical treatment is cheap: an office visit with a physician costs $25–$40, and a teeth cleaning by a dentist will be $35–$45.

Things to buy: Belize is not a shopper's paradise unless you want the ubiquitous T-shirts and beach souvenirs found the world over. Even when you find authentic, high-quality crafts, they're twice as expensive as similar items in Mexico or Guatemala. One exception worth purchasing: fine, handmade Garifuna drums.

Resources

Guidebooks include the usual publishers, such as Lonely Planet, Rough Guides, Frommer's, and the like. Check the publishing date, because many publishers go years between editions. The Fodor's guide is updated annually, and *Moon Handbooks Belize* was updated in 2007. Both are written by authors who know the country well and have covered it for years, so either is a good bet.

Understanding Belize: A Historical Guide and *Belize: A Concise History* are good for those who want deeper understanding of the country's history.

Several guides to diving and snorkeling in Belize come out on sporadic schedules. Again, check the publication date.

Internet resources on Belize are very helpful:

The official tourism site is **www.travelbelize.org.** It maintains an excellent list of affordable, independent lodging choices at its Toucan Trail link (**www.toucan trail.com**).

The Belize Hotel Association (**www.belizehotels.org**) lists its member hotels and resorts.

Belize First (**www.belizefirst.com**) is run by the author of several books on Belize and is an in-depth guide to the country.

Belize Forum (**www.belizeforum.com**) is a message board with discussions about different topics.

Belize Journeys (**www.belizejourneys.com**) has articles about Belize that are more in-depth than what you find in mainstream travel publications.

Belize by Naturalight (**www.belizenet.com**) is a good basic portal with varied resources.

Belize News (**www.belizenews.net**) has links to all local media outlets.

> The Thousand Foot Falls, which are actually 1,600 feet, are the highest in Central America. The volume of falling water is even greater at nearby Big Rock Falls. Both are near the upscale Blancaneaux Lodge.

For Placencia information and accommodations, see **www.placencia.com**.

The *San Pedro Sun* newspaper on Ambergris Caye maintains an online version at **www.sanpedrosun.net**.

Retirement Opportunities

Belize doesn't get much press as a retirement destination, but it receives a steady stream of expatriates. Its "live and let live" atmosphere is attractive, as is the use of English as the dominant language. The legal system is English-based as well.

Belize City is only a two-hour flight from Miami and a two-and-a-half-hour flight from Houston. Thus, while medical care is good in Belize, an emergency trip to the States isn't a major ordeal.

If you are 45 or older and place $2,000 a month in a Belize bank, you qualify for duty-free importation of goods (including a car or boat) and pay no income tax. You can't legally work for someone else, but you can open your own business and do what you want with the income.

The most current guidebook to making a new home in the country is *Living Abroad in Belize,* available from Moon Handbooks. *International Living*

> **Bliss from a Baron**
>
> Henry Edward Ernest Victor Bliss spent several months cruising around the waters of Belize (then British Honduras) on his yacht in 1926 after suffering food poisoning contracted in Trinidad. The British businessman with a Portuguese title fished, explored, and soaked in the beauty of the coast while trying to recuperate. He never fully recovered and died in March 1926 without ever setting foot ashore. Nevertheless, he'd somehow been so impressed by the country that he left a trust fund of more than 1.3 million Belize dollars, a vast sum at the time, for its people. The compounding fund continues to finance public projects. The date of his death is a national holiday.

(**www.internationalliving.com**) and EscapeArtist (**www.escapeartist.com**) both advertise e-book reports that can be helpful for those considering life in the tropics.

Helping Out

Those who take an interest in the environment and ecological balance will find plenty of worthy organizations in Belize that could use some help. Many large environmental organizations work here, but also consider donating to local operations directly. Local branches or groups include Belize Eco-Tourism Association (**www.bzecotourism.org**), the Belize Audubon Society (**www.belizeaudubon .org**), and Programme for Belize (**www.pfbelize.org**).

For a comprehensive list of volunteer opportunities in Belize, go to **www .belizefirst.com/indexvolunteer.html.**

The Toledo Ecotourism Association arranges trips near Punta Gorda, where each participating village has built a guesthouse (sleeping up to eight in bunk beds) for visitors. Prices include two meals. Proceeds benefit the local villages. See more at **www.southernbelize.com/tea.html.**

Teachers for a Better Belize (**www.tfabb.org**) offers teacher-training opportunities for experienced educators. If you want to make a lasting difference, try to make spending decisions that aid the local economy instead of putting more money into the hands of foreign corporations. Hire local guides, eat in family-owned restaurants, stay in independent hotels, and buy handicrafts close to the source. These actions can have a far more lasting impact on people trying to better their life than a check sent to an aid organization.

GUATEMALA

If life were fair, Guatemala would be one of the world's most-heralded tourist destinations. Most countries can only dream of having the natural and cultural attractions you'll enjoy in Guatemala. The problem has been that a harsh struggle between the haves and have-nots started in the early 1960s and continued until 1996. During those years, the welcome light in the window was flickering, and tourist magnets such as Tikal, Lake Atitlán, and Antigua slumbered in hibernation. But now Guatemala is at peace, and the welcome mat is out.

Visitors, including tour groups, now feel safe and are eager to explore this wonderful country. In places such as Chichicastenango, Antigua, Tikal, and Panajachel, you'll see lots of gringos, but that's still not true elsewhere. Facilities are in place to welcome travelers, and it's easy to get around and find a nice place to sleep and eat. There are point-to-point shuttle bus services to almost anywhere a tourist would venture and quite a few comfortable and attractive mid-range hotels. Yet you can still feel like an explorer discovering an exotic treasure just a short plane trip south of the U.S. border.

Guatemala is a mountainous country filled with volcanoes and impressive panoramas at every turn. Tikal, the astounding, stony remains of one of the largest cities in the powerful Maya empire, is in the northern jungle. That area alone is home to more than 350 kinds of birds, 105 types of reptiles, and more than 100 types of mammals. The wildlife variety in the rest of the country is equally mind-boggling.

Cobbled streets and impressive architecture help make the 16th-century town of Antigua one of the most enchanting Spanish colonial settlements in all of Latin America. To stunning Lake Atitlán, surrounded by volcanoes, add the black-sand beaches on the Pacific shore, fishing expeditions, jungle walks, raft trips, and the funky community of Livingston on the Caribbean.

Many visitors are drawn to Guatemala because it has by far the largest intact indigenous population in the Americas. These are people who strongly adhere to their centuries-old traditions, including those regarding dress. Many towns are filled with men and women wearing intricate, handwoven clothing dyed in a neon rainbow of bright colors. These aren't costumes to create photo ops for tourists—they're the real thing.

Guatemala is an outstanding value for travelers. Many prices are 30 percent to 50 percent less than in Belize or Costa Rica, especially for hotels and adventure activities. In fact, many travelers spend months wandering around Guatemala on the cheap—and they never get bored.

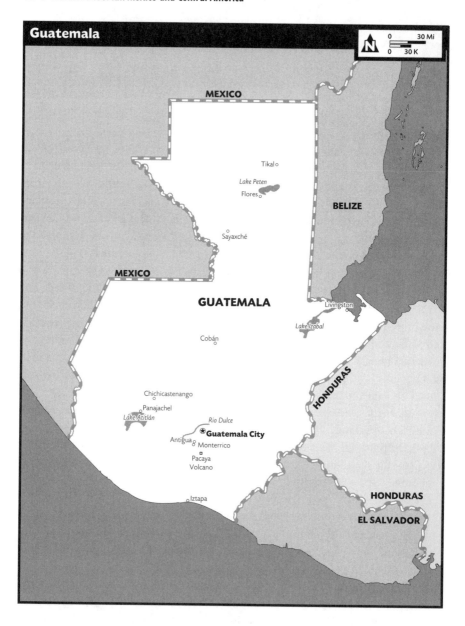

Lots of travelers visit because it's one of the least expensive places to take a Spanish-immersion course. You can receive high-quality one-on-one language instruction for less than $200 a week, including room and board with a local family.

Guatemala is shaped vaguely like Texas, with the "panhandle" (including Tikal) projecting far into Mexico. Relatively, Guatemala City is about where Austin is in Texas. This most-populated Central American country borders

Belize on the northeast and El Salvador and Honduras on the southeast. It's about the size of Tennessee, though the many mountains make it feel a lot bigger. The Pacific shore is mostly mangroves and black-sand beaches, while the mouth of the tranquil Río Dulce bisects the small patch of coastline on the Caribbean side. The elevation ranges from sea level to a chilly 13,845-foot summit. Earthquakes, volcanic eruptions, massive mudslides, and hurricanes all take their toll on the land and the people.

Guatemala became independent from Spain in 1821 and, after many years of dictatorships, is a constitutional democratic republic. Two-thirds of its exports are agricultural (coffee, sugar, bananas) plus some apparel and petroleum, 53 percent of which go to the United States.

> Guatemala has 33 volcanoes (some active, some dormant) that beg to be climbed as well as photographed. Santiaguito, the country's youngest and most unpredictable volcano, emerged with a fierce eruption in 1902 near the city of Quetzaltenango.

Guatemala's People

More than 40 percent of the population of 13 million is considered indigenous, tracing its lineage to the Maya. About 60 percent of the population lives below the poverty line. Sadly, there is almost complete overlap between these two groups. As in much of Latin America, descendants of Europeans have most of the rich farmland, wealth, and power while the indigenous people eke out a livelihood on steep terraces, often living in one-room houses with dirt floors. On a raw per-capita basis, Guatemalans appear wealthier than Hondurans and Nicaraguans. However, most of that wealth is concentrated at the very top, and much of it is in Guatemala City. For perspective, Guatemala's per-capita gross domestic product is a little more than half that of Brazil.

The good news: now that the fighting has stopped, people have returned to taking care of business. Economically, things are looking up. Expanding tourism is a boon for many indigenous families who make a living as guides, drivers, and makers and sellers of handicrafts.

Visitors often ask where the Maya people disappeared to. What disappeared was not the people; it was the empire. The people are still here, stubbornly holding on to their authentic traditions. When you think of Guatemala, think of vibrant colors. On market days, picture hundreds of patterns and hues coming together in ensembles of up to eight different pieces of clothing worn by each woman. In many areas, the men still don traditional, handwoven clothing as well. By the way, a small Garifuna community on the Caribbean coast (of mixed Caribbean and African origin) has a completely different set of traditions and lifestyles.

The percentage of Catholics here (70) is lower than in many Latin American countries. In addition, there are local forms of the religion that the Pope would barely recognize. Evangelical Protestants have made major headway here, claiming some 25 percent of the faithful.

Guatemalans have a reputation for being friendly, polite, and patient. Reciprocate, and your travels will be smooth as silk.

Highlights

- **Antigua**, framed by volcanic mountains and dotted with impressive, Spanish-style homes and churches (some intact, some in ruins), is perhaps the most magical and attractive city in Central America. Some of the former grand homes have been converted into inviting inns. The town is small enough that you can easily see it all by strolling on cobblestone streets—or opt for horse-drawn carriage rides. Although this is ground zero for Spanish-language schools, it's also a good base for excursions to a live volcano or nearby coffee farms.

- The towering Maya pyramids of **Tikal**, rising out of dense jungle just beyond Lake Peten, are some of the most magnificent, as well as mysterious and somehow brooding, structures in the Americas. While it flourished, this site might have been the center of power for the entire Maya empire. As of now, hundreds, maybe thousands, of structures remain to be unveiled from beneath the jungle shroud. Those who truly appreciate the Maya can visit other sites in the area that are also still emerging, including Yaxhá and Uaxactún. There are several small hotels next to the entrance of Tikal and many more around Lake Peten.

- **Lake Atitlán** is an 11-mile-long lake formed by a massive volcanic eruption 85,000 years ago. It is one of the deepest lakes in the world: more than 900 feet. Surrounded by steep ridges and extinct volcanic cones, it's a beautiful, captivating spot. Hippies who never got around to leaving share the streets with indigenous people hustling their handicrafts. The half-dozen or so villages along the lakeshore are easily accessible by regular boat-taxis. With the exception of Panajachel and San Pedro la Laguna, which are pretty busy, they're fine places to chill out and hang with local folks. When you're in the mood, hike up a volcano, trek off into the forest, swim, paddle a kayak, or just cruise the lake.

> You will notice a lot of children in Guatemala. The average is 3.7 children per woman, and the median age of the population is slightly younger than 19. As a result, many people adopt children from there.

- You can't really get the sense of any place in Latin America unless you visit its markets. In Guatemala, that means you don't want to miss the giant, twice-weekly market days in **Chichicastenango** (an easy trip from Panajachel). There are tourists, of course, but this market is for local people who make long trips bringing their wares from remote villages. You can buy trinkets, high-quality souvenirs, indigenous clothing, or bolts of handwoven cloth, or just stroll around watching folks haggle over the value of chickens, vegetables, and homemade hooch.

- **Cobán**, not to be confused with Copán in Honduras, is a mountain town that is usually misty or downright rainy, but it's a major adventure-travel base for the region. The most popular excursions are to the Grutas de Lanquin caves (where an army of bats departs each night) and the Semuc Champey collection of natural pools and waterfalls in a serene setting.
- **Guatemala City** is not a major highlight of the country, and most travelers choose to stay for no more than a night, but it does have a children's museum, an outstanding zoo, and an excellent archaeological museum.
- **Livingston**, a small port town on the east coast, has an authentic Caribbean culture very different from the rest of the country. It's a fine place to drink a brew under an umbrella and talk with local fishermen, assorted old-timers, and travelers passing through. It's also the place to hire a small boat for a trip through the canyon of the **Río Dulce** and the Castillo de San Felipe fort on Lake Izabal. Most trips stop at the manatee reserve on the way. Río Dulce town is a secluded haven for world-traveling yachts, so the cuisine is outstanding.
- The waters off the Pacific coast are home to the highest concentration of **billfish** in the world. Anglers reel in record marlin and yellow fin tuna. **Iztapa** is the center for deep-sea fishing trips. The black-sand beaches may not be the subject of gushing Travel Channel reviews, but their charms are an absence of crowds and plenty of opportunities to gorge on fresh seafood, then doze in a shaded hammock. **Monterrico** is the best spot for mellow beach life.

Itineraries

If You Have a Week in Guatemala

For a "Highlights of Guatemala" tour when arriving in Guatemala City by air, use Antigua as a base, taking a one- or two-night trip (by plane) up to Tikal and the region around Lake Peten. Then split the rest of the week between Antigua and Lake Atitlán, perhaps making time for side trips to a rural market and to Pacaya volcano.

If arriving from the Copán ruins in Honduras, from Mexico, or from El Salvador, follow the same itinerary, shuttling to Antigua after taking an international bus trip across the border to Guatemala City. Or, if you've had enough of visiting ruins, venture past Atitlán and hike near Quetzaltenango or hit the beach at Monterrico.

If arriving overland from Belize, head straight to Tikal, then catch a bus to Cobán and explore that region for a day or two, or fly to Antigua. Split the remaining time between Lake Atitlán and Antigua.

If arriving by boat from Belize and landing at Livingston, take a boat trip up the Río Dulce. With only a week, you'd need to choose between Tikal and Antigua unless you hop on some well-coordinated flights.

Diving into Lake Atitlán, Guatemala

If You Have Two Weeks or More in Guatemala

Two weeks allows you take the "highlights" circuit outlined on page 62 and add either Livingston on the Caribbean or Monterrico on the Pacific. Or you'd have time to escape the tourist trail and go exploring more deeply into the boonies. Or choose from among all these options and take a one-week Spanish-immersion course in Antigua.

If going for the "exploring more deeply" option, consider one or more of the less visited indigenous areas around Quetzaltenango or the Ixil Triangle west of

Cobán. If you are especially interested in ruins, visit the sites north of Tikal and the three partially excavated sites near Sayaxché, off the highway between Tikal and Cobán.

Why not visit a neighboring country? From Río Dulce town, catch a boat down the river to the Caribbean and on to the Belize islands and back. Alternatively, just over the Honduran border are the famous Maya ruins at Copán. You also may be beckoned by the Pacific beaches and the colonial hill town of Suchitoto in El Salvador.

And for learning Spanish via immersion, if one week is good, two weeks are better—maybe one week in Antigua, with its bars and international restaurants, but the second week in some place much more remote.

And with two weeks, can you afford to miss the world-class fishing off the Pacific coast?

Cost Comparisons

Guatemala is a good value for everyone, from shoestring backpackers to those with a fat budget. Most travelers consider this the best "bang for the buck" in the region. Over time, expect to spend 30 to 50 percent less than you would in Costa Rica, a Mexican resort area, or Ambergris Caye in Belize. The following are representative costs across Guatemala and do not include places where prices are inflated, such as deluxe hotels and fine-dining establishments.

> Guatemala has 92 national parks and protected areas, making up 28 percent of the total land area.

- Liter of water in a convenience store: 80 cents–$2
- Bottle of beer in a bar or restaurant: $1.20–$3
- Bottle of beer in a store: 75 cents–$1
- Meal of the day in a locals' restaurant: $1.20–$3.50
- Half kilo of oranges, in season: 40 cents
- 1 hour of Internet access in a cafe: 70 cents–$2
- Cup of coffee, juice, or soda in a restaurant: 75 cents–$1.50
- 10-minute taxi ride across town: $2.50–$5
- Taxi from main international airport to hotel: $3.50–$7.50
- 3-star or equivalent hotel: $35–$70

Accommodations

If you like hotels that exude history, are aesthetically pleasing, and have a real sense of place, Guatemala delivers. In Antigua, most of the lodging consists of colonial-era homes converted into family-run inns. Throughout the country, expect appealing architectural touches and décor that makes ample use of local fabrics and crafts. Best of all, you don't spend a fortune. Even the cheapie $15-for-a-double places often have a central garden filled with plants and flowers. In the $35 to $70 range, you find very nice hotels nearly anywhere. The only spot

The Grandest Archaeological Site

Tikal is billed as "the largest excavated site in the American continent." That claim could be disputed, but there's no denying that this UNESCO World Heritage site is huge and certainly the largest city of the Maya empire. The site has been developed well by the archaeologists, and the government has created a vast buffer of land around it—222 square miles of jungle. That buffer land undoubtedly contains foliage-wrapped secrets waiting to be discovered. Mercifully, no luxury hotels have crowded in to spoil the atmosphere. From your lodging, the main ruins are a 20- or 30-minute trek on a path through the jungle. Along the way you see awe-inspiring mahogany and ceiba trees with huge trunks and sprawling roots half-above the ground. Colorful toucans and screeching orioles share tree space with spider monkeys and howler monkeys. Finally, you enter a clearing and see an ancient pyramid rising high into the sky. It's easy to imagine the admiration early visitors must have felt soon after the structures were rediscovered in the 1800s.

Some of the impressive stone buildings of Tikal are more than 2,000 years old. Just think of that compared to the primitive, mound-like structures that existed in North America when the first Europeans arrived—and how long after that it took the new arrivals to build anything approaching these pyramids in importance. The Maya empire was a very big deal in the history of this continent. Tikal was at its zenith from AD 200 to AD 850, with a population that at one time may have been 200,000. It was abandoned in the tenth century and lay dormant for another thousand years while a colossus developed in the north.

Temple IV, at 212 feet (64 meters), is the tallest structure. If you visit outside rainy season and get up early, the summit of Temple IV is the place to watch the sun rise. Up to 1,500 people visit the park daily during peak periods, so get there early to miss the rush of day-trippers and allow plenty of time to get around the sprawling site. Right now, you can treat yourself to a neat 3-D map of all the excavated structures at **www.tikalpark.com** (click on "Tikal Map").

that feels overpriced is inside the national park at Tikal, where there are only three small hotels. That's where many travelers want to stay, so demand drives the prices up.

So far, the country is refreshingly free of cookie-cutter international chain hotels, but there are some near the airport in Guatemala City, catering mostly to business travelers. In the rest of the country, small inns are the norm. A town will seldom have more than two or three hotels with more than 40 rooms.

At the bottom end, a fair number of hostels cater to single travelers, with a bed costing from $4 to $10. Where there's competition, this price will include some kind of breakfast and free Internet access. Some of them are 20-something party haunts with no hot water. (Of course, this isn't exactly a cold country.) A couple who've outgrown that phase are better off renting a double room for $10 to $20. For as little as $20, you can usually get a double with hot water, a private bath, and maid service. Note that the hot-water system is not what you are used to at home. It may be a gas system where you have to fiddle with the knobs to get it right. More often, it's an electrical attachment to the showerhead. The water gets heated as it passes through coils. A little scary, but it's common around the world.

The middle range is where the real values are in Guatemala. A $60 room at La Casa del Mundo, perched on the shore of Lake Atitlán, included the best view I've ever had from a hotel. In Antigua, the same amount paid for a two-room suite. On the Pacific coast, it gets a beachfront bungalow with a sprawling, furnished veranda. In some of the smaller villages, $50 buys the best room in town. This is all much more economical for two people than for one. A single room is usually only $5 to $10 less than the price of a double.

Despite great values and a recovering tourism business, the luxury hotel scene is still in its infancy. Even in Antigua, there are only a few hotels catering to an upscale

Temple One at Tikal, Guatemala, capital of the Maya empire

clientele. That's also true anywhere else outside the capital. If you're addicted to going first class, you should either wait a few years or downgrade your expectations. On the plus side, Francis Ford Coppola's La Lancha Resort near Tikal tops out at $240 a night for the best room in high season, and Casa Santo Domingo in Antigua is $170 for a standard double in peak periods. For links to hotel sites in various locations, see the "Resources" section later in this chapter.

Note that the best times to visit Guatemala coincide with the important local holidays of Christmas and Easter, when locals with enough money are filling buses and booking available hotel rooms for the week. Reserve ahead for these periods and the other holidays listed in "Holidays and Festivals," below.

Food and Drink

A left-handed compliment about Guatemalan food is that it's "Mexican with less spice." It shares many ingredients with its northern neighbor, but dishes seem less complex and less spicy. In tourist restaurants, native Guatemalan cuisine is usually drowned out by international options: Italian, Asian, Mexican, Chinese, or fried chicken-burgers-fries. An unadventurous tourist could spend two weeks without biting into a tortilla or getting a fork full of fried plantains.

If you find the food too bland, reach for the omnipresent bottle of hot sauce on the table, or ask for salsa. Typical local dishes include *chiles rellenos* and thin steak with salsa, as well as a variety of chicken and fish dishes. Various vegetable and meat dishes show up on "meal of the day" options. Breakfast is usually robust with eggs, black beans, plantains, white cheese, and tortillas or bread. And some fine coffee.

Holidays and Festivals
- December 31–Jan. 1: New Year holiday
- January 6: Day of the Three Kings (family celebrations)
- March or April: Semana Santa (Holy Week, Easter)
- May 1: Labor Day
- May 2–3: Day of the Cross at Lake Atitlán
- June 30: Army Day
- July 25: Town fair in Antigua
- July 27: Rabin Ajau beauty pageant festival in Cobán
- August 15: Assumption Day
- September 15: Independence Day (largest fair is in Quetzaltenango)
- October 12: Discovery of America Day
- October 20: Revolution Day
- November 1 and 2: All Saints' Day and All Souls' Day
- December 14–21: Town fair in Chichicastenango
- December 25: Christmas

Beverages are a highlight of any meal. Seasonal juices and *licuados* (blended fruit drinks), widely available in restaurants and stalls, are served straight up, with water, or with milk (a big hit with kids). Most menus also include freshly made orange or lime soda, and some juice combined with soda water and a bit of sugar—just the ticket on a hot day. Of course there are the usual American bottled soda brands, plus a few less popular local brands.

In most coffee shops you can get a really good brew from local beans. Be sure to try hot chocolate, which is noticeably different from any you've had at home.

There are plenty of beer choices in Guatemala, though the Gallo brand seems to outnumber the roosters it is named after. El Dorado and Monte Carlo represent the upper tier of beer, but the price premium seems to pay for foil wrappers and prettier labels. Beer lovers prefer Moza, an authentic and tasty black, German-style bock beer. High-end Guatemalan rum (Ron Zacapa Centenario) is among the best in the world, but you're more likely to see cheaper local varieties or Nicaraguan rum in most bars. A bottle of rum in local stores will run $2 to $8 depending on age, with the very best still a bargain at $20. Except at wine bars, the vino is overpriced jug wine from South America.

> The locals are so crazy for ice cream that there's a shop on every other block, a freezer in most convenience stores, and pushcart vendors in most town squares. Helados Marylena in Guatemala City wins the prize for originality, with flavors including yucca, maize, cauliflower, and beer. Hmmm, it would have to be a very hot day.

Transportation

There are three classes of **buses** in Guatemala: the regular "chicken buses," van shuttles for tourists, and deluxe buses that are used mostly for destinations in another country. For most routes, it's worth paying the premium for a shuttle because it runs point-to-point, picking you up where you specify. This keeps you from having to haul your luggage across town to a chaotic bus station, where your bags may be tossed onto the roof. Most of the executive buses to neighboring countries are run by Hedman Alas or one of the Mexican companies and are quite comfortable, with a bathroom on board.

The regular buses have the same lineage as those in other Central American countries: hot, crowded converted school buses built before emissions controls. Some are painted with bright colors, while others might still read something like "Springfield County Schools" on the side. They're fine for a short trip and cost only

> Guatemalans can't make up their minds about units of measurement. Expect to see land and distances measured in the metric system but gas for sale by the gallon. In the grocery store, some food items are sold by the kilo, some by the pound, and some by the *mano* (handful).

about a dollar an hour, but are no fun as a way to get from the capital to somewhere as far away as Lake Peten.

Sample bus routes and costs (highest class available):

City 1	City 2	Travel Time	Cost
Guatemala City	Antigua	1.5 hours	$10
Panajachel	Antigua	3.5 hours	$7–$12
Flores (Tikal)	Guatemala City	9 hours	$30
Flores (Tikal)	Belize City (Belize)	5 hours	$25
Cobán	Guatemala City	4.5 hours	$15
Guatemala City	Copán (Honduras)	6 hours	$40
Monterrico	Antigua	2.5 hour	$14

If you are a family or group, consider hiring a **private shuttle**. A private van from Antigua to the Guatemala City airport, for example, costs $20 to $30. One from the Santa Elena airport to the hotels next to Tikal is $35 to $50.

With such reasonable public-transportation rates, it doesn't make sense to **rent a car** in Guatemala. The main roads are okay, but the surface gets worse off the beaten path. You'll find familiar rental-car brand names in the capital, but they charge more than at home (especially for an automatic with air-conditioning).

A revamped school bus in Guatemala

This is a very mountainous country, so have a very good reason for taking the wheel rather than letting someone who knows the lay of the land do it for roughly the same price.

Internal **flights** are good for longer jaunts in Guatemala, especially the trip from the capital to Tikal. A lot of people on vacation are very willing to pay $200 round-trip to avoid the long, winding bus ride. It's also reasonable to go by air to Belize City, Honduras, or Mexico. You can reach all these neighboring countries overland easily on a comfortable bus, but for an extra $100 to $200, flying can save a day (or night) of traveling.

At one time, Guatemala had extensive **passenger-train** service. It's all gone now.

Whether it's a normal **taxi**, a **shuttle van**, or a three-wheel *tuk-tuk* (similar to those in India and Thailand), charges are quite reasonable. To cross town, you'll pay somewhere between $1.50 and $4. A request for more than $6 means you're really being "taken for a ride." Meters are rare outside the capital, so agree on the fare before you start moving. Ask at your hotel how much a trip should cost.

Small **ferries** circle Lake Atitlán to all villages ($1.50 to $4). Scheduled ferries go between Livingston and Puerto Barrio on the Caribbean coast.

Activity Costs

If you wait until after arrival to book organized tours and adventures, you find major bargains. Competition is heavy, so prices are about half what they would be for similar activities in Costa Rica or Belize. Most of the following options will likely cost two to four times the rate listed if you set them up through a U.S. travel agency or as a cruise-ship excursion. As in much of the world, anything booked from a luxury hotel costs far more than it would anywhere else in town. Where applicable, ask about the type of vehicle and the language proficiency of the driver or guide.

- Tikal admission: about $13. An official guide for several hours costs $25.
- 2-day, 1-night trip to Tikal from Antigua, including hotel, round-trip air-fare, and all other transportation: $280–$320
- Pacaya active volcano day tour from Antigua, with transportation and guide: $5–$12
- Day tour of villages around Antigua or tour of a coffee farm: $15–$25, including lunch
- 2-day, 1-night tour of villages around Lake Atitlán from Panajachel: $30–$60, depending on lodging
- 7-day sailing trip from Fronteras down the Río Dulce and around the islands off Belize: $400, including meals
- 4-day sailing trip down the Río Dulce to Livingston and transportation back to Fronteras: $200 or less, including meals

- Deep-sea fishing trips from the Pacific town of Iztapa vary from a basic 1-day trip for $150–$200 to professionally run packages that cost $500–$1,000 per day, all-inclusive (makes you wonder who's taking the hook).

Tour Companies

Many responsible small-group North American operators lead trips to Guatemala. For example, G.A.P Adventures (**www.gapadventures.com**) offers more than 20 trips. Adventure Life (**www.adventure-life.com**) runs well-regarded 6- to 12-day trips. Adventure Center (**www.adventurecenter.com**) runs 8- to 60-day trips (the latter as part of a multicountry trip). Djoser (**www.djoser usa.com**) and Intrepid Travel (**www.intrepidtravel.com**) include Guatemala in several long, multicountry trips. International student agency STA Travel (**www .statravel.com**) has several offices in-country.

Because there are hundreds of travel agencies and tour companies in Guatemala, consult a current guidebook and ask other travelers for recommendations. Keep an eye on reports in *International Travel News*. The following are not endorsed by Traveler's Tool Kit, but here are a few of the best-known operators:

- Turansa (**www.turansa.com**) is one of the largest full-service agencies based in Guatemala. It's been in business since 1988 and has offices in the capital and Antigua.
- Sin Fronteras (**www.sinfront.com**) is an Antigua-based agency with English-speaking personnel and a Web site in four languages.
- ViaVenture (**www.viaventure.com**), run by three expatriates living in Antigua, specializes in personalized, high-end tours that feature only Guatemala's best hotels.
- Aventuras Vacacionales (**www.sailing-diving-guatemala.com**) runs sailing and diving trips in eastern Guatemala and into Belize.
- Maya Expeditions (**www.mayaexpeditions.com**) is one of the most professional adventure outfitters, running trips for rafting, caving, hiking, paragliding, kayaking, and more.

Useful Details

Getting there and away: Air connections are available to Guatemala City from the United States and Canada on American, Delta, Continental, Taca, United, and Aeromexico.

Many travelers arrive in Guatemala overland or combine two or more countries on one trip. See the overland options following, under "border crossings."

Flights to all other countries in the region are available from Guatemala City. Some flights to Flores (for Tikal) go on to Belize City or Cancún.

Border crossings: Good roads and bus connections lead to multiple crossings into Mexico, El Salvador, Honduras, and Belize. Overland crossings are usually quick and painless unless it's the end of a hot day and the crew has knocked off early. Try to cross early in the day.

Many visitors come from Honduras through Copán or two other points. There are three entry points from Campeche or Chiapas states in Mexico. There are four crossings from El Salvador. One of the busiest crossings for tourists is on the road that goes from northern Belize to Flores, on Lake Peten near Tikal.

Scheduled ferries shuttle between Punta Gorda in Belize and Livingston and Puerto Barrios in Guatemala. Tour agencies offer pleasure-boat trips down the Río Dulce to the islands of Belize (see the "Activity Costs" section, page 71).

Some people get so excited by Tikal that they want to go straight up to the great Maya lands of Mexico. Given the dense jungle along the border north of Tikal, it's much easier to get to the Mexico's Yucatán Peninsula via Belize.

Driving into Guatemala from a neighboring country requires a lot of paperwork and patience, and a new insurance policy. Be prepared to sacrifice most of the day when crossing.

Visas: Most foreigners, including those from the United States and Canada, do not need a visa to visit Guatemala and are able to stay up to 90 days. One tourist

stamp and fee allows you to travel overland among Guatemala, Honduras, El Salvador, and Nicaragua without again paying or getting stamped.

Currency: The Guatemalan currency is the quetzal (named after the large, brilliantly colored bird with long tail feathers that was also a Maya symbol) and generally trades at between 7 and 8 to the U.S. dollar. American dollars are widely accepted at hotels and restaurants in tourist areas, but elsewhere you will need local currency. Euros and Canadian dollars are seldom accepted. Ideally, bring a mix of U.S. bills and make sure your $100 bills are relatively new (so they won't be considered counterfeit).

Departure tax: Twenty quetzales (less than $3) per person for every flight leg, whether domestic or international. An additional $27 international departure tax should be included in your airline ticket. Departure tax for land crossings is minimal or nonexistent.

Weather and when to go: December through May is the high season. Late May through November is the rainy season. Confusingly to North Americans, the high season is called summer (*verano*), and the rainy season is called winter (*invierno*). While June through August should be low season because of the weather, those months actually see an influx of visitors from the United States, Canada, and

Europe—a number of them coming to study Spanish. Antigua especially gets very busy at this time despite regular rains. The downpours usually don't last all day, but when they do, you may have to turn back on some mountainous rural roads.

Packing for a trip to Guatemala can be a challenge if you are including varied topography. Tikal is humid and can hit 100°F, while in the mountains you'll need a jacket at night. High-elevation hiking trips can get downright frosty.

Electricity: Current and outlet shapes are the same as in the United States.

Internet access and telephones: Telephone connections are good, though calls will cost a dollar a minute or more from spots such as the hotels near Tikal. Elsewhere, you can choose from phone kiosks, pay phones that use scratch-off cards, and phones where you insert a prepaid card from Ladatel, the telecom company. Expect to pay 20 to 50 cents a minute at these places. Least expensive are VoIP phones at Internet cafes. Considering the connection speeds and the ubiquity of Skype (for free or close-to-free calls), it's cheap to stay connected from Guatemala.

Internet cafes are abundant, and "high-speed Internet" usually really is. Wi-Fi is available in many hotels and tourist coffee shops.

Language: Spanish is the primary language, and this is a major destination for intensive Spanish courses. However, Spanish is the second language for many rural Guatemalans. There are 23 post-Maya languages, such as Quiché, Cakchiquel, and Xinca. These are people who honor their traditions.

In the main tourist spots, many people speak English. In fact, don't be surprised if the hotel or restaurant owner is a transplant from New Zealand, Finland, Switzerland, or Canada. In Antigua, although you can easily get by speaking only English, half the foreigners in town are trying to practice the Spanish they've learned in their language courses.

Safety: During the long civil war, some parts of Guatemala were very rough. However, I was there in the early 1990s before the peace agreement and didn't feel threatened—but I also avoided the rural northwestern regions. Even though the peace has held firm since 1996, most North Americans still have no idea who was fighting or what they were fighting about—or that it has been over for a long time. As more and more happy travelers return home, that's changing. Now you only have to keep alert for the usual safety issues and take commonsense precautions. I won't say that crime isn't an issue here—the murder rate is distressingly high—but the serious crime usually involves rival gangs and score-settling. Tourists are seldom victims or witnesses of major crime.

When additional caution is needed, such as in big cities, on isolated hikes, or on rural roads, ask around for advice. Hotel owners are usually well versed on which areas require extra vigilance. In some areas, carry a minimum of cash and leave the fancy watch and expensive camera back in the room. (For more, please see Chapter 17, Safety and Security.)

Health care: Health care is generally good in cities and abysmal in remote rural areas. If you will be spending a lot of time in the mountains, medical-evacuation insurance would provide peace of mind. City hospitals are clean and well run, often with staff doctors who have trained abroad and can speak some English.

Guatemala is starting to become a "medical tourism" destination, especially for dental work. The prices for crowns, fillings, and whitening treatments are one-fifth to one-third the rates commonly charged in the United States.

For a review of health issues to be aware of in Guatemala, please see Chapter 12, Keeping Healthy.

Things to buy: Guatemala is by far the best place for shopping in Central America. The selection and quality are superior to what is found in most parts of Mexico as well. A high percentage of textile items are expertly handwoven or embroidered. You see far fewer tacky, machine-made tourist items than in most destinations.

Some of the textile color combinations may be too wild for a tourist's tastes, but they make eye-catching wall hangings, pillow covers, and tablecloths. Place settings and napkins make good gifts, as do wood carvings, masks, and pottery. Silver and beaded jewelry are abundant and attractively priced. Among consumables, consider fine rum, coffee beans, and chocolate—from the region that popularized cocoa.

Resources

Guidebooks and other references: Guidebooks for Guatemala are published by the usual companies, including Lonely Planet, Frommer's, and Moon Handbooks, which put out updates in 2007. A 2008 *Fodor's Guatemala* guide will be updated annually. The Rough Guide edition is reasonably current. Check the copyright date on others. Insight Guides, Footprint, and others combine Guatemala and neighboring countries in a single guidebook. *The Rough Guide to the Maya World* covers the whole Maya region.

There are many fine recent books pertaining to Guatemala, including beautiful coffee-table books such as the magnificent *¡Viva Colores!* by Paola Gianturco and David Hill, and *Guatemala Revealed* by Cristobal von Rothkirch and Harris Whitbeck. *Tramping Through Mexico, Guatemala and Honduras* covers just what the title states.

Numerous historic titles report the tragic civil war. A good guidebook will provide a list for browsing.

Web sites: The Spanish version of Guatemala's official tourism site (**www .visitguatemala.com**) is far more extensive than its English counterpart.

EnjoyGuatemala (**www.enjoyguatemala.com**), run by a tour company, has first-rate write-ups on key tourist areas and useful links and lists of resources.

A well-connected hotel owner has put together a useful site at Guatemalaweb (**www.guatemalaweb.com**).

La Ruta Maya Online (**www.larutamayaonline.com**) offers photos, articles, and an excellent set of information links, including links to local newspapers, embassy offices, and dozens of language schools.

Atitlan.com (**www.atitlan.com**) is a fine guide to the Lake Atitlán region, with a comprehensive listing of hotels in all budget ranges and some useful travel articles.

The Tikal National Park Web site (**www.tikalpark.com**) is loaded with information about Tikal-area transportation, flights, hotels, and the park site itself. Also see Maya Traveler (**www.maya-traveler.com**).

Mesoweb (**www.mesoweb.com**) is a thorough resource on the Maya world, including sites in Guatemala.

Take a look at Revue (**www.revuemag.com**), which makes its content available in English in PDF form so you can peruse a copy before you arrive. Very good for scoping out hotel ideas.

Retirement Opportunities

Because Guatemala was mired in civil war until 1996, it hasn't had throngs of retirees lining up at the immigration office. That's changing. Real-estate offices catering to foreigners are popping up at Antigua and Lake Atitlán, and you see ads for coffee farms, building lots, homes, and even a few condos.

Apart from cheap prices, Guatemala doesn't offer any incentives to retirees. The government does make it relatively easy to qualify for a residency permit, though. To receive retired-resident status, you need to go through the usual paperwork drills and prove total pension or investment income of $1,000 per month, plus an additional $200 per month for each dependent.

Foreigners are barred from owning waterfront land or building a home within 15 miles of an international border. There are two ways around these restrictions: establishing a corporation to own the property or buying the property with a local partner. Or you can do what many expatriates have done: marry your local sweetheart, and put the purchase in the spouse's name.

Helping Out

Guatemala's fledgling democratic government has a reputation for limited effectiveness when it comes to social programs, local infrastructure development, medical care, and environmental stewardship. As a result, hundreds of nongovernmental organizations have stepped in to offer aid and improve conditions. These range from good-hearted groups on "mission trips" that zoom in for a week, delivering medical or dental care, to international organizations such as Doctors Without Borders (**www.doctorswithoutborders.org**), Habitat for Humanity (**www.habitat.org**), and Heifer International (**www.heifer.org**).

Guatemala's Civil War

Beginning in the 1960s, Guatemala's industry began growing, and unions organized. It wasn't long before Guatemala started sliding into conflict between the have-nots and the wealthy elite. Most expected the troubles to stay small and isolated, but by the end of the 1970s, Amnesty International estimated that more than 60,000 people had died. When brutal General Efraín Ríos Montt came to power in 1982, he began a reign of terror against the rural communities that supported insurgents, killing at least 15,000 citizens, razing more than 400 villages, and causing thousands of destitute people to flee the country. Meanwhile, the have-nots (called "rebels") were carrying out their own atrocities and reprisals.

Despite a return to democratic rule in the mid-1980s and continuing peace negotiations, the tit-for-tat killings continued. In 1996, after 36 years of fighting, the government and rebels signed a peace agreement formally ending the conflict. The government promised to make changes to recognize more rights of the downtrodden, but some have still not been enacted. After 36 years, there had been neither industrial growth nor equity. There had been only death. By the time the conflict was over, more than 100,000 were dead, and some 1 million had become refugees.

Nearly all of them would be glad to accept your help, especially if you have skills in demand. Listed below are two clearinghouse organizations that post their needs. If you haven't lined up something before you arrive, just look around when you get there. Numerous volunteers in Guatemala are working at a clinic or school they discovered during their travels. If you can donate money, hundreds of charities and other nongovernmental organizations can make it have a real impact.

Project Mosaic Guatemala (**www.promosaico.org**), based in Antigua, is another effective nonprofit that matches volunteers to local needs.

EntreMundos (**www.entremundos.org**), based in Quetzaltenango, works on up to 100 development projects throughout the year, matching volunteers with the appropriate projects. Upcoming projects are listed on the site.

Check Charity Navigator (**www.charitynavigator.org**) to research global organizations that operate in Guatemala. Search the *Transitions Abroad* site (**www.transitionsabroad.com**) for articles on volunteer programs in Guatemala. Some U.S. organizations, such as Cultural Embrace (**www.culturalembrace .com**), combine two-week volunteer projects with morning Spanish classes.

Many Spanish-language schools, and even some travel agencies, also function as English-speaking representatives of organizations needing volunteer work. If you can teach English or help with medical needs, you will be especially in demand. Whatever your skills and interests, there is a local organization that is a good fit, provided you learn to communicate in Spanish.

EL SALVADOR

Ask an international surfer about El Salvador, and you'll hear nothing but super-latives. It has one of the best collections of surfing spots in the world along its Pacific coastline. Elsewhere along the seashore, soothing waters caress miles of almost-deserted beaches.

Inland, attractions range from volcanic slopes with spectacular views to Spanish colonial towns such as Suchitoto, often compared with Antigua, Guatemala, because of its architecture and mountain setting.

Nevertheless, there have been few articles about El Salvador in glossy travel magazines, and few splashy advertisements for foreign-owned resorts—at least so far. Most of this country's 1 million annual visitors are either just passing through or traveling on business from other Central American countries. There are a number of American business travelers because the United States receives more than 60 percent of El Salvador's exports.

Mention El Salvador to North Americans, and, depending on the age of the person, you'll get either a blank stare or a hazy recollection of a war. But what war? Actually, it was a civil war (in which the United States involved itself) that ended in 1992. Though that conflict is long gone, its cloud lingers vaguely in the public consciousness. That's one reason El Salvador attracts the fewest tourists in the region. And that's a major plus if you like visiting a place still largely undis-covered by tourists.

In reality, there's nothing mysterious about contemporary El Salvador. Bordered by Guatemala, Honduras, and the Pacific Ocean, it's the smallest country in Central America (about the size of Massachusetts) and the most densely populated. There are problems in this country of 7 million, but it's no economic backwater. The Heritage Foundation's Index of Economic Freedom gave El Salvador the high ranking of 29th in the world. The foundation cited low inflation (less than 5 percent), relatively low official unemployment (6.5 percent), and low tax rates. The country won high marks for encouraging entrepreneurs and investors. It's a robust market where enterprising people have opportunities to build successful businesses. When tourism demand finally gets moving, it won't take long for services to catch up.

Salvadorans buck the Central American trend by lacking interest in baseball. They're much more interested in basketball and the NBA.

El Salvador's People

The Olmecs, whose stone sculptures and ruins are most prevalent in the Tabasco area of Mexico, occupied part of what is now El Salvador as early as 2000 BC. The area was an important trading center, so many cultures, including the Maya, influenced and blended with the local population. The Pipil, descendants of the Toltecs and Aztecs, occupied most of the region when the Spanish invaded in the 16th century.

A mere 14 European families (mostly Spanish) controlled the bulk of the land throughout the 1700s, increasing agricultural output through widespread slavery. After several revolts and church interventions, El Salvador broke free from Spain in 1821 and then from the Central American Federation in 1839, becoming a sovereign, independent nation.

The 20th century was bloody in El Salvador. Civil wars, insurrections, and brutal government clampdowns marked nearly every decade. Finally, in 1992, a peace agreement took hold. And refugees who have been away for a decade or two are now trickling back home. El Salvador in the 21st century is—thankfully—a very different country than it once was.

Those who have traveled around Central America comment on the generosity and warmth of El Salvador's people, who are also known as industrious workers and savvy business owners. So visitors wonder how such a kind and friendly people could be capable of such destruction. It seems to have stemmed from poverty and unemployment, both of which are still problems, especially in the capital.

Although the civil war is over and the political process stable, the proliferation of guns in the capital has an impact on the crime stats. Whether San Salvador is any more dangerous than any other big city—or your own hometown—is debatable because the bad neighborhoods and the tourist zones don't intertwine. Nevertheless, seeing a guard with a rifle in front of a restaurant or hotel can come as a shock.

This is a churchgoing country where 83 percent of the population is Catholic, though Protestant evangelicals are working hard to recruit members.

For a harrowing glimpse into El Salvador's civil war as seen through the story of an unhinged photojournalist, see the 1986 movie *Salvador,* starring James Wood and directed by Oliver Stone.

Highlights

- The colonial city of **Suchitoto** has been populated for more than 1,000 years and was briefly the capital of the Spanish colony in the early 1500s. Its tranquility is a nice contrast to the bustle of San Salvador. In a beautiful countryside sprinkled with volcanoes and overlooking an azure lake,

El Salvador's Civil War

From the 1930s on, El Salvador was politically turbulent, with coups, armed power struggles, and insurgencies. Beginning in the early 1970s, intense social discontent grew into confrontations between the people and the government. By the end of the decade it had become a full-fledged civil war that lasted 12 years. Leftists killed government soldiers, and rightist vigilante death squads killed thousands of citizens. In 1981, an archbishop was executed on orders of the military intelligence chief. In December of that year, 900 civilians were slaughtered by the Salvadoran Armed Forces in the El Mozote massacre.

Despite outrageous abuses by El Salvador's leaders, the U.S. government gave them billions of dollars in aid to "stop the communists." The chaotic situation did not improve.

In 1989, a government death squad killed six Jesuit priests and their two employees. International outrage followed, and the United States finally cut off its military aid. The guilty men went to prison, and the United Nations began work on mediation talks. In late 1991, a peace agreement was signed. A ceasefire took effect on February 1, 1992. A ceremony on December 15, 1992, marked the official end of the conflict, and the leftist leaders became part of the political process.

this city of red-tile roofs and cobbled streets has become a key center for artists. It has more interesting hotels and restaurants than any other area in the country and is a great place to relax. Many wealthy families moved here after an earthquake struck San Salvador in 1854, so Suchitoto has also been a cultural capital for 150 years, with many concerts, indoors and out, throughout the year.

- El Salvador is part of the "Ring of Fire" that stretches the length of the west coast of the Americas. With **25 volcanoes** scattered around, it usually has dramatic scenery within sight. From the town of Miramundo on the slopes of 8,957-foot El Pital mountain, you can see most of the country on a clear day.
- The shoreline is among the most free of commercial development on the entire Pacific coast of Central America. Paths to the **many good beaches** are not always well marked, so you either have to get directions or search.
- Many of El Salvador's tourists are surfers, lured by the **big waves** near the beach towns of La Libertad, El Sunzal, and El Zonte.
- El Salvador shares several **nature reserves** with neighboring countries, including Montecristo National Park at the northern tip and Bosque El Imposible National Park in the far west. Besides the abundant birds (such as striped owls, quetzals, toucans, eagles, and parrots), wildlife in the parks includes anteaters, pumas, and spider monkeys. The small islands in the **Gulf of Fonseca** between El Salvador and Honduras are worth a trip for mountainous panoramas and sea vistas, hiking, and beaches. There are two hotels on the largest island, Meanguera, and a few places to eat on Meanguerita for a day trip.
- The colonial town of **Ahuachapán** is in a pleasant highland setting near the Guatemalan border, surrounded by high peaks and coffee plantations.
- The **Coatepeque crater lake** is one of the country's major attractions for residents as well as tourists. The drive to the rim of the caldera is easy, and the viewpoints are spectacular. The caldera is 7 miles long by 4 miles across, and the lake below is about half that size. Private homes surround the deep water, but there are also two hotels. There is no evidence of current volcanic activity—well, if you don't count a number of fumaroles and a few hot springs. There are several villages in the nearby mountains and lots of hiking trails, so visitors usually stay longer than they had planned.
- In the northeast is **Ruta de la Paz**, a series of walking trails connect villages. Among the attractions are caves outside the towns of Corinto and Cacaopera that contain paintings dating from 8000 BC. They convey perspective on how long humans have inhabited this region.
- The city of **Chalchuapa** is about two hours from the capital. **Tazumal**, on its outskirts, is the country's main Maya site. The ruins won't wow you like

the major Maya sites farther north, but the 75-foot main pyramid and surrounding structures are worth a visit.

- **San Salvador**, the capital, has a population of 2.2 million in a smog-filled valley. It may not be a real highlight, but you'll probably spend at least one night there if you fly or your bus connection requires it. The city has been hit by 14 earthquakes over recent centuries—the last one in 2001—so many notable sites have been damaged. Still, there's a historic center worth a stroll, with some buildings from the 16th and 17th centuries. Many visitors find the city to be more developed than they expected, with lots of shopping malls, movie theaters, and attractive restaurants providing diversion from the muggy afternoon heat, exhaust fumes, and dense traffic.

> El Salvador is the only Central American country without a Caribbean coast.

Itineraries

If You Have a Week in El Salvador

If arriving overland from Guatemala, start in Santa Ana, then spend a couple of nights soaking up the scenery at Ahuachapán and Coatepeque Lake. Head to the Spanish colonial hillside city of Suchitoto, then either head north to the Montecristo Cloud Forest and El Pital Mountain (with a stop in the craft center of La Palma) or go straight to the coast. Spend a night or two at one of the beaches east or west of La Libertad, then the last day and night in San Salvador.

If arriving overland from Honduras, start in the craft center of La Palma and use it as a base for exploring the Bosque Montecristo National Park. Spend a night or two in Suchitoto, then a night in San Salvador before catching a bus to Coatepeque Lake and Ahuachapán for hiking and appealing scenery. End your trip at one of the beaches, and then either head to the airport or move overland to the next destination.

If flying into San Salvador, spend a night there, then travel to Coatepeque Lake and Ahuachapán. Spend a night or two in Suchitoto, and then end the trip either on the coast or in the highlands around La Palma if going on to Honduras.

If your next destination is southern Honduras or Nicaragua, end your visit at the eastern end of El Salvador, perhaps spending some time on Meanguera Island. If your next destination is Guatemala, switch the itinerary around to spend the last night in Santa Ana, the country's second-largest city.

There are plenty of destinations for easy day trips from San Salvador, including Cihuatán, an archaeological park on the site of the largest city in Mesoamerica in the time of the Toltecs, and Joya de Cerén, an ancient Maya village that was buried under 18 feet of volcanic ash about AD 600. (The latter is the country's sole UNESCO World Heritage site.) Some travelers take a day to hike to the crater of Volcán San Salvador, not far from the capital.

If You Have Two Weeks or More in El Salvador

In two weeks, you can cover all of the country without rushing and have time to explore various beaches and hike up a few volcanoes. You can also visit the islands in the Gulf of Fonseca and the villages and cave art of the Ruta de la Paz in the northeast.

If you begin your visit at Coatepeque Lake, you'll have easy access to three natural parks, each with a distinctive landscape: Cerro Verde, El Imposible, and Barra de Santiago. The last one encompasses a coastal mangrove region, with beaches nearby. The colonial town of Izalco, with a colorful market and festivals, is worth a stop. Spend an extra night or two in San Salvador, taking day trips to buried Joya de Cerén and Cihuatán archaeological park.

Cost Comparisons

Prices in El Salvador are somewhat higher than in neighboring countries. Lodging choices at the low end can be slim, and taxis are expensive. The following are representative costs across El Salvador but don't include places where prices are inflated, such as deluxe hotels and fine-dining restaurants:

Holidays and Festivals

- January 1: New Year's Day
- March or April: Semana Santa, the week before Easter, is a major vacation and celebration time. Most businesses close for three days, but government shuts down for ten!
- May 1: Labor Day
- May 3: Day of the Cross
- May 7: Armed Forces' Day
- May 10: Mother's Day
- June 17: Father's Day
- June 22: Teacher's Day
- First week of August: Festivals celebrate El Salvador del Mundo (the Savior of the World), the country's patron saint, in San Salvador.
- September 15: Independence Day
- October 12: Columbus Day
- Most of November: Carnival, San Miguel, honoring the city's patron saint, the Virgen de la Paz
- November 2: All Souls' Day and Day of the Dead
- November 5: First Cry of Independence Day
- December 12: Virgin of Guadalupe Day
- December 24: Christmas Eve
- December 25: Christmas
- December 31: New Year's Eve

- Liter of water in a convenience store: 50 cents–$1
- Bottle of beer in a bar or restaurant: $1–$2
- Bottle of beer in a store: 40 cents–$1
- Meal of the day in a locals' restaurant: $1.25–$4
- Half kilo of oranges, in season: 50 cents
- 1 hour of Internet access in a cafe: $1–$1.50
- Cup of coffee, juice, or soda in a restaurant: 50–90 cents
- 10-minute taxi ride across town: $5–$7
- Taxi from airport to hotel: $16–$20
- 3-star or equivalent city hotel: $40–$75

Accommodations

Overall, hotel prices are quite reasonable throughout El Salvador, but finding hotels with character is not always easy, especially at the low end. Because there's not a lot of tourism, the lodging industry is geared more to business travelers and domestic groups. The exception is Suchitoto, where two excellent boutique hotels—La Posada de Suchitlán and Los Almendros de San Lorenzo—wow travelers for $100 a night or less.

To serve domestic travelers, the government has set up many campgrounds. These *turicentros* are the only option in some park and beach areas.

A basic hotel room with a shared bath will range from $6 to $15 a night. Spending $20 to $40 will get you a decent room with maid service, a private bath, and hot water. At this price, you will often also get air-conditioning, breakfast, and free Internet access. The problem is that apart from the highlight areas listed in this section, there may be only one hotel in town. Keep some extra cash for nights when choices are slim. Be aware that an "auto hotel" is not a roadside motel. It's a "love hotel" for couples trying to be discreet.

Paying more than $60 a night generally gets you into the deluxe range, usually a business-oriented, three-star hotel with a bar, restaurant, elevator, and bellhop. The best international hotels, such as the Hilton and InterContinental in San Salvador, list standard rooms for less than $150 a night. If you don't mind staying at typical business hotels, there are plenty to pick from in the larger towns and cities.

The beachfront is relatively undeveloped, but there are a few resorts. The Royal Decameron Salinitas, just 45 minutes from the capital, follows the typical all-inclusive mold, but at half what you would pay in most other locations: as little as $140 a night for two. Otherwise, expect to stay in small, motel-like places that cater to domestic families. Often, these will have a kitchenette and swimming pool.

> Remittances to relatives from the many Salvadorans living abroad make up a key element of the country's economy, equivalent to more than 16 percent of the gross domestic product.

Food and Drink

Pupusas are the national dish: pancake-thick cornmeal or rice-meal tortillas stuffed with pork cracklings, cheese, or whatever meat and vegetables are handy. They are served at humble street stalls, nice restaurants, and *pupuserías*. They come with cabbage salad and spicy tomato sauce.

Other typical menu choices include baked chicken with gravy, black bean soup, seafood soup, baked plantains stuffed with minced meat and white cheese, and a type of turkey sandwich. Variations of dishes from elsewhere in the region, including tamales, ceviche, and chilis rellenos, appear in slightly different form.

Salvadorans eat lots of rice, beans, and plantains, so finding vegetarian food is seldom difficult. The capital has vegetarian restaurants. Seafood—especially fish and shrimp—is prominent along the coast. Locals love fast food as well. Some blocks in San Salvador look as if they were transplanted from the United States, with typical American franchises lining both sides of the street.

With so many of El Salvador's residents being descendants of immigrants or Salvadorans who have returned from living elsewhere, there's a wide variety of ethnic food, especially in San Salvador and Santa Ana. If you crave Chinese, Italian, Middle Eastern, or Peruvian food, you'll be satisfied.

Because there are wealthy Salvadorans in the cities, you can enjoy fine dining—and at a much lower price than at home. Figure on less than $50 per person at the best restaurants for several courses and a few drinks.

The quiet life, El Salvador

Lunch can last for a couple of hours, so restaurants stay open well into the afternoon. In the capital, dinner is served late, with restaurants at their busiest about 8 or 9 p.m. A standard tip is 10 to 15 percent.

El Salvador's main beer brands are Suprema, Pilsener of El Salvador, Rio Clara, and Caguama (which tastes very similar to Mexico's Corona and can sometimes be found in U.S. stores). Otherwise, there are the usual bland lagers that are hard to tell apart—okay on a hot day, but nothing to get excited about.

The country grows some good coffee beans, so ask for the local coffee. Fresh fruit juices are easy to find. Whatever is in season will cost less than $1 for a big glass.

Transportation

Riding El Salvador's **buses** is cheaper than it is comfortable. No ride normally takes more than five hours, so there's not much demand for executive buses like those in many other countries. There are a few first-class buses and shuttle vans for some routes. Otherwise, rich people take their cars, and everyone else crowds into regular buses. Unless you are on a tour bus, you will be crammed into what used to be a school bus. If you go this route, be prepared to see the real Central America. I wouldn't miss it.

The bus system is like the hub-and-spoke airline system: you can seldom get from Point A to Point B without going through San Salvador. There is no centralized bus system, so different companies ply different routes. Ask at your hotel or at the station about departure times for specific destinations. The regular buses are the only ones serving most routes, but at least they're cheap. The ride from San Salvador to Santa Ana (2 hours 30 minutes) costs less than $1, while a four-hour *directo* bus with fewer stops will seldom top $4 for anywhere in the country from San Salvador. You can find private shuttles from the capital to La Libertad, Santa Ana, and Suchitoto, with rates of $3 to $8.

If you have a few people in a group, it is economical and far more comfortable to pay $30 to $50 to hire a **car and driver** for all-day excursions. You'll see a lot more than if you rely on public transportation. It can be worth hiring a **taxi or van driver** for short trips from the capital as well: a taxi to La Libertad usually costs about $20 one-way, $35 round-trip.

Destinations are close together, and there are no distant islands to reach, so there's no domestic **airline** service. Airlines do connect to other Central American countries. From the United States, direct flights are available on Continental, Delta, United, TACA, and American. It's an easy three hours in the air from Houston, two and a half from Miami.

The country has no **passenger trains.**

Taxis are plentiful except in rural areas. Few trips will cost more than $10 within a city. It is not the custom to tip drivers.

Renting a car can cost 10 to 50 percent more than at home, and local insurance is mandatory (at $10 to $15 a day), but El Salvador's compact size and lack of upscale buses make it a good place to have your own wheels. Driving opens up exploration options and eliminates time-wasting trips back to the capital to change buses. Several international rental-car companies have offices here, and there are numerous local operators. Try to drive only during daytime to avoid the risks of driving on unfamiliar roads at night. The main roads are paved, but back roads may be gravel or dirt, with few signs. Allow plenty of time.

Gas costs slightly more than in the United States, but distances are so short it's hard to go through more than a tank a week.

Activity Costs

- Rent a surfboard at La Libertad for $15 a day.
- Take a deep-sea fishing trip for one of the lowest rates in the Americas: a half day for six people costs about $200.
- Hiring a boat and captain for a day's sightseeing around Isla Tasajera runs $80.
- One of the best spots for scuba diving is the coral reef near Los Cóbanos. Expect to pay $60 to $100 for a day of diving. Dive shops in San Salvador also arrange diving trips to Coatepeque or Ilopango lakes.

Surfing in La Libertad, El Salvador

- At any national park or archaeological site, you can hire a guide for a few dollars an hour. Ask at your hotel or the entrance booth.

Tour Companies

Only a few companies run organized tours to El Salvador. There's just not enough demand to create a lot of competition. G.A.P Adventures (**www.gapadventures.com**) operates one trip that also includes Guatemala. MILA Tours (**www.milatours.com**) and Gate Travel (**www.gate-travel.org**) are among the few companies offering standard guided trips to El Salvador alone. For surfing trips, try Access Tours (**www.accesstrips.com**), Punta Mango (**www.puntamango.com**), or Wavehunters Surf Travel (**www.wavehunters.com**).

One other option is to purchase a package deal to one of the Pacific beach resorts, such as Royal Decameron Salinitas, and strike out from there on day trips or overnight journeys.

Eva Tours (**www.evatours.com.sv**), based in San Salvador, can set up nearly any excursion or customize a whole vacation itinerary.

Useful Details

Getting there and away: Airlines connect El Salvador to a variety of U.S. gateways and many cities in Mexico and elsewhere in Central America.

Visas: Citizens of the United States, Canada, and Mexico don't need a visa for El Salvador but must purchase a tourist card for $10 when entering the country. The standard length of stay is 30 days, but on entry, you can request up to 90 days at no extra charge. Citizens of some countries—including the United Kingdom, Israel, neighboring Central American nations, and many European Union countries—don't need a visa and do not pay a fee,

One tourist stamp and fee allows you to travel overland among Guatemala, Honduras, El Salvador, and Nicaragua without additional payments, stamps, or another tourist card. But you do need your passport.

Border crossings: On land, you can cross to and from neighboring nations with a minimum of delays and hassles. Bus lines in Honduras, Guatemala, and Nicaragua serve various El Salvador destinations—in very nice buses—for $30 to $80, depending on distance.

There are four crossings into Guatemala, including one on the Pan-American Highway at San Cristóbal. Three border posts allow crossings into southern Honduras.

You can travel the short distance from southwest El Salvador to northwest Nicaragua by boat, but connections are not always reliable. Most travelers go overland through Honduras or fly between the capitals.

Currency: The dollar rules. American travelers don't have to exchange money because El Salvador adopted the American greenback and coins as its own in 2001. You may occasionally still see prices in the old currency, colones (for which the rate is 8.75 to the dollar).

Departure tax: It's $32 for those departing by air, which is often included in your ticket price.

Weather and when to go: El Salvador doesn't get as hot as some of its neighbors. The average daytime high throughout the year is 85°F. Temperatures vary only a few degrees, rarely getting much above 90.

The coolest and driest months are November through January, so this is the most pleasant time to visit, though most tourists arrive from December through April. The hottest months are March through May. Although the air is humid, things can get quite dusty then because the rains haven't arrived. The rainy season, May through October, is the least desirable time for trekking and hiking volcanoes. Some parks are closed because roads can get washed out.

Electricity: Current and outlet shapes are the same as in the United States.

Internet and telephone access: Internet cafes are abundant in urban areas, especially in shopping centers and malls. Logging on is dirt cheap: seldom more than $1.50 an hour. Competition rules here, so a variety of phone companies fight for business, each having its own pay phones and corresponding phone cards.

Rates to call the U.S. are half those of other countries in this book: 15 to 25 cents a minute.

Language: Spanish is the primary language. Because a large number of Salvadorans have lived in the United States, English is more prevalent than you would expect in a country with so few tourists.

Safety: Although El Salvador's homicide rate is higher than that of some neighboring countries, travelers are generally not at risk because most of the violence occurs in the inner cities. Exercise special caution at night in San Salvador, San Miguel, Sonsonate, La Unión, and La Libertad. Leave valuables locked up at your hotel. At night, skip the bus and avoid the temptation to take a long stroll. Spend a few extra dollars to take a taxi.

Otherwise, follow the precautions outlined in Chapter 17, Safety and Security.

Health care: Several hospitals and clinics provide some of the best health-care services in Central America—often from doctors who were educated in the United States. Health care can be rudimentary outside San Salvador because half the country's wealth is in the capital (but you're never far from there). If you come down with a bug, a house call to your hotel room will rarely top $40.

The standard inoculations for Central America should be up to date. (See Chapter 12, Keeping Healthy.) There's some malaria and dengue-fever risk in rural areas, including the coast.

Things to buy: El Salvador's handicrafts are better than those of many neighboring countries, reflecting the people's industrious nature and good business sense. A lot of high-quality crafts are good enough to export. A long-established textile industry produces good work.

A wide variety of handicrafts is available in stores and markets, but certain areas are known for specific crafts. Nahuizalco is the place for baskets and wicker. San Sebastián is known for hammocks. La Palma produces painted wooden boxes and wood carvings. Panchimalco is the main weaving center, and Ilobasco is the ceramics center. Getting to these places is not always quick or easy by public transportation. If you plan to do a lot of shopping, budget some money for a driver or car rental.

Resources

The only guidebook covering the country in depth is *Lonely Planet Nicaragua & El Salvador*—but watch the publication date. Otherwise, you'll have to depend on guidebooks published by Footprint, Rough Guides, Lonely Planet, or Fodor's that cover all of Central America. If you're a surfer, check out *Wavefinder: Central America,* by Terry Gibson.

Trying to find reliable travel information about El Salvador on the Internet is frustrating. Because the country draws so few tourists from outside Central America, there's not much incentive to build extensive resource sites, and few local tour groups put a major effort into publicity. The Other El Salvador (**www .theotherelsalvador.com**) and Gateway El Salvador (**www.gatewayelsalvador .com**) have helpful links and information for exploring the country. Tim's El Salvador Blog offers insight (in English) about what's happening in the country: **luterano.blogspot.com.**

Suchitoto has an official site in English (**www.suchitoto-el-salvador.com/ english**) as well as a commercial one with additional information and hotel links (**www.gaesuchitoto.com**).

For surf conditions and maps, see Punta Mango Surf Trips at **www.punta mango.com**. (Punta Mango also books surfing packages.)

Retirement Opportunities

Few books, magazines, or Web sites offer information about El Salvador as a retirement location. On the other hand, foreigners can own land in El Salvador, including beachfront property, without restrictions, and there are plenty of bargain prices. For example: gated-community building lots for $18,000, a three-bedroom beachfront house with a pool for $69,000, and a five-bedroom luxury house with an acre of land and two pools for $225,000. Hard to beat!

Helping Out

Many organizations run development projects, and there's no shortage of volunteer opportunities. English teachers, medical workers, and reconstruction experts are all in high demand. International groups operating here include Habitat for Humanity (**www.habitat.org**) and Heifer International (**www.heifer.org**).

CRISPAZ, or Christians for Peace in El Salvador, works with local partner organizations regarding the environment, food security, community organizing, and organic farming: **www.crispaz.org.**

The Global Volunteer Network has a local office in San Salvador and has placements in several cities: **www.volunteer.org.nz/elsalvador.**

Seeds of Learning (**www.seedsoflearning.org**) is involved in building schools and communities.

HONDURAS

Honduras offers postcard-perfect island beaches, some of the best scuba diving and snorkeling in the hemisphere, vast nature reserves, and Copán—one of the most impressive Maya ruins. Before final independence in 1838, it was known as Spanish Honduras, to differentiate it from British Honduras (now Belize). This mountainous country with a long coast on the Caribbean Sea borders Guatemala on the west, El Salvador on the southwest, and Nicaragua on the southeast.

Tourism in this second-largest Central American country (slightly larger than Tennessee) has been rising at a double-digit rate each year, with most tourists heading to the Bay Islands of Roatán and Utila, or to the Maya site of Copán. In fact, Roatán looks like a different country, much more luxurious than the mainland. Outside those areas, you're unlikely to run into many other travelers. Much of the country is undeveloped or set aside as nature reserves, including all land above 6,000 feet.

Honduras means "the depths" in Spanish, but it's more often thought of as the original "banana republic." That somewhat derogatory name came from the days when banana crops represented 70 percent of the country's economy. It has often been under the thumb of external governments and big businesses, both as a banana producer and as a pawn of the U.S. armed forces during conflicts in Nicaragua. This history, and the devastation from Hurricane Mitch in 1998, have helped make Honduras one of the poorest countries in the hemisphere (just a tad wealthier than Haiti and Nicaragua). If there's a bright side, it's that foreign funds have caused roads and some other public infrastructure to be in better condition than in most other countries in the region. Happily, in recent years Honduras has escaped the bloody civil wars and coups that have plagued some other Central American countries, and it has held several peaceful, democratic elections.

Adventurous travelers can have a great time hiking the lengthy trails, rafting good whitewater spots, sea kayaking, and diving and snorkeling around the huge barrier reef.

Honduras is one of the least expensive places in the Americas. Backpackers can coast on $15 to $20 per day. Travelers who want more comfort should plan on $20 to $60 per person. For $200 a day, travelers can afford everything offered on mainland Honduras. Expect to pay twice that much for a luxury-hotel scuba-diving package on Roatán during high season.

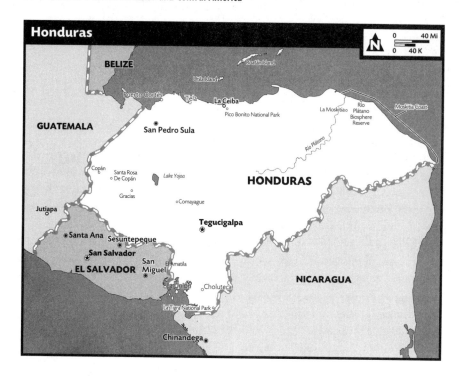

Honduras's People

The area now known as Honduras has a rich multiethnic history. The Mayas occupied the area of Copán in western Honduras from around 1000 BC until AD 900. Other indigenous peoples, such as the Lencas, lived near Copán and in other parts of the country.

Christopher Columbus reached the Bay Islands in 1502 and then landed near Trujillo. The local people fought occupation, and it took several decades for Spain to control the region.

The Spanish ruled for approximately three centuries, bringing the Garifuna people into the ethnic mix.

After gold and silver were discovered near Tegucigalpa in 1570, pirates stormed the coast seeking plunder. British buccaneers enjoyed Roatán so much that by 1600 some 5,000 of them had moved in. Dutch pirates sacked Trujillo so thoroughly in 1643 that it wasn't resettled by the Spanish for more than a century.

Honduras and the rest of the Central American provinces asserted independence from Spain on September 15, 1821. In 1838, Honduras became an independent nation. After a long period of military rule, a democratic government took power in 1982. Transfers of power have been peaceful since.

Most Hondurans are classified as *mestizo* (a mix of Spanish and indigenous heritage). The rest are Garifuna; descendants of English settlers; expatriates from North America; and immigrants from East Asia, Palestine, and Syria.

The Garifuna

The Garifuna people living along the coasts and on the islands of Honduras, Belize, and Guatemala have African roots. Most are descended from a group of 2,248 Garifunas who were settled on the Honduran coast and Bay Islands in 1797 because they were aligned with the French against the British in the battle for Caribbean territory. Their exodus spread farther up the coast of Honduras and eventually into Guatemala and Belize, at times with the support of the Spanish, who were seeking a labor force.

Ninety-seven percent of Hondurans are Roman Catholic, with virtually all the rest Protestant. About one-third of the population works in agriculture. Reliance on commodity exports (chiefly bananas, pineapples, and coffee) makes the economy dependent on world market prices, subjecting it to wild swings. Unemployment, more than 25 percent, is a major problem.

Highlights

- Long, skinny **Roatán Island** is a major diving destination with everything from low-key hotels and rental homes to luxury resorts. Unlike nearby Belize, this island has great beaches—but you may need plenty of bug spray to ward off sand flies at dusk. The West End neighborhood is known as Gringo Central because of the many foreign retirees and the businesses that serve them. Now that cruise ships are docking at Coxen Hole, that town is, unfortunately, developing the aura of other commercialized cruise ports. Top-end rooms and meals reach a higher standard than elsewhere on the Central American coast south of Belize. Upscale rooms can top $300 a night. Gourmet meals cost $20 and up per person. However, the lengthy coral reef and superior scuba diving and snorkeling may still make this a better value than the rest of the Caribbean. Not all the lodging is top-tier. Roatán has many simple diving lodges—some right on the water—and budget hotels with relatively basic standards.
- The nearby island of **Utila** is a smaller, more budget-oriented diving hot spot with plenty of easygoing hotels and rental apartments. Off both islands (and nearby smaller ones), divers and snorkelers encounter a wide variety of marine life, including manta rays, parrot fish, and harmless whale sharks. Bottlenose dolphins often frolic near the beaches.
- The **Copán** ruins are nearly on a par with Guatemala's Tikal and Mexico's Chichén Itzá as a must-see Maya site. Copán is not as large or spectacular as the other two but has the most

Honduras is a biological hot spot. It has about 250 species of reptiles and amphibians, more than 700 bird species, and 110 mammal species (half of which are bats).

The Betrayed Lempira

Why is the monetary unit called the lempira? To honor a great leader and warrior who died, so the story goes, because of a foreign deceiver.

During the early Spanish attempts to form a colony in Honduras, the Lenca chief, Lempira, was a constant thorn in the Spaniards' side, repeatedly attacking outposts with his men. In 1537, he unified more than 200 tribes that had been ancient rivals in order to fight the Spaniards. He gathered all the tribes on top of the great rock of Cerquín and built fortifications. For six months, the Spanish tried and failed to defeat them.

At the same time, Lempira continued to incite trouble elsewhere. Comayagua was set on fire. Gracias was threatened by surrounding tribes, and other native groups attacked San Pedro de Puerto Caballos and Trujillo. In desperation, Captain Alonso de Cáceres resorted to treachery. He invited Lempira to a meeting, indicating it was for a peace settlement. During the meeting, an unseen marksman shot Lempira in the head in view of his men. With their leader gone, an estimated 30,000 men dispersed, and the revolt was lost.

extensive and best-preserved carvings and inscriptions in the Maya world. (See "Exploring Copán" in this chapter.)

- The town of **Santa Rosa de Copán**, near the archaeological site, is a center for coffee and cigars. You can tour a coffee plantation and see a factory where high-quality cigars are hand-rolled. Check out the birds at the nearby Macaw Mountain Bird Park & Nature Reserve (**www.macawmountain.com**).

- Travelers who wish they'd been born in the age of explorers can see what those folks experienced at one of the huge protected **rain forests and cloud forests** inhabited by indigenous people. Village guides charge very reasonable prices. Visitors travel by foot or canoe. You'll take a tent, a water purifier, insect repellent, and food, and can expect to see plenty of wildlife, including tropical birds, monkeys, crocodiles, and butterflies. Jaguars see you much more often than you see them.

- The **Moskitia Coast** was made famous in the Paul Theroux book *The Mosquito Coast* and the subsequent movie of the same name. However, *Moskitia* comes from the name of the indigenous Miskito tribe, not the insect. Much of this "little Amazon" is still unexplored, a wild area with far more creatures than people. Some companies lead trips through the jungle, first on foot, then on rafts down the Río Plátano. The Río Plátano Biosphere Reserve is designated as a UNESCO World Heritage site.

Exploring Copán

Copán Ruinas is a perfect walking town, with cobbled streets, old buildings being restored, an active central plaza, a bustling market, good restaurants and bars, and the proper laid-back attitude for this latitude. Cowboys stroll the streets in their jeans, white shirts, boots, and distinctive sombreros. Bright red three-wheeled *tuk-tuks* (imported from India) will give you a ride most anywhere for a bit more than 50 cents a person. Try Twisted Tanya's for open-air dining and delightful food. Always carry a flashlight because the electricity in Copán Ruinas seems to be off as much as on. No electricity means no running water, so fill a couple of containers for washing and flushing. Nevertheless, the low cost of living and the warm ambience are attracting North American retirees to settle here.

The Museo Regional de Arqueología, adjacent to the town plaza, features a collection well worth an hour of your time. The originals of two glyph-covered altars are here, along with stelae (carved stone pillars) and two re-created tombs.

The ruins of Copán are in the open so, unless heat doesn't bother you, arrive early. It's possible to explore the ruins in a morning and actually get a good feel for the place. Expect to walk on groomed trails through the forest, and up, down, and around the pyramids on narrow steps. The ruins are known for the beauty of their deep-relief carving, much of it in quite good condition. Don't miss the fine carvings on the stelae, the grandeur of the glyph staircase that records 400 years of history of the Copán dynasty, the vistas from the tops of the pyramids, and the destruction wrought by gnarled kapok trees growing out of ruined temples. The ball court here is in excellent condition, with rooms from which kings and priests watched the brutal contests.

Opposite the visitor center, you enter the dramatic new Museum of Maya Sculpture through a jaguar's mouth. It opens into a tunnel that symbolically represents the entrance to the underworld. In a courtyard inside, you'll enjoy a reconstruction of the Rosalia Temple in its plastered and painted glory. Stelae and carvings are dramatically displayed around the sides of the courtyard. Check out the bold sculpture of a leaf-nosed bat, the symbol of Copán. You see how the Maya defined status by the sculpture on a scribe's house, a noble's domicile, and a king's palace. With explanations in English and Spanish, this museum is a visual tour de force.

- You don't have to hit the Moskitia Coast to get into the wilderness. The 429-square-mile **Pico Bonito** National Park offers abundant room to roam. The entrance is near the city of La Ceiba. Take a canoe trip among the mangroves, a wild whitewater-rafting trip through gorges on the Cangrejal River (Classes III and IV), or hike around Pico Bonito Mountain, which tops 8,000 feet.

- The capital of **Tegucigalpa** (often shortened to "Tegus") won't win any awards as Latin America's prettiest city, but it does compare favorably with the other main city of San Pedro Sula. The historic center of the city has survived natural disasters and provides dramatic views of surrounding mountains.

> Honduras boasts the oldest functioning clock in the Americas. It was built by Moors in the 12th century and transferred to the Cathedral of Comayagua in 1636.

- Just 7 miles from the capital is the entrance to **La Tigra National Park**. You won't see any tigers, but this cloud forest is one of the richest wildlife habitats in the world, including more than 200 bird species. Hiking trails wind through the park, one passing a waterfall that is spectacular in the rainy season.

- **Comayagua**, some 50 miles northwest of Tegucigalpa on the highway to San Pedro Sula, attracts many visitors to see its Spanish Colonial architecture and centuries-old clock. Comayagua was founded in 1537 and chartered Central America's first university in 1632. The first capital of Honduras after independence, it's now a pleasant town of 60,000.

- **Gracias** is another colonial town and former capital. Visitors come to see churches and a fort that date back 400 years and to admire nearby mountains, including the highest point in Honduras—**Mount Celaque** (9,347 feet). You can hike the mountain independently or book a trip with a guide for a reasonable rate.

Itineraries

If You Have a Week in Honduras

If you're a fan of the Maya, visiting Copán is a must. If you're committed to hiking, biking, river rafting, or sea kayaking, you have lots of choices. But if you're a passionate scuba diver or snorkeler, you'll head straight to Roatán in the Bay Islands, where you'll spend most of your week on or under the water and then head happily home. Some spend a few days in Roatán and move to the neighboring island of Utila for more of the same. Many visitors take advantage of one of the package deals that include lodging, dive certification, and

Hurricane Mitch

Hurricane Mitch caused such widespread damage in 1998 that officials estimated 50 years of development had been destroyed in a few days. Some 70 percent of the country's crops and transportation infrastructure was ruined. The hurricane and resulting high waters wiped out nearly all bridges and secondary roads. At least 33,000 homes were leveled and 50,000 damaged, and about 5,000 people were killed. Total damage was pegged at $3 billion, which is greater than an entire year of Honduran government revenues today.

reliable dive gear for a terrific low price. (See the "Activity Costs" section of this chapter.)

If you get a little waterlogged, you might take a plane or ferry to the mainland and spend a day or two near La Ceiba doing some mountain biking, hiking, or rafting. The terms of your plane ticket will determine if you can fly home from a mainland airport or have to return to Roatán for your departure.

If you're arriving overland from Guatemala, Copán will be the first stop. If arriving by air in San Pedro Sula, again, head for Copán. Spend a few days among the ruins, the 16th-century town of Gracias, and Santa Rosa de Copán. Visit a cigar factory, hike, and do some tropical-bird watching. Take a bus to La Ceiba, on the Caribbean coast, which offers many outdoor-adventure activities in addition to a beach. Catch a flight from La Ceiba to Roatán or Utila for diving or beach bumming. Fly back to your departure airport of San Pedro Sula or Tegucigalpa.

If arriving by air in Tegucigalpa, you can follow a similar itinerary, but Gracias will be the first stop on the way to Copán. If you're arriving from El Salvador or Nicaragua, follow the itinerary starting in Tegucigalpa.

If you arrive by boat from Belize or Livingston, Guatemala, leave the docking area of Puerto Barrios, Guatemala, and take a bus into Honduras to the western beach area of Tela. Work your way along the coast to La Ceiba and on to the Bay Islands, then take a flight to Copán. You could make it from Belize to Roatán or Utila in one day, skipping the rest of the coast. Or proceed overland from Livingston through northeastern Guatemala and arrive in Copán, following the itinerary described above.

If You Have Two Weeks or More in Honduras

With two weeks or more, you can add more beach and dive time, more visits to mountain towns (adding Comayagua), or some time in the jungle in La Moskitia or elsewhere. You might visit volcanic Lake Yojoa south of San Pedro Sula. The other option is to follow the one-week itinerary at a more leisurely pace, spending more time enjoying each area. Perhaps visit other beach areas or Comayagua on day trips and take advantage of overnight hiking or rafting trips. Spend some time in the small towns and craft villages that you discover.

The minimum time for exploring the Río Plátano Biosphere Reserve is four days, but seven to nine days will better allow you to get deep into the jungle on a river trip. If this is high on your list, give it adequate time.

Cost Comparisons

For backpackers and independent travelers watching the budget, Honduras vies with Nicaragua for the distinction of being the cheapest destination around. The

Always wanted to see 10,000 butterflies in one place? You can do that at La Ceiba's Butterfly and Insect Museum (**www .hondurasbutterfly .com**), along with 3,000 other insects from 112 countries.

following are representative costs across Honduras and do not include places where prices are inflated, such as deluxe hotels and fine-dining establishments:

- Liter of water in a convenience store: 30–60 cents
- Bottle of beer in a bar or restaurant: 50 cents–$1
- Bottle of beer in a store: 25–60 cents
- Meal of the day in a working-people's restaurant: $2–$3
- Half kilo of oranges, in season: 25 cents
- 1 hour of Internet access in a cafe: $2–$4.50
- Cup of coffee, juice, or soda in a restaurant: 40–60 cents
- 10-minute taxi ride across town: $4
- Taxi from main international airport to hotel: $7–$9
- 3-star or equivalent hotel: $40–$80

Accommodations

The cities have plenty of midrange and four-star-equivalent hotels, mainly for business travelers and tourists in transit. High-end chain hotels, such as Hilton and InterContinental, usually cost $100 to $175 in the cities. There are few

Holidays and Festivals

- January 1: New Year's Day
- January 19–25: Guancasco Festival (honoring Saint Sebastian), Gracias
- First week of February: Virgin of Suyapa Fiesta, Suyapa, outside Tegucigalpa
- March or April: Semana Santa, the week before Easter
- April 14: Pan American Day (Day of the Americas)
- May 1: Labor Day
- Late May: La Ceiba Carnaval
- June: Fiesta de San Antonio, Tela
- June: Fiesta de San Juan Bautista, Trujillo
- Last week in June: June Fair, San Pedro Sula
- July: Lempira Festival, Gracias
- Late July: Utila Carnaval, Utila Island
- September: Folkloric Festival, San Pedro Sula
- September 10: Día del Niño (Day of the Child—a nationwide children's birthday party)
- September 15: Independence Day
- October 3: Francisco Morazán Day. He was a 19th-century statesman and president of the short-lived Federal Republic of Central America.
- October 12: Columbus Day
- October 21: Army Day
- December 6–16: Central American Tourism and Artisans' Fair, Tegucigalpa
- December 15–21: Cultural fair, Copán
- December 25: Christmas

expensive hotels on the mainland but plenty on Roatán. A three-star hotel or equivalent goes for $40 to $80, though in Roatán you'll spend far more when occupancy is high. If you're not picky, you can often find a nice clean, basic hotel room with air-conditioning for $20 to $40 in most spots.

There's a good chance you'll see "Made in Honduras" on the tag inside your underwear or jeans. Global brands manufactured around San Pedro Sula include Fruit of the Loom, Maidenform, Wrangler, Hanes, and OshKosh B'Gosh.

Budget travelers can find a dorm bed or basic single room for $2 to $8 in many areas. A basic double is $4 to $10 with a shared bath, $6 to $15 with a private bath. (Yes, this is one of those countries where the sub-$5 hotel room still exists.) Long-term rentals are available in many areas for $100 to $300 a month. Some of the best values are on Utila, where it's simple to find a bed for a few dollars or a private room with a shared hot-water bath for less than $20. The tourist infrastructure is limited outside the most popular areas. Off the beaten path, most rooms are pretty basic.

A dive package (rooms, meals, and diving) on the Bay Islands is the best value in the Caribbean. Whatever you choose, the livin' is easy.

On Roatán and Utila, book ahead or be prepared to shuttle around looking for a place to stay. Despite a building boom, the better places fill up fast during high season. As in most Latin America countries, hotels are packed during festival periods and holidays. See "Holidays and Festivals" elsewhere in this chapter. If traveling during such an event, book ahead.

Get hotel information from Web sites listed in the "Resources" section later in this chapter.

Food and Drink

Expect tortillas, beans, rice, eggs, and potatoes, plus excellent seafood near the coast (including lobster dishes for considerably less than $10). Fish soup with coconut milk is a standard dish, as is a similar concoction with vegetables served over rice. Yucca finds its way into a lot of dishes here. Look for Honduran versions of burritos, called *baleadas*, as well as Salvadoran *pupusas* (stuffed tortillas). Other local specialties are simple but filling, such as *tajadas*: fried plantain chips topped with cabbage and meat.

There are many fast-food options in the cities, including burgers, pizza, and kebabs, and full international menus in tourist spots and the capital—even Middle Eastern, Japanese, and Czech. Vegetarians will be easily satisfied in tourist centers, especially on the islands. The influx of expatriates to the Bay Islands has inspired the addition of a huge variety of international cuisines there, with great breads and desserts.

Breakfast is usually a tortillas-eggs-beans creation, often with fruit, for less than $1.50. Other meals range from $1 for a quick burger or burrito to $6 for a three- or four-course meal or pizza at a local eatery.

A cheap *comida corriente* (midday "meal of the day") at a simple restaurant costs about $2. Splurge on the *comida típica* for another dollar or two. The difference is the quality of the main dish. The sides will include tortillas and some combination of beans, rice, plantains, eggs, vegetables in season, cabbage salad, or cheese.

In the coastal town of La Ceiba, some open-air seaside restaurants and bars require you to deposit your firearms in lockers by the entrance before going farther. Wyatt Earp would love it!

Eating outside of deluxe hotels, you have to order lobster to spend more than $20 on dinner. A steak dinner at a high-end restaurant will exceed $10 only if you add wine. Restaurants will sometimes add a service charge to your bill, sometimes not. If you want your server to receive a tip, hand it to him or her.

A beer in a restaurant or bar will average $1 (50 cents during the numerous happy hours). Salva Vida has more malt than the Central American norm and is the best of the local crop. There is no local wine industry.

Good rum is a better bet. Rum-and-fruit cocktails commonly cost $2 along the coast. The popular Flor de Caña rum comes in several tiers of aging and quality, with the 12-year-old product demanding serious appreciation. Most wine in Honduras is imported from Chile or Argentina and sells for $5 to $8 a bottle in a restaurant.

Refreshing mixtures of water and fruit are popular, but ensure that it's bottled or filtered water. *Licuados* consist of fruit blended with milk. (Be sure it's pasteurized milk, not fresh off the farm.) Soft drinks are available everywhere, and it's easier to get a good cup of coffee than in neighboring countries.

Transportation

Many of the roads were built by U.S. contractors (to facilitate U.S. involvement in El Salvador and Nicaragua), but maintenance is now spotty. Roads rebuilt after the last hurricane are in the best shape.

The **bus** system is extensive, and it's easy to find connections. Away from the main routes, finding a comfortable bus may be tough. The cheapest ticket usually buys a seat on an ancient yellow U.S. school bus. The rules governing the school children's behavior are sometimes still posted inside—in English. These buses stop for everyone who waves at them along the way, doubling the driving time. Fares are about $1 an hour.

Between major cities, you'll have your choice of several classes of express or "executive" buses. Expect comfy seats and, in the top class, snacks and drinks. It's well worth the premium to ride on the best bus available, especially for longer trips. The lowest express buses cost $2 or $3 an hour, compared with $6 to $8 for the top "Ejecutivo Plus" class.

Sample bus routes and costs (highest class available):

City 1	City 2	Travel Time	Cost
Tegucigalpa	San Pedro Sula	3.5 hours	$10
Tegucigalpa	La Ceiba	6.5 hours	$7–$12
Copán	San Pedro Sula	3 hours	$30
La Ceiba	San Pedro Sula	3 hours	$25
La Ceiba	Tela	2 hours	$15
Copán	Guatemala City, Guatemala	5 hours	$46
Tegucigalpa	Guatemala City	10 hour	$68

Local bus rides are practically free. It's rare to pay more than 25 cents, and some hops are 10 cents. Of course, you have to figure out which bus will take you where you want to go, and when. Great way to meet local people.

A city **taxi** ride across town will rarely top $4. Many taxis are not metered, so agree on the fare up front. Hiring a taxi for an out-of-town excursion can be well worth it. A cab from Tegucigalpa to La Tigre National Park, for example, costs less than $15 after a little haggling.

Internal **flights** have a reputation for being the cheapest in Central America ($20 to $100). The robust local airline industry includes Sosa, Isleña, and Atlantic. The twice-a-day **boat** trip between the mainland and Roatán or Utila costs $16 to $22—but you can fly for only about $10 more. Island-hopping boats run regular trips, or you can hitch a ride with someone making a supply run.

The last intercity **train** was canceled in 2003. The only place to ride the rails now is a suburban line of less than 2 miles in La Ceiba. The fare is about 17 cents.

Avis, Budget, Hertz, and other **rental-car** agencies operate in the major cities, in the Copán area, and on Roatán. Rental rates are higher than at home—plus $5 to $10 per day for liability insurance. Main roads are in decent shape, but it's safer to drive only during the day.

Activity Costs

- If you arrange an all-day whitewater-rafting trip on the Cangrejal River through The Lodge at Pico Bonito (**www.picobonito.com**), it will cost $80 per person, including lunch. Book it through an independent agency in La Ceiba for about $60.
- La Ruta Moskitia (**www.larutamoskitia.com**) runs four- to nine-day trips into the Moskitia region. The shorter ones include internal flights, while the longest are mostly overland. Rates vary greatly depending on group size, starting at less than $60 per day per person for land-only groups of four or more.

- Honduras is the cheapest place in the Western Hemisphere, maybe in the world, to get certified as a scuba diver. The standard fee is $179 for a five-day, open-water course. If you're already certified, plan on a paltry $15 to $20 per dive, with volume discounts available.
- You can rent snorkeling equipment for $5 to $10 a day on the Bay Islands. If you go on a boat trip ($20 to $30), equipment is often included in the price.
- Many spots in Central America feature ziplining—zipping through the jungle canopy while suspended by a wire. While you might be charged big money in Costa Rica, costs in Honduras are as low as $20, including transportation (which may be on a horse) to the site. A more organized trip, including a lunch, costs about $30.
- In most areas, you can hire a guide for $4 to $10 an hour, depending on group size and the guide's expertise. This is a good investment for hiking trips because trails are almost never well marked.

Tour Companies

Very few U.S. or Canadian tour companies lead trips solely to Honduras. Most include Honduras in multicountry trips. One exception is Mountain Travel Sobek (**www.mtsobek.com**). The trips are pricey (nine-day land-only cost is $2,990 to $3,290), but the company has an excellent reputation.

Traveler's Tool Kit does not endorse any of the following local operators, but all have been around awhile and have solid reputations.

School band in Coxen Hole, Roatán, Honduras

Relaxing at a small hotel near Copán, Honduras

- Omega Tours (**www.omegatours.info/index2.htm**), based in La Ceiba and associated with a jungle lodge, is one of the best operators for outdoor adventures. The company offers kayaking trips, whitewater rafting on Rio Cangrejal, horseback riding, and trips into the Moskitia region.
- La Ruta Moskitia (**www.larutamoskitia.com**), an alliance of groups owned and operated by local communities, offers trips in the Moskitia region at reasonable prices.
- La Moskitia Ecoaventuras (**www.honduras.com/moskitia**) runs a wide variety of rafting trips, from half-day to 14-day adventures, in the Río Plátano Biosphere Reserve.
- Tourist Options (**www.touristoptionshonduras.com**), based in La Ceiba, provides English-speaking guides for day trips and city tours.
- Team Marin Honduras Fishing (**www.teammarinhondurasfishing.com**) offers nine-day, all-inclusive fishing trips for slightly less than $2,000.

Useful Details

Getting there and away: It's only a two-hour flight from Miami to San Pedro Sula or the capital on American or TACA. Continental flies nonstop from Houston to San Pedro Sula, Tegucigalpa, or Roatán in three hours. Delta flies nonstop to Roatán once a week from Atlanta, and budget carrier Spirit Airlines flies to San Pedro Sula several times a week from Fort Lauderdale, Florida.

Fairly frequent flights link three Honduran cities to other countries in Central America and Mexico.

A ferry runs twice a week between Dangriga in Belize and Puerto Cortés in Honduras (**www.belizenet.com/boatcharters**).

If you use the Hedman Alas bus service between Guatemala City, Guatemala, and San Pedro Sula, Tegucigalpa, La Ceiba, or Tela in Honduras, you can opt for a free stopover at the Copán Ruins. (**www.hedmanalas.com**).

Visas: U.S. and Canadian citizens do not require a visa or tourist card to visit Honduras. Upon arrival, you fill out a form and can stay for 30 days without renewal. You can easily extend this to 90 days on request after you arrive.

One tourist stamp and fee allows you to travel overland among Guatemala, Honduras, El Salvador, and Nicaragua without again paying or getting stamped.

Border crossings: If you're driving, you'll pay at least $30 at the border (not including "extra charges" that may arise), and you'll have to sit through paperwork and baggage inspections.

Currency: The Honduran lempira stays relatively stable at 19 per 1 U.S. dollar. ATMs are prevalent in the cities but sparse where there are few tourists. Carry some cash in rural areas. As in many developing countries, it may be hard to get change for big bills, so keep small bills handy.

A friendly family in the port city of La Ceiba, Honduras

Credit cards are widely accepted in the cities and at tourist establishments, but it's common for merchants to add 3 to 6 percent if you use one. It's not legal, but good luck making that point. Many merchants, hotels, and restaurants accept U.S. dollars, especially on Roatán and Utila.

Departure tax: It's $30 per person, often included in the airline ticket.

Weather and when to go: Temperatures and rainfall vary drastically depending on location and altitude. Tegucigalpa is more than 3,000 feet above sea level, so it's pleasant most of the year, with a mean temperature of 74°F. This is true for most of the highland areas, which get cool enough for a sweater at night in the winter. Coastal regions are hot and humid.

Expect rain at any time. The rainiest months are August through December on the coast, while the interior sees the most rain from May through October.

The ideal time to visit is January through March, when the climate is relatively dry but vegetation is green.

Electricity: Current and outlet shapes are the same as in the United States.

Internet access and telephones: Internet cafes are common in cities and other places where tourists gather. Prices are higher than in many neighboring countries because the government monopoly, Hondutel, likes it that way. Even so, logging on seldom costs more than $4 an hour for a relatively fast connection. Telephone calls to home are expensive and inconvenient, given the absence of easy phone cards and kiosks. Use e-mail to communicate when possible, or take advantage of a place set up with Skype phones.

Language: Spanish is the primary language throughout the mainland. On the Bay Islands of Roatán and Utila, English is the main language because of early English buccaneers and, more recently, English-speaking tourists and expatriates. The Garifuna along the coast and other people who cater to tourists are likely to speak English well enough to converse.

Safety: Where tourists gather, especially on Roatán, safety is not much of an issue because tourist police are in place. However, when Hurricane Mitch knocked down buildings a decade ago, it also knocked down a lot of jobs. At least partly because of unemployment, the cities of Tegucigalpa, Tela, La Ceiba, and San Pedro Sula all have rough areas that should be avoided. Drug gangs and smugglers are a serious presence, so be especially careful at night, and don't venture too far alone on foot.

Some beach areas are also better explored with a partner or group. This is not a good country for a woman traveling solo to stroll around late at night while carrying a purse. If in doubt, ask for advice about particular areas of town.

Put it all in perspective though: the vast majority of visitors don't experience any more trouble than they would walking around their own hometowns.

Maya carvings, Copán, Honduras

Health care: Honduras has good hospitals and clinics in the cities, though it's a long way to a city from some jungle areas. Evacuation insurance would make sense if you're going into remote regions. Costs for local care are a minuscule fraction of what you'd pay at home. Even on Roatán Island, an appointment with the doctor will run you less than $20, and prescription medicines cost about 40 percent of U.S. prices.

There's a risk of mosquito-borne diseases, especially in the jungle. Occasional cases of cholera mean you should avoid tap water and undercooked food. And don't forget the bug spray. Talk with a travel-medicine doctor to assess current conditions, and consult Chapter 12, Keeping Healthy.

Things to buy: If you're a cigar smoker, Honduras is heaven. Many of the world's top cigars are rolled here. Conveniently for tourists, one of the main production areas is near the ruins of Copán.

Carved wood items are popular, and woven baskets are well made if you look for the good ones. Seek out Garifuna musical instruments on the coast and ceramic items in the western highlands. Coffee is another good gift item. Beans are commonly about $2 a pound.

Resources

Moon Handbooks Honduras stands out among the few Honduras guidebooks. Lonely Planet's *Honduras & the Bay Islands* guide is also good. Other current guides include Hunter's *Adventure Guide Honduras & The Bay Islands* and *Open Road's Best of Honduras*. Honduras is featured in the Central America guides put out by various other publishers, such as Rough Guides and Footprint.

If you're a diver, check out Lonely Planet's *Honduras' Bay Islands: Diving & Snorkeling*.

A variety of Web sites do a good job of covering the bases for Honduras and linking to hotels and other resources. Try the following for a start.

The English-language newspaper *Honduras This Week* maintains a good Web site (**www.marrder.com/htw**) that will keep you up on local happenings.

Honduras Tips (**hondurastips.honduras.com**) has extensive information on all areas of the country, with thorough hotel listings, including prices, in English and Spanish. It also has the best bus route guide.

Honduras.com (**www.honduras.com**) is not pretty, but it contains plenty of solid information on travel options, some current news, and the weather in Tegucigalpa, Santa Rosa de Copán, Roatán, and La Ceiba.

The Honduras Travel Guide (**www.sidewalkmystic.com**) is one traveler's ad-free labor of love about Honduras, also available as a downloadable PDF file.

About Utila (**www.aboututila.com**), an official tourism site, tells you everything you need to know about the island, including all lodging options and registered dive shops.

Roatan OnLine (**www.roatanonline.com**) offers comprehensive links to hotels and dive shops and has good info on what to do in the area. Travel Roatan (**www.travel-roatan.com**) also has good general information. The Roatan and Bay Islands Visitors and Travel Guide (**www.roatanet.com**) is more commercial but also has useful links. For timely news, see the site for the monthly newspaper *Bay Islands Voice* (**www.bayislandsvoice.com**).

A local restaurant owner maintains the useful Santa Rosa de Copán site (**snow .prohosting.com/srcopan/src**), with plenty of tips and useful links.

Retirement Opportunities

Roatán has become one of the most popular destinations in Central America for expats and retirees from North America. Like certain sections of Costa Rica, it's hardly undiscovered, but prices are still far lower than in the rest of the Caribbean. If you're looking for a place to move that's already well established and mostly English-speaking, this could be a good choice. Otherwise, there are nearly 400 miles of mainland coastal land east and west of La Ceiba, not to mention highland towns in the interior. Unfortunately, you can't expect much in the way of cultural attractions and nightlife (except in the cities).

You can get a retirement residency permit when you either prove $1,500 a month in independent income or you invest $50,000 in an approved business project. Acquiring the permit takes as little as two months. Once you

A pier in the Honduran town of San Lorenzo

have it, you can import all your personal and household goods, including one car, duty-free. If you don't work locally, you won't owe any income tax. If you start a tourism business, such as a restaurant or hotel, you owe no taxes on the income for 20 years.

International Living magazine reports that retirees on Roatán spend $1,000 to $3,000 a month, depending on how extravagantly they live and the size of their house. Anywhere else in the country, it's possible to live comfortably on even less.

Helping Out

If you have a special skill, money to spare, or time to help out, there's no shortage of aid groups or opportunities for volunteers to help struggling Hondurans. These range from well-funded organizations that are making a huge difference (for example, Habitat for Humanity, **www.habitat.org;** Heifer International, **www.heifer .org;** and CARE, **www.care.org**) to more-modest efforts that have a big impact on a single community.

Project Honduras (**www.projecthonduras.com**) is an online community that collects ideas and reports on aid projects across the country. A handy map allows you to search by region of the country for projects or organizations. More than 100 organizations are listed as active in Honduras. Here are a few examples:

- Niños de la Luz, or Children of the Light (**www.thechildrenofthelight.org**) helps homeless children.
- Prolansate (**www.prolansate.org;** Spanish only) is a nonprofit ecotourism group based in Tela set up by Peace Corps volunteers. The Adelante Foundation (**www.adelantefoundation.org**), based in La Ceiba, provides microloans to female small-business owners who otherwise can't get credit. It also provides business training and health workshops.
- La Clinica Esperanza (**www.missionroatan.org/PeggyAssist.htm**) provides low-cost or free health-care services to poor communities on Roatán, relying primarily on donations. It always needs medical and dental professionals who can volunteer some time.

In poor soil, tree roots strike out on their own to survive.

NICARAGUA

Think of Nicaragua in terms of sparkling lakes, endless beaches, dramatic volcanoes, tropical jungles, and hundreds of exotic bird species. The same things that draw millions to visit Costa Rica also abound in Nicaragua. You won't come to Nicaragua to enjoy ruins from ancient civilizations or go sightseeing in the traditional sense. Instead, come and take pleasure in the great, unspoiled outdoors.

> Lake Nicaragua is the largest lake in Central America and the largest between the Great Lakes and Lake Titicaca in Bolivia and Peru.

Nicaragua also features Granada, a town that's a lakefront showpiece where a wave of restoration is taking place, plus the cobblestone colonial atmosphere of León.

Although it's the largest country in Central America—roughly the size of New York State—Nicaragua is one of the least visited and least expensive. It's at the north-south midpoint of the Americas, with the Pacific on one side, the Caribbean on the other.

While most Nicaraguans have limited means, they love life and possess a strong spirit, enjoying each day in a way many in the developed world have forgotten. If you slow down and take things at their pace, you will be rewarded.

Many who hear the word "Nicaragua" think of civil war, Sandinistas, and Contras (maybe not quite knowing what those words stood for or what the fighting was about). Well, the right-wing Contras are defunct. The populist Sandinista "rebels" are an active political party—and their leader, Daniel Ortega, has become president. Fortunately, the days of the Iran-Contra scandal are long gone, and fighting in the mountains ended in 1990. It's time to take a fresh look at Nicaragua.

This is a tourist destination on the rise: think Puerto Vallarta in the 1950s or Costa Rica in the 1970s. It's not the place for those who need to go first class all the way, but for adventure travel without high prices and big crowds, it's hard to top this destination.

> Nature reserves occupy 22 percent of Nicaragua's land area.

With *International Living,* the *Wall Street Journal, National Geographic Traveler,* and the *New York Times* all having talked up the place up in travel features, forward-looking investors are opening inns and restaurants at a rapid pace, especially in the colonial city of Granada.

As Nicaragua shows up in even the swankiest magazines, tourism is growing by double-digit percentages

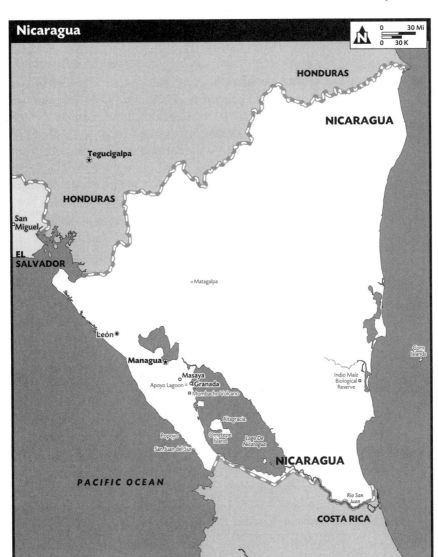

each year. New businesses are popping up each month to meet demand. Positive word of mouth is spreading.

The government of Nicaragua has aggressively wooed foreign tourism investment and has put a lot of effort into improving the roads. However, there's still a long way to go when it comes to infrastructure. The country is the second-poorest in the Americas, behind Haiti. Don't expect five-star hotels and gourmet restaurants in every town. Instead, expect all the natural wonders that Nicaragua's neighbors have to offer—and then some. What you won't find are throngs of tourists on a package vacation. You can stroll down an empty beach for miles without seeing another person.

Nicaragua's People

The 6 million people of Nicaragua have been through a lot of disasters, both man-made and natural, but still manage to be gregarious, fun-loving, and full of life. Most Nicaraguans are descended from indigenous people, Spaniards, or other Europeans—often with a mixture of two or three bloodlines. On the Caribbean coast, there is more African and Creole influence.

> Unlike most Latin American countries, where soccer is a national obsession, baseball is by far the most popular sport in Nicaragua. Some young players wind up playing pro ball in the United States.

The country is more than 70 percent Catholic, with a strong evangelical Protestant presence on the Caribbean coast. The population is very young: four of every ten residents are younger than 18. Elementary-school education is free and compulsory.

The economy is based on agriculture. Much of the working population is involved in the export of cash crops such as bananas, coffee, and tobacco, and the processing of sugarcane into rum. Income from tourism has started to improve living standards. There's still quite a gulf between rich and poor, with the top echelon having a vast amount of wealth.

Among internationally famous Nicaraguans are Bianca Jagger—Mick Jagger's first wife—and the poet Rubén Darío, known for his influence on Latin American literature. Nine Nicaraguan baseball players have made it to the U.S. major leagues.

Highlights

- The town of **Masaya**, about 40 minutes from Granada, is the country's popular handicrafts center. It's easy to get here on a day trip, and everything on offer anywhere in the country is in the stalls. Take time to inspect the quality, and bargain patiently. The nearby **Masaya Volcano National**

William Walker

A Tennessean named William Walker earned an odd footnote in Nicaragua's history. A megalomaniac adventurer who was quite possibly insane, he took over Granada with a force of 60 mercenaries in 1855. He then rigged an election to make himself ruler of the whole country. After he made a series of unpopular proclamations (including those legalizing slavery and making English the official language), Costa Rica, Guatemala, U.S. businessman Cornelius Vanderbilt, and the U.S. government all worked to unseat him two years after he took power. Walker tried to return three years later and was eventually executed in Honduras.

Park has a road leading up to the rim of the crater of an active volcano. There are also hiking trails where you can spot sulfur-resistant parakeets.

- Near Masaya are a few **lake beaches**. You can laze the days away on pristine Pacific and Caribbean beaches, too.

Nicaragua has only one major golf course.

- **Big Corn Island** and **Little Corn Island** in the Caribbean will be on the cover of every travel magazine in another five or ten years when a few upscale resorts are in place. Visiting these two rather undeveloped islands is like taking a step back into the Caribbean past, when they served as bases for pirates, smugglers, and hunters of contraband turtles. Today they're becoming popular with travelers who want to get away and enjoy the unspoiled beaches. For now, these are sleepy getaways with rustic hotels. On the big island you can rent a bike for $2 an hour and explore the whole thing on its 6-mile road. The island of **Ometepe** has two volcanoes—one active, one not—that rise to more than 4,000 and 5,000 feet above Lake Nicaragua. The larger volcano, Concepción, the active one, has been called the most perfectly formed volcanic cone in Central America and erupted in 2007. The small towns here are a great base for hiking through virgin forest and enjoying panoramic vistas. Parakeets and monkeys far outnumber the residents.

- **San Juan del Sur** is the most popular Pacific beach area for foreigners and the ideal base for surfing, sailing, or fishing. With a perfect crescent beach lined by black-rock cliffs, it's easy to get lulled into staying longer than you planned.

Nicaragua claims to have 7 percent of the world's plant and animal species— including more than 700 bird species.

- The college town of **León** is known for its cathedrals, but visitors also like its Spanish colonial atmosphere, as well as its bustling dining and cafe scene. The beautiful Hotel El Convento is built on the grounds of a 17th-century convent. A riverboat trip into the **Indio Maíz Biological Reserve** is a journey into a world that few tourists experience. The dense jungle is home to jaguars, tapirs, and a wide variety of tropical birds.

- The **coffee plantations** in the highlands offer tours and the opportunity for a homestay or a night in a simple inn.

- Nicaragua is a paradise for **bird-watchers**. Here's a sample of what will be flying overhead: quetzals, goldfinches, hummingbirds, eagles, toucans, parakeets, and macaws.

Itineraries

If You Have a Week in Nicaragua

Most likely, you'll arrive in Managua. Stay overnight only if you arrive too late to move on. Immediately take an *expreso* bus, "microbus" minivan, or hired taxi to the picturesque colonial city of Granada, an hour and a half away.

At 485 miles long, Río Coco is the longest river in Central America.

Spend two or three nights in Granada, with day trips to the handicrafts town of Masaya and an adventure excursion to Mombacho Volcano or one of the nearby lake islands. Or spend a day or night on the shores of Apoyo Lagoon at the Norome Resort & Villas.

Take a ferry to Ometepe Island, and spend a night or two on this large, twin-coned volcanic island in a lake. Take a guided hike or horseback ride to explore the lush vegetation, serene scenery, and varied wildlife.

Pass through Managua and head north to the vibrant college town of León, home of the largest cathedral in Central America.

Spend a night or two at one of the Pacific beach resorts, such as the Barceló Montelimar Beach Resort and Casino or Morgan's Rock Hacienda & Ecolodge. Or kick back in a hammock with a rum drink in one of the smaller beach-hut places, such as Los Cardones Surf Lodge or the surfer camps at Popoyo.

If You Have Two Weeks or More in Nicaragua

Add a short flight to the Corn Islands on the Caribbean side, 40 miles offshore.

Add adventure activities such as jungle explorations, mountain biking, volcano hikes, or rafting trips. Take a jungle riverboat trip through the Indio Maíz Biological Reserve.

Visit the cool mountain town of Matagalpa, home of coffee plantations, nearby cloud-forest wildlife areas, Finca Esperanza Verde (an ecolodge, organic coffee farm, and nature preserve), and the venerable Selva Negra Mountain Resort.

Cost Comparisons

Nicaragua is heaven for backpackers on a shoestring budget. Rates for everyday items are a bargain. The following are representative costs across Nicaragua and do not include places where prices are inflated, such as deluxe hotels and fine-dining establishments:

- Liter of water in a convenience store: 40–60 cents
- Bottle of beer in a bar or restaurant: 90 cents–$1.50
- Bottle of beer in a store: 50–90 cents
- Meal of the day in a locals' restaurant: $2–$4
- Half kilo of oranges, in season: 40–70 cents
- 1 hour of Internet access in a cafe: $1–$2
- Cup of coffee, juice, or soda in a restaurant: 50 cents–$1.20
- 10-minute taxi ride across town: $3–$6
- Taxi from airport to hotel: $8–$12
- 3-star or equivalent hotel: $30–$70

Nicaragua has the largest area of primary-growth rain forest north of the Amazon.

Accommodations

In most towns and cities, it is hard to find anything approaching a fancy boutique hotel, but Granada is an exception. There, you can now find half a dozen places, most run by foreign expatriates or elite Granadans, that combine friendly service and nice amenities for about $40 to $120 for a double room, usually including breakfast.

Any town where there's some backpacker traffic will have many choices for basic rooms in the $6 to $20 range for two. For this price, you won't usually get hot water or air-conditioning. In the $25 to $60 range, however, those amenities will be joined by cable TV and maybe a swimming pool or bar. Don't drop in at an "auto motel" by mistake: these are love hotels rented by the hour.

Holidays and Festivals

Nicaragua observes the usual Catholic holidays prevalent in Latin America, and several festivals center on local events or saint's-day parties. Following are the main ones. Be advised that around Christmas and Easter, airline prices go up, and there is high local demand for transportation and hotel rooms. Getting any help from a government official the week before Easter is usually a lost cause.

- January 1: New Year's Day
- January 19–21: Fiesta de San Sebastian, Diriamba, near the Pacific coast
- February 1: Air Force Day
- Third week in March: Granada's handicraft festival
- March or April: Semana Santa, the week before Easter. The biggest festival is in León.
- May 1: Labor Day
- May 27: Army Day
- July 19: Liberation Day
- August 1 and 10: Managua's patron saint parades
- August 15: Assumption of Mary festival, Granada
- Third week of August: Music and dance festival, Estelí
- August 27-28: Crab Soup Festival, Corn Islands
- September 14: Battle of San Jacinto
- September 15: Independence Day
- Last Sunday of October: Fiesta del Toro Venado, Masaya
- November 2: All Souls' Day
- November 3-5: Equestrian Festival, Ometepe Island
- November 12-18: Patron saint festival, Altagracia
- December 8 (December 7 in León): Immaculate Conception
- December 25: Christmas. Christmas celebrations start about December 18 and don't quit until after January 7.
- December 31: New Year's Eve

Performance of El Güegüense, *Nicaragua's signature folkloric drama*

A few villa-rental options are starting to pop up, with foreign owners renting out their homes while they are away. Most of these rental homes are in the city of Granada or on the Pacific coast. If you want to stay in one place for a while and need a kitchen, say for a family, these can be just the ticket. In a few spots, such as Playa Coco south of San Juan del Sur, these villas are the only option for accommodation.

So far, you can't blow more than $150 a night on a hotel even if you want to. Often, $75 to $100 will be plenty for the best hotel in town, including on the Corn Islands. The exceptions are the few major all-inclusive beach resorts on the Pacific coast, which offer pampering at prices that are still relatively low in international terms. The best are Barceló Montelimar Beach Resort and Casino near Pochomíl and Morgan's Rock Hacienda & Ecolodge near San Juan del Sur.

Especially in beach areas, expect to pay a premium when demand is high. Local holiday times, such as Christmas and Easter Week (Semana Santa), are the worst, but any peak time can cause even the most basic rooms to double or triple in price. See the "Holidays and Festivals" list in this chapter, and consult your guidebook for local holiday periods if you have some flexibility when making plans.

There are ten casinos among Managua, Masaya, Bluefields, and the Barceló Montelimar Beach Resort and Casino.

Get direct links to hotels from the links listed on page 125 in the "Resources" section.

A crater lake in Nicaragua

Food and Drink

Nicaraguan food is straightforward and not spicy. At market stalls or basic lunch-counter places (*comedores*), $1 to $3 will cover a hearty meal with several set items. A common lunch might include fried rice, beans, plantains, and fresh corn tortillas. Some kind of meat, often chicken, will also be available (but watch out for the locally popular tripe, or *mondongo*). *Fritanga* barbecue places supply a heap of meat for a few dollars. Vegetarians may not find great variety in larger towns unless they go for "foreign" food, but in rural areas where there is less money, there will be far less meat and plenty of vegetables. Portion sizes are more than ample.

The tab at the hippest places in León will be less than $10 per person, including several courses and a beer or two. It's hard to go much above this anywhere except in restaurants catering to business travelers in Managua and upscale tourists in Granada. Outside these two cities, spending more than $15 per person on dinner requires going to the fanciest restaurant in town. Granada has experienced a recent foreign investment boom, so trendy new eateries catering to the *Condé Nast Traveler* crowd are starting to move into restored colonial mansions.

Bodies of water are always nearby, so a whole fish for dinner will often cost only $2 or $3.

Managua has the widest variety of foreign food, but in most towns it is easy to find Chinese, Mexican, or American food (the latter all too often being burgers, pizza, and *papas fritas*). A large pizza usually costs $4 to $6.

Nicaragua's rum is superior, and the Flor de Caña brand is known the world over. It's a great bargain here, with the 7-year old version available in a bar for less than $5 a half liter—glasses, ice, limes, and cola included.

Unfortunately the beer won't win any prizes: pale, boring pseudo-pilsners, all made by a single brewery. In the heat, however, any cold beer is welcome. Cans are more expensive than bottles and don't get recycled. If you don't understand what the clerk is saying about a deposit on the bottles, you may get a surprise: your beer will be handed to you in a plastic bag—the clerk keeping the bottle after pouring. Otherwise, you pay a deposit of 20 to 30 cents on each bottle.

Fresh fruit juice is available anywhere, and fruit is abundant at stands all over. Bananas are less than $1 a kilo (2.2 pounds).

Most of the good coffee has traditionally been exported. Search for places that are working to raise the bar domestically. Usually that means a gringo-owned cafe.

Transportation

Most of the **buses** in Nicaragua are converted school buses well past their glory days, discarded by first-world countries for a second life here. Get an express (*expreso*) bus when possible, since in theory it won't stop at every little station along the way or pick up people waving alongside the road.

A **minibus** is a much better choice. It may cost twice as much as a local bus and one-third more than the *expreso*. It's worth every córdoba. They are more comfortable and far less crowded, and they save a lot of time. A slow bus from

Taking it easy, Nicaragua

León to Managua, for instance, can take two or three hours and cost about $1. A minibus will take an hour and a half and will cost about $1.75. If you need air-conditioning, you'll probably want to arrange a top-end car with a driver or take an organized tour.

Nicaragua has about 40 volcanic cones, 7 of which are still active. Cerro Negro began forming as recently as the mid-1800s and has now grown to more than 1,400 feet.

You can take a **long-distance bus** to the nearest large city in Costa Rica, Guatemala, El Salvador, or Honduras for $10 to $35.

Taxi rides start at less than 50 cents in most cities, and it seldom costs more than a couple of dollars to get across town. In Managua, trip rates start at about $1 and top out at about $6. Taxi rates often fluctuate with the price of petroleum, which can reach double what it is in North America.

Boat transportation is required in some areas, with prices ranging from $1 to $3 per hour on a long trip. Ferries across Lake Nicaragua are a bargain. A first-class cabin on the overnight trip from Granada to San Miguelito costs less than $7. Schedules can be erratic, with wind, waves, and poor management contributing to uncertainty, especially March through May. The most expensive ferry option from Bluefields to Big Corn Island is $15.

Sample bus and ferry routes and costs (highest class available):

City 1	City 2	Travel Time	Cost
Managua	Granada	1.5 hours	$1.75
Managua	León	3.5 hours	$1.80
León	Matagalpa	9 hours	$3.50
Granada	Masaya	5 hours	$1.00
Granada	Altagracia (Ometepe Island)	2 hours	$2.20
Granada	San Juan del Sur	2.5 hours	$3.00
San Juan del Sur	Costa Rica border	2 hour	$3.00

Renting a car is as expensive as at home, and the danger factor is twice as high. For the same amount of money or less, hire a car and driver. It's much safer, and you have someone who knows where he's going. The driver is also less likely to be pulled over by police with a fabricated excuse to hand out a ticket. Note that you generally can't take a rental car across an international border, so don't expect to rent a car in Nicaragua and drive it into Costa Rica. However, you can cross the border in your own vehicle. See Chapter 20, Transportation, for more about renting a car.

Internal flights are well worth the cost for long distances. Prices are reasonable in international terms. For example, it costs about $100 for a round-trip flight from Managua to the Corn Islands.

Nicaragua has no **passenger trains.**

Activity Costs

- Organized tours and hikes booked locally commonly cost $15 to $30 per day, per person.

> Over 12 percent of the country's electricity is generated by "clean energy" sources, much of it from a volcano (at a geothermal plant at the base of Momotombo).

- A zipline "canopy tour" near Rivas costs about $10 per person, plus a few dollars to get there.
- Fishing trips out of San Juan del Sur cost $130 to $275 for a group of four to six and last up to six hours.
- Private tours of the country in a four-wheel-drive Land Cruiser with an English-speaking driver will generally cost $50 to $150 per person, including accommodations.
- Feeling rich? Tour the country by helicopter for about $1,500 per day, all-inclusive.

Tour Companies

If you're an adventurous traveler, or you become one after you've read *Traveler's Tool Kit,* you can certainly experience Nicaragua on your own. However, of the countries profiled in this book, Nicaragua is the one where travelers would benefit most from the guidance of a knowledgeable tour operator—if not for the entire trip, then at least for adventure excursions such as volcano hikes, bike trips, coffee-plantation tours, and helicopter tours. Several companies run overland trips through Central America that include several days in Nicaragua. See Chapter 6, The Organized Tour, for general recommendations on tour companies in this region.

It's not our role to endorse any of the following tour companies beyond saying that they have good reputations for their English-language tours in Nicaragua and have been around long enough to know what they're doing. See Chapter 6 for detailed information on how to choose a good tour operator.

- Nicaragua Adventures: **www.nica-adventures.com**
- Careli Tours: **www.carelitours.com**

Hurricane Mitch

When Mitch struck Nicaragua in 1998, it was the worst hurricane in 200 years. A year's worth of rain poured down in a few days, and rivers swelled to 10 times their normal size. Volcanic lakes overflowed, joining the rivers in washing away houses, bridges, factories, and farmland. Thousands died, and property damage exceeded $1 billion. The storm made a poor country even poorer. The silver lining is that hundreds of millions of dollars in international aid poured in, leading to improved infrastructure, including better roads and bridges, and better disaster-preparation plans.

Horse and cart on a street in Granada, Nicaragua

- ORO Travel: **www.orotravel.com**
- JB Fun Tours: **www.jbfuntours.com**
- Tours Nicaragua: **www.toursnicaragua.com**
- Solentiname Tours: **www.solentiname.com.ni/english**

Useful Details

Getting there and away: Delta flies via Atlanta and Los Angeles, American via Miami, Continental via Houston, TACA via Miami, and Copa via several other Central American cities.

It's simple to cross overland from Costa Rica or Honduras, or to catch a regional flight from those and other Central American countries. You can even get a bus from Mexico City if you're feeling hardy.

Visas: No one from North America or Europe needs a visa for Nicaragua. You buy an automatic three-month permit on entry for $7.

Border crossings: Going overland to or from Costa Rica requires a passport and a fee of $4 to $10, depending on direction.

Currency: The córdoba has been declining a little each year in relation to the U.S. dollar. In 2007, $1 bought 18 córdobas.

> Before the opening of the Panama Canal, Nicaragua was a popular crossing point for people heading to California to participate in the gold rush and for those returning home with or without gold in their pockets.

Memorial to Sandinista soldiers and civilians killed circa 1977, Condega, Nicaragua

Departure tax: It's $35 per person at the airport and may be included in your flight ticket.

Weather and when to go: The temperature doesn't vary much throughout the year. Daytime temperatures seldom go lower than 80°F, and it's not uncommon for them to hit 95. Except for the highlands near Matagalpa and the mountain slopes, expect tropical heat. The main variable is the level of humidity. The worst months to visit are generally April through May (the dusty, dry season) and September through October (the wettest months, with possible hurricanes). Best choice from a weather standpoint: December and January, when it's clear, slightly cooler, and not as humid.

Electricity: Voltage is the same as in the United States, and nonpolarized plugs (with pins of equal size, as is standard on many new electronics) will fit. Otherwise, you'll need an adapter. Laptop users should bring a portable surge protector, because the electricity supply is erratic. Because power outages are common, bring a flashlight and a travel candle.

Internet access and telephones: There are many Internet cafes in Nicaragua, but not many wireless hot spots for a laptop (though they are increasing in number). Here's why: monopoly-run broadband Internet is so expensive in Nicaraguan income terms that there are comparatively few high-speed connections.

Telephone calls go through one company, Enitel, unless you are making a VoIP call through the Internet. The latter is the best bet for calling home, via an Internet cafe, because regular phone calls cost 40 to 60 cents per minute. You can call through an Enitel office or use a pay phone that accepts a prepaid card you can buy at most convenience stores.

Language: Spanish is the primary language of approximately 90 percent of the population. English is the first language along much of the Caribbean coast. English is also fairly common in tourist and business centers. Please refer to the section in Chapter 19, Language, that describes how to minimize inconvenience related to language.

Safety: Nicaragua is one of the safest countries in Latin America. Homicide statistics are so low they make the United States look like the lawless Wild West. Tourists are more likely to be hassled by a curious drunk than to be robbed. Take the common precautions against pickpockets that you would anywhere, and avoid urban buses in Managua. Leave flashy jewelry at home. Avoid *El Triángula Minero,* in the Jinotega area of the northeast, where bandits occasionally, well, act like bandits. For comprehensive information on how to have a safe trip, please see Chapter 17, Safety and Security.

The usual safe-eating advice applies here (see Chapter 16, Eating and Drinking). Nicaragua is still a developing country, so more caution in eating is necessary than in Costa Rica, in much of Mexico, and on the Honduran island of Roatán.

Health care: Outside Managua, medical facilities are basic and understaffed. Evacuation insurance is fairly inexpensive and could be a worthwhile investment. On the plus side, the cost of medical treatment ranges from free to cheap. You can pay with a credit card at larger hospitals and clinics.

Things to buy: Nicaragua is not known as a handicrafts center, partly because there's not an indigenous population with a thousand years of craftsmanship under its woven belt. The best choices are hammocks, ceramics, embroidered blouses, wood carvings, leather goods, rum, and cigars. The fine rum is very fine indeed.

Resources

Because only a few hundred thousand visitors a year come here, there are only a few guidebooks for Nicaragua. The most comprehensive is *Moon Handbooks Nicaragua.* The same authors wrote the *Moon Living Abroad in Nicaragua* guide. The only other current guidebooks are one from Footprint Handbooks and one from Lonely Planet that covers Nicaragua and El Salvador. With the country getting increased media attention, however, the selection will almost certainly expand soon.

Square in Granada during Nicaragua's Independence Day

Any guide to Central America covers Nicaragua, including those from Lonely Planet, Rough Guides, Fodor's, and Footprint.

Good books include the practical *Living and Investing in the New Nicaragua* and the narrative titles *The Sharks of Lake Nicaragua* by Randy Wayne Wright, *Meet Me in Managua* by Wendy Zoba, and *The Inhabited Woman* by Gioconda Belli. One of Salman Rushdie's lesser-known books is *The Jaguar Smile: A Nicaraguan Journey*. The title character of the 1996 British film *Carla's Song* is a Nicaraguan refugee who returns to the country during the 1980s civil war.

Few Internet resources deal with Nicaragua, partly because there's not much money to be made yet.

The official Nicaraguan tourism site looks pretty but so far is only in Spanish: **www.intur.gob.ni**.

Go To Nicaragua (**www.gotonicaragua.com**) offers news, links, and a thoughtful user forum, created by the authors of the Moon guidebooks.

Nicaragua Living has the inside scoop from expatriates: **www.nicaliving.com**.

ViaNica has a lot of solid country information: **www.vianica.com**.

IBW has a lot of varied Nicaragua links (some in Spanish only): **www.ibw .com.ni**.

San Juan del Sur tourism information is available at **www.sanjuandelsur .org.ni**.

Retirement Opportunities

For those in the know, Nicaragua has been a retirement destination for quite a few years because real estate is still relatively cheap and the government has provided a lot of incentives. If you are older than 45, can verify a monthly income or pension of at least $400, and can prove you're not a criminal, you qualify. It is relatively straightforward to get a residency visa and import up to $10,000 of personal goods and a car tax-free. You don't pay any tax on out-of-country earnings.

This is also an attractive country for setting up your own business. Nicaragua has enacted one of the most aggressive tourism-incentive laws in Latin America. If your business qualifies, you are exempt from business-income taxes and real-estate taxes for up to ten years. You can also import or locally buy your supplies tax- and duty-free.

Helping Out

More than a dozen agencies and companies operate organized volunteer programs in the country, and countless more carry out aid and charity programs. These range from international operations such as the Peace Corps (**www .peacecorps.gov**), Habitat for Humanity (**www.habitat.org**), and the Red Cross (**www.redcross.org**) to many small local groups doing good work with scarce resources. If you are interested in volunteering or donating, see the listings in the *Living Abroad in Nicaragua* book, or check the volunteering section of TransitionsAbroad.com (**www.transitionsabroad.com**).

COSTA RICA

Costa Rica is buzzing—and humming, chirping, and chattering.

To put that another way, nature and Costa Ricans have pooled efforts to create and maintain a paradise of zoological and botanical diversity. You start with a landscape of sea-level jungles, cloud forests, and volcanic peaks topping out above 11,000 feet. Then you populate it with specimens of, some say, 5 to 10 percent of all the creatures found anywhere in the world. And, finally, you make a national commitment to preserve it all.

Costa Rica shelters as many bird species as the United States and Canada combined, has more reptiles than all of Europe, and more butterflies than Australia. Costa Ricans proudly say it's the most dense collection of species of any country in the world.

Not surprisingly, people who flock to Costa Rica for the wildlife are not disappointed. In terms of its popularity with tourists, this country the size of West Virginia ranks below only vastly larger Mexico in the region.

What will you see here? Visitors rave about toucans, macaws, parrots, sloths, sea turtles, frogs, monkeys, reptiles, alligators, tapirs, ocelots, anteaters, and enough hummingbirds to pollinate a small planet. Not to mention the countless varieties of tropical plants. Look at "Nature by the Numbers" for the stats. Not all of these wonders are obvious. Seeing them takes some patient observation, letting nature unfold and ripple around you.

Tourism officials are not paid to be altruistic. They're very aware that guarding the ecology has commercial value. The example set in Costa Rica has become a model and stimulus to other countries to clean up their acts—and create a lure to dangle in front of tourists like a fly in front of a largemouth bass. In a few places, real-estate development has gotten a little frenzied—such as the areas around Jacó and Guanacaste now sprouting retirement homes for gringos—but the government understands the fable about killing the goose that lays the golden eggs. "Green" hotels pay more than lip service to conservation. Recycling bins are used. And while streets aren't as pristine as in Singapore, there's not a lot of litter either.

A visit is not just about "seeing." There are many opportunities to play as well.

Raft some good whitewater rivers, ride through the forest canopy on a zipline, windsurf—get your heart pumping. If you can think of an adventure, someone will try to make it happen for you. Prefer a "soft" adventure? How about horseback riding, easy hiking, and floats through the jungle on a serene river?

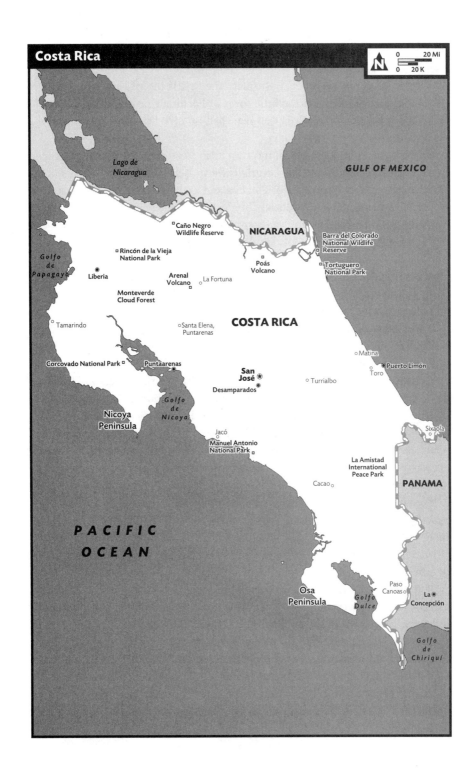

All this takes place in a country of 4.2 million people located between Nicaragua on the north and Panama on the south. It's so small you can travel from sea level to 11,300 feet in a couple of hours, or from the Caribbean to the Pacific and back in a day.

Sure, there are a couple of downsides. The first is the risk of reaching tourist saturation. For example, the little town of Fortuna near the Arenal Volcano receives some 600,000 visitors per year, half of the visitors who come to the entire country.

Second, prices in some of the most popular areas are on a par with those at Mexican beach resorts and Ambergris Caye in Belize. In other words, double what you'd spend in Nicaragua or Panama and not much cheaper than vacation prices in the United States. In fairness, you usually do get what you pay for. Things normally go smoothly, and you can communicate in English. This peaceful country has been hosting tourists for decades and has it down very well.

Costa Rica's People

Costa Ricans have by far the highest standard of living, literacy rate (96 percent), and life expectancy (77.2 years) in Central America.

These achievements are no accident. A major contributing factor is that the people have made peace a fundamental value and have avoided fighting each other or their neighbors. If only everyone in the Americas would learn from them!

Costa Rica has had inspired leadership from Oscar Arias Sánchez, who holds a doctorate in political science and was first elected president in 1986. He immediately intervened against activities of the U.S.-backed Nicaraguan Contras in Costa Rica and launched a major effort involving all governments in Central America to achieve democracy and peace (including the ending of civil wars). He was awarded the Nobel Peace Prize in 1987 and was elected to a second term as president in 2006.

Because Costa Rica abolished its army in the 1940s, it has been able to invest heavily in education and other social values. Workers contribute 9 percent of their salaries to a social-security program that provides universal health care and education. The elimination of an army has had positive ramifications throughout the population.

Perhaps because explorers discovered long ago that Costa Rica had little gold and silver, the country was never effectively colonized. Still, because of Spanish influence, 76 percent of the population is Roman Catholic.

Tourism is king of the economy, but agriculture still plays a big role. This is the world's leading producer of fresh pineapples, one of the largest producers of coffee, and a major exporter of papayas, bananas, melons, vanilla, and plantains. It has benefited from globalization, with international call centers and other outsourced businesses drawing on its educated workforce. Land ownership is widespread.

Nature by the Numbers

Costa Rica consists of just 0.03 percent of the earth's landmass but contains about 5 percent of the earth's plant and animal species. Among other reasons for this is that the country is the northern migration limit of some species, the southern limit of others, and a stop along the way for yet others. Here are a few statistics:

- 137 species of snakes (22 are venomous)
- 175 types of amphibians
- 894 species of birds (more than the United States and Canada combined)
- 1,250 species of butterflies
- 360,000 species of insects
- More than 8,000 species of moths
- As many as 1,500 species of orchids

The Monteverde Cloud Forest alone contains more than 400 types of birds and more than 100 species of mammals.

The per-capita gross domestic product is $12,500 per year, the highest in Central America. The minimum wage is about $1 an hour, though, so many at the bottom are still struggling to get by. A large number of the roughly 20 percent of the population below the poverty line are refugees from Nicaragua living here legally or illegally.

Costa Ricans (who call themselves "ticas" or "ticos," depending on gender) are proud of what their small country has accomplished economically but try hard to keep work and life in balance. The phrase you hear most is *pura vida*— "pure life."

Highlights

Visitors don't come to Costa Rica to see the "sites" or the "sights" in the traditional sense. There are few must-see historic monuments or colonial cities. Instead, travelers come for the splendid landscapes and flora and fauna beyond compare.

- **Arenal Volcano,** a dramatic cone rising out of the forest, is a *very* live volcano. It fires rocks, flame, and lava high into the sky day and night. It's a fascinating show, especially at night. To give warning of a really big blow, 4,000 sensors around the volcano monitor seismic activity. Three hot springs provide a lot of commercial revenue. In the nearby town of Fortuna, more than 40 companies offer dozens of adventures from canopy tours to horseback riding.
- The **Monteverde Cloud Forest** is one of the world's most interesting and well-preserved ecosystems, a primary forest luxuriant in plant life and

Golden Beans

While Costa Rica now depends on tourism, it was coffee that vaulted the country into its position of relative prosperity. Coffee plants cover the rich volcanic soil in the Central Valley.

President Juan Mora Fernandez began encouraging citizens to plant the imported crop in the 1830s. As international demand grew, prices rose to a level far above that of bananas and pineapples. The coffee farms fueled the rise of a middle class larger than that in most of Latin America. Costa Rica is also a leading player in the production of organic and "shade-grown" types of coffee, which are fetching the highest prices in the U.S. market. Of course, those who live by fluctuating commodity prices can die by those prices as well.

In contrast to many coffee-producing countries, Costa Rica also enjoys the bean. Taking a coffee break is serious business here, and a lot of business gets discussed over a savored cup.

home to abundant animals and birds. Because of the altitude, the forest literally exists within the clouds. The resplendent quetzal, a grand bird with impressive plumage, may be hard to spot elsewhere, but it is a common sight here. (Quetzal feathers were considered so beautiful and spiritual that only kings and chieftains could wear them in centuries past.)

- The **Osa Peninsula** and the primary rain forest at **Corcovado National Park** offer some of the most untouched coastal land in the country. You'll find pristine Pacific beaches with great snorkeling, and scarlet macaws filling the air.
- **Manuel Antonio National Park** and the nearby Pacific Ocean beaches attract nature lovers, beach bums, and surfers.
- The **Nicoya Peninsula,** also on the Pacific, is like a private paradise for beach lovers. There's a rambling Four Seasons complex in Punta Islita and Tamarindo, as well as a lively beach popular with both backpackers and package tourists. Beyond those and a few upscale resorts, you're on your own for mile after mile of clean sand. Well, except for an occasional iguana.
- Most of the **Cordillera de Talamanca** mountain range consists of protected nature reserves, including the forest covering Cerro Chirripó, the country's highest mountain.
- The dry northwest **Guanacaste** region, containing **Liberia** and volcanic **Rincón de la Vieja National Park,** is a land of hot springs, mud baths, and Pacific beaches. Liberia is regarded as the country's most attractive city, with more colonial architecture than elsewhere.
- The wetlands of **Caño Negro Wildlife Reserve,** easily reached from Fortuna, offer a display of birds you can see on a leisurely boat trip.

Topiary near San José, Costa Rica

- **Barra del Colorado National Wildlife Reserve** and **Tortuguero National Park** on the Caribbean coast are best explored by boat along narrow canals that run parallel to the sea. These are protected nesting sites of green, hawksbill, loggerhead, and leatherback turtles. The rain forest along the canals is home to sloths, monkeys, alligators, tapirs, ocelots, anteaters, and half the bird species in Costa Rica. A vigilant visitor may even see manatees swimming past.
- **Poás Volcano** gives you the opportunity to hike right up to the edge of a volcano's crater, where swirling smoke steams out of vents that run toward the core of the earth.
- The **Pacuare River** (near Turrialba) is considered by some to rank among the ten best **river-rafting** runs in the world—and there are at least ten other good whitewater challenges around the country. I rafted the Savegre River with Amigos del Río (**www.amigosdelrio.net**) and had a blast. Check a guidebook for the best time to run each river and departure points for trips. In general, the dry season is a good bet because exposed boulders make better rapids. But if it's *too* dry, you'll be dragging your tail. The toughest runs may be at the beginning and end of the rainy season. You'll be soaked anyway, so who minds a little rain?
- **La Amistad International Peace Park**—the name means the "the friendship"—is the largest park in Costa Rica and is shared with friendly

Rockin' Hot Lava

"There's a Rolling Stones concert every night," the guides joke to groups arriving at the Arenal Observatory Lodge (which once was an observatory for Smithsonian Institution volcanologists). Guests at this and other hotels with views of the correct side of Arenal Volcano have an amazing show each clear night as molten lava and glowing rocks are blasted heavenward. Red and orange streaks flare and fade. Even when clouds obscure the volcano's mouth, you hear a sound like thunder as rocks tumble down the slope, colliding and shattering. If you're staying in one of the hotels, pull back the curtains and watch the show as you fall asleep. You awaken to a cacophony created by howler monkeys, flocks of birds, and . . . more rocks tumbling down the mountain. This is one rolling stones concert that never ends.

Panama. The altitude in La Amistad Biosphere Reserve, which includes the international park and several other parks and reserves, ranges from 475 feet to 11,644 feet, with miles of hiking trails through wilderness. Many hire a guide for a rugged three-day hike and stay in rustic park lodges or campsites.

- Overall, the **adventure-tour** industry is professional, experienced, and loaded with good equipment. Those characteristics are worth paying for. If there's an adventure you've wanted to try, from bungee jumping to a three-day horseback trip, you can find someone offering it.

Itineraries

If You Have a Week in Costa Rica

Don't expect to see everything Costa Rica offers in one week. It would take four weeks just to hit all the highlights listed in the previous section. For one thing, getting from one place to another takes far longer than you might guess. As my van driver swerved to miss ruts and potholes, he cheerfully said, "You could take this road all the way to Panama!" Consider picking an area, and don't try to cram too much in. Otherwise you'll spend most of your time bumping along in a van or bus, wondering what's moving in those trees in the distance.

Some tour groups spend a week visiting the Arenal Volcano area, one or two national parks, and one beach. Even that still involves a fair amount of all-day travel.

Others head straight for Costa Rica's Pacific-northwest region, then work their way down the coast and the Monteverde Cloud Forest, ending up at Manuel Antonio National Park and the beach.

Another option is to see Poás Volcano, then visit a highland nature reserve and after that Barra del Colorado National Wildlife Reserve and Tortuguero National Park on the Caribbean coast.

Or, in one week you could explore the nature reserves in Cordillera de Talamanca mountain range and then spend a few nights on the ruggedly beautiful Osa Peninsula.

If arriving overland from Nicaragua, consider a trip down the Pacific coast, perhaps veering inland to Rincón de la Vieja National Park, the Monteverde Cloud Forest, and the Arenal Volcano region.

If arriving from the Pacific side of Panama, the logical path would be the Osa Peninsula, the Cordillera de Talamanca, and perhaps Turrialba for a white-knuckle rafting trip before catching a flight from San José. If arriving from the Caribbean side of Panama, you'll bump slowly along the sole Caribbean coast road before it veers inland to San José. Go from there to whichever itinerary fits the time you have.

If You Have Two Weeks or More in Costa Rica

With two weeks or more, you can string together any of the previous itineraries or spend more time in an area that matches your interest. Some people base themselves in Santa Elena (near Monteverde) or Fortuna (near Arenal) for a week and try a different activity every day. Others spend two weeks or more on a bird-watching circuit, traveling from one nature reserve to another, exploring different elevations and microclimates. Some people hit a dozen surfing hot spots or go ocean fishing. Others attempt to raft every whitewater river. Whatever you want, you can have.

A few travelers following the Central American isthmus north or south treat themselves to a couple of weeks in Costa Rica. It's important to know that you move much more quickly on the Pan-American Highway than when following the roads that weave along the coasts.

Cost Comparisons

Costa Rica has become a vacation playground for short-stay tourists (mostly Americans) and is priced accordingly. There are few visitors from other Latin American countries and not many backpackers, maybe because costs for tourists are similar to those at home. As with resort towns in Mexico, expect restaurant, adventure, and hotel prices in tourist areas to test what the market will bear. However, it's still possible to travel cheaply, especially if you stay mostly in one area and cook for yourself now and then.

> Of the many volcanoes in Costa Rica, five still breath fire and brimstone. Two active ones are close to San José. One, Irazú, erupted in the early 1960s and caused quite a bit of destruction. Arenal's last major eruption was in 1968, leading to the creation of an extensive monitoring system. For now, anyway, they're more an attraction than a threat.

The following are representative costs across Costa Rica and don't include places where prices are inflated, such as deluxe hotels and fine-dining establishments:

- Liter of water in a convenience store: 75 cents–$2
- Bottle of beer in a bar or restaurant: $1.50–$2.50
- Bottle of beer in a store: 75 cents–$1
- Meal of the day in a working-people's restaurant: $2–$5
- Half kilo of oranges, in season: 50 cents*
- 1 hour of Internet access in a cafe: $2–$4
- Cup of coffee, juice, or soda in a restaurant: 75 cents–$1.25
- 10-minute taxi ride across town: $3–$8
- Taxi from main international airport to hotel: $12–$25
- 3-star or equivalent hotel: $70–$150

*Fruit is abundant and cheap. A whole pineapple or papaya averages $1.25, and $1 buys about 25 bananas.

Accommodations

For the vast majority of tourists looking for middle-range lodging, there are a lot of good values even if the entry level is higher than in neighboring countries. From $50 up, you can expect a clean and spacious room with maid service, a hot shower, a sitting area, and often a balcony or terrace. Many are family inns with lush gardens and a pool.

The fictional Costa Rican "Isla Nubar" of the book and movie *Jurassic Park* was supposedly modeled after the real Isla del Coco. The island has no hotels or other facilities for visitors, but it is a major dive attraction because of the profusion of hammerhead sharks. Much of the movie *Congo*, based on another Michael Crichton novel, was filmed in Costa Rica.

Where tourist traffic competing for rooms is intense, luxury hotels can charge sky-high prices. Costa Rica has a dozen or so truly world-class hotels scattered around the country. Some are collections of upscale villas, such as the Four Seasons Resort, while others, such as Villa Blanca Cloud Forest Hotel and Spa, try to reconcile upscale service with a strong ecotourism focus.

Low-budget travelers can find a dorm bed or basic double room for $6 to $12 per person in most areas that cater to adventure travelers. That may include breakfast, an hour or two of Internet access, hot showers, and maybe daily happy-hour specials. Finding a nice *and* cheap double room for less than $30 can be a challenge, however, except in areas such as Fortuna where lower-budget travelers congregate.

Coming in by cab from the San José airport, close your eyes unless you have a fondness for Hampton Inns, Best Westerns, Sleep Inns, Marriott Courtyard, and the like.

For information on hotels, see the Web sites listed in the "Resources" section on page 145.

Food and Drink

If you don't expect much more than fresh food prepared simply, you will be okay. A typical basic meal for Costa Ricans may be plantains, rice, and beans. Few visitors ask for recipes to take home, and many travelers complain that the prices are often higher than the quality. If you expect artistic presentation and complex dishes, you're out of luck beyond the upscale hotels.

A typical "meal of the day" consists of a small salad, a soup, a meat or fish dish, and some mix of rice, beans, and plantains. Fresh fruit and vegetables are abundant, so it's easy to stay healthy. With altitude ranging from sea level to more than 11,000 feet, local produce runs the gamut from tropical fruits and yucca to plums, potatoes, tomatoes, and cherries.

Because of the number of tourists, there is plenty of international food. Spaghetti is almost as common as black beans, and you can always find a burger, fried-chicken plate, or sandwich. The larger cities offer Chinese, Japanese, Mexican, and more exotic cuisines.

The good news is that you can eat almost anything you want without worrying about bad water and stomach bugs. Few travelers experience problems here, though it's prudent to avoid street food when you're straight off the plane.

Holidays and Festivals

- January 1: New Year's Day
- March 19: St. Joseph's Day (patron saint of San José province)
- March or April: Easter Week (Semana Santa)
- April 11: Juan Santamaria Day. Santamaria was a national hero who fought at the Battle of Rivas against invader William Walker in 1856. See the Nicaragua section for more on Walker.
- May 1: Labor Day
- Late May or June: Corpus Christi
- June 29: St. Peter and St. Paul's Day
- July 25: Guanacaste Day (marks the annexation of Guanacaste from Nicaragua in 1824)
- August 2: Virgin of the Angels Day (patron saint of Costa Rica)
- August 15: Mother's Day and Assumption Day
- Last weekend of August: Saint Ramón Day (colorful processions in San Ramón)
- September 15: Independence Day
- October 12: Columbus Day and Cultures Day. In Limón Province, there is a carnival the week before, culminating on the day itself.
- November 2: All Soul's Day
- December 8: Immaculate Conception of the Virgin Mary Day
- December 24: Christmas Eve
- December 25: Christmas Day

> Forget asking for anyone's address in Costa Rica. Very few streets have names, and most houses don't have numbers. Most people don't bother mailing anything. Bills are paid in person. Driving directions require lots of description and landmarks. Government officials estimate it would take two decades to name all the streets and number the buildings. Not a high priority in the languid tropics.

The main beer brands are Bavaria, Pilsen, and Imperial. Bavaria makes a nice black lager, while the others are as generic as their names—basic light lagers with just a bit more body than usual.

Good rum is a comparative bargain. A 7-year-old Flor de Caña from Nicaragua has the highest quality-to-price ratio, but locally produced Ron Centenario is very good as well. What you'll normally be served in your fruity cocktail, however, is lower-level Ronrico. (But when it's mixed with pineapple, papaya, or whatever, do you really care?) Taking another step down, the favorite local firewater is guaro (Cacique is the most popular brand), best mixed with sugary soft drinks. There's no local wine industry. All wine is imported—and that shows up in the prices.

Fruit juices are abundant and reasonably priced, with something good in season anytime. With the variety available, you can have strawberry juice one day and mango juice the next. You can get them mixed with milk or water and ice, or blended into a smoothie. Soft drinks are widely available.

Costa Rica is a major coffee producer, and plenty of the good stuff stays in the country. It's easy to find a fantastic cup of coffee, even in a small hotel or basic restaurant. The beans by the pound are barely cheaper than prices at home, though: good for gifts but not really worth hauling home otherwise. Because cocoa beans are a big crop, mouthwatering chocolate is plentiful.

Transportation

Roads in Costa Rica are a mixed bag. It's not unusual to be cruising nicely on a wide, paved road that suddenly turns into rutted gravel with pothole craters for the next 5 miles. In some cases, this is intentional. The community around the Monteverde Cloud Forest has famously refused to allow the access road to be paved in order to limit crowds and development. In other areas, it's just a matter of bad weather and a lack of initiative. Further complicating driving is the fact there are almost no road signs. On the one hand, renting a car allows more freedom to explore, but it can get frustrating to find the places you're trying to go.

The **bus system** is not really tourist-friendly. It's possible to reach the main towns and cities by bus, but to reach most activities and nature reserves, it's usually necessary to have your own transportation or to book a group tour. Several companies have filled in the gaps with private shuttle service, including Fantasy Gray Line (**www.graylinecostarica.com**), which serves 15 destinations, including 2 in Nicaragua. Quality Transfers (**www.qualitytransferscr.com**),

Whitewater rafting in Costa Rica

based in Monteverde, provides shuttles to and from various Pacific-coast locations, Arenal, and San José, among others.

The prices below are for a small shuttle that goes point to point. An upscale bus may cost slightly less for popular routes, especially from San José. Sample bus routes and costs (highest class available):

City 1	City 2	Travel Time	Cost
San José	Monteverde region	4.5 hours	$30
San José	Jacó	2.5 hours	$21
Jacó	Monteverde region	5.5 hours	$38
Monteverde	Arenal region	3 hours	$25
Arenal region	Golfo Papagayo	6.5 hours	$38
Liberia	Tamarindo	3 hours	$15
Manuel Antonio	Rincón de la Vieja	7 hour	$38

A **taxi** ride is one of the few bargains, from less than $2 dollars for a short trip to less than $10 to get nearly anywhere as long as you are outside San José.

The large number of **internal flights** can save a huge amount of travel time. Two companies operate most of the flights: Nature Air (**www.natureair.com**) has regularly scheduled flights to 16 locations. Paradise Air (**www.flywithparadise .com**) covers even more, serving groups with special requests on a charter basis.

Note that most flights run in the morning, when visibility is best. Luggage limits are tight on the turboprop planes—pack light! Prices are quite reasonable, with one-way rates ranging from $50 to $155. If you have a group, you can charter a 7- or 12-passenger plane through Paradise Air and pay by the planeload, making it more economical than the per-person charges. Regular **train service** is limited to suburban commuter trains from San José to San Pedro, Universidad Latina, and Pavas. The Tico Train Tour (**www.americatravelcr.com**) is a tourist trip from San José to the Caribbean coast at Caldera (91 kilometers).

Avis, Budget, Hertz, Alamo, and other **rental-car** agencies operate in tourist zones around the country. Rental rates are at least what you would pay at home, plus insurance. You should spring for a rugged vehicle or four-wheel drive. While many roads are paved and well maintained, some that are unbelievably bad in the dry season actually get worse in the rainy season.

Getting around with your own car can be trying. Even Costa Ricans say, "Ask three people which way to go, and if two give the same answer, go that way." There are almost no directional signs off the main highways and even fewer street signs. If you are not comfortable asking directions in Spanish several times a day, don't rent a car.

Activity Costs

Most people come to Costa Rica for outdoor adventure and nature activities. These can be a big part of the overall expenses, so include them in your budget.

- Admission to many national parks is $7–$15, but figure on $30–$40 per person if you go in with a guide—which you should because they are vastly better at finding wildlife than you are. You'll never know how much you didn't see.
- Whitewater rafting trip on the Naranjo or Savegre river: $65–$100, including lunch
- Most zipline canopy adventures (traveling through the rain-forest canopy while suspended from a cable) in Costa Rica consist of an extensive series of platforms and lines, rather than just one or two. Budget $45–$75 per person.
- The hot springs near Arenal Volcano include many pools of varying temperatures (some with bars): $20–$55, depending on facility and time of day.
- Half-day coastal kayaking trip through the mangroves: $60–$90
- Half-day horseback-riding excursion: $45–$70
- Half-day boating and snorkeling trip: $60–$75

Tour Companies

Dozens of U.S. and Canadian tour companies lead trips to Costa Rica, with new ones popping up every month or two. All the small-group companies listed in

Chapter 6, The Organized Tour, operate in Costa Rica. I traveled with Adventure Life (**www.adventure-life.com**) and highly recommend the company. Its excellent guides go out of their way to make sure group members are happy. This operator tends to use smaller, family-run hotels and small restaurants off the main drag.

Others based in the United States that lead a lot of small-group tours in the country include the following:

- Costa Rica Experts (**www.costaricaexperts.com**)
- Costa Rica Rios (**www.costaricarios.com**)
- Tico Travel (**www.ticotravel.com**)

It would take a whole chapter to list all the local operators based in Costa Rica. *Traveler's Tool Kit* does not endorse the following local operators, but all have been around a while and have solid reputations with travelers:

- Horizontes (**www.horizontes.com**): Has guided visitors since 1984; heralded for its sustainable-tourism practices
- Travel Excellence (**www.travelexcellence.com**): In business for more than a decade
- Costa Rica Expeditions (**www.costaricaexpeditions.com**): Active since 1981; gets good marks in several guidebooks
- Costa Rica Tours (**www.costaricatours.com**): Active since 1986
- Swiss Travel Service (**www.swisstravelcr.com**): Caters to the upper end of the spectrum, with a desk in most of the top hotels in San José

Ziplining in the Costa Rican jungle

Useful Details

Getting there and away: There are direct flights to San José from 11 airports in the United States: the hub cities of Delta, Continental, American, Spirit, US Airways, and Frontier Airlines. TACA, based in El Salvador, flies to San José from Miami, Los Angeles, and New York. The airport in Liberia is a better bet for those heading to the north of the country.

Air Canada offers direct flights to San José from Toronto. There are also frequent flight connections from Mexico and other countries in Central America.

Overland, Tica Bus (**www.ticabus.com**) has comfortable bus trips from Panama, Nicaragua, and farther afield.

Border crossings: The Pan-American Highway crosses the border from Nicaragua at Peñas Blancas. The main land crossing to Panama is at Paso Canoas, near the Pacific coast.

To get to the Bocas del Toro islands in Panama, you would cross the border at Sixaola and then take a ferry from Changuinola in Panama.

In general, even the secondary crossings are quick and painless if you arrive early in the day. By late afternoon, posts may be deserted, leaving you stuck in a border town until the next day.

Visas: U.S., EU, and Canadian citizens do not require a visa or tourist card. Upon arrival you receive a stamp good for 90 days. Citizens of Australia, New Zealand, and some other nations receive only 30 days automatically.

Currency: The colón is the national currency, generally worth between 500 and 600 to the dollar. U.S. dollars are widely accepted, as are credit cards. Outside of rural markets and the like, you can rely on dollars or plastic plus maybe $100 worth of colones for a week. ATMs are hard to find, especially outside the cities. Even in major tourist areas, you may have to take a taxi to get to one, so withdraw an ample amount.

Departure tax: It's $26 per person, which must be paid at the airport and is not included in your airline ticket price.

Weather and when to go: The ideal time to visit is December through February, the coolest part of the dry season, with temperate days, low humidity, and few rainstorms. The next-best months are March and April, when it's getting hotter but is still reasonably dry. Temperatures and rainfall vary greatly depending on location and altitude.

Outside these months, expect some rain. It may be a quick afternoon shower, but it could be a daylong downpour—no fun if your scheduled activity was birdwatching and hiking through a national park. How much rain are we talking about? Buckets. The La Paz Waterfall Gardens receive 14.5 *feet* of rain per year, compared with 2.5 feet in London and 3 feet in Seattle.

If you do come during the rainy season, expect much better weather on the drier Pacific coast. The Caribbean coast is almost always rainy, but the precipitation does slack off a bit from May through September. That's not the case in the rest of the country. (See the Web sites in the "Resources" section for local weather forecasts.)

Electricity: Current and outlet shapes are the same as in the United States, and you'll find three-prong outlets in many hotels. The electrical supply is more stable than in most other Central American countries. Think air-conditioning and ice.

Internet access and telephones: The telephone system is laughably bad in most areas, with exorbitant charges. There are card phones but no cards for sale, and none of the handy phone kiosks so common in the rest of Latin America. Your cell phone will not work in most areas, and if it does you'll pay several dollars a minute to call home. You could rent a mobile phone locally, but that's not easy, either. There are temporary, prepaid numbers, and you basically have to go through a special agent and pay dearly to get one. Local people avoid all this with annual contracts, but they complain that coverage is hit-and-miss almost anywhere outside San José.

Kayakers near Manuel Antonio National Park, Costa Rica

Exploring the jungle in Costa Rica

Internet cafes are common in cities and tourist areas, but the connections are almost always achingly slow. While waiting to finally log on, thank the government telephone monopoly, which also happens to be the electric-utility monopoly. Wi-Fi is rare outside upscale hotels and the airport.

Language: Spanish is the primary language, but English-speaking tourists have had a huge impact. Many local people are fluent in English, and you could navigate for a week on the tourist circuit without speaking a word of Spanish. Of course, you will meet a wider range of people if you can speak some Spanish. Off the main "gringo trail," English will not always be understood.

Safety: Costa Rica has a reputation as being safe. Most areas probably have less crime than your hometown does, but it's still not a place to let your guard down foolishly. Petty theft is a problem in places with lots of tourists, so leave the jewelry at home, and lock away your valuables and passport, especially at the beaches. Taxis are cheap, so don't walk in poorly lighted areas at night. Please see Chapter 17, Safety and Security.

Prostitution and gambling are legal in Costa Rica, so you may see both, especially in the capital. There's a well-defined red-light district in San José that is definitely high risk at night.

Health care: Costa Rica is a major "medical tourism" destination, with people coming for dental work, elective surgery, or assorted nips and tucks. Most of this is done at private hospitals and clinics, where the doctors are well trained and professional. The country has a national health-care system, so the regular public facilities can involve a lot of waiting. Rural areas are underserved, especially by medical specialists, so get to a city if you have a real problem.

The lowlands have plenty of mosquitoes, so there is some risk of malaria and dengue fever, especially near the borders of Panama and Nicaragua. Take precautions. Oh, and watch for the snakes. Fortunately, there are few other nasty diseases or critters to worry about. Please see Chapter 12, Keeping Healthy.

Things to buy: Shopping in Costa Rica can be summed up by a statement from a tourist in Manuel Antonio: "I wouldn't want this stuff if it were free." There are some decent wood carvings, but in general the rest is pretty poor. Even the imports from Nicaragua or Guatemala are far from their best yet carry prices comparable to those in U.S. stores. Save your shopping money for some other trip.

As gifts, consider the excellent coffee beans, local chocolate, rum, or vanilla.

Resources

Guidebooks and other references: More than 20 publishers put out new editions every year or two. Some rival publishers even share the same authors. Guides from Lonely Planet, Moon, and Fodor's are reliable and current, but browse the choices to see which best fits your style and budget. Please see the section on choosing guidebooks in Chapter 4, How to Plan Your Trip.

There are also some titles that aren't put out by the big corporations, including *Adventure Guide to Costa Rica* and *Explore Costa Rica.*

If birding is your passion, see *The Birds of Costa Rica: A Field Guide* or *Site Guides: Costa Rica; A Guide to the Best Birding Locations.* Some attractive coffee-table books include *Hummingbirds of Costa Rica* and *100 Butterflies and Moths: Portraits from the Tropical Forests of Costa Rica.* Other nature guides include *Tropical Plants of Costa Rica: A Guide to Native and Exotic Flora, The Amphibians and Reptiles of Costa Rica: A Herpetofauna between Two Continents, between Two Seas, The Mammals of Costa Rica: A Natural History and Field Guide,* and *Costa Rican Wildlife: An Introduction to Familiar Species.*

Some of the most popular books pertaining to moving to Costa Rica are *Living Abroad in Costa Rica, The New Golden Door to Retirement and Living in Costa Rica,* and *Choose Costa Rica for Retirement: Information for Travel, Retirement, Investment, and Affordable Living.* For etiquette, consider *Culture Shock! Costa Rica: A Survival Guide to Customs and Etiquette* and *Costa Rica: Culture Smart! A Quick Guide to Customs and Etiquette.*

The Surfer's Guide to Costa Rica & SW Nicaragua gives the lowdown on the big waves.

For more insight into the culture, read *Costa Rica: A Traveler's Literary Companion.*

Web sites: The official site of the Costa Rica Tourism Board is **www.visit costarica.com.**

The Tico Times (**www.ticotimes.net**) is the weekly English-language newspaper.

Inside Costa Rica (**www.insidecostarica.com**) is another good online news source.

MyCostaRicanGuide.com (**www.mycostaricanguide.com**) has lots of facts and other resources.

InfoCostaRica (**www.infocostarica.com**), run by a tour agency, has maps of each section of the country.

Fortuna Welcome (**www.fortunawelcome.com**), run by a tour agency, has good background and useful hotel links for the Fortuna/Arenal region.

MAQBeach (**www.maqbeach.com**) has info for the Manuel Antonio and Quepos area.

Monteverde Info (**www.monteverdeinfo.com**) has been covering the Monteverde Cloud Forest area well since 1998.

The Costa Rica section of Boomers Abroad stuffs more than 100 useful links on one page (**www.boomersabroad.com**).

The Costa Rican Hotel Association site (**www.costaricanhotels.com**) has listings with detailed information and maps for more than 250 member hotels throughout the country.

Luxury Latin America (**www.luxurylatinamerica.com**) has detailed reviews of the best upscale hotels in the country.

Retirement Opportunities

Costa Rica was pegged as a hot retirement destination in the early 1980s. Anyone who got in then is probably feeling very smug and wealthy now. Some early investors have seen their land values go up by a factor of 20. It's a very different story now, especially on the Pacific coast, where it's not unusual to see condominium ads stating, "Prices starting in the $500s." At half a million dollars, a condo is no longer a "steal." Compared with prices in Florida or California, that may not seem outrageous, but the word *bubble* is being whispered these days.

The government offers very few incentives to foreign residents. It doesn't need to bother. Wealthy Americans keep following their friends here, and some developments sell out before the first cement trucks have even been dispatched. The bandwagon effect is in full swing, even though prices are several times what they are a short hop away in Panama, where incentives are far greater.

Prices aren't nearly as high in the interior. There are still plenty of true bargains in the Central Valley, including around Arenal Volcano. These are also popular tourist areas, so opportunities to combine a residence with a business are numerous. You could buy a turnkey inn and hit the ground running.

Helping Out

Given the focus in Costa Rica on environmental stewardship, there are plenty of opportunities to help as a donor or volunteer. Nearly all the global environmental groups, such as the World Wide Fund for Nature–World Wildlife Fund (**www.panda.org**), the Rainforest Alliance (**www.rainforest-alliance.org**), and Conservation International (**www.conservation.org**) are present. They are joined by dozens of regional groups, such as the Caribbean Conservation Corporation (**www.cccturtle.org**) and Talamancan Association of Ecotourism and Conservation (**www.greencoast.com/atec.htm**).

Keeping your eyes sharp while traveling will lead you to organizations that can use your help. To set up something in advance, see the extensive listings on the Transitions Abroad site (**www.transitionsabroad.com**), which cover everything from protecting sea turtles to teaching English.

PANAMA

Think of Panama as one of the world's key crossroads. It's the land bridge between North America and South America and the waterway between the Atlantic–Caribbean and the Pacific. The country is an S-shaped isthmus lying on its side east to west, with a land area slightly smaller than South Carolina. Here's the counterintuitive part: the Caribbean Sea is to the north, the Pacific Ocean to the south.

But, honestly, what do you think of when you hear the word "Panama"? Maybe the stylish Panama hat, or Panama Red? Certainly the Panama Canal. But none of these has been a magnet for tourists.

Furthermore, Panama hats are actually made in Ecuador. It's been decades since Panama was a competitor in the marijuana trade. And watching a ship pass through the canal is only slightly more exciting than watching paint dry.

Unlike the energetic tourism offices in nearby countries such as Costa Rica and Mexico, the Panamanian tourism folks have taken a distinctly *que sera, sera* approach. Which explains why you won't be bumping into crowds of tourists filling the cafes and driving up prices.

Now here's the real Panama: stunning beaches, world-class fishing, great scuba diving, fascinating jungle excursions, and a bustling metropolis that serves as an international banking center. At the same time, some describe Panama as "like Costa Rica was 20 years ago," meaning a tranquil pace—on a busy day.

Certainly, this is a nature-lover's paradise, with a biodiversity reportedly greater than that of even Costa Rica. An amazing 29 percent of the land is protected as national parks, forest reserves, and wildlife sanctuaries. More than 900 species of birds call Panama home, as do 220 species of mammals and 354 species of reptiles and amphibians. Plus, the offshore area hosts hundreds of islands and miles of protected coral reef, sheltering a wide diversity of marine life. The Smithsonian Tropical Research Institute, a place for scientists to study Panama's unique ecology, is located there.

Panama City, founded in 1519, was the first European settlement on the Pacific Ocean. Immense fortunes in gold and silver from South America (mostly Bolivia and Peru) passed overland through Panama on their way to Europe.

Panama won't stay undiscovered, but in all of Central America, it's the best opportunity to beat the crowds—without having to rough it as a trailblazing pioneer. At some point, the spotlights of glossy travel magazines will light the way, and the throngs will follow.

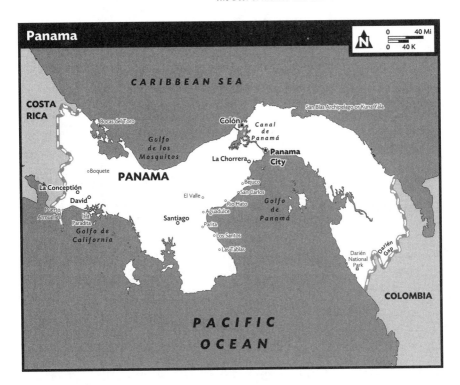

In addition to other attractions, Panama is an easy place in which to travel. Because of the long U.S. presence, English is fairly common. And the U.S. dollar has been the Panamanian currency since 1903.

Panama's People

Panamanians are proud of having a great diversity of cultures and people. In fact, Panama City is more international than most cities in the melting pot of the United States.

The indigenous Kuna people are Central America's least assimilated ethnic group. They maintain their centuries-old traditions, including clothing that they don't don just for tourist photos. You can visit some of the islands only if there's a spot open for you; villages cap the number of nonnative guests at just a handful.

Panama's economy is growing by 6 to 8 percent per year, and the inflation rate has averaged less than 2 percent for the past 40 years. The International Monetary Fund has cited the country as a top performer in Latin America in terms of growth. It has the third-highest per-capita income in Central America, but, unfortunately, prosperity has not spread evenly, and too many Panamanians are still struggling. However, you may see "working girls" but very few beggars.

Much of the wilderness is still wilderness because the population is quite concentrated. In the same way that Egyptians hug the Nile, Panamanians hug the canal. More than 40 percent of the population lives in Panama City and Colón—the two access points to the canal.

Highlights

- The **Panama Canal** is one of mankind's great works that changed the way the world operated. It replaced the lengthy and dangerous journey around Cape Horn at the southern tip of South America with a 50-mile trip between the oceans. On a map of the hemisphere, it's easy to see why the French and then the Americans salivated at the idea of creating such a shortcut. Because the canal connects the Caribbean Sea with the Pacific Ocean, logic suggests that it would run east–west—but it doesn't. The cut runs diagonally, but more north–south, with Colón on the Caribbean side and Panama City on the Pacific side. It carries a huge amount of shipping traffic through narrow locks (which raise or lower the water level) and man-made Lake Gatún. Many cruise companies offer trips through the canal. You can also arrange passage locally or visit the three major locks (Miraflores, Pedro Miguel, and Gatún) by road. Another alternative is a leisurely trip on the Panama Canal Railway between Corazal, at the southern end (near Panama City), and Colón, at the northern end. Several hotels and resorts are next to the canal, so you can sit on a balcony and watch the ships go by. (See "The Panama Canal," on facing page, for more info.)

  > Central America has no suburbs in the Kansas City sense—except for the Canal Zone of Panama. Americans operated the canal for more than 80 years, and they re-created a bit of home to live in. Instead of dense apartment blocks or homes hidden behind high concrete walls, you'll find single-family homes with gardens, grassy front yards, and garages.

- **Panama City** is hot and humid all year and somewhat rough around the edges, but it's also the most vibrant and cosmopolitan city in Central America, full of gleaming high-rises, active nightlife, and good restaurants serving food from around the world. Explore the Columbus-era ruins of Old Panama (sacked by Captain Morgan, the infamous pirate). Soak up the atmosphere of Casco Viejo, the city's historic district, founded in the 1600s, and see the entrance to the canal from several vantage points around town. Take a stroll out to the Amador Causeway, stretching nearly 2 miles into the Pacific Ocean and offering a nice skyline vantage point. Or take a ferry 12 miles to Isla Taboga for an easy beach break.

- The **Bocas del Toro Archipelago** in the Caribbean consists of 9 islands and 52 smaller keys, plus a capital that is a laid-back, ramshackle collection of houses and small inns on stilts. Fishing boats are the main mode

The Panama Canal

Even before the Panama Canal was built, much of the cargo from the eastern United States bound for the U.S. West Coast moved through this area. It used a combination of riverboats, mule trains, human labor, and an expensive train line. (Another route went through Nicaragua.) In 1880, a French company led by Suez Canal construction leader Ferdinand de Lesseps started digging a canal through the narrow isthmus. Disaster followed disaster, and an estimated 20,000 workers died (mostly from malaria and various other diseases). The company went bankrupt and almost crippled France at the same time.

The United States wanted to buy the French concession but soon sparred with Colombia, since at that time Panama was a province of Colombia. President Teddy Roosevelt, as usual, sent gunboats. Panama soon declared independence, without bloodshed, and signed a treaty with the United States so the canal could move forward. The lopsided treaty provided for one-time payments of $10 million to Panama and $40 million to the French, and annual payments of $250,000 to the Panamanian government. In return, the United States got control over the canal "in perpetuity."

Completion of the canal, which among other challenges required cutting through 9 miles of mountains, cost $352 million (in early 1900s dollars). It opened in 1914, under budget and ahead of schedule, with the major side benefit of the near-eradication of yellow fever, malaria, and cholera in the Canal Zone.

Panama Canal trivia:

- The average trip through the canal by ship takes eight to ten hours.
- A ship going from New York to San Francisco through the canal instead of around South America saves 7,900 miles.
- Panamanians didn't build the canal (only 357 worked on it). Most of the workers were imported, especially from the Caribbean.
- In late 2006, Panamanian voters approved spending $5.25 billion to add a third channel that will double the canal's capacity, allowing giant container ships to pass through.
- The record for most transits in a single day is 65, set in 1968.

of transportation, and most of the good beaches require a water-taxi ride. This area is popular with expats and is a prime spot for snorkeling and diving. Much of it is protected, including the Isla Bastimentos National Marine Park and, on land, La Amistad Biosphere Reserve. Besides the array of bright-hued fish, there are turtle-nesting zones, a variety of sloths, and frogs in neon colors.

- For a very different island experience, head to the **San Blas Archipelago**, part of the **Kuna Yala** region that stretches nearly 250 miles along the

Caribbean coast. This is the home of the indigenous, self-governed Kuna people. They have staked out their paradise of isolated coral islands as a place where they can keep their traditional culture alive and aligned with nature. You can reach the area by boat or small plane. The Kuna run rustic facilities for visitors.

> To discover buried pirate treasure, your best bet is Isla Toboga, where pirate Henry Morgan and other plunderers created a trading base and hideout. In 1998, construction workers unearthed 1,000 pieces of silver dating to the 17th century.

- **Mainland beaches** southwest of the capital feature only a few major hotels, but there are plenty of small hotels, rental villas, and vacation homes. An area known as Arco Seco, starting just 50 miles from Panama City, consists of 40 miles of beaches on the Pacific coast. During midweek, you have the beaches almost to yourself. There are a few major resorts—including Coronado Golf & Beach Resort and the 820-room, all-inclusive Royal Decameron Beach Resort—and many less expensive alternatives.

- Many favor **Boquete**, at the base of Barú, the country's highest mountain (11,400 feet), because of its "eternal spring" climate. The dramatic scenery features mountains covered by fruit trees and wildflowers. Activities include hiking, horseback riding, fishing, and biking. Two rivers provide Class III and IV whitewater rapids for rafting through canyons and jungle. Nearby **La Amistad International Peace Park** is a 479,000-acre park shared with Costa Rica.

- **David** has an airport that serves people visiting the Chiriquí highlands and Boquete. It's a humid lowland city that's just a stopover for most people but it has good hotels and restaurants and a grand central square. It is the nearest sizable city to the Costa Rican border crossing of Paso Canoas. From here, you depart for an adventure on remote and eco-friendly **Isla Paradita**. This is 1 of 50 small islands in the Gulf of Chiriquí, part of Panama's national park system near Costa Rica.

From McDonald's Manager to President

The current president of Panama, Martín Torrijos, went to the United States in his teens and earned degrees in economics and political science from Texas A&M. After working as a manager for a major McDonald's franchise in Chicago, he returned to Panama and entered politics.

His is no "out of nowhere" story, however. His father was General Omar Torrijos, the Panamanian dictator who negotiated the handover of the Panama Canal with President Jimmy Carter. Martín ran for the presidency in 1999 and lost (no wonder his father didn't like democracy). Undeterred, he ran again and is serving a five-year term running to 2009.

- **Colón**, at the Caribbean end of the Panama Canal, is universally panned as a nasty city for a tourist, but its Zona Libre is the second-largest free-trade zone in the world. If you are a dedicated shopper (or need to get goodies for a new home in Panama), come here to stock up.
- The **Darién Gap** is one of the rawest and wildest regions in the Americas. This huge, almost uninhabited national park is so dense that the Pan-American Highway stops at the gap and restarts on the other side in Colombia. It is one of the best bird-watching regions in the world, and there are enough other creepy-crawlies and four-legged creatures to keep a botanist busy for decades. In addition to the rugged terrain, there's another reason it's not for the faint of heart: bandits and smugglers from Colombia. Whether you're traveling on foot or by river, an experienced guide is essential.
- **El Valle** in the Anton Valley has long been a highland vacation area for Panama City's elite. The cool, misty air and pine trees offer a major change from the lowlands. The town, in a huge crater of a dormant volcano, and its surroundings host morpho butterflies, stone petroglyphs, and trails to cascading waterfalls.

Itineraries

If You Have a Week in Panama: Mainland Only

Arrive in Panama City, and spend a day or two, perhaps with a side trip to the Metropolitan National Park (right outside town) for wildlife, and visit the Miraflores Locks to see the ships passing through. Continue along the canal by train, ship, or road (stopping at the Gamboa Rainforest if not traversing the waterway by ship). Fly or bus to the city of David from Panama City or Colón and proceed to Boquete. Spend one or two days enjoying the mountain climate, coffee plantations, and such local adventure activities as hiking, rafting, or horseback riding. Fly back to Panama City, and enjoy the remainder of your time in the city or on one of the Pacific beaches of the Azuero Peninsula.

If You Have a Week in Panama: Mainland and Islands

Arrive in Panama City, and explore the canal region with a night in the Gamboa Rainforest and its resort. Return to Panama City, and fly or take a boat to Bocas del Toro or the San Blas Islands for diving, fishing, snorkeling, or wildlife watching. Return to Panama City before heading home.

If You Have Two Weeks or More in Panama

A two-week trip lets you see most of the highlights without rushing. You can spend more time in the national parks, traverse the canal, do some scuba diving, or just lounge on a beach. Many people find they don't want to leave the Boquete area.

Alternatively, a span of two weeks or more allows getting off the beaten path more often (though no path is all that "beaten" in Panama) and exploring the San Blas or Bocas del Toro islands in more depth—perhaps visiting both. Or, for tropical paradise seclusion, get your hammock time on eco-friendly Isla Paradita and around the Gulf of Chiriquí. Another option is to strike out for parts of the mainland that get very few visitors, such as the Darién Gap.

Cost Comparisons

Overall, Panama occupies the middle ground in Central America in terms of costs. It is noticeably less expensive than Costa Rica or Belize, but not as rock-bottom cheap as Nicaragua or mainland Honduras. Note that Panama is not a big destination for overland backpackers, so values are better for those on a vacation budget than for those on a shoestring budget.

- Liter of water in a convenience store: 50–80 cents (but tap water is potable)
- Bottle of beer in a bar or restaurant: 75–$2
- Bottle of beer in a store: 50–90 cents
- Meal of the day in a locals' restaurant: $2–$4
- Half kilo of oranges, in season: 50–80 cents
- 1 hour of Internet access in a cafe: $1.50–$3
- Cup of coffee, juice, or soda in a restaurant: 40–90 cents
- 10-minute taxi ride across town: $1–$4
- Taxi from main international airport to hotel: $20–$30
- 3-star or equivalent hotel: $30–$75

> Panama City's Metropolitan Cathedral took 108 years to complete, finally being finished in 1796. It's encrusted with mother-of-pearl and contains tower bells from the older cathedral in Panamá la Vieja (Old Panama).

Accommodations

Extremely low room rates are in short supply, but it's possible to find places to sleep for less than $10 outside the cities (a hostel-type bed and communal bathrooms). Otherwise, plan on $12–$20 for a clean double room with ceiling fan and bath. Now the good news: Comfortable accommodations priced in the midrange are plentiful. Many family-run midrange hotels cost $30 to $75 a night. They are probably where you'll stay most of the time if on vacation or on a package tour. You'll have a private, hot-water bath, air-conditioning, maid service, and often a pool and TV.

At the luxury end, Panama is not nearly as developed as Costa Rica, Belize, or Mexico. The few big beach resorts follow the typical all-inclusive, group-oriented template. Many all-inclusive deals for a couple go for less than $200 per night outside high season. The Bristol in Panama City is the only hotel on the mainland that charges more than $300 a night for a regular room. Donald Trump has announced development of the $220 million Trump Ocean Club condominiums, so things will surely change.

As in all Latin American countries, pay attention to the holidays. (See "Holidays and Festivals" in this chapter.) During Semana Santa, or the week before Easter, you can expect hotels to be packed.

Food and Drink

Panama is known for its good hygiene. For example, you can safely drink the water in most towns and cities. As a result, food-borne illnesses are rarely a worry. Though reasonable caution makes sense, especially upon arrival, sampling the local cuisine in restaurants shouldn't get you into any trouble except in the most remote areas. Food is seldom spicy here; you need to load on the hot sauce to give it punch.

Inexpensive meals are easy to find if you eat where the locals do. A big helping of tamales or fried plantains costs $1 at any market. *Sancocho,* the national dish, is a hearty meat stew (usually chicken) with avocado, yucca, plantains, corn, and aromatic seasonings, including *culantro,* a flavorful cousin of cilantro. You can find *sancocho* almost everywhere for less than $2. Other simple local fare includes coconut rice, ceviche, and a shredded-beef-and-veggies dish called *ropa vieja* ("old clothes").

A Giant Rat

One of Panama's wildlife oddities is the web-footed capybara ("water hog"), a semi-aquatic animal that resembles a guinea pig—except that at 4 feet long and 125 pounds, it's a giant: the world's largest rodent.

Holidays and Festivals

- January 1: New Year's Day
- January 9: Martyrs' Day
- February 25: Anniversary of the Kuna Yala Revolution (celebrated on the more traditional islands in Kuna Yala)
- February or March: Carnival, the week before Lent
- March or April: Semana Santa (week before Easter)
- May 1: Labor Day
- August 15: Founding of Old Panama
- November 1: National Anthem Day and Children's Day
- November 2: All Souls' Day
- November 3: Independence from Colombia Day
- November 4: Flag Day
- November 5: Independence Day (Colón only)
- November 10: First Call for Independence
- November 28: Independence from Spain Day
- December 8: Mother's Day
- December 24: Christmas Eve
- December 25: Christmas

The USS Missouri *passing through the Panama Canal shortly after WWII*

Most basic restaurants serve a *comida corriente* (meal of the day) for $1.50 to $4. It consists of meat or fish, rice, and some vegetables. Breakfast is usually a choice of some egg-and-meat combination with bread. Good pastry shops are plentiful.

The larger cities offer a wide range of ethnic foods, including Middle Eastern, Mediterranean, Japanese, and northern European—as well as the omnipresent American fast food. You'll also find plenty of fancy restaurants with servers in crisp, white shirts and bow ties. Prices are often half what they would be in Costa Rica.

Cheap firewater is similar in most Central American countries—a rough, rumlike drink made from distilled sugarcane. In Panama, it's called *seco*. Many locals like to drink it as *seco con leche* (with milk). At only $2 or $3 for a bottle in a store, this stuff flies off the shelves. It should be taken with caution.

Real rum is plentiful, of course, and is preferable to Panama and Soberana, the weak local beers. There's no local wine industry, so most wine is imported from Argentina or Chile.

Dozens of different fruit drinks and juices are available, made from a wide variety of tropical fruits and even corn and sweet potatoes. Take advantage of the fresh juice drinks. Here, you don't have to worry about the water, ice, or milk in them.

The best coffee is from the region around Boquete. Some of the good stuff makes its way to cafes in the cities.

Transportation

Bus travel in Panama won't hit your wallet very hard. A comfortable, two-hour bus trip from Panama City to the beach resort areas of Farallón costs $5. You can get anywhere in the country on a bus for $20 or less. On main routes, you have your choice of classes and comforts. On less frequented routes, you may have to take the "chicken bus." Figure on less than a dollar an hour for these. In general, though, buses are newer and better maintained than in less developed Central American countries.

Sample bus routes and costs (highest class available):

City 1	City 2	Travel Time	Cost
Panama City	Almirante	10 hours	$24
Panama City	David	6.5 hours	$15
Panama City	Colón	1.5 hours	$3
Panama City	Los Santos Beaches	5 hours	$10
Panama City	San José, Costa Rica	16 hours	$30
Colón	David (via Panama City)	8.5 hours	$18
Boquete	Panama City (via David)	7.5 hour	$17

Taxis are inexpensive—as little as $1 for a short trip in David—and tipping is not expected. The charge for the trip from any airport is inflated, however, so be prepared to cough up more upon arrival. There are no meters, so negotiate the fare before getting in. Or, if you want a little excitement, try negotiating at the trip's end. Hiring a driver for a day's excursion out of the city is often less expensive than an organized tour—and gives you much more flexibility.

Local city buses can be hot, crowded, and confusing, but some routes are better: the bus from central Panama City to the international airport costs 75 cents and is air-conditioned.

Walking in Panama City is no picnic. If the exhaust fumes don't get you, the crazy drivers will. Outside the big cities, pedestrians have an easier time.

Oddly, travel by **boat** is uncommon. Only the Bocas del Toro Archipelago has plenty of scheduled, inexpensive boat transportation. Two ferry services carry passengers between Panama City and Isla Taboga daily. The two-hour Expreso Del Pacifico ferry runs on weekends to Contadora Island from the capital. In other areas, including the San Blas (Kuna Yala) islands and the Darién, you work out something with a private-boat captain.

The main **train** option is the Panama Canal Railway (**www.panarail.com**), a one-hour experience that is worthwhile for the novelty as much as it is for the transportation. The view often features the canal on one side and the rain forest on the other. A slow banana train runs 13 miles between Changuinola and Almirante in the Bocas del Toro region. It doesn't take you anywhere you need to go, but it can be an interesting ride for the cultural interaction. Go ahead: blow $1.

Internal flights are quite reasonable and can be a good investment if time is limited. For example, a flight from the capital to David, Contadora Island, or Bocas del Toro generally costs less than $75 one way.

Driving in Panama City is daunting, with horns honking constantly and traffic at walking speed during rush hours. If **renting a car** in Panama City, try to leave the city midmorning or midafternoon. Once outside the capital, driving is pleasant on relatively good, well-marked, uncrowded roads. Rental companies do not permit cars to be driven into Costa Rica. Cross the border by public transportation, and then rent a car. Most expatriates do what locals do and take the bus.

Activity Costs

- Chiriqui River Rafting (**www.panama-rafting.com**) runs one-day rafting trips from Boquete on the Class III and IV rivers in the Barú Volcano National Park for $60 to $105 per person, including transportation and lunch.
- The fee is $40 for a rain-forest canopy tour in El Valle that involves hiking and four zipline rides from different platforms. If you book the trip in Panama City, figure on about $100, including transportation and lunch.
- Soak in the Pozos Termales hot springs (just off the main road in El Valle) for a mere $5. Five hot mineral pools and a batch of therapeutic mud provide a do-it-yourself spa experience. Go early to beat the crowds.
- A one-night tour to the Kuna Yala region from Panama City runs about $175, including flight and lodging.
- A boat transit of the Panama Canal booked locally runs $115 to $250, depending on the operator and whether it covers all or part of the canal.
- Half-day whale-watching tours from Panama City run $60 to $80 per person.
- Chartering a deep-sea fishing boat for the day from the capital or one of the islands usually costs $500 to $700 for a boat that holds six to eight passengers.

Kuna woman of the San Blas Islands, off the Panama coast

Tour Companies

Some very reputable North American operators lead trips to Panama, including Adventure Life (**www.adventure-life.com**), G.A.P Adventures (**www.gap adventures.com**), Adventure Center (**www.adventurecenter.com**), and Djoser (**www.djoserusa.com**). Smaller companies that specialize in Panama or are based there include Enjoy Panama (**www.enjoypanama.com**) and Aventuras Panamá (**www.adventuresinpanama.com**). Panama Explorer Club (**www.pex club.com**) offers reasonably priced hiking, rafting, rock climbing, and other outdoor activities led by experienced guides. Ancon Expeditions (**www.ancon expeditions.com**), a large local operator, runs adventure trips and has its own lodge in the Darién.

Panama Private Tours (**www.panamaprivatetours.com**), a group of more than 30 travel agents, can set up customized experiences throughout the country.

Panama Travel Experts (**www.panamatravelexperts.com**) can arrange full-country tours or local excursions booked in the capital.

Useful Details

Getting there and away: More than 100 flights a day go in and out of Panama's Tocumen International Airport near Panama City. Tocumen is the hub for Copa Airlines (a partner of Continental) and therefore has direct flights from Miami, Orlando, New York, Los Angeles, and the District of Columbia.

Altogether, you can get to Panama nonstop from eight U.S. airports. If you're not at one of these (all are major hub airports except Orlando), you'll need to change planes at a hub. The same is true for anyone flying out of Canada except on package charter deals.

Some package deals from Canada and the United States range from $1,000 to $1,300 per person for a one-week, all-inclusive beach trip, including airfare. An eight- or nine-day "Highlights of Panama" trip usually costs less than $2,000 with airfare. With a good operator (see the "Resources" section in this chapter), the latter can be a tremendous value for an introductory trip.

There are also flights to Panama from Mexico and the capital cities of most other Central American and South American countries.

Overland: Crossing into Panama from Costa Rica is easy at any point along the border. It's also common to arrive by boat in Bocas del Toro. There is no scheduled ferry service around the Darién Gap to Colombia, and going through the gap overland is a bad idea. First, it's an incredibly arduous trip. Second, you're likely to encounter drug traffickers in the jungle. Make it easy on yourself: fly, or hire a private boat captain.

Buses run from Panama City to other capitals in Central America and Mexico. This is a good adventure, one that will cost you more time than money. You can take a bus to Managua, Nicaragua, for about $40, for instance, but it will take you 30 hours. Some bus companies allow you to make overnight stops along the way if you specify the dates when purchasing a ticket. In theory, you could make your way from the U.S.–Mexico border all the way to Panama City by public bus, but bring a seat cushion, good humor, and plenty of time!

Visas: For those of most nationalities (including U.S. and Canadian), a $5 tourist card issued on landing is all you need for a 30-day stay. This can be extended without much hassle. You will need a passport.

Currency: Panama uses the U.S. dollar as its currency. Officially, it's called the balboa. While the coins are the same size and value as U.S. ones, they have local designs.

World Heritage Sites in Panama

Panama is home to five UNESCO World Heritage sites. One encompasses two sections of Panama City: the ruins of Panamá la Vieja (Old Panama) and the walled settlement of Casco Viejo (colonial Panama; the name literally means "old helmet"). The others are the colonial structures and stone fortresses of Portobelo, a major transit point on the Caribbean coast; Darién National Park; La Amistad International Peace Park and associated areas; and Coiba National Park and its marine protection zone.

ATMs are surprisingly hard to find considering that Panama is an international banking center, so load up on cash when you can. Credit cards are widely accepted. This is one of the few places in the Americas where you can freely exchange any major currency. Do your conversions here if you're carrying pounds, yen, or leftover pesos.

Departure tax: The tax at the airport is $20, which is sometimes included in your ticket.

Weather and when to go: Panama has two seasons: wet and dry. Temperatures don't change much throughout the year. In general, the most desirable time to visit is December through April, when the weather is slightly cooler and it rains the least. This is about the only time Panama City is not steaming-hot and humid. July through November is wet and rainy in most of the country, and visibility is reduced.

On the Caribbean coast, including the islands of Bocas del Toro, afternoon downpours are common any time of year. The Pacific coast is much drier.

In the lowlands, expect temperatures reaching 80 to 95°F in daytime most of the year and seldom dropping below 70 at night. The weather is far more temperate in the highlands, including the area around Boquete, where daytime highs rarely get above 80 and a sweater or jacket comes in handy in the evenings.

Electricity: Current and outlet shapes are the same as in the United States.

Internet access and telephones: The telephone system in Panama is good, though charges for an international call are high. The best bet is an Internet cafe that has Skype or a similar Web-based calling system. Internet cafes are abundant, and speeds are fast.

Language: When the United States managed the canal, English was more common than it is today. Apparently, after the turnover, there has been less need to speak English, at least in the Canal Zone. There's also a desire to honor the Spanish heritage. Among educated businesspeople, however, English remains essential for banking, global commerce, and tourism. Tour operators know, from observing Costa Rica, that proficiency in English is vital to attracting international visitors.

In Panama City, Boquete, Gamboa, and Bocas del Toro, you may go for days speaking only English. Outside those areas, however, some knowledge of Spanish or a good phrase book comes in handy.

Safety: Panama is considered a safe destination, though the normal commonsense precautions are in order. (See Chapter 17, Safety and Security.) Notwithstanding the gleaming high-rises in Panama City, many Panamanians barely have enough food to eat. Some of them want visitors to share. Leave the Rolex at home.

The Darién Gap is a haven for drug smugglers, so hire a reputable outfitter and guide if you want to explore that area. The guides know which patches to avoid.

Health care: Panama has one of the best health-care systems in Latin America. In fact, it's a "medical tourism" hot spot where people come for competent medical procedures done on the cheap. Many Panamanian doctors are U.S.-trained, and the standards at the top hospitals are high. Should you need medical attention while in a rural area, get to a city. Panama has tropical-disease risks, so know what shots and medicines are needed before departing. (See Chapter 12, Keeping Healthy.)

Things to buy: Even though fine "Panama" hats were never made here, you can buy them in Panama anyway. Locally made hats tend to be coarse or middle-grade; the top-end ones are from Ecuador. Masks and ceramics from the Azuero Peninsula are popular, as are straw baskets and leather goods. Colorful embroidery from the Kuna people of the San Blas Islands is an extension of their traditional clothing. The country's most highly regarded handicrafts are the intricate baskets woven by the Wounaan and Embera indigenous women of the Darién Rain Forest. They also create ceremonial masks made the same way. The men there stick to wood carvings, which are also works of art.

Surprisingly, some of the best buys are electronics, perfume, watches, and clothing in the duty-free zone around Colón (a city best avoided if you're not going there to shop).

Resources

Guidebooks for Panama are available from Frommer's, Lonely Planet, Ulysses, Bradt, Moon Handbooks, and *National Geographic Traveler*. The Moon Handbook has a good reputation, but buy the 2008 edition or later. Panama is included in guidebooks covering all of Central America, such as those by Rough Guides and Footprint. *Pocket Adventures Panama* covers a variety of excursions. Also consider *A Guide to the Birds of Panama*.

Narrative travel books focused on Panama include *99 Days to Panama: An Exploration of Central America by Motorhome*, by Dr. John and Harriet Halkyard; *Is There a Hole in the Boat?: Tales of Travel in Panama without a Car*, by Darrin DuFord; and *Don't Kill the Cow Too Quick: An Englishman's Adventures Homesteading in Panama*, by Malcolm Henderson. There are two books simply titled *Panama*: the historical novel set in the 1800s, by Eric Zencey, and the nonfiction book about the Noriega period, by Kevin Buckley. You may remember the John le Carré novel *The Tailor of Panama*, which was made into a movie starring Pierce Brosnan and Geoffrey Rush.

Several books cover living or retiring in the country, including *Living and Investing in Panama, Living in Panama,* and *Choose Panama . . . the Perfect*

Retirement Haven. International Living magazine and EscapeArtist.com (**www .escapeartist.com**) both advertise e-books written by knowledgeable expats. To navigate the local culture, pick up *Panama: Culture Smart! A Quick Guide to Customs and Etiquette.*

Also, try these Web sites:

- Official Panama tourism site (**www.visitpanama.com**)
- PanamaRide (**www.panamaride.com**)
- Panamainfo (**www.panamainfo.com**)
- Panama Tours (**www.panamatours.com**)
- Explore Panama (**www.explorepanama.com**)
- The Panama News has current reports in English: **www.thepanamanews.com.**
- The Panama Report (**www.thepanamareport.com**) covers real estate, culture, and travel.
- Isla Taboga (**taboga.panamanow.com**) is the best resource for that island.
- See the Boquete Times site (**www.theboquetetimes.com**) for info on the highlands.
- Ads make up most of **www.bocas.com,** but it does have some useful facts and links about the Bocas del Toro Archipelago.

Retirement Opportunities

International Living magazine named Panama the world's top retirement haven for six years running. This doesn't mean the country is perfect for retirees—no place is, of course—but Panama does offer an impressive number of incentives. No matter your age, if you can document a mere $500 a month (plus $100 per dependent) of pension or investment income, here are a few of the perks that you will enjoy:

- Exemption from import duty on household goods, plus the ability to import a new car every two years
- 50 percent off certain entertainment costs and weekday hotel stays, 30 percent off domestic transportation, 25 percent off domestic airfares, and 25 percent off restaurant bills
- 50 percent reduction in closing costs on home loans
- 25 percent discount on utility bills
- Sizable discounts on hospital bills, prescription medicines, doctor visits, dental exams, and eye exams

This is on top of prices that are almost always lower than those in the United States and Canada, especially for real estate and house rentals. In addition, charges for domestic help are so low that most retirees can afford to hire a regular gardener, maid, or cook.

It's obvious that Panamanians want you to spend your golden years with them. An estimated 50,000 Americans have already made their home in Panama for at least part of the year.

Visit for a while to check the place out before making a commitment. If you'd be there full time, experience the hottest and rainiest periods. For example, even the idyllic Chiriquí Highlands receive torrential downpours part of the year, and there's almost no nightlife for a diversion when outdoor activities aren't possible.

Why did Panama finally drop off the top spot at *International Living* in 2007, bumped down by Mexico and Malaysia? Rising prices in Panama City, for a start, but the country reduced the tourist visa period to one month—a major problem for those testing the waters before settling down. This seems to be a classic case of a government shooting itself in the foot, however, so the decision may be reversed. Check the resources listed in this section for the current status.

Helping Out

Hundreds of nongovernmental organizations and volunteer groups operate in Panama. Opportunities to help with your time or donations include schooling street children and indigenous communities, teaching English, aiding conservation programs, supporting historic preservation, and more. Many global aid or assistance organizations are active here, such as the Peace Corps (**www.peacecorpsonline.org**) and Habitat for Humanity (**www.habitat.org**). Many global volunteer-placement agencies, such as Volunteers for Peace (**www.vfp.org**), have multiple placements here throughout the year. For the most comprehensive list of options, search for "Panama" at **www.idealist.org** or **www.volunteerabroad.com.**

Rather than giving to a child who may be part of an organized begging ring (with the money going to the adult boss), give directly to a recognized local charity instead.

PART TWO: Planning Your Trip

CHAPTER 4

How to Plan Your Trip

All journeys have secret destinations
of which the traveler is unaware.
—Martin Buber

THE CHANGING WORLD

Sure, we have to consider practical issues such as where to go and how much to spend, and we'll do that, but first I want to make the case for going *now*.

Wildness is disappearing. Distinct cultures are blending together into a shapeless mass. Diversity is being sacrificed to relentless increases in population. Where millions of people plant crops and burn forests to survive, elephants, lemurs, and gorillas in the wild are condemned to extinction. Where multinational greed levels forests and spews toxic chemicals across the earth, how can any species survive in the long run?

It is far too late for us to share with intrepid explorers such as Stanley and Livingstone, or Burton and Speke, the experience of forging trails across massive lands never before traversed. In fact, it wouldn't surprise me today to find a new Pizza Hut at one of their old campsites. We can no longer cross Arabian deserts to encounter the nomadic cultures about which Wilfred Thesiger wrote with such respect and affection. Those same deserts are now crisscrossed by oily black ribbons of asphalt. Camels, the ships of the desert, have been replaced by tanker trucks.

The great coral reef off the coast of Belize, one of the longest in the world, is under threat. The manatees that used to thrive in Guatemala's Río Dulce are diminishing in number.

Only a few years ago, in Keoladeo National Park in India, I sat quietly in a small rowboat, my hands motionless on the oars. Majestic Siberian cranes swept into sight like a flight of snow-white arrows. Ending a 3,000-mile migration, they dropped gracefully from a great height to hover on seven-foot wings above the marsh, then settled as softly as giant snowflakes. That sight will always remain in my memory. Their ancestors had made the annual migration from Siberia to India for millennia.

Over recent years, though, affected by human encroachment and pollution, their number has steadily dwindled from thousands to a few hundred. Three

On the beach in Costa Rica

years ago, only five cranes arrived in Keoladeo. Next year, who knows? In Africa, some of the national game reserves are turning into little more than open-air zoos. Rangers who try to corral packs of Toyota tourist vans by day must try to intercept deadly poachers at night. Distant, exotic Kathmandu, once a magnet for mystics, trekkers and hard-core travelers, has become a routine stop promoted by hundreds of tour operators. All around the world, traditional dress is being discarded, along with cultural identity, giving way to T-shirts and blue jeans.

Paradoxically, wonderful television documentaries sometimes mask what is really happening to our planet. When they bring the Serengeti migration, mountain gorillas, and the Papua New Guinea "sing-sing" to us in our armchairs, they imply that cultures are stable, that nature is thriving. Behind the scenes, however, directors shield evidence of modernization from the camera lens. They're well intentioned in focusing on what remains, but doing so leads us to underestimate the ferocious rate at which the world is changing.

Nevertheless, many have sensed or observed the changes and tried to stem the tide. We'll probably manage to keep a few exotic specimens alive, but the leopard in a cage is not the leopard of the jungle—any more than a river "turned on" for a few hours by the keeper of the dam is a wild river. How great can our sense of accomplishment be when the price paid for seeing such specimens is no greater than crosstown taxi fare? The message is simple: dust off that passport, and hit the road sooner rather than later. Travel lightly so as not to add to the problem. Let your trips inspire you to become part of the solution.

It's worth noting, by the way, that Costa Rica has a very advanced ecotourism orientation and that countries in Central America, except for Honduras, have set aside between 20 percent and 47 percent of their land for preservation. In fact, one of the greatest attractions of the entire region is its unspoiled nature.

The world is waiting. See it for yourself.

CHOOSING THE DESTINATIONS RIGHT FOR YOU

Choosing the destinations right for you is essential to a fulfilling trip, so it's odd that so many people make those decisions so lightly. In choosing, look inside first. Answer two questions: what kinds of experiences do you want, and what do you want to gain from the trip?

What would you like to be doing? Would the days be peaceful, or would they be full of activities? Would you be alone or meeting lots of other people? Do you lust for fine food, sensuous beaches, unfamiliar wildlife, spectacular landscapes, and physical challenges—or do you seek insights and internal change, perhaps a new direction for your life? Choosing a purpose for your trip requires getting in touch with your feelings. Your answers enable you to think about where to go without being influenced by the popularity of a destination or a desire to impress people.

The moment you've chosen the right destination, the most important part of planning the trip is behind you.

Because this book focuses on Mexico and Central America, perhaps you're already drawn to that region. But let's take a broader look. Forget being practical. Start with a dream. Close your eyes, and conjure up the names of places that make your heart beat fast—or the activities that really get you excited. Brainstorm. Think of cultures that appeal to you, places that have beckoned you since childhood.

Study maps, photos, travel books to stimulate your imagination. Skim back copies of *National Geographic, Outside, International Travel News, Transitions Abroad,* and *Condé Nast Traveler.* Visit travel Web sites listed in this book and on the *Traveler's Tool Kit* Web site. Attend meetings of local travel groups. Watch the Travel Channel, the Discovery Channel, and the National Geographic Channel. Seek out travel tales from friends and experts in the region. Keep in mind that the countries spending the most on PR and marketing get the most coverage. Even when a magazine article touts country A as "the new hot place to go," country B may suit you better.

Use this book to zero in on the destinations that rise to the top of your list. Post this list on the refrigerator or anywhere that will keep it in your consciousness.

FACTORS TO CONSIDER

Now you're ready to be practical and think about affordability, health, sanitation, safety, weather, local

> I wanted to sail beyond the sunset. I wanted to follow Ulysses' example and fill life once more to overflowing.
> —Richard Halliburton, *The Glorious Adventure* (1927)

language, timing, and the rest. We'll discuss those and other practical considerations. The point is: listen to your heart, and don't settle for some destination just because it's practical.

One Country—or Many?

The differences between a survey trip through many countries and a trip that focuses on a single country or region are substantial. If you have just a week or two, a tightly focused trip dealing with only one language, one transportation system, and one culture may be ideal. In general, your daily costs of transportation, lodging, and food are lower when you spend more time in one place. On the other hand, a multicountry trip is like a buffet table loaded with rich and varied dishes, many of which will be new to your palate. It requires more effort and a faster pace to sample everything on the table.

Political Conditions

Research the political situation at destinations you're considering. It was risky to visit Nicaragua in the 1980s, but it's now an emerging—and safe—tourist destination. There were clashes in Guatemala in the past, mostly in the northwest, but not now. Chiapas in Mexico, once a no-go zone, is now considered safe. Political differences flared up for a while in Oaxaca, Mexico, and Mexico City, but now they're back to normal. Keep in mind that television and newspaper reports tend to sensationalize any friction in other countries, and that the U.S. State Department travel advisories are notoriously conservative. The most reliable solution? Read reports from recent travelers in travel magazines and on the Web. Read magazines that really cover international news well, such as The Economist and The Week, or the BBC Web site.

Mental and Physical Fitness

There are times on the road when you won't know exactly what's happening, or why, or what will happen next. Ask yourself how much input you can handle from cultures different from your own, and for how long. If your tolerance for ambiguity is low, you may prefer staying on the beaten track until you're a more seasoned traveler.

Physical fitness should also affect your decisions. For some, the rigors of daily treks through museums and local crafts markets can be substantial, let alone climbing a half dozen Maya pyramids or a couple of Nicaraguan volcanoes. Where heat or exertion will be factors, be honest with yourself about the physical condition required. Don't think in terms of how fit you were when you were 18 or how fit you could be if you worked out for six months. Think of how fit you actually will be when you board the plane.

> You wouldn't have time. You would always mean to go, but you never would go.
> —Henry James, *The American* (1877)

Hilltop view of Antigua, Guatemala

For some, making a strenuous effort is part of the reward. The achievement of a goal and the ensuing fitness are worth a little pain. Others prefer a more languorous trip. Early in your international travel life, err on the side of caution, and stay well within your capacity. After a trip or two, you'll know much more about what you can, and choose to, handle.

As departure date approaches, step up your physical conditioning a notch. Consider walking a brisk 3 miles three times a week for eight weeks before you go. If you have a gym membership, use it three or four days a week. Like preparing for the ski season, it's mostly a matter of building up your legs and stamina.

To the extent age is connected to fitness, it's a consideration but need not be a deterrent. Aboard a bus in steamy Tamil Nadu, India, I leaned across the aisle and struck up a conversation with a sturdy, white-haired Englishwoman who looked to be at least 65 years old. As we got off the bus, I swung my backpack down from the overhead rack and asked if I might get hers as well. She thanked me and suggested we have tea. I was amazed when she told me she'd just completed a solo bicycle ride the entire length of India and, several years earlier, had ridden more or less around the world. Hiking the Annapurna circuit in the mountains of Nepal, I walked for a while with a man celebrating his 74th birthday. Age need not be a disqualification when the flame is burning brightly. Ben Franklin said, "Travel is one way of lengthening life." Few activities keep a person feeling as young as does independent travel.

The more remote reaches of the world are not very accommodating to people with physical disabilities. Nevertheless, I've met people traveling successfully with what seemed to be fairly severe physical disabilities. It's more of a hassle, but it can be done.

Local Languages

Because we humans use more than 5,800 different languages and dialects, some prospective travelers may worry about their inability to communicate. They needn't. First, English is rapidly becoming a global language. Second, where English is not spoken, there's plenty of help available in the form of pocket-size dictionaries and phrase books with functional sections containing words for shopping, asking directions, ordering meals, and changing money. Third, language-training courses on cassettes or CDs and accelerated language classes in community colleges can bring you up to speed quickly. Fourth, even when people have absolutely no language in common, it's amazing how much can be communicated nonverbally. Lack of familiarity with a foreign language should not deter you from going somewhere you really want to go.

In Mexico and Central America, lack of knowledge of Spanish can make handling daily details a bit difficult, but a few phrases and a couple of dozen words will get you by.

> I cannot rest from travel; I will drink / Life to the lees; all times have I enjoyed / Greatly, have suffered greatly, both with those / That loved me, and alone . . . I am become a name; / For always roaming with a hungry heart / Much have I seen and known . . .
> —Alfred Tennyson, *Ulysses* (1842)

We'll talk about language at greater length in Chapter 19.

Timing

If you feel locked into taking a trip during a specified period—by an employer, kids, school, or whatever—the following factors may influence your choice of destinations. If you've already chosen a destination, they'll help you know what to expect. If you have flexibility about when you go, these factors should definitely affect your choice of destinations.

Weather: In a region where hot temperatures, heavy rainy seasons, and tropical storms are an issue, weather may influence your timing. If you can't go when the weather is ideal, at least avoid extremes in temperature and rainfall. Find out what weather to expect and be prepared.

Does continual rain get you down? A rousing thunderstorm may be exciting, but dark skies day after day dampen most spirits. In many countries, heavy rains close the roads and transform trails into slick, muddy chutes.

In Mexico and Central America, keep your eye on heat and hurricanes. Pay special attention to "when to go" because "when *not* to go" can be as long as

Hurricane Planning

The Caribbean coasts of Mexico and Central America are susceptible to hurricanes between late July and early November. Hurricane risk is lower on the Gulf Coast of Mexico because storms usually head north toward the United States instead. Hurricanes along the Pacific coast are generally smaller and less deadly. Given the narrowness of Central America in some spots, a hurricane developing in the Caribbean can occasionally rip across the whole width of a country.

seven months in some spots. Thirty days can be the difference between beautiful, sunny weather and torrential rain.

In the past it wasn't unusual for resorts to shut down during hurricane season. Today, travelers can book a stay for any time of year. However, that doesn't mean you should. Consider scheduling your visit, to anywhere in the region, outside the August to October period.

Otherwise, get trip-cancellation insurance for your flights or tours in case you have to cancel, or suffer other loss, because of a hurricane. Reckless travelers should note that if the storm heading for your destination is already "named" (e.g., "Tropical Storm Rosie") when you make your booking, most insurance companies won't cover you. Gee, wonder why?

The cautious option is to avoid the Caribbean coast during late summer and early autumn, heading to the interior or the Pacific coast instead. The weather will probably be better and you won't have to worry about hunkering down in a shelter with 100 newfound friends.

To track current storms developing in the region, go to the National Weather Service site (see below).

A traveler with a passion for a certain place will go when the opportunity arises, even if that may mean hell and high water. Sure, most people living there get through it, but why suffer if you have a choice?

Because the timing of wet and dry seasons, as well as the temperature, differs area by area, you need specific information. The following are useful resources:

- See **www.weather.com**, **www.wunderground.com**, and **www.weatherpost.com.** For hurricane Information, see the National Weather Service (National Hurricane Center) site at **nhc.noaa.gov.**
- The U.S. Department of Commerce provides two useful sites, **www.ncdc .noaa.gov** (National Climate Data Center) and **www.noaa.gov** (National Oceanic and Atmospheric Administration), which offer numerous publications on weather. Keep in mind that average-temperature reports are not as helpful as they appear. What you need are highs and lows.

- Most country-specific guidebooks contain good information on weather, including the best and worst times to visit.
- Good travel agents and tour operators are familiar with international weather, particularly if they specialize in a certain region.
- American Express members can call American Express Global Assist at (800) 554-2639 and receive worldwide weather reports and forecasts.
- National tourist offices can be good sources, but, because they promote tourism, it's wise to be a little skeptical of their reports. For example, the tourist offices in Panama and Costa Rica have been known to deny the existence of a rainy season. They admit only to a "green season." Similarly, you'll seldom see any reference to hurricane season in the Cancún or Riviera Maya literature, even though three separate hurricanes pummeled the area in 2004 and 2005.

Tourist seasons: Because crowds of tourists rank with monsoons as things to avoid, know when the tourist high season begins and ends at a potential destination. In general, it's June through September in the Northern Hemisphere, but there are exceptions. Please see Chapter 3, Destinations, which identifies high season in Mexico and each country in Central America. The tourist high season may not always coincide with the best weather. Instead, it may reflect the time of year when most people are free to travel. May and June are perfectly good times to visit the Riviera Maya of Mexico and the Caribbean beaches of Central America. Because U.S. spring break is over and Canada has thawed, fewer travelers visit these warmer destinations during that time.

> Seeing new places always brings up the possibility of other new places.
> —Frances Mayes,
> *Under the Tuscan Sun*
> (1997)

Crowds change every travel experience—always for the worse. Limited facilities become crowded in high season, and local people become noticeably less congenial. Prices go up, sometimes tripling. Avoiding tourist high season should be a major factor in planning.

If you can't avoid high season, keep your sanity by visiting popular tourist sights very early in the morning or as late as permitted in the evening. Take a leisurely stroll while other tourists are still wolfing down heavy breakfasts, then hole up in a museum during the heat of the day.

Shoulder seasons, a few weeks on either side of high and low, are often the best times to visit.

Local holidays, school recesses, and special events: Local holidays and school recesses create their own high seasons, with the majority of travelers being local people. The moment school is out, young people and families hit the road. Because local people know those dates, they book transportation and accommodations far in advance.

Watch for major events, such as festivals, so you can adjust your planning. If you choose to attend some major event, prepare well in advance. Find out about special events on the Web and through tour brochures, guidebooks, national tourism offices, and travel agents.

Chapter 3 lists holidays for each country it covers. As a rule, expect hotels and buses everywhere to be packed the week before Easter (Semana Santa).

DECIDING HOW MUCH TIME TO TAKE

The typical vacation is usually not long enough to fully disengage from work, friends, and habits and become immersed in where you are. A trip of short duration carries other limitations. The countdown to return begins almost as soon as you walk out the door. You may spend most of your time in big cities, seeing only the most well-known sites. You travel at a hectic pace, always on the move, struggling to absorb what's around you. When you're rushed, it's hard to be flexible, to change your route with your mood or fall in with other travelers for a side trip. The three- and four-night getaways advertised for Latin American destinations barely allow enough time to unpack and look around before heading home.

As you think about allotting time for your trip, don't accept the idea of a two-week vacation as natural or inevitable. Working people in most other developed countries routinely take more than two weeks away from their jobs. Austrians and Portuguese get seven weeks a year; Germans, French, Spaniards, Italians, Belgians, and Finns get six weeks. Even industrious Swedes may take five weeks a year. Other Europeans expect no less than five weeks. On average, a European takes three times as much time away from work as an American does. As Europeans put it: we work to live, while Americans live to work. European employers believe that time off improves efficiency, productivity, and morale. Several scientific studies confirm that overworked employees are inefficient, less engaged, and short on groundbreaking ideas.

Negotiate with your employer. Can you get more time off if part of it is unpaid? Can you trade some overtime work for time off? Or can you take an unpaid leave of absence? Life is too short to limit ourselves to two-week bursts of interaction with the rest of the world. Do everything you can, including loosening restrictions you place on yourself, to take long trips—the ultimate trip being open-ended.

Having said all that, if time or money or other constraints mean that you can absolutely get away for only 14 days, or 10, or 5—do it! Every bit of the world you see will motivate you to experience more next time. Draw as much juice from those days as you can. Just don't accept one or two weeks quietly if you can have more.

HOW MUCH DO YOU WANT TO SPEND?

Here are two ways to decide how much you want to spend:

1. Review how much money you have available and what else has claims on it—then choose an amount you're comfortable spending on a trip. In other

words, set a maximum, and then select destinations. When choosing the amount, consider all the money you won't be spending at home for food, entertainment, utilities, and so on. If this is your approach, and it's a rational one, I'll wager that you'll raise the figure as you come to recognize that travel is an investment that pays rich dividends.

Obviously, the amount you set influences your choice of destinations. If a destination is far away and the cost of living there is high, you won't be able to stay very long. Use the Checklist in Chapter 9, How to Prepare a Reliable Budget, to estimate local daily costs of traveling. If that allows too little time, you may have to go somewhere else.

2. Here's the other approach. Choose your favorite destination, and figure out how many days it will take to experience everything you want to. Next, use the Checklist in Chapter 9 to calculate how much that many days will cost. Now persuade yourself to spend that amount. If you absolutely can't make the case or the cupboard is too bare for the grandest scheme, cut back where you must, even the amount of time, until you have a match. Or decide which region(s) or attraction(s) would be best to cut. Keep in mind that moving every day or two quickly increases expenses. The main point is this: persuade yourself that you can afford to do what you really want to do. *Traveler's Tool Kit* will help empower you to go wherever you want.

Your choice of destinations will greatly affects the cost of your trip. A week touring Japan or Norway can easily cost more than a month or two traveling in Guatemala. Fortunately, much of Latin America is a relative bargain compared to the United States, but there are still major variations between, for example, Mexican beach resort areas and a small town in Nicaragua or mainland Honduras.

Traveling in Mexico and Central America can be moderately expensive if you stay in international chain hotels, eat at tourist restaurants, and routinely hire private transportation. But for thoughtful travelers, these countries can be very inexpensive. By the way, if someone says that a certain place is inexpensive, be sure you and that person agree on what "inexpensive" means—and that the information is current. When I say "inexpensive," I'm thinking of a private room for two, and usually a private bath, for less than $25 a night.

The cost of travel in a given country also depends in part on the strength of your currency in relation to that country's. In the 1960s, when the U.S. dollar was strong and European currencies were weak, students carried Arthur Frommer's book *Europe on $5 a Day* and it was possible to travel for that. Today, a Coca-Cola could cost $4 in Germany. Because a martini can cost $25 in some European capitals, imagine what you'd spend for a serious night on the town. A haircut that costs $4 in Panama City costs $50 in Tokyo. A rum and Coke that's $1.50 in Nicaragua could cost $15 in Oslo.

While the U.S. dollar is still holding its own against the Mexican peso and the currencies of other Latin American countries, now is a good time to travel to this region.

DRAFTING AN ITINERARY

An itinerary is the foundation for your trip, and you can't draft a good one without doing your homework. When you know where you want to go, what you want to experience, how much time you have, and how much money you're willing to spend, link it all together to create an itinerary.

We've provided sample itineraries in chapters on individual countries, but think of them only as starting points. Make each trip your own.

At first, the idea of a detailed itinerary may seem restrictive. Believe me, it's not. Once you're out the door with a thoughtful itinerary in hand, you're free to indulge whatever spontaneous urges arise. Having done the research, you understand the costs and benefits of each change you consider making on the road. If you were winging it, you could easily underestimate the chaos a spontaneous side trip might cause later on in your journey. Drafting an itinerary also uncovers opportunities to explore along the way. People who pride themselves on winging it, which sounds appealing, miss a lot.

Here are five principles that apply to drafting an itinerary:

1. If you have a choice, schedule destinations most like your own country early in your trip so culture shock will be minimal. Having grown "salty" by the time you reach more exotic destinations, you'll cope with them easily.

2. Schedule countries with higher health risks toward the end of your trip. The odds are greatly against your getting sick, but, if it happens, it's convenient for home to be on the horizon.

3. If you can handle the crowds, include music, art, and religious festivals in your plan. The best resources I've seen are Rough Guides' *World Party* book and the Web site **www.whatsonwhen.com**. And, of course, we list festivals in Mexico and Central America in Chapter 3.

4. Expect delays. Obstacles come in unlimited variety. Some are serendipitous: scuba diving so great you can't tear yourself away or the friend's friend who insists on taking you to visit the family cabin on a lake in the mountains. Others are unwelcome surprises, such as picking up a stomach bug and needing a couple of days out of action. After calculating the time your trip should take, add 10 to 20 percent, depending on your destination, as a fudge factor to cover unexpected events, good and bad.

5. When scheduling connecting flights, leave enough time between them to keep a minor delay along the way from toppling your entire flight plan. Anytime you have a choice, avoid changing planes and airports notorious for foul-weather shutdowns (for example, Chicago and Boston).

When you've come up with an itinerary that works, calculate how many days it will take, including obstacles and rest days, and compare that with the time you have.

SAVE Money Learning to create an itinerary will also help you save money because many travel agents now charge a fee to draft a detailed itinerary for a client. And you wind up with their ideas, not yours. Do it yourself, and spend that money on some faraway adventure.

An easy way to do it:

1. On a good map, circle your intended stops, and choose the cities abroad where your travels will start and end. Make the most commonsense connections among your circled destinations, avoiding doubling back when possible.

2. Once you've selected a preliminary route, adjust it to take into account factors such as available transport, tourist seasons, temperatures, rain, festivals, national holidays, costs, and your objectives. Now you have your basic itinerary.

3. Decide how you'll get from place to place, and determine approximately how long each trip will take. A good guidebook makes this easy. If you must estimate time and you know the distance involved but have no further guidance, err on the generous side.

4. List things you want to do or see along the way, and attach time values to each. This brings your trip to life. Be realistic. Rushing every day just to squeeze in an extra country, or even one more city, is seldom worth it.

Build in time for rest, a missed connection, or a little longer stay in some wonderful place. And always remind yourself of your reasons for traveling.

When the days add up to more than your budgeted time, think first about granting yourself more time. When you've stretched that as far as you can, make your route more efficient, and cut some destinations. But leave time to enjoy each place rather than rush, rush, rush. You have a lifetime for travel.

Drafting an itinerary motivates you to assemble information you ought to have anyway. It's a servant, not a master.

If you are thinking of traveling on an organized tour, drafting a dream itinerary can still be a worthwhile exercise. After all, why go on a tour that skips places you really want to visit? Or one that spends one night in a place where you want to spend three? Or one that is in such a hurry to check sites off some invisible checklist that you never have time to wander around on your own?

HOW TO CHOOSE AND WORK WITH A TRAVEL AGENT

For decades, travel agents provided their services without direct charge to the consumer. Instead, they received commissions from those whose services they sold (including airlines, tour operators, car-rental agencies, and hotels). Thus, using a travel agent cost you nothing unless the agent was not competent or not objective in choosing among providers. In fact, a good travel agent could save you money and time and provide valuable advice.

However, in 1995 a volcano erupted in the world of travel agencies when airlines set a maximum dollar amount they would pay in commissions no matter how high the price of the ticket. Then the Internet expanded and made it easier to buy tickets directly. Many travel agencies soon closed or merged. In general, the agents who survived the shakeout were the most professional and most passionate. Also, more travel agencies now specialize in specific types of travel.

On the other hand, consumers now feel the pinch in the form of service fees when using an agent. Though many consumers avoid those fees by dealing directly with the airlines, that can be problematic for complicated or multi-airline itineraries. Plus, you may wind up navigating a call-center phone tree from abroad if there's a problem. Just when you need an advocate, you may have an adversary.

It's now common for agencies to charge for preparing a complex, customized itinerary, for reissuing a ticket, for making a refund, and for retrieving travel records. In practice, the situation is flexible, with established customers receiving the best treatment.

Keep in mind that information from a travel agent will affect your biggest travel expenditures (airfare, tour-operator fees, lodging, and so on). A good travel agent can find the best (cheapest, if that's what you ask for) airline tickets, negotiate upgrades, get a ticket on a supposedly sold-out flight, locate discounts, and provide reliable advice.

With big commissions gone, you can expect an agent to charge for spending time finding domestic and many international airline tickets. For international tickets, a good agent may search out the best deal, buy the ticket wholesale, mark the price up, and resell it to you. If the markup is minimal, you'll get a good deal. To know whether it's fair, you have to do some homework and learn what the ticket ought to cost. Because Internet resources are plentiful and competitive, that's not a big problem.

A good specialist agent also knows reputable in-country providers of services, such as tour operators. Dealing with such providers directly rather than through some big-name, big-advertising U.S. middlemen can save you big bucks, often 50 percent or more.

No matter how complex the trip, you can plan your own itinerary. However, when it's really complex or you're traveling with children or a group of friends, you may prefer to put the variables and choices in the hands of a qualified agent. If in doubt, ask yourself how much your own time is worth. Agents who specialize in a specific region can save you hours or days of searching for ideal hotels, especially if they have access to lodging information not available on the Internet.

If you decide to travel on a tour, *Traveler's Tool Kit* shows you how to evaluate tour operators (see Chapter 6, The Organized Tour), and the individual country sections in Chapter 3 provide names and other resources. Still, knowing the best tour operators is another strength of a good agent. Simply pulling names of operators off the Internet is risky because there's a lot of, shall we say, exaggeration.

To find the best agent to suit your needs, start by seeking recommendations from friends and from magazine or newspaper articles. Look in online directories, newspapers, and magazines for advertisements from agents that suggest a good fit with your travel plans—though an ad is not a substitute for a recommendation or evaluation. Unless you live in a major city, agents are probably dedicated to corporate business, package trips, and cruises. They may not be much help regarding your own destination. When you have a few names, ask questions. This seems obvious, but most prospective travelers don't make the effort. Those are the ones who also enjoy Russian roulette. It may make sense to use the same agent for multiple trips if he or she is good, but most of the best travel agents are specialists who add value by knowing a territory or specific kind of journey inside out.

Evaluating Travel Agencies

Ask a lot of questions, such as:

- Do the agency's personnel know about the kind of travel that interests you? This is especially important if you're considering adventure travel.
- What fees does the agency charge?
- Can the agency do better on airfares than you could on your own?
- Be cautious about paying an agency to prepay hotels, car-rental companies, and so on. If an agency asks you to pay it directly, ensure that the money will be held in an escrow account (and know where). If you pay a deposit, get a receipt. Protect yourself by paying with a credit card. Also ask whether the agency has IATA (International Air Transport Association) approval. To get it, the agency must be bonded. If it is, your funds are protected.
- Does the agency have a staff person who understands complicated international fares? If not, it may have to depend on the fares that airlines post on the Internet, reflecting the airlines' interests more than yours.
- If you need help while abroad, can you reach the agency by fax and e-mail?
- Can the agency direct you to resources (for example, useful Internet sites) for information such as lists of things to do, important holidays, etc.?
- Will it maintain a file on you so you won't have to repeat your seating and other preferences every time you book a trip? Will someone remember your interests and let you know when good deals come up?

Evaluating Travel Agents

Finding a reliable travel agency is only the first step. Next, you must choose the most appropriate agent in that company. Again, ask questions:

- Is the agent a traveler? If this sounds like a silly question, remember that there are deskbound members of every organization. You want someone who thinks like a traveler.

> The traveler sees what he sees; the tripper sees what he has come to see.
> —G. K. Chesterton

- How much traveling has the agent done to the areas in which you're interested?
- Does he or she seem bright and well organized? Seek someone who listens and pays attention to details, gets excited by travel, and makes an extra effort on your behalf.
- Does the agent try to learn what you like and don't like?
- Do your personalities seem compatible?
- How much experience does the agent have? Is he or she a Certified Travel Counselor (meaning someone with at least five years' experience who regularly participates in professional training)?
- Can the agent give you relevant information about the recent experiences of other clients?
- Is the agent knowledgeable about exchanging money, purchasing travel insurance, and ordering visas?
- Is the agent paid a salary or paid by commission?
- In seeking the best fares and connections, it's reasonable to expect an agent to look on his or her in-house computer reservations system, check airlines' Web sites, check fare-comparison sites such as Kayak and SideStep, and check with a wholesaler. Does this agent take all those steps? You want an agent willing to dig relentlessly for the best deal.
- Does the agent work with "preferred" suppliers? If so, he or she may receive additional compensation for steering business to those airlines, tour operators, hotels, etc. That may be okay if it's the most desirable product and the supplier is reliable. If not, you may wind up with inferior or more-expensive arrangements.
- Will the agent give you the names of clients as references?

What Else Can You Expect from a Travel Agent?

An agent should:

- reserve the seat you want (if the airline will cooperate).
- tell you about penalties associated with your tickets.
- ask the airline to accommodate your dietary preferences.
- advise you of current baggage weight, size, and content limits.
- find affordable lodging for stop-over passengers (something especially useful when you're stuck with an overnight layover in high-priced places). If rooms are available by the hour in or near the airport, the agent should know and tell you about it.

- tell you about weather at your destinations.
- tell you about frequent-flier procedures before you fly.

When you've given instructions to your agent, you need to follow through to make sure everything is done to get your trip under way smoothly. Remember the lesson of the squeaky wheel.

> Most travelers content themselves with what they may chance to see from car-windows, hotel verandahs, or the deck of a steamer . . . clinging to the battered highways like drowning sailors to a life raft.
> —John Muir, American naturalist

It's not realistic to expect a travel agent to plan your trip for the fun of it. He or she expects compensation from you and perhaps from suppliers of products sold to you. Therefore, the amount you ask an agent to do should be proportional to what you're buying. If you're not going to purchase commissionable items (such as hotel or rental-car reservations, a cruise, guided tours, an expensive safari, etc.), there's a limit on how much time he or she can devote to you. Some specialist agents deal with this by charging you a percentage of the dollar amount you spend, then making a bit more from the commissionable items such as hotel stays (which may not cost you any more than if you had booked them yourself). If you want someone with experience to take care of all the details for you, this is money well spent.

Explore the Options

What you want from your agent is the full range of options so you can choose the ones you prefer. Don't passively accept the first suggestion. If you're willing to endure some inconvenience in return for lower fares, say so. Ask whether the fare would be lower if you flew on a different day of the week. Or at a different time of day. Or if you moved the departure date a few days one way or the other (which might move you into a less expensive "season"). Ask whether any special promotional deals are available (or coming up). Be clear about what is important to you and when you're willing to spend a little more to upgrade to a better hotel room, for instance. The agent may not mention such opportunities if you've specified that everything has to be as cheap as possible. It's probably worth it to pay more for a direct flight that shaves six hours off travel time, or for a flight that arrives in the afternoon instead of the middle of the night.

HOW TO CHOOSE A GUIDEBOOK

Traveler's Tool Kit will empower you in most aspects of travel, but it should be supplemented by a guidebook for each trip. A good guidebook can become a trusted friend that saves time and money and avoids frustration, building your confidence by arming you with information. It can also become a silken cord that binds without being noticed, inhibiting you from experimenting. The trick is to benefit from a guidebook without being constrained by it. It is a guide, not a bible. Ensure that your feet find their own path, or you'll find yourself too often in the midst of familiar faces.

Evaluating Guidebooks

A traveler needs facts, not fluff—solid information on how a country works. By "works," I mean recommendations concerning transportation, lodging, and restaurants (and prices for all). I also mean opinions. For example, is local public transportation reliable? Are local bureaucrats a problem? What current scams are being pulled on careless travelers? What behaviors would offend local customs?

Here's what to look for in a guidebook:

- By far the most important characteristic is whether the guidebook was written with travelers like you in mind. That is, does it address your budget and your degree of traveling experience? You can't safely assume it does even if you've used another guide from the same publisher in the past.
- Is the edition current enough that prices, schedules, and so on are still accurate (meaning not more than a year old)? If not, you'll be repeatedly frustrated.
- If you're going to rely on it for lodging and restaurants, see how many recommendations it offers. If there are only a few, put it back. Do the same if they are not in your budget range.
- Does it provide information on the nuts and bolts of daily life, such as transportation, entertainment, and sightseeing? Unless you intend to stay on the beaten track, does it recommend various adventures? If you like cultural and historical information, is it there? Guidebooks differ widely on this last one.
- Consider style and tone. Does the author's voice please your ear? If the author is a spectator, rushing from sight to sight (rather than offering insights), return the book to the shelf. There's a Swahili saying: "Mwenye pupa hadriki kula tamu," or, "A hasty person misses the sweet things."
- Are there plenty of maps, and are they readable? Are there enough photos to give you an idea of what to expect?
- Is it well organized and easy to use, with a sizable index?

While there's no guarantee that the most expensive book is best for you, choosing a book because it costs the least could be very expensive.

The best guidebooks are not always the lightest or smallest. If you are concerned about weight, cut out any sections of a guidebook that cover areas where you won't be traveling. Leave them at home for another trip.

If you lose a guidebook or become unhappy with the one you have, it's fairly easy to find another as long as you're on the "tourist trail." Otherwise, they're hard to find, expensive, or both—so try to get one from a departing traveler.

The Guidebooks

Years ago, many travelers automatically picked up a copy of the Lonely Planet guidebook relevant to their itinerary. Others, perhaps more affluent at the time, might have chosen Fodor's or a Michelin Guide. In those days, each guidebook had a distinctive personality—and often an attitude. Each was created for a niche market that usually coincided with the founder's travel preferences. Each was written with great enthusiasm by people who loved the country about which they wrote and who knew it well. Now, many guidebooks have become part of very big businesses and are aimed at the great middle market. Some writers are far less experienced, having become revisers and updaters.

Quite a few guidebook series offer information about Mexico and Central America. These include Berlitz, Bradt, DK Eyewitness, Fodor's, Footprint, Frommer's, Hidden Guides, Hunter, Let's Go, Lonely Planet, Moon Handbooks, National Geographic Traveler, Open Road, Rough Guides, Unofficial Guides, and *The People's Guide to Mexico,* among others.

Now a few words about specific guidebooks, but keep in mind that the prime directive is to choose one written to serve your particular needs and preferences.

Fodor's Travel Guides have undergone a major revamp in recent years, shedding the stodgy bent that endeared them mainly to wealthy retirees. For travelers well above the shoestring level, the Fodor's guides often do the best at covering restaurants and hotels. They have added more practical information and nightlife info, making them more appealing to a wider audience. The books are updated every year without fail, so they are seldom far out of date.

The Frommer's series now numbers more than 100 volumes counting the basic guides (to a specific country), $ A Day, Memorable Walks, city guides, phrase books, and its "For Dummies" guides. Frommer's is now an imprint of the huge Wiley publishing conglomerate. Its sometimes-inexperienced writers can be fun and refreshingly opinionated, but the quality of the information can be hit-and-miss. The company has ten titles for Mexico and also covers Belize, Costa Rica, Guatemala, and Panama. The regular Frommer's books are at their best when describing restaurants, hotels, and nightlife.

Several series of books were traditionally designed for travelers with low to moderate budgets. All of them are now trying to appeal to a wider readership except for Let's Go, which faithfully goes after the party-hearty college-age crowd.

The Lonely Planet series, colloquially referred to as the LP, has earned a fine reputation in the realm of worldwide budget and independent travel. Born in Australia and now the world's biggest independently owned guidebook publisher, the company covers every corner of the globe. It offers several series, including Shoestring Guides (anything from a region to a continent for low-budget travelers), City Guides, Walking Guides (about hiking and trekking in various global locales), and Phrasebooks (for about 50 languages). LP guides are generally dependable for a range of budgets outside the highest end, though as the company has grown and has begun using less experienced writers, some of its books have become the second- or third-best guide in some countries rather than the automatic best choice. The guides are always solid on practicalities, however, and the city maps are generally the best of all the guidebooks. In countries that are not well traveled, the LP guide can be the only choice. For El Salvador, for instance, there is currently no other option.

LP books are written in a personal, opinionated tone. In fact, authors of some editions have opined on local politics with sufficient candor that the book has been temporarily banned in the country covered. One caution: LP updates individual books only every few years, so check the publication date.

The Handbook series published by Moon Travel Guides is comprehensive and accurate. Its tone is fairly dry and reportorial, but the books often carry the most authority because they are written by long-term experts in the region. The titles for Belize and Nicaragua, for instance, are the clear standouts for those countries. The books themselves are durable and compact, though travelers who feel lost without a good map will find these frustrating. Moon also publishes a Living Abroad series that currently covers Belize, Nicaragua, Mexico, and Costa Rica.

The Rough Guides series, published in the United Kingdom, was for many years an also-ran for budget travelers alongside Lonely Planet. The series has matured and branched off, however, deciding to compete on better background information rather than being the best at practicalities. A Rough Guide will usually be the longest guide available for that country because of extensive cultural information, including information on music, art, literature, and film related to that country or region. While budget travelers chafe at the almost useless price information provided for hotels and restaurants, the information on entertainment and transportation is more reliable. Rough Guides are available for Mexico, Belize, Guatemala, and Costa Rica and Panama. The company also publishes a general Central America guide.

The Footprint Guides are popular for some countries in Latin America. One general guide covers Mexico and Central America, and another deals with Belize, Guatemala, and southern Mexico. Specific guides spotlight Mexico, Costa Rica, and Nicaragua. They are comprehensive and well written, though there are long stretches between updates, and much of the information on the Web site hasn't been updated in years. Make sure the publication date is very recent. Also, study it to see if it fits your style. As with the Rough Guides, you have to refer to a key to figure out prices for meals and hotels, the organization is baffling, and the practical information is sometimes not as thorough as it should be.

Insight Guides generally contain the greatest number of photos, so they may be the best choice for those who love to make plans by looking at beautiful images. On the road, however, they are far less useful. A single guide covers Guatemala, Belize, and the Yucatán, and individual guides deal with Belize, Costa Rica, and Mexico.

Other Guidebooks

The following cover only specific spots in Mexico and Central America:

- *The Unofficial Guide to Mexico's Best Beach Resorts* is very good.
- The Hidden Guides, published by Ulysses, cover Belize and two regions of Mexico. Ulysses also publishes the excellent eco-oriented guide *The New Key to Costa Rica.*
- *National Geographic Traveler* publishes a series of guidebooks accompanied by stunning photography, including guides for Mexico and Costa Rica.
- The DK Eyewitness Guides, which many travelers love for their great illustrated maps and cutaway architectural renderings, are available for Costa Rica and Mexico.
- Bradt publishes guides to Costa Rica and Panama, with a goal of getting people beyond the main tourist sites and off the beaten path.
- Open Road's guides to Costa Rica and Honduras recommend specific itineraries for varying budgets and lengths of trip.
- Hunter Travel Guides publishes five regional guides for Mexico as well as regular or "pocket adventure" guides to Costa Rica, Guatemala, Honduras, and Belize.
- Try **www.americanexpress.com** and click on "Travel," then on "Local Color." The reward is destination information from Lonely Planet, *Travel + Leisure,* and IgoUgo.

It's worth repeating that there's a downside to guidebooks. After you've been on the road awhile, you realize that many people are carrying the same guidebook you are and, therefore, going to the same places. Because some of your most powerful memories are likely to come from your time away from the tourist trail, don't let a guidebook become a tether. Get off the bus or train on impulse at a village that has no cathedral that rates a mention in anyone's guidebook. Take local transport, rent a bike, or walk. Get into the interior of the country, into the small places where village life is still unaffected by clicking cameras or streams of gringos. Use the guidebook as a guide—not as a crutch.

PLANNING ADVENTURES

SAVE Money Part of the exhilaration of travel is doing new things, unusual things, challenging things. In other words, having adventures. I'm thinking of rafting, diving, snorkeling, renting a bike, drifting in a hot-air balloon, taking a short safari, renting a boat or helicopter, and so on. Assuming that cost is a consideration, let's discuss how to save money on adventures.

SAVE Money The guiding principal is that paying someone at home to make arrangements in some faraway place is more expensive than doing it yourself. The service for which you pay $200 in Costa Rica may cost $400 in the United States, plus an agent's commission. The message: save money by doing it yourself.

Here's an example. By arranging my own trip to Rwanda, I paid less than $350 to visit the mountain gorillas. This included round-trip airfare from Kenya to Rwanda, the park permit, food, lodging, and local transportation. If a U.S. travel agent had arranged a similar trip, the price could have exceeded $2,000. From home, I called the Kinigi Park Administrative Office in Rwanda (the telephone number was in an Africa guidebook, but I could have gotten it from the embassy) and chose a date on which a permit was available to visit the gorillas. Next, I got a Rwandan visa, specifying the dates I wanted it to be effective. The Rwandan visa is unusual in that you must arrive in the country on the date your visa becomes effective. Because of the time constraints of the visa and the permit, I booked the Kenya-to-Rwanda flight while still in the United States to avoid delays in Kenya. I waited until I arrived in Rwanda to arrange for local lodging and transportation. *Hakuna matata*—"no problem."

Whether you're hiking the Inca trail, rafting a river in Costa Rica, or going on safari in Africa, consider booking directly from home with an on-site company. Better yet, book it on the spot. You'll get an even lower price and be better able to assess the quality of the local operation. It's worth a little shoe leather to visit several offices to compare services, prices, and personnel. To avoid this small effort, or for the comfort of certainty, many people book the trip through an agency at home and pay much more.

If you plan to organize your adventure when you arrive, gather information before you leave. Guidebooks identify potential adventures and list reputable operators. And there's always the Web.

TRAVEL RESOURCES ON THE INTERNET

The Internet has become a powerful information-gathering tool for travelers, a vital supplement to traditional sources of information. You can find out what temperatures to expect in the Nicaraguan highlands or look at a photo of a seaside lodge in the Honduras Bay Islands.

Log on to a travel forum or chat room with people who've just visited destinations you're dreaming about; get tips and answers to your questions. Ask for comments on your proposed itinerary, view videos and photographs, and even interview potential travel partners. Just keep in mind that there is no guarantee that Internet information is accurate.

Look to the Internet for electronic versions of travel magazines and guides, information about prospective destinations, and lists of restaurants and hotels. Make airline and car-rental reservations.

New sites appear on the Web like daisies in the spring—and many wither about as quickly. That's why some published lists of travel-related sites are, unless periodically updated, less useful than they appear. It's important to learn how to fish on the Internet for information that's relevant, accurate, current, and comprehensive.

If you're just starting your "surfing" career, you might check out a book or two, make frequent use of the "help" button, and get comfortable following your intuition. Or you can just ask any savvy teenager to show you how it's done.

At first, seeking information on the Internet can be like wandering in the desert; you don't know where you are, and you can't find your way back. As you develop skills, you cut down dramatically on frustration and wasted time.

Search Engines

Here's the really good news. Everyone who's established a resource on the Internet wants you to find it. To help you, each scatters its site's address (called a Uniform Resource Locator, or URL) like bread crumbs around the Internet. All you have to do is recognize and follow the trail. You do that with the help of certain essential tools. One of them is called a search engine. Here's the Webopedia (**webopedia.internet.com**) definition:

"A program that searches documents for specified keywords and returns a list of the documents where the keywords were found. Although 'search engine' is really a general class of programs, the term is often used specifically to describe systems like AltaVista and Excite that enable users to search for documents on the World Wide Web and USENET newsgroups."

Google (**www.google.com**), Yahoo (**www.yahoo.com**), and MSN (**www.msn.com**) are generally acknowledged as the best and most popular search engines, but if you don't find what you need, check others such as Ask (**www.ask.com**).

Adventure Travel E-zines and Sites

- Travelroads—information about adventure-travel tour companies, destinations, and gear: **www.travelroads.com**
- *Backpacker* magazine online—forums, news, and advice: **www.bpbasecamp.com**
- *Condé Nast Traveler*: **www.concierge.com**
- GoNomad—alternative travel stories from around the world: **www.gonomad.com**
- *High On Adventure*—adventurous travel; articles on city and country destinations: **www.highonadventure.com**

- Lonely Planet—fact sheets, newsletter, and travel tips: **www.lonelyplanet.com**
- *National Geographic Traveler* and *National Geographic Adventure:* **www.nationalgeographic.com**
- *OneWorld*—environmental, cultural, and exploration issues; features stories, travelogues, and photo essays: **www.oneworldmagazine.org**
- *Outside* Online and GORP—resources and feature stories regarding worldwide adventure travel: **www.away.com**
- *Perceptive Travel*—award-winning online magazine with travel stories by book authors: **www.perceptivetravel.com**
- Specialty Travel Index—lists more than 600 special-interest tour operators by destination and activity: **www.spectrav.com**
- World Hum—well-regarded literary travel site that is a partner of The Travel Channel: **www.worldhum.com**
- 21st Century Adventures—adventure stories, travel articles, discussions, photos: **www.21stcenturyadventures.com**

Want to Chat?
- BootsnAll Travel: **www.bootsnall.com**
- Chowhound—where foodies unite: **www.chowhound.com**
- Family Travel Forum—travel with children: **www.familytravelforum.com**
- Fodor's: **www.fodors.com**
- GORP—huge site designed to benefit outdoors-oriented men and women; expert advice on travel, gear, hiking, climbing, biking, and much more: **www.gorp.com**
- IgoUgo—reviews, destination reports, and message boards: **www.igougo.com**
- Lonely Planet: **www.lonelyplanet.com**

Airlines
Please see Chapter 20, Transportation.

Books, Guides, and Literature
- Alibris—offers out-of-print travel books: **www.alibris.com**
- BootsnAll Travel—jam-packed with stories, blogs, and an active message board: **www.bootsnall.com**
- Contrarian Traveler—links on traveling better for less: **www.contrariantraveler.com**
- Fodor's—active message board for travelers: **www.fodors.com**
- Globe Corner Bookstores and Powell's Bookstore—high-quality bookstores with large travel selections: **www.globecorner.com** and **www.powells.com**

- Johnny Jet—one of the most comprehensive sets of travel-resource links on the Web: **www.johnnyjet.com**
- Planeta—the best resource for responsible tourism and ecotourism: **www.planeta.com**
- *The World's Cheapest Destinations*—travel articles and pages of resource links on bargain destinations: **www.worldscheapestdestinations.com**
- *Transitions Abroad*—extremely useful, especially for travelers seeking an extended intercultural experience: **www.transitionsabroad.com**
- TravelPage directory: **www.travelpage.com**
- *International Travel News*—one of the most current and useful nuts-and-bolts sources of travel info: **www.intltravelnews.com**

> He did not think of himself as a tourist; he was a traveler. The difference is partly one of time, he would explain. Whereas the tourist generally hurries back home at the end of a few weeks or months, the traveler, belonging no more to one place than to the next, moves slowly over periods of years, from one part of the earth to another.
> —Paul Bowles,
> *The Sheltering Sky*
> (1949)

Clothing and Luggage

Please see Chapter 11, Travel Gear.

Educational Travel

- Elderhostel—educational adventures for older adults: **www.elderhostel.org**
- International Student Travel Confederation: **www.istc.org**
- Servas International: **www.servas.org**
- STA Travel—specializing in student travel: **www.sta-travel.com**
- *Transitions Abroad*—Web site has extensive resources on studying abroad and language learning: **www.transitionsabroad.com**

Hotels, Hostels, and Inns

Please see Chapter 15, Lodging.

Rail

Please see Chapter 20, Transportation.

Weather

- AccuWeather: **www.accuweather.com**
- Intellicast—Weather reports, forecasts, links: **www.intellicast.com**
- National Oceanic and Atmospheric Administration—United States only, but useful for tracking hurricanes affecting Mexico and Central America: **www.noaa.org**
- The Weather Channel—detailed local and international forecasts: **www.weather.com**
- *USA Today* worldwide weather: **www.usatoday.com/weather**

General

- GreenNet—contributions from environmental, peace, and human-rights groups: **www.gn.apc.org**
- Infobel World—telephone directories for Central America: **www.infobel.com/en/world/index.aspx**
- InfoHub—very good specialty-travel guide: **www.infohub.com**
- InfoSpace—world directories, including Mexico: **www.infospace.com**
- LatinWorld—good search engine for Latin America: **www.latinworld.com**
- SmarterTravel—excellent e-mail reports on discounts and deals: **www.smartertravel.com**
- The Travel Channel—Rewarding site for places, events, and cuisine: **travel.discovery.com**
- *The Travel Web* by Randolph Hoch (**www.extremesearcher.com**) provides comprehensive lists of sites pertaining to lodging; dining; adventure and educational travel; travel by seniors, families, gays, lesbians, and handicapped/disabled persons; and museums, festivals, translation tools, country guides, and maps.

> They shall beat their swords into plowshares, and their spears into pruning hooks; nation shall not lift up sword against nation, neither shall they learn war any more.
> —Isaiah 2:4

- Many online travel-resource guides provide multiple links to other sites. These include *Forbes*'s list of what it considers the best travel sites on the Web (**www.forbes.com/bow/b2c/section.jhtml?id=3**); the self-explanatory 100 Top Travel Sites (**www.100toptravelsites.com**); the Yahoo directory to travel sites (**dir.yahoo.com/Recreation/Travel**); the PlanetRider Travel Directory, including sites about Costa Rica and Yucatan (**www.planetrider.com**); and the Librarian's Internet Index (**www.lii.org;** enter "Travel").
- *Travel Weekly*—the national newspaper for the travel industry: **www.twcrossroads.com**
- World Fact Book—information about destinations, courtesy of the CIA: **www.odci.gov/cia/publications/factbook**
- World Travel Guide—vast amounts of geographical info: **www.worldtravelguide.net**
- U.S. Department of State (see page 193)
- Yahoo—country-specific travel resource listings: **www.yahoo.com/regional/countries**

OTHER SOURCES OF TRAVEL INFORMATION

National Tourist Offices

Look up the official tourism sites of the places you want to visit, and request materials by e-mail or phone. They'll be delighted to send you information

Periodicals

- *Abroad View* Magazine: This unique semiannual magazine focuses on experiences of people, especially young people, who are studying abroad. The contributors relate life-changing incidents and insights, and they voice their views on important cultural, environmental, political, and social issues and ideas, both global and regional.

- *Arthur Frommer's Budget Travel:* This magazine has become an essential read for the bargain hunter. It is now focused less on package tours and more on independent travel—but it doesn't look down its nose at comfort, either.

- *International Living:* It relentlessly tries to sell you something—usually its other publications or foreign real estate. If you can wade through the self-promotions, it has valuable advice for anyone who wants to retire overseas or live abroad for an extended period.

- *International Travel News:* Proving that function can triumph over form, this black-and-white-on-newsprint magazine is an excellent resource for all travelers, especially those who prefer tours but want to get beyond package tours that treat you like a number.

- *National Geographic:* It may put more boots on the trail than any other stimulus. It invests immense resources in the highest-quality photography and reporting. It is attuned to ecological issues and produces a stream of influential articles that help shape debates.

- *National Geographic Traveler:* Extends the *National Geo* tradition and offers flashes of luxury as well as stories that please a hard-core traveler. Notable for the high quality of the writing.

- *Outpost:* One of the best travel magazines in North America for thoughtful independent travelers. Insightful, culturally sensitive writing, with a view from the ground, not from the Four Seasons balcony. And all with a Canadian perspective.

- *Outside:* Covers the planet, specializing in adventures in remote destinations. Some consider its writers the best in the business.

- *Condé Nast Traveler, Travel + Leisure,* and *Town & Country Travel* are the heavyweight glossies. Directed to readers with more money than time, they please the eye, span the globe, and occasionally offer sound advice. But their impact is about as lasting as that of Chinese food.

presenting their countries in their best light. Ask about late-breaking information or permit requirements. Many countries also have an extensive network of tourist offices in-country that can make your travels much easier.

Traveler's Tool Kit Web Site

We maintain a list of ever-evolving travel resources on our Web site (**www.travelers-tool-kit.com**). We invite you to visit.

Conversations

Bring up pending travel plans in conversation. You'll frequently find people who've been where you're thinking of going or know someone who's been there. Even scraps of information can change and enrich your trip. Naturally, make sure the information is current, and take into account the personality of whoever gave it to you. Ask for names of people to contact abroad, no matter how tenuous the relationship. You can make great acquaintances by calling friends of friends.

Public Libraries

Check out books, videotapes, CDs, and DVDs about destinations. You can find materials for learning Spanish while you are at it.

Travel Bookstores

Travel bookstores specialize in travel books, maps, and related materials. They often have experienced travelers on staff who will gladly talk with you about destinations.

Videos

TravelVideoStore.com (**www.travelvideostore.com**) offers 60- to 90-minute videotapes and DVDs of sites around the world, produced by *Reader's Digest*, Video Visits, Fodor's, and Rand McNally, among others.

U.S. State Department

The State Department, **travel.state.gov,** provides information on passports, visas, embassies, travel advisories, and much more. It also has several useful online brochures, including *Your Trip Abroad,* with basic advice for travelers; *Safe Trip Abroad;* and *Travel Tips for Older Americans.* Check out "Contact Us" on the Web site for phone numbers for various services.

Literature

Understand the people of a country by reading its literature, both fiction and nonfiction. A good guidebook lists books set in a country as well as its best authors.

Draw on the wealth of travel CD-ROMs, including *The Traveler,* from the Magellan Corporation, which offers presentations on more than 100 destinations and 25 activities. The CD is free, but there's a shipping fee. Call (800) 561-3114.

Maps

There's no reason to plan a trip using only a small map when fine maps are available from AAA, *National Geographic,* travel bookstores, and even many regular bookstores. A good 11-by-15-inch atlas is a great investment.

Consider Google Maps (**maps.google.com**), Maps.com (**www.maps.com**), Map Link (**www.maplink.com**), MapQuest (**www.mapquest.com**), Moon Handbooks' itinerary-planning maps (**www.moon.com/travelplanner**), Rand McNally (**www.randmcnally.com**), and the Perry-Castañeda Library Map Collection at the University of Texas (**www.lib.utexas.edu/maps**).

CHAPTER 5

How to Choose the Ideal Travel Partner

There ain't no surer way to find out whether you like
people or you hate them than to travel with them.
—Mark Twain
Tom Sawyer Abroad (1894)

The solo traveler is an icon. He's the guy playing guitar for a group of locals in a Nicaraguan restaurant. She's the woman with a backpack striding up some volcanic slope. Solo travelers set their own itinerary, choose their own pace, and make decisions to suit only themselves.

Local people are likely to invite him for a meal or a stay in their home. She solves problems and learns new skills—because she has to—and builds her self-confidence in the bargain.

On their own, they don't have to deal with someone else's mood swings and are free to meet someone who might turn out to be very important in their lives.

> To be sure that your friend is a friend, you must go with him on a journey.
> —Angolan proverb

Cornelia Parker wrote, "What is your thrill may be my bore. I cannot imagine what fire and pillage I would commit if someone were in a position to keep me looking at things longer than I wanted to look."

Then There's Reality

Traveling solo offers generous rewards, but the fact is, most people won't consider leaving home without a partner. That's fine, of course, so long as they know what they're getting into. Ignore Mark Twain's insight at your peril.

Traveling with a partner is like paddling a canoe together. If not synchronized, paddles are likely to clash, and the canoe might capsize. Best take a short trip together before tackling heavy whitewater. Even traveling with someone you think you know well may reveal how superficial your relationship has been. Conflict on the road can fracture a relationship, even a marriage. So choose a partner with great care.

THE IDEAL TRAVEL PARTNER

Finding the ideal travel partner is easier than finding the source of the Nile or safe passage around Cape Horn—but not much.

The ideal travel partner is:

- Someone with whom you agree on the *vision for the trip.* Do you like the same destinations? Is one of you thinking of an adventure-seeking trip while the other dreams of long afternoons lying on the beach? Does one love to hike while the other wants a taxi if the restaurant is two blocks away? Do you like to search out new places, while your partner would rather return every day to a familiar cafe? It's not a question of who's right; it's a matter of being certain the trip has the same shape for both of you. Identify and reconcile differences before leaving home.
- Someone with the same *tolerance for risk.* How do you both feel about riding on top of the bus, hiking without a guide, spending the night at the top of a Maya pyramid, or visiting areas that may not be completely safe?
- Someone who feels the same way you do about *intimacy.* Is romance on the agenda? Do you feel okay about sharing a room, or a bed? Make the wrong assumptions about this one, and it may be a very long trip.
- Someone with whom you agree about *the budget.* Reasonable people can become very weird when it comes to money. Are you thinking of paying $12 a night for a hotel room, but your prospective partner won't be comfortable for less than $112?

On Gili Trawangan, an easygoing tropical island near Bali, I met a couple who had barely started their honeymoon. They'd just moved into a clean bungalow with a bathroom, decent beds, and a fan—only 50 feet from the gentle waves—all for $15 a night. He was delighted by the place and the price. A few hours later, they stood on the front deck arguing about her desire to return to the mainland and the comforts of a beach resort hotel at $150 per night. That's a reminder of the risks in traveling with a significant other, especially when romance is in first bloom.

> Discuss how you and your partner will handle money.

You'll both be consuming medical supplies, meals, groceries, and possibly liquor, but not in equal quantities. Do you prefer to split things evenly or to pay for exactly what you consume? One approach is to pool enough money for meals and incidentals for a week and pay joint expenses from this common wallet. You may settle up every country or two, or after returning home. Just be sure you're both satisfied. Talk about money in advance, keep it in perspective, and adjust as you go.

- Someone who operates on a *similar clock.* The day person–night person issue has plagued more than a few travelers. As Thoreau put it, "The man who goes alone can start today; but he who travels with another must wait till that other is ready." Would one of you become crazed if the other took an hour to dress? A stickler for punctuality and orderliness could lose his mind in the occasional chaos of the less developed world, or even a messy hotel room. If one partner dedicates himself to late-night partying and the other prefers visiting local markets at dawn, there's a problem on the horizon.

Partners can also fall out over the timing of meals. You might wake up ravenous, but your partner prefers to have breakfast in midmorning. You may want three meals a day while your partner would rather wing it, snacking out of the day pack.

- Someone whose *energy level* and pace are similar to yours. If you don't have compatible degrees of fitness, you may not be able to travel well as a team.
- Someone who's realistic about *health problems.* That means leveling with each other about health issues and considering the implications, especially for an arduous trip, in advance. The important thing is that both partners share the same expectations.
- Someone who has a *flexible, even-tempered personality.* There are bumps in the road that will jostle anyone's cart. Travel requires dealing with uncertainties and solving problems. If you're considering traveling with someone who blows up easily or criticizes and complains nonstop at home, take a cold shower and start over. Look for a partner with a sense of humor, one who understands that most frustrations arise from the very differences in culture that make a place worth visiting.
- Someone whose *personal habits* are compatible with yours. Do you have similar feelings about alcohol? Cigarettes? Illegal drugs? If one partner spreads his gear over every available surface, will the other flip out? If one of you snores like a chain saw . . . well, then what? No judgments, just a reality check before the plane rolls down the runway.
- Someone who will *share the load* and keep agreements; someone you can count on.
- Someone who *recognizes the need for "quiet time."* Most of us aren't used to spending 24 hours a day within 50 feet of the same person, so too little privacy can lead to a contagious case of crankiness. If one partner needs an occasional meal alone, a solitary walk, a solo day, or some parallel travel, the other partner should respect that need without feeling rejected.
- Someone who will *communicate.* If there's a problem, a molehill of small resentments can become volcanic if not dealt with immediately. Agree to express, calmly and immediately, your feelings about each other's behavior or whatever the issue is.
- Someone who *can solve problems in creative ways.* Choose some regular time, such as Sunday breakfast, to discuss candidly how you both feel the trip is going. Are you spending money at about the right

> "I learned one thing."
> "What?"
> "Never go on trips with anyone you do not love."
> —Ernest Hemingway,
> *A Moveable Feast*
> (1964)

rate? Does the pace make you both happy? Is it time to alter the itinerary or make any other changes? Are you having fun?

• *Someone you like!* Nothing is more important.

Finally, a cardinal rule about partners: never expect that someone will change for the better just because he or she is on a trip.

What's the Point?

What do people get from traveling with a partner?

Travel *costs less* with a partner. Because a single room usually costs at least 80 percent of the price of a double room, your lodging costs drop when you split room rent 50-50. The same is true for expenses such as taxis, guidebooks, medicine, and reading material. If you're on a tour, having a partner keeps you from paying a stiff supplement charge for singles.

It can be a relief to *divide daily chores* such as changing money, buying tickets, finding a room, or figuring out how to get across town to hear a local band.

You're *safer* when traveling with someone. Even walking down the street is considerably safer for two or more. Having a partner is especially helpful to women for repelling unwanted advances.

If the *lonesome, homesick blues* show up, a partner can be a cheerful presence.

Traveling with someone who speaks the *local language* makes daily life much easier.

If a *health problem* arises, a partner assumes the attributes of an angel.

Partners create a *synergy* that leads to unexpected pleasures. On a cold, drizzly afternoon in Paris, I was thinking of settling down for a few hours of writing and coffee in a neighborhood cafe. But my partner suggested we call a local couple who were friends of a friend (the kind of phone number you accept before you leave, never intending to use it). They invited us for dinner. As it turned out, he headed a major European news service, and she ran an international modeling agency. We became friends, and they loaded us up with fantastic contacts that improved the quality of the rest of the three-month trip. For years after that, every one of her models who came to California for a shoot arrived with my law firm's business card in her pocket.

When the trip is history, the two of you can *reminisce* over dinner.

Expectations

Here's an example of mismatched expectations. An acquaintance who held the *Guinness Book of World Records* title as the world's most-traveled man has been married and divorced six times. But he had an explanation: "During courtship, each of my wives said she loved travel, but every one of them was thinking about the *QE II* and the Ritz, not about riding some dirty ship from one godforsaken island to another."

How to Find Your Travel Partner

There are thousands, maybe millions, of potential travelers who are divorced, are between romantic involvements, or have friends and family unable or unwilling to join in their adventures. The result? They stay home and grump. Consistent with my anti-grump campaign, I have some suggestions. Look at bulletin boards in colleges and bookstores. You may find a note from someone who's looking for a travel partner. Review *International Travel News* and other travel periodicals in which travelers seeking partners list where and when they'd like to go. Ask the travel editor of your newspaper whether a local travel club organizes trips for singles.

You can even leave home alone, hoping to find one or more partners along the way. It's easy to meet travelers in museums, on day tours, on trains, at the beach, on the trail, in hostels, and in restaurants. If one of these spur-of-the-moment partnerships doesn't work out, it's also easy to move on alone.

Numerous Web sites such as Match.com happily—for a fee—serve as massive virtual markets for people seeking . . . well, I guess that varies. I have no opinion about them, but, as you can tell from the criteria I suggested earlier in this chapter, finding an ideal travel partner requires a special effort. The profiles on most sites just don't elicit the information you need. Competent, comprehensive profiles provide basic personal statistics, of course, but you also need

Coauthor Tim Leffel and his perfect partner

information on preferred travel style and budget, preference in accommodations and handling expenses, and the specific reason someone is seeking a companion. For those reasons, I'd prefer a site whose profiles are specifically oriented toward identifying your ideal travel companion.

After reading a person's profile, you've learned a lot about who he or she is and whether that person fits what you're looking for. Once you've found several prospective travel partners, it is essential to make the right choice. Read those answers carefully. Don't ignore red flags. If he loves bullfights and she's an ardent member of the SPCA, she should take the hint. As good as these questionnaires are, they may not cover everything you want to know. Don't be embarrassed to ask.

Almost 80 percent of the profiles indicate a definite preference for traveling with a person of the opposite gender. Of these, 85 percent prefer to share accommodations. If the Leaning Tower of Pisa is not the only thing on the minds of some, that fact is made clear in the profiles.

Whether you're looking for a partner so you can avoid paying the brutal single-supplement charge on a tour through the south of France or so you can share an independent trip to Greece, there's help around.

Connecting: Solo Travel Network, based in Vancouver, British Columbia, has been in operation since 1990 (call [800] 557-1757 or [604] 886-9099, or see **www.cstn.org**). Membership includes a subscription to a bimonthly newsletter full of travel advice, readers' reports, travel tales, and short personal notices that give intended destinations, budgets, interests, and preferred characteristics in a travel companion. Members receive the *Single-Friendly Travel Directory,* which lists tour operators, outfitters, resorts, cruise lines, and singles clubs whose services and pricing policies are directed toward the solo traveler.

Golden Age Travellers Club (call [800] 258-8880 or [800] 628-0136, or see **www.gatclub.com**), in business since 1969, specializes in serving people older than 50. It will either find you a roommate for its tours, most of which are to Europe, or waive the single supplement.

CHAPTER 6

The Organized Tour

Tourists capture the image of a well-known place in a
photo but miss its essence; the anti-tourist dismisses
the place as a cliché and misses the whole thing;
while the traveler grasps its majesty.
—John Thorn

Effortless transportation has inspired some tourists to think they're intrepid travelers as they're shepherded safely to places previously accessible only to daring adventurers.

Paul Fussell opined, "An explorer seeks the undiscovered; a traveler seeks that which has been discovered by the mind working in history; and the tourist seeks that which has been discovered by entrepreneurship and prepared for him by the arts of mass publicity." Another critic described tourists as people who travel primarily to raise their social status at home, to realize fantasies of freedom, or to pose as members of a social class above their own.

In my opinion, the distinction between traveler and tourist goes beyond who did the planning for the trip or even whether someone else takes your luggage down to a bus each morning. It's based on your objectives and state of mind. A traveler intends to merge with a place and its people in a way that a tourist does not wish to.

To me, the word *tourist* has a connotation different from merely describing people who travel on an organized tour. It identifies people who see the well-known sights but leave a place understanding the culture only superficially. They have few friendly contacts with local people and are little changed by their trip. A tourist is a person who, whether with a tour group or not, is primarily along for the ride and doesn't get actively involved.

From that perspective, it would be inaccurate to categorize everyone on an organized tour as a tourist. Tour participants can be far more than tourists if they educate themselves about what they'll see, interact with local people as meaningfully as possible, and choose their tour operator wisely.

Independent travel requires self-confidence, the ability to organize, and adequate health. Uncertain about meeting these requirements, many people hook up with a tour, especially for their first major trip, and have a great time. If anxiety about coping with distant parts of the world might cause you to stay home, you'd be doing yourself a disservice to dismiss tours. It's far better to explore the world in whatever vehicle feels comfortable than to mildew in an armchair at home.

If taking a tour seems like a good way to get under way, the trick is to select the tour that will meet the objectives you set. That's what this chapter is about. Even if you are not interested in tours today, it's possible you'll travel with an organized tour group in the future.

REASONS TO TRAVEL WITH A TOUR OPERATOR

- Decide to travel with a tour group, and that's one of the last decisions required. Someone else makes the logistical arrangements. Before long, the mailman delivers a glossy brochure bulging with superlatives, an itinerary, a list of what to bring, an orange plastic luggage tag, and detailed instructions. Under way, courteous guides answer every question, adequate hotels and restaurants appear when wanted, and scenic vistas flow by without misadventure. If there are hassles, you probably won't even hear about them, much less have to deal with them. It's about peace of mind. Participating in a tour can teach you a lot about planning your own itinerary the next time out.
- The requirement in some countries that visitors travel only with a tour group has been generally abandoned, although permission to travel independently in Myanmar, North Korea, and a few other places phases in and out. Countries with limited tourist facilities want to be sure that big spenders are given priority. It's also easier for an inquisitive government to keep tabs on groups than on independent travelers.
- In several countries, traveling with a tour group is not mandatory, but logistics can be daunting for an independent traveler. For example, consider a group if you want to travel hassle-free in Mongolia.
- Some tour operators include considerable educational value in their trips. In those cases, you're likely to be accompanied by an art historian, a geologist, or some other appropriate expert to help satisfy your curious mind.
- A tour can be an efficient way of moving from place to place. Because independent travel, especially in the Third World, can be very time-consuming, a tour may be a good fit for a traveler with limited time. If you don't want company, an "air and accommodations only" tour package may be useful.
- Some people prize the company of others. In fact, meeting like-minded people may be part of the reason for the trip. It is not unusual to travel repeatedly with people with whom you've formed friendships on a tour. You may also meet future travel partners for independent travel.
- Most tours insulate tour members from meaningful contact with local people. In contrast, some are organized specifically to permit or encourage contacts with local people from across the spectrum. Travelers ought to insist that tour operators work harder to provide such contacts. It's a

sure-fire way to begin reducing the mutual ignorance that underlies so much of the conflict on our planet.

- **SAVE Money** Some tours actually save money. If you don't mind staying in the places, eating the type of food, and seeing the sights that tour groups do, you can sometimes save money by joining tours and taking advantage of group rates (available because tour operators purchase in bulk), including big discounts on air fare. If the tour group stays at four- or five-star hotels, it will cost you considerably less than if you were on your own. On the other hand, it will cost you much more than if you chose your own two- or three-star hotel. You can save money in other ways using a tour. For example, you can deal directly with a local tour operator in a foreign country rather than a U.S. operator. Similarly, joining a group—say, a scuba-diving group in Belize—will cost you much less after you've arrived in the country. Another money-saving approach is to book an off-season tour not long before departure.

- A tour may be ideal for persons with less than robust health. The availability of assistance may enable someone to travel who doesn't have the stamina required for independent travel.

- A tour provides the opportunity to combine high adventure with low risk. The expertise of experienced guides enables people to make difficult trips in comparative safety. Similarly, a tour may provide an additional feeling of personal security.

After reading a stack of tour brochures, you will realize that tourist trails around the world are deeply worn. On the other hand, if you read brochures put out by a few companies, such as Geographic Expeditions, Mountain Travel Sobek, and Turtle Tours, you may be amazed at how many remote corners of the world still await your visit. Companies such as these have sought out nearly inaccessible hideaways from Mongolia to Indochina, from the sub-Sahara to Antarctica. They'll take you to Lunana in northern Bhutan, to the fabled Inner Dolpo region of northwest Nepal, across the Himalayas from Manali to Ladakh, or on an icebreaker out of Cape Town bound for the far side of Antarctica. Yes, you could arrange almost all these trips on your own, but you'd have to do extensive research and overcome formidable logistical problems.

> As a member of an escorted tour you don't even have to know that the Matterhorn isn't a tuba.
> —Temple Fielding, Fielding's Guide to Europe (1963)

REASONS NOT TO TRAVEL WITH A TOUR OPERATOR

Some of the reasons that persuade people to sign on with a tour group are the very reasons that persuade other people not to. Tours come with trade-offs. Very aware of this, many tour operators work hard to combat the disadvantages I mention subsequently, but to some extent they are inherent in tours.

- **SAVE Money** Many tours are expensive compared to independent travel. For single travelers, part of the extra expense of a tour is the single supplement, the substantial charge often added to cruise, hotel, or tour prices for people traveling alone. Save money by seeking tour operators who don't impose this charge or who waive it if you're willing to accept a roommate. Negotiate. Tell the tour operator you'll sign up only if the charge is waived. As the departure date approaches, the operator may see it your way. If not, consider finding a partner. (Please see Chapter 5, How to Choose the Ideal Travel Partner.)

Some tours cost much more than independent travel because the tour operator, anticipating the preferences of prospective clients, builds upscale amenities into trips. The company may lodge clients in the most expensive hotels and furnish a sociable, educated, English-speaking guide. On your own, you might stay in less expensive lodgings and get along without a guide (or with one whose English is only somewhat better than your command of his language). The operator also pays for other helpers, local permits, fuel, equipment, food, transportation, and insurance. On your own, you might eat more simply and rely on public transportation.

Then there's overhead. The tour operator maintains a staff to provide all those pre-trip services to you. To the high cost of producing that gorgeous brochure, add the costs of finding you and mailing it to you. At least 10 percent of the trip price may be paid as a commission by the tour operator to the travel agency. And then there's the profit.

A good operator spends as much money as it takes to ensure that the trip is flawless—because that's what people expect. The independent traveler, on the other hand, is prepared to accept a glitch or two. It's up to you to understand and choose what you want.

- Regimentation is the rule. On a typical tour, you board the daily transportation at a prescribed time, travel a fixed path selected by others, and eat as a group when the bell rings. If the pace is significantly different from your own, you can go bananas. There is seldom any downtime. You're expected to eat, and enjoy, everything on the plate. You can struggle against the routine by skipping some of the planned activities, substituting your own, and hitting the streets every time there's a free period on the schedule. In the end, however, you're still aboard a guided missile.
- Being with a tour group changes the nature of any experience. A cloud-wrapped monastery, memorable when seen alone, feels different when 25 people pile through the low door and the monks scramble to peddle their crafts.
- Unprofessional tour guides can drive anyone crazy. Manifestations of unprofessionalism range from not knowing the subject to paying no attention to group preferences to hitting on the clients.

- Your companions can make or break the tour, and possibly you in the bargain. Noel Coward referred to tourists as "monumental bores who travel in groups and herds and troupes." As a generalization, that's unfair, but bores are not nearly the worst human peril you encounter on tour. A mysterious metamorphosis lies dormant in some people, seemingly triggered by paying a lot of money to a tour operator. Failing to ask the tour operator in advance for an honest profile of the group could be a serious error.

Richard Bangs, founding partner of Mountain Travel Sobek, has listed some of the clients his guides dread: The Stud, who's out to conquer the landscape and anything else available; The Ignoramus, who learned nothing about the tour destinations ahead of time and didn't bring the proper gear; The Inflexible Retentive, who has memorized the brochure and explodes when local conditions force the slightest deviation (even an otherwise understanding person may cast her cape aside and emerge as a chronic complainer); The Peacock, whose primary pleasure is parading around in the most expensive clothing available; The Snipe, who snarfs up far more than his share of whatever goodies are available; and The Grunge, who violates all rules of hygiene, endangering everyone else's health. And Bangs didn't even mention the loners, the whiners, the loudmouths, the chatterboxes, the professors, the question askers, the perpetually tardy, and those who'd rather stop for coffee than enter the cathedral.

- Food and hotels selected by tour operators are typically Americanized. You could miss much of the flavor of the country.
- You meet few local people. Those you encounter are lecturers very familiar with tourists or are hardened traders whose primary goal is to sell you as much as possible during the brief moments you are together. They're very good at it, but it's not what you would call a fulfilling experience for you.
- People on tour see restaurant workers, taxi drivers, and beggars who gather outside their hotel (precisely because it is a tourist hotel) but have little interaction with the general populace. They don't hang out with local artists, soldiers, or politicians. An invisible cocoon forms around a tour, difficult to penetrate in either direction.
- You're likely to become dependent on the lifeline of bus and guide. Travel becomes too easy. Someone else has the answers, and you become timid about venturing out on your own.

> I was drunk with travel, dizzy with the import of it all, and indifferent to thoughts of home and family.
> —Charles Kuralt
> A Life on the Road
> (1990)

Some independent travelers may look down their noses a bit as they see a tour bus pulling up in front of yet another temple. However, there's another way to view it. First, that tour bus is taking people to places they would not, or could not, otherwise go—and that's good. Second, tour groups pay in hard currency, vitally needed by the host country—and that's good. Third, I remember standing in a blazing-hot, dusty, chaotic bus yard, trying to figure out what the name of my destination might look like in Hindi. Overwhelmed by noxious fumes and the sound of roaring engines, my eye caught an air-conditioned luxury tour bus gliding by, stereo playing, hostess already pouring ice-cold beers. I promise you, I wasn't looking down my nose at tour groups at that moment. And that's good.

If you feel uncertain about what you'll encounter in some faraway land, recognize that you're not quite as fit as you'd like to be, don't want to take the time to organize a trip on your own, or just want to be coddled, consider a tour. If going on a tour will initiate a lifetime of traveling, give it a try. If you decide to take a tour, don't drag your feet. Hit the road with optimism and a cheerful spirit. Make it your trip—and don't sweat the small stuff.

TYPES OF TOURS: HIGH COST TO LOW COST

Before investigating any particular tour, decide where you want to go, how long you want to travel, what time of year you prefer, how much you want to spend, and what kind of people you want to travel with. In other words, set the initial agenda yourself. If you choose to make adjustments later to meet the specifics of available tours, at least you're following your own path.

You learn quickly that tours don't come just in vanilla. There are four general types: escorted, package, independent, and charter. Here are thumbnail descriptions:

- *Escorted tour:* Tour director; group travel; set itinerary with lodging, activities, and most meals included; minimum of hassles; a measure of security; learning; some free time.
- *Package tour:* No organized group and no tour director; fixed itinerary with air and ground transportation and lodging booked in advance; services you buy from the tour operator are affordable because of bulk purchases, but you pay all other expenses; you're free to wander at will.
- *Independent tour:* No group; no guide; no fixed itinerary; you buy selected components such as airline tickets or lodging (reservations or vouchers) from the tour operator; can also add local "hosts" who help with planning.
- *Charter tour:* The tour operator rents a plane and sells seats at a 10 to 30 percent discount from regular airfare.

Tours vary widely in cost, services, and objectives. Itineraries, multiplying like a computer network, are now a great spiderweb covering the globe. To make wise choices, you need to understand what is available:

- *Upscale:* On some fully escorted tours, you never lift a hand; in fact, your feet may barely touch the ground. The accommodations are five-star, and the food is gourmet (although being served chicken cordon bleu in Beijing may strike you as a little weird). An imported expert guides you through the sights of the day and lectures at night. After a nightcap, you tuck yourself into a crisp, clean bed. (Yes, you generally have to do the tucking yourself.)

- *Standard:* On the majority of tours, you're accompanied by an escort, stay in good hotels, eat well, and listen to local guides reel off a galaxy of details. Every morning, you're rousted early to line up your bags in the hall, ready for the next lap. These tours generally last 10 to 30 days, and prices vary accordingly.

- *Locally hosted packages:* A guide meets you or your group as you arrive at a destination, takes care of you for a few days, and then sees you safely onto transport to your next destination—where you meet your next guide-for-a-day.

- *Special focus:* Some tours distinguish themselves with a special focus, such as Chinese celadon, butterflies along the Tambopata, French wines, or the Namibian system of jurisprudence. Special-focus tours are often organized by zoological societies, museums, cultural groups, and the like.

The North Acropolis in Tikal, Guatemala

- *Adventure travel:* The popularity of this type of special-interest tour is rapidly expanding. I'll discuss it at greater length in the next section.
- *Affinity groups:* These can be anything from accountants to zydeco musicians to redheaded people named Smith. Shoppers, feeding wildly in country after country, are a common affinity group.
- *Package:* You initiate a package tour by stepping into a travel agency with a general idea of where you'd like to go. You leave the agency with a package of airline–hotel–overland-transport reservations and travel on your own within that framework. No escorts are provided. Hotels, airlines, and rental-car companies sell blocks of space to package operators (sometimes called wholesalers) at a discount, so the cost to you can be significantly less than if you bought the individual components separately. You get the group discount without the group; not a bad deal. The accommodations will be somewhat upscale and westernized, but at least you're on your own. A foreign independent tour (FIT) is similar, usually unescorted but occasionally with guide service.
- *Disability groups:* Because international travel can be difficult for persons with significant disabilities, it's worth getting advice and assistance in advance. The Society for Accessible Travel & Hospitality (**www.sath.org**) has a list of tour operators who make special efforts to assist travelers with disabilities. Susan Gersten and Jacqueline Freedman have written a helpful book titled *Traveling Like Everybody Else: A Practical Guide for Disabled Travelers.*

Not specifically fitting the standard concept of a tour are two other situations in which you employ someone else to show you the sights. Although many travelers pass up local tours and local guides, each has merits.

Local Tours

Units of government or private tour operators offer inexpensive local tours. Most commonly, they are bus trips around a city or region lasting for one long day, although some continue for a week or more. There's usually no problem boarding just before departure, but it's safer to sign up a day ahead. A local day tour saves you from having to figure out how to get to and from a dozen remote sites in a city new to you. The driver or guide explains what you're seeing and is usually willing to answer questions having little to do with the tour. By the end of the day, you've identified places to which you want to return, and you may have met interesting people in the bargain. I often take a local tour on my first day in a large city new to me.

> The tourist travels in his own atmosphere like a snail in his shell and stands, as it were, on his own perambulating doorstep to look at the continents of the world.
> —Freya Stark, *Baghdad Sketches* (1932)

It would be logical to assume that everyone on the bus paid the same—and it would be wrong. Those who asked their hotel or a local travel agency to book them almost certainly paid much more than those who booked directly with the tour operator. If you book through your hotel, ask for a discount. If someone tries to switch you from a tour you requested to a different one, it's probably because he or she gets a higher commission from the latter.

Local Guides

Wherever your elbow is in the world, a would-be guide will touch it to commend himself to your attention. He may dress in a shiny suit and speak melodic upper-school English, or he may be a 14-year-old in a scruffy djellaba. Whichever, he is certain to be tenacious. He will also probably be knowledgeable, which he'll attempt to demonstrate by bombarding you with arcane info-bits before you can say, "No, thank you." He'll offer to guide you safely through the maze of the souks of Marrakech, protect you from being cheated by merchants, and shield you from his "not honest" competitors who are also seeking your attention.

After several experiences with guides who told me much more than I wanted to know and always seemed to have an uncle whose carpet shop just happened to be on our route, I responded by turning away every applicant. I remember one guide I turned down in a Prague museum who then ran ahead of me and turned off the lights in each room one by one to make sure I got his point. Before long, I regained perspective and began accepting guide services. In addition to what they've programmed themselves to tell me, guides provide answers that help satisfy my curiosity as no guidebook can. With encouragement, they take me to remote corners I would otherwise miss. As a bonus, beneath the routine patter, many guides are interesting—proud of their knowledge and their fluency in foreign languages.

If you think a person would expect to be compensated for performing such services, you would be right. The question is, how much? Starting without an agreement almost assures that one or both parties will be unhappy at the end. However, before discussing price, agree on exactly what services the guide will provide. That done, if he's failed to state a price, raise the subject yourself. He's likely to respond, "Nothing, sir. Nothing at all. If you do not like my services, you pay me nothing. If I am helpful, you pay whatever you decide." Sounds fair, eh? Yes, it does—but it's a trap. Your conscience will never permit "nothing," and the guide knows it. If you pay anything less than a year's income, the guide will protest that it is too little. His protest may be quiet and courteous, as if embarrassed that you don't know any better, or he may feign shock or grief. You are vastly better off reaching agreement in advance. If you wish, talk with several prospective guides, comparing their merits and their asking prices. Or decide what a guide's services would be worth to you and offer a take-it-or-leave-it price. The price of a guide is, to put it mildly, highly elastic, depending on how many guides there are and how many prospective clients. Only if the trip involves some strenuous activity such as climbing with you to the top of the four highest pyramids at Tikal is there likely to be an irreducible minimum price.

You often see a little knot of tourists being towed passively through a site by a fast-talking guide. Within minutes, a few become hostile, but most lapse into glassy-eyed boredom. In contrast, when I set off with a guide, I immediately try to engage him as a person and get him to see me as an individual traveler. I let him know my special interests in the site. As we walk, I ensure that we proceed at my pace so I can understand what I'm seeing, take photographs if I choose, and ask questions. If the guide makes a special effort, I pay him more than we agreed on—and we're both happy.

HOW TO CHOOSE THE BEST TOUR OPERATOR

Check Out the Tour Operator

Some tour operators are experienced travelers who entered the business to put their happily acquired knowledge to profitable use. Others are deskbound managers who have spent years assembling mountains of information. And a few operators are simply unqualified, relying on untested local contractors and shipping people to any destination for which they'll pay. Overall, though, tour operators are an excellent source of information about destinations.

Evaluating tour operators is a good way to avoid aggravation, and yet an amazing number of people don't bother. A man was recently indicted in Alexandria, Virginia, for ripping off more than 2,000 people in 43 states. He used telemarketing to sell cheap vacation packages (for example, $199 for two people to the Caribbean and Cancún). Requiring the would-be traveler to pay the full price in advance, he would then deliver "promotional vouchers" with so many restrictions that virtually no one could use the trips. Here's the kicker: Among the aliases he used were Dusty Rhodes and Skip Town! It must be true; it was reported in *Travel Weekly*.

Several magazines, such as *International Travel News* and *Consumer Reports*, periodically publish ratings of major tour operators. Contact the American Society of Travel Agents (call [800] 275-2782, or see **www.travelsense.org**) or the United States Tour Operators Association (call [212] 599-6599, or see **www.ustoa.com**) to check credentials of travel agents and tour operators. ASTA, for example, will tell you if a travel agency is a member, whether there have been complaints against it, and whether they've been resolved.

> The old hunger for voyages fed at his heart . . . to go alone . . . into strange cities; to meet strange people and to pass again before they could know him; to wander, like his own legend, across the earth—it seemed to him there could be no better thing than that.
> —Thomas Wolfe, *Look Homeward, Angel* (1929)

What You Want to Know about the Tour Operator

- *Priorities and values:* The tour operator should provide a clear statement of its philosophy. Sure, it will be self-serving, but at least you can see if it includes the buzz words you want to see.
- *Operator's experience:* How long has the tour operator been in business? How many tours does it handle annually? How many trips has it sponsored to the area that interests you?
- *Price:* Exactly what does the price of the tour include? On the European Plan, no meals are included in the price. On the American Plan, three meals a day are included, whether you are hungry or not. Modified American Plan (MAP) means that breakfast and lunch or dinner are included. If it's the Continental Plan, you'll get a bread-and-beverage breakfast that may leave an echo in your stomach. Is the price firm, or does the tour operator retain the right to increase the fare after you've signed the contract? An increase of more than 10 percent or a significant change in departure date should entitle you to a refund. Are there any extra charges for side trips, tipping, taxes, and so on that are not included in the price? Will the operator provide a roommate so you don't have to pay a single supplement? To compare prices of various trips, take the total price; subtract your estimate of the airfare, if it is included; and then divide the remaining amount by the number of nights. That will give you a price-per-night figure for each trip.
- *Firsthand experience:* Has anyone in the travel agent's office traveled with the tour operator the agent is recommending? Was that person satisfied? Have any of the agency's clients traveled with the operator? Were they satisfied? Get the names of some with whom you can speak.
- *Trip difficulty:* Many tour brochures grade the trips they offer in terms of physical difficulty. Seek a match with your own energy level. Don't hesitate to ask; you're in this for fun. An active person could be climbing the walls after two weeks of sitting on a bus. On the other hand, if a trip is billed as "strenuous trekking" or "high altitude," don't sign up without understanding what that means.
- *Guides:* Who will accompany the tour group? Who exactly will be the guide? There's nothing wrong with using local subcontractors if they're well trained and reliable. When they're not, that's when the glossy brochure turns into toilet paper. What is the ratio of guides to group members? How long have the guides been with the company?
- *Accommodations:* Think about what level of comfort you want and are willing to pay for. What's the quality of the scheduled accommodations? Ask for specifics about location of the lodging. If it's at the edge of the city, it's likely to be far from the attractions you want to visit and you'll waste a lot of time commuting.

- *Group demographics:* What are the maximum and minimum numbers of persons in the group? There may be a situation in which a large group would be preferable to a small one, but I can't imagine what it would be. Ask about the demographics of people who have already signed up. Do you care about the backgrounds of others on the trip? If you have an interest in romance, find out if there are appropriate singles on the manifest.

- *Pace:* What will the pace of the trip be? Do you want continual activities, or a laid-back pace with lots of free time? Do you prefer to change hotels frequently or stay for several days at a time in the same place?

- *Independence:* Will there be time to explore on your own? To me, this is essential. Some of your strongest memories will come from time spent on your own. And there may be times when you just need to be away from the group.

- *Contacts:* Will there be opportunities to connect with local people? In my opinion, a traveler ought to give high marks to any tour operator for arranging opportunities to talk seriously with local people. I'm thinking of conversations about culture, religion, conflict, and values. The idea is not to persuade one another—a genuinely bad objective—but to increase understanding.

- *Shopping:* What is the operator's policy about integrating shopping into daily activities? This policy is far more important than it sounds. Frequent "shopping" stops may provide handsome kickbacks to the guide and tour operator but cut deeply into your sightseeing time.

- *Materials:* What materials will the tour operator provide in advance (gear lists, maps, readings, and so on)? You'll want to do a lot of research on destinations before the trip so you can appreciate what you're seeing.

- *Atmosphere:* How casual or formal will the trip be?

- *Extensions:* Are there side trips or extensions you can take rather than returning home with the group? By the end of a tour, you'll be feeling confident of your ability to navigate on your own and eager to experience more of the country you've been touring.

- *Lifestyle choices.* Will dietary, religious, smoking, and other personal preferences be accommodated?

- *Local relations:* How does the operator ensure that local support-staff members are adequately clothed, fed, and housed? In what ways are the guides sensitive to local cultures? Does the operator purchase goods and services locally?

- *Free trip:* If you deliver a certain number of other people who sign up for a tour, will the tour operator give you a free trip, including airfare, room, and board? If so, how many people would it take?

- *Tipping policy:* Rather than building fair wages into the price of a tour, it is common practice for tour operators to extract tips from clients to supplement income to guides, drivers, and so on. Because tips can add substantially to the cost of a trip, the tour operator's tipping policy should be fully disclosed early on in trip materials. Otherwise, uncertainty about appropriate tipping is a source of anxiety, even conflict, for many travelers. A tour operator's suggestions that seem excessive need not be followed.

- *Cancellation.* What are the cancellation penalties? Are there situations in which either you or the tour operator may cancel without penalty?
- *Financial protection.* Because you'll want your money back if the tour operator cancels the trip or goes bankrupt, you'll want to know whether it's financially responsible. Does it have liability insurance? Is it bonded? Does it belong to the consumer-protection program (a fund available to reimburse consumers in the event of bankruptcy) of the United States Tour Operators Association? Does your payment go into a trust account or escrow held by a third party? Can you pay by credit card? What penalties are there if you cancel? Have any complaints been filed against the tour operator? Naturally, you won't pay any tour operator until you've carefully read the terms of the contract.

ECOLOGICAL RESPONSIBILITY

In the real world, few travelers are likely to select a tour operator solely or even primarily because it treats the environment gently. However, in choosing among otherwise-qualified companies, ecological responsibility could be the deciding factor. Not surprisingly, you'll have to look beyond mere inclusion of some form of "eco" in a company's title. That word is meant to appeal to the public but may mean little in practice.

Ask questions such as: Do you provide predeparture information about the ecology of the destination? Do you use low-impact transportation when practical? Are your local facilities designed to minimize environmental damage? Do you donate money or equipment to help the local environment or protect natural resources? Do you use wood or alternative fuel for fires? How do you dispose of waste?

Because these are "have you stopped beating your wife?" questions, not all tour operators may be candid, but their answers will give you a chance to form an opinion. Further, even a few inquiries may motivate operators to be more ecologically responsible.

Some tour operators, listed in the table later in this chapter, are well regarded for their efforts to provide travelers with environmentally sensitive experiences.

Other good resources on ecotourism include the International Ecotourism Society (**www.ecotourism.org**); the book *Handle with Care: A Guide to Responsible Travel in Developing Countries*; the International Centre for Responsible Tourism (**www.icrtourism.org**); and the Archaeological Institute of America, which lists hundreds of sites where you can assist with archaeological work (**www.archaeo logical.org**).

The Ecumenical Coalition on Third World Tourism has published some considerations for travelers to keep in mind. Among them are the following:

travel with a genuine desire to learn more about people and be aware of their feelings; listen and observe; realize that your personal time concepts and thought patterns are not universal; learn local customs; ask questions; don't expect special privileges; don't make promises you can't or won't keep; and reflect on the experiences of each day.

Environmentally Responsible Tour Operators

The following are some tour operators and other companies that provide services in Mexico and Central America and have signed on to a code of conduct that commits them to follow guidelines of responsible ecotourism travel:

Adventure Life Journeys (**www.adventure-life.com**), AdventureSmith Explorations (**www.adventuresmithexplorations.com**), ExpeditionTrips (**www.expeditiontrips.com**), Forestour (**www.forestour.com**), G.A.P Adventures (**www.gapadventures.com**), International Expeditions (**www.ietravel.com**), Maya Expeditions (**www.mayaexpeditions.com**), and Wilderness Travel (**www.wildernesstravel.com**)

The following are other tour operators who have gained a solid reputation for ecological sensitivity. They are good companies to know about even if they don't offer trips in Mexico or Central America: Above the Clouds Trekking ([800] 233-4499; **www.aboveclouds.com**), Costa Rica Expeditions (**costaricaexpeditions.com**), Earth River Expeditions ([800] 643-2784; **www.earthriver.com**), Earthwatch Institute (**www.earthwatch.org**), International Expeditions ([800] 633-4734; **www.ietravel.com**); Mountain Travel Sobek (**www.mtsobek.com**), Overseas Adventure Travel (**www.oattravel.com**), the Plowshares Institute ([203] 651-4304; **www.plowsharesinstitute.org**), the Sierra Club (**www.sierraclub.org**), and Wildland Adventures (**www.wildland.com**).

Tourspeak

One of the most helpful foreign languages to learn is "tourspeak." To have a shot at understanding what an agent is saying, you need to know what the words mean in context. Here are some samples: If an agent (or brochure) says you will "visit" someplace, it means the bus will stop, and you'll have time to get off and look around. If the word is "view," however, there will be only a brief opportunity to take a photo or two. "See" means the bus might slow down as it whizzes by the attraction. If a brochure says you "can" play golf or "will be able" to visit an amusement park, these activities are probably not included in the price. Another tricky word is "near," as in "your little cottage is near the beach." It may be near only via a taxi. Listen and read with care so you'll know what to expect.

"Options galore" means not much is included in the price. "Spacious quarters" may mean "sparsely furnished," while "airy" means no air-conditioning. "Carefree natives" may be a euphemism for terrible service. "No extra fees" probably means no extras at all.

Resources

So how do you find tour operators? Naturally, they swamp the Web. Enter a destination, and the borders of your monitor will be lined with promotions. If you have an activity in mind, such as a safari, enter that as well. Look at ads in the travel sections of major newspapers, in travel magazines, and in special-interest magazines (scuba diving, photography, and so on). Call their toll-free telephone numbers for brochures, and visit their Web sites. These brochures and Web sites are very helpful, even when filled with wildly enthusiastic descriptions.

You seldom get a discount if you book directly with the tour operator, so you lose nothing by dealing with a good travel agent. However, when the travel agent is paid by tour operators, not by you, there is some potential for a conflict of interest. See Chapter 4, How to Plan Your Trip, for tips on how to choose the best agent.

The U.S. Tour Operators Association (**www.ustoa.com**) provides useful information such as the Find Your Vacation Personality Quiz on its home page. It produced accurate results for me. It will also steer you to tour operators that provide the services that match your preferences. Very clever. This guide lists all member companies and the areas of the world in which each specializes.

Local and national business and philanthropic organizations promote tours all over the globe, as do many universities. Watch for their ads.

The American Association of Retired Persons (AARP; **www.aarp.org**) and other "seniors" organizations, such as Grand Circle Travel (**www.gct.com**) and the National Active and Retired Federal Employees (**www.narfe.org**), sponsor tours offering discounts of 10 to 50 percent on many hotel and tour rates.

UNUSUAL TOUR OPPORTUNITIES

Although many tours follow a basic pattern, the creativity of some tour operators has resulted in magnificent exceptions. These exceptions demand a little more of participants, provide contact with local people, and inevitably have a deeper impact on those who choose them.

Political-consciousness or Reality Tours

Several organizations offer tours specifically intended to interact gently with local cultures while enhancing the political consciousness of travelers. Perhaps the most prominent provider of "reality tours" is the Center for Global Education (**www.globaled.us**). It specializes in trips to Latin America and other parts of the "Two-Thirds World" (which includes two-thirds of the human population, land mass, and resources). Its objective is to expose participants to poverty, injustice, political instability, unequal allocation of resources, and the dynamics of international social change. Participants talk with poor people as well as with traditional decision-makers. These are intense trips, intended to educate through frequent meetings with everyone from campesinos to refugees, clerics to ambassadors. Trips have included meetings with refugees returning to El Salvador and

Guatemala, stints as election observers in El Salvador, and explorations of causes and effects of violence in other countries. The overall goal is to foster awareness, cooperation, and understanding.

People to People International (**www.ptpi.org**) was founded in 1956 by then-President Dwight D. Eisenhower as a new path to International understanding. Its programs send thousands of American teenagers abroad as student ambassadors. It also arranges for adults to meet professional peers (scientists, doctors, teachers, lawyers, farmers, and so on) and participate in seminars. The idea is to explore common interests through personal contacts. Inquire about its potentially life-changing Global Peace Initiative. Also ask about People to People's Citizen Ambassador Programs (**www.ambassadorprograms.org**).

Franciscan nuns operate Global Awareness Through Experience (GATE) (**www.gate-travel.org**), which offers cultural-immersion programs and women's spiritual quests. It attempts to promote change, especially with respect to equality and justice, in Latin America and Europe. Participants meet spokespersons for the poor and attend meetings of reform movements.

Plowshares Institute (**www.plowsharesinstitute.org**) considers itself a catalyst for social change and sponsors projects that address social justice issues. It offers short-term (e.g., two-and-a-half week) "immersion seminars" and cross-cultural experiences to promote global understanding on the part of North Americans. Trip members meet religious, business, and government leaders. The goal is for participants to return and act on what they learned about issues of global peace and justice. Even though Plowshares is not presently active in Central America and seminar space is always limited, I mention it here because the rewarding nature of the experience makes it worth checking into at some time.

The goals of Global Exchange (**www.globalexchange.org**) include linking people north and south of the equator who are promoting social justice, democracy, and disarmament. Their trips visit Central America, Cuba, Mexico, Vietnam, Brazil, and southern Africa, among other places. Global Exchange is active in efforts such as a literacy project in Honduras.

Trips for Women

To provide opportunities for women to travel in the company of other women, some tour operators specialize in trips for women only. They run the spectrum from relaxing to challenging adventures. I've listed here only some of those whose international trips include Mexico or Central America.

- A*Broad Adventure (**www.abroadadventure.com**): Mexico
- Adventure Associates (**www.adventureassociates.net**): Mexico and Costa Rica
- Adventures in Good Company (**www.adventuresingoodcompany.com**): affordable outdoor and wilderness trips for women, including Mexico (beaches, castles, caves) and the Caribbean (sea kayaking)

- Adventure Women (**www.adventurewomen.com**): adventure trips for active women, including Mexico (sea kayaking), the Caribbean (sailing, snorkeling, scuba), and Costa Rica (nature safari)
- Canyon Calling Tours (**www.canyoncalling.com**): multiactivity adventure trips, including Costa Rica
- Global Awareness Through Experience (**www.gate-travel.org**): offers insight into implications of global economies and politics, including spiritual quest trips to Mexico
- Journey Weavers (**www.journeyweavers.com**): adventure and cultural trips in Costa Rica
- Mariah Wilderness Expeditions (**www.mariahwomen.com**): Costa Rica and Baja (sea kayaking, rafting, hiking, birding, relaxation)
- Women Traveling Together (**www.womentraveling.com**): trips to Mexico and Belize
- Woman's World Travel (**www.womansworldtravel.com**): cultural, gourmet, and adventure trips, including Costa Rica

Trips Designed for Seniors

A reasonably fit older person is safe choosing from among the thousands of tours offered for all ages. That is, as long as he or she reads the tour specs carefully in terms of required fitness. If the brochure is not clear, ask someone on the tour operator's staff. Be honest with yourself about what you prefer and can handle.

Despite the aging population, few tour operators offer trips specifically designed for seniors. However, AARP (**www.aarp.org**) has an Escorted Tours Collection (which includes Central America) for members. The tours are actually operated by established companies such as General Tours and Globus. AARP membership provides a discount in the range of $50 to $300. Although AARP actively markets its activities and products to seniors, its airfare prices are seldom better than general any-age public fares on the big airline sites. However, it sometimes has a 10-percent-off rate on flights to Mexico.

For international trips with great educational value and specifically designed for seniors, consider Elderhostel (**www.elderhostel.org**). Eldertreks (**www.eldertreks.com**) offers "soft adventure tours" (including Costa Rica) but, as always, check the activity level. Grand Circle Travel (**www.gct.com**) is also known to tailor its itineraries for seniors (and includes Mexico, Costa Rica, and Guatemala).

When evaluating any tour brochure check whether the itinerary and pace are suitable for seniors and whether there's a discount for having achieved senior status. Senior discounts still exist, mostly for hotels, but they are fewer and smaller than in the past. That means seniors should learn how to compete for the best deals in the all-ages market. In addition to *Traveler's Tool Kit*, take a look at **www.seniorsomething.com** (see the "Travel" section for information and links), **www.suite101.com** (see "Travel"), and **www.smartertravel.com** (see the "Senior" section and the monthly newsletter).

A final thought. Anyone with limited mobility ought to ask the tour operator whether climbing stairs in hotels will be necessary.

Adventure Travel

Adventure-travel trips, fairly expensive and often physically demanding, appeal primarily to comparatively affluent people in their late 20s to late 40s. Trips range from "gravity adventures," such as whitewater rafting, bungee jumping, and tandem skydiving, to "soft adventures" that combine the exploration of wilderness with considerable creature comforts. One operator, reflecting the spirit of many, bills itself as a "broker of your dreams."

Adventure-travel tour operators, of whom there are more than 10,000 in the United States alone, offer trips through some areas so remote or undeveloped that arranging a journey on your own would be a logistical nightmare. Some trips involve real danger, but more often guides work hard to convey the feeling of adventure and challenge without placing clients at undue risk.

Most tour operators grade their trips in terms of physical demands. Because getting in over your head guarantees an unhappy trip, pay attention to these grades. If a trip isn't graded, ask. When considering an adventure trip, get opinions from several people who have taken that specific trip.

I'll mention a few adventure-tour operators that, in my experience, offer especially high-quality trips. Mountain Travel Sobek (**www.mtsobek.com**) has built a fine reputation for its mountain and river trips (and its brochure is a visual treat). It charges more than most of its competitors, but superior equipment, experience, and services may justify the price. The company sometimes invites you to join it on an "exploratory" expedition (such as the first descent of a wild river). Of course, you return the compliment by paying a considerable fee. Unfortunately, you've missed the opportunity to join its first circumnavigation of Greenland: 25 days on an icebreaker for only $19,900. (I wonder if the company thought a flat $20,000 looked like too much?)

Wilderness Travel (**www.wildernesstravel.com**) offers more than 100 trips on five continents, including some to Mexico and Central America. It holds its group size to a maximum of 15.

Journeys International (**www.journeys.travel**) offers more than 300 trips in 35 countries (including Mexico, Guatemala, Belize, Panama, and Costa Rica). Journeys also sponsors trail-cleanup, monastery-restoration, and solar-heating projects. Wildland Adventures (**www.wildland.com**) established the Travelers Conservation Trust, which supports community projects promoting environmental or cultural preservation.

Many other fine companies emphasize a specific geographic or activity niche. For example, Earth River Expeditions (**www.earthriver.com**) pioneered the world-class whitewater run down the Futaleufu River in Chile and is considering expanding into Central America. Outdoor Adventure River Specialists, better known as OARS (**www.oars.com**), specializes in highly challenging white-water-river trips and, like Earth River, is respected for its commitment to preserving ecosystems.

You can organize many of these trips by yourself, possibly at a lower cost, but doing so requires considerable effort and a high tolerance for ambiguity (because some arrangements can't be made until you're on the ground near where the adventure starts). You can also join local tours. Safaris in Africa are an excellent example. Joining a safari locally is not difficult—and the savings are great. In contrast, whitewater and mountaineering trips are particularly difficult to arrange on your own. In addition to logistical issues, risk goes up greatly in the absence of guides expert in the ways of the river or mountain.

The adventure-travel business is generally unregulated, so it's up to you to separate experienced, reliable operators from underfinanced, uninsured companies run out of someone's basement. Ask questions, and ask for references.

Work

I haven't set out on the road specifically for a work experience, but thousands of travelers have. An English friend traveled for three years, stopping to take jobs once in a while to pay for her trip. She's picked fruit in New Zealand, worked in a restaurant in Hong Kong, and acted as a nanny in India. She always earned enough to finance her forward progress.

The Archaeological Institute of America (**www.archaeological.org**) will send you its Archeological Fieldwork Opportunities Bulletin, which lists scores of domestic and overseas digs. The Web site also contains an online version of the bulletin. Be aware that the location affects your opportunities to meet local people, so choose carefully. You may pay something for room and board, but you may also receive a small salary. No experience in archaeology is required. Before you sign up, be clear on the nature of the work—and how hot it's likely to be.

Earthwatch Institute (**www.earthwatch.org**) will, for a fee, volunteer your services for work on a worthwhile project. These expeditions typically involve hard work, sometimes in challenging surroundings, but require no specialized skills. Trips include digging for woolly mammoth, camel, and giant armadillo fossils in Mexico in order to learn about migrations between continents, and analyzing artifacts to learn the role of ceremonial caves in the religion of the Maya. I met Earthwatch volunteers measuring water quality on the island of Roatán off the coast of Honduras. Although the volunteers seemed to be minoring in scuba diving, their valuable work may lead to a reduction in waterborne diseases among the island's population.

If you're interested in overseas employment, take copies of your résumé as you travel and plant them where they might mature into a full-time job. You can get a job overseas while at home, but it's far more effective to introduce yourself as you're passing through. If you're interested in working abroad, review the discussion on work permits in Chapter 7, Going into Action.

Homestays

World Learning, operating in 77 countries, arranges homestays (**www.world learning.org**). Let them know the dates and country you prefer. The opportunity to stay in a family home, long available to students during the summer, is now available to adults throughout the year. During a homestay of one to four weeks, you gain understanding quite different from that available to a traveler staying in commercial lodging, hopping from place to place. There's a fee to the organization (averaging less than $500 for a two-week stay), but little or nothing goes to the family with whom you stay. The family offers its hospitality for the same reasons you would.

Servas (**www.servas.org**) organizes a network of hosts and travelers with the objective of facilitating world peace and understanding. It can put you in touch with host families in 125 countries for free homestays of 2 to 14 days. In turn, you have an opportunity to act as a host for international travelers under the same program. People rave about these experiences.

The Friendship Force (**www.friendshipforce.org**), actively supported by Jimmy and Rosalynn Carter, sends groups of 15 to 30 people to various countries to spend a week with host families (more than 500,000 people have gone to 55 countries since 1977). Participants spend a second week traveling in-country. The emphasis is on personal contact or, as the group puts it, "faces, not places."

TOUR OPERATORS ACTIVE IN MEXICO AND CENTRAL AMERICA

Hundreds of tour operators are eager to sign up prospective clients to visit Mexico and Central America. Here's a short list of tour companies that have strong reputations for responsible travel and that don't spend the days shuttling 45 clients around in buses as guides point at passing wonders. This is only a sampling, and there are undoubtedly other fine organizations. (Please also see the lists of tour operators for each country in Chapter 3, Destinations.)

- Adventure Life (**www.adventure-life.com**) runs small-group tours in four Central American countries, with a variety of choices in each. It employs qualified local guides, emphasizes eco-friendly practices, and makes sure money goes to locally owned inns and restaurants.
- G.A.P Adventures (**www.gapadventures.com**), based in Canada, began by operating "sustainable tourism" trips to Latin America. It now covers much of the world but is still very active in Mexico and all of Central America, taking travelers on low-impact, reasonably priced trips that put money into local communities.

Code of Ethics for Nature and Culture Travelers

1. Aspire to invisibility (observe but do not disturb natural systems);
2. Vanish without a trace (minimize your impact on the environment);
3. Seize the power of your experience (act directly to accomplish conservation); and
4. Reverse missionary zeal (respect local cultures).

- Intrepid Travel (**www.intrepidtravel.com**) has been active since 1989 with a mission to enrich clients' lives by creating unique, interactive travel experiences.
- Adventure Center (**www.adventurecenter.com**) is committed to affordable, ecologically sound trips that benefit local communities economically. It runs immersion trips throughout Central America.
- Culture Xplorers (**www.culturexplorers.com**) operates trips to Mexico and Guatemala, encouraging cultural interaction and making a positive impact on communities it visits.
- Djoser (**www.djoser.com**) is a Dutch company operating affordable, active tours in Costa Rica, Panama, and Mexico.
- Global Exchange (**www.globalexchange.org**) provides "reality-based tours" in impoverished areas of Mexico, Guatemala, Honduras, Nicaragua, and Costa Rica. As the company puts it in one document: "As we travel across Honduras we will examine the repercussions of neo-liberal globalization in different sectors of society." Its trips will stir you up.
- For a list of adventure (and educational) tour operators, see **www.extremesearcher.com/travel/chap7.html**.

PART THREE: Getting Ready to Go

CHAPTER 7

Going into Action

A journey of a thousand miles must
begin with a single step.
—Lao-tzu
The Way of Lao-tzu

You've decided where you're going, the amount of time you'll take, how much money you'll probably spend, and what time of year you'll leave. Now you're ready to deal with passports, visas, plane tickets, reservations, and the other nuts and bolts of travel. This process, which feels like finding your way through a labyrinth the first time around, will soon be a familiar routine. This chapter will help you solve the puzzle forever.

DOCUMENTS YOU WILL NEED

Passport

What It Is

A passport is a form of identification, issued by a government, that permits the holder to enter and leave his or her own country. However, if you want to enter almost any foreign country, its government will also require that you carry a valid passport issued by your home country. In other words, without a passport, you're tethered to home base. Once you have one, it's like a chocolate bar full of crunchy almonds in your pocket—very hard to resist.

Crossing borders between the United States and Canada or Mexico used to be very informal. It was sufficient to slow down a bit and wave a driver's license at the guard as you crossed. Well, those days are gone, and, sorrowfully, may not return. For reasons related to perceived security, the rules have changed concerning when a passport is required for travel between the United States and Canada, Mexico, Central and South America, and the Caribbean. As of January 23, 2007, all persons, including U.S. citizens, traveling by air between these countries have been required to present a valid passport (or an Air NEXUS card or U.S. Coast Guard Merchant Mariner document). The next step is expansion of that requirement to apply to all persons, including U.S. citizens, traveling between these countries

> When you look like your passport photo, it's time to go home.
> —Erma Bombeck (1975)

by land or sea (including ferries). The timing for that is in the hands of the sometimes-unpredictable Department of Homeland Security.

How to Get Your Passport

To obtain a passport for the first time, go in person to one of more than 9,000 passport-acceptance facilities throughout the United States. Take two photographs of yourself, proof of U.S. citizenship, and a valid form of photo identification, such as a driver's license.

Acceptance facilities include many federal, state, and probate courts, post offices, some public libraries, and a number of county and municipal offices. There are also 13 regional passport agencies that serve customers who are traveling within 14 days or who need foreign visas. Appointments are required in such cases.

You must apply in person if you no longer have your expired passport, or if your previous passport has expired and was issued more than 15 years ago, or if your previous passport was issued when you were younger than 16, or if your currently valid passport has been lost or stolen. To do so:

1. Fill in an "Application for a U.S. Passport" (Form DS-11), which you can get from a passport agency office, post office, or travel agent. This and other passport forms and information are also available at **travel.state.gov.**
2. Show proof of U.S. citizenship in the form of a certified copy of your birth certificate, a naturalization certificate, or a citizenship certificate, or proof that you are a U.S. citizen born abroad. If you can't locate the necessary documents, the passport agency and **travel.state.gov** can suggest substitutes.
3. Provide proof of identity (such as a driver's license or a government or military ID card).
4. Submit two identical 2-by-2-inch photographs (color, front view, no hat or sunglasses, with a plain light background). Vending-machine photos will not be accepted, but there are many alternatives, including those from drugstores, copy shops, camera stores, AAA, and some department stores. Because passport photos convey an impression of your status to a foreign official whose cooperation you may need, it's worth dressing nicely.
5. Pay the correct fee, the amount of which will be on the form.

Make certain that your paperwork is filled out correctly and that you've provided all information requested. Otherwise, your application will be returned, and you will have to resubmit the forms just when you may be running out of time.

If you were issued a passport within the past 15 years and were older than 16 at that time, you may renew using Form DS-82, which you obtain at any of the places from which you can obtain a first-time application. Simply send the application, your old passport, two photos, and the fee to the address on the form. In the past, the normal time required to issue a passport by mail was six weeks, sometimes more. Because situations in which a passport is required have increased, the waiting time now may be 10 to 12 weeks with routine service. When planning a trip, check with the Department of State on current processing times (**travel.state.gov/passport/get/processing/processing_1740.html**). If you become worried and want to check on the status of your application, contact the National Passport Information Center (call [877] 487-2778 or see **travel.state.gov**). Payment of an extra fee gets your application processed within two to three weeks but you may have to demonstrate necessity, rather than procrastination, as the reason. If you're in a bind and have a ticket showing departure within 48 hours, show up in person and throw yourself on some clerk's mercy. If you have good travel karma, you may get almost immediate service, but that's become much less likely. If you have time, send in your application at least three months before your planned departure date. Applications pour in from January through July. Getting your passport isn't optional; why risk disappointment?

It's important to get this message: obtaining a passport takes even longer than it used to. Start early.

A travel agent can handle the passport-application process for you, or you can hire a professional service. If you use a service, the charge would be $35 or more for seven-day service and $100 or more for same-day service. Plan ahead and spend the extra money on a tour through the Costa Rica cloud forest instead.

Passport pages provide spaces for visas, some of which take up a full page. Furthermore, when you enter most countries—whether they require a visa or not—your passport will be vigorously hand-stamped, perhaps more than once. You may collect additional stamp imprints as you travel within a country, and the stamp will strike again on your way out. To make it worse, some officials disdain

> Request a passport with the greatest number of pages allowed.

putting their country's stamp anywhere except on a blank page. The result is that visa pages of those who visit many different countries will fill up quickly, requiring application for a new passport well before the current one expires.

SAVE Money Here are a couple of ways to save money by delaying purchase of a new passport. First, when your visa pages are mostly filled, use an Application for Additional Visa Pages (Form DS-4085) to extend the life of your passport. You can also pick up extra pages at any U.S. consulate while you travel. Second, do your best to guide the person with the stamp to minimize the space he or she uses.

Expiration

Don't let yourself be surprised by a sharp-eyed immigration officer who discovers that your passport has just expired. If you'll be on the road when your passport expires, renew before you leave. Some countries will not issue a visa unless your passport has at least six months of life remaining at the time of entry. I've heard of an occasional immigration officer raising this objection and then happily waiving it upon receipt of a small gratuity. If you arrive home with an expired passport, you may be subject to a fine. For more information about passports, go to **travel.state.gov/passport.**

Visas

What They Are

A visa is a document issued by a foreign government permitting the holder to enter its country and stay for a limited period of time. A visa usually takes the form of a rubber-stamp impression inked on a page of a passport, but may also be a postage-type stamp or a sheet of paper stapled or glued into the passport.

Who Needs Them

At the moment, about 90 countries require nationals of at least some other countries to obtain a visa. It's common for a country to require nationals of some countries to obtain a visa while permitting nationals from other countries to enter without one.

At present, Canada, Mexico, Caribbean, and western-European countries do not require U.S. citizens to have a visa to enter. Within Central America, a relatively new agreement among El Salvador, Nicaragua, Honduras, and Guatemala allows travelers to cross those borders freely after paying a single entry fee. If a border official doesn't volunteer this information and asks for an additional fee, just remind him gently of the agreement.

It would be a disservice to provide a list of countries that require visas because requirements change frequently, and out-of-date information could create serious inconvenience. To find out if a country requires a visa and what its conditions are, see **travel.state.gov/travel/cis_pa_tw/cis/cis_1765.html.** This site also includes links and contact information for the countries' embassies in Washington, D.C.

Check whether special permits are required for internal travel. If you contemplate an extended stay, see if an HIV test is required (it is in more than 40 countries). The American Automobile Association (AAA) is another reliable source of information about visa requirements.

If you ask your travel agent which countries on your itinerary require visas, be sure the answer is based on fact, not assumption. Of course, travelers make assumptions too. An experienced travel agent told me that any time a client of hers bought an airline ticket to a country that required a visa, she would write on the ticket: "Don't forget your visa." That worked until one client, upon arriving in Taiwan, reached into his wallet and produced—what else?—his VISA credit card.

If you ask other travelers about visa requirements, it's better not to rely on their answers. The information may be out of date or involve special circumstances of which you are unaware. You don't want to be standing at the border when you hear the bad news.

At the Border

Even having a visa in hand does not guarantee entry into a country. Some countries require that you also have sufficient funds to pay for your stay and an outbound ticket in hand. These seemingly inhospitable requirements were usually reactions to impoverished students and hippies who streamed around the world in the 1960s. Bureaucrats wanted to make sure these joyful visitors had the means to move on. Now they may also be motivated by concern about immigrant workers who cross the border and forget to leave. These requirements can come up anywhere from Zimbabwe to Great Britain when authorities suspect you may intend to set up housekeeping. If you don't have an onward ticket, be prepared to make the case that you have the intention and means to keep going.

Ask your travel agent to check the Internet to see whether you will run into an onward-ticket requirement. If so, purchase a fully refundable plane ticket for a short leg out of the country. If you decide not to use it, cash it in later. Alternatively, a few travelers carry a Miscellaneous Change Order (MCO). An MCO is not a ticket. It's more like a cashier's check, showing that you have a guaranteed credit in a specified amount that can be used to pay for a plane ticket. An MCO is easily converted into cash when you return. If you want an MCO, ask your travel agent, or get it directly from an airline.

Another inexpensive alternative is to buy a bus ticket to another country. This is an "onward ticket," and you can get most of the cost refunded if you cancel a few days in advance.

Although immigration officials have discretionary authority to bar a traveler from entry, that happens rarely. When it does, it's almost always at an overland border crossing rather than an airport. For that reason, I think of a border crossing as a one-act play and dress for the part by wearing my most normal clothes and being as well groomed as circumstances permit. I approach with a smile, say something courteous, and am prepared to be patient. On the other hand, anyone with an urge to spend a few hours broiling in the sun outside a crumbling, concrete guard shack on some remote border crossing should challenge the guard's authority, throw in some vulgar language, and assert his own importance back home.

Should there be a problem, stay calm, and follow any reasonable instruction, such as to open your luggage. If the situation is prolonged or threatens to get out of hand, ask for the guard's superior officer.

At a checkpoint entrance to West Sikkim, in the state of Sikkim, India, a young, smartly uniformed guard sitting at a scarred table under a tree pointed out that the visa in my passport permitted travel to Gangtok, the capital of Sikkim, but said nothing about traveling into West Sikkim. He had me, and we both knew it. After flipping through my passport for a full three minutes, he tossed it aside on his desk without comment and dismissed me with a lackadaisical backhand flip of his wrist. I sat at the base of a tree, staying within sight but not pressing him. After about 20 minutes, I approached his table again. This time, I mentioned that I was actually *leaving* Sikkim by a circuitous route that only at the moment happened to be going away from the border. Satisfied that he had demonstrated his authority, he stamped my passport vehemently and held it out to me without a glance. I'd played the game properly, and he was satisfied.

Different Types of Visas

Visas come in several versions: transit, business, student, resident, immigration, employment, and tourist. The two most important to travelers are transit and tourist. A transit visa permits only a short-term visit. Its purpose is to give you time to dash into a principal city or visit a particular sight, then continue your journey. The longer-term tourist visa is what most travelers need.

Each visa indicates its type, its length or dates of validity, and the number of times you are permitted to enter the country. Normally, a visa permits a single entry. If you foresee entering, leaving, and returning to the same country, you'll need a multiple-entry visa. If you don't have a multiple-entry visa, you may be able to purchase a new visa at the border. If not, you'll have to backtrack to a major city in another country. The fee for multiple entry is greater than for a single-visa entry, but less than you would pay if you bought a new visa for each entry.

> In the Middle Ages people were tourists because of their religion, whereas now they are tourists because tourism is their religion.
> —Robert Runcie, Archbishop of Canterbury

Visas are valid only for a specified length of time, usually 30 to 90 days, but that figure can range from a week to a year. If the period starts on the date the visa is issued, and you won't get to the country for a while, the time limit could pose a problem.

If you'd like to stay put for a while, retiring in sunny Mexico or Panama, you will eventually need a residency visa or permit. Most people arrive on a tourist visa, then sort out the residency requirements. That may require leaving the country to start the visa clock ticking again. The retirement-opportunities guides listed in the country sections in Chapter 3 cover these requirements in detail.

Applying for a Visa

A government wants some idea why you're entering its country and where you want to go. When answering questions on a visa application, I recommend against listing your occupation as writer or reporter, or stating affiliation with any military, government, or international organization, or anything else that could be interpreted as meaning you would be inspecting their country. Any

Store It in Your Mind-safe

Memorize your passport number, the city in which it was issued, and the dates of issue and expiration. Otherwise, you have to pull out your money belt every time you fill out an immigration or hotel-registration form.

remotely prestigious occupation is enough to establish credibility; ones such as "teacher" and "manager" seem to make officials happy.

If forms ask for a local address, officials are satisfied with the name of any moderately upscale hotel. Even "hotel" is usually sufficient. When it inquires about "religion," the question may be loaded in some countries. You have a choice. If answering "none" feels okay, that's probably safest. You could finesse the issue by putting "nondenominational" or leaving it blank. If a form asks about your itinerary, list everywhere you might possibly go. Under "length of stay," ask for the maximum the visa allows. Give yourself the widest latitude in case the official limits you to what you asked for. Have a passport photo handy just in case the form requires it.

Don't underestimate how long it may take to obtain visas. While some are issued automatically, obtaining others can be time-consuming. You might get it in a few days, or it might take several weeks. If a country is reluctant to admit visitors or is especially bureaucratic, you can be in for a challenging experience. It may reduce your frustration if you realize that the United States is notorious for making it difficult for foreigners to obtain visas to visit. Here's the kicker: when you've sent your passport to one embassy with your visa application, you may not be able to apply for visas from other countries.

Fortunately, U.S. and Canadian citizens visiting Mexico and Central America don't need to obtain visas in advance unless staying beyond the permitted period—30 days to six months.

SAVE Money If you need a fast turnaround, expect to pay more. Plan ahead and save money.

If you apply in person, a clerk will tell you when to return for the visa. If you apply by mail, the issue date is less certain. Although travel agents and tour operators are usually reliable in obtaining visas, it's your responsibility to follow up relentlessly until the visas are in hand.

In the great majority of cases, it's much easier to obtain a visa before leaving home than while on the road. You have plenty of time and don't have to deal with a foreign language muddled by bureaucratese. In fact, unless you're certain of the practice, it's risky to arrive at a border without a visa hoping

> It's usually easier to obtain a visa at home than on the road.

that some official will issue a point-of-entry visa on the spot. It's possible to obtain most visas abroad, but you may have to detour to a city where the visa can be issued—and the office may be closed when you get there. In any case, your forward motion will stop while you wait (and wait and wait) for the visa to be issued. You may even discover that you just can't get the visa you want, or you can get it only by complying with some requirement, such as joining a tour group. If there is a restriction, discover it at home when you have plenty of time to dance the bureaucratic break dance rather than on the road in the turmoil of a crowded visa office.

When you give up your passport abroad when applying for a visa or for any other reason, always ask for a receipt.

If you decide to get your visas as you travel, find out from the appropriate consulates exactly where to get their visas abroad. Some guidebooks provide this information. Bring extra photos in case the application requires one.

Fees

Fees for visas vary greatly. While most fees range from $15 to $50, they may soon emulate the price of gas. Call ahead to ensure that you send the correct fee. If you send the wrong fee, your application may be returned unprocessed.

Visa Services

Another approach in obtaining a visa is to employ a professional service. If you search the Internet for "visa services," most sites you find will tell you the visa requirements for each country. You pay generously for their assistance. They charge $30 to $100 per visa, plus postage and the cost of the visa itself. These services fill in the forms and hand-carry them, with your photos, International Health Certificate (if required), and passport, from embassy to embassy. Knowing embassy personnel helps them speed up the process.

Tell the service the date you want each visa to become effective. As I mentioned earlier, a visa has a time boundary, so don't let it become effective so far in advance of your arrival that you have to cut your visit short. Give the service a date by which you want the visas returned to you. Follow up periodically to monitor its progress. When it returns your passport and visas, check to ensure you received all the visas you requested.

Search the Web for "visa services," or check the Yellow Pages under "Passport and Visa Services."

Visa Expiration

Rather than overstay the expiration date of a visa, pay a fee and get an extension, or, if you must, leave the country and return with a new visa. If you overstay, you become an illegal alien, subject to fine, deportation, and arrest. You might be lucky enough to blow by the border official on the way out without being noticed, but if they catch you, there will probably be a fine.

Special Permits

At present, travelers are unlikely to need a special permit to visit any locations or to undertake any activities in Mexico or Central America. However, because special permits are sometimes required elsewhere, they merit a few words of explanation. For example, because authorities want to keep track of who is wandering where, many treks on Himalayan trails require a permit. If you don't reappear, they know, more or less, where to look for you. Sometimes a permit is required to take photographs. The fee is small for regular cameras but is often high for video cameras.

Some permits are a bureaucratic way of enforcing an unofficial policy. Suppose a government doesn't want visitors to a certain part of its country. Rather than say that, it simply requires a permit and then makes it impossible to get one.

Permits also are used to protect natural resources. The Rwandan government permits only a few people a day, usually about two dozen, to climb the mountainsides to see gorilla families. Travelers who reach Rwanda without this permit in hand are likely to find all permits sold.

> Some countries require you to register with police upon arrival.

To sustain Milford Track's reputation as "the finest walk in the world," New Zealand officials regulate the number of people on trails and in huts. The permit is expensive, and months may pass before it's issued. Peru does the same to protect the Inca Trail hike to Machu Picchu.

Another type of permit is the requirement in a few countries that you register with the police within 24 hours of arrival. This requirement is noted in guidebooks and is usually brought to your attention by a point-of-entry official. Your hotel clerk will probably take care of it for you. That service should be a freebie, but an appropriate tip is a good investment. To avoid a fine when you're ready to leave the country, follow up to ensure that the registration occurred.

Many permits can be obtained only on the spot, but those that can be acquired at home should be. If your travel plans include any place or activity out of the norm, check with a travel agent or the country's consulate to see whether a permit is required.

Work Permits

For a professional looking for permanent employment abroad, the job search is very different from that of someone on an extended vacation seeking low-skilled, seasonal work. For one thing, it's almost impossible to conduct a successful country-specific job search before leaving home. That's one reason professionals are most often hired by U.S.-based organizations that send Americans abroad: private-sector companies, nongovernmental organizations, or government departments. Such employers choose the country where they need you and will take care of your work visa.

International employers are rarely multinational manufacturing companies, such as General Motors, but more often organizations involved in resource extraction, management consulting, international finance, trade promotion, diplomacy, and international development.

For such jobs, entrance requirements are stiff. In many cases, these are career-track jobs where you may be expected to understand cross-cultural negotiations, be able to communicate effectively in a cross-cultural work environment, and be aware of the business cultures of specific countries.

Travelers Looking for Work Abroad

For the backpacking world traveler who wants to find work in a specific country or for the retiree looking for extra income while living abroad, getting a work permit is always a challenge. Before you leave home, find out what's required. Because it's so difficult to get a permit and maybe an extended visa as well, it would be unwise to depend on earning money you'll need as you travel.

Many countries are flooded by refugees seeking work. To protect jobs for their own citizens, regions with depressed economies often simply exclude outside labor. At least in theory, employers can be heavily penalized for hiring people who lack official work permits.

Your best chance of getting a work permit is to possess a specialized skill that's in short supply and high demand in the country where you want to work. In addition, before you arrive, you may have to find an employer who will give you a written offer of employment. Not many travelers can pull that off in advance.

There Are Other Ways

There are alternative ways to earn income abroad. Organizations can secure a short-term visa for work in many of the most popular destinations. Sponsors of these "work abroad" programs include the British Universities North American Club (**www.bunac.org**), the Council on International Education Exchange (**www.ciee.org**) and, for Canadians, the Canadian Federation of Students' SWAP Working Holidays (**www.swap.ca**). Originally offering programs for students or persons under the age of 30, organizations such as these are increasingly offering programs with no age restrictions. For a reasonable fee, the organization will obtain your authorization to work and give you a list of potential employers, general tips on employment, and information on living in the country. There will often be a representative on-site to assist your hunt for a job and lodging. If you're willing to take a subsistence-level job to support yourself and cover costs of some local travel, you will most likely be successful with this approach.

While in your chosen country with a short-term work visa in hand (usually valid for six months), you research the domestic job market and write one or more résumés specifically for that market. These jobs tend to be in the retail and service sectors and are often seasonal or tourist oriented. Working in a pub or

National Institute of Statistics, Flores, Guatemala

hotel and picking grapes are examples. Take the initiative and make face-to-face contact with potential employers. In these circumstances, communicating with employers at a distance, say by e-mail, is not very effective. Impress employers with your charm and personality through an in-person sales pitch.

Many organizations also offer summer work camps, or volunteer and internship programs, in countries throughout the Americas. As odd as it sounds, you usually must pay a fee to volunteer to work on a local project, although room and board may be supplied. In addition to supporting the project, you meet people from other countries, learn a foreign language, and experience another culture. Typical projects include historical-site restoration, well-digging, housing rehabilitation, an archaeological dig, historic preservation, forestry, and working with children, elderly persons, and people with disabilities.

Now, let's be honest. An awful lot of people with a tourist visa but no work permit find off-the-books, temporary jobs. Although the usual employers of travelers are tourist establishments, restaurants, and farms, you may be able to land an unofficial job of almost any kind: working as a nanny, working for other foreigners living abroad, applying some specialized knowledge you have by contacting employers in your field. Many travelers have at least one skill they can market in any economy: knowledge about business at home, potentially valuable to someone wanting to export goods to your home market.

These jobs are short term and require little or no paperwork. As with so many things in life, success depends on taking the initiative. For example, watch for English-language menus, brochures, store-window signs, and other forms of advertising that contain incorrect grammar or spelling. Step up and offer your services as an editor. Travelers regularly trade meals in return for correcting a restaurant's menu. Connect with the expatriate community, and job leads may pop up.

Study abroad at a university for one semester, and make enough contacts to find employment. In some countries, rules are relaxed for foreign students, making it easier to get a job legally. Studying language abroad is another way of making local job contacts. Besides earning the income, you're learning the language and perhaps moving toward career goals.

For example, an environmentalist might study Spanish in Costa Rica for four months and then backpack through neighboring countries offering English-translation services and environmental expertise to ecotourism companies writing trail guides. Or a business student might set up an accounting system on Quicken for a nongovernmental organization.

A practical way to subsidize your travels is by teaching English while abroad. A billion or more people in the world want to learn English, and many of them are in Latin America. You're very employable if you have a bachelor's degree (although a couple of years of college will often suffice) and have completed a one-week TESOL (Teaching English to Speakers of Other Languages) or TEFL (Teaching English as a Foreign Language) course. You can easily find work as a teacher in a language school, as an independent private instructor, as a nanny teaching English to children, or as a professor at an international school catering to foreigners (this last case requires top credentials). In a few countries, it's very easy to get a work permit to teach English. In most countries, it is easy to teach unofficially without a work permit.

A very good reference on the subject of working overseas is *The BIG Guide to Living and Working Overseas* by Jean-Marc Hachey (**www.workingoverseas .com**). Another fine resource is *Transitions Abroad* magazine (**www.transitions abroad.com**), including its Directory to Overseas Employment. Then there are: *Teaching English Abroad* and *Work Your Way around the World,* both by Susan Griffith; *Jobs and Careers Abroad,* current edition by Guy Hobbs; and *Jobs for People Who Love to Travel,* both by Ron and Caryl Krannich.

English-language newspapers published abroad list job opportunities (please see "Resources" listed for specific countries in Chapter 3).

When you see ads in North American newspapers promising high-paying jobs abroad, be skeptical. They may be legitimate—or the first move in a scam intended to extract money from you. If you line up a job through correspondence, satisfy yourself, perhaps through a reconnaissance trip, that you know enough about the foreign country to be sure it's worth making the commitment.

Or ask to speak to others already working there. That friendly recruiter is usually a sales rep working on commission.

Airline Tickets

SAVE Money Airfare is such a major part of travel costs that it's one of the best opportunities to use your knowledge to save money. Most people—from habit, caution, or whatever—buy all their tickets before they leave home. However, doing that deprives you of the opportunity to buy tickets abroad at lower prices. It also commits you to be at certain airports on certain dates, curtailing flexibility and freedom. Whether to pack that albatross in your luggage deserves serious thought.

There are several situations in which you should buy your airline tickets before leaving home:

- When you're going to an area where flights are infrequent, which means they're often fully booked. One approach is to buy fully refundable tickets in the United States for the entire itinerary, treating the extra cost of refundability as an insurance premium. If you can buy a segment cheaper as you travel, do so, and get a refund on that segment when you get home. If you can't buy a significantly cheaper ticket, at least you won't be left standing in the airport.
- When an air pass must be bought before arriving in the country in which you'll use it. TACA offers an ever-changing air pass for its routes in Mexico and Central America. Check its Web site (**www.taca.com**) for details.
- When you'll be traveling to or from a popular resort area in high season.

For much more information on buying airline tickets, please see Chapter 4, How to Plan Your Trip, and Chapter 8, How to Save Money.

HOTEL RESERVATIONS

Many travelers venturing for the first time to foreign countries take it for granted they should make hotel reservations before leaving home. Travel agents say many of their clients make reservations for every night of the trip, while others reserve a hotel room for at least their first night out and the night before they fly home. Making reservations is common for travelers heading for an event likely to fill a city. Others make reservations because they've heard that a certain hotel is so splendid, they're determined to stay there.

The bottom line: most people make reservations to reduce concern about the unknown. A reservation is a security blanket, ensuring that there will be a room in a safe location at an acceptable price. It also eliminates the need to spend time selecting lodgings on arrival, perhaps while struggling with an unfamiliar language.

If you decide to make reservations, please see the criteria discussed in Chapter 15, Lodging.

How to Make Reservations

If a standard-brand hotel is okay, and you don't care much about the cost, it's probably easiest to let your travel agent handle the reservation. If you prefer to have a hand in the process, you need information.

All U.S.-based hotel chains with international operations have toll-free numbers and Web sites. However, you won't get the best deals by talking to a central operator staring at a computer screen full of standard prices that don't reflect how eager a certain hotel is for your business. Nor is the operator likely to know many of the particulars of the hotel, such as the best rooms or views (let alone the location of noisy ice machines).

Instead, check the Web site or do an Internet search for the direct-dial number of the hotel location you want. Many of the international chains based in other countries also have toll-free numbers in the United States. If not, look up the local number on the Internet. After the hotel quotes a rate, ask about special package deals, corporate rates, and other discounts. Say you're willing to pay a certain amount and ask what the hotel has available. By the way, if you're quoted a "double occupancy" rate or a "double room" rate for lodging outside the United States, be clear on the definition of the term. The former often means that *each* of two people pays the quoted amount (and that's always the case when it's "per person, double occupancy"). "Double room" is the total price of the room.

There are many sources of information about hotels around the world. Here are a few ideas:

- The Internet pulsates with organizations dedicated to finding you a place to sleep. One is Utell Hotels & Resorts (**www.utell.com**), a reservation service with nearly 4,000 member hotels in more than 140 countries. Its hotels range from small independents to international chains and from tourist class to deluxe. It charges no fee. Hotel Reservation Service offers thousands of hotels worldwide, many of which can be reviewed at **www.hrs.com.**

- Use the Internet to contact tourism offices abroad. Furthermore, almost any site related to tourism will be flooded with ads for hotels, inns, bed-and-breakfasts, and so on. The owners of a lot of cozy lodgings around the world have learned to make themselves visible on the Internet, so, with a little effort, you can find a place almost anywhere. However, booking online may not get you the best prices (and may cost you a surcharge). Also, online reservations have been known not to "take," so get a confirmation.

- Professional Travel Guide (**www.professionaltravelguide.com**) covers more than 160,000 hotels, including reviews by professionals, and posts international travel guides and travel news. It doesn't book trips, so it's unbiased.

- Good guidebooks give you information on locally owned hotels and list phone numbers and Web addresses of recommended hotels.

- Check out lodging used by small-tour operators (because they obviously approve of the property and the management). For example, the Backroads brochure (**www.backroads.com**) lists a fine group of inns at which its bicycle tours stop.
- Travel agencies have lists of thousands of hotels at home and overseas. Asking a travel agent at your destination to suggest hotels can sometimes lead to great recommendations.
- Fax machines minimize language barriers and let you exchange information with foreign hotels quickly and easily.
- Draw from other travelers (including reports in *International Travel News* and on Internet chat sites).

Reasons Not to Make Reservations

Travelers suggest five main arguments against making hotel reservations in advance:

- If a hotel abroad has spent enough on advertising to be known here, its rates are likely to be pretty high. According to the *Wall Street Journal,* rates at "name" international hotels are setting records. You can't assume that reasonably priced domestic hotel chains are equally reasonable overseas—just one more reason to stay away from the big hotel chains. As a rule, you'll spend a lot more on hotel rooms if you make reservations from home.
- Upscale hotels overseas tend to be cocoons for well-heeled tourists, insulating them from the rich texture of local life.
- Using reservations to ensure that you aren't shut out by NO VACANCY signs is unnecessary except in a few very popular destinations or during large special events.
- If you reserve and do not or cannot show up, you will lose your deposit, and maybe more, if you don't cancel well ahead of scheduled arrival. Similarly, if you check out early, you still may have to pay for the entire period reserved. Try to avoid reserving with a credit-card number (say you'll be paying cash).
- Most important, a reservation is a commitment to be at a certain place on a specified date. That may not sound bad before you leave home, but it can become a serious restriction on your freedom once you're on the road.

After you've been traveling for a while, the security of having a reservation no longer feels necessary. You know what to expect. You've learned that lodging is easy to find locally by using guidebooks, tourist-information offices, tips from other travelers, and your own common sense. Throughout the world, hotels, lodges, inns, guesthouses, pensions, bungalows, youth hostels, and a dozen other forms of lodging compete vigorously for your business. Something will be available with the amenities and price that suit you. As you reminisce years from now, you'll remember the funky, family-style lodging and its proprietors, not international chains.

Exceptions

A few circumstances might lead even an experienced traveler to make advance reservations:

- If you'll be flying into a city late at night and flying out early the next day
- If lodging is in short supply
- If your destination is a specific resort
- If you're a woman arriving solo, especially late in the evening

Otherwise, I always opt for the freedom of winging it.

SAVE Money To save money when booking rooms, please see Chapter 8, How to Save Money. Please also see Chapter 15, Lodging, for tips on how to find superior, affordable lodging anywhere in the world while paying a fair price.

ADVENTURES

By "adventures," I mean activities such as safaris, whitewater-river trips, treks, and so on. During the planning phase, you decide whether to make arrangements at home through a U.S. tour operator, at home through a tour operator based in the destination country, or after reaching that country.

The first option usually means you'll get a reliable, high-quality product and you'll be traveling with other Americans. Many people routinely do this, paying for advertising, intermediaries, and upscale amenities. The second option can also result in a high-quality product, but you must carefully research the reputation of the tour operator. The group with which you travel is likely to be more international—and the price may be considerably lower. The Internet has made this option very viable.

People pay higher prices to avoid uncertainty when arriving in a foreign country. That's understandable. Time is also a factor. If you make the arrangements at home, you hit the ground running when you get there. Otherwise, you may burn a day or two getting something organized locally. For example, raft trips in Costa Rica may leave only on set days of the week.

On the other hand, if you book an adventure from home to begin on a specific date, that's your date—foul weather or not. But if you book locally, you can probably move departure up or back fairly easily.

SAVE Money Arranging an adventure when you're at or near the local site is also an excellent way to save money. I've saved 50 percent or more compared to what I'd have paid for a similar, though sometimes more luxurious, trip I could have booked at home through a tour operator or travel agent. Often, the local company actually running the trip is the same in both cases.

Arranging adventures while abroad requires a little effort, but it's not nearly as difficult as it might seem from a distance. In foreign countries, outfitters and tour operators seek you out and are often willing to tailor their services to your desires.

SAVE Money If cost is the controlling factor, you're better off making arrangements locally. Please see Chapter 8 for tips on how to save money when arranging an adventure.

TRAVEL INSURANCE

Let's face it: insurance is not a fun topic. Not only are policy terms complicated, but insurance decisions also require thinking about things that could go wrong—and no one wants to do that when planning a great trip. Nevertheless, I suggest considering insurance because a few people do experience losses while traveling. A camera disappears, there's a bill for medical services in a foreign hospital, or it becomes necessary to cancel a trip after sending in a large deposit. Odds are good that none of this will happen, and in later chapters we'll discuss how to make the odds even better. Still, a prudent traveler should at least understand insurance options.

As with other forms of insurance, terms of travel insurance are understood by practically no one, at least not until after a loss. Let's improve our understanding by dividing travel insurance into three types of coverage: personal property, trip interruption or cancellation, and medical or evacuation. There are also three types of trips—tour, cruise, and independent travel—and insurance coverage differs for each.

A typical cruise package might cover trip cancellation or interruption, lost luggage, evacuation, health care onboard, and hospitalization onboard. Cruise-related insurance does not depend on age.

For tours as well as cruises, the operator will likely offer insurance packages. Premiums for tour insurance are often based upon the cost of the trip and the age of the client.

Ask if your policy covers losses overseas.

An increasing number of operators even require that clients buy insurance. They promote insurance for a couple of reasons. First, they get paid a commission. Second, if there's a problem and it's covered by insurance, you are not likely to go after the operator or travel agent.

When you travel independently, you have to put together an insurance package yourself. Using an online search engine, you can type in "travel insurance," "evacuation insurance," and so on, and be swamped with pitches from companies wanting your business. Your task is to decide whether you need additional coverage and, if so, what questions to ask about coverages. So that's what we'll discuss on the following pages.

Personal Property

You may already have some personal-property coverage for losses overseas. Check your homeowners, renters, or automobile insurance and your credit-card agreements. Even if you're not covered, many insurance companies offer low-cost riders to existing policies.

If you're not covered, should you buy insurance? The answer depends on how insurance-conscious you are at home, how inherently risky your trip will be, which risks would be covered, which would be excluded, and what premium you would pay.

The insurance industry reports that half of all claims relate to loss of baggage and personal effects. Airlines accept only limited liability for luggage they lose. If you have coverage, it has a deductible. On balance, insurance that covers lost baggage alone seems disproportionately expensive, especially considering the exclusions.

Terms of insurance policies vary widely from company to company. Ask exactly what would be covered. Lost luggage? Lost cash? What about the loss of specific items, such as a camera, jewelry, or other valuables? Would you need a police report to make a claim? What about costs incurred by delays? Would you be covered for harm you cause to others and their possessions, perhaps through use of a motor vehicle? What exclusions are there (for example, losses while traveling through certain territories)?

The scope of coverage matters. For example, a standard policy covers luggage only if you can prove it was stolen, while an "all risks" policy covers you whatever the cause of loss.

Trip Interruption or Cancellation

The National Tour Association says that only 1 in 100,000 individuals who book tours might be affected by failure of the tour company. On the other hand, the U.S. Tour Operators Association estimates that those odds are as short as 1 in 20. Figure that one out. AIG Travel Guard, a major insurer, reports that approximately 3 percent of people who buy trip-cancellation insurance actually cancel a trip.

Most travelers who cancel a trip just before departure might lose hotel-reservation deposits or the cost of a nonrefundable airline ticket. The bigger loser would be someone who had made a nonrefundable payment for a cruise or tour. If you have to change your flight schedule midtrip, the extra cost also could be substantial. Only you know how likely it is that health or business obligations might interfere with your trip and whether the odds suggest buying cancellation or interruption insurance.

Some policies bury exclusions as if they were land mines, so read the fine print. To do that, you need a copy of the complete policy, not a summary prepared by the marketing department. Take it for granted that an insurer will interpret the policy strictly against you. So will most courts.

Here's what you want to know. If a travel agent can't answer your questions satisfactorily, call the insurance company yourself.

- When would coverage begin and end? Coverage under some policies (especially for cruises) ends 72 hours before the trip starts. If you were forced to cancel after that, you'd be out of luck.
- Under what conditions would the policy reimburse you for penalties and deposits if you canceled after your deposit with the tour operator became nonrefundable? Would a personal or business conflict, or a change of heart, qualify? What about missing the trip for weather-related reasons, such as a hurricane? A policy that would reimburse you in case of voluntary cancellation could be extremely expensive.
- Would you be covered if illness, injury, or death (yours or your companion's) or some other major problem at home caused cancellation or interruption of your trip? Would proof of medical reasons be required? Would you be covered for extra trip costs incurred as a result of disaster striking a close family member?
- Would the policy cover you if a preexisting medical condition forced you to cancel the trip? A typical definition of such a condition is "any ailment for which a person was treated by a doctor, or for which he took prescribed medication, during a specific time period." Some policies will not reimburse you if the preexisting condition that caused the loss was known between 30 and 180 days before you purchased the policy. If you have a preexisting condition, look for a policy that will cover you if that condition has been controlled by medication. Application of the preexisting-condition exclusion has prompted so many complaints that companies are abandoning it.
- Would you be covered if an unexpected problem along your route, such as a hurricane, terrorism, or a communicable disease, interfered with the trip?
- Are there other exclusions (for example, drug use, hazardous activities, or war)?
- Would you be required to have a doctor certify your illness before you canceled a trip? What about after you canceled?
- Could you extend the policy if you extend your trip?
- What sort of failure by the tour or cruise operator would result in payment to you? Exactly which of your expenses would be covered if the tour operator canceled? You want protection against failure to perform, not merely against bankruptcy. By the way, you may get free protection against operator failure simply by paying with a credit card. If the operator fails, the charge can be removed from your account.

If an interruption is caused by the airline (because of a mechanical problem or a pilot failing to show up sober, that sort of thing), the airline may or may not be required to make any special effort on your behalf. If, however, the delay is caused by weather or heavy air traffic, airlines uniformly disclaim responsibility.

Some trip-cancellation or trip-interruption insurance also bundles coverage for accidents, certain medical problems, and evacuation costs. Some even cover lost or stolen baggage (Access America, Travel Guard Group, Travel Insured International, and Travelex Insurance Service. See several paragraphs on page 242 for details). Other policies treat these various coverages separately.

Trip-cancellation or -interruption insurance is expensive. Premiums range from $5.50 to $8 for every $100 of coverage. Balance the premium for temporary coverage against what you have at stake in up-front money.

I've read letters to travel columnists praising trip-cancellation or -interruption insurance, but I've also read angry complaints that one policy or another didn't pay off.

Also available is package insurance that covers everything for a fee of about 7 percent of your prepaid expenses. If there are no tour costs involved, that means airfare, rail passes, and not much else. For tours, the premium for package insurance may be reasonable.

Tour operators assert that insurance supplied by them is somewhat less expensive and has more generous terms than individually purchased policies. Compare prices.

Health

Whether overseas health-insurance coverage is a good investment is a personal decision. The State Department reports that of the 16 million adult U.S. citizens who flew overseas in a recent year, 23,000 were hospitalized abroad. That's 1 out of every 696 travelers, or 0.14 percent.

Existing coverage: If you already have health insurance, call the carrier to see what your policy covers overseas and what it doesn't. For example, most Blue Cross and Blue Shield plans cover some emergency care overseas, and bills are sent directly to the insurer. Medicare, on the other hand, does not cover anyone overseas.

What is covered: Travel medical insurance typically pays for treatment of an illness suffered abroad, including prescription drugs. It may or may not pay for dental care. Virtually no insurance covers emergency medical evacuation overseas.

If you consider buying coverage for overseas medical expenses, ask first about premiums, deductibles, and copayments, then about possible exclusions such as preexisting conditions, sexually transmitted diseases, injuries arising from civil war, and problems related to illegal drugs, pregnancy, and self-inflicted injuries. Ask whether travel in specific countries is excluded.

If you have what might be considered a preexisting medical condition, discuss the situation with the insurer. Some insurers won't pay if you had a health problem during a specified time period before your trip and that condition was responsible for your later claim. Most companies that retain this exclusion use a 60-day period (although some use 90 days or more, and some even exclude conditions controlled by medication).

> Does the policy cover risk sports like scuba diving or skiing?

Most policies provide coverage for preexisting conditions if neither symptoms nor treatments have occurred within the stated period before the trip. In other words, they cover conditions that are stable or controlled. An increasing number of companies are waiving the exclusion for preexisting conditions.

Insurers often require that coverage be purchased within 24 hours of payment of the first deposit on your trip. Therefore, if you want insurance coverage, you should identify an insurance company before you book the trip. Keep documentation of the timing in case you need to make a claim.

Ask the insurer whether you must call home to pre-certify an elective or surgical procedure. You probably will have to, at least for nonemergencies. Ask whether the insurer requires a second opinion. Naturally, if you claim a loss due to health, you'll have to prove that health was the cause.

Some policies exclude coverage for injuries that arise from sports such as scuba diving, mountain climbing, and skiing. Some will include them if you pay an additional premium.

If you decide to buy travel medical insurance, the amount of coverage should depend on whether your primary medical insurance will be in force. If it will, a policy to cover its deductible should be sufficient. For a small additional fee, you may be able to buy lost-luggage and trip-cancellation or -interruption riders to medical insurance.

Reimbursement or direct payment: Payment by an insurance company comes in two forms. The company either reimburses you for expenses you've already paid or pays the medical-care provider directly. This is an important distinction because if you incur medical expenses, you will likely be required to pay them on the spot—which will require cash, a direct-payment insurance policy, or possibly a credit card. Carrying evidence of reimbursement insurance may help delay payment, but don't count on it. If you plan to seek reimbursement for expenses, collect receipts for payments and documentation of diagnosis and treatments (these records will also assist your doctor at home).

Other Health-related Coverage

Emergency evacuation: If you will be taking above-average risks or will be off the beaten track, consider emergency-evacuation coverage. Although most medical care abroad is fairly inexpensive, evacuation is not. From relatively remote areas of South America, Africa, Asia, and the Pacific, air evacuation back to the United States could cost $30,000 to $100,000. Obviously, the cost is less from Mexico and Central America, but you still have to balance your known risk factors against the premium.

Most emergency-evacuation policies cover evacuation because of illness or injury more than 100 miles from home, repatriation (bringing you home if you've had medical care abroad), and repatriation of remains (when the medical care didn't work out so well). They will also arrange reputable medical assistance (which you pay for), which can be every bit as valuable as airlifting you off the mountain. If you'll be hospitalized abroad for more than a week, some will pay round-trip expenses for someone you choose to fly to your side. Typically, preexisting conditions are irrelevant. *Note:* In order for coverage to apply, the insurer must arrange the assistance.

SAVE Money Diver's Alert Network (DAN; call [800] 446-2671, or see **www .diversalertnetwork.org**) was established to cover divers for the costs of treatment and evacuation pertaining to a diving accident. However, non-divers can purchase a membership in DAN that provides coverage for evacuation and some other expenses, not including coverage for medical treatment. The latter requires purchase of a separate insurance plan at an additional charge. DAN will evacuate regardless of preexisting conditions. The cost of the basic membership is $29 a year for an individual, $44 for a family. It's a great way to save money.

The Traveler's Emergency Network (call [800] 275-4836, or see **www.ask4ten .com**) will provide and pay for emergency evacuation up to $100,000. MEDEX (call [800] 732-5309, or see **www.medexassist.com**) offers SafeTrip coverage with no benefit maximum for only $3.50 per day of travel. International SOS (call [800] 523-8930, or see **www.internationalsos.com**) offers $1 million coverage for about $8 per day for trips of up to 49 days. MedJet Assist (call [800] 527-7478, or see **www.medjetassistance.com**) covers medical evacuation for all trips for a whole family for $350 a year, no matter where you go, as long as no trip exceeds 90 consecutive days.

If you have a health problem that's not obvious, consider wearing a MedicAlert tag that signals medical personnel about allergies and special health conditions. The tag includes a telephone number that can be called for information about your condition. Membership in the MedicAlert Foundation (call [888] 633-4298, or see **www.medicalert.org**) is $40 for the first year and $25 for subsequent years, plus the cost of the stainless-steel tag (as little as $10).

Where to Buy Insurance

Insurance companies sell travel-coverage policies directly, through travel agencies, or through tour or cruise operators (sometimes under the operator's name even though the operator is not the insurer). Don't decide on price alone.

Take a close look at the breadth of coverage, the terms, and the extras. A good company will let you call collect if you need medical assistance and will provide direction to nearby medical care (and a translator if needed). It will also contact your family if you ask it to. If you decide you want health insurance, ask your travel agent's opinion as to the best carrier. Ask other travelers about their experiences.

Medicare won't cover you abroad, but most "Medigap" policies will. The extent of coverage for "medically necessary emergency care" depends on which level of policy you purchase. Perhaps typical is payment of 80 percent of Medicare-eligible bills after a deductible (say, $250). It may be that the care must be given during the first 60 consecutive days you've been out of the United States. Medigap does not cover emergency evacuation.

HTH Worldwide (call [866] 979-6753, or e-mail **dan@travelinsurancecenter .com**) offers a Travelgap Multi-Trip plan for an annual premium of around $280. This policy provides accident and medical benefits, as well as emergency evacuation services. Preexisting conditions are not excluded.

STA Travel (call [800] 777-0112, or see **www.statravel.com**) offers a very good, inexpensive trip policy with no upper age limits and no preexisting-conditions exclusion. It offers full coverage for medical expenses as well as interruption or cancellation. For a two- or three-week trip, the premium might be $100.

The following are a few more of the many travel-insurance companies I've used or had recommendations for: Access America (call [800] 284-8300, or see **www.accessamerica.com**), BerkelyCare (call [800] 645-2424, or see **www .berkely.net**), AIG Travel Guard (call [800] 826-4919, or see **www.travelguard .com**), RBC (Royal Bank of Canada) Insurance (call [866] 305-5757, or see **www.rbcinsurance.com**), TravelEx Insurance (call [800] 228–9792, or see **www .travelex-insurance.com**), and Nationwide (call [800] 335-0611, or see **www .nationwide.com**).

Others in the field include International SOS (call [800] 523-8930, or see **www.internationalsos.com**); American Express Global Travel Shield (call [800] 332-4899, or see **americanexpress.com/travel**); CSA (call [800] 873-9855, or see **www.csatravelprotection.com**); Global Health Insurance, a broker that works with several insurance companies (call [866] 383-0476, or see **www .global-health-insurance.com**); Wallach & Company (call [800] 237-6615, or see **www.wallach.com**); Safe Passage International, another broker (call [800] 777-7665, or see **www.spibrokers.com**); Travel Assistance International, (call [800] 821-2828, or see **www.travelassistance.com**); Travel Insured International (call [800] 243-3174, or see **www.travelinsured.com**); and MEDEX (call [800] 732-5309, or see **www.medexassist.com**).

Figuring out what to do about insurance may be a minor hassle the first time around, but from then on it's easy.

Car-rental Insurance
Please see Chapter 20, Transportation.

CHECKLIST: WHAT NEEDS TO BE DONE WHEN
12 months before D (Departure) Date
_____ Choose a destination and start trip planning.
_____ Start collecting information.
_____ Start studying languages, if needed.
_____ Start talking with other travelers.
6 months before D Date
_____ Rough out your itinerary and the length and cost of your trip.
_____ Select a travel agent.
_____ Research airfares, tour options, and insurance.
_____ Have passport photos taken, and start the process of getting a passport.
_____ Read literature from and about countries you may visit.
_____ Review guidebooks.
_____ Determine what shots you'll want and when the sequence should start.
(Please see Chapter 12, Keeping Healthy.)
_____ Begin increasing your physical activity.
3 months before D Date
_____ Firm up your itinerary.
_____ Start getting visas.
_____ Make decisions about your gear and begin assembling it.
_____ Add to your travel-information file.
_____ Collect addresses of people to contact abroad.
_____ Increase your physical activity; build your stamina.
_____ Choose someone to look after your affairs while you're away.
2 months before D Date
_____ Have medical and dental exams.
_____ Start inoculations.
_____ Complete research.
_____ Make airline reservations and get seat assignments.
_____ Buy any new clothing and equipment you need.
_____ Decide whether additional insurance is appropriate.
_____ Test new equipment, especially shoes and cameras.
_____ Start organizing travel gear.
1 month before D Date
_____ Buy medical supplies.
_____ Make photocopies of appropriate documents, and distribute them.
_____ Complete inoculations.
_____ Prepare for closing your home.

_____ Make financial arrangements (someone to pay credit-card charges and other bills).

_____ Give necessary documents to the person who will be taking care of things.

2 weeks before D Date

_____ Organize gear for packing; see if it will fit in your luggage.

_____ Schedule suspension of utilities, subscriptions, and other services.

_____ Arrange for mail to be dealt with.

Final week

_____ Ready your home to be closed. (Please see Chapter 13, When It's Time to Go.)

_____ Send your itinerary to those who should have it.

_____ Finish packing at least three days before departure.

_____ Confirm all flights; ensure you have all tickets and other documents.

CHECKLIST: TRAVEL-INFORMATION LIST

(Leave a copy at home, and take one with you.)

1. Credit-card numbers:
2. Driver's license number:
3. Traveler's-check numbers:
4. Contacts abroad:
5. Medical information:
6. Airline-ticket information:
7. Address of bank:
8. Travel- or medical-insurance policy:
9. Copies of first two pages of passport:
10. Copy of itinerary:

CHAPTER 8

How to Save Money

> Not all those who wander are lost.
> —J. R. R. Tolkien
> *The Fellowship of the Ring*

If you assume that it costs a fortune to travel internationally, and money matters, you may conclude that you can't afford to travel. Unless you know what you're doing, you might be right. It's rough out there for the unwary—but a well-informed traveler can avoid outrageous prices at home and abroad.

SAVE Money As we suggest ways to save money, consider these thoughts:

- If you have a choice, it would be a mistake to travel in the cheapest way possible. A miserly trip can exact a high price on your health and state of mind.
- Some people assume that traveling on a low-to-moderate budget assures a meaningful trip. Not true. It provides many opportunities for personal contact with local people, but it's up to you to take advantage of those opportunities.
- When we discuss getting the most for your money, it is always in the context of accomplishing your goals for the trip and having a great time, not of saving money just for the sake of saving money.

AIRFARE

Picture yourself running across the airport tarmac as fast as you can. You're heading for a sleek, twin-jet Cessna Citation parked there because you've heard it's the cheapest way to get to your destination. Next to it is an old-fashioned, single-prop Cessna Skyhawk. When you get close, you see a sign on the Citation that reads, OUT OF ORDER. Disappointed, you walk up to the Skyhawk anyway to see what it can do for you. The meaning of this little tale will be clear in a moment.

Making airline reservations used to seem simple. Not so long ago, travelers had little independent access to information about flight schedules, fares, and so on. We called a travel agent or an airline and took the best of what we were given. Since those ignorance-is-bliss days, a technological revolution has dramatically affected the way we buy tickets—and changed the participants in that process. That revolution took place, of course, on the Internet.

Here are the players in the ticket-selling game today: mammoth online ticket sites, consolidators and bucket shops, the airlines, and travel agencies.

Online Sites

SAVE Money The Internet has created new opportunities for informed travelers to save money in air travel—and to get far better flight schedules. All airlines now have Web sites offering standard ticket prices and schedules. These sites contain a universe full of information provided by each airline. If we studied this information carefully, we might come up with an acceptable flight schedule and get a competitive price. We soon learned, however, that looking only at the offerings from one airline meant we had little chance of getting the best deal. So, we looked at sites of other airlines and tried to compare them. That was very tedious until the resources listed below came into being to enable us to view the entire field before calling the play.

Even now, no single Web site has the solution. You must invest some time and creativity. To get something acceptable, we often have to experiment with different airports, hours, and maybe even days. When stringing flights together for an international trip, it's necessary to be conservative about the time we allow for making connections. An hour for a connection is risky if you and your luggage have to change planes, especially if you have to hustle to a faraway concourse or must survive another round with customs and security. Any delay en route, and you're stranded in Mexico City rather than basking on an Acapulco beach. When you find the combination you can live with, be prepared to book it immediately because you're fishing in a fast-moving stream.

In what now seem like the good old days, I thought arriving for a flight 45 minutes before departing was overly cautious. Now, grumbling all the way, I arrive at least two and a half hours ahead for an international departure. That's because of delays due to tightened security and the time it takes to pack passengers into airplanes like martini olives in a jar.

So, here's an overview of the online supermarket:

- There's not much difference in offerings on Expedia (**www.expedia.com**), Orbitz (**www.orbitz.com**), and Travelocity (**www.travelocity.com**), the big online entities that offer rates on airfares, hotels, car rental, cruises, and so on. However, when one offers a "fare alert"—meaning you set a price you're willing to pay for a ticket, and if the price drops to that level, you receive an e-mail alert—sign up for it.
- Don't stop there. Use the "aggregators" to compare fares across all these entities. For example, Kayak (**www.kayak.com**), Mobissimo (**www.mobissimo.com**) and SideStep (**www.sidestep.com**) aggregate airline flight, hotel, and car-rental information from other Web sites, in theory presenting you with the best options. ITA Software (**www.itasoftware.com**)

does the same thing, supposedly with less commercial bias. It will also warn you of long layovers, but you can't make a booking through this site. Be aware that many smaller, regional airlines aren't included in the listings (and neither is Southwest for domestic flights), so you must search them separately.

- Are the fares you're seeing a good deal? You can check historical highs and lows by using Farecast (**www.farecast.com**) or FareCompare (**www.farecompare.com**). They will show you whether the ticket price you're considering is merely in line with averages or a great deal. On some routes, the price rarely changes, so when you travel won't make much difference in price. On others, the price may bounce around like a SuperBall. On FareCompare, you can also check the price of so-called Y-up or Q-up tickets that can be automatically upgraded to first or business class if space is available.

- Yellowpages (**www.yellowpages.travel**) is a useful tool that enables you to enter your travel preferences once and search most of the major travel services providers to compare prices and schedules. It's also a directory of travel businesses.

- Hotwire (**www.hotwire.com**) is like a modern, automated version of an old-fashioned consolidator. It offers unsold seats on flights, with better deals close to departure. You don't know which airline you'll fly until booking, and you can't cancel once you've paid. Read the fine print, and add up the full charges. Priceline (**www.priceline.com**) offers a similar service, except you bid whatever price you're willing to pay instead of knowing what it is up front. If no airline accepts your bid, nothing's lost. If your price is accepted, you buy the ticket immediately, and your credit card is charged. This works best for last-minute purchases. Understand the rules, the risks, and the strategies before getting into this game. SkyAuction (**www.skyauction.com**) sells excess airline seats on routes to resort destinations in an auction format, but be sure to add up all the extra fees.

- SmarterTravel (**www.smartertravel.com**) is a great resource for airfare sales and articles highlighting specials, plus you can sign up for an e-mail alert that sends you sale fares on flights from your home airport each week. It sometimes offers sale flights to Mexico and Central America. SmarterTravel also has a feature that lets you compare fares across several booking sites.

- Charter airline companies, such as those run by the big vacation-package agencies, will often sell vacant seats to independent travelers at a discount (for example, a round-trip flight from the United States to Mexico for $200). Watch for advertisements in your Sunday newspaper travel section. Look for such names as USA 3000, Vacation Express, Worry-Free Vacations, and Apple Vacations.

- Ticket prices bounce up and down daily, even hourly. Travelocity's FareWatcher feature (**www.travelocity.com**) offers guidance on when fares to your chosen destinations are likely to drop. You can get help in choosing your plane seat through SeatGuru (**www.seatguru.com**) or ExpertFlyer (**www.expertflyer.com**).
- Consider downloading the free Yapta program (**www.yapta.com**). When you're shopping for a ticket on the sites previously mentioned, including airline sites, Yapta will track specific flights for you and send an e-mail if the price drops. After you've made a purchase, it will keep tracking. If the price drops and you hold a refundable ticket, you can claim the savings from the airline. If your ticket is nonrefundable, you can probably change it by paying a fee (but make sure doing so doesn't lose your seat assignment).
- Telephone numbers for all U.S. airlines: **www.airlinenumbers.com.**

Consolidators and Bucket Shops

Now we're ready for the rest of the story concerning the Citation and the Skyhawk. The Citation represents airline consolidators and bucket shops. Until just a few years ago, they were the traveler's best friend as far as saving money was concerned. Many of them are grounded now, but there's just enough life left in some of them to make it worth explaining what they are, how to find them, and how to use them.

A consolidator buys wholesale from one or more airlines, while a bucket shop is a retailer that gets its tickets from consolidators and sells them to the public. The expertise of bucket shops is in dealing with complicated itineraries. Regardless of what the business calls itself, both provide airline seats to knowledgeable travelers at much less than published prices.

Consolidator tickets aren't sold behind the airlines' backs. They are part of overall yield-management strategies by the airlines to maximize profits. From experience, airlines know when to expect large numbers of empty seats. Since an unfilled seat is worth nothing to them, they allocate blocks of tickets to consolidators to sell at below-market prices. Or they give consolidators a commission that increases with the volume they sell. In either case, consolidators pass on most of the saving to travelers. To avoid offending full-fare flyers, airlines don't advertise this practice.

That arrangement worked well for many years but is declining for two main reasons. First, airlines no longer need consolidators as a backup because they no longer have as many seat vacancies. That's happened because they've reduced routes and frequency of flights since 9/11, they've started flying smaller planes, and they've seen far more people flying (especially Asians and Europeans taking advantage of the wounded U.S. dollar). So, airlines are doing to consolidators what they did to travel agents: changing the game even thought that will put most of them out of business.

Another factor is that so much of the flying public has become Internet-savvy, and fares have become much more transparent. Thus, travelers buy tickets online without even thinking of using an intermediary.

All consolidators sell to travel agencies, but far fewer now sell to individuals as well. Those consolidators that specialize in particular destinations or regions will typically sell directly to individuals. Those who sell to individuals offer little in the way of service and may charge a retail customer slightly more than they'd charge a travel agent. Despite that, these tickets are still cheaper than the best published fares available from the airlines themselves.

Here's an important tip: if you use a travel agent, ask him or her to buy from a consolidator. In case the agent is not experienced in doing that, you'll find a list of consolidators on the next page that you can give your agent.

> Price wars can make consolidator's tickets less appealing.

Consolidators that exist only online may undercut everyone else because of high volume and low overhead. However, I prefer a consolidator that also has a physical address and lists a telephone number.

Note that airlines in the midst of a price war or major promotion may temporarily make prices of certain tickets competitive with consolidator prices. However, as we've all learned, tickets available at "price war" prices may be as plentiful as hens' teeth.

Unfortunately, some consolidators follow the same practice. When you ask for the ticket at the price they've advertised, they can't deliver. I understand that they have a limited number of tickets and may sell out quickly, but if I sense a bait-and-switch, that consolidator never hears from me again. If you see an ad, call the consolidator or take the ad to a travel agency and ask the agent to get the ticket for you at the advertised price.

In the past, many travel agents didn't take advantage of consolidator tickets, even though that would benefit clients, because they wanted to maintain their relationships with the airlines. Now that airlines have given travel agents a stiff-arm, that loyalty has disappeared. However, you need to make sure an agent knows how the system works.

The terms of a consolidator's tickets are frequently better than those of standard tickets, but be sure you understand any restrictions and penalties. For example, consolidator tickets usually don't require a Saturday stay-over and remain valid up to a year. In addition, there's no advance-purchase requirement, so they are ideal for spur-of-the-moment trips. The major disadvantage is that a consolidator ticket on airline A will not be accepted by airline B. If airline A's flight is canceled, you can get a refund for the ticket, but you can't just hop on someone else's plane. You may not earn frequent-flier miles and may have to pay a fee to use a credit card. Fees for making changes, for example in departure date, vary widely, so check them out.

Similarly, a bucket shop's rules regarding routes, stopovers, and so on are governed by the contract between bucket shop and airline (or consolidator), not by the rules that govern a published fare. (See "Dealing with Consolidators and Bucket Shops," page 258.)

If the available ticket happens to be for an airline you haven't heard of, check it out. The National Transportation Safety Board (**www.ntsb.gov**) lists airline accident statistics.

Because profit to the consolidators and bucket shops is thin, customer service may be thin as well. Don't expect time-consuming hand-holding. If you're not sure what you want, consider paying a little more to get good advice from a travel agent. At the same time, be cautious about planning a complicated international itinerary with an inexperienced travel agent.

The bottom line is that the Citation is gone, but the Skyhawk can still give you a lift.

The list of consolidators and bucket shops below is merely a sampling. Unfortunately, the availability of consolidator fares to Latin America has declined because Delta has terminated all its contracts with consolidators. United has only a few remaining, and American has none. This list does not constitute an endorsement of any consolidator.

- Airline Consolidator.com (call [888] 468-5385, or see **www.airline consolidator.com**). International flights.
- Air Treks (call [877] 247-8735, or see **www.airtreks.com**). Deals mostly with round-the-world and multiple-stop trips. Serves individuals, and buys consolidator tickets on your behalf.
- C & H International (call [866] 266-5264, or see **www.cnhintl.com**). International flights; 23 locations, 300 employees, 40 airlines. Travel agents only.
- Economy Travel (call [888] 222-2110, or see **www.economytravel.com**). This consolidator deals with individuals but offers very few flights to Central America.
- EZTicketSales (call [866] 835-5797, or see **www.ezticketsales.com**). Domestic and international flights.
- Flights.com (**www.flights.com**). Domestic and international flights.
- GTT Global and USA Gateway Travel (**www.gttglobal.com**). Calls itself the largest U.S. consolidator (40 offices, 46 airlines). Offers international flights, including some to Mexico and Central America. GTT Global and USA Gateway deals only with travel agents, but you can steer your agent to the company.
- Hotwire (call [866] 468-9473, or see **www.hotwire.com**). Lists price, but doesn't reveal airline until booking. International and some domestic flights.

- Mill-Run (**www.millrun.com**). Serves 600 domestic and international cities; 30 years in business, 200 employees, 10 branches. Again, travel agents only, so you know what to do.
- Priceline (**www.priceline.com**). Doesn't reveal its selling prices. You have to guess what Priceline will accept, and that gives the house an edge. See also LowestFare.com (**www.lowestfare.com**), which Priceline owns.
- STA Travel (call [800] 781-4040, or see **www.statravel.com**). Specializes in but not limited to students. Domestic and international flights, including to Mexico and Central America.
- Trans Am Travel (call [800] 822-7600, or see **www.transamtravel.com**). Another of the heavyweights. International flights, including to Mexico and Central America. Travel agents only.
- Up and Away Travel (call [800] 275-8001, or see **www.upandaway.com**)

Bucket shops and consolidators are usually in large cities, especially those with plenty of immigrants. They exist primarily to give neighborhood folks low airfares to visit their home countries. The national airlines of those countries may give them extra-low prices on excess tickets to help make this happen.

To find a consolidator or bucket shop in your hometown that serves destinations in Latin America, look in the local Spanish-language newspaper. Even if you don't read Spanish, it's not hard to find the airfare ads for your destination.

Also check the Sunday travel sections of major newspapers, such as the *New York Times, San Francisco Chronicle, Chicago Tribune, Los Angeles Times, Houston Chronicle,* and *Miami Herald.* The last three are especially good for flights to Latin America. *USA Today, LA Weekly,* and the *Village Voice* also have consolidator and bucket-shop ads.

Buying Abroad

If you can't find the discounted tickets you want at home, buy them on the road. For one complicated trip, I bought a ticket in the United States for only the first leg of the trip, then purchased the rest of my tickets at bucket shops along the way. I saved $800 compared with what I would have paid in the States.

Another example: a ticket from Guatemala to Costa Rica might cost $300 in the United States but only $100 in Guatemala. Check it out.

There are bucket shops in most Latin American capitals. Just ask around. You'll also find them in Amsterdam, Athens, Bangkok, Bombay, Brussels, Cairo, Delhi, Hong Kong, Istanbul, Kuala Lumpur, London, Penang (in Malaysia), Sydney, and Tel Aviv (in Israel), among other places.

When you walk into a bucket shop abroad, you're unlikely to mistake it for the American Express office. The decor is usually spartan. They know you're there because of price, not pretty paintings on the wall or small talk. The bucket shop I use in Calcutta is in a budget hotel and consists of two desks and a computer on a landing halfway up the first flight of stairs. That seems more than a little shaky, but they always hand me authentic tickets in return for my money.

Dealing with Consolidators and Bucket Shops

Caveat emptor. As with many businesses, reliability varies. Before paying for anything, make sure you agree with the choice of airline, flight times, and cancellation and change fees. Ask about taxes, service fees, and so-called incidentals. Ask for the total price. If you pay anything before the ticket is issued, try to limit the amount to a deposit, say 25 percent. Until the company gets to know you, it has to question your reliability as well.

You can usually pay for tickets purchased in the United States with a credit card, even though that may entail an additional charge of 2 percent or more. Paying by credit card enables you to cancel the charge if the ticket doesn't arrive. If a U.S. company insists on payment in cash or by check, I'd be very cautious. In most of the rest of the world, however, you may have to pay in cash. If so, you're at risk until you have the ticket in hand.

After you've made your reservation, wait a day, then confirm directly with the airline that it holds a reservation in your name. If it doesn't, call the consolidator at once. Avoid anxiety by insisting on a ticket or confirmation well ahead of your departure date. When you receive it, check that flight numbers, times, and dates are correct. Ensure that your status is shown as "okay," which means you have a confirmed seat (rather than being waitlisted). Again, confirm directly with the airline.

When you've verified your reservations, request seat assignments and enter frequent-flier numbers. Unfortunately, some discounted-fare tickets restrict or prohibit both.

The rare problems I've read about in the United States generally concern a consolidator or bucket shop that went bankrupt, having received payments without issuing the tickets. Of course, travel agencies, cruise lines, and airlines go bankrupt from time to time as well. And so do travelers. Use common sense, trust your intuition, and ask questions:

- Where is your office (street address, not a post-office box)?
- How long have you been in business?
- With what airlines do you have contracts?
- Is your firm accredited with the Airlines Reporting Corporation (ARC) and International Airlines Travel Agent Network (IATAN)? (Both have standards for financial stability and experience.)
- Are you bonded? If so, for how much?

If you have doubts, call the Better Business Bureau in the company's hometown, or contact the American Society of Travel Agents consumer-affairs department (**www.astanet.com/about/consumercomplaint.asp**). If you buy from a consolidator or bucket shop used or recommended by another traveler or a travel agent, the consolidator will be of known quality.

Buying Direct from Airlines

Ticket prices on booking sites such as Travelocity differ little from prices listed on sites sponsored directly by the airlines. They're all using the same reservation systems. That's true for prices obtained through travel agents as well (except for agents who use consolidators). It's still worth investing a few minutes to shop around, especially because you can do it quickly using a site such as Kayak, but significant differences in fares are more fleeting oddities than regular practice. Several exhaustive tests by magazine writers have found better deals at site A or site B for various destinations, but rarely is the difference more than 5 or 10 percent. You may be able to save more than that researching discount prices for hotels and ground transportation for your trip. In other words, you should shop hard to find the flight times and other flight characteristics that suit you best, but you'll seldom find the much lower fares that used to be possible.

If you've checked all the booking sites and found that airfares for your itinerary are about the same, you may be better off buying direct from the airline. First, you usually won't pay a fee for booking online. However, some stingy U.S.

airlines, such as Delta, charge $10 to make a phone reservation through an agent. Southwest, on the other hand, will gladly book your ticket by phone for no extra charge.

Second, many airlines will award you a frequent-flier mileage bonus for booking online direct with them rather than through a site such as Expedia (which also will charge a fee). Third, if you book direct with the airline, you're sure to be in its system and to get proper mileage credit without a hassle. Remember the benefits of their alliances as well. For example, you can get United credit for booking on TACA, or Continental credit for booking on Copa.

If you use an airline Web site, sign up to be notified by e-mail of cheap specials.

In recent years, most airlines have lost or squandered so much goodwill that we now assume that whether you book by phone or on their Internet sites, they will charge the highest possible price they can get you to pay. Maybe the best strategy is to treat the ticket agent with great courtesy—as if you hadn't been kept on hold for an hour—and hope for kindness to strangers.

Buying from Travel Agents

It's a waste of time and money to ask a travel agent to book a simple airfare. However, when you have a complicated itinerary—and perhaps want hotel, ground transportation, and tours as well—consider using a travel agent.

If you want a discounted ticket, ask the travel agent clearly whether the agency can buy discounted tickets for your itinerary. If the answer is "no," try another agency. When no consolidator tickets are available, ask specifically for the lowest fare. Not all agents are equally competent or motivated to find the lowest fare, so insist that you want discounted tickets, not merely the lowest published fares.

Unfortunately, many travel agents who are not expert in dealing with consolidators may conceal that fact. Unless a travel agency advertises that it can beat airline fares or that it offers consolidator prices, the best it will do is get you the lowest of the computer reservations system's published fares. There's no guarantee you'll do even that well. To get discounts, use an agency that deals in discounts.

Many experienced travelers describe their planned trip to more than one agency and ask for a proposal. This will flush out how knowledgeable the agents are and how well they know the consolidator market. Tell the agencies that whoever comes up with the best deal will get your business. Don't abuse an agent's time if you don't intend to buy from someone.

> Not bound to swear allegiance to any master, wherever the wind takes me I travel as a visitor.
> —Horace,
> Roman Poet

On balance, sound advice from a good travel agent can more than offset the fees they now charge—so long as they get you discounted tickets or provide other services that save you time and hassle and improve your travels.

Foreign Airlines

SAVE Money You may save money by flying on foreign-flag airlines. Even when less familiar to you, many are excellent carriers. If you're working with a travel agent, you may have to make a specific request. However, you may not receive usable frequent-flier miles unless the foreign carrier has a reciprocal arrangement with American or Canadian carriers.

Many of these foreign airlines offer more comfort and amenities than their U.S. or Canadian counterparts. As airlines such as Delta and American cut services to the bone and squeeze in more seats on international flights, they've fallen to the bottom of the heap in consumer surveys. Airlines such as Aeromexico, Copa, and Mexicana will usually be a more pleasant option.

Charter Flights

A charter tour operator leases an airplane for a specific time period and route, say, San Francisco to Panama City, and then sells the seats. The prices are usually good and sometimes get better as flight time approaches. The problem is that if the operator doesn't sell enough seats, it is likely to cancel the flight. You should get your money back, but you'll have been left hanging. Other airlines will not honor your charter ticket.

Many airplanes can also be chartered for flights within a country or region. This is certainly true in Mexico and Central America. Most travelers don't use them because there's no reliable way to evaluate aircraft maintenance and pilot skill from afar.

Frequent-flier Programs

The frequent-flier program is not aging well. Intended as a marketing ploy to inspire brand loyalty, it worked so much better than imagined that it's been converted into a house of mirrors. Feeling ill-used, tens of millions of frequent fliers have turned against the very airlines that sought their business. After drawing consumers into their programs, airlines restricted frequent-flier seats to an average of only 5 percent of capacity of each flight. They also limited frequent-flier seats to odd routes at odd hours. As a result, many customers have to make reservations almost a year ahead of departure and fly thousands of miles out of their way at inconvenient times.

The airlines keep changing the redemption formula, never in your favor. Suddenly, you learn that an airline requires far more mile credits than it required for the same route last year. Then there's the matter of vanishing miles. While you're earning some, others are expiring.

The key is to accumulate the most miles possible on just one or two airlines. If you play the game well and are creative, you can earn regular free flights or upgrades and get the most value out of those miles.

How to Earn Credits

The original way to earn frequent-flier points was by—what else?—flying. However, the nonflying ways in which you can increase your frequent-flier credits are growing daily. First, phone companies offered credits, then rental-car companies and grocery chains. Many airlines sponsor MasterCard or VISA credit cards, issued by various banks, that earn frequent-flier mileage credits. Some credit-card programs—for which you pay an annual fee—get around the blackout dates and limited seat allocations imposed by the airlines. Flying on many foreign airlines earns frequent-flier miles on the program of one of the U.S.-based airlines.

You can earn frequent-flier miles with some calling cards or credit cards.

When forced to concentrate their mileage on one or two airlines to accumulate the minimum mileage required to earn a free flight before their miles start expiring, some travelers wind up resenting the airlines. And you know what? The airlines don't care because their goal has changed. Airlines reap huge profits by selling mile credits to all sorts of businesses that, in turn, use them to attract customers to buy their vacuum cleaners or recliners.

Cashing In

You can exchange your frequent-flier miles for a ticket directly with the airline. Use the credit to buy an expensive ticket, not a cheap one. At present, one frequent-flier mile is worth about one penny. Thus, a 25,000-mile credit will earn you a $250 gift certificate with a merchant or, depending on the airline, one domestic flight. If you can buy a ticket for significantly less cash than the value of the mileage credit the flight would require, hold on to the credit. On the other hand, some suggest using your miles as soon as you can, before the value of the programs to you deteriorates further.

In general, using your miles for an international flight or an upgrade to business class will get you the most bang for your miles. Most airlines require 30,000 or 35,000 miles for a flight to Mexico or Central America, only slightly more than a domestic flight. But because published fares on those international routes are routinely $400 to $600, you are often getting 1.5 cents or more per mile in value.

Most programs encourage you to cash in your miles for all sorts of products or services. Out of disgust, that's what many would-be travelers do even though they would get a better return keeping credits to get free tickets (if they could just find available seats).

Some airlines offer to let frequent fliers "buy" their way out of blackout dates and other restrictions, using additional frequent-flier points. What makes that offer particularly offensive is that the restrictions were imposed by the airlines in the first place. How many times can they milk one cow? In general, this is a poor use of the credits unless you're loaded with mileage credits, or avoiding a restriction or flying on a certain date is essential to you.

Even though they cram in so many seats that only munchkins have adequate legroom, airlines aren't heartless. To enable passengers to prevent thrombosis and claustrophobia, they'll let you buy a few extra centimeters of space. If you want to reserve an aisle seat to avoid inconveniencing other passengers when you desperately need to stretch your legs, some airlines will charge extra for that, too.

Many elite-level frequent fliers (generally those who fly at least 25,000 miles on one airline in a calendar year) use their miles for upgrades to get extra legroom and better amenities, especially for long flights.

If you are trying to get a frequent-flier ticket for specific dates to a specific place during a holiday weekend, you are probably out of luck. To avoid being shut out, be creative. You may have to take off-peak dates, avoid hub cities, fly to cities near your real destination, or pay a big premium in miles. But flexibility pays. One knowledgeable traveler got frequent-flier tickets for himself, his wife, and his child to Acapulco and back. His only cost was $68 per ticket in taxes. He made it work by being willing to return home on a different flight from his wife and child.

Money-saving Tips

Check the ads in the travel sections of the *New York Times,* the *Washington Post,* the *Los Angeles Times,* and your local paper for specials from foreign countries' national airlines. These airlines often cut prices sharply to encourage travelers to visit.

Ask a travel agent about air-and-hotel package deals. Special promotions offer airfare and several nights' lodging for less than you might pay for regular airfare alone. Some packages are priced so low that they're worth it even if you don't stay in the hotel. These deals are common for hot spots such as Jamaica and Cancún, but you'll find some for more adventure-filled destinations as well. Most of these packages are legitimate; only a few offer poorly located or poorly maintained facilities.

Many airlines used to offer fare discounts to seniors (age 65 and older). This benefit has fallen to the airlines' relentless erosion of special fares for travelers. The remaining exception—no surprise—is Southwest. Still, even those who hate the idea of being considered a "senior" should ask about a senior discount—just in case pigs grow wings.

Some hotels and car-rental agencies also offer discounts of 10 to 15 percent to those as young as 50 or 55. In some cases, these discounts are available only to AAA or AARP members. Your companion may receive a discount regardless of age.

Sources of Information

There are so many frequent-flier programs, and the rules change so often, that you may have to buy a scorecard to keep them straight. The following are some sources of help:

- Expert Flyer (**www.expertflyer.com**): a paid service that helps you maximize your miles for trips and upgrades
- First Class Flyer (**www.firstclassflyer.com**): a subscription service that provides "in the know" details on getting upgrades and reaching elite status
- FlyerTalk (**www.flyertalk.com**): free frequent-flier message boards on every related topic
- InsideFlyer (**www.insideflyer.com**): Monthly magazine; $45 a year
- *Mileage Pro: The Insider's Guide to Frequent Flyer Programs* **www .mileageprobook.com**): The definitive book on the subject
- Points.com (**www.points.com**): This free site for managing your reward programs includes a marketplace for trading mileage credits. Use it as a last resort because you'll get a poor return.
- Mileage Manager (**www.mileagemanager.com**): A place to keep track of your frequent-flier programs

Make sure the travel agent knows you are flexible (or check the "Flexible Dates" option when booking online). For example, are you willing to:

- leave on any day within a period of several days?
- stay at your destination over a Saturday night?
- depart from a nearby airport rather than your hometown's?
- accept an intermediate stop or a change of planes?
- accept an alternative destination? For example, you may save a lot by flying into Louisville instead of Cincinnati, or Colorado Springs instead of Denver, or Toledo instead of Detroit, or Birmingham instead of Atlanta, among others. Public or private transportation usually connects the airports.
- fly during off-peak hours (especially overnight)?
- fly during the off-season? (For high seasons in specific countries, see Chapter 3.)

Some believe airlines often raise ticket prices on Saturday and Sunday and post sales on Tuesday night at midnight.

Fare wars often follow a major holiday. Be ready.

When you've tentatively selected an airline, dates, and route, review the restrictions carefully:

- Are you permitted to make changes or cancel the ticket? If so, what is the charge? If not, be certain you're ready to make the deal final.
- Does the ticket permit you to add a stopover without charge?

- Is there a minimum or maximum stay?
- Can you make the whole trip on one airline? If so, it may be cheaper than using several airlines.

LODGING

SAVE Money If you choose to find lodging as you travel, see Chapter 15, Lodging, for suggestions on how to find the lodging best for you and how to negotiate the best prices. If you prefer to make hotel reservations before leaving home and want to save money, here are some ideas:

- First stop is the Web. When you enter "discount hotels" in a search engine, you'll come up with a zillion choices. Some of the more credible sites include: Expedia (**www.expedia.com**), Hotwire (**www.hotwire.com**), Orbitz (**www.orbitz.com**), HotelConXions (**www.hotelconxions.com**), Travelocity (**www.travelocity.com**), Travelzoo (**www.travelzoo.com**), hotels.com (**www.hotels.com**), Priceline (**www.priceline.com**), ShermansTravel.com (**www.shermanstravel.com**), and CheapTickets (**www.cheaptickets.com**).

These big sites will beat rack rates, but they tend to focus on upscale and mid-range hotels, so you'll still be well above the prices charged by budget hotels. The sites differ in terms of information detail, photos, reviews, ratings, and number of client hotels. Some, such as Hotwire, want you to make the reservation before it gives you the name and location of the hotel you've just reserved.

- For small, locally owned hotels, your best bet is to consult local sites focused on the country or city you are visiting. These will have a far greater selection, especially at the budget and midrange level. See the "Resources" listings in specific country sections in Chapter 3.
- **SAVE Money** When making a reservation, save money by asking for a discount on grounds of being an employee of a specific corporation or the government, a student, a travel writer, a frequent flier, a senior, a member of the military or the clergy, or a member of an organization such as AAA, AARP, or anything else that seems remotely defensible. The hotel may ask for some identification, but a business card is usually sufficient to capture the corporate rate (which may be up to 20 percent off the rack rate).
- If you are a senior, say so. The minimum age for a senior discount varies from 50 to 65. In addition, many hotel chains have "clubs" for seniors with discounts in the 10 to 25 percent range (though some go up to 50 percent). Membership in some is free; others charge $10 to $50 a year. For $12.50 a year, anyone age 50 or older may join AARP (**www.aarp.org**) and take advantage of its discount arrangements with hotel chains.
- Ask about a hotel's promotional discounts for weekends, room-and-breakfast packages, the summer season, or whatever. Ask about a discount

for making a reservation 30 days in advance (as much as 30 percent). See if the hotel has a package deal with an airline. Don't ask whether the hotel has such a discount; just ask for it. If the hotel clerk expects vacancies, which is often, he or she will work with you to get your business. It may not be as good a deal as you could make in person, but you should get some break.

- Some travel agents sell vouchers for hotel rooms. You buy as many vouchers as you expect to need before your trip, then use them as you travel. You're supposed to receive significant discounts. In some cases, you do; in others, you pay even more than the rack rate. Vouchers are good for travel agents and great for hotels, but not so good for travelers.

- "Half-price" discount programs sound good, but the rate from which the discount is calculated (the rack rate) may be an inflated rate that almost no one actually pays. You may not be able to reserve a room on the dates you want, and the programs have membership fees ranging from $30 to $125. Because the programs are designed to fill empty hotel rooms during slack periods, you probably won't get a room when the hotel expects to be able to rent it for a higher price. You can find these programs, such as the International Travel Card and the Privilege Card International on the Web, but it's not clear they are a good value.

- You may be able to obtain "preferred" hotel rates through your travel agent. A preferred rate is one negotiated with a hotel by a local travel agency, by a national or international travel agency (for example, Carlson Wagonlit, American Express, U.S. Travel), or by a travel club (for example, the International Airline Passengers Association). Even small travel agencies may offer a preferred-rate program. Discounts average about 20 percent. Most of the hotels that participate are midrange to expensive.

> Ask if your travel agent can get you a preferred hotel rate.

In evaluating these discount programs, remember that the rack rate may be fictional. Therefore, the discount may not be as good as what you could negotiate on the spot with these hotels or with a smaller, independent hotel.

By the way, if you can prove you made a reservation and the hotel won't honor it (because of overbooking or any other reason), the custom is to give you a free night at a comparable hotel and transport you there. Act as though both you and the clerk take it for granted that that is the least the hotel can do.

Toucan perched alertly in the Guatemalan rain forest

Ziplining through the canopy of the Costa Rican cloud forest

Lake Atitlan, Guatemala—one of the deepest lakes in the world—
surrounded by steep ridges, extinct volcanoes, and colorful villages

Carved wooden masks for dance, pageants, mystical rites—even scaring away evil spirits

Logging is big business in Nicaragua, but environmentalists worry,

Tropical foliage

An unbeatable combination: secluded beach, lapping waves,
and leisurely lunch, followed by a siesta

Tranquility measured by the mile, Mexico

Street musicians playing for their supper,
San Pedro la Laguna, Guatemala

CHAPTER 9

How to Prepare a Reliable Budget

> Twenty years from now you will be more
> disappointed by the things that you didn't do than
> by the ones you did do. So throw off the bowlines.
> Sail away from the safe harbor. Catch the trade
> winds in your sails. Explore. Dream. Discover."
> —Mark Twain

Picture yourself just after dawn, standing in a wicker basket below a red-and-yellow-striped hot-air balloon. After the chuff-chuff-chuffing burner fills the balloon, you ascend majestically, sipping chilled Champagne as you drift above the magnificent Maya ruins of Chichén Itzá. Now picture yourself left behind, standing on the ground, gazing up with envy, wishing you'd budgeted money for this adventure.

As college-age backpackers, many of us traveled on a bare-bones basis and kept going until our money ran out. That sort of trip required eating on the margins of nutrition and hygiene, living occasionally in barely habitable accommodations, and forgoing most treats.

Sound like fun? It was back then, but now time, health, and love of adventure are more important than a few dollars. After all, one major reason to travel is pleasure. If you make informed choices, bargain a bit, and skip overpriced tourist frills, you can easily have a fine trip within a reasonable budget—one that includes hot-air balloon rides.

Most people are about as fond of figuring budgets as they are of calculating their taxes. But, as with taxes, you'll pay a penalty if you don't do it right. Let's find out how it's done.

Holland Isn't Guatemala

We'll begin by acknowledging one of life's realities: travel costs vary wildly around the world, and your choice of destinations must take that into account. That may cause many travelers to write off Japan, most of Europe, and a few other high-cost destinations until the U.S. government stops running up huge deficits and the dollar becomes more robust.

A week touring Norway can easily cost more than a month in Guatemala. Fortunately, much of Latin America is a relative bargain, even inexpensive. For example, a private room for two, with a private bath, can cost less than $25 a night. But there are major cost variations between, for example, a highly promoted Mexican beach resort and a Nicaraguan seaside village.

Hotel entryway in Antigua, Guatemala

The cost of travel in a given country also depends in part on the strength of your currency in relation to that country's. In the 1960s, when the U.S. dollar had some muscle, Europe on $5 a day was very possible. Today, when a martini can cost $25 in some European capitals, imagine what you'd spend for a serious night on the town.

You think New York City is expensive? According to Mercer Human Resource Consulting, it ranked only 15th among the world's most expensive cities. Moscow (where a cup of coffee is $5.60) heads the list, followed by London, Seoul, Tokyo, Hong Kong, Copenhagen, Geneva, Osaka, Zurich, and Oslo. Los Angeles was 42nd, San Francisco 54th.

A nice, three-star, double hotel room is easy to find for $50 in Antigua, Guatemala, but you'd pay that in Amsterdam or London for two dorm beds in a noisy hostel. That $10 taxi ride from the airport in Mérida, Mexico, will run more than $100 in Madrid. A haircut that goes for $5 in Colón, Panama, will set you back $65 in Tokyo. A simple fast-food meal that costs only $3.60 in Mexico City will zap you for $13 in Oslo.

The Accountant's Budget

Which is the chicken; which is the egg? Do you plan your trip by choosing a destination first, or do you start by drafting a budget? That's actually a trick question. Obviously, the destination matters most, so, if money didn't matter, that's what you'd focus on first. But if money *does* matter, you'll have to bother with a budget. One way to draft that budget, perhaps the one a responsible accountant might take, is to choose the maximum amount you're comfortable spending on a trip. Then bump that up a bit because of all the money you won't be spending at home for food, entertainment, utilities, and so on.

Let's suppose you choose to spend $2,500, and your round-trip transportation will cost $900. That leaves you $1,600 to spend on the ground. Use the Checklist in this chapter to estimate local daily costs, and divide that amount into $1,600. If that allows you 14 days, great. But suppose it permits only eight days, and that's just not enough time to see everything you want to see. Does that mean you're condemned to yet another trip to Destin, Florida?

The Romantic's Budget

Not at all—because there's another way to approach a budget, one a romantic would prefer. Choose your favorite destination, and figure out how many days it will take to experience everything on your must-see list. Next, use the Checklist to calculate how much that number of days will cost. Now persuade yourself to spend that amount. If you absolutely can't do it, cut back on the level of accommodations, and figure out which areas or attractions you can cut—until you have a cost you can live with. The romantic will find a way to afford what she or he really wants.

Constructing the Budget

List all the things you expect to spend money on, then plug in the length of the trip and local cost estimates. Let's practice by assuming certain expenses for a hypothetical 30-day trip in Central America:

Pre-departure expenses: These include the costs of visas, film and other photographic equipment, medical protection (for example, shots and prescription and over-the-counter medicines), guidebooks, new clothing, and other gear. Let's estimate predeparture expenses for this trip at $450.

Airfare: Assume an airfare cost (getting there, traveling around, and returning home) of $900.

Other transportation: This includes local buses, taxis, and other nonair transport. Your working itinerary shows how often you'll need local transport, and guidebooks give you a reasonable idea of the costs. Estimate $100.

Lodging and meal expenses: The best cost estimates come from the Internet, current guidebooks, and people who've recently returned from your destinations. Of course, before you're actually there, it's hard to know exactly how much you'll spend for meals and lodging that will make you happy. Nevertheless, here's the process for estimating these costs for a 30-day trip in Central America.

- Subtract the number of days when you'll pay no separate charge for lodging, such as when you'll be trekking, living aboard a dive boat, and the like. Let's say there are five of those days, leaving 25 days. An average cost of $40 per day (easy to do in Central America) times 25 gives you $1,000. Adjust that upward by 15 percent to cover price escalation and an occasional splurge, and budget $1,150 for lodging.

CHECKLIST: BUDGET

Predeparture Expenses

$_____ Passport, visas, and photos

$_____ Guidebooks

$_____ Camera, film or memory cards, filters, other photo equipment

$_____ Luggage, day pack

$_____ New clothes

$_____ Travel insurance

$_____ Gear (binoculars, money belt, etc.)

$_____ Health care (medicine, shots)

$_____ Toiletries

$_____ Reading material

Transportation

$_____ Airfares

$_____ Other (trains, buses, etc.)

Lodging and Meals

$_____ En route

$_____ Daily lodging

$_____ Daily meals

Special Experiences

$_____ Scuba diving, rafting, etc.

$_____ Entertainment (sightseeing tours, etc.)

Miscellaneous

$_____ Souvenirs, gifts, tips, laundry

- An average cost of $20 per day for meals times 30 gives you $600. Adjust that upward 15 percent, and budget $690. Remember that you'd spend at least that much in 30 days at home.

Special experiences: If you don't plan for them, paying for special experiences can wreck your budget. I'm referring to such things as the cost of scuba diving, sailing, trekking, rafting, and so on. Most of these opportunities will surface during your research, but you won't recognize some as *musts* until you get there.

How much do these special experiences cost? Check the Internet and guidebooks, call national tourism offices, ask a knowledgeable travel agent or someone who has been there recently. If you can't turn up anything, guess. I suggest three rules of thumb. First, special experiences in developed countries cost more than you might expect, and in developing countries, even less than you expect. Second, if modern technology is involved, such as a helicopter, the experiences will be fairly expensive even in developing countries. Third, prices quoted by a travel agent for special experiences will almost certainly be higher than you'll pay if you make your own arrangements abroad.

For our hypothetical trip, assume four days of scuba diving and several day trips with guides. Estimate: $550.

Miscellaneous: This category includes odds and ends: clothing you buy on the road, souvenirs, toiletries, beverages, books, postcards, postage, tips, and so on. Your estimate here is a matter of personal preference and available money. Whatever you estimate, add 25 percent. For this hypothetical trip, budget $400.

If you want to fine-tune your budget, find out whether your own currency has grown significantly stronger or weaker since the information you've gathered was published. Stockbrokers have this information. For current exchange rates, check the Internet (**www.oanda.com/converter/classic** or **www.xe.net/ ucc**) or the currency trading table in the *Wall Street Journal*. In recent years, the weakness of the dollar has made Mexico and Central America very attractive when contrasted with Europe. To view historic exchange-rate trends, see **www.fxtop.com.**

To be even more conservative, add up all the categories and add an additional 15 percent to the total to cover surprises and spontaneous splurges.

If the grand total is more money than you have, don't skip a beat. The purpose of your estimated budget is to simulate reality ahead of time and, if necessary, to put you on notice that you have to cut some expenses or redesign the trip.

In summary, avoid an absolutely bare-bones budget if you can. Leave room for decent food and shelter, small pleasures, and special experiences. Before you cut back on your trip, consider investing just a bit more in your lifelong memories.

CHAPTER 10

How to Manage Money Successfully

When preparing to travel,
lay out all your clothes and all your money.
Take half the clothes and twice the money.
—Susan Heller

This chapter is about money in the various forms that matter to travelers, including how to trade yours for theirs and, the fun part, how to bargain like a pro.

CURRENCY

Explorers and early travelers carried their funds in the form of precious metals or other minerals. Everyone was relieved when paper currency came along, but, though it's convenient, it's still bulky, vulnerable to loss, and uninsurable. Given the options available today, it would be a major mistake to carry all the money you need in the form of currency.

How Much Currency?

There are two issues: how much U.S. currency to take with you when you leave, and how much local currency to carry on the road. Even where I will have reasonable access to ATMs and can use my credit card for many purposes, I still take perhaps $300 with me where there's a chance it will be accepted. Where ATMs are scarce and credit cards often useless, as in many less developed parts of the world, I take in cash a higher percentage of what I expect to spend.

Although carrying $1 bills for gifts or tips makes sense, carrying change does not. Tip someone with a quarter, and the local bank won't give him anything for it unless he accumulates buckets full. Even then, the exchange rate is poor because banks don't want to transport heavy foreign coins.

Personal checks are almost useless except, maybe, as a way to get cash from American Express.

TRAVELER'S CHECKS

Traveler's checks are a safe way to transport money, don't take up much room, and protect you in case of theft or loss. So why not take traveler's checks and forget everything else? There are several good reasons:

- There may be nowhere to exchange a traveler's check for cash at the moment you need to pay for something (such as on a weekend when banks are closed). Many banks in less developed countries won't accept traveler's checks. Many merchants won't, either.
- You may pay a fee when you buy traveler's checks, and you will pay a fee when you exchange them for local currency.
- You may get a less favorable exchange rate for traveler's checks than for cash.
- Traveler's checks aren't accepted on the black market, so without cash, you lose the opportunity for creative financing.
- The vast increase in the number of cash-dispensing machines has made traveler's checks almost obsolete.

The Fee

SAVE Money Most issuers of traveler's checks will try to charge a fee, usually 1 percent of the amount you want to purchase. Even if they imply that a fee is automatic, negotiate, and you'll save money. When buying checks from a bank, assert your status as a customer. It doesn't take much to get the fee waived. If you belong to an organization that dispenses traveler's checks (such as AAA), you won't pay a fee.

Another Option

There are now prepaid traveler's check cards. For example, American Express charges $15 to issue a reloadable card with a minimum deposit of $300 and a maximum of $2,750. It isn't linked to your bank account and will be replaced if lost. You use the card at stores like a debit card or in an ATM machine to make a withdrawal. It's much less bulky than traveler's checks and is an easier way to obtain local currency. However, it has no real advantage over regular debit cards and may be more expensive to use.

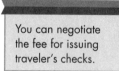

You can negotiate the fee for issuing traveler's checks.

Which Brands and What Denominations?

Carry only widely accepted brands of traveler's checks, such as American Express, Thomas Cook, Citicorp, and VISA.

In deciding what denominations of traveler's checks to carry, the issue is bulk versus flexibility. Carrying packs of $10 checks gives you the greatest flexibility but chokes your money belt. If you take only $100 checks, you run the risk of being stuck with more local currency than you want as you're about to leave a country. If you carry traveler's checks, consider mostly $20 checks, a few $50 checks, and only enough $100 checks to pay for airline tickets and special events.

In Case of Loss or Theft

Never *countersign* a traveler's check until you're in front of the person accepting it—or it may not be accepted. If a check you've reported missing shows up bearing your countersignature, you'll have some explaining to do.

When you purchase the checks, ask how the replacement process works, request a list of local representatives where you will be traveling, and get a telephone hotline number.

When you cash a traveler's check, record the number, amount, date, and place of the transaction. If you don't keep track, a clever thief could steal a few checks, and you wouldn't discover it immediately. You might even lose some checks yourself and fail to report them for replacement. Review your remaining checks once in a while to ensure that none are missing. If some are, you have to figure out whether you simply failed to record a transaction or they were lost or stolen.

When you report a lost or stolen traveler's check abroad, you can expect quick replacement if you have the check numbers and denominations. Without this information, you'll wait while it's obtained.

Take the receipts on the trip, but keep them separate from the checks. I also give a copy of the receipts to my travel partner and to someone at home.

CREDIT CARDS

Can a traveler survive on plastic alone? Even though credit cards are accepted in Tegucigalpa, Honduras, and you'll find ATM machines on street corners in Mérida, Mexico, the answer is "no." In some of the most fascinating parts of the world, credit cards are still not accepted. Even where they are, you may not want to patronize the upscale hotel or restaurant that is the only place that will accept payment by charge card. Some merchants (especially in Guatemala) will charge a 4-to-5.5-percent "service fee" if you use plastic.

> Back up your credit cards with alternate sources of funds.

Nevertheless, expanding acceptance of credit cards has transformed traveler's checks into a backup source of payment. In a growing number of countries, many expenses can be charged on VISA, MasterCard, American Express, and, to a lesser extent, Diners Club and Discover. In fact, it may make sense to put everything on your credit card if you can do so without changing the nature of your trip and if you pay off the balance when you return. Back up credit cards with an alternative source of funds.

Credit-card benefits include at least some of the following (depending on the specific card):

- Charging purchases
- Obtaining cash advances as you go so you can carry less cash at any one time

- Doubling the manufacturer's warranty on products you purchase
- Obtaining protections that may include assistance with legal and medical issues, and insurance covering accidental death, rental-car damage, and shipping from overseas
- Obtaining "purchase security," meaning that the issuer will replace, repair, or reimburse you (usually up to $500) for eligible items of personal property in the event of theft, fire, vandalism, weather damage, and so on (when the items are bought with the credit card and claims are filed within 90 days)
- Avoiding the spread (in essence, a fee) and commission charged when converting cash or traveler's checks into local currency (but see page 280 regarding fees charged by credit-card issuers)
- Getting a good currency-exchange rate. The international corporate rate is more favorable than the rate you get from a local bank or currency dealer. However, credit-card issuers are beginning to take some of this for themselves (on top of an added fee of 2 or 3 percent),
- Having some protection should there be a problem with the purchase
- Frequent-flier mileage or other rewards-program credit

Credit-card tips:

- Two things that sometimes cause a credit-card issuer to block access to your card are changes in spending habits and charges coming from foreign countries. To avoid having your credit strangled, call the issuer at least three days before you leave and let it know when you're leaving and when you'll return.
- Before using a credit card to get cash, be sure you understand the fees (that keep being increased). At present, MasterCard and VISA networks charge a 1 percent "currency exchange fee" for processing and converting foreign-currency credit-card transactions. Credit-card issuers, mostly banks, now charge an additional 1 to 3 percent. At the moment, only Capital One and some local credit unions issue cards with no fees for foreign-currency transactions. Consider these fees when choosing which credit card to use.
- If you use credit cards to help finance your trip, carry more than one. Don't let a technological glitch or plastic-eating machine halt your trip. In case of loss, have cash or traveler's checks ready as backup.
- To avoid a late charge, you may need to arrange for your credit-card bill to be paid while you're away. You may also need to make payments to keep sufficient credit available as you travel. Ask the issuer how to handle it. The most efficient way is to authorize the credit-card issuer to withdraw electronically from your money-market fund or bank account.
- Ensure that the bill is correct before signing the slip, and keep your copy.

- If your credit card disappears, you will probably have no liability as long as you report the loss at once. Any merchant who accepts the card can help you report its loss.
- Using a credit card does not free you from paying for an item if you are simply dissatisfied with it, if the goods turn out to be worth less than you thought, or if the vendor ships you the wrong item. You can complain to the credit-card issuer and withhold payment while your claim is investigated, but you must file your complaint within the time limit stated by the issuer of the card, usually 30 or 60 days. When goods are defective, the credit card usually provides protection only if you purchased the item in your home state or within 100 miles of home. In other words, the credit-card company isn't required to investigate that sort of claim with respect to items you bought abroad. Although many issuers at least attempt to investigate the dispute, the facts are often impossible to determine, in which case the issuer rules against the cardholder.
- To reduce fees for using credit cards (as well as ATM cards), you are usually much better off making fewer and larger exchanges rather than a lot of small exchanges.
- Capital One cardholders pay the lowest fees. American Express cardholders can call on local amex offices for help in almost every foreign country.

ATM CASH CARDS

All over this planet, automatic teller machines are eagerly waiting to put cash in your hand as soon as you whisper your PIN in their ears.

It sounds so simple. Slip the card in your wallet, and you're off. But hold on. There's more to it:

- As with credit cards, the issuer of an ATM card may block access to your money if it detects changes in spending habits and charges coming from foreign countries. To avoid that, call the issuer at least three days before you leave and let it know when you're leaving and when you'll return.
- There is probably a daily limit on how much you can withdraw. Know what it is.
- Transaction fees used to be a mere nibble, but the banks are now taking a larger mouthful. One card issuer charges a fee of 2.5 percent of the amount of cash you withdraw and starts charging 7.9 percent interest the moment the cash comes down the chute. At least that issuer does not charge an additional currency-conversion fee of 1 or 2 percent. Some do. If you'll be traveling for a while, shop around and find the lowest total charges.
- Call the international number for the issuer and ask whether ATMs at your destination require personal identification numbers (PINs) with more or fewer digits than your usual PIN. Four digits is the common standard.

- Card issuers have numbers you can call collect from overseas when you need help. Look them up before you leave.
- Determine ATM locations at your destinations. MasterCard and VISA systems have hundreds of thousands of locations in more than 200 countries and territories. See **www.mastercard.com** and **www.visa.com** for ATM locations worldwide and guides to benefits of using the respective cards. Of course, you can also do what most travelers do: ask around on-site. If you can find one associated with your own bank, it will cost you less.
- Becoming dependent on ATMs can penalize you. A given ATM may not accept your card. Or you may not be able to read the machine's instructions. It may be out of money. Or you may not be able to find one—which is most likely in the most interesting parts of our planet. Draw on ATMs when you're in bigger cities because you may be without access to one in areas where banks and technology are sparse.

DEBIT CARDS

When you use an ATM to obtain cash, you are directly debiting your bank account. However, if you lose a debit card that does not require a PIN, the underlying account could be emptied by the finder. Not so good when you're far from home.

You can also get a prepaid card, say, a MasterCard, that operates on the same debiting principle. You deposit a certain amount of money before you leave and draw down that amount with the MasterCard as you travel. It's a way to reduce transaction costs and serves those without easy access to credit cards.

RECEIVING MONEY OVERSEAS

If you're on the road and your wallet needs refueling from home, you can ask someone to wire money. However, fees are very high. Also, even though the source will be paying in hard currency, you'll likely be given local currency in exchange. In a pinch, you can use Western Union (**www.westernunion.com**). It has offices everywhere in Mexico and Central America because so many remittances come in from relatives working in the United States. Note that money sent instantly incurs higher fees than payments that can wait a day or two.

TAKING FOREIGN CURRENCY ALONG

If you decide to take foreign currency along, International Currency Express (call [888] 278-6628, or see **www.foreignmoney.com**) can provide currency from 60 countries, including Mexico and every Central American country except Nicaragua. It can also issue money orders in many foreign currencies. But see the comment in "Where to Exchange Your Money," at right.

EXCHANGING MONEY

How Much Local Currency Should You Buy?

If you buy too much local currency, you waste money on the exchange transaction in both directions, buying and selling. If you're stuck with the currency after you leave the country, it's probably a total loss.

I seldom travel with more than the equivalent of a few hundred dollars in local currency unless I anticipate some large expense.

Be aware of weekends and holidays coming up. If you won't have ready access to an exchange window or machine, exchange enough to avoid standing with an empty wallet in front of a closed bank. You may find someone on the street who will exchange money, but if you're in a bind, the rate will reflect your situation.

Don't Always Exchange Your Money

In some countries, the U.S. dollar is accepted as readily as local currency, with no exchange penalty. In Central America, this is true in El Salvador, Panama, and the tourist areas of Belize and Honduras. In some other countries, you can make purchases in dollars, but you will be given, with no mention of it, a very poor exchange rate. There are still a few countries where you have more bargaining power when you pay in U.S. dollars. These are usually where the local currency is very unstable or merchants are collecting dollars to spend on their own travel.

Where to Exchange Your Money

Where you'll find the worst exchange rates:

- Outside the country. If you arrive in a country between midnight and dawn, when the money-exchange office at your point of entry may be closed, it might be nice to have a little local currency in hand. But few sources outside the country are likely to stock its currency. If they do, they'll charge a hefty fee and give a poor exchange rate in the bargain. In my opinion, it's not worth the trouble.
- At points of entry. If you fly into a country, there will be an exchange window or machine in the airport. If you arrive by train, there will probably be an opportunity to exchange in the station just after the border or in the first large city. If arriving on foot or by automobile, you should be able to make an exchange just beyond the immigration office. Where no official money exchange is available, there are often informal bankers on the street.
- From hustlers at borders, including the guys outside airports and train stations. They try to con you into exchanging money with them before you know what rate you should get. If you have to exchange money at an entry point, change only the amount you need to get into town and pay for a night's lodging and a couple of meals.

> Wait to trade money until you know the fair exchange rate.

- At the cash register. The sellers of products or services, including hotels, restaurants, and souvenir shops, will often give you a poor exchange rate. Some will even zap you with a fee on top of that. Fortunately, many spots in Central America are an exception. Be aware of the prevailing bank rate at your destination so you will know if the rate your hotel or shop is quoting is favorable.

Where to get better exchange rates:

- From travelers who have left the place you're going. You'll get a great rate because the currency is worth zero to them.
- At automatic currency-exchange machines, which resemble ATMs. They usually spit out local currency, but some can make exchanges among many currencies. You feed the machine your currency and tell it what currency you want back. In some places, the machine's exchange rates are better than bank rates (taking bank commissions, fees, and stamps into account). They're fun to play with—kind of like slot machines where you win every time.
- From private dealers. In some countries, only banks can legally exchange money. Others have government-sanctioned, privately owned currency-exchange dealers who operate in small offices along the main streets. Their rates differ from one another but are generally better than bank rates. Shop around.
- To pay no foreign transaction fee at all, use a VISA card from Capital One or USAA, or a MasterCard or VISA from some credit unions or small banks. Check with them first. Some travelers also recommend the Bank of America card that allows you to withdraw cash at ATMs of many different banks without paying a fee.

To pay the lowest fees (probably 1%), use a VISA card from Capital One or USAA, or a MasterCard or VISA from some credit unions or small banks. Check with them first. Some travelers also recommend the Bank of America card that allows you to withdraw cash at ATMs of many different banks without paying a fee.

Making the Exchange

Before you approach a currency-exchange window, calculate roughly how much money you should receive in an exchange. Learn the rough relationship between your currency and that of your destination country, and the calculation becomes second nature. That will keep you from being the victim of a misplaced decimal. It happens.

Things get a little complicated when you reach the window. Each foreign currency in which the dealer trades is listed, followed by several columns. When you're using your cash to buy the local currency, the figure that matters is in the "Buying Cash" column. When

> A transaction fee may be charged when you buy local currency.

you are selling local currency to the dealer, the rate you'll get is in the "Selling Cash" column. You'll always have to pay the difference, called the "spread," between the buying and the selling rates. In other words, the rate you pay for the peso you buy when you arrive is higher than what you'll get when it's time to sell it back. This spread is like the house percentage in a casino.

Besides comparing exchange rates, you must also compare transaction fees often charged in addition to the spread. That fee may be based on what the total amount of the transaction is or whether you're exchanging cash or traveler's checks. If the difference between dealers is small, it's not worth walking back across town to chase a few pennies.

Not all currency-exchange clerks are honest. The amount given you may not just be incorrect—it may not even be close! Some clerks play tricks, so count the money before taking even one step away. Don't feel pressured by the people in line behind you. Count the money in plain view of the clerk but not the crowd. If the total is correct, tuck it out of sight before you leave the window. Because someone may be watching, the money is at risk as long as it's in your hand or in an accessible pocket.

THE MERCHANT SHUFFLE

In some Central American countries, it's almost a surprise to receive correct change when paying for something. The clerk or waiter may make a small personal deduction or even give you coins from a nearby country that are worth less. I think of this practice as an informal foreign-aid program.

Merchants sometimes play an interesting game of monetary musical chairs. When a bank note becomes torn or worn, banks will no longer accept it—which means that merchants will not accept it from you. But, oh, will they try to give it to you! Take a look at your change. If there is a seriously battered bill, simply hand it back with a smile. The merchant will replace it. It was just a little test to see if you heard the music stop.

Also be advised that many countries have chronic shortages of small change, and many merchants have the baffling habit of opening the store with no money in the till. If you try to pay with a large bill—even if it's only worth $10 in local currency—expect to wait while the merchant tries to borrow change from someone else. How do you avoid this? Act like a local and hoard your change!

BARGAINING: WHEN AND HOW

Most Westerners are convinced they don't like bargaining, at least not "street" bargaining. Perhaps underlying that cultural hang-up is the belief that they don't know how to do it. Except for unhappy episodes when attempting to buy a car, most Westerners don't do much one-on-one bargaining.

SAVE Money   In most of the world, bargaining is part of daily life. Certainly in Mexico and Central America, anyone who doesn't bargain is regarded as so foolish that he or she deserves to be charged a penalty. Even in Europe, it's far more common than most Western tourists realize. It would be a shame to let inhibitions or cultural differences interfere with experiencing the art and sport of bargaining. Besides, if you use tips from this chapter, you'll save money wherever you travel. Bargaining is a skill that can also help you save money when you return home.

In less developed countries, prices in restaurants are fixed, but be prepared to bargain for almost everything else, including hotel rates, taxis, guides, treks, clothing, art, crafts, and souvenirs. You may occasionally walk into a shop and see price tags on items, maybe even a sign that says "fixed prices." Sometimes prices really are fixed, but those signs are more likely the first move in bargaining chess.

Surely you can't bargain over airfare? Oh, but you can! The sales agents of most major airlines won't bargain, as far as I know, but many travel agencies abroad have some latitude in what they charge for a ticket. There's a spread between what they get from you and what they remit to the airline. Because you don't bargain with travel agents at home, you may feel reluctant, but give it a try. You'll be surprised at how often the agent comes up with a previously unmentioned "special." You'll never get it without asking.

To begin the bargaining process, start with your own state of mind. Loosen up. Have a sense of humor about it. Think of yourself as writing your own lines in an amusing play.

Ideally, you should decide what an item is worth to you before you start bargaining. That's easier said than done with spontaneous purchases, especially when it's something you've never seen or heard of before. Have you given much thought to how much an antique Mexican army sword is worth to you? If there's a price tag, ignore it. If the merchant calls out a price, ignore it. Think for a moment what you would pay to have that particular object in your home. Only then should you investigate what the item is worth in the local market. Ask several people who've bought something similar. If you ask just one person, it may be someone who paid way too much.

Don't fall in love with an item the first time you see it. Check other shops. The colorful carved-fish mobile that caught your eye has counterparts in a dozen shops—and they differ in quality as well as in the shopkeeper's opinion of its value. Initial prices vary from merchant to merchant. Do some preliminary bargaining to get feedback from the market. After a round or two of light sparring, you'll know the neighborhood of the outcome. More than anything, successful bargaining takes patience.

The bargaining process begins as you enter the shop.

See what local buyers pay for what you want. As you walk through the market, look over their shoulders. You may not get the item for the same price, but you'll know what the merchant can sell it for and still make a profit. That's a big edge.

Recognize that the bargaining process begins earlier in a transaction than you think. While you're wandering around the shop, the vendor is sizing up your clothes and noting the amount of attention you give particular items. As she approaches, you'll hear: "You are from what country?" She may inquire about your occupation and where you're staying. Her bargaining strategy will be based on your responses, starting with the language in which you answer. As charming as she may be, her questions do not spring from friendly curiosity. They're part of a highly developed socioeconomic evaluation that would make Northwestern's Kellogg Graduate School of Management proud. Answering her questions would be like showing your hole card in the middle of a hand of poker. Instead, just smile, mumble, respond with a question of your own, or act as if you didn't understand her.

It would be an expensive error to show enthusiasm for the thing you want, so bargain first for something else. Let your attention wander from one item to another, patiently letting the vendor guess what might interest you. The more time she invests, the greater her eagerness to conclude a sale at some price.

Because I don't know what effect the presence of other shoppers may have on the merchant, I try to avoid bargaining in front of anyone else.

She may try to hand you the item in which she thinks you have an interest. Just smile and nod, hands in pockets. If you accept it, you may have a difficult time getting her to take it back.

Don't hesitate to courteously criticize the item for which you're bargaining, pointing out real or imagined defects. Indicate aspects that aren't quite right for you or mention features of similar products elsewhere that this one doesn't have. However, I avoid implying that the shopkeeper or artisan is intentionally selling something undesirable or worthless. There's always "face" involved, and it's better to maintain a courteous relationship. Keep the tone light, never angry. I cringe when a tourist bargains loudly and aggressively, heaping scorn on some object. Whatever the outcome, it's a disgraceful way for a visitor to behave. Similarly, if the vendor gets too aggressive, I'm out of there. I don't mind a skillful pitch, but I'm not there to be hassled. When I'm absolutely certain I don't want to carry an eight-by-ten-foot carpet in my luggage and I can't get the merchant to stop trying to sell it to me, I leave.

Always let the merchant make the first offer. Don't respond when pressed for a counteroffer. Be cool. Keep looking around. See if the price will drop before you respond. The merchant's first price may be twice to ten times what will be accepted, so don't think of just knocking 10 or 20 percent off it. If you pay more than 60 percent of the asking price at the famous Sunday market in Chichicastenango, Guatemala, the shopkeeper might light a candle in your memory. In other words, don't buy into the asking price as being related to actual value. If interested, mention a figure you might pay—perhaps 20 percent of the reduced asking price. State your tentative counteroffer with reluctance and expect a response somewhere between incredulity and feigned personal affront. In rare cases, your sanity may be challenged. Keep in mind that merchants are also actors with their own scripts.

If you have any expertise concerning an item, don't reveal it until you can use it to your advantage as you near the climax.

Tell the shopkeeper that you aren't a rich tourist and can't afford her price. If you're staying at an inexpensive hotel, say so. If what you say is consistent with how the shopkeeper has sized you up, perhaps a smaller profit will be more acceptable than loss of the sale.

Two people can be an effective team in a bargaining situation by playing a variation of the old "good guy, bad guy" routine. As one person bargains, the other begins to fidget, expresses lack of interest in the item, checks the time, moves toward the door, and exerts pressure on the bargainer to come along. At that point, the prospective buyer mentions a price considerably lower than that at which the negotiation has stalled.

> Remember that the shopkeeper is a pro at bargaining.

The merchant, having only a few moments in which to make the deal, may yield a bit more.

If you're by yourself, suggest that you're going to leave and "look around," perhaps mentioning a competitor's prices, real or mythical. These words strike dread into the heart of any merchant. Or say, "I'm going to see what my friend thinks." More grim words. Be sure to give the merchant a chance to make another "final" offer. If it doesn't come, step out the door. If a merchant won't drop the price any lower as you walk out and doesn't follow you, you're close to a fair price.

If you've reached an impasse on something you really want, tell the seller you'll pay the price if something else is included.

If you're planning to buy several of one item, such as scarves, first negotiate a price for a single item. Then introduce the possibility of buying several. Ask for a further discount of, say, 30 percent. Or buy several different items from the same merchant if possible rather than cherry-picking from separate shops.

It sometimes helps to pull money out of your pocket and hold it in your hand. Psychologically, it may make the seller want to reach for it—by meeting your price. More than once, I've put the amount of my target price in one pocket, pulling it out at the last moment and saying, "This is what I have." It sometimes works. If it doesn't and I still want to play, I check another pocket and discover a bit more money. Remember, timing is important—and the merchant has been through this scene thousands of times.

> You won't have to look for the black market—it will find you.

In countries in which hard currency has special value, you may break an impasse by offering to pay your price, but in an equivalent amount of U.S. dollars.

Prices vary from season to season. In the tourist off-season, great deals are available. When the market pulses with acquisitive tourists, you'll pay closer to the top of the range (but still less than the asking price). After all, the vendor knows there will be an innocent coming through the door right behind you, eager to be sheared.

It's easy to lose perspective during the bargaining process. You could find yourself getting hung up over $2, or even 50 cents. If you feel ambivalent about purchasing the item, hold firm or walk away. If it's something you want to own and walking off doesn't produce a last-minute concession, walk back and pay the shopkeeper's last price—perhaps with a sheepish smile. Don't let your own "face" stand in your way. Why chastise yourself later over having left behind something you really wanted?

What if the asking price is so cheap that you're willing to pay it without discussion? If you're talking about a few cents, it's not worth your time to bargain. But if you want to make a contribution, why not choose an appropriate charity or a needy person? Why make a donation to a shopkeeper who, in that economy, is seldom one of the needier people?

If you accept something from the merchant, such as a cup of tea or a cold drink, be aware that her primary motive is to make you feel indebted or friendly. I'm not disparaging her motive, only saying that acceptance of a cup of tea creates no obligation on your part. If you don't reach agreement, leave with a courteous "thank you anyway." Under the rules of engagement, negotiating, no matter how lengthy, commits you to nothing. You're ethically free to walk away anytime. If you and the merchant place a different value on something, and you can't resolve the difference, that's okay. However, when a merchant accepts a price you've offered, you should pay that price. It would be bad karma to walk away at that point.

As you bargain for anything, remember that your adversary is a pro, much more experienced at this than you are. She knows her costs and the quality of the item. She won't close a sale if she won't come out all right, so don't hesitate to do your best. Stay lighthearted and friendly, never intense. Because sitting for many hours in a market stall on a steamy day isn't anyone's idea of a great time, a good bargaining bout may be fun for the seller.

> Prepare for black-market exchanges as you would legitimate ones.

Bargain hard, but never, given the great disparity between your income and that of the merchant, sharply. Don't try to cut it too close. However the deal goes, leave one another with a pleasant memory.

Here's a final thought about "after the sale." If it later appears that your purchase wasn't all that shrewd because of price or quality, learn what you can from the experience and forget self-recriminations. If somebody claims to have bought the same thing for less, think of it as a reminder of price elasticity that you can use to your advantage next time. And realize that people have been known to shade the truth more than a little when discussing their own astute bargaining.

All this may seem complicated at first, but it isn't in practice. In no time, you'll be improving on these strategies with your own flourishes.

For more on bargaining, please see Chapter 15, Lodging, and Chapter 25, Shopping and Shipping.

A Curious Exchange

One of my most remarkable bargaining experiences took place in New Delhi. Because I was heading to the high altitudes of Ladakh, I wanted to buy a warm jacket. After looking around, I spotted a coat with great character. The shop owner asked $55, a considerable sum in India. I looked dubious. He dropped the price to $40. I declined. He poured tea and we talked for an hour or so about politics. Then he said, "Okay, pay me $30, take the coat, bring it back, and I'll give you the money back." I was considering his unusual offer when he said, "No, never mind, just take the coat. Promise to bring it back some day and tell me all about Ladakh. I've always wanted to go, but I never will." And so, many weeks later, I told him my tales of the Kingdom of Ladakh.

CHAPTER 11

Travel Gear

I had grown into my clothes, the way travelers do
who haven't looked into a mirror for weeks.
—Colin Thubron
"Night in Vietnam"
Granta magazine

I used to know it all.

When I recommended travel gear in years past—from backpacks to boots, clothing to cameras—I did so with confidence. That was because only a few manufacturers consistently offered high-quality products. Furthermore, my friends and I had road-tested most of it and knew what worked and what didn't. Well, now I've grown reluctant to recommend specific products. For one thing, many other reputable suppliers have entered the field, offering diverse and sophisticated travel gear. For another, budding travelers are not some homogeneous group of good folk setting off to see the world. Fact is, they differ widely in terms of age, physical condition, destination, and a dozen other characteristics. The choice of gear is also affected by the intended use: adventure, tour, cruise, or whatever. Therefore, each person is in a much better position to make choices for himself or herself than I am.

Finally, any prospective traveler can use the Internet to access endless details (including evaluations) of available products. So I'll stop recommending my battered Kelty Kathmandu convertible backpack. My contribution will be to suggest the issues you should consider to make the best choices to meet your needs.

I suggest you start your search with the Internet. Every significant manufacturer has a Web site, but you may find some of the more comprehensive sites, such as that of *Outside* magazine (**outside.away.com**), more useful in the beginning because they cut across so many brands and prices.

There's no point in wasting money buying trendy labels, and the fancier the gear looks the more it becomes a target for thieves. It's best to buy high-quality, durable, lightweight clothing and equipment, but don't let the prices of the optimum gear keep you at home. Cutting corners could become expensive if something important fails on the road, but some people travel with the cheapest gear available, and good fortune usually carries them through.

Let's start with a theme that should influence every choice of gear you make. It's a state of mind.

TRAVEL LIGHT!

That's easy to say—and hard to do. Choosing the right travel gear requires time and research. Proceeding in haste, an inexperienced traveler will always carry too much. But let's get to bedrock. Why should you care about the weight or size of what you bring with you? Two reasons. First, you or someone has to move it repeatedly from one place to another, sometimes under less-than-ideal conditions. Second, airlines have discovered yet another way to turn you into a profit center. They've tightened luggage weight and size limits and instructed their check-in people to collect penalties without mercy. And why would you expect mercy from someone who may get a bonus for nailing you?

I've heard people claim they can slide everything they need for a three-month trip under their plane seat every time. Or fit it all, plus the *Collected Works of Shakespeare,* into a day pack. But let's talk about normal human beings, people who want to travel with a camera, shower shoes, maybe even a snorkel; people traveling to have fun. They too can travel light, but it takes some thought.

For my first long trip (which turned out to be seven months), I wanted to be prepared to dress up, so I actually carried a blue blazer along. The predictable result: overload. It was a greenhorn's mistake, not knowing that local people are aesthetically forgiving about travelers. If you look clean and smile, they don't expect high fashion. Randy Wayne White, whose excellent articles appear in *Outside* magazine, observed that inexperienced travelers take too much of what they don't need, and experienced travelers take too much of what they do need. Instead of throwing or giving it away, they lug the extra stuff mile after mile, to be returned unused to the closet.

There's a better way. Don't include an item just because it might come in handy (what I call the deadly "just in case" syndrome). You can almost always do without it. If not, you can probably find some local equivalent. Limit yourself to what you're willing to carry without complaint up a steep hill on a hot day. If you're traveling with a partner, travel light enough that either of you can carry most of the luggage, leaving the other free to sprint ahead of the crowd to find a good room or the best seats on a bus.

In general, that means trying to limit your load to 25 pounds; 30 to 35 is still bearable. If you leave home with more than 50 pounds, I guarantee you'll cut down for the next trip. A few extra pounds may not seem to matter much at home, but they will on the road.

BAGGAGE LIMITS

Guess who's stepped up to help you travel light? It's the airlines. As we know all too well, airlines have created a labyrinth of regulations governing the amount, size, and weight of luggage with which you may travel. Exceed those limits, and you'll pay heavy penalties.

Variables that affect these limits are: whether it's a U.S. or foreign airline, whether the route is domestic or international, whether the plane is large or small, whether the luggage is checked or carry-on, what class of ticket is being used, and, of course, what the whims of the particular airline may be.

For checked luggage, a total size of 62 linear inches (length plus width plus height) for one piece is common for economy class, and some airlines further restrict the size of a second or third bag (if they even allow a third checked bag). Carry-on luggage is restricted to one main bag, with total linear dimensions not to exceed 45 to 50 inches, depending on the airline. It must fit under your seat or in the overhead bin.

Some airlines have a simple test. They place a box near the check-in counter. If you can stuff your bag into it, you may carry it on board. If not, it must be checked. I've heard passengers scream in rage when told their bags full of fragile items were too large to be carried aboard. That was even before they received the bill for the luggage being overweight.

In addition to the carry-on bag, you can bring the equivalent of a purse or day pack. Because of the erratic nature of security rules, ask early on about a purse, briefcase, laptop, collapsible luggage cart, reading material, camera, binoculars, umbrella, coat, and similar items. Overseas, these items may also be subject to weight limits and other rules.

> Check the airline's size and weight limits before you go.

Limits usually get tighter on small feeder airlines. The trip you start on a large Delta jet may connect with its partner airline flying a much smaller plane. Ask about the lowest limits.

Penalties for violating these rules are not amusing. If you're over the limit on the number of checked bags, think $50 to more than $100 per extra bag. If a bag is oversize or overweight, think $25 to more than $100.

I offer this information reluctantly, and you must not rely on it. Don't assume that these limits or the ones you used to follow are still in effect. Don't generalize, hope, or guess. The variables that follow result in many different numbers—and every one may change by edict of an airline. *Call the airline for each flight, or be certain you understand the rules on its Web site.*

If you're about to get socked for an overweight-baggage penalty, be creative. Reclaim your luggage. Unpack and wear as much as you need to. There's no limit on that yet. Ask someone to treat one of your bags as theirs (which a cautious person certainly won't do).

At the moment, exceptions (that don't have to be in the zip-top bag but still must be declared) include:

- Reasonable quantities (which can be more than 3 ounces) of prescription medications and baby formula, breast milk, and juice for a companion infant or toddler. The medication must be in the name of the person holding the ticket.

Items Prohibited for Carry-on Air Travel

Regulations change often. When there's a new security concern, a new "solution" emerges. Because new regulations usually mean new restrictions, your safe course of action is to obtain current information.

Your guide is the Transportation Security Administration and its volatile list of "permitted and prohibited items" for carry-on luggage (call [866] 289-9673, or see www.tsa.gov). The "3-1-1" rule currently covers liquids, gels, creams, and aerosols. Here it is:

- **3-1-1 for carry-ons** = 3 ounce or less bottles; 1 quart-sized, clear, plastic, zip-top bag; 1 bag per passenger. The one-quart bag must be removed from carry-on luggage and placed in the screening bin or on the conveyor belt.
- **Consolidate** bottles into one bag to speed screening.
- **Be prepared.** TSA searches slow down the line. Practicing 3-1-1 will ensure a faster checkpoint experience.
- **3-1-1 is for short trips.** If you must carry greater quantities, put them in checked luggage.

> I cannot go so fast as I would, by reason of this burden that is on my back.
> —John Bunyan, *The Pilgrim's Progress* (1678)

- Nonprescription medicines in their original containers or daily-dosage dispensers.
- Liquids or gels for treatment of diabetes or other medical conditions.
- Gel-filled bras and other prosthetics worn for medical reasons.

Note that these "exception" items must be kept separate and be declared to the TSA officer. Aerosol insect repellents are prohibited. Although you can't bring bottled water through security, you can take aboard water and food purchased after passing security.

CHOOSING LUGGAGE

My criteria for luggage are:

- Transportability: Will it qualify as carry-on luggage in terms of size and weight? Can I handle it easily while under way?
- Durability: Will it survive brutal baggage handling?
- Accessibility: Is it easy to find packed items? And easy to repack?
- Security: Can it be securely locked? And not easily sliced open?

Because carry-on luggage is much more protected from theft, loss, and rough handling than is checked luggage, it's by far the best choice. In any case, try never to travel with more than one main bag, a day pack, and, if it's essential, one more small piece.

Luggage that works fine when heaved about by taxi drivers, porters, and bell-hops may become a real burden when you're handling it yourself. Think about muscling it around on subways and buses. Or, at the end of a long day, up three flights of steep stairs in a charming bed-and-breakfast. Or on a long trek uphill on rough paving stones on a summer afternoon. As you explore more deeply into rural Mexico and Central America, distances seem to grow longer and the sun hotter.

A major transformation in luggage was an astounding technological break-through called . . . wheels. Formerly rare on luggage, they are now common. (I won-der what that says about our society?) But not all wheels are created equal. Some are thin and can't handle rough pavement, let alone cobblestones. Some are fragile; others are attached in a way that invites the luggage to tip over every few feet.

Carefully examine brand-name bags on sale in discount stores. Those bags are often inferior in quality to similar models sold in luggage shops at higher prices. If you choose a shoddy bag and then stuff it to its limits, don't be surprised if it fails along the way. At least improve your odds by binding cheap luggage with a couple of tough, webbed luggage straps.

Reputable periodicals such as *Consumer Reports* provide important compari-sons of products, and most multibrand luggage sites on the Internet offer con-sumer ratings. Some comments raise good points. Others seem to be marketing pitches used to stuff the ballot box.

Now let's review various types of luggage. It's tempting to recommend spe-cific brands and styles, but it's also pointless. Characteristics and prices change too frequently. Some mergers have turned old reliables into cheap knockoffs. Examine potential choices closely. Don't rely on brand names or assume that a high price guarantees better quality.

Hard-sided Luggage

After watching poor-quality, overstuffed luggage disintegrate in transit, bag-gage handlers recommend hard-sided luggage because it's tough. Of course, durability is important partly *because* of baggage handlers. However, I don't recommend a standard hard-sided suitcase for anything but a trip during which you go to one place, stop, and return—a typical business trip. Weight is the major reason. A hard-sided suitcase adds an extra ten pounds or so more than soft-sided luggage.

If it's dead weight dangling at the end of one arm, you'll be ready to aban-don it after the first mile. Adding wheels eases the burden but adds even more weight—which you'll notice every time you can't use the wheels.

Soft-sided Luggage

Many people prefer not to carry a backpack. Maybe it's a back problem, maybe an image problem, or maybe just habit. If soft-sided, non-backpack luggage is your choice, look for 1,000-denier fabric—either Cordura nylon or polyester. If

Tim's choice of gear makes his load bearable.

it has wheels, make sure they're wide and sturdy, partly recessed or protected by housings. Dainty little wheels won't stand up to rough surfaces or long distances. A sturdy, retractable handle is far preferable to a leash. It should also have a hand grip you can use when wheels won't work. Some of the best designs include a pair of hidden shoulder straps so you can sling the whole thing onto your back when you need to.

Look for a waterproof pocket and compression straps inside (to keep your clothes from shifting). Good construction is important. Rivets are more durable than D-rings or screws for connecting shoulder straps and handles. Seams are usually encased in plastic for water resistance, but casings of leather, shell fabric, or wide, woven tape resist abrasion better. Many travelers like luggage that includes a small pack that can be zipped off to use as a day pack.

Another form of soft-sided luggage that may work well for some trips is a garment (hanging) bag—especially if it will fold enough to be eligible as a carry-on. Be certain it has a sturdy, padded, over-the-shoulder strap. Look for good quality, and be sure all compartments can be locked.

Duffel Bags

Some people are fanatically fond of traveling with a duffel bag. I'm not normally one of them, but I traveled with a BAD BAG (Best American Duffel;

www.badbags.com) to Antarctica because it had the capacity to carry all the foul-weather and photographic gear I needed. The regular BAD BAG, which has the best workmanship I've seen in duffels, comes in five sizes ranging up to 7,800 cubic inches and is made of 1,000-denier Cordura Plus with a urethane coating for water resistance. Mine has two inside pockets, tie-downs, an expandable outside pocket, a leather handle, a seat-belt-style nylon shoulder strap, two grab loops, and heavy-duty hardware. Will Steger chose the largest model for his seven-month dogsled trip across Antarctica. An *Outside* magazine writer wrote that "BAD BAGS are the best all-around duffel bags available." I've heard good things about Eagle Creek (**www.eaglecreek.com**) and Eddie Bauer (**www.eddiebauer.com**) duffels as well.

Because duffel bags hold so much, we tend to keep filling them until they're about as mobile as tombstones. To address that problem, an interesting hybrid has recessed rubber wheels on one end and a leash on the other (which make it heavier still—but movable).

Traveling with a large, fully loaded duffel is like towing a sea lion, so the larger duffels are best used for transporting a lot of gear to a single destination rather than from place to place. Once I set mine down aboard ship, I didn't move it for 18 days.

Backpacks

The days when only hard-core hikers or hippies carried backpacks are long gone. Backpacks are now the choice of many travelers from across the economic spectrum. I confess to never having grown fond of carrying a heavy weight on my back, but I consider a backpack the best choice for the type of travel I enjoy most. It lets me take my gear where I want to go farther and easier than any other form of luggage.

The first step is to buy from an outfitter with a good reputation. I can't resist one comment about my Kelty Kathmandu (which Kelty has long since succeeded with newer models). When the main zipper finally failed after ten years, Kelty took the pack and replaced all the zippers and the back panel without charge. That's standing behind your product.

To meet the criteria of transportability, durability, accessibility, and security, I recommend a convertible, interior-frame backpack. "Convertible" means that the harness suspension system can be tucked out of sight behind a panel. In that mode, it resembles normal luggage rather than a backpack, so you can walk into a hotel or a bureaucrat's office without being stereotyped as a backpacker. Oh, the concierge in a five-star hotel will probably notice, but if he's as good as he should be, he'll never raise an eyebrow. Besides, who wants to plan a trip around the expectations of a concierge?

It was inevitable that backpacks would also metamorphose into wheelies. Some models come with built-in rubber wheels and a pull-frame. While convenient, those wheels add several pounds to the weight—which you must carry on occasion and which may cost you an overweight baggage charge at the check-in counter.

If you're going on a lengthy wilderness excursion over moderate terrain, you may prefer a backpack with an exterior frame to which a sleeping bag, climbing equipment, and other odds and ends can be attached. Otherwise, an interior-frame pack is superior because it's lighter, less susceptible to damage, and unlikely to get hung up on an airport carousel.

I'm not plugging any brand—again, because things change—but Eagle Creek (**www.eaglecreek.com**), Kelty (**www.kelty.com**), L.L.Bean (**www.llbean.com**), JanSport (**www.jansport.com**), REI (**www.rei.com**), and The North Face (**www .thenorthface.com**) consistently receive good marks from travelers.

Summary of Pack Characteristics

I recommend that a pack have the following characteristics (most of which are equally applicable to a suitcase, carry-on, or duffel bag). Many pieces of luggage fail to meet one or more of these criteria.

- **Color.** Any pack will get dirty on a train-station platform, the open deck of a boat, the roof of a bus, or an oxcart, where it's serving as your seat. A dark color makes the dirt less obvious.
- **Fabric.** For durability, one of the best materials is 1,000-denier Cordura nylon with a light urethane coating. Plain Cordura is tough but not water-proof, so Scotchgard it before each trip. If your pack will be exposed to water, consider an inexpensive rain cover. (A large plastic trash bag works in a pinch.)
- **Construction.** Seams should be double- or triple-stitched and reinforced at stress points. Inside seams should be taped or finished. Raw edges will soon begin to fray—and those little stringlets seek zippers like a Sidewinder missile seeks heat.
- **Handle.** There should be one, and it should be padded.
- **Shoulder strap.** It should be padded and wide.
- **Suspension harness.** It should be strong and easily adjustable. Stays should be aluminum so they can be fitted to the contour of your back.
- **Lumbar pad.** It should be large enough to provide a cushion where the pack rests against your lower back.
- **Waist belt.** It should be strong and padded.
- **Compression straps.** They keep the load from shifting and help reduce the size to meet airline baggage limits.
- **Zippers.** Plastic zippers seem to last longer than metal and work more smoothly in very cold temperatures. Ensure that zippers are sturdy (such as #10 YKK) and well sewn into the pack. See if the zipper will reseat itself

Pack Protection

Many gear manufacturers build in some features to protect against snatch-and-run theft, slashing, and so on. Pacsafe (**www.pacsafe.com**) is one of the masters at this. Its packs and bags have lockable zippers, a cable for locking the bag to a secure fixture, slash-proof straps, and panels protected by very tough removable or built-in mesh. These things are almost bulletproof.

on its tracks if it splits open. There should be a flap over the zipper to keep rain out.

- **Compartments.** I prefer a large, front-opening compartment (for easy access to contents) plus several smaller, lockable compartments that let me separate contents on the basis of function. In a single-compartment pack, contents can become a hopeless jumble after you paw through them a couple of times. If a pack has just one compartment, use smaller "stuff bags" of different colors to create mobile compartments and make things easier to find. Some people like packs with a zip-off compartment that can serve as a day pack, but I prefer a day pack designed solely to be a day pack.
- **Expandability.** Some packs have a soft bottom that opens to increase capacity by up to 1,000 cubic centimeters. This feature is handy toward the end of your trip if purchases become irresistible. It would be a great error to fill it up as you start the trip.

Day Packs

In addition to carrying one principal piece of luggage, I use a day pack to carry a book, a journal, pens, maps, fruit, sunglasses, a camera, medical supplies such as Band-Aids and sunscreen, and, usually, a bottle of water—things to which I want easy access. I avoid the temptation of using it to carry things that belong in my money belt. My day pack has one main compartment and two smaller ones, all with lockable zippers. It's a dark color and leaves home well treated with Scotchgard. Apply the same standards of quality for a day pack as for a backpack. You'll rely on it for years, so it's no place to economize.

If you need a carrying case for a small computer, find one that doesn't scream, "Computer inside!" There are several excellent laptop backpacks that look no different from a college student's book bag. However, they're padded on the inside for extra protection.

Some women prefer a purse-equivalent instead of a day pack. Be sure it's sturdy, with a secure clasp and a tough strap.

Now, let's consider the fanny pack. It should never be used as a storage place for valuables. It's better for carrying nonvaluables than a purse is, but a thief may strike anyway because he won't know what you have in it. L.L.Bean offers some of the most ingenious fanny packs. Modular-system fanny packs now come with zip-off gear pouches, mesh water-bottle holsters, urethane-coated cloth to repel water, external tie-downs (for such things as a wind shell), a padded back panel, and a reflective strip on the back. What would Daniel Boone think?

Where to Buy Luggage

Where will you find the luggage you want? Department and "big box" stores, luggage shops, local outdoors outfitters, catalogs, or Internet merchants.

If you prefer a standard suitcase, department stores and luggage shops have a wide selection. If you're considering a duffel or backpack, educate yourself about what's available and how much it costs.

Review catalogues, including those of L.L.Bean (**www.llbean.com**), Campmor (**www.campmor.com**), Magellan's (**www.magellans.com**), Patagonia (**www .patagonia.com**), REI (**www.rei.com**), Eagle Creek (**www.eaglecreek.com**), Sierra Trading Post (**www.sierratradingpost.com**), and TravelSmith (**www .travelsmith.com**). Scan outdoors and travel-oriented magazines.

Search the Internet, and you'll be exposed to an almost infinite selection at good prices along with what may or may not be valid reviews. One place to start might be **www.ebags.com**.

When you have a feeling for features and prices, stop by a local outdoors-gear store to find packs with the features you want. By visiting a local store, you can see and touch the product; discuss fit, quality, and characteristics with a knowledgeable person; and compare competing products.

Try on different packs with the assistance of a salesperson who knows how they should fit. Learn how to adjust the suspension harness properly for your body. When you've found a pack that feels right, examine its construction and features closely.

Resist the temptation to buy a pack that's too big for you. Given the compulsion to fill empty space, think about the maximum weight you want to carry, and keep airline size limits in mind. One traveler I admire hasn't checked a piece of luggage for years. She travels for weeks with only a carry-on that fits under the seat or in the overhead compartment. Besides frustrating those baggage handlers who send luggage into outer space, the small bag disciplines her to travel light.

Ask for recommendations from the salesperson, especially if he or she is an experienced traveler. What are the strengths and weaknesses of the various types of luggage? Which ones have other customers liked the most? When you've made your choice, load it up and walk around the neighborhood so you know what to expect.

Shop for the best price for the luggage you want, but be cautious about buying something cheap. Quality matters. It's no bargain if you wind up with luggage that starts to disintegrate in the boonies. Good luggage will last a long time.

So where do you buy it? It's a kind of ethical issue. Surf the Net for sure. The variety is amazing, and prices are probably lower than at your neighborhood outfitters. But good information about proper fit, use, and care come from the local person. When I'm buying something about which local advice is valuable, I'll pay a bit more to buy locally. I want to help keep that option alive.

Locks

Luggage must be lockable, but now the locks must accommodate two different circumstances. The first is when your luggage passes through a security process, which means allowing access for inspection. If you're standing there with a key, no problem. Otherwise, if officials decide to inspect they'll try their "magic keys." If those keys don't work, they will force your lock open. If you choose to accept that risk, bring an extra lock or two along. For details about approved locks that security personnel can open and relock, contact the Transportation Security Administration (**www.tsa.gov**). You can buy TSA-recognized locks in most luggage stores or from outlets such as Magellan's (**www.magellans.com**) or The Sharper Image (**www.sharperimage.com**). They include Travel Sentry and Safe Skies luggage locks.

The alternative is an array of cheap, temporary devices (such as a $2 pack of 30 nylon ties from Radio Shack) that keep no one out but do alert you that someone has been in your bag. If you claim your bag at an airport carousel and see that it's been opened, check immediately to see if anything is missing. If so, raise hell on the spot.

This is a good time to make the point about not overstuffing your luggage. If a crammed-full bag is inspected, re-closing it will take longer—maybe just long enough for it to miss your flight.

The second circumstance is the rest of your trip. During that time, your locks should make it hard for an intruder to get inside and immediately obvious if someone has.

If an opening has only one zipper tab, there should be a ring to which it can be locked. If there are two zipper tabs, they should be designed so that one can be locked to the other. The zipper tab, which should be metal, typically has a large hole at the top and a small hole at the bottom. Buy a lock with a shackle small enough to fit through the small hole. If you lock the zippers using the large holes, the compartment can be opened enough to allow a hand to reach inside. Try it and you'll see.

Few zipper locks are very strong, but avoid the cheapest ones. They're easy to force or pick. Small combination locks are better because thieves are less familiar with them.

A lightweight, plastic-coated bicycle-locking cable makes it easy to secure your luggage to something immovable. Several companies combine a retractable cable with a combination lock.

Even the best lock doesn't prevent someone from slashing your luggage or stealing it, but it foils the opportunist, the sneak thief who has only a few seconds to get inside and doesn't want you to know he's been there. Locks signal an observer that you are aware of his presence. Like any wolf, he'll prey on the weakest in the flock—and that won't be you.

> Use a distinctive mark on your luggage so it's easily identified.

Luggage Tags

Buy sturdy luggage tags, perhaps with a leather flap to hide the name and address from prying eyes. Otherwise, put a piece of paper (not a business card) bearing only your name in the window of the tag. Your address goes on the back to prevent passersby from knowing where your empty home is. Some travelers use an office address or a friend's name and address. Include your country with the rest of the address.

Because baggage handling can detach any luggage tag, tape your name and address and a friend's telephone number to the inside of your luggage. I strongly recommend also tagging, or otherwise marking, your camera, day pack, and anything else from which you may become separated.

If a misrouted bag is located, the airline sends it to the address on the tag. If that's your home, that might not be your first choice when you're in the middle of a trip. A new type of tag asks the airline agent who locates your lost bag to read the enclosed itinerary and forward your bag to the appropriate destination. It's worth considering (available from Magellan's and others).

Unless your luggage looks very distinctive, you might mark it with a strip of bright tape or a colorful ribbon. Besides being a signal to you, it keeps an inattentive fellow passenger from inadvertently taking your luggage from the baggage carousel. It happens.

Most people get a kick out of airline routing tags from exotic places, but it's better to pull them off your bags as you go if you don't want your luggage to accidentally visit one of those places without you.

HOW TO PACK

For an extended trip, start assembling clothing and equipment weeks before departure and—this is the key—complete packing at least three days before you leave. Don't fudge on that date. Almost no one does that, but do it once, and you'll be a convert. Details, double-checking, and last-minute purchases can be stressful. By finishing early, you avoid mistakes and walk out of the house feeling comparatively peaceful. Laying things out early allows time to figure out what you can do without. I urge you to leave home with some room in your luggage, but few can resist filling it up. Fortunately, everything settles after a while.

Packing tips:

- Pack little or nothing of real value in checked baggage. Never check important documents.
- Pack essential medications in carry-on luggage (or split them between checked and carry-on).
- Divide your belongings among your luggage so that if one bag goes astray, you won't lose all of something.
- Pack film in your carry-on luggage because the radiation that zaps checked luggage is much more powerful than at carry-on checkpoints. The TSA Web site says flatly not to put film in checked baggage, regardless of ISO.
- Travel with gifts unwrapped in case inspectors want to look at them. Saves time and anguish.
- Clothes are like calories; they all add weight. After laying out all the clothes you think you'll need, let a few days pass. Then subtract at least one-fourth of the pile.
- Use a list, and check things off as you put them in the bag. Keep this list. It will be valuable in making a claim if the airline causes your bag to vanish. Because of the current behind-the-scenes chaos in many baggage handling operations, I also suggest taking a picture of your luggage.
- Many travelers roll shirts, pants, underwear, and all other clothing into cylinders, each secured with a stout rubber band. Rolling saves space and keeps clothes relatively unwrinkled (don't even think about lugging a travel iron along). When everything is rolled, searching for an elusive shirt doesn't scramble the contents of your bag. Some who don't roll their clothes wrap them in plastic bags from the cleaners to keep them separated.
- Zip or button clothing to help it hold its shape better.
- Pack no glass containers or containers with spout tops that open easily under pressure.
- Protect breakables by surrounding them with cushions of clothing.
- Keep sharp edges away from luggage fabric to avoid a tear under pressure.
- To minimize shifting, put the heaviest things in the bottom.
- Stuff small items (socks, belts, etc.) inside shoes.
- Pack only small quantities of things, such as soap, that you'll consume as you travel. They're easy to replace, so there's no reason to leave home with a supply for the whole trip.
- Figure out what you can share with a partner so you don't duplicate items.
- Leave home with your luggage partly empty so you have space for things acquired along the way. Of course, when you're disciplined enough to do this, you're a candidate for the Traveler's Hall of Fame.
- Put things in approximately the same places each time you repack on the road.

- Valuables belong in your money belt, not in checked luggage. Semi-precious valuables, such as a journal, belong in carry-on luggage.

Lots of sources, such as **www.smartpacking.com**, describe multistep details of where to place every item in your luggage and in what sequence. It's probably sound advice but seems like overkill. You're not likely to carry pages of packing instructions with you, and even if you took the time to follow all that advice at first, you wouldn't on the road.

CHOOSING CLOTHING

These guidelines will minimize the weight of the clothing you take, help you stay clean and comfortable, and reduce potential problems on the road.

> Your true traveler will not feel he has had his money's worth unless he brings back a few scars.
> —Lawrence Durrell

Choose function over fashion: Some travelers feel secure only when they're prepared to dress conventionally for any event that might come up. In a situation where dressing up is integral to the trip—some cruises or a tour that stays at five-star hotels—then that's the way it is. Every country has some flashy restaurants where diners spiff up, so I always carry at least one shirt that can pass as a dress shirt. Maybe even a tie. Otherwise, it's okay to be a little behind the fashion curve when the alternative is to carry a blue blazer through the rain forest. In other words, forget about packing clothes for every contingency.

Dress for the weather: A travel wardrobe should reflect the climate at your destinations. However, temperatures can differ quite a bit within a small area, especially when you change altitude. Research what high and low temperatures (average temperatures are useless) and rainfall to expect. This information is available on the Internet, in some guidebooks, in libraries, from embassies, and from other travelers. By the way, the Weather Channel (**www.weather.com/travel**) has a tool that offers packing suggestions based on weather conditions in more than 400 locations.

Layer: Layering can greatly reduce the bulk and weight of your wardrobe when visiting cool or cold climates. The inner layer is a thermal (warming) layer that also draws perspiration away from your skin rather than trapping it, and allows it to evaporate. A synthetic material such as Capilene or polypropylene works very well. The middle layer is for insulation. Many materials work fine, and they need not be bulky. The outer layer is to protect you from rain, snow, and wind. It should be lightweight and breathable, and have pockets, a hood, and zippers for ventilation. I like some combination of a light synthetic undershirt or thermal underwear, a turtleneck, a warm canvas or corduroy shirt, maybe a down vest, and a Gore-Tex shell.

Dressing in layers makes it easy to adjust to changes in exertion, temperature, precipitation, or wind. Best of all, layering means you don't have to lug around a parka or other heavy outer garment.

Work on timing: When you absolutely need bulky clothing for severe cold weather, try to arrange things so the coldest part comes at the beginning of the trip. I'm referring to such things as winter high-altitude journeys or hikes that require heavy boots and specialized gear. Use the heavy stuff, then ship it home inexpensively via sea freight—or give it to someone who needs it. If you'll need cold- or foul-weather gear (for example, a wool cap, gloves, a sweater) for only a short time later in a long trip, consider buying it when you need it.

Match the pieces: Ensure that all tops and bottoms match (meaning color and pattern) well enough that they can be worn interchangeably. That cuts down on what you pack and helps keep you from getting bored with what you're wearing. Consider concentrating on two or three colors. Take bottoms that match well with several tops.

Consider colors: Colors such as maroon, blue, red, black, and green don't show the grime and wounds of travel as dramatically as light colors do. Except in a very hot climate or on a very urban trip, packing a lot of white clothes would be a mistake. Even khaki shows dirt easily.

Avoid the military look: A potentially serious mistake would be wearing clothing that looks as if it were military-issue. Olive-drab or camouflage cloth makes a statement you might not want to make as an American abroad.

Check for condition: Examine all clothing to be sure it's in good shape. Otherwise, a loose button or a worn elbow will make itself known at the most inopportune time.

Choose easy-to-clean clothes: Pack clothes that resist wrinkling and are easy to care for. We all like wool and 100 percent cotton, but synthetics have recently found more defenders. A wet cotton shirt or sock stays cold and damp much longer than something made of polypropylene or synthetic blends. The latter are lighter, wash and dry more quickly, and look better after being rolled up in your pack. Leave at home anything that requires dry cleaning.

Check the price of laundry service before sending anything off. It's generally not as inexpensive as you expect. Sometimes the charge is based on weight, sometimes on the number and type of pieces. And sometimes—could this be true?—it's based on presumed ability to pay. It's worth taking along a small container of concentrated laundry detergent.

Try to take clothes that will air-dry overnight, and try to avoid those that can't be washed until you'll be in one place for several days. A zip-top bag works well for transporting things that haven't quite dried. If you're trekking, fasten the zip-top bag to the outside of your pack.

Clothes wrinkle less if you shake them, roll them in a towel, then hang them up. If you hang rumpled clothes in the bathroom, steam from the shower eliminates most of the wrinkles.

When I tired of starting from scratch each time I got ready for a trip, I made a list of everything I'd taken on past trips and evaluated each item in terms of whether or not I'd needed it. Then I made a list of what had been worthwhile. That list, tweaked to take climate and special activities into account, makes packing a snap.

CHECKLIST: CLOTHING

Obviously, no list of clothing can serve all purposes. The following list contemplates an informal trip of several weeks. Your adjustments will reflect personal tastes, the length of your trip, and anticipated climates and activities.

For Men

1. Shirts

_____ Two short-sleeve outdoor shirts. Consider 100-percent-cotton-mesh polo shirts with collars. They are cool, wash easily, and hold up well.

_____ Two long-sleeve shirts with collars (depending on the weather). My favorites have front pockets that button. Depending on the trip, you may want one or two dressier, wrinkle-proof shirts.

_____ Two or three cotton T-shirts. Buy more as souvenirs.

_____ One long-sleeve turtleneck for cool weather.

_____ One vest. Optional, but can provide both warmth and a little dressiness.

2. Pants

_____ Usually two pairs, seldom more than three. One pair might be a tough, 100 percent cotton twill, suitable for rough parts of the trip. L.L.Bean (**www.llbean.com**) offers these in several colors. If the weather will be very cold, I substitute 80 percent wool pants made by Woolrich (**www.woolrich.com**).

The second pair should be lighter weight but very durable. One useful style has legs that zip off at midthigh (creating a good pair of shorts for use when the sun rises high). TravelSmith (**www.travelsmith.com**) and others offer these convertible pants. The third pair should be a potentially dressy pair of khakis. For big-city trips, add a pair of dress slacks.

Avoid pants in which the side or slash pockets do not swing freely. Those in which the pockets are sewn to the pants leg dump change, keys, and everything else each time you put your feet up. For security, look for pockets that button, snap, zip, or close with Velcro, or sew metal snaps into the tops of the pockets.

_____ One or two pairs of hiking or gym shorts. To reduce weight, one pair ought to double as a swimsuit.

_____ On the road, consider buying colorful, lightweight pants made in the local style. They're fun to wear even though they may look a little weird or fall apart by the time you get home.

Perhaps contrary to expectations, blue jeans don't make great travel companions. They're heavy, have no dress-up potential, dry slowly, and can bind fiercely on a long bus trip.

3. Underwear

_____ Cotton or cotton-blend briefs in dark colors. How many pairs you take depends on how often you'll be able to wash them. Taking nylon underwear that doesn't breathe to the tropics would invite a fungal infection.

For Women

1. Shirts

_____ Two T-shirts.

_____ Three shirts or blouses, as dressy or basic as appropriate. Long-sleeve or short-sleeve, depending on the weather (but not no-sleeve). Avoid plunging necklines. A jogging top can serve as a shirt, a swimsuit top, and even sleepwear.

_____ Whether you bring a wool shirt depends on the weather; the same for a blue-jean shirt. Either layers well over a blouse.

_____ One turtleneck for cool weather.

_____ A vest provides warmth, dressiness, and an extra bit of modesty in conservative countries.

2. Pants

_____ One or two lightweight pairs of loose-fitting pants (possibly substituting one heavier pair, depending on expected weather). Buy casual pants on the road.

_____ One or two regular skirts for slightly dressier wear. Skirts should fit loosely and extend below the knee. In some countries, especially in the Muslim world, women are expected to keep their legs covered. Local standards of modesty should guide choices everywhere.

_____ Some women recommend a pair of sturdy leotards or ballet tights for warmth.

_____ At least one pair of shorts.

The comments I've heard about one-piece pants suits or body suits have been uniformly negative on grounds that they stifle variety and are incompatible with using basic toilet facilities.

3. Underwear

_____ Cotton or cotton-blend panties and brassieres. Although silk underwear dries quickly, it's inappropriate for warm climates. In many places, the no-bra look would offend local mores and attract unwanted attention.

For Men and Women

4. Socks

_____ Three or four pairs of high-quality socks. You may want some wool socks (with a little nylon) heavy enough for hiking, as well as some that are lighter but still sturdy enough for sock-footed temple visits. Some argue that the best socks are made of hydrophobic (water-hating) synthetics that wick sweat away from the foot. Two favorites are Wigwam Ultimax (**www.wigwam.com**) and the Thorlo (**www.thorlo.com**) hiking model. Colors, even gym gray, conceal road grime better than white. Taking several identical pairs of socks works well. Depending on the trip a man might want one pair of dress socks, a woman one pair of knee-high stockings.

5. Shoes

_____ One pair of sandals. Cheap rubber sandals or plastic flip-flops are fine for showers and the beach, but you need sturdy sandals to cushion the feet and protect them from debris. Many brands work fine so long as they are well made and have an ankle strap and fairly thick soles. Wear sandals for a while before you leave so the straps won't rub raw patches on your feet when it matters.

I used to travel with good hiking boots, but no longer. They're heavy and space-consuming. Affordable, lightweight trail/walking shoes have improved dramatically. They're a good investment and work well for all but strenuous hiking. Dark brown, gray, and black don't show dirt and look fairly dressy. Ordinary tennis shoes are okay, but they usually provide less arch and lateral support than do good walking shoes.

Rub in Sno-Seal to waterproof shoes. I've been told that the aerosol in at least some waterproofing sprays dissolves the glue between the sole and the upper.

Whatever your choice in shoes, give them a good workout before you travel so you don't get under way with a pair that doesn't fit. Your feet are your wheels; pamper them a little.

For women: My recommendations are the same as for men with, perhaps, the addition of ballet-type slippers or light leather flats for dressier wear. They're light and compress well in a pack.

6. Belt

_____ Take one sturdy belt that fits the loops of all your pants. Consider one with a secret zipper pouch for currency.

7. Nightshirt

_____ You need some covering, at least for hostels, overnight trains, lodgings with bathrooms down the hall, and the strict standards of modesty in some countries. A gym warm-up suit works fine but is bulkier than a nightshirt. In tropical countries, consider a khanga, lavalava, lunghi, pareu, sarong, or whatever it's called locally. It's a rectangular piece of cloth that you wrap around your waist or chest to provide modesty consistent with local custom. It also serves as a beach blanket or towel.

8. Swimsuit

_____ On some beaches, skimpy suits are not welcome. On others, suits are not necessary at all. If you bring a suit, it should be more modest than not and be made of quick-drying material.

9. Rain gear

_____ Consider a Gore-Tex shell or a light, waterproof poncho. The latter, which takes less room, should be long enough to cover a pack on your back. Although hot and not very durable, a cheap raincoat or rain suit that stuffs into a pocket may be sufficient.

10. Extra warmth

_____ Light, warm synthetics are a good place to start. A lightweight windbreaker, which needn't be expensive or fancy, can be extremely useful. A polyester-cotton or polypropylene-pile jacket works well. Fleece jackets come in wondrous variety, many using Polartec (a warm, textured fleece with a soft hand). For extra warmth, consider a model with a windproof membrane inside the fleece. Don't buy one that will roast you. Layer instead.

A down vest provides warmth in a small package. Depending on the climate, it may be worth taking a light sweater (but that's the case less often than you might think). Buy a heavy sweater on-site if needed rather than carrying it all the way. Find warmth through layering or endure a little chill rather than lug a heavy jacket around the world. If the weather will be really chilly, take thermal underwear.

11. Towel

_____ Don't expect to be furnished a towel or washcloth in every budget hotel. If you take a towel, it should be small and thin to save space and drying time.

12. Bandannas

_____ They make good sweatbands and are generally useful, especially for women. They're plentiful in local markets.

13. Scarves

_____ A scarf makes you snug in raw weather and can dress up an otherwise road-weary outfit. In certain cultures, women are expected to cover their heads with a scarf.

14. Hat or sun visor

_____ Take one or the other, or buy one on the road.

15. Gloves

_____ For a very cold climate, take insulated gloves. For less-than-bitter cold, a pair of wool knit gloves is fine. To protect your hands when warmth isn't a factor, cheap cotton gloves are sufficient.

16. Tie

_____ A tie is the easiest way for a man to dress up. Bring one along or buy one locally. If you can't do the latter, ties aren't the custom—so forget it.

17. Blazer

_____ If you'll be doing business or visiting places where upscale dress is imperative, tuck a wrinkle-proof blazer into the bottom of your bag. However, it's not worth carrying one on the chance you might want it.

CHECKLIST: TOILETRIES

We all know what toiletries we want, so why bother with a list for something so personal? Because it's easy to overlook something.

I prefer a leak-proof, soft-sided, see-through toiletries container instead of a heavy leather kit. Catalogs, especially Magellan's (**www.magellans.com**), offer many versions.

Unless you are on your way to a month in the Darién Gap in Panama, you needn't take sufficient quantities of everything to last your whole trip. Buy travel-size products (in most drugstores or at a Web site such as **www.minimus.biz,** where the product line is oriented toward meeting Transportation Security Administration regulations). Take small sizes, and treat yourself to shopping in local stores to restock as you go. And, of course, you can address restrictions on carry-on fluids and gels by replacing them with solid alternatives (deodorant sticks, shampoo bars, shaving soaps, sunscreen sticks).

Here's what to take:

_____ Antiseptic hand-cleaning gel

_____ Band-Aids

_____ Comb or brush

_____ Deodorant (not aerosol)

_____ Dental-care items, including a toothbrush (preferably a travel type with its own storage container or cap), toothpaste, and dental floss

_____ Insect repellent. DEET is very effective, but because it is absorbed into the bloodstream, a solution of no more than 30 percent is preferable for a long trip. UltraThon, a DEET solution using a controlled-release polymer suspension, is very popular. I also recommend permethrin clothing spray. (See Chapter 12, Keeping Healthy.)

_____ Laundry detergent

_____ Lip balm with sunscreen

_____ Moleskin (to prevent blisters from bringing your trip to a halt)

_____ Mosquito coils

_____ Nail clippers or emery boards

_____ Razor and blades. Ordinary soap or shampoo can serve as shaving lather. Some travelers prefer a battery-powered, rechargeable electric razor.

_____ Safety pins (to pin keys in your pocket, pin a pocket closed, replace a button, etc.)

_____ Sanitary napkins or tampons (not universally available)

_____ Sewing kit

_____ Shampoo (can serve as shaving lather and laundry detergent)

_____ Soap (small) in a plastic container

_____ Sunscreen (waterproof; SPF 30 or higher)

_____ Thermometer (in a plastic case)

_____ Toilet paper (take out the cardboard tube). Don't leave home without it. Keep some in your day pack, more in your luggage. TP is for sale most places, but it's a rarity in bathrooms, even in some hotel rooms, in less developed countries. Ignore this advice only if you intend to follow the local custom.

_____ Tweezers and scissors (in your checked luggage)

Chapter 12, Keeping Healthy, discusses prescription and other medicines as well as first-aid supplies.

CHECKLIST: MISCELLANEOUS GEAR

Here's where the devil really tries to tempt you. Swarms of eager merchants offer luggage accessories, travel appliances, organizers (for documents, grooming, hanging, etc.), health and hygiene stuff, travel comforts, security products, packing aids, clocks, adapters and converters, electronic gadgets, and on and on. Just remember what happens to those who accept temptation—well, at least too often. Among the temptations, consider these:

_____ Airplane stuff—a pillow, an eyeshade, earplugs. A new industry is springing up to deal with some airlines' shortcomings in, among other things, keeping the seats clean. Consider paper headrest covers with Velcro strips to keep them in place.

_____ Bags. Take a couple of sturdy plastic garbage bags, large enough to protect your pack from a downpour or salt spray, and a few sturdy, freezer-grade zip-top bags (for leaky toiletries, a wet swimsuit, etc.). Plastic bags, such as dry-cleaning bags, keep muddy shoes from soiling their neighbors in your luggage. Light nylon stuff sacks, with drawstrings and cord locks, are useful for organizing small items.

_____ Camera gear. Remember extra batteries, plenty of memory, and a lens-cleaning kit.

_____ Clock. Take a reliable, durable, compact alarm clock that ticks quietly—but has a loud alarm. If you need an especially loud wake-up call, consider the Braun, whose alarm increases in volume until it hits 82 decibels. I carry a clock that illuminates the face with a push of a button. Start the trip with fresh batteries.

_____ Eyeglasses. Because many sunglasses for sale abroad provide little protection, bring a decent-quality pair of sunglasses (with unbreakable lenses and ultraviolet protection). Whether or not it's worthwhile to bring a second pair of prescription glasses depends on how much you rely on them. At least bring an up-to-date prescription in case you need a replacement. A hard plastic travel case keeps glasses from being crushed in your pack. TravelSmith, **www.travelsmith.com,** offers a "bombproof" case. Also consider a retainer strap for glasses.

Airborne dust and sand sometimes cause problems for contact-lens wearers. Because standard contact-lens supplies are bulky and often unavailable on the road, some travelers use disposable lenses. Don't forget lens solution.

_____ Flashlight. Take only a flashlight with a switch that can't turn on in your pack. Batteries are sold almost everywhere, so one extra set should suffice. A compact Mini Maglite or a key-chain flashlight saves space. Consider the Maglite Solitaire, which is about the size of a fat cigarette, weighs only a few ounces, and is available in any gear shop. If you need something more substantial, there's an Energizer model (the 2 in 1) on which the case slides up for a lanternlike effect.

What about a flashlight with neither batteries nor a crank? Shake it for about 3 minutes to charge it to shine for 20 to 30 minutes. It uses a coil and magnet, not magic. It's available many places, including REI (Nightstar CS; **www.rei.com**).

_____ Guidebooks. See Chapter 4, How to Plan Your Trip.

_____ Journal. A five-by-eight-inch journal fits easily into a day pack.

_____ Locks. With the Transportation Security Administration safeguarding airports, you must keep current on its rules pertaining to locks (**www.tsa.gov**). For luggage, small, sturdy locks are better than super-cheapies that can be picked in a second. Take enough for luggage and day-pack zippers. Give a duplicate set of keys to your travel partner. Code each key to match the corresponding lock (with dots of paint or nail polish) to avoid fumbling. Some locks, when open, retain their keys.

To avoid the problem of dealing with multiple keys, consider small combination locks. Using the first numbers of your zip code, your birthday, or something equally obvious helps you recall the combinations. Three-number locks on which you set the combination yourself start at $5 at a discount or hardware store and go up to $13 a pair in catalogs.

You definitely should have a light cable lock to attach your luggage to something solid and stationary. It's good for a hotel room but essential for getting some sleep in airports or bus or train stations. On some, the cable pulls out of a small case to deploy, then retracts when not needed. REI has a good one (the PacSafe RetractaSafe; **www.rei.com**), but there are many around.

For security in hotel rooms, some travelers carry a battery-powered doorstop alarm, a wedge that fits under a hotel door. If the door moves, a shrill siren alarm goes off. A low-tech door wedge also works fine. A Travelock locks dresser drawers as well as hotel doors.

A Jammer is a device that jams a sliding window or door to prevent entry.

_____ Maps. Some guidebook maps are good, but they're small. Buy large-scale maps to help in planning your trip, and take them along to assist in rerouting. Travel bookstores and AAA are good sources. Tourist offices abroad also have adequate maps.

_____ Money belt and wallet. The traditional favorite money belt is a flat, ten-inch-long pocket designed to be worn around the waist under the clothes. The better ones have two or three zippered pockets. For travelers who prefer something less bulky around the waist, consider shoulder-holster, hanging-from-the-neck, pin-on-the-bra, zipper-pouch-in-a-belt, and around-the-calf styles. They provide security, but their capacity may be too limited. My choice is a hidden pouch that hangs inside the front of the pants from a belt loop. It's much easier to reach than the around-the-waist type—and much cooler to wear. Whatever your choice, make sure it will hold all the things you must keep secure.

If you carry a wallet, Cordura is preferable to leather because the rough Cordura surface makes it less likely to slip or be slipped out of a pocket. Some people prefer a trifold wallet that attaches to the belt with a light chain. They can be purchased in motorcycle shops and at truck stops.

_____ Reading material. Starting your trip with enough reading material for the entire journey means carrying a heavy burden. New books are often more expensive abroad than at home, but you'll find plenty of used-book shops that will trade two of your books for one of theirs. Readers recognize one another, so it's also easy to trade with other travelers.

Reading the literature of a country as you travel through it—whether fiction, philosophy, politics, history, art, architecture, or culture—brings greater depth of meaning to the words and to the trip. In terms of price, variety of contents, and weight, Norton Anthologies of short fiction, literature, essays, or poetry are an excellent value. Thousands of tissue-thin pages provide hundreds of hours of pleasure.

_____ Rubber bands. Take a couple dozen for fastening your rolled-up clothes and all kinds of unexpected uses.

_____ Swiss Army knife. A knife with a couple of blades is adequate, but it's the rest of the collection that makes Swiss Army knives indispensable. One version includes scissors, a corkscrew, tweezers, a can opener, a bottle opener, and a screwdriver. One caution: a knife will be confiscated by airport security if carried in your day pack or pocket.

_____ Water-purification kit.

_____ Wristwatch. Desirable features include a display of the date and day, an alarm, a light for the face, and water resistance. Whatever you wear, it shouldn't look expensive.

_____ Writing materials. A couple of yellow pads, plus a few ballpoint pens (which are easy to replace while traveling). If you have room, pens make nice gifts.

CHECKLIST: DOCUMENTS TO TAKE ALONG

_____ Airline tickets (and a copy)

_____ American Automobile Association membership card (definitely optional). Foreign automobile associations may extend reciprocal benefits to AAA members, including maps and travel information. You may even get free road service if you've rented a vehicle.

_____ ATM card. Take more than one.

_____ Certificate of Registration (for registering expensive items with customs on departure; see Chapter 25, Shopping and Shipping)

_____ Credit cards (including a list of card numbers and telephone numbers for reporting a loss). Take more than one.

_____ Driver's license. It serves as general identification and may be required to rent cars.

_____ Insurance. Carry proof of automobile insurance and your agent's telephone number.

_____ International Certificate of Vaccination ("yellow card"). See Chapter 12, Keeping Healthy.

_____ Student ID card. Verification of student status can make you eligible for many discounts abroad.

_____ Itinerary

_____ Long-distance phone charge card(s)

_____ Medical information. Blood type (even though you want to avoid receiving blood abroad), description of special medical conditions, list of allergies, personal physician's phone number, health insurance information.

_____ Names, addresses, and telephone and fax numbers of people to be contacted in case of emergency and people to contact on the road and at home

_____ Passport (plus copies of the first two pages) and extra passport photos in case you must replace a lost passport

_____ Permits (trails, game watching, work, etc.)

_____ Photo ID (for times when your passport isn't available or appropriate)

_____ Prescriptions and extra copies of essential prescriptions

_____ Reservations (for hotels, etc.)

_____ Traveler's checks (and a separate copy of check numbers)

_____ Visas

_____ Youth-hostel membership card

CHECKLIST: OPTIONAL EQUIPMENT

Everything on this list could add to the pleasure of your trip, and I've taken most of the items at one time or another. You could take them all at once—as long as you plan to travel with an elephant and bearers. The issues are weight, space, and simplicity.

_____ Binoculars. Good ones are expensive—and attractive to thieves. Powerful binoculars are essential for wild-game viewing, but for most other purposes, a camera's zoom lens works well enough.

_____ Briefcase. Eastern Mountain Sports (**www.ems.com**), Eagle Creek (**www.eaglecreek.com**), and others sell a soft Cordura briefcase for keeping papers and documents collected inside your pack. This is surprisingly useful.

_____ Business cards (or travel cards you've designed for the trip). Cards make a good impression on officials and are an easy way for travel friends to keep track of your name and number.

_____ Calculator. Simple solar-powered calculators sell for $2. For a very reasonable price, consider a combination calculator, currency converter, metric converter, and translator between English and a selected language (40,000 or more words, phrases, and idioms). Although very small, it has sufficient memory to store traveler's check numbers, flight information, telephone numbers, and so on. Seiko makes good ones, and there are others.

_____ Carabiners. These small, locking rings, used by climbers, are unexpectedly handy for keeping things from getting lost. No need to buy the high-quality type unless your life will be hanging from one.

_____ Contraceptives. They can be purchased abroad, but the brands may not be ones you recognize.

_____Duct tape. About three feet (wound around a piece of cardboard) is enough to fix a lot of what breaks on the road.

_____ Eating utensils. A knife, fork, and spoon kit is nice when your hands are filthy or you don't feel like eating with them.

_____ Electrical gadgets. Another reason, beyond weight, space, cost, and karma, not to take electrical appliances that have to be plugged in is that they may not work. For one thing, your plug may not fit in the local socket. If your trip is geographically limited, you may get away with one adapter plug. Otherwise, consider an adapter plug set. Note that any battery charger may need an adapter.

Because electrical current in much of the world is different (220–240 volts) from that used in the United States (110–120 volts), you are likely to need a current converter as well. The type of converter depends on where you're going, what kind of equipment you will use (camcorder, razor, laptop computer, etc.), and how heavy your usage will be. Converters range from $15 to $28 and weigh up to 13 ounces. Magellan's catalog tells you what converter you would need—but you have to decide whether you really need the appliance. Note that this is not an issue in Mexico and Central America because they use the same voltage as the United States.

_____ Immersion heater. Plug one end of this device into a wall socket and dip the other in your tea or coffee cup, heating the water in minutes. It's lightweight, inexpensive, convenient, and pays for itself quickly. Choose 220 or 110 volts, depending on where you'll be traveling.

_____ Mace. Be aware that carrying self-defense sprays such as Mace is forbidden on airlines.

_____ Mask and snorkel. Although both are usually available for rent at dive sites, you can't always find a mask that fits well and has a clear lens. Fins available for rent are often weary and sized for small feet. Still, think twice before carrying bulky fins around the world. Scuba-diving equipment is always available on-site, but quality varies. Inspect it closely. If you doubt it, try elsewhere.

_____ Music maker. The MP3 player has displaced the cassette and CD player. In addition to providing good company, the MP3 device can hold scanned documents, photos, and more. Plug it in at a cybercafe, and you're good to go. Some even have recording capacity so you can capture local music to add magic to your memories. If you're planning to write about your travel experiences and may be interviewing people, a recorder is a great help.

_____ Musical instruments. Shared music is an instant introduction. I envied a Canadian with whom I traveled who had a wonderful time playing his fiddle with local bands. I carry a tenor recorder for my own amusement.

_____ Nylon clothesline. Potentially useful, seldom necessary.

_____ Pillow. It sounds wimpy, but you'll love it while enduring long overnighters on a bouncing bus—and trips on tight-fisted airlines. Consider a covered, inflatable pillow (less than $10) that tucks under your chin and curves around to rest on your shoulder.

_____ Radio. A shortwave radio, such as the Grundig, will pull in the BBC and music from around the world. If you're more interested in local music and local language, a simple AM-FM radio will do. Consider a small, hand-cranked radio-flashlight. Portability is everything, so avoid clunky ones. The Highgear SmartDynamo (about $30) is very compact and can also charge a cell phone.

_____ Sewing kit. A small one, including a few safety pins, can be useful.

_____ Sheet sack. Because beds in hostels don't come with linen, you must use a sheet sack (essentially, a very lightweight sleeping bag). Some hostels rent them, but the cumulative expense would be considerable for anyone staying in hostels frequently. They're bulky, so take one only if you must. You can make one, buy one from a hostel, or order one in a catalog.

_____ Sink stopper. A flat rubber sink stopper can be handy, especially when washing clothes.

_____ Sleeping bag. Seldom necessary; carry only if you're certain to use it.

_____ Slippers. If you want something other than socks or sandals for showers, down-the-hall toilet trips, or the beach, consider Ultra Soles, sold by Magellan's (**www.magellans.com**). Partially net, they come in a pouch and weigh only four ounces.

_____ Travel games. When there's nothing going on and you're not creatively inspired, break out the cards and start a first-to-10,000-points game of gin rummy. If you draw a curious crowd, use the opportunity to meet people and learn local card games. Chess, backgammon, and Scrabble are available in miniature travel versions. Amuse yourself and others with any of the versions of

Trivial Pursuit or its imitators (especially ones that focus on travel). A Frisbee is great for a playful spirit and a little exercise. A plastic jar of soap-bubble fluid is an easy way to involve a group of local kids.

_____ Umbrella. I buy a cheapie on the road if I need one. If you'd rather start with one, stick with an eight-inch compact version.

_____ Water bottle. Choose a tough plastic bottle with a secure top (preferably with the top attached to the bottle). It should hold at least a liter but not more than two liters (or it will be very heavy when full). A wineskin served me well for several months in South America. The reason I consider a water bottle optional is that in most of the world, clean water is sold in plastic bottles (in such volume that they've become a hazard to the environment). It's also increasingly common to see travelers wearing a CamelBak hydration pack (**www.camelbak.com**).

_____ Whistle. This could be useful for summoning help on a wilderness trek—or for security.

CHECKLIST: WHAT NOT TO TAKE
_____ Breakable or leaky containers
_____ Jewelry
_____ Illegal drugs
_____ Illegal drugs
_____ Illegal drugs
_____ Problems from home
_____ Anything you absolutely cannot stand to lose

MEDICINE
Chapter 12, Keeping Healthy, covers medicine and first-aid items.

JEWELRY
As I was checking into a small hotel on Ipanema Beach in Rio de Janeiro, a woman burst in through the front door, crying, blood streaming from her forehead and one elbow. A thief had knocked her to the sidewalk as he ripped a heavy gold necklace from her throat. She was wearing a gold necklace in Rio? Good jewelry and watches, and expensive-looking fakes, are a magnet for thieves worldwide. Instead, consider buying inexpensive jewelry from local artists. Thieves know how little these things cost and leave them alone. If you buy expensive jewelry while traveling, it's safer locked up.

CAMPING
Carrying a full set of camping equipment is cumbersome and unnecessary. I've had no difficulty renting what I needed as I went along (inexpensively, at that). For whitewater trips, safaris, and similar events, equipment is available at the

Where to Buy Stuff

Most of the gear you want is available, at low cost, in most general-merchandise stores. For harder-to-find items, try your local travel outfitters. If you're still looking, the **Magellan's** catalog and Web site (**www.magellans .com**) are filled with what the company calls "essentials for the international traveler." As travelers themselves, Magellan's telephone operators (call [800] 962-4943) have used much of the equipment listed in the catalog, so they can discuss it accurately. If you're looking for something not in stock, they'll call you back when it turns up, even a year later. That's good service.

But don't stop there: go online where every merchant is represented. Here are some useful sites:

- Backcountry: **www.backcountry.com**
- Best American Duffel (BAD): **www.badbags.com**
- Eagle Creek: **www.eaglecreek.com**
- eBags: **www.ebags.com**
- ExOfficio: **www.exofficio.com**
- JanSport: **www.jansport.com**
- Kelty: **www.kelty.com**
- L.L.Bean: **www.llbean.com**
- Patagonia: **www.patagonia.com**
- REI: **www.rei.com**
- Royal Robbins: **www.royalrobbins.com**
- Sierra Trading Post: **www.sierratradingpost.com**
- TravelSmith: **www.travelsmith.com**

And keep going—for discounts. For example, you'll find excellent travel deals on the Backcountry site (above). Click on "Outlet" for discounts of up to 90 percent. If you're on the hunt for something, tell the company to e-mail you the day's specials. Also look at **www.rei-outlet.com** for discounts of 50 percent or more on everything from backpacks to socks. And try **www.sierratrading post.com**, which claims savings of 35 to 70 percent as an online outlet mall.

departure point. On most independent treks, you can find food and lodging in villages along the way, so you needn't worry about a tent, foam pad, tarp, stove, and the rest. If you need cooking equipment, it's certainly better to rent it than carry it halfway around the world. In places where a hammock would be desirable, there are plenty for sale locally.

Sleeping bags are so heavy and bulky that I've never wanted to carry one very far. If you do, synthetic is better than down if there's any chance the bag will get wet.

Keeping Healthy

I have traveled widely in my lifetime, having been struck
by the virus at an early age and having, as yet, developed
no antibodies to harden my resistance or immunity.
—Caskie Stinnett
Grand and Private Pleasures

We hear reports of avian flu in Asia, malaria in Africa, even Montezuma's revenge in Mexico, and we have to wonder: should we international travelers be concerned about possible threats to our health? The answer is yes—at least enough so that we're prompted to learn what the risks are and what basic preventive measures to take.

That emphatically does not mean exaggerating the risks and staying home.

Consumers' Association in England (**www.which.co.uk**), which conducts probably the most extensive travel health surveys in the world, reports that only about 15 percent of all travelers get sick, and that only 4 percent get sick enough to seek medical attention. Those numbers would be even lower if the much higher percentages in parts of India and many Africa countries were excluded.

At least as important as knowing the low rate of health challenges is realizing what is actually affecting travelers. More than half who experience any health issues have only stomach problems and diarrhea. Next in line are sunburn, coughs, colds, ear infections, and motion sickness. Of those who do get some bug, the overwhelming majority are healthy again by the time they get home. Overall, it's a very small price for the vast rewards of travel.

About one-quarter of travelers' deaths are related to injuries, not diseases. Deaths often involve motor vehicles and alcohol. Another substantial percentage of deaths result from underlying medical problems, such as cardiovascular disease. The risk of being affected by a major health problem while traveling is greater than the risk of being impaled by a unicorn, but it's certainly tolerable.

The potential health problems discussed in this chapter affect only a very small number of travelers. For example, of more than 140,000 Peace Corps volunteers, only 3 have died of tropical diseases in 34 years.

Nevertheless, I address health issues at some length precisely because knowledge and preparation are essential to enable us to travel without undue concern about getting sick. Knowledge is a fine antidote for anxiety.

Acknowledgment

Dr. Emily McClure is a family-medicine practitioner, travel-medicine guru, and former Centers for Disease Control and Prevention staff doctor whose experience includes Central America. She generously critiqued and contributed to this chapter.

Discussing these things with some care is also necessary because the behavior of some travelers is breathtakingly baffling. They are the ones who assume they're bulletproof and won't get sick no matter what they do. They read an article on health risks, throw a couple of all-purpose medicines in their toiletries kit, and never give another thought to health. Perhaps some believe that signing on with a tour group encloses them in a magic bubble. Others convince themselves that the only way to truly experience a country is to live as the locals do, eating street food and drinking tap water. These attitudes court disaster.

Good health depends on factors such as where you go, whether you take effective preventive measures, how careful you are, what risks you take, and what your health was like when you left home—plus your attitude and a little luck.

PREVENTION

I'm a naturally healthy person and have had good luck along the way, but simple defensive behavior has been the major factor in keeping me free from health problems on the road. Prevention consists of doing some research, getting a checkup before leaving for an extended period, following a few guidelines, and exercising common sense and a touch of self-discipline.

Start by considering honestly whether you have any disabilities or illnesses that should deter you from traveling independently to the countries you've selected. Evaluate the physical demands of the trip in the context of your general fitness. Keep in mind the availability of health services. Discuss your trip with a doctor, preferably one who specializes in travel medicine. Remember that travel doesn't suddenly neutralize things that make you sick at home, such as heart disease, upper-respiratory infections, and such chronic diseases as diabetes, gout, and arthritis.

Instead of staying home or taking unnecessary risks, learn:

- which health hazards may exist on a particular trip,
- what to do to avoid those hazards, and
- what to do should a problem occur.

This chapter is filled with that information.

Risk usually accompanies expansion of our horizons, but that didn't keep our ancestors at home, and it shouldn't keep us at home either. I'll take Guatemala anytime over fast food and freeway driving.

Research

As soon as I have an itinerary, I contact the Centers for Disease Control and Prevention (CDC) in Atlanta (**www.cdc.gov**; click on "Travelers' Health," and you'll find information on specific destinations, vaccinations, diseases, mosquitoes, safe food and water, and illness and injury, along with a list of travel-medicine clinics). The CDC also provides current information on malaria and other diseases in every country. Call (404) 332-4559 for the international travelers' hotline. You'll be dealing with recorded messages, so be prepared to take notes. You can even find sanitation reports on cruise ships.

Advice from a good travel-medicine clinic, of which there are more than 500, is usually superior to advice from general practitioners. To find a clinic, check the CDC listing. You can also see the Yellow Pages for the "Travel Medicine" or "Infectious Diseases" subheading under the main listing for physicians. Or call your local hospital for the name of a travel-medicine specialist.

Prices vary considerably, but most clinics simply charge a reasonable consultation fee (which may include one or more vaccinations).

Most local public-health services have exotic immunoglobulins and vaccines on hand (which doctors in private practice often do not). Their charges are reasonable, and their nurses are expert at giving shots. However, many health departments do not prescribe medications such as malaria prophylaxis.

You should ask whether any countries on your itinerary require that you've had specific vaccinations as a precondition to entry. These requirements are listed in *Health Information for International Travel*, available online at **www .cdc.gov/travel/contentYellowBook.aspx**. The U.S. Government Printing Office (**www.gpo.gov**) is another excellent source for travel-medicine information.

If you'll be traveling anywhere exotic, you'll probably need immunizations. Some consist of a series of two or three shots, and some cannot be given at the same time as other shots. That means you can't wait until the last minute. Tell the health service where you're going and which shots you want, and it will give you a schedule. Ask whether you ought to get booster shots for measles, mumps, chicken pox, diphtheria, tetanus, pneumonia, and influenza. If you're pregnant, ask whether each vaccine is safe for you. If you have the time, call three months before your planned departure. If you're in a hurry, a month may be enough. Even if you've waited until the last minute, some vaccines may still be worthwhile.

Travelers are occasionally stopped at a border and asked to provide proof of some immunization or another. An International Certificate of Vaccination (known as the "yellow card," even though it's a booklet of several pages) is accepted as proof. If you don't have it, you may be turned back or required to get an inoculation on the spot under conditions that certainly would not be your first choice. Your local public-health department, or whoever gives the inoculations, has the certificate and will list the required vaccinations, other shots you've received, your blood type, allergies, and the person to notify in case of an emergency. The card lets you know how long each vaccine is effective. Because the yellow card is typically the only record of your shots, leave a copy at home.

I haven't suggested asking a primary-care doctor in private practice for information pertaining to international health issues because many don't have it. They usually weren't trained for these illnesses and don't encounter them regularly. You can't afford information that's out of date or just plain wrong. And you can't count on most docs to recognize some rare bug you brought home. See a specialist.

> Don't wait to get your immunization shots

Medical Help Abroad

The International Association for Medical Assistance to Travellers (IAMAT) (**www.iamat.org**) provides a world directory of English- or French-speaking doctors abroad (in more than 500 cities) who meet its standards and have agreed to charge an established schedule of fees. IAMAT also provides a World Malaria Risk Chart, a booklet titled *How to Protect Yourself against Malaria*, and a World Immunization Chart. It even sells a freestanding mosquito net for beds. There is no charge for the information, but a donation is suggested (and needed). When you see the material, you'll feel like donating.

You can also sign up for the International Society for Infectious Diseases' free Pro-MED e-mail service for information regarding emerging infectious diseases (**www.promedmail.org**).

Many credit cards have services that recommend hospitals and provide the names of English-speaking doctors abroad. They may even furnish an American doctor to consult with you or your foreign doctor.

Consider taking this chapter with you as you travel. If a problem develops, this information will help connect the symptoms with the probable disease—and thus with the appropriate medicine and other remedies.

13 PRACTICAL TIPS

These tips seem obvious, yet so many travelers ignore them.

1. Keep well rested. Every traveler feels worn out once in a while from an overnight bus trip, several days of trekking in the cloud forests, or any number of other things. Being immersed in a culture different from your own can be surprisingly wearing, especially early in a trip. You have daily tasks in a new environment, you're often in the midst of more people than at home, and you may feel a little homesick. All this, plus a fast pace, can catch up with you physically or psychologically. If that happens, shut down for a day or two, or longer if that's what it takes. Being run-down makes you more susceptible to illness and undermines the positive attitude that helps ward off oncoming disease. Taking time to rest is a trade-off, an investment in preventing future sick days. In planning an itinerary, schedule a few days on a beach or in some other peaceful place after an especially demanding adventure.

Getting enough sleep usually isn't a problem on the road. There will be days when you're out at dawn to catch a bus or train or you stay up for late-night conversations and parties, but generally you turn in much earlier than at home. Away from cities, nightlife is pretty quiet. Where there is no electricity, yawns come early, and most local people have to be in the fields or at the market at sunrise.

To ensure decent rest, find hotel rooms shielded from noise. Keep in mind that three sounds can penetrate the most determined slumber. The first sound is the raucous screeching of roosters. Some think that roosters crow only at dawn. They don't: they hold challenge matches all night long. The second is the honking of impatient drivers in the early morning. The third is the sound of shrieking laughter from dancers and drinkers in nearby nightclubs—or the driving drumbeat from an all-night rock band.

2. Improve your fitness before you leave, then stay within your limits. Get into shape to walk 3–5 miles without discomfort. If health permits, lift weights for a few weeks to build upper-body strength. Extend your limits as the trip progresses, but don't try to do too much early on. It's easy to tear up a knee by plunging down a steep, rocky mountain trail before your thighs have strengthened to take the load.

3. If you feel more than a little sick, get help. Seems obvious, doesn't it? Still, I keep meeting such people as a German woman who fell ill in Nepal and stayed miserably, painfully sick for a month. When she finally went to a doctor, her dysentery was cured in a few days. Why suffer? Get help.

4. Do not consume local water or food unless you are certain it is uncontaminated. Assumptions aren't good enough, especially because they tend to be wishful thinking when you're thirsty or hungry. By following the guidelines in Chapter 16, Eating and Drinking, you greatly improve the odds in your favor.

5. Eat nutritiously, drink plenty of clean water, and take vitamins daily. When making unusual demands on your body, eat well (even when it means eating unfamiliar foods) to keep up strength and resistance. If your diet becomes unbalanced, especially due to a shortage of greens, consider multivitamins with minerals, folic acid, and vitamins C and E. (*Note:* Taking more than 400 international units of vitamin E per day may interfere with ability of blood to clot.) Some believe that acidophilus tablets are a good diarrhea preventive in general and may prevent or resolve diarrhea caused by taking antibiotics, but that is uncertain. Clean water is a necessary investment; drink plenty of it. Don't risk dehydration or a bladder infection.

6. Keep clean. Dress in combinations of clothes purchased in the last three countries you've visited, let your hair grow, do whatever helps you feel free—but get clean regularly. It's not for someone else or for the sake of convention, but

because staying clean affects your health and state of mind. After a day in a gritty city or on a dusty trail, a shower lifts the spirits. Opportunities to shower "later" evaporate all too often, so I've learned to take a shower when I have the chance.

Keeping your body clean helps keep cuts from getting infected or jungle rot from getting a foothold. No one likes taking a cold shower in cold weather or washing out of a bucket, but it's worth gritting your teeth once in a while to get clean.

Because diseases communicated by touch are common on the road, wash your hands much more frequently than at home. A good way to avoid colds as well as fecal–oral transfer is to keep your fingers out of your mouth and avoid rubbing your eyes or nose. In public toilets, surfaces have been touched by many hands, so don't touch anything you don't have to. Wash your hands in the morning, wash before eating, and wash after visiting the bathroom. We still may not wash as much as we should, but we can train ourselves to wash more than at home.

7. Treat cuts and sores immediately. The possibility of infection is higher when you're traveling, especially in the tropics. When skin is constantly moist, microbes flourish, and small cuts and sores become infected quickly. When something needs first aid, tend to it right away.

8. If you must receive a blood transfusion, exercise great caution. Tainted blood supplies spread HIV and other germs. If the need for a transfusion is foreseeable, consider flying, or being evacuated, to where the blood supply is safer. If that's not possible, call an embassy to see if it has a registry of screened donors. Make the medical facility aware of your concern. Insist on sterile needles, and get someone trustworthy to supervise the process.

9. Shield yourself from people coughing and sneezing. You'll be in crowds in train stations, on buses, and on city streets. Even if you feel like a hypo-chondriac, protect yourself by turning away, moving away, or covering your mouth and nose. Those little droplets travel faster and farther than you think. Respiratory diseases are common, so being a little defensive is better than being a lot sick.

10. Protect yourself from mosquitoes (not to mention sand flies, blackflies, ticks, mites, and tsetse flies). This is one of the most important ways to protect your health. If biting insects are a problem, tuck your pants legs into your socks, and wear a long-sleeve shirt. Stay away from stagnant water, including rivers and lakes, around dawn and dusk, when mosquitoes are most active. Sleep under a mosquito net.

Use an effective repellent. Although a persistent rumor suggests that Avon's Skin So Soft lotion works as a repellent, tests do not indicate that it deters mosquitoes. Anything based on DEET works best. However, DEET has a toxic quality and should be used with care, especially if use will be prolonged. For children, consider concentrations of as low as 10 percent (and ask a doctor before using it on infants). Do not apply DEET to a child's hands if it could be transferred to the mouth. Consider applying over sunscreen to reduce absorption. Because pregnant women are generally advised to avoid insecticides, check first with a knowledgeable doctor. Doctors usually recommend that pregnant women avoid malarial areas entirely because the risk of causing problems is high.

My personal preference is a concentration of 35 percent or less. I add protection by spraying permethrin on my clothing and mosquito net (careful not to spray it directly on skin). It should remain effective on clothing through four washings.

Some mosquito repellents will eat through your toilet kit if they spill, so transport them in watertight containers. When I look at the way they dissolve plastic, it makes me wonder what they do to skin.

Adjust the precautions you take according to the level of risk. Don't get spooked every time you hear a nasty whine, but do make an extra effort to avoid those little biters and suckers.

Because even the best prevention may not succeed every time, we'll discuss treatment for malaria later in this chapter. Chapter 15, Lodging, also discusses mosquito warfare.

11. Carry good medical identification, including your blood type, allergies, and other special health information (relevant medical or surgical history and names and doses of critical medication). List the name of a person to contact should you be in need. If you have medical insurance, carry evidence of it (though in some countries, medical facilities may still require payment in cash).

12. First aid. The Red Cross offers a worthwhile first-aid course and issues a useful first-aid instruction card for travelers. It can also teach you how to perform cardiopulmonary resuscitation (CPR) and the Heimlich maneuver, important skills at home or abroad.

13. Coming home. If you took mefloquine, doxycycline, or chloroquine, remember to keep taking them for four weeks after leaving the malarial area. (For Malarone, it's seven days.) During your first weeks back, keep an eye on your health. If there's a problem, don't ignore it. Get a checkup, and tell the physician exactly where you've been (including time spent in rural areas or on the water) and whether you ate anything risky. If the doctor isn't knowledgeable about diseases from that area, find a specialist.

The book *Patients Beyond Borders* (**www.patientsbeyondborders.com**) identifies medical facilities around the world popular among "medical tourists"—people seeking high-quality health care at prices one-third to one-half those in the United States. Locations include Costa Rica, Mexico, Brazil, and many others.

The rest of this chapter contains some information that will be most important for those traveling somewhat off the beaten track, in the countryside, and away from competent medical help. Most of it, however, is knowledge every traveler should have. It's not an overstatement to say that it's about a way of life designed to keep you healthy wherever you are.

MINOR HEALTH PROBLEMS: HOW TO AVOID AND HOW TO FIX

Minimize the effect of the relatively minor health problems on this list by washing frequently, buying into the tips on page 319, and dealing with problems before they become serious. Where I have mentioned medications, I've indicated whether the item is available over the counter (OTC) or only by prescription (P) in the United States.

Allergies

> Always go to the bathroom when you have a chance.
> —George V (1899)

Even if not troubled by allergies at home, you might encounter something on the road that pushes an allergy button. Antihistamines such as Benadryl (OTC), Atarax (OTC), and Chlor-Trimeton (OTC) could help, but they have a sedative effect. Claritin (OTC), Allegra (P), and Zyrtec (P) are all less sedating. If you have a history of asthma, bring your medicine, and don't let your travel schedule interfere with taking it regularly. As you travel in urban areas, vehicle exhaust and general air pollution may affect your respiratory condition.

Athlete's Foot, Fungal Infections, Blisters

Everyone's dealt with these issues at one time or another, so why cover them here? Because foot problems are frequent on the road and can put you out of action for days. Because high humidity and barefoot bathroom visits can lead to foot fungus and plantar warts, wear shower shoes and dry your feet thoroughly. Don't let your socks get too grungy; change them every day if possible.

If your feet will be constantly wet, coat them with Vaseline. It's messy, but it works.

If painful cracks develop between toes, treat them immediately with Tinactin (OTC), Desenex (OTC), or Monistat-Derm (OTC). If you're prone to problems with foot fungi, sprinkle Mexsana (OTC) powder in your shoes to absorb perspiration in which fungi thrive. Powders are best for prevention. Cream or liquid forms are best for active cases.

Wearing two pairs of socks helps prevent blisters. If you feel a blister developing, put on a Band-Aid with a patch of moleskin (OTC) over it. If you pop a blister voluntarily, you're inviting infection, a bigger problem. If a blister pops by itself, treat it as you would a cut. Wash it often, and apply Neosporin (OTC) antibiotic. If you're allergic to neomycin, apply some other topical antibiotic, such as Polysporin (OTC). Many people are allergic to neomycin. When in doubt, I would use nothing. Cover the blister when you need to do so to keep it clean. The rest of the time, such as in bed, leave it exposed to the air. Watch for infection. See if you can find and fix whatever caused the blister.

Bites, Prickly Heat

Most bug bites, excluding those of malarial mosquitoes, are little more than a temporary irritation. If there are dozens of bites, which may be the case if that nice-looking bungalow turned out to have bedbugs or you've run into a swarm of sand flies on the trail, it takes superhuman willpower not to scratch, even though you know scratching makes the situation worse. An application of Mexsana (OTC), Benadryl gel (OTC), or calamine lotion (OTC) helps hold down the itching.

If bites are in danger of becoming open sores that can become infected, try a 1 percent hydrocortisone cream (OTC) (a topical anti-inflammatory drug that helps control the compulsion to scratch) or oral Benadryl (OTC) (an antihistamine) for three or four days. If you do scratch a little, use something other than fingernails, something softer and less likely to transmit germs.

Spraying your clothes with permethrin adds protection against pests such as chiggers, mosquitoes, bedbugs, and ticks and remains active through four washings. Sporting-goods stores sell one such spray, Permanone Tick Repellent (OTC).

I've read about a dermatologist who recommends wearing dog tick and flea collars around your ankles to ward off sand flies and other insects. Until they do more for my dog, I'll pass on that idea. Besides, the package says not to let the collar stay in contact with human skin.

Lice love to play in your hair, but they don't mind making themselves at home elsewhere on your body as well. They'll come to your attention as you begin to itch or, the fates forbid, experience a kind of indefinable crawling sensation. Plenty of shampoos that poison lice are available abroad, so it's not worth taking anything with you. A new, nontoxic product (50 percent isopropyl myristate), available in Canada as Resultz and in Britain as Full Marks, is safer for children and pregnant women than other louse products.

> The ability to see the bright side when times are rough may be an asset more valuable than physical conditioning.
> —John Walden, *Jungle Travel and Survival* (2001)

To make sure the lice are gone, wash your clothes thoroughly with hot water and detergent. The little devils like to hide in the seams, so scrub vigorously.

Keep an eye out for ticks. They seem to be the penance for a great walk through the bush. In tick country, check your hair and skin each evening. If one has already burrowed into your skin and is gorging on your blood, you must remove it. If you leave the head behind, it can cause an infection. First choice: apply a dab of liquid soap on a cotton ball to the tick for 30 seconds, and it should let go. If that's not feasible, there are alternatives. Use the tip of a hot match, a spot of gasoline or alcohol, insect repellent, or iodine to make the tick want to let go. When the tick is gone, wash the site thoroughly with soap and perhaps apply an antibiotic cream, such as Neosporin (OTC). If you later notice a rash, swollen lymph nodes, malaise, or a fever, and no medical help is readily available, consider taking an antibiotic such as doxycycline (P).

Who hasn't winced at the sight of Humphrey Bogart on the deck of the *African Queen* recoiling as leeches suck his blood? We think of leeches in water, but the land-based variety found in tropical rain forests is more common. Check your shoes and legs. If a leech has attached itself, use heat, iodine, alcohol, or salt to make it let go in a hurry. Wash the wound with soap and water. If it bleeds for a while because of the anticoagulant injected by the leech, apply pressure to stop the flow.

Fleas may await in even the nicest-looking bed, but DEET will keep them away. The CDC recommends sleeping without repellents on skin, so you must make a risk–benefit decision. If you don't have DEET, wad up the bedding, toss it into the hall, and hope the mattress is not infested.

Blackflies, mosquitoes, and sand flies spread unpleasant diseases through their bites. If the risk is significant, spray your clothing with permethrin, and use DEET on exposed skin. Reapply after swimming or sweating profusely. It may be better not to use extensive applications of DEET for more than a week at a time, but doing so seems better than picking up one of these insect-transmitted diseases.

Prickly heat, caused by sweat glands getting plugged, consists of a field of red bumps that itch like the devil. A common cause is clothing that doesn't let sweat evaporate into the air, especially in the sultry tropics. To avoid it, keep dry, wear loose cotton clothing, and apply talcum powder. Air-conditioning should help.

A few other things may take a bite out of a traveler. For example, it's best not to assume that all dogs are friendly. They are often guards rather than pets, which means they are very territorial and may move in for a nip if you intrude on their space (more on this subject under "Rabies" later in this chapter). If there's reason for concern, carry a stick or a handful of rocks. Monkeys are notorious biters, and humans should stay clear of them. Snakes are more common in the Third World landscape than in your yard, but they'll do everything they can to avoid you. Just watch where you step. Contrary to what you see in the movies, most wild animals will flee from you (although hippos do attack humans, and they take no small bites). If an animal does take a bite, follow the recommendations in the section on rabies later in this chapter.

Burns

Immediately apply cool cloth or a cloth-wrapped ice pack, or immerse the burned area in cool water. Remove clothing unless it is stuck to the burn, and cover the burned area to keep it clean. Do not apply butter or other grease. Good burn creams are available locally, but when you need one, you need it immediately, so it's worth carrying one along. Silvadene (P; watch for sulfa allergy) is one of the best. Small burns will normally heal without further medical attention, but a large burn deserves medical help. Some cultures apply a poultice of dirt and dung over a burn. While I respect traditional medicine, I'd think twice about that particular remedy.

Colds and Coughs

Cold viruses live in the upper nasal passages and are usually spread from the nose to the hand of an infected person, then to the hand and nose of the victim, often through intermediaries such as a doorknob or telephone receiver. Improve your odds of avoiding a cold by staying away from people with colds (easier said than done), washing your hands frequently, and keeping your hands away from your nose and eyes. You are more resistant to colds if you keep rested and eat well.

We haven't done well at curing a cold, but there's plenty of help available to reduce symptoms, such as a stuffy nose. Sudafed (OTC), Advil Cold & Sinus (OTC), and Dristan Nasal Spray (OTC) are decongestants that shrink mucous membranes and open nasal passages to make your nose run (the fluid takes the

Medical help is readily available in San Pedro Sula, Honduras.

cold virus with it). Aspirin (OTC) or Tylenol (OTC) help reduce the headache. Note that aspirin is not advisable for children and teenagers, and Advil Cold & Sinus may not be suitable for lactating women.

For a cough that is interfering with sleep, consider Mucinex DM (OTC), a tablet that is both an expectorant and a cough suppressant. Water is also an effective expectorant, as are hot beverages and soups. If the cough is not interfering with sleep, concentrate on an expectorant only. For a dry, persistent cough, the problem may be small airway spasms requiring an albuterol inhaler (P), often used for asthma or emphysema.

Fever and thick green or yellow sputum accompanying a cough may be signs of bronchitis or pneumonia (discussed later in this chapter).

Constipation

Drinking ample fluids and eating washed, peeled fruits (especially apples, dates, figs, and mangoes), veggies, and other fiber-rich foods help prevent constipation. Should constipation not resolve itself naturally, try Colace (OTC) or Dulcolax (OTC) for one or two days. Use constipation remedies for a short time only. Some are sufficiently addictive that after a while your bowels won't work properly without them.

When constipated, don't just lie around. Exercise is a strong stimulant to bowel activity. Suspend taking narcotic pain medicines (because they slow bowel activity).

Cuts

Have a doctor look at serious cuts or punctures. For the nicks that come with everyday living, start with a thorough washing with soap and clean water. Betadine (OTC) or hydrogen peroxide (OTC) are good antiseptic solutions for the initial cleansing only. Unless you're allergic to neomycin, apply Neosporin (OTC) ointment. The ointment will prevent the dressing from sticking to the cut and will keep the cut moist. To keep a cut clean, cover it with a bandage during the day. Because exposure to air helps the healing process, leave the cut uncovered at night. By the way, mosquito repellent in a cut won't make you smile.

If bleeding is severe, apply direct pressure, preferably with your hand on a thick, clean compress—without delay. Raise the bleeding area above the heart, but only if there is no fracture or neck injury. Apply a cold compress (ice wrapped in cloth). Apply pressure to arterial pressure points in the groin and upper arms. A tourniquet may cause loss of the limb, so use it only in an emergency. If a cut requires stitches, clean it, close it as much as possible (perhaps with a butterfly bandage), keep it moist, and get to a doctor within 24 hours. Start antibiotic treatment, and continue it for as long as the doctor prescribes.

Because a cut, especially in the sweaty tropics, is a magnet for infection, you should change a dirty bandage right away. If an infection starts, you'll probably see red streaks around the cut. If the streaks run in the direction of the torso, amoxicillin–clavulanate (P) is a reasonable choice for those who tolerate penicillins, although azithromycin (P) should work as well. The area will probably feel unnaturally warm, swollen, and tender, and you may run a low fever. If these symptoms appear, see a doctor at once.

Treat a minor abscess by puncturing it with a flame-sterilized needle after cleaning the area with alcohol or iodine. Wash it thoroughly, and apply antibacterial ointment. Leave it open to the air part of the time, and keep it clean.

You've probably heard that there is something different about coral cuts. It's true. Infection probably comes from microorganisms living on the coral or in the salt water. If you clean the cut immediately and thoroughly (alcohol or hydrogen peroxide, which bubble the coral fragments to the surface, are good) and treat it as a cut (for example, with Neosporin) and not just a scratch, you should have no problem. If you don't treat it, infection is possible. Not long ago, I was with a friend who didn't tend to a coral nick on her knee. Within 48 hours, her knee became enormously swollen and so painful she couldn't sleep. It's worth being careful.

Dehydration

Dehydration is insidious. You would expect it to be a problem in the Sahara, but it can happen anywhere, including at sea, at high altitude, and during sickness. At home, drinking two or three pints of fluid each day may be enough, but during a hike in the tropics, you could lose that much through perspiration in two hours. If you lose fluid equal to 5 percent of your body weight, you'll feel very thirsty. Lose 6 to 10 percent, and you'll experience headache and difficulty walking or performing any work. Lose more, and you're heading for delirium, unconsciousness, and possible death. Put another way, a person working outdoors in extremely hot weather should be drinking 10 to 16 pints of fluid a day. That's a lot! Most people fall far short and unknowingly risk the consequences.

Water, juices, broths, and caffeine-free colas are good. Coffee, tea, and alcohol increase urine output, contributing to dehydration. It may help your state of mind to bolt down a cold beer after a long day in the sun, but you need to follow it with nonalcoholic fluids. Increasing salt intake helps retain fluids.

Even better is drinking clean water into which a packet of oral rehydration salts, sometimes called just ORS (OTC), has been mixed. For diarrhea-induced dehydration, you need ORS to replace the electrolytes (or salts) and water that your body is losing. Prolonged diarrhea can lead to serious dehydration and even death. ORS packets are available in countries where they're needed. Yes, it tastes nasty—and it can save your life.

Diarrhea

How to get it: So many things cause traveler's diarrhea, including bacteria, viruses, food poisoning, and stress, that it's tough to avoid them all. Microbes that cause diarrhea are transferred by personal contact or via contaminated food or water. The usual reason travelers are affected is that digestive-system bacteria at their destination are different from familiar domestic bacteria. Not better or worse, just different. In addition, taking antibiotics tends to destroy friendly bacteria. This leads to diarrhea that should cease when you stop the medication or when "good bacteria," such as acidophilus from capsules or active-culture yogurt, are consumed.

Symptoms: Diarrhea is the symptom. The problem is actually gastroenteritis (inflammation of the digestive tract), which accompanies many diseases. Diarrhea's intensity varies, and it is usually self-limiting, meaning it will go away by itself. One person may feel a little queasy for a couple of days while another may have vomiting, stomach cramps, and mild fever. Simple diarrhea should clear up without treatment in two days to a week (only 10 percent of cases last longer than one week). If it doesn't, see the doc.

How to avoid it: The best way to avoid diarrhea is to be healthy and practice good personal hygiene. Then make a continuous effort to avoid contaminated food and water. Eat only peeled fresh fruits and veggies, eat well-cooked foods, and don't drink water that might be contaminated. (See Chapter 16, Eating and Drinking.) Some of the pathogens that cause diarrhea will enter your system no matter what you do, but following precautions concerning food, drink, and cleanliness greatly increases the odds in your favor.

To prevent diarrhea, some doctors suggest taking a preventive such as trimethoprim–sulfamethoxazole (Bactrim, Septra; P), doxycycline (P), or ciprofloxacin (Cipro; P). However, in some cases these medicines can cause adverse reactions such as blood and liver disorders, photosensitivity, or a severe rash and can actually contribute to diarrhea. They also help make invading pathogens more resistant to antibiotics. For these reasons, most doctors don't recommend preventive medicine for ordinary diarrhea; save the antibiotics for treating persistent diarrhea.

A less aggressive preventive would include taking two bismuth subsalicylate tablets (the old standby, Pepto-Bismol; OTC) four times a day (but it's not for pregnant or aspirin-allergic persons). Don't take aspirin at the same time, and don't be surprised if your tongue and stool turn black. If you also hear a ringing in your ears, take no more. Some people are convinced that acidophilus tablets and buttermilk also help prevent diarrhea.

If you are with a group and someone gets diarrhea, concentrate on your personal hygiene, and avoid contact with the affected person.

Also, vaccinations against hepatitis A, typhoid, and polio help avoid some gastrointestinal infections.

Treatment: Take no medicine, but drink plenty of clean water or other nonalcoholic (and, preferably, caffeine-free) fluids to avoid dehydration. Fruit juice and bananas replace lost potassium; honey and sugar replace lost glucose.

Bottled soft drinks are fine, especially those that are caffeine-free, because they also replace glucose. To replace salts, add a little table salt to food, juice, or soda. Alcohol is not recommended during diarrhea.

In many places throughout the world, oral rehydration salts (OTC) are readily available in pharmacies and general stores. Taken with clean water, they are an excellent replacement for lost salts, glucose, and minerals. You can make a rough equivalent as follows: three tablespoons sugar (or honey), three-quarters of a teaspoon salt, one-half teaspoon baking soda, one cup fruit juice, and enough water to make one liter. It's not too tasty, but it works.

Eat nondairy foods, especially carbohydrates that are easy to digest. Avoid milk and ice cream. Take aspirin, rest, and let your system have a day or two (sometimes up to a week) to clean itself out. Keep fluids coming in, even beyond the point at which you stop being thirsty. The goal is replacement. As you tentatively start eating solid foods again, remember BRAT. The acronym stands for "bananas, rice, apples, and toast." Your intestines will appreciate it.

Circumstances, such as an upcoming all-day bus trip, may make it temporarily preferable to prevent diarrhea from running its course, so to speak. For that purpose, Kaopectate (OTC) will give more body to the stool, but it doesn't reduce other symptoms, such as cramps, or reduce the frequency of the diarrhea events. For additional relief, there is Pepto-Bismol. If you want certainty of relief from the primary symptom, the leading antimotility drug is Imodium (OTC). Lomotil (P) is equally effective but more likely to cause drowsiness and retention of urine. Either will contain the problem, but neither is a cure. To the contrary, both retard completion of the cycle because they cause the body to retain the pathogens. Nevertheless, take Imodium along. When you need it, you definitely need it.

Another treatment is a general antibiotic such as ciprofloxacin (Cipro; P), ofloxacin (Floxin; P), or Bactrim or Septra (P). Some physicians feel it's better not to take antibiotics unless fever accompanies the diarrhea. Those who recommend antibiotics are divided on whether it's better to take antimotility drugs before taking antibiotics, or better to start with antibiotics, or better to take both together. A small majority seems to favor taking the antibiotic first, permitting the diarrhea to flush out your system. Xifaxin (P) is a new antibiotic for travelers' diarrhea—not necessarily better, just another option.

Enterovioform and Mexaform are used to treat diarrhea in some other countries, but the U.S. Food and Drug Administration considers both dangerous and has not approved them.

Diarrhea accompanies quite a few illnesses, including dysentery. If the diarrhea doesn't disappear after a week or there are other symptoms (such as fever, severe cramps, blood or mucus in the stool, light sensitivity, or a stiff neck), the cause may be more serious than unfamiliar bacteria. In such cases, do your best not to use the antimotility agents, such as Imodium. Try Cipro or Bactrim, and get medical attention.

Prolonged diarrhea may also indicate giardia or other parasites (discussed later in this chapter). In that case, you might try metronidazole (Flagyl; P), but be aware that it causes nausea and vomiting in some people if they drink alcohol within several days of their last dose. Tinidazole (P), now available in the United States, is considered an excellent choice, though quite expensive.

Fatigue, Stress

The stress of travel burns considerable energy. The length of time a person can travel without feeling physically or mentally exhausted depends on personality as well as physical and mental resilience. If you shed stress easily and have a light heart, you may coast through an entire trip without feeling fatigued. If you're less flexible, sleeping too little, or a little off your feed, daily demands can get to you. Weather can be a factor, too. A string of gray days causes most heads to droop.

Learn to recognize such symptoms as crankiness, withdrawal, and lassitude for what they may indicate. Notice when little bumps in the road that would normally make you laugh don't seem amusing at all. A series of minor illnesses or accidents may be stress- or fatigue-related. You may find yourself thinking you should cut the trip a little short.

The remedy is simple: Stop! Chill out. Spend extra money for a while. Find a place to stay that's a notch or two up from your budgeted norm. Eat well. Play. Forget errands. Get shined up. After a few days, you'll probably be your high-spirited self again.

I've never gotten so fatigued that a good break didn't restore my energy, but if that happened, I'd take a close look at my health and nutrition. I'd certainly try several remedies before calling it quits and going home early. Besides, I like to go home feeling strong, with that last burst of speed you summon at the end of a race.

If you recognize that fatigue or stress may affect your travel partner also, you'll be sought after as a person with whom to travel.

Fever

Start with acetaminophen (Tylenol; OTC) or ibuprofen (OTC), except for small children, to lower body temperature. Remove excess clothing. Increase fluid intake. If you don't know what's causing the fever, consult a doctor. If that's not possible, and the fever is accompanied by headache, chills, and fatigue, and you are in an area where malaria is possible, consider treating first for malaria (discussed later in this chapter). If there is also bloody diarrhea, treat for bacterial dysentery (also discussed later in this chapter). If your temperature tops 104 degrees, you must take stronger action: cool the body with water, ice, and moving air. Get a doctor.

Food Poisoning

This section might be lumped together with traveler's diarrhea because they are often similar. Symptoms are usually vomiting and diarrhea, sometimes with cramps. They may start within an hour after eating the contaminated food—but may take a day or more to manifest. Take ample fluids, and symptoms should disappear within 24 hours. Contaminated seafood can make you more ill, possibly with neurological symptoms and respiratory failure. Along with vomiting and diarrhea, you might experience a peppery or metallic taste in your mouth and loss of coordination. If that happens, get medical help.

Headache

For a mild painkiller and fever reducer, many people choose acetaminophen (Tylenol; OTC), aspirin (OTC), ibuprofen (Advil or Motrin; OTC), or naproxen (Aleve; OTC). All are painkillers and anti-inflammatory drugs (that is, they help relieve inflammation and muscle aches). You can achieve a Motrin-like result by increasing the dosage of Advil. Like aspirin, they carry some risks for people suffering from ulcers and gastritis. It is better not to take acetaminophen for pain relief while consuming alcohol or suffering a hangover because the combination may overtax your liver.

If a headache is accompanied by a distinctly stiff neck, fever, sensitivity to light, and general feeling of malaise, consider the possibility of meningitis (discussed later in this chapter), and seek medical attention immediately.

Heat Exhaustion

It takes several days to acclimate to an unusually hot, humid environment. It's common sense to avoid exposure during the hottest part of the day and wear a head cover. Wear loose-fitting, light-colored natural fabrics that enable perspiration to evaporate quickly.

When working or exercising in the hot sun or high humidity, make an effort to drink clean, nonalcoholic fluids and take in extra salt. If your urine turns darker yellow, it's a sign to drink more water.

When approaching heat exhaustion, you sweat heavily, but your skin feels clammy and looks pale. You may feel nauseated or throw up. Your muscles may cramp, and you may have a headache. Your heart rate is higher than normal, but blood pressure may drop. At this point, your temperature may still be only slightly above normal. Stop what you're doing, get into the shade, rest, cool yourself, and drink as much fluid as you can hold (including oral rehydration salts, if available; OTC).

If you respond properly, heat exhaustion shouldn't be a severe problem, but it can progress to heat stroke, which can be fatal. (Heat stroke is discussed later in this chapter.) I recall a huge sign on the pier at Hagåtña (formerly Agaña), Guam, that read, "The Sun Is VERY Hot in Guam!" Tired of watching visitors keel over at midday, the authorities were putting arriving travelers on notice.

Motion Sickness

A week of scuba diving off the Bay Islands of Honduras is a memorable experience, but it means spending time in a small boat at sea. Some great bus trips through the mountains in several Central America countries can be like riding a dragon's tail for hours. If trips like these challenge your tummy, you're susceptible to motion sickness. Despite what you may have heard, it's not all in your head. Motion sickness occurs when there is a breakdown in the signal between the motion-sensing parts of the body (inner ear, eyes, and limbs) and the brain. However, your expectation of becoming sick from motion can increase the probability that you will be affected. Motion-sickness symptoms include lightheadedness, dizziness, sweat, pallor, nausea, and, as we know all too well, vomiting.

The solution is simple. Dimenhydrinate (Dramamine; OTC) or meclizine (Bonine; OTC) will stabilize your innards and your mind. Take one pill an hour or so before the onset of motion. Adults may prefer a scopolamine patch (P), which, applied 8 hours before any tummy twisting, remains effective for up to 72 hours. These medications can make you a bit sleepy, but that's a lot better than hanging over the rail or out the window. Some physicians recommend that pregnant women, asthmatics, and anyone being treated for glaucoma avoid these drugs. Phenergan or even Benadryl can also be tried.

On a more naturalistic level, try ginger root in the form of hard candy, gingerbread, or, better yet, powdered ginger root capsules, to settle your stomach. It works. Green olives, green apples, and crackers also help, as does Coca-Cola, and none of them make you drowsy. Many people swear by the effectiveness of a wristband based on the principle of acupressure. Its small beads pressing on the wrist do the job for many travelers. A German firm sells earrings with titanium electrodes that deliver a small electrical current to an acupressure point in the ear. Neither I nor the Food and Drug Administration vouches for their effectiveness.

Whatever vehicle you're aboard, choose a seat that will move the least, usually one in the middle. Get fresh air blowing in your face. Keep your eyes on a steady reference point, such as an object in the vehicle itself, rather than watching scenery rushing by to the side. You can't fool your inner ear, but there is no need to reinforce the sensations by watching endless switchbacks of a mountain road whiz by. If the vehicle stops, get off and walk around.

Perhaps most effective, other than medication, is diverting your mind (I know that's easier said than done). Make yourself as comfortable as possible, and try to sleep. If you can't do that, focus your mind on something else, or talk with the person next to you. Invite cigarette smokers to desist (pantomime the potential consequences if they don't). Watching someone else get sick is enough to put almost anyone over the edge.

Parasites

Worms and various other parasites tend to arrive via contaminated water, insect bites, and undercooked fish and meat (especially pork). You probably won't see them, but their presence may be advertised by diarrhea, bloody urine, muscle pain, coughing, headache, and fever. Another sign may be rectal itching, most noticeable at night. Among the diseases they cause are amebiasis, bilharzia (also called schistosomiasis), Chagas's disease (also called American trypano-somiasis), filariasis, giardiasis, leishmaniasis, malaria, and more. How's that for a charming lineup? If you suspect a problem, have a laboratory test your blood and a stool sample to determine whether parasites are sharing your travels and, if so, what you should do. Correct treatment, which depends on the type of disease, is usually effective.

Because you can also pick up certain parasitic worms through your feet, resist the pleasures of going barefoot, especially on dirt. Keep shoes between you and those little augers. If you wear open sandals, consider wearing socks as well.

As usual, the best prevention is good hygiene (especially hand washing before eating) and caution with food and water. Run-of-the-mill worms shouldn't cause much of a problem so long as you prevent re-infection, which you can do easily after returning home.

Strains, Sprains

A strain is an injury to a muscle, while a sprain is a tearing or stretching of the ligaments that hold bones together across a joint (as in a twisted ankle). Treat either by icing the area, preferably for at least a full day, and elevating it above your heart if practical. Wear an elastic bandage if you have one. Take an anti-inflammatory drug, such as ibuprofen (OTC), to reduce swelling and pain, and prepare to get some involuntary rest. If pain persists, have an X-ray to check for a fracture.

Sunburn

Sunburn can bring a trip to a painful halt. I spent a full day snorkeling in a series of six spectacular bays off the island of Ko Tao in the Gulf of Thailand. To avoid sunburn, I wore a tank top and plenty of sunscreen. That night, I discovered I'd overlooked a couple of spots. The backs of both of my ankles were inflamed and swollen, practically glowing. Along with the pain, severe blistering developed, bringing considerable chance for infection. A friend wrapped ice cubes in a cloth and held them on the blisters to minimize the swelling. I immediately applied aloe vera and kept the burned area moist. Later, I treated the burns as if they were cuts, applied Neosporin, and took aspirin for the anti-inflammatory effect. Because I was returning to the mainland the next day, the burns didn't interrupt my travel, but I wouldn't have been putting scuba boots on over those inflamed heels any time soon. I learned my lesson.

Because one of my reasons for making a trip is to be outdoors, I don't expect to stay out of the sun while I travel. Nevertheless, I keep in mind that when the sun is high, a clear atmosphere lets through a lot of burning rays—as does a white T-shirt. On a boat or the beach, water reflecting the sun's rays multiplies the effect. The remedy: cut the time of exposure, cover up, wear a hat or a visor, and use a good sunscreen (rated SPF 15 or higher). Even a waterproof sunscreen must be reapplied frequently—and use plenty of it. It's cheap compared to the alternatives. Before you go, treat your shirts with a sunblock for fabrics, which greatly decreases the ultraviolet rays that get through, even when the shirt is wet. One product is called U-V-Block Sun Protection, UPF 30+ (**www.atsko.com**). It will stick to the fibers through several washings.

Does this sound a little wimpish? Well, consider the Australians. Notorious sun-lovers in the past, they are now notorious for their incidence of skin cancer. You no longer see many who are not fully protecting themselves against sun damage.

Upset Stomach, Abdominal Pain

Unfamiliar foods, robust spices, poor sanitation, lack of refrigeration, stress, or even just bacteria new to your system may give you digestive problems. For effective relief, try Pepto-Bismol (OTC). It comes in chewable tablets (anyone who puts a bottle of that pink liquid inside a pack deserves what will inevitably happen sometime during the trip). Pepto-Bismol contains an aspirin-related compound, which I mention because some people have ulcers or are allergic to aspirin. It may not be suitable for young children. As an antacid, consider Maalox or Mylanta (both OTC). Ranitidine (Zantac; OTC) or famotidine (Pepcid; OTC) are effective and can be taken for prolonged periods. Check to make sure that your other essential medications do not require an acidic stomach for their absorption.

If abdominal pain is severe, accompanied by vomiting or cramps and fever, stop eating and drink a little clean water. If you have a high fever, consider taking an antibiotic.

Also, check the right lower part of the abdomen. If it is very tender, you may have appendicitis, which requires prompt surgical treatment!

If the left side is tender, diverticulitis is a possible cause. If no doctor is available, treat at least seven days with ciprofloxacin (Cipro; P) plus metronidazole (Flagyl; P).

Severe abdominal pain can accompany a multitude of other problems, some of which are surgical emergencies. Get medical help.

CHECKLIST: MATCHING MEDICINES WITH MINOR ANNOYANCES

_____ Aches, headache: aspirin, acetaminophen, ibuprofen

_____ Acid stomach: Maalox, Mylanta, or Gelusil

_____ Allergies, poison ivy, rash, etc.: hydrocortisone cream, diphenhydramine (Benadryl), chlorpheniramine (Chlor-Trimeton)

_____ Altitude sickness: acetazolamide (Diamox)—do *not* take if allergic to sulfa drugs; dexamethasone (for severe symptoms); ibuprofen; acetaminophen

_____ Athlete's foot: tolnaftate (Tinactin powder), clotrimazole (Lotrimin AF), undecylenic acid (Desenex), Mexsana, Lotrisone

_____ Blisters: moleskin, Band-Aids

_____ Burns: Silvadene

_____ Chapped lips: Blistex, Vaseline, or ChapStick

_____ Colds: Advil Cold & Sinus for chest congestion; pseudoephedrine (Sudafed), Benzedrex Inhaler, Afrin, or Dristan for nasal congestion; acetaminophen for pain and fever

_____ Constipation: docusate (Colace), bran tablets, or natural bran

_____ Contaminated water: iodine tablets

_____ Cough: Robitussin DM syrup (or guaifenesin capsules), cough lozenges

_____ Cuts, blisters: Neosporin, Betadine (liquid antiseptic), or aloe vera gel; Cipro for infections; Band-Aids, gauze squares, adhesive tape, wound-closure strips

_____ Diarrhea: Pepto-Bismol (bismuth subsalicylate), Kaopectate, Lomotil, or Imodium; Oralyte (oral rehydration salts)

_____ Eye problems: eyedrops; for contact-lens wearers, contact-lens solution and Sodium Sulamyd antibiotic eyedrops

_____ Fever: acetaminophen, aspirin; thermometer

_____ Headache and general cold symptoms: aspirin, acetaminophen, or ibuprofen

_____ Herpes sores: Anbesol gel; acyclovir (Zovirax)

_____ Infection: Neosporin

_____ Insect bites: 1 percent hydrocortisone cream, Benadryl

_____ Motion sickness: Dramamine, Bonine, Phenergan, or scopolamine patches; acupressure wristbands

_____ Sleeplessness: Benadryl, Serax, melatonin

_____ Strains and sprains: elastic bandage

_____ Sunburn and other minor burns: SPF 15 (or higher) waterproof sunscreen and aloe vera; Silvadene; Neosporin; ibuprofen

_____ Toothache: eugenol (oil of cloves)

_____ Unbalanced diet: vitamins

_____ Upset stomach: Pepto-Bismol tablets

_____ Urinary-tract infections: Cipro, Ampicillin, or cotrimoxazole (Bactrim or Septra)

_____ Vaginal yeast infection: nystatin vaginal tablets, vaginal suppositories

MAJOR HEALTH PROBLEMS AND WHAT TO DO ABOUT THEM

Major medical problems mentioned here include some from which you are generally sheltered at home but which you might encounter as you travel in Mexico and Central America. You don't want to experience them—and you don't have to if you make a reasonable effort.

Bronchitis and Related Respiratory Diseases

Bronchitis, an inflammation of the air tubes between the throat and the air sacs in the lungs, is commonly caused by an infection (viral or bacterial), an allergy, or an irritation. If untreated, it may go away in a week or so—or it can lead to pneumonia.

How to get it: Usually by inhaling airborne bacteria, smoke, dust, or viruses.

Symptoms: Because airways have narrowed, the chest feels constricted. Green, yellow, or white sputum develops, but it's the fever and persistent, wracking cough that get your attention.

How to avoid it: Don't smoke, and don't breathe air polluted by smokers! Avoid urban areas with heavy industrial fumes and vehicle exhaust or rural areas with "slash-and-burn" agricultural practices and indoor fire pits for cooking. Good luck is the best ally, although general fitness helps by keeping immune levels high. Treat colds and flu early. Certain people have a predisposition to bronchitis: smokers, alcoholics, asthmatics, and people especially susceptible to allergies.

How to treat it: Many cases are viral and require mucus mobilization with guaifenesin (Mucinex; OTC) and humidification with warm steam and hot beverages. You may need to find an albuterol inhaler (P) to decrease airway spasms that cause persistent or deep coughing or wheezing. Azithromycin (P), Bactrim (P), or Septra (P) is a good bet if the cause is bacterial, as indicated by several days of yellow, green, or thick white sputum. If the infection is viral, antibiotics won't help. In either case, breathing hot vapors may help break up the sputum and reduce coughing. Keep a vaporizer or teakettle going if you can find one. Try Robitussin (OTC), and drink lots of water.

Chagas's Disease

This disease is a significant cause of death in parts of Central and South America. It arrives via nocturnal insects (sometimes called "kissing" or "assassin" bugs) that emerge from the walls and ceilings of rustic rural lodgings. They look much like a North American stinkbug but have a long snout. Typically, they drop from a thatch roof (or palm tree if you're sleeping outside) to feed on you as you sleep. When they bite, they poop, and it's the feces entering through eyes, mouth, or the bite wound that introduces the parasite. The first sign is a small, red bump at the bite site, followed in a week or two by fever and a firm swelling at the spot.

Chagas's disease can result in congestive heart failure 10 to 20 years after infection. The best defenses are insect repellent and mosquito nets. Although the disease rarely affects travelers, I mention it because the symptoms would be difficult for a general practitioner to diagnose. If you think you may have been bitten while asleep in a Chagas-endemic area, see a travel-medicine specialist.

Cholera

How to get it: Cholera, currently present in more than 40 countries, is caused by a toxin produced by cholerae bacteria. Few travelers get it because when there's a cholera outbreak, the word spreads quickly, and most people become supercautious. Humans get it most frequently via contaminated salt water and food, especially raw seafood such as shellfish (in which the bacteria concentrate), or via infected food handlers who use inadequate hygiene. Fortunately, it is not spread by inhalation. Because it usually erupts as an epidemic, travelers hear about it and can easily avoid infected areas. In the absence of an outbreak, the risk of contracting cholera is very low. However, where cholera is endemic, there is some risk of transmission by carriers not showing symptoms. Check with the Centers for Disease Control and Prevention (**www.cdc.gov**) before you travel.

Symptoms: Cholera attacks the lining of the intestines and sucks vast quantities of fluid from the cells. The victim experiences copious diarrhea, often accompanied by vomiting and cramps. This massive loss of fluids and salts destroys the victim's electrolyte balance, prevents retention of nutrients, and causes collapse of the circulatory system. If untreated, death from dehydration is a possibility.

How to avoid it: The best protection is to stay away from current outbreaks. The cholera vaccine previously available in the United States is no longer produced because its effectiveness was limited. Outside the United States, some travelers may receive Dukoral, the Swedish oral vaccine (see **www.sblvaccines .se**). There is a new strain of cholera in India and a few other Asian countries for which there is as yet no approved vaccine. The World Health Organization is testing an inexpensive vaccine that may be effective for up to one year.

Vaccinated or not, follow hygienic precautions in any area with known cases of cholera. Don't drink untreated water or ice, and don't eat raw seafood (specifically shellfish), uncooked fruits or vegetables, or food prepared under unsanitary conditions.

How to treat it: See a doctor immediately, and have a stool sample tested for cholera. Some cases of cholera clear up by themselves, but don't wait it out. Severe dehydration, especially in small children, results in circulatory collapse. The real lifesaver is oral rehydration salts, or ORS (OTC), in sanitized water to replace salt, potassium, bicarbonate, sugar, and fluid volume. ORS are available from many health-food stores and at many pharmacies abroad. If the salts are not available, follow the recipe in the section on diarrhea earlier in this chapter. If even that is not possible, offer water, broth, caffeine-free soda, and sugary juices.

A victim should rest and take nothing by mouth except fluids (no food) until the diarrhea stops. After that, starches are fine. It is essential to drink clean hydration formula and get sufficient rest. Avoid milk and drinks containing caffeine. Several antibiotics, such as Cipro (P) and Floxin (P), help reduce the length of a cholera attack, but they kill beneficial bacteria as well as the ones causing cholera. The drug of choice is tetracycline (P).

Dengue Fever

How to get it: The colloquial name, "breakbone fever," tells you right away that it's something you'd just as soon skip. Its most serious form is dengue hemorrhagic fever. It's found in Central America, South America, the Caribbean, Africa, and tropical Asian countries. North Americans don't hear a lot about it, but there have been epidemics in some Latin American countries in the past ten years, and it is a growing public-health threat. It is brought into your life by a female mosquito who takes her nips and transmits the virus, usually during the day when you may not be expecting mosquitoes. Dengue-carrying mosquitoes hang out in urban areas and often venture indoors.

Symptoms: The symptoms may not show up for five to seven days. There are at least two stages. First, a fever develops, along with chills, headaches, and vomiting. These symptoms last three to five days before disappearing. They then return, accompanied by abdominal pains and wracking aches in joints and muscles. This round, which can last ten days, may be misdiagnosed as malaria until a diffuse rash appears on the trunk of the body, the palms of the hands, and the soles of the feet. Remission may be followed by a relapse, and full recovery may take weeks. The good news is that it's seldom fatal.

How to avoid it: There is no preventive antibiotic or vaccine. The best defense is similar to that against malaria: avoid all mosquitoes—but with increased vigilance during the day. If you hear of an outbreak of dengue fever, move on.

How to treat it: No antibiotics or vaccines are known to cure it. Take acetaminophen (OTC); do not take aspirin or ibuprofen. Keep taking fluids to avoid dehydration, and get plenty of rest. If you're not sure whether you have dengue or malaria, treat it as if it were malaria until you can get expert medical attention.

Dysentery

How to get it: Amoebic dysentery (or amoebiasis) is caused by a protozoan, *Entamoeba histolytica*. Bacillary dysentery may be caused by *Shigella* bacteria. Both generally enter through one's mouth as a result of careless hygiene or consumption of contaminated food or water. Use of human waste as fertilizer and failure to wash one's hands after defecating contribute to contamination. Both types of dysentery can be spread by a food handler who doesn't wash his hands, by human contact, and by insects who have stepped in human waste before dropping by their favorite kitchen or outdoor market. The odds are that you won't encounter dysentery if you are careful about sanitation and hygiene.

Symptoms: On the road, it is difficult to distinguish between amoebic and bacillary dysentery. In fact, it may be initially difficult to tell the difference between dysentery and simple diarrhea. Amoebic dysentery may produce mild abdominal discomfort and constipation with bouts of bloody diarrhea. Some *Shigella* infections are quite mild and have few definitive symptoms, while others can be fatal. For a reliable diagnosis, the stool must be checked. The clues that point to dysentery rather than simple diarrhea are fever, and blood or pus in the stool.

In amoebic dysentery, abscesses may form in the liver, lungs, or brain. Not surprisingly, amoebic dysentery can be lethal, but with basic treatment there is little to fear. It is, however, a high price to pay for impulsively drinking tap water or being careless about personal hygiene.

How to avoid it: Choose with care the places you eat and drink. Wash your hands frequently, and don't put your fingers in your mouth. Remember that dysentery can be spread from one person to another by touch. Avoid food that may have been in contact with insects.

How to treat it: If you're concerned by the symptoms, send a stool sample to a laboratory for analysis. If it is dysentery, take oral rehydration salts (OTC), and drink extra fluids to offset losses through diarrhea. If you have or seriously suspect amoebic dysentery, take metronidazole (Flagyl; P), followed by iodoquinol (P). Women in their first trimester of pregnancy should avoid Flagyl. Anyone taking it should also avoid alcohol for three days after the last dose. Many use tinidazole (Tindamax; P) for killing amoebas in abscesses or the intestine. The FDA approved it in 2004.

Bacillary dysentery may go away in a week or so, even without treatment. Drink plenty of fluids to prevent dehydration. Rest, and eat light, nongreasy meals. Take Bactrim (P), Septra (P), or ciprofloxacin (Cipro; P). If the strain has developed resistance to these antibiotics, drop into a hospital. Treated, the bacteria should be out of the body within several days. Untreated, a person could continue to shed bacteria in stools for several weeks.

In practical terms, it will be almost impossible for travelers to distinguish among simple diarrhea, food poisoning, dysentery, and giardia, so get to a doctor.

Giardiasis

How to get it: When excreted by human or animal carriers, the parasite *Giardia lamblia* can survive for months, during which it can wash into a water supply. That's why even the apparently pristine rivers in the Sierra Madre Mountains of California carry danger downstream from the snowy wilderness. Besides being spread via feces in food or water, giardiasis can spread from person to person via poor hygiene.

Symptoms: Fewer than half the people who drink water heavily contaminated by giardia develop infestations. Most of those who do show no obvious symptoms. Whether one gets infected may be a function of the number of parasites consumed. The minority experience diarrhea, stomach cramps, excessive intestinal gas, and lack of energy. If the stool is foul-smelling and the victim starts burping and experiencing a taste like rotten eggs, giardiasis is a likely culprit. If diarrhea lasts for more than a couple of weeks, suspect giardiasis.

How to avoid it: Drink only clean water, and eat hygienically prepared food.

How to treat it: Even without treatment, symptoms disappear in seven to ten days—but may recur. With treatment, symptoms should disappear for good in about a week. If not treated, the victim may become a symptom-free carrier for years, capable of transmitting the disease to others.

Diagnosis is usually based on a test of the stool. The accuracy of the test depends on the number of cysts present at the time of the test, and the cyst count can vary hour to hour. Giardiasis can be treated with metronidazole (Flagyl; P), also used to combat amoebic dysentery. However, according to the Centers for Disease Control and Prevention, giardiasis has been increasing its resistance to metronidazole. In any case, the drug should not be taken by anyone in her first trimester of pregnancy, or in conjunction with alcohol. If there is a relapse after treatment, consult a doctor.

Heatstroke

How to get it: Heatstroke (or sunstroke) is a risk when you spend too much time in the sun without replacing perspiration with fluid intake. Exercise or exertion contributes to the problem, especially in high humidity, when sweat doesn't evaporate efficiently to cool the body. Antipsychotic medications also confer considerable risk in hot climates by interfering with the body's ability to regulate its temperature. With heat stroke, the control system that regulates body temperature stops working. Temperature escalates, leading to possible kidney damage, brain damage, and death.

Symptoms: You feel feverish and confused, and your skin is dry, flushed, and hot to the touch. Unlike someone suffering from heat exhaustion, the victim has a high temperature and does not sweat. Pulse and breathing rates increase. Unconsciousness is possible.

How to avoid it: Drink plenty of fluids in conditions of intense sun and high temperature, especially when exercising. Reduce exercise when humidity is high, and pay attention to your body. If your pulse becomes unusually rapid or you begin to feel faint, stop! Get out of the sun. Drink something, and consume some salt.

How to treat it: Get the victim out of the sun immediately, and lower the body temperature quickly. Undress the victim, and put cold packs on the groin, armpits, head, and neck. Fan vigorously. Some recommend giving the victim a little to drink, very slowly. Others, to avoid the risk of vomiting or aspiration, prefer to give nothing. Best is saline solution administered intravenously in a hospital. When fever has subsided, cover the victim to prevent chilling, and seek medical help. After the event, the victim should rest for several days, drink plenty of fluids, and, oh yes, avoid similar circumstances.

Hepatitis

Although hepatitis is casually referred to as if it were a single disease, it comes in several versions. All attack the liver, but they differ in how they're transmitted and in their effects. Those afflicted typically recover completely from types A and E, but B, C, and D can become chronic and possibly fatal.

Hepatitis A

How to get it: Hepatitis A virus (formerly known as infectious hepatitis), the least serious of the hepatitis infections, is usually spread by consuming food or water contaminated with human or animal waste. Shellfish and raw fish are common sources. It's also transferred by contaminated needles and occasionally by sexual intimacy. The incubation period is two to seven weeks. Hep A is probably more common than all the more exotic diseases combined.

Symptoms: The symptoms are headache, nausea, and fatigue, like those of a case of flu that won't go away. Other symptoms include generalized aches and pains, fever, vomiting, lack of appetite, diarrhea, and upper abdominal pain. Here's the telltale: urine becomes golden-orange. In most cases, jaundice ensues, meaning the skin and whites of the eyes turn a yellow hue in five to ten days. This happens because the liver is under attack, failing to dispose of old red blood cells properly. At this point, the liver, in the upper abdomen on the right side, is extremely tender to the touch. Lymph nodes also become enlarged. You're likely to feel sick for a couple of weeks and weak for one to three months. To check for hepatitis, get a blood test. Some who get hepatitis A, especially children, don't show symptoms. After recovering from a hepatitis A infection, you have lifelong immunity against a later infection.

While recovering, be kind to your liver. Drink clean water, avoid alcohol, and avoid acetaminophen and other nonessential medications.

How to avoid it: For decades, many doctors have recommended an immune globulin (IG) shot just before departure. This provides some protection but not immunity. The duration of the effectiveness of the shot depends to some extent on the dosage. A two-milliliter dose is supposed to be effective for two or three months, while a five-milliliter dose is effective for about five months. Health departments routinely give the smaller dose, so if you want longer protection, ask for it. The vaccine should be the prevention of choice.

The Food and Drug Administration has approved Havrix (or Vaqta; both P), a vaccine already in wide use abroad, which appears to give immunity for 10 to 25 years. The first shot should be received four weeks before travel, followed by a booster 6 to 12 months later. Protection is estimated at 90 percent. If you'll be traveling to a high-risk area in less than four weeks, receive IG simultaneously with the vaccine. Because 100 percent immunity is seldom certain, continue to avoid food and water that may be contaminated. The Centers for Disease Control and Prevention and the National Foundation for Infectious Diseases recommend this vaccine.

Avoidance of hepatitis A should become part of your daily routine on the road. Check out cleanliness when choosing a restaurant, drink only clean water, avoid ice, eat only thoroughly cooked foods, avoid raw shellfish, and wash your hands more frequently than at home. (You must be getting tired of hearing this.) Even if food and water are not contaminated, the container they're in may be. By the way, the rumor that an alcoholic beverage will neutralize the hep A virus is wishful thinking.

How to treat it: If you're exposed to hepatitis A while traveling but you're not yet showing symptoms, consider getting an IG shot immediately (but only if you can be certain the needle is new and clean). Antibiotics will not help; this is a virus. There is no cure for hepatitis A, but it's self-limiting rather than chronic. However, the elderly, carriers of hepatitis B or C viruses, or chronically ill persons may be affected much more seriously. If you get it, be as certain as you can that your sources of clean food and water are reliable. Then settle in for a good rest, eat well, drink lots of fluids (except alcohol until tests show your liver has recovered), and be careful not to pass it on to anyone else through contact.

Hepatitis B

How to get it: The hepatitis B virus (also formerly known as infectious hepatitis) is extremely contagious. The example sometimes given is that a single drop of hepatitis B–infected blood in a large swimming pool filled with unchlorinated water is enough to infect a swimmer. Think of it as 100 times as infectious as AIDS. The hepatitis B virus is transmitted most commonly in the same ways, and sometimes at the same time, as HIV: by sexual contact, razors, toothbrushes, tattoo ink and needles, piercings, nose pipes, contaminated blood products, infected hypodermic needles, or even open sores on an infected person.

In some parts of the world (especially Southeast Asia, China, sub-Saharan Africa, the Amazon Basin, and several Caribbean islands), transfusions and inoculations are risky because not all donated blood has been thoroughly tested for HIV, hepatitis B, malaria, and other diseases, and not all disposable needles are disposed of.

Symptoms: The disease manifests itself one to six months after exposure with gradual onset of abdominal pain and loss of appetite. Jaundice, similar to that caused by hepatitis A, occurs in about half of all cases of hepatitis B. Symptoms can last several months, but it's common to carry hepatitis B and show none of the usual symptoms.

How to avoid it: Recombivax-HB and Engerix-B are vaccines effective against hepatitis B. They are given as a series of three shots, ideally over six months, although they can be given within two or three months if need be. Most young children in the United States have received a hepatitis B vaccination before school admission. Some authorities recommend it for travelers who expect to work in health care, have sexual contact, or stay for more than six months in areas where hepatitis B is endemic. The six-month boundary seems a little arbitrary, so you might want to receive the vaccine even for shorter trips. The chance of infection on a short trip for those not engaging in high-risk activities is low.

Avoid getting injections (including those for drugs, tattoos, body piercing, and acupuncture) or sharing razors or toothbrushes. Practice good hygiene, and avoid unprotected sex.

How to treat it: Receive hepatitis B immune globulin as soon as you know you've been exposed. Avoid raw shellfish, alcohol, acetaminophen, and nonessential medications that must be processed by the liver. Don't push yourself. Antiviral medications in combination with interferon (P) may be helpful. Adults have a 90 percent probability of complete recovery and immunity, but for the rest, hepatitis B becomes a chronic infection, causing cirrhosis and possibly liver cancer. Anyone with troubling symptoms after returning from a trip should mention the possibility of hepatitis B to the doctor.

Consider the TWINRIX series, which combines hepatitis A and B vaccines. After the first injection, a second follows in four weeks, and a third five months after that.

Hepatitis C

Hepatitis C is widespread throughout the world, including the United States. Check with your local health department or travel doctor. It is transmitted in the same ways as hepatitis B and HIV (for example, through infected needles or blood, and through sex). Tests have been developed to distinguish this type of hepatitis from the others and to screen infected blood products.

Hepatitis C is particularly dangerous because the virus remains alive and active in approximately 85 percent of the people infected They remain carriers at risk for chronic active hepatitis. About half the carriers get cirrhosis or scarring of the liver that can lead to liver cancer. Several antiviral regimens are available and are best administered by an infectious-disease physician or a hepatologist or gastroenterologist.

Hepatitis D

The hep D virus becomes active only in combination with the hepatitis B virus and is spread in the same ways as the latter. The combination leads to severe liver damage and a mortality rate of 20 percent. Symptoms are similar to those of hepatitis A, including headache, nausea, fatigue, aches and pains, fever, vomiting, lack of appetite, diarrhea, upper abdominal pain, and golden-orange urine. In most cases, jaundice ensues. Avoid it by getting a hep B vaccination and avoiding the risky behavior that transmits the virus. If you have hep D, you also have hep B and must treat that as outlined previously. In addition, you may need interferon-alfa and even a liver transplant. In other words, head for home and expert care.

Hepatitis E

Hepatitis E is transmitted primarily by contaminated drinking water, but it can also be spread in the same other ways as hepatitis A. There is no vaccine, and immune globulin probably offers no protection. The most important method of prevention is avoiding contaminated water. Those infected generally recover without any problems. However, pregnant women can be severely affected.

Leishmaniasis

How to get it: Leishmaniasis is present in Central America (also South America, Africa, central Asia, the Middle East, and northern China). A quick nip from an infected female sand fly injects a tiny parasite that invades lymphoid cells in internal organs such as the spleen and liver, as well as bone marrow or mucous membranes.

Symptoms: You may not even notice the bite until weeks or months later, when it becomes a painful ulcer. Because it's difficult to distinguish leishmaniasis from quite a few other diseases, it's important to realize that a skin ulcer may be a signal.

How to avoid it: Prevention being preferable to cure, take the usual precautions, such as using insect repellent, wearing long pants, using fine-mesh netting, and so on. (See the section on malaria later in this chapter.)

How to treat it: If left untreated, leishmaniasis can be fatal. Most infected people wait months before seeking treatment, and then their doctor may not diagnose it properly because of lack of familiarity with the disease. Tell your physician exactly where you've been traveling, because treatment varies with the species of parasite and form of the disease you've contracted. See someone with experience treating the disease.

Malaria

Malaria is present in more than 100 countries. Almost 2 million people die from it each year. However, of the 350 to 500 million people infected every year, only about 30,000 are travelers. Of those, fewer than 800 are American. That's because, although there's no absolute immunity against malaria, most American travelers take proper precautions and, if infected, have access to prompt treatment.

Amazingly, though, some travelers in areas of known risk ignore even the basic precautions of taking preventive tablets (chemoprophylaxis) and following simple routines to avoid being bitten by mosquitoes, the carriers of the disease. Given the risks to the fetus and alterations in a mother's immune system and liver with pregnancy, pregnant women should not travel to malarial areas unless it's necessary.

Although early treatment of malaria is usually effective, consequences can be very serious if treatment is delayed. People living in highly malarial areas may develop partial immunity after repeated attacks of malaria, but unprotected travelers are at risk.

According to the Centers for Disease Control and Prevention (CDC), the risk is highest in tropical Africa, Amazonian South America, and parts of Central America, Mexico, India, the Caribbean, southern Asia, Indonesia, and New Guinea. The chance of getting malaria in Africa is estimated as 2,000 times greater than in Latin America.

How to get it: Physicians used to believe that something about the air in swamps and sewers caused the disease. Hence the name, from the Italian *mala aria,* or "bad air." Turns out they weren't far off. We now know that it is the female *Anopheles* (a Greek word meaning "hurtful") mosquito, a lover of swamps and sewers, that delivers malaria to us. She is merely a carrier, picking up one-cell parasites from an infected person and transmitting them, via the saliva accompanying her pesky bite, to the next person. The parasites travel to the liver of the new host, multiply, and escape into the bloodstream. There, they invade red blood cells and multiply, causing the cells to burst and the parasites to flood the system like bloodthirsty pirates searching for more cells to invade.

Symptoms: Malaria symptoms usually appear between a week and a month after exposure but can take longer. The first round includes chills that may last from 15 minutes to an hour, even up to eight hours. High fever follows for several hours, then heavy sweating. Fatigue, severe headache, muscle pains, dizziness, and increasing weakness usually accompany these symptoms. When an attack of malaria subsides, the patient feels weary but much better. Symptoms may recur every one to three days, depending on which species of parasite is roaming around in the blood. The parasites can also damage the brain, lungs, and kidneys (when malaria affects the kidneys, it's called blackwater fever because bursting red blood cells darken the urine), which can be lethal.

Only a minority of malaria cases include any intestinal uproar, so a person who has some or all the symptoms listed previously plus nausea, vomiting, cramps, or diarrhea may have typhoid, cholera, dysentery, dengue fever, or hepatitis rather than malaria. (Now there are some great choices!) If you have an unexplained fever while in an area in which malaria is common, get a blood test immediately.

How to avoid it: Prevention is the best answer. Don't get bitten. Before you leave home, review the World Malaria Risk Chart and How to Protect Yourself against Malaria, both available from the International Association for Medical Assistance to Travellers (**www.iamat.org**). The IAMAT material is so helpful, it's almost reckless not to use it. The Malaria Branch of the CDC publishes a useful booklet called *Preventing Malaria in Travelers,* available online at **www.cdc.gov/ malaria/pdf/travelers.pdf**.

There are a number of ways to minimize the likelihood of mosquito bites (and they don't include staying home). Be more vigilant when mosquitoes are most active—during warm months and at dawn and dusk. Be wary of water, especially if it's slow-moving or stagnant. Strong scents and body odors attract mosquitoes, so a shower at the end of a hot day is practical as well as pleasurable. For anyone disposed to take hair spray, perfume, or perfumed cosmetics on their travels, the mosquito's keen nose is one more incentive to leave those things at home. Unfortunately, mosquitoes are even attracted by the carbon dioxide we exhale— and there's not much we can do about that.

Definitely use an insect repellent. Among those available, DEET is amazingly effective, and no traveler should be without it in a malarial area. The recommended concentration is 30 percent (10 percent for children), and it should be combined with sunscreen. In addition, spray permethrin (sold as Permanone) on your bed net and clothing (not on skin). Permethrin does more than repel; it actually kills the mosquitoes. It won't melt synthetic materials and remains effective even after the clothing has been washed several times. Rub DEET on thoroughly, and reapply it every few hours—more frequently if you sweat heavily or otherwise get wet. DEET on one part of your body does not deter mosquitoes from biting untreated skin nearby. Tuck your pants into your shoes, especially if ticks are a problem.

Ultrathon insect repellent uses a polymer suspension to achieve controlled release of a 34 percent DEET solution with very low absorption through the skin. It's supposed to keep mosquitoes, ticks, flies, chiggers, gnats, and fleas at bay for up to 12 hours, and it resists water and perspiration. Whatever you select, use it. Not getting bitten is by far your most effective protection. We'll discuss this further in Chapter 15, Lodging.

For those for whom DEET is not acceptable, Picaridin is an alternative, though protection lasts only one to four hours.

Clothing fends off mosquitoes fairly effectively, so at prime time in malaria-land, wear long pants and shirts with long sleeves. Protect your neck. Army-surplus stores sell light, inexpensive hats with mosquito-proof mesh that covers the head and neck (don't worry if you salute when an officer of the French Foreign Legion strides by).

Where mosquito nets are needed, you'll usually find them provided in your hotel room or for sale on the street. The most common type of net hangs from overhead, covering the entire bed. Tape any holes or tears closed, or tie the net around them into a small knot. If you can't seal the holes, ask the clerk for a better net. You can take a net with you; some good ones weigh less than a pound and cost about $30.

When mosquitoes are around, light mosquito coils at the head and foot of the bed. Some people prefer putting oil of citronella on themselves and the corners of the bed. After you're in, tuck the net under the mattress all around. Think of yourself as the favorite entrée on some mosquito's evening menu, and act accordingly.

Because, at present, no drug regimen guarantees complete protection against malaria, virtually all knowledgeable travelers take a malaria prophylactic (I know you know that we're not talking about a condom here). The available drugs simply suppress multiplication of the parasites in the liver, thus preventing their spread through the body to become full-scale malaria.

Even a person who's taken no antimalarial pills is unlikely to contract malaria from a single bite, so don't panic if one little dive bomber slips through. We seem to have at least a limited natural immunity, but, because that immunity is minimal, protection remains very important.

Quinine protected Enrico Caruso when he sang grand opera 1,500 miles up the Amazon at the turn of the last century and Dr. David Livingstone as he trudged through the jungle trying to find the headwaters of the Nile. In India, the officials of the British raj quaffed endless gin and tonics (tonic water contains quinine), but that probably won't work for you.

Because malaria parasites are always changing in their susceptibility to antimalarial drugs, it's impossible to specify any one therapy with certainty. Before departing on your trip, review the CDC Web site's section on malaria (**www.cdc.gov/malaria**).

In many parts of the world, malaria parasites have mutated, acquiring resistance to chloroquine phosphate (P), the drug everyone used to take. Although some degree of chloroquine resistance has been reported almost everywhere malaria occurs, chloroquine is still effective in Mexico and Central America north of Panama. Not long ago, the CDC was suggesting that where parasites are resistant to chloroquine, one ought to take mefloquine (Lariam; P). Doxycycline (P) is also widely used.

The CDC recommends Fansidar (P) as a means of suppressing malaria symptoms long enough to reach proper medical treatment, and as a treatment as well, but doesn't recommend it as a prophylactic.

Some well-regarded antimalarial pills are not sold in certain countries. For a trip I took to central Africa, the most appropriate antimalarial drug appeared to be proguanil (Paludrine). It wasn't sold in the United States but was available over the counter in England. I took a daily proguanil and a weekly chloroquine pill and didn't get malaria. Of course, a friend relied on Chinese herbs during the same trip, and she didn't get malaria, either. What can we conclude from that?

Because a malaria prophylactic may have side effects, ask a doctor what to expect. For example, some users have reported serious side effects from Lariam (for example, nightmares and panic attacks). If my palms and the soles of my feet started scaling, I'd feel better if I knew it was just a rare side effect of proguanil.

Malarone (P) has been cleared by the Food and Drug Administration and is now available as a preventive treatment. It has fewer side effects than Lariam for many people.

Again, I do not recommend a specific antimalarial pill because that choice should be determined by what's effective where you're going, how much time you'll be spending in rural areas (where mosquitoes are most dense), and what drug allergies you have. You need current medical information to connect the best protection with your itinerary. Again, see **www.iamat.org** and **www.cdc.gov.**

The usual drill is to begin taking the pills two weeks (for Malarone or doxycycline, it's two days) before you enter an area of a malaria risk. As perhaps slight evidence of global consciousness, almost every traveler I know who takes a weekly pill takes it on Sunday. To avoid an upset stomach, follow your pharmacist's directions (usually, to take it after a meal). Continue taking the pills at prescribed intervals during your travels and for the specified number of weeks after you are last exposed to any risk of acquiring malaria. The objective is to kill any parasites that may still be lounging around your liver.

Women in their first trimester of pregnancy should be cautious of antimalarial drugs. Neither they nor young children should take these drugs without advice from a knowledgeable doctor.

Blood donations are not tested for malaria. Therefore, a person who has malaria or who has lived or traveled in a country where malaria is present must not donate blood until enough time has passed to be certain that he or she is not infected—three years for someone who has completed treatment or has lived in a country where malaria is found, one year for a person returning from a trip to a country where malaria is found. Describe your status, including travel destinations and dates, to the blood bank or hospital.

A few words about what does not work: studies do not support the belief that vitamin B1 is an effective mosquito repellent. Gadgets that project sound waves do not work. Avon's Skin So Soft acts as a temporary physical barrier because of its mineral oil but is only about 50 percent effective, and only if reapplied every ten minutes or so. As a Saint Joseph's Hospital (Atlanta) Travel Advisory put it, none of these alternatives will hurt you, but relying on any of them to prevent malaria "would border on lunacy."

How to treat it: In the 1700s, South American natives taught strangers how to use powder made from the bark of a certain tree to relieve malaria symptoms. That was good advice at the time, but if you believe you have the symptoms of malaria, forget those gin and tonics and see a doctor. If you must minister to yourself until you reach a doctor, take an increased dose of whatever prophylactic medicine you've been taking. The number of pills you should take depends on the dosage and contents of your tablets. When you buy the drug, ask, "What dosage should I take if I experience symptoms of malaria?"

If you get malaria, a blood test will determine the type of parasite. You then take a drug designed to kill that specific parasite, and there should be no recurrence of the symptoms. In other words, malaria is curable. The danger is in failing to get treatment. Without treatment, one type of malaria parasite can be lethal. Other types are unlikely to be lethal but can cause recurrence of the symptoms and damage to assorted internal organs if untreated.

If you see a doctor after you return from a trip during which you took anti-malarial drugs, be sure to mention that fact. If you think you may have malaria, tell the doctor where you've traveled. Also ask him or her to consider the other diseases your research suggests you might have encountered. If you're concerned that your doctor may not be current on malaria and these other diseases, find a travel-medicine or infectious-disease specialist right away.

The bottom line: with reasonable efforts, you can probably avoid mosquitoes and thus avoid malaria; protective medicine greatly reduces the chances that full-scale malaria will develop; and if you get malaria, proper treatment should cure it.

Rabies

Rabies (also known as hydrophobia) can cause prolonged suffering and death. It's present in most areas of the world, including Europe and the United States. Rabies is found in raccoons, jackals, wolves, bats, cattle, cats, and dogs, among other animals.

Although symptoms usually appear within two to eight weeks, one nasty characteristic of rabies is that it can take up to seven years to show up—long after the victim has forgotten the incident that caused it (which could have been merely getting infected saliva in a wound). To be cautious, receive the Imovax (Human Diploid Cell Vaccine; P) in three not particularly painful injections beginning a month before you travel.

As you travel, don't pet an animal that can bite you, and get out of the way if you see an animal behaving strangely (erratic motions, howling bark, frothing mouth, and jaws fixed open). Rabid animals are fearless and will attack without provocation. However, an animal infected with "dumb" rabies will be docile and show none of this behavior.

If bitten, or even licked on a wound by an infected animal (the virus travels in the animal's saliva), wash the wound immediately with soap and clean water. Pour in some hydrogen peroxide. If no clean water is available, use alcohol, tea, or even carbonated soda. You are attempting to wash the virus from the wound, so wash vigorously and repeatedly. See a doctor to help you decide whether to receive the vaccine (if you haven't had it) or an injection of rabies immune globulin at the bite site. The decision will be much easier if the offending animal is caught and tested.

Schistosomiasis (Bilharzia)

More than 200 million people carry this parasite, which exists primarily in sub-Saharan Africa, the Middle East, Japan, China, the Philippines, Indonesia, Thailand, tropical South America, and the Caribbean islands. If you'll be traveling in one or more of these places, you should know the precautions to take.

How to get it: Schistosomiasis is caused by trematode parasites that live inside freshwater snails. After metamorphosis, they enter the water, seeking their next host (and humans are very hospitable). If these parasites are present, a person is at risk when swimming in, bathing in, drinking, or even just walking through water. Parasites can enter a host through the skin (a break in the skin, such as a cut, isn't required) or when swallowed. They reproduce and attack the bowel, bladder, liver, and colon, ultimately appearing in the stool or urine. When parasite-contaminated excrement later enters the water source, the process begins again as the parasite seeks out the snail.

Symptoms: The first sign might be a brief rash where the parasite entered the body. Appearing three to ten weeks after infection, symptoms include abdominal pain, tender and enlarged spleen and liver, headache, chills, fever, diarrhea, blood in the stool or urine, nausea, aches, body rash, coughing, and weight loss. Remission may occur two to eight weeks thereafter. In advanced cases, schisto has caused blindness, epilepsy, and even death. The diversity of symptoms makes it very hard to diagnose.

How to avoid it: Where schistosomiasis is a possibility, don't swim in rivers or lakes, in stagnant water, or immediately downstream from a city. Even brief exposure can result in infection. If you must cross freshwater in a schisto-infected area, wear shoes, and cover your ankles. If you get wet, rub your skin dry immediately; apply alcohol if you have it. You want to remove or kill the parasite before it can penetrate the skin. Boil (for at least one minute, per the CDC), filter, or treat water to disinfect it before drinking or bathing. If you can do nothing else, wash with soap. Prevention is important because schisto can do considerable damage before being detected.

How to treat it: You may need to be tested more than once because a test soon after exposure may be misleadingly negative. Schisto can be diagnosed by a urine or stool test and can be cured by an antiparasitic drug regimen. Check with your travel-medicine specialist or the CDC about what drugs have been effective in the area where you have traveled.

Severe Pain (Broken Bones, Kidney Stones, and Other Fun Things)
If you're going to be days away from outside medical help, take a heavy-duty painkiller along in case of serious injury. It won't cure anything, but it makes the pain easier to endure until you can reach help. Don't take it in conjunction with alcohol. The bottle containing pain medication should be labeled to avoid any problem with customs.

Sexually Transmitted Diseases

Acquired Immunodeficiency Syndrome (AIDS)

How to get it: AIDS, caused by the human immunodeficiency virus (HIV), is epidemic in at least ten African countries, India, Thailand, and the Philippines, and is a growing problem in many other countries. Good news: you do not contract AIDS just from being in certain places. Nor is it spread by casual contact, coughs or sneezes, bad food or water, toilets, mosquitoes, or any of the other usual culprits that propagate many diseases. Whether you contract AIDS is determined primarily by your own behavior; it is not an inherent peril of being on the road.

AIDS is transmitted for the most part by sexual intercourse or, euphemistically, by transfer of body fluids. It can be contracted during a single sexual contact, and you get no free swings. HIV infection can also be transmitted via a needle—while taking intravenous drugs, getting inoculations, getting a tattoo or a body piercing, undergoing acupuncture or a blood transfusion, or suffering an accidental jab.

Symptoms: The symptoms are too complex—and well known—to need repeating here.

How to avoid it: To avoid deterring tourists and businesspeople, some governments low-ball the number of known HIV-positive cases in their countries. That means you should not rely on published information about the prevalence of AIDS in a given country. Unless you're skiing across Antarctica, assume HIV is present.

The local people whom travelers meet most frequently are those who make their living around the tourist trail. Unfortunately, this makes them a high-risk group. Among those at highest risk are intravenous drug users, prostitutes, and guys who prowl tourist

> Your next sexual partner could be that very special person. The one that gives you AIDS.
> —Public-health notice in Zimbabwe

areas hoping to seduce travelers. Other travelers who have sex with local people can, if infected, pass the virus on to you.

It's pathetic that your life may be on the line when you're considering a sexual relationship with an enchanting person as you travel—but that's the way it is. How many unexpected births must there be before we concede that condoms are not fail-safe as protection? You must not let blood, semen, or vaginal secretions from an infected person enter your body.

If you haven't traveled extensively in faraway places, you may not be able to predict how you'll respond to the stimuli of romantic settings and attractive companions (about whom, unfortunately, you may not know a lot). A prospective partner may be unaware of, or unwilling to admit, his or her AIDS status. Or someone may lie to you about his or her status or sexual behavior. If you are uncertain about what choices you might make as you travel, you would be well advised to take along latex condoms with nonoxynol-9 spermicide. Although latex doesn't remain impervious to tropical heat for long, animal-skin condoms are too porous.

Anyone who uses a questionable needle to inject recreational drugs or otherwise pierce one's skin in a foreign country has a death wish, one that may be accommodated. Stay away from tattoos and acupuncture unless you're certain the equipment is sterile (which is highly unlikely). If you require an inoculation, be certain that a new, still-in-the-package, disposable needle is used. Don't take anyone's word for it. See the package opened—or go elsewhere. Some travelers carry a packaged syringe and needle in case of injury in countries where AIDS is common.

A related issue is whether the blood available for transfusions is contaminated. Most underdeveloped and developing countries still can't ensure that their blood supply is free from hepatitis, AIDS, or other diseases, so travelers should do everything possible to avoid receiving a transfusion. In an emergency, consider plasma extenders. If you're traveling with a partner or a small group, you might compare your blood types and HIV status to determine who could donate to whom should the need arise. If the need for a transfusion arises and you have the choice, buy a plane ticket. Fortunately, the odds against needing a transfusion when you are in a high-AIDS-risk country are massively in your favor.

How to treat it: There is no known vaccine for protection against AIDS. Expensive, multidrug therapy that must continue for the rest of your life may control the disease but does not cure it.

Syphilis, Gonorrhea, Chlamydia, and Other Sexually Transmitted Diseases

Even though sexually transmitted diseases (STDs) are more prevalent in developing countries than in developed countries, more than a few travelers roll the dice, making an intimate decision based on a spontaneous evaluation of someone's personality or appearance. Abstinence is the best preventive medicine, followed by having sex only with a partner who has tested negative for sexually transmitted diseases. Condoms come in a distant third. If you decide to go forward, use a latex condom and a vaginal spermicide. In addition, check for sores or discharge, wash the genitals of a prospective partner with soap and water, and urinate after intercourse. Sounds pretty romantic, doesn't it?

Common STD symptoms include penile or vaginal discharge, urination that causes a burning sensation, and lower-abdominal pain. There may also be an ulcer, rash, and fever. Men generally experience the first symptoms of gonorrhea within two to seven days, but it may be weeks before a woman feels symptoms, if ever. Some STDs have no symptoms. It would be prudent to assume that you might have been infected and to practice safer sex with a condom until both you and your prospective or established partner receive negative results on blood tests. If you think you may have an STD, let partners know, avoid sexual contact, and start medication immediately.

In 2007, the CDC announced that gonorrhea has become resistant to ciprofloxacin, ofloxacin, and levofloxacin. It had already become resistant to penicillin, sulfa drugs, and tetracycline. The CDC recommends an injection of ceftriaxone (Rocephin; P) as the drug of choice.

Treatment for chlamydia, which may be the leading cause of infertility and pelvic inflammatory disease, includes doxycycline (P) or azithromycin (P). Some doctors recommend rythromycin (P) and Levaquin (P), but those are not the current CDC Web site recommendations.

Women may experience a pelvic inflammatory disease, often caused by gonorrhea or chlamydia. Treatment usually includes ciprofloxacin, cefixime (P), and doxycycline (for nonpregnant women only).

Syphilis announces its presence 10 to 90 days after infection with a sore on the genitals or the lips, fingers, or anus. Although the sore is painless, it is highly contagious. It disappears without treatment, but the disease continues to grow in the person affected. If untreated, syphilis may cause serious problems, including heart disease and insanity. When an unexplained sore appears in one of these areas two to ten weeks after sexual contact, get medical help. Treatment for STDs can be complicated, so see a doctor as soon as you can.

Shock

Symptoms of shock include a weak, fast pulse; a pale face; perspiration; fainting; clammy skin; dull eyes; and nausea. Blood pressure drops so low that vital organs do not receive adequate blood. Shock often accompanies major trauma (for example, a large burn, severe illness, or extensive blood loss) but can occur even after relatively minor injuries or serious infections. Keep the victim lying down and, if injuries permit, elevate the legs higher than the head. Use blankets to conserve body heat. Giving the victim water or oral rehydration salts (not alcohol) may help, but there is some risk of vomiting or aspiration. If the victim is unconscious, turn him on his side so he won't choke. Keep the mouth and throat clear. Because blood is not flowing to vital organs, shock can kill. It is essential to get medical help, especially intravenous fluids, immediately.

Tetanus

How to get it: Tetanus (sometimes called lockjaw) microorganisms are omnipresent and can infect through any break in the skin. Tetanus may invade through puncture wounds from splinters, thorns, or almost anything else. Remember your mom warning you not to step on a nail? It's a serious problem but one that can largely be prevented through immunization.

How to avoid it: In 2006, the tetanus vaccine was combined with the diphtheria and pertussis (whooping cough) vaccine for everyone under age 65. That combination provides a high degree of immunity. Almost everyone gets this vaccination as a child, but a booster is necessary every ten years (or within five years of your last immunization if you've had a dirty scrape, cut, or skin ulcer). Because tetanus germs are so common, this immunization is important whether you travel or not. Clean and cover any wound. If it's large, get medical attention.

Thrombosis, Blood Clots

How to get it: Deep-vein thrombosis can occur in a variety of ways, but for travelers it has become known as "economy-class syndrome." When people sit for hours in a cramped space—certainly including airplane seats with demonically truncated legroom—blood begins to pool in their lower legs. This can also occur on long car or bus trips. A blood clot forms in a deep vein, usually in the legs. If the clot breaks free and travels through the bloodstream, it can block a blood vessel in the lungs. This is known as a pulmonary embolism, and it can be fatal.

How to avoid it: At higher risk are people older than 60, smokers, those who are overweight or have cancer, and anyone taking birth-control pills or hormone therapy. Preventive measures include doing small exercises while seated and getting up regularly to stretch and stroll down the aisle. If that draws a frown from a fellow passenger or the flight attendant, well, that's the way it has to be.

How to treat it: There may be no obvious symptoms but there might be swelling in a leg, and the area might feel warm or be discolored. If uncertain, see a doctor for an ultrasound or venogram.

Trauma

Trauma is a wound or shock produced by an extensive physical injury. Travelers are more at risk of experiencing traumatic injury than of being affected by almost any of the other health threats on this list. If a problem occurs that requires quick, effective first aid, a traveler can't count on finding help quickly (most countries have no 911 service). Emotions or pain at the time of injury can create confusion. That's why it might be wise to take a first-aid course before you travel—or read and take along one of the excellent small-format first-aid booklets.

Studies have identified certain factors associated with higher risk of trauma: being male, being elderly, riding high-risk vehicles (such as motorcycles or small aircraft), drinking alcohol, and being in less developed countries. However, following three suggestions will provide some protection.

First, be careful in traffic abroad. The traffic flow may be the reverse of what you're used to, and the pedestrian seldom has the right of way. Look both ways before stepping into the street. Too often, drivers, especially drivers of big trucks, are careless of human life.

Second, if you're riding in a vehicle and the driver seems drunk, get out— or off. It's amazing how many canyons are littered with the remnants of buses because a cannonballing driver didn't see a curve in time. Don't assume, as you might at home, that the driver must know what he's doing and will get you safely to the barn. A high correlation between alcohol and accidents prevails around the world. Listen to your intuition.

> There's no doubt about it: the easier it becomes to travel, the harder it is to be a traveler.
> —John Julius Norwich, *A Taste for Travel* (1985)

Third, don't drive in developing countries when you can avoid it. It's like trying to dance when you don't know the steps.

If someone is injured in an accident, see if he or she is breathing, then check for a pulse. If CPR seems necessary, use those lessons you took before leaving home. If you think there's a broken bone, apply ice, immobilize the area with a splint, elevate it, and find a doctor. Be careful not to aggravate a neck or back injury by unnecessary movement. If movement is unavoidable, immobilize the injured area with a splint first. You can splint an arm by strapping it to the chest. Bind legs together. Use a tree limb, anything, to keep broken pieces from moving freely.

If there is serious bleeding, elevate and apply pressure to the wound or to the artery supplying blood to that extremity. If a person is unconscious and there is chance of a neck injury, moving the victim is very dangerous. If you must do so, use a backboard, and immobilize the head and neck.

Try to ensure that fluids drain from the mouth to prevent aspiration or suffocation. Call for help, and be prepared to administer CPR.

If a traumatic injury causes you to be taken to a local hospital, you or your partner must remain very alert. Serious pathogens (hepatitis B, C, or D; hemorrhagic fevers; HIV; and so on) can be transmitted, partly because reuse of needles for injections may be as high as 25 percent. This is why travelers ought to consider evacuation insurance.

Tuberculosis

Though seldom present in the United States, tuberculosis (TB) has never ceased being a problem in many other countries. Recently, it has been spread by people who got it as a result of diminished immunity due to AIDS. New forms of TB are increasingly resistant to standard drug treatment. You can do three things to reduce risk: keep yourself in good health, avoid letting people cough on you, and get a TB skin test if you may have been exposed. A BCG (bacille Calmette-Guérin) shot is sometimes given to children to decrease risk of TB meningitis, but it's not normally prescribed for adults. Trials of other vaccines have produced inconsistent results so far.

Typhoid Fever

> When I was very young and the rage to be someplace was on me, I was assured by mature people that maturity would cure the itch . . . Now that I am fifty-eight perhaps senility will do that job. Nothing has worked. In other words, I don't improve, in further words, once a bum always a bum.
> —John Steinbeck

How to get it: Consuming food or water contaminated by *Salmonella typhi* bacteria is the usual way. High-risk areas for typhoid, which is highly infectious, include parts of Central and South America.

Symptoms: It begins like a cold or the flu and progresses to extreme fatigue, chills, high fever, coughs, bloody diarrhea, constipation, headaches, and loss of appetite. A telltale sign is that your pulse gets slower when your fever increases. After a week or so, there may be pink spots on the body and some delirium.

How to avoid it: Be alert to sanitation in places you eat and drink, especially in villages and rural areas. Typhim Vi (P), a single-dose vaccine, is said to be effective, with minimal side effects. A booster is required every two years. A live oral vaccine, which provides five-year immunity, has been reported to be as effective as the injection and is, of course, painless. Avoid combining the oral vaccine with antibiotics and proguanil antimalarials. Typhoid is still common in underdeveloped countries, so it's worth keeping this immunity current.

How to treat it: There should be no long-term complications if you get extended rest and take one of several antibiotics such as ciprofloxacin (P), trimethoprim–sulfamethoxazole (Bactrim or Septra; P), or ampicillin (P).

Typhus

How to get it: Bites or ingestion of contaminated feces from lice, fleas, and mites are the primary sources of infection. Typhus exists mostly in the highland areas of Mexico, Peru, Ecuador, Africa, Asia, and the Middle East.

Symptoms: There may be days or weeks of fever, chills, severe headache, coughing, and pains in the chest and back. There may also be a rash on the trunk of the body that lasts for up to a week. Typhus carried by lice and mites may progress to pneumonia after about a week. The severity of typhus depends on the specific bacteria involved.

How to avoid it: Watch out for lice, fleas, mites, ticks, and rats. Bathe frequently, and wash your clothes in very hot water. Use insect repellents. If you find the insects, use an insecticidal shampoo such as Kwell (P). Or consider the less toxic isopropyl myristate (sold under the name Resultz in Canada; OTC) or phenothrin (Full Marks products in the United Kingdom; OTC). If you hear of an outbreak, go somewhere else.

How to treat it: Tetracycline (P) and doxycycline (P) are considered effective.

Yellow Fever

How to get it: As with malaria, yellow fever is brought into your life by a mosquito. However, like the mosquito carrying dengue fever, this one bites during the day.

Symptoms: Jaundice (yellow skin and eyes) gives this illness its name. There is an initial fever with rapid pulse. The fever ebbs, then returns with a rapid pulse, perhaps accompanied by bleeding from the mouth and stomach, headache, loss of rationality, and possibly coma.

How to avoid it: Yellow fever is still present in South America and the Caribbean, especially in rural areas. If you may be in a yellow-fever area, get a single shot of live virus vaccine before you go, then a booster every ten years. If a country requires, as a condition of entry, evidence that you've had this vaccination, you must have received it at least ten days before your arrival and had it entered on your yellow card. Countries that require evidence of the vaccination are all in Central and West Africa, plus French Guiana. Note that the yellow-fever vaccination must be separated from a cholera vaccination by at least three weeks. Check with the CDC (**www.cdc.gov**) for information.

How to treat it: There is no effective treatment, but medical assistance is necessary to provide intravenous fluids, monitor kidney functioning, and control gastrointestinal bleeding.

CHECKLIST: MATCHING MEDICINES WITH MORE-SERIOUS PROBLEMS

_____ Bronchitis: amoxicillin (avoid if allergic to penicillin), cotrimoxazole (Bactrim or Septra), erythromycin, ciprofloxacin (Cipro)

_____ Dehydration: oral rehydration salts

_____ Dysentery: metronidazole (Flagyl), ciprofloxacin (Cipro), cotrimoxazole (Bactrim or Septra)

_____ Giardiasis: metronidazole (Flagyl)

_____ Malaria: mefloquine (Lariam), sulfadoxine (Fansidar), chloroquine phosphate, or doxycycline; DEET, Ultrathon, permethrin (one version is sold as Permanone Tick Repellent), mosquito coils. *Note:* It is essential that your malaria-related regimen be based on the places you visit and resistance patterns at that time.

_____ Severe pain: Demerol; ibuprofen or acetaminophen for lesser pain

_____ Sexually transmitted diseases: Preventive measures include condoms treated with nonoxynol-9, disposable needles

_____ Typhus: tetracycline

TRAVEL-MEDICINE KIT

With this litany of unpleasantness in mind, it's obvious why a traveler is well advised to carry a thoughtfully prepared travel-medicine kit. I'm far from being a hypochondriac, but I carry more medicine when I leave the country than I ever keep on hand at home. I've never had to use even one of the major treatments and don't expect to.

Consider including some backup prescription medicines in the event some overzealous customs official snatches your main supply.

If you don't take this chapter with you on your trip, consider taking at least the medical checklists to help properly match the remedy with the problem.

You may have seen ready-made portable medicine kits for sale. Some may be okay for minor first aid, but I don't use or recommend them. Because they're designed for general use, they're incomplete and expensive. It's better to think carefully about what you might encounter and design your own kit.

Medicine-kit Tips

- Transport medicine in a watertight case or sturdy zip-top bag.
- Leave glass containers at home.
- Consider taking a brief first-aid manual.
- Transfer pills from large containers into smaller ones, along with the prescription information. Clearly label all containers.
- When you have a choice, take a capsule or pill rather than a liquid.
- Symptoms don't announce themselves with labels, so you have to be able to connect them with the appropriate remedy. Write on separate slips of paper what illness each medicine treats and the illness's major symptoms. Put each slip in the appropriate container.
- Take copies of prescriptions and the generic names of the medications. Have the pharmacist include the expiration date of each medicine on the label. Don't rely on prescription medicine that is nearing its expiration date.
- If prescriptions are filled abroad, ensure that the proper weights, presumably metric, are used.
- If you buy abroad, beware of "brand name" drugs being sold at absurdly low prices. Make sure the label looks authentic. Misspellings, for example, don't inspire confidence. Some drugs sold abroad may contain impurities.

- Take most medicines along rather than planning to buy them while traveling. Otherwise, you might need a medicine where there is no source or when you have a problem communicating.
- Take some or all of your essential medications in your carry-on luggage (so you won't lose everything if your checked bag is lost). Some travelers make two complete sets and carry them separately.
- Confer with your doctor before buying the components of a travel-medicine kit. This is especially true for pregnant women; mothers who are breast-feeding; persons with asthma, glaucoma, diabetes, or high blood pressure; persons with kidney, heart, thyroid, or prostate disease; and persons with autoimmune or chronic diseases. Review all drug doses and the circumstances in which you should take them with the doctor who prescribes them.

If you develop a significant health problem while abroad:

- Ask for recommendations from a consulate (yours or anyone's).
- Discuss it with a local pharmacist.
- Call your credit-card company if it offers medical assistance to travelers.
- Consult your International Association for Medical Assistance to Travellers directory of physicians (**www.iamat.org**).
- Check with volunteer organizations on-site, such as the Peace Corps.
- Contact the State Department Office of Overseas Citizen Services at (202) 501-4444.
- Ask expatriates.
- Get advice from other travelers.
- Get assistance from local people.
- Get to a big city, where the standard of care is higher than in the countryside.
- Hop on a plane for home.

CHECKLIST: SHOTS TO GET BEFORE YOU LEAVE

What shots you need depends on where you're going, the current status of your inoculations, and the requirements of the countries you'll be visiting. Obtain annual information on the prevalence of specific diseases in specific countries, along with immunization requirements, from the CDC. Call the agency's 24-hour information line at (404) 332-4559, or visit **www.cdc.gov**.

Because some shots interfere with others and some shots are given as a series, you can't drop into the health department at the last minute to get all your immunizations at once. Besides, it's nice to have some time to recover from any adverse reaction. It would be ideal to receive the full series of immunizations over a four-week to four-month period, but the pace can be accelerated if need be.

_____ Cholera: Vaccine (if desired and if available) four to six weeks before you leave. If practical, it should not be received at the same time as the yellow-fever vaccine. Protection is only partial. Check with the CDC to determine whether a cholera certificate of vaccination is required to enter any country on your itinerary. In practice, few doctors give this vaccine anymore.

_____ Diphtheria: Vaccine six weeks before you leave. Booster every ten years, in the same shot with tetanus and pertussis boosters.

_____ Hepatitis A: Vaccine is the primary option now over immune globulin, although it's substantially more expensive. Havrix and Vaqta offer very long-term immunity, possibly lifelong. The first shot is taken two to four weeks before departure; the second, six months later.

_____ Hepatitis B: Ideally, the three-shot vaccine series (Recombivax) takes six months.

_____ Influenza: Vaccine any time (but it's not usually available in the United States except in fall and winter). Especially important for people older than 65 and anyone with chronic heart or lung disease.

_____ Measles, mumps, rubella: Vaccines six weeks before you leave. If you were born after 1956, it is recommended that you receive a measles booster even if you've had an earlier shot.

_____ Rabies: Begin Imovax series four to six weeks before you leave. It may be repeated every two years if indicated by a decrease in antibody levels.

_____ Tetanus: Vaccine (combined with diphtheria and pertussis vaccine) six weeks before you leave. Booster every ten years or after a puncture wound or major laceration.

_____ Typhoid: If you take the standard injectable Typhim Vi, get the shot at least two weeks before departure, with a booster every three years. The oral vaccine may be preferable but should be kept refrigerated and must be taken as directed, with a booster every fifth year.

_____ Yellow fever: Vaccine three weeks before you leave. Booster every ten years.

Enter each shot on your yellow card. Keep a copy in a safe place because it's probably the only record of what shots you've had and when.

Health Reminder

If a health problem emerges after your return, including unexplained weight loss, which you suspect might be related to your travels, tell your doctor where you've been and what your ideas may be about possible causes. If symptoms are severe or recurring, find a specialist.

Caveat

Neither of the authors is a doctor, and nothing in this chapter or this book can be relied on as medical advice. Nor are those who reviewed various sections of this chapter responsible for the final contents thereof. Even if we seem to state something definitively, we're simply sharing with you the results of our research and the choices we make for ourselves. You must do your own research at the time you're going to travel, applicable to the specific regions you expect to visit. We are not a substitute for your doctor. If you consult one or more doctors, ensure that they are qualified to answer the questions you ask. A doctor may be expert in his or her field but inexperienced or not up to date concerning your foreign-travel questions.

When a product is mentioned by brand name, it's because it is currently considered to be an effective choice. We have no interest in promoting any particular product. Any medicine should be taken only by a person who is aware of its risks and possible interactions with other medicines. Be cautious about buying drugs over the counter abroad that are sold only by prescription in the United States. Ensure that you understand clearly what the possible side effects might be.

CHAPTER 13

When It's Time to Go

I travel not to go anywhere, but to go.
I travel for travel's sake. The great affair is to move.
—Robert Louis Stevenson
Travels with a Donkey in the Cévennes (1879)

I'm good at getting ready for a long trip, but stress creeps in as the departure date grows close. There's too much to do; I can't get ready in time. Fortunately, I get a grip and make the plane every time.

When you're stressed, you tend to forget things. Even when you've packed your clothing and equipment, you still have to remember all your last-minute tasks and make arrangements for everything that someone else has to do for you while you're away. I've solved that problem by creating two checklists: one for me, one for my Guardian Angels.

"Guardian Angels" is what I call the relatives, friends, business associates, and significant others who care for my home, pay my bills, screen the mail, handle taxes, care for the dog, and do the other tasks that keep things together while I'm away.

Guardian Angels have a lot of responsibility if a problem arises. For that reason, I bring them exotic presents, thank them repeatedly, and pay them if that is appropriate. I'll always be in their debt.

These checklists are intended to avoid that moment when, lying on the perfect beach on Roatán, I snap my fingers, and say, "Damn, I forgot to . . ."

CHECKLIST: LAST-MINUTE TASKS

This comprehensive checklist is designed for trips of a couple of weeks or longer, but many items apply to travel of any length.

_____ Appliances. Turn off, set, or unplug everything that runs on electricity. Check whether your brand of refrigerator should be unplugged. Don't let a power surge zap your computer and other tools and toys.

_____ Bills. Pay all your outstanding bills, and put as much as possible on automatic-payment plans. If you'll have Internet access on the road, you can pay other bills online. For whatever is left—and that shouldn't be much—open a special checking account with a Guardian Angel as a signatory, and put enough money in it to cover all expected, and some unforeseeable, bills. (See "Checklist: Guardian Angel.")

_____ Cable TV. Depending on the length of your trip, you may save money by suspending cable service.

_____ Car. Save money by transferring your car to "storage status" for insurance purposes (meaning you retain comprehensive but not liability coverage). For a long trip, consider disconnecting the battery. (See "Checklist: Guardian Angel.")

_____ Computer. Back up your computer hard drive. If you use an external hard drive, CDs, or DVDs, consider tucking the disks away in a safe-deposit box.

_____ Fireplace. Empty the ashes, and close the damper.

_____ Keys. Hide a set of house and car keys outside.

_____ Legal matters. Consider giving someone a General Power of Attorney, enabling him or her to take action necessary on your behalf. Tell someone where your will is.

_____ Mail. File a change-of-address form with the post office, redirecting mail to a safe haven. Don't discuss your absence with post-office personnel or indicate a return date on the form.

_____ Personal care. Get travel clothes cleaned and mended. Consider a last-minute haircut.

_____ Security. Well before you leave, you might invite the police to inspect your home and give you a security checklist. You needn't mention that you're leaving. Use double-key dead-bolt locks, and don't hide keys in obvious places. Use several automatic timers with multiple on and off settings for a light or two, a radio (the best justification for talk radio), and perhaps exterior lights. Make sure all accessible windows are locked or fastened by screws. Check all locks just before you walk out the door.

If you have a burglar alarm, let the operator know you'll be on a trip until further notice, and tell him or her whom to notify in the event of a signal.

Put new bulbs in the lights just before you leave (with spares nearby). Close side curtains, but leave some open in front. Close some doors leading from one room to another. Leave some clutter to make your home look lived-in.

Tell your neighbors you'll be away, and ask them to keep watch. Invite someone to park in your driveway once in a while.

People differ on whether to notify the police that they'll be away. I don't, nor do I let tradespeople know. I'm less worried that someone will guess that the house is unoccupied than I would be if strangers knew for certain.

_____ Subscriptions. Suspend newspaper and magazine subscriptions unless you really plan to plow through the pile on your return.

_____ Taxes. If property taxes are your responsibility and will become due while you're away, arrange to prepay or to have them paid rather than suffer a penalty. Arrange for an income-tax extension if necessary.

$AVE Money _____ Telephone. If an answering machine works for you, fine. Otherwise, consider forwarding calls to some other number. Or you might use the answering services offered by the telephone company. If you subscribe to other special services, such as call waiting, save money by suspending them.

_____ Trash. Anything not dumped could be a health hazard by the time you return.

_____ Utilities. Depending on manufacturers' recommendations, unplug the refrigerator and freezer, or turn settings to a high temperature. Those innocuous-looking boxes gulp electricity like a parched camel hitting a water hole.

Don't leave the water heater standing ready to provide steaming-hot water on demand. Turn it off, or set it to its lowest setting. Turn heating and air-conditioning systems off unless the weather is likely to be extreme. If you leave them on, set the thermostat at a level that will prevent extremes in temperature.

A courtyard in Antigua, Guatemala

Turn off inside water taps tightly. In case of very cold weather, ask your Guardian Angel to let the faucets drip.

Make sure utility bills will be paid in your absence. Consider an automatic bill-payment plan, or leave money on deposit with the utility company

_____ Valuables. Hide them, store them with someone, or drop them into a safe-deposit box. If concerned, store your computer, TV, and stereo elsewhere.

_____ Water pipes. Insurance companies fear water leakage that continues unnoticed. Because burst pipes are often the culprit, if you haven't drained your water lines, there may be a requirement that your house be visited every four to seven days in order to keep the insurance coverage active. Check your policy.

_____ Final check. Confirm that you've packed everything on your checklist, and have tickets, passport, cash, credit cards, and traveler's checks ready to go.

Remember to line up someone to take you to the airport.

Confirm your reservation a couple of days before departure. A couple of hours before your flight (or earlier if it's an international flight), check whether the plane will depart on time. Plan for traffic, and allow extra time to get to the airport.

The amount of time required to pass through security has increased. Do not underestimate how long it can take. Check with the airline to find out how many hours ahead of time you should check in—and when it will close the counter. Take a good book, grumble a little about the system, and avoid jangled nerves or, much worse, missing the first flight in a series.

When your ticket envelope is handed back, check that all the correct tickets are in it. Check that the destination airport code put on your luggage is correct. Then take a deep breath, and stride toward your adventure with a bounce in your step.

CHECKLIST: GUARDIAN ANGEL

_____ Bills. I've opened a special checking account (# _____ at _____ Bank), and you are a signatory. Please deposit incoming checks and pay incoming bills. Please mail, on the ____ of each month, one of the signed and dated checks for my monthly mortgage (or rent) payment. Pay the full balance (or the minimum amount due) on each credit card. I left extra money in this account for you to use as a source of petty cash for unforeseen expenses.

_____ Car. Please start my car every two weeks and let it run for a while. (Or, "I've disconnected the battery in my car.") Since this car is in "storage status" for insurance purposes (meaning it has no liability coverage), it must not be driven.

_____ Contact Info. I've given you a list of my reservations (with telephone numbers and e-mail addresses; my itinerary; my cell-phone number, _____; and my e-mail address, _____.

_____ Documents. I've given you copies of the first two pages of my passport;

numbers of my traveler's checks, credit cards, and ATM card; a list of telephone numbers of repair shops to call if there's a problem; and phone numbers for my lawyer and accountant. My homeowner's insurance carrier is _____ (at _____), and the policy number is _____.

_____ Freezing weather. Please let the water faucets drip if freezing weather hits. If freezing will be severe, consider draining the pipes.

_____ Growing things. I've put my indoor plants in your care and have arranged for _____ (at _____) to cut and water the lawn and other green things. If there's a problem, please hire someone else to keep things well tended. Please fill food and water bowls for _____ each morning. I've left an adequate supply of food. If _____ needs care, the vet is Dr. _____ (at _____). You have my full authority to obtain whatever care is needed.

_____ Keys. I've given you two sets of my house and car keys.

_____ Legal matters. I've given you a General Power of Attorney, which gives you authority to take any action necessary on my behalf.

_____ Mail. Please trash junk mail, set personal letters aside, pay the bills, and open anything that looks as if it might deserve attention.

_____ Security. Please don't discuss my absence unless it's someone you know well. Please occasionally change the settings on the _____ automatic timers to conform to sunset, and reset everything if there's a power outage. The burglar alarm is activated (please keep it on), and I've given you the code to get in (and the security code in case you accidentally trip it). If you need to reach the operator, the number is _____. Please replace any lightbulbs that burn out (spares are in the kitchen cabinet). I've intentionally left the doors and curtains as they are. Please make sure no signs of absence accumulate outside (such as doorknob hangers and shoppers' newspapers). Feel free to park in my driveway.

_____ Subscriptions. I think I've suspended all subscriptions, but if anything arrives please call and have it suspended.

_____ Taxes. If I'm not back, please mail the income-tax extension I've given you. Please pay the property-tax bills when due.

_____ Telephone. If my answering machine memory fills up with calls, please make a list of calls received and empty it.

_____ Valuables. I've stored my _____, so don't be alarmed if you notice they're missing.

PART FOUR: On the Road ("Go!")

CHAPTER 14

The Day You Get There

One of the gladdest moments in human life, methinks, is the departure upon a distant journey into unknown lands. Shaking off with one mighty effort the fetters of Habit, the leaden weight of Routine, the cloak of many Cares and the slavery of Home, man feels once more Happy.
—Sir Richard Francis Burton
Journal entry, December 2, 1856

THROUGH THE AIRPORT

The immigration officer smiles pleasantly, examines your passport, and looks for a visa if one is required. She may ask to see a ticket proving you have the means to move on, but that's rare. After a discreet glance down at her computer screen that reassures her you're not on Interpol's "most wanted" list, she welcomes you to her country and you're on your way.

Your next stop is the customs officer, who will review the customs-declaration form you've already filled in. If he hands it back, you're expected to keep it to show when you leave the country. Most countries are concerned about people secretly bringing in items they might sell to local citizens. Some countries also have prohibitions against bringing in items such as alcohol, explosives, pornography, and anything that might carry a plant or animal disease. Unless smuggling is your game, don't enter a country without declaring weapons or unusual amounts of drugs, currency, or valuables. The customs officer may ask you to fill in a currency-declaration form, especially if there's an active local black market. Most people are a little nervous about going through customs, but it's generally painless. Before you know it, you're waved along.

One caveat: everyone is edgy these days, so don't joke with officials in the airport—about anything.

Even if you can't read the signs, follow the crowd to the baggage area. When you've claimed your gear, and assuming your bag doesn't get tagged for inspection, you're ready to start on a few tasks. The first stop is the ATM or the currency-exchange counter, where you change just enough money to last a day or two (because exchange rates are poor in airports). If there's a tourist-information counter, collect information that might be useful. Then stop by the airline counter if you need to reconfirm a flight, get a seat assignment, or do any other business.

As soon as you're ready to head for town, you need to shift into traveler's mode. You'll seldom be as vulnerable to theft as you are at this moment. Your self-protective reflexes, soon to be fine-tuned and automatic, are still untested. Up shields!

THE RIDE INTO TOWN

The intense beehive hum just outside the terminal comes from a zillion transport entrepreneurs seeking your business. Each one of those taxi drivers is hoping you have no idea of the fair price for a ride into town. Your job is to educate yourself on the correct price before you get to the curb. Ask people on the plane. Ask at Tourist Information. Ask a friendly local person. Before leaving the baggage-claim area, try to line up a small group to ride together and split the fare.

If an airport has a system through which you buy taxi tickets at a booth inside the terminal, use it. Otherwise, a taxi driver will know he has a greenhorn who is about to help him pay for a new television set.

Ask at the airport about bus transportation. See whether there's an airport shuttle bus or local bus that stops near your destination. Either may cost less than one-tenth as much as a taxi. No matter where the bus drops you in town, the cost of transport from there to the hotel you choose will be far less than airport taxi rates.

At the curb, take advantage of competition. Get quotes from several drivers, then invite everyone to beat the best offer. Nine times out of ten, someone's self-interest will overcome the group's attempt to maintain a monopoly price. As you bargain, keep in mind that if the taxi driver doesn't get your business, he may have to drive back to town empty. After you get an acceptable price, climb in and enjoy the ride.

Some travelers relax the moment they see a meter. No bargaining, they think, just pay what the meter says. Things are seldom that simple when there's a taxi involved. First, the mere presence of a meter doesn't mean the driver intends to use it. He might prefer to start bargaining with you somewhere away from the airport. Second, if the meter is working, make sure it wasn't "accidentally" already running before you got in. Third, if the meter is "broken," there's a reason—and you won't like it. Strike a deal before the wheels roll. And last, even if the driver flips the meter on as your ride starts, and it works, make sure you aren't charged a night rate for a day ride.

Some cities fix the rates taxi drivers can charge to take you to certain destinations. Those rates are supposed to be posted in the taxi. Unfortunately, some taxi drivers print their own official-looking cards showing inflated fares. If a rate card looks homemade, climb right back out.

In a large airport with separate departure and arrival points, try scouting the area where departing passengers are dropped off. After dropping off a passenger, a taxi driver must go to the end of a long line waiting to take arriving passengers back into town. Or he can pick you up immediately—for a considerably discounted fare.

As a final word on taxis: don't let yourself be separated from your bag before getting into your chosen taxi, and never get into a taxi before you've settled on a fare.

$AVE Money Master this simple process of getting into town on a cost-effective basis, and you'll save money at every stop.

TOURIST INFORMATION

After you get to town, make your hotel arrangements (please see Chapter 15, Lodging), and then visit the local tourist-information office. Its location is probably in your guidebook. If not, your desk clerk or a police officer or someone on the street will know where to find it. Watch for the international "i" or "?" symbol on street signs.

Someone in the tourist office will probably speak some English and will gladly answer your questions. Even if no one speaks a language you know, you'll find brochures, posters, and maps—a gold mine of information. If you give the tourist officer a list of places you'd like to see, she can help organize your visits and suggest additions. She'll tell you about special events and may even sell you tickets and arrange transportation. Friendly tourist-information officers have told me about a ceremonial burial that was about to take place in a village in central Sulawesi, Indonesia; an elegantly costumed performance celebrating the Hindu poet Rabindranath Tagore's birthday in Calcutta; a gathering of tribes performing ritual dances in northeast Botswana; and, in Prague, the best chamber music I've ever heard.

If you have time, climb aboard one of those see-it-all-in-a-day tour buses. They're an inexpensive, efficient way to cover long distances in a new town to find what merits a longer visit. When you get tired of being herded, hop off. If you're lucky, you'll meet another traveler using the tour the same way.

Overcome the temptation to take taxis everywhere. They cut you off from local people and spontaneous experiences. Instead, learn to use local public transportation right away. Before long, you'll be flagging down brightly decorated *colectivos,* or whatever the public-transit vehicles are called where you are. Getting around the way local people do is definitely the way to go.

> Afoot and lighthearted I take to the open road, / Healthy, free, the world before me, / The long brown path before me leading wherever I choose. / Henceforth I ask not good fortune, I myself am good fortune, / Henceforth I whimper no more, postpone no more, need nothing, / Done with indoor complaints, libraries, querulous criticisms, / Strong and content I travel the open road.
> —Walt Whitman, *Song of the Open Road* (1856)

> Everything is going to be different; life is never going to be the same after your passport has been stamped.
> —Graham Greene, *Another Mexico* (1939)

CHAPTER 15

Lodging

You fly off to a strange land, eagerly abandoning all the
comforts of home, and then expend vast quantities of
time and money in a largely futile effort to recapture
the comforts that you wouldn't have lost if you
hadn't left home in the first place.
—Bill Bryson
Neither Here Nor There: Travels in Europe (2001)

You seldom forget places where you lay your head as you travel. Some are wonderful; some make you laugh. And there are always a few that, well, make great stories. In this chapter, you'll learn how to find lodging that will please you in Mexico, Central America, and elsewhere. The reality is that providing lodging for hire is a leading means of economic survival in most of the world. Good lodging abounds, and there's plenty of competition for your business.

In major cities and tourist centers everywhere, you'll find upscale hotels that equal or exceed the opulence of those in your home country. Most of these are nationality-neutral, and English is commonly spoken. You can't miss the logos of international hotel chains with their cookie-cutter amenities. They charge extraordinarily high prices because they provide a reassuring cocoon and know that most travelers, especially those on business or on tour, expect to pay high prices. These are "world" prices, usually in dollars, that have no relation to prices in the local economy.

Virtually everywhere you'll also find pleasant, locally owned midrange hotels in which comfort and character outweigh occasional dings. Although their prices may be above the budgets of some independent travelers, they're very reasonable by North American and European standards.

Then there are the legions of lower-priced hotels with which many travelers become intimately familiar. They range from a concrete box ruled over by Quasimodo's ill-tempered brother to an architectural masterpiece gently supervised by an elderly couple whose mission in life is your daily happiness. At the lowest end of the rate scale, some hotels are best enjoyed with a measure of good humor and recognition of where you are. You may be pleased to know that shortcomings are more often in the nature of rickety furniture or fixtures that don't work rather than dirt or bugs.

Satisfaction with lodging depends in part on a good state of mind and realistic expectations. Here's an example: in the early 1980s, when China had just reopened to strangers, tourist facilities were not highly developed. We stayed at the venerable Peking Hotel. Although it had a distinctly Addams Family ambience, it was the best hotel in Beijing at that time and had an excellent location near the Imperial Palace. It turned out that there were a few, although generally small, holes in the walls. Some in the group were outraged by the holes and complained regularly. The rest hardly noticed and had a great time. It was a matter of state of mind. Now, of course, there are hotels in China that rival the most opulent in the world.

Many North Americans leave home with a mental image of two queen-size beds, a private bath with a tub and shower, air-conditioning, good soundproofing, and reasonable prices, all in a large room with a view. Internationally, these expectations will be met and exceeded at the higher end of the price scale. Overall, however, expect some differences. For example, you'll find one large bed or two monastic singles, but seldom two large beds. Air-conditioning is more the exception than the rule. Tubs become a distant memory. Soundproofing? Maybe if you block the window with a pillow. What you often get is character and an exciting new world just outside the door.

> I dislike feeling at home when I'm abroad.
> —George Bernard Shaw

Even if you are determined to start off with hotel reservations in hand, this chapter will be of benefit. After a few days on the road, you may decide to choose lodging that has more local character or better suits your pocketbook. Or you may find that the flexibility of traveling without reservations has become more important than it seemed at home.

HOW TO FIND GREAT PLACES TO SPEND THE NIGHT

It used to be that our access to lodging resources was very limited. Travel agents, friends, and guidebooks offered a few suggestions, usually restricted to the tourist trails, and we started a trip with little idea of the real breadth of lodging opportunities. Now, the Internet has overthrown the tyrant of ignorance and we can approach your destinations brimming with knowledge.

Don't just review information generated in the United States. Go to sites originating at the destination. For example, if you're heading to Mexico, look on Web sites of the national and local tourist bureaus. Look up the city and search for lodging. In Chapter 3, we list hotel Web sites for each country. Here are a few general sites that should be of use. We haven't listed hotel chains because there are too many, and they're easy to find. Usually, you just type "www." and then the hotel name, then ".com."

- Hotel aggregators: Kayak (**www.kayak.com**), Mobissimo (**www.mobissimo .com**), CheapAccommodation.com (**www.cheapaccommodation.com**), and SideStep (**www.sidestep.com**)
- For auctions on resort or upscale hotels: SkyAuction.com (**www.skyauction .com**) and Luxury Link (**www.luxurylink.com**)

- For international low-budget options and hostels, check with HostelBookers (**www.hostelbookers.com**), Hostelling International (**www.hihostels.com**), Hostelz.com (**www.hostelz.com**), or Hostels.com (**www.hostels.com**).
- Bed-and-breakfasts: BedandBreakfast.com (**www.bedandbreakfast.com**), BnBFinder.com (**www.bnbfinder.com**), Bed and Breakfast Explorer (**www.bbexplorer.com**), Bed & Breakfast Inns Online (**www.bbonline .com**), and International Bed and Breakfast Pages (**www.ibbp.com**)
- Luxury Latin America provides detailed reviews of the best upscale hotels in Mexico and Central America: **www.luxurylatinamerica.com**
- Mexico Boutique Hotels lists small, locally owned boutique hotels across Mexico: **www.mexicoboutiquehotels.com**
- For a comprehensive list of lodging sites: **www.extremesearcher.com/ travel/chap6.html**

$AVE Money Please see Chapter 8, How to Save Money, for a full discussion of how to save money on lodging.

When I stepped off the launch at a tiny, remote island in the Gulf of Thailand some years ago, I got some guidance from a couple of people in the village and walked along a sandy path until I found a great bungalow at the edge of the beach. It had a bathroom, fan, verandah, and world-class view, and it cost $8 a night. It's gone up to $14 now. I know that because I entered "Ko Tao, Thailand— lodging" into a search engine. I also got lists of dozens of other lodging options on the island, including descriptions and prices.

But suppose the Internet is not your thing. Or that you alter your itinerary while on the road and head for an impromptu destination. Will you have a problem finding good accommodations?

No problem at all; they often find you—through a tug on your sleeve. When you arrive in a new place, people representing low- and midrange hotels approach you. If you're at the airport, touts spring forward to solicit your business, flashing photographs of hotels and rooms. They may offer free transportation into town in return for your agreement to "just take a look" at the hotel. Ask questions. If a hotel sounds attractive and is near where you want to stay, the offer is at least a good way to get into town and may result in a good room.

Your trusty guidebook is more reliable than the eager tout, at least as to quality. Providing some information on hotel prices, amenities, and management is one of the ways a good guidebook justifies its price. It sometimes suggests real treasures and keeps you from running around town looking at dogs. On the other side of the ledger, guidebook favorites fill up early: they raised their rates as soon as they were mentioned in the book.

Don't fall into the trap of thinking there are no alternatives to guidebook suggestions. Once you have your travel legs, you'll be perfectly capable of finding

> To awaken in a strange town is one of the pleasant sensations in the world. You are surrounded by adventure. You have no idea what is in store for you, but you will, if you are wise and know the art of travel, let yourself go on the stream of the unknown and accept whatever comes in the spirit in which the gods may offer it. The tourist travels in his own atmosphere like a snail in his shell and stands, as it were, on his own perambulating doorstep to look at the continents of the world. But if you discard all this, and sally forth with a blank leisurely mind, there is no knowing what may happen to you.
> —Freya Stark, *Baghdad Sketches* (1933)

your own special places. Pretend you're writing a guide-book for a friend. Just go out and look around.

Ask other travelers. A strongly positive recommendation usually leads to a memorable stay. On only a few occasions have I reached a hotel someone raved about and wondered if the guy had been taking hallucinogenic drugs. On the other hand, always pay attention to a warning about a specific hotel.

Many tourist-information booths located in or near airports, train stations, and bus depots offer a room-finding service. You may pay something for this service, either as a fee at the booth or in a slightly higher room rate, but it can be very helpful on a cold, drizzly night. Unfortunately, the least expensive lodgings in town are seldom on lists provided by these booths. However, the clerk knows places that have yet to appear in any guidebook.

Ask a hotel clerk. If you've stopped into a place that has no vacancy, or you just can't agree on price, tell the clerk what you're looking for. It's common to get helpful directions.

If you have several possibilities in mind, call to check for availability and prices. Crisscrossing town after a long day on the road is no one's idea of fun. Telephoning is particularly useful if you're competing with a group of arriving passengers for scarce space in choice lodgings.

If no assistance materializes, it's no big deal. You can discover that special place all by yourself.

HOW TO CHOOSE LODGING THAT'S BEST FOR YOU

According to surveys, what most travelers look for in lodging is clean appearance, reasonable price, convenient location, good service, and security—in that order. When travelers have complaints, what they remember most are dirt, lack of security, and noise.

Location

When you arrive in a country, you may want to choose a hotel that has a reputation as an information node, a gathering place for travelers with interests similar to yours. These hotels are usually reasonably priced, but more important is the opportunity to learn quickly how the country works from people with current experience. Guidebooks sometimes note such hotels; if not, ask around.

If gathering information is not the primary objective, look for lodging near some of the sights you'll be visiting, near public transportation, and within shouting distance of a restaurant.

If reserving from abroad, guard against winding up far away from the action. I want to live in the midst of the "character" of a place and don't want to cap off a fine dinner and great music with an hour-long trip back to the nest.

Amenities

Memories grow from quiet courtyards and views from your balcony. Of course, sometimes the amenity that matters most is a "vacancy" sign.

Here's what to consider:

- **$AVE Money** What's the shower situation? For openers, is there a shower in the room? In upper- and midpriced rooms, of course there is. In less expensive places, it may be down the hall. In lower-priced lodging, a private bathroom can double the room rate, so the more frequently you do without a shower in your room, the more money you save. Is there hot water? Don't take anyone's word for it. Test the temperature. That will also tell you if the water pressure is more than a symbolic drizzle. Don't assume that hot water is available 24 hours a day. In fact, it may be available for only six to eight hours a day. Forget to check these hours, and icy water will greet you at a moment guaranteed to make you unhappy. When the plumbing doesn't work as represented, at least you'll hear some wonderfully inventive excuses.
- When I checked my room at a lovely, two-story stone lodge on the crest of a mountain ridge in Kalimpong, India, no water flowed from the shower nozzle. However, the charming proprietress assured me that hot water would be available at 7 p.m. Given the chill Himalayan air, I watched the clock eagerly. Right at 7, the hot water arrived as promised—at my door, in a bucket.

You may be startled to see water being heated by electric coils bolted loosely to the wall above the showerhead. This arrangement seems a little dangerous, but I haven't heard of anyone being fried.

- Are the beds clean? Are they soft enough? Finding a firm bed is seldom a problem.
- Are the lobby and the room clean? Is there evidence that bugs might be a problem?
- Is the room secure? For information on hotel security, please see Chapter 17, Safety and Security.
- Will the room be quiet enough for sleep? Don't trust the hotel clerk on this one. Either he's genuinely stopped hearing the racket, or he's not going to tell you. It may be stone quiet when you check

> The bedrooms are just large enough for a well-behaved dwarf and a greyhound on a diet.
> —John Russell, on modern European hotels (1977)

Public Toilets

If you think a public toilet is hard to find in Los Angeles, wait until you look for one in most of the rest of the world. Before a moment of supreme need, watch for facilities in museums, expensive hotels, and restaurants. It's the custom in some places to tip the public-restroom attendant. Even if you are not used to tipping in that situation and can't see that the attendant has performed any service, leave a small tip with grace. We're guests.

---

in at dusk. Then, about the time you're settling in, the disco next door roars to life for an all-nighter. Check out nearby bars, road traffic, roosters, and thin walls—and hope there aren't too many noisy guests. If you suspect a problem, ask for a
quieter room higher up or at the back of the building. Don't wait until 4 a.m. to discover the truck depot below your window.

- Any discussion of amenities must include toilets. I know one person who won't leave the United States because of her aversion to any toilet she believes to be inferior to what she's used to. Given the strength of her feeling, she's made the right choice. Fortunately, most people are more flexible.

The toilet may be in your room, down the hall, or in a different building, and the price of the lodging will reflect the proximity of the toilet every time. Toilets come in quite a few forms. At the low end, so to speak, the toilet is a hole in the floor of a small room, and waste drops into a fertilizer-collection room below. Okay, this is really rare, and such squat toilets are not found in Mexico or Central America.

Modern toilets are common in hotels that cater to international travelers. Of course, in some of the least expensive places, toilet seats are sometimes missing, and toilet paper is a rumor. If the room you're considering has a Western-style toilet that's supposed to flush, see if it does. The flushing device may not be the familiar handle; look for a knob, a push button, a pull chain, a pedal, or even a bucket of water. If it doesn't flush, ask the clerk to help.

Not all toilets are plumbed to accept paper. If there's a trash can nearby, that's where used paper should go. Otherwise, it will probably clog the pipes, distressing everyone. If toilet paper hasn't been provided, ask for it. The clerk may smile and say, "Sure," but you may have to follow up. A sizable portion of the world's population doesn't use toilet paper, which is the main reason you don't see people eating with their left hand. Your best bet is to carry your own supply of TP (including the high-quality stuff you "borrowed" from the upscale hotel where you stopped for a beer).

- When traveling through an area in which malaria is a problem, ensure that there is some barrier between you and mosquitoes. This usually means screens on the windows or a mosquito net over the bed. If you take a mosquito net with you, buy one impregnated with Permethrin, or spray it yourself. If there are neither screens nor a net, you may have to sleep with the windows closed. Although that turns a tolerable night in the tropics into a sweat bath, a hot night is a lot cooler than malarial fever.

On some tropical islands, windows may be fitted only with rough hurricane shutters and no glass. That's part of the charm. About all you can do is fire up a green mosquito coil at both ends of your bed and sleep under a light sheet. I take a couple of packets of coils with me, but they're brittle and hard to use when broken. When you're in mosquito-land, coils are generally available in stores (if there are stores).

Speaking of insects, hold your shoes upside down and shake them before putting them on. Give bugs, scorpions, spiders, or whatever a chance to live another day.

- Ask whether the price includes breakfast and, if so, what is on the menu. You're likely to find the fare surprisingly spare, usually of the bread and coffee variety. Sometimes, though, it's sumptuous. Find out where and when it's served. It's no fun to drop into the dining room with high expectations just after service has ended. If breakfast doesn't appeal to you, perhaps you can negotiate a slightly lower room rate.

Terrace of a hacienda hotel room near Chichén Itzá, Mexico

- Air-conditioning is not standard internationally, so if you're interested, be sure to ask. In tropical latitudes, a ceiling fan greatly aids a good night's sleep. Even a small, oscillating table fan can make a humid night bearable. Besides cooling your body, the breeze from a fan keeps mosquitoes away.

  - A great view out the window or from your balcony is a fine way to start any day.

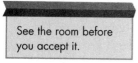

See the room before you accept it.

  - A smiling, knowledgeable owner or clerk who looks me in the eye and makes me feel welcome overcomes shortcomings elsewhere.

Price

Lodging that ranges from satisfactory to terrific is available at reasonable prices almost anywhere. But what's a "reasonable" price? The place I chose in Antigua, Guatemala, has a formal sitting room with a stately grandfather clock and a stylishly furnished, wood-paneled dining room. Each morning, I ate breakfast on a sunny flagstone patio with a view of two volcanoes. That double room cost $35. In picturesque Ouro Prêto, Brazil, a room with a garden view might cost $16. My en suite (meaning it has a bathroom) room in Cuzco, Peru, has a 15-foot vaulted ceiling and skylight and came with breakfast, room service, and Internet access. It overlooks a courtyard containing a fountain and orange blossoms. It's about $20 today.

There's no shortage of pleasant, affordable lodging in Latin America, and much of it even has style. In contrast, there's wonderful variety in Europe, but prices in large cities may leave you eating a lot of bagels.

Especially regarding lower-priced lodging, here's a cardinal rule: see the room before you accept it. For one thing, the reality may be very different from the clerk's description. For another, you can't bargain as effectively until you've seen the room. If you are traveling with a partner, one of you checks the room while the other watches the gear. If a clerk goes with you, she'll probably be carrying keys to more than one room. No matter what you've said you want, the clerk will open the bidding by showing a traveler the hotel's most expensive room, the local equivalent of the Emperor's Suite. Even if tatty, it's sure to be huge. Although the air conditioner pumps out more noise than cool air and the radio receives only one station, that room will cost at least 500 percent more than the room you said you wanted. After all, the clerk knows that some travelers are crazy enough to take it. No problem; just smile and ask to see other rooms.

Cheap rooms don't always start out cheap. The clerk states the room rate as if it were fixed, but that doesn't mean it is. Feel free to bargain on the rate:

- when you'll be staying three or more nights;
- in the off-season or when something (bad weather, a riot, a coup) has curtailed tourism;

- when you see a lot of room keys hanging on hooks behind the desk;
- or maybe every time, unless it's clearly inappropriate.

SAVE Money The cost of lodging is a large part of your budget. If you bargain effectively on lodging prices, you'll definitely save money. If you don't, lodging will still be affordable, but you'll spend more than you need to.

When the clerk states a price, you say it's too expensive, that you'd like a room that costs no more than "X" pesos, quetzals, lempiras, or whatever. Actually, you have even more leverage if you call ahead and say you'd like a room for "X." At that point, the clerk has no chance for your business unless she agrees. Cite prices at a competitor's lodging. Ask for a special rate on grounds of being a student, a teacher, an archaeologist, an old person, a young person, or anything else you can think of. If you have a business card or a membership card, lay it on the counter. Reality doesn't matter; the desk clerk doesn't care. The point is to persuade her that you won't stay in her hotel unless you get a discount of some kind. Then give her a theoretical reason for granting it.

Try not to look too exhausted from the day's travel, and never let your luggage go to a room until you've agreed on a price. As she calculates her offer, the desk clerk is evaluating whether you have enough energy to try another hotel. If she senses that you're pooped, she'll become the Rock of Gibraltar.

Be firm but pleasant, never argumentative. It's poor strategy to disparage the accommodations being offered. Why behave like a person the clerk wouldn't want under her roof? Furthermore, the clerk probably lives in worse conditions than the room you're discussing.

If you can't get the room rate reduced, ask for a better room at the same price. If the clerk offers a lower rate for a less desirable room, offer to pay the lower price for the room you really want.

If you're one of a group of people traveling together, occupying several rooms, insist on a group-rate discount, all or none. You should receive an almost automatic discount of 10 to 30 percent if you'll be staying at one place for three or more days.

> Be certain you and the clerk agree on the final price.

If you've reached a temporary impasse, ask if the clerk "can do any better." If nothing happens, and you're not satisfied, say you've decided to look around at other hotels, but leave slowly enough that she has a chance to make another offer. You're likely to hear a call from over your shoulder. On the other hand, if your bargaining doesn't achieve what you want, don't let pride send you away if you really want to stay there.

Make sure the room will be available for as long as you want it or at least until a certain date. Otherwise, you could be evicted unexpectedly.

In the end, be certain to agree with the clerk on a total price. Don't set yourself up for miscellaneous charges and taxes that were never mentioned. At the upper end of the price scale, it is becoming more the rule than the exception to add various luxury taxes and service charges. Ask the clerk to write down the total price on a piece of paper or enter it on the ledger to ensure that no misunderstanding arises at checkout time. Be certain what time period the price covers. Get it all straight on the front end so you can part friends when you leave.

When you've reached an agreement, pick up a hotel business card. Some have a map on the back, and all have the address in the local language—which is how you get home after you've forgotten the name of the hotel and how to get to it. One night I took a series of buses across Beijing, guided through two transfers by a Chinese acquaintance. She showed me where to get off to attend a performance by a famous troupe of acrobats and continued on her way. When I emerged from the theater hours later, I realized I had no idea which bus to take, let alone how the transfers worked. If I hadn't had the hotel card, I'd probably still be circling Beijing like Charlie on the MTA.

On that subject, when you're leaving the hotel, ask the clerk to write your destination on a piece of paper. The taxi driver will appreciate it—and you may get where you want to go.

A last thought: always check behind before you check out. Look under the bed, in the closets, on the shelves, everywhere. Did you leave anything drying on an outside line? Even if you find an about-to-be-forgotten piece only once every 20 times, it's worth checking. Do the same thing in a restaurant. As you're about to leave, check for day pack, camera, and journal. It's an easy routine. If you leave something behind, either you won't be able to get back for it or it won't be there when you do. Take the easier way.

> Hostels are a great way to meet fellow travelers.

OTHER INNOVATIVE CHOICES

SAVE Money Hostels, elderhostels, YMCAS, YWCAS, backpacker hotels, and homestays were designed to help you save money. They're also fine places to meet other travelers and local people.

Hostels

Hostels can be the financial salvation of budget travelers. However, many people who can afford to pay more seek out hostels because of the ambience. They're good places to meet like-minded travelers, find a temporary traveling partner, and gather information.

Where will you find hostels? They're everywhere in Europe and scattered elsewhere around the world, although there are comparatively few in the States.

How much do hostels cost? In Mexico, you'll pay $11 to $14 a night. That's also a common price range in Central America. Compare that with France at

$20 to $26. Many hostels offer excellent family rates as well. One of the best sources for information about hostels and other budget accommodations is **www.hostels.com.** It devotes a special section to hostels in Mexico and Central America.

Also look at Hostelling International (**www.hihostels.org** and **www.hiusa .org**) for locations and descriptions of its more than 4,000 members in more than 80 countries. You can book at both sites. You don't have to be a member to stay at a hostel in the Hostelling International network, but membership does bring discounts. You can join before you leave home or at a hostel when you check in. A 12-month membership is free for those younger than 18, $28 for those 18 through 54, and $18 for those older. As a nonmember, you can stay at a hostel simply by paying a supplement (maybe $3), but membership has other benefits, such as discounts on some travel and entertainment purchases, entrance fees, goods at retail outlets, or even rental cars (5 to 10 percent at Hertz). Naturally, members receive priority over nonmembers for beds.

Despite the word "youth," there is no maximum age limit. More than 10 percent of hostelers are older than 55.

Hostels range from clean, basic shelter to architectural or cultural marvels. For example, you can stay in a castle in Altena, Germany, or aboard a three-masted schooner in Stockholm. In the United States, there's a hostel in a Spanish village built as a bohemian artists' community in Miami, in an old longshoremen's hall in Seattle, and in a lighthouse in Cape Vincent, New York.

$AVE Money Some hostels serve hearty, inexpensive meals, whereas others permit you to cook your own meals. Besides being a great way to save money, hanging out in the kitchen is a good way to meet other travelers. It's not unusual to find a pool table, a library full of well-worn books, or a piano with which to amuse yourself.

Traditionally, sleeping accommodations have been dormitory-style, segregated by sex, although the trend is toward rooms with four to six beds, and many have private rooms.

Making advance reservations at popular hostels may be a good idea during peak seasons in Europe. In most other places, it usually isn't necessary. If you choose to book ahead, make contact via e-mail a few weeks before your arrival, giving the date of arrival, number of beds (or private rooms) desired, and length of stay. You can also make reservations abroad through any Hostelling International-American Youth Hostels office. The majority of travelers just drop in with their fingers crossed.

Elderhostel

Elderhostel programs are for people older than 55 (who may be accompanied by a younger spouse or companion, even grandchildren). These programs combine education, comfortable lodging, camaraderie—and good value—in 90 countries (including all U.S. states and Canadian provinces). The emphasis is on studying interesting subjects and meeting like-minded people. In Elderhostel's Service Learning programs, the participants provide volunteer service to worthwhile causes around the world. Its Road Scholar program, open to all ages, combines hands-on learning, independent exploration, and worthwhile projects. See **www .roadscholar.org.**

Elderhostel has many programs in Mexico and Central America. See **www .elderhostel.org.** Call (800) 454-5768 for a free Elderhostel catalog.

YMCAs and YWCAs

The Ys offer lodging in almost 3,000 locations in nearly 100 countries. They are often a little higher-priced than most budget places but are consistently clean and friendly. Unlike hostels, they seldom permit cooking. To find information about YMCA lodging around the world, see the World Alliance of YMCAs Web site, **www.ymca.it.** For information about the YWCA, see **www.worldywca.org.**

Backpacker Hotels

An extensive network of excellent backpacker hotels has sprung up. Most of them are old, centrally located hotels that have been spruced up and given new amenities. They often radiate charm and good vibes—and you can sometimes stroll downstairs to a pub or restaurant. Double rooms range from $10 to $20, and you needn't arrive with a backpack. On the Internet, search for "backpacker hotels" plus your destination.

Homestays

When you have an opportunity to stay with a family, whether for free or a fee, take the chance. If you'd like to set up something before you hit the road, try one of the organizations described in Chapter 6, The Organized Tour, that specialize in arranging homestay trips. If you haven't arranged anything in advance, ask around for a family that will take you in for a while. Don't let uncertainty about what it might be like dissuade you from accepting a family's invitation. The odds are good that it will be an experience you'll remember with affection.

Turnabout

When you meet people from faraway places traveling in your home country, remember the hospitality you received when you were on the road. Be sensitive to how expensive it is for many people to travel in developed countries. (Think of the feeling you get when you price a new car—or new tennies, for that matter.) Be generous. Pick up that tab. Take them to see your local wonders. Provide a secure pillow when you can.

If an opportunity to stay with a family arises from hospitality rather than a commercial motive, be sensitive to fitting in. Despite its good intentions, the host family may not really be able to afford the food and drink it lavishes on you. Some travelers become sponges, accepting hospitality as though it were their due and overstaying their welcome. Instead, reciprocate by making some contribution. The family probably needs money, but you may feel awkward offering it. If a gift seems okay, buy something such as groceries, fabric, or tools. In some situations, it may be better to do some tutoring or other useful work for the family. Ask others about the local customs concerning hospitality. Without fail, send a card or letter to the family when you get home.

The Hospitality Club (**www.hospitalityclub.org**) is a global community offering free accommodations all over the world. You commit to be a host as well as a guest.

A final note: we've been talking about choosing lodging that pleases you at a price you're willing to pay. If price doesn't matter or you feel an urge to splurge, arm yourself before you go with the results of polls that rate "the world's best" hotels (see *Condé Nast Traveler* online at **www.cntraveler.com,** and click on "lists + polls").

CHAPTER 16

Eating and Drinking

If you reject the food, ignore the customs, fear the religion,
and avoid the people, you might better stay home.
—James Michener

What you see is not always what you get.

Pleased to see a sign advertising a Mexican restaurant, I dropped in for a meal. The first clue that I wasn't in Acapulco came when the waiter urged me to "try the enchilada with our special monkey-gland sauce." That restaurant was owned by a Maltese and a South African, neither of whom had been within 4,000 miles of Mexico.

Even though the local version of some dish isn't prepared the same as it is at home, can you find food you like as you travel? The answer is an emphatic "yes." In fact, good food is one of the rewards of travel. You'll find high-quality restaurants throughout the world. If local cuisine isn't to your taste, Chinese, Indian, and Italian foods are almost universal. In one country after another, you'll discover a new symphony of tastes. Many local dishes are so delicious you'll seek them out when you return home. That's important to know, because if we're worried about whether we'll find what we like to eat in some faraway place, we may not go there.

HOW TO FIND FOOD YOU REALLY LIKE

Good food in Latin America is plentiful and often quite inexpensive. For example, on Roatán, oa marinated tuna filet, French-fried potatoes, salad, and a couple of Salva Vida beers, served on a deck extending over the moonlit Caribbean, might run $7.

For dining tips before departure, clip references from travel magazines. Once you're abroad, check your guidebook and ask other travelers. Hotel clerks and taxi drivers eagerly offer recommendations, but the kickback they get may be more appealing to them than the food. Glance through windows of places filled with smiling local diners. Many restaurants post their menus outside, making it easy to check out dishes and prices as you stroll.

"Street food," not common in the United States, consists of snacks, a single dish, or a simple meal that you buy from a street-side stall or cart. Often, the food is fried or grilled as you watch. Street food can be tasty, cheap, fast, convenient, and ethnically authentic. It may also be hazardous to your health. Food may sit on greasy plates in the sun for hours while flies feast. The hands that go with the smiling face may not have been washed all day.

Considering that the gastronomic pyramid ranges from street stalls with plumbing and a roof to establishments that serve the finest cuisine, I offer two cautions. Although some hotel food ranks among the finest in the world, too often you get only high prices and little character. Why stay cooped up in the hotel when you can have dinner in an open-air cafe overlooking Lake Atitlán? Similarly, avoid restaurants that market themselves vigorously to tourists. Why settle for the same food and faces you find at home?

Shopping in local markets can provide good, cheap meals. If prices are not posted, watch what local people pay for what you want. Don't be bothered by being charged a small premium, but avoid being badly ripped off. It could be a mistake to hold out a handful of money and invite the lady to take what she wants for her tomatoes. If you have no idea, hand her what you think might be right. If a little more is due, she'll say so. After you've stocked up, you're ready for a terrific picnic.

For a little more guidance, consider *Eating and Drinking in Latin America,* by Andy Herbach and Michael Dillon (Open Road Publishing).

Finding food you like becomes easier as you add appropriate food words to your vocabulary. Draw on a phrase book, ask questions, and take notes.

How to Order

You've found the perfect restaurant, but the menu is in a language you can't read. Now what? The daily special is always popular and cheap, but until you're certain

Dutch restaurateur on the shore of Lake Atitlán, Guatemala

of your tummy's tolerance, review the ingredients before placing an order. If you see someone else eating a meal that looks appetizing, stroll over to that table. After a friendly greeting, ask what's on the plate. If there's a language problem but the food looks good, take a chance.

If communication is a problem, point to an item on the menu as you pronounce it. Be sure you and the waiter understand each other. If in doubt, ask that your order be repeated back to you.

Check prices carefully. Before you receive the bill, figure out roughly how much your meal should cost. You may be surprised how frequently there are "mistakes." Just in case the cashier assumes you are unfamiliar with the currency or are fabulously wealthy, count your change. No point in getting annoyed. It's part of the game.

Exotic Dishes

I'll admit that there are many local favorites my mind can't take. How about roasted locust, toasted silkworm, stewed grasshopper, dog kabob, roasted tarantula, bull-penis soup, stir-fried termite, newborn mouse, deep-fried scorpion, broiled rat, roasted walrus, pig snout, anaconda head, yak lung, pan-fried palm grub, and sea slug? Makes chocolate-covered ants sound almost appetizing. Becoming a part-time vegetarian as you travel shields you from giving offense if you decline well-intentioned offers of food that you find too challenging.

HOW TO EAT AND STAY HEALTHY

It's far better to return home raving about newly discovered spices and food preparations than to start raving on the road as a result of what you ate. Travelers find delicious-looking food almost everywhere in the world, yet, as in the melancholy folk song about the lemon tree, not all is as edible as it appears. Fortunately, this paradox is easily resolved. If you understand the risks and know what to look for, eating will be a pleasure to remember. Be careless, even once, and you may be, as was that balladeer from the 1960s, "a sadder man but wiser now."

Throughout Latin America, you'll find plenty of luxurious restaurants, ones in which you think, surely, the food here is safe. And it very well may be. So you'll be making lots of judgment calls. Or you'll be careless. Or you'll be cautious—as I am.

The rule in Latin America is: If it's not boiled, peeled, or cooked, forget it. While that's easy to remember, it's also a little simplistic. It takes more than that to safeguard your health on the road. How cautious you should be varies greatly from country to country. Outside developed countries, you must limit your food choices. Virtually all travelers who follow a few basic rules come home in perfect health. The major issues to consider are preservation and sanitation.

> Lemon tree very pretty, and the lemon flower is sweet. But the fruit of the poor lemon is impossible to eat.
> —Will Holt

Preservation

Restaurants should store perishable food at temperatures of less than 45°F or more than 140°F and keep dairy products refrigerated. However, in many countries, scant attention is given to proper preservation, sometimes even in upscale restaurants. Consequently, meat and fish spoil quickly, exposing unwary diners to parasites, dysentery, hepatitis, and other food-borne diseases. Because local people eat food not kept at proper temperatures, they often have the problems you want to avoid.

Where proper refrigeration is improbable, seek very hot food, such as food cooked as you watch. Avoid food that has been sitting around for more than a few minutes. If everything were cooked well done and served immediately, most of the risk would be eliminated. Too often, that isn't what happens.

If you choose meat, be certain it's cooked well done. Beef (or pork, venison, etc.) may be a higher risk than chicken because the chicken may at least have been killed on the same day it's served.

If seafood is sold soon after being caught or has been dried so thoroughly it looks like shoemaker's scraps, it's relatively safe. However, many travelers wisely skip raw fish and shellfish because those foods are often associated with outbreaks of cholera or concentrations of toxins. Perhaps it's a blessing that so much seafood around the world is served fried.

Sanitation

Poor sanitation practices are another health concern. In street stalls, there is seldom even a gesture toward sanitation (not too surprising because there's no running water), which raises the risk of contaminating serving utensils as well as the food. It's also hard to become comfortable with the sight of a stringy length of unidentifiable flesh dangling above a bloody counter, swinging from a rusty hook like a slow pendulum in the sun, a mobile buffet for flies.

Food handlers may themselves be transmitters of diseases, especially hepatitis. The farther away the source of clean water, the less likely it is that hands get washed during the course of a day.

If a cook uses a knife to cut a raw fish and then to slice your potato, you may be about to ingest anything that was wrong with the fish. Similarly, if your tea is served in a cup that was only swirled around in a pail of murky water after being used by someone else, you may be about to swallow someone else's problem. The solution: keep your eyes open. Carry your own cup or utensils if you prefer. I hate to say this, but it's better to be impolite than sick.

When you eat street food, choose your spots carefully. Ask a local to point out a favorite street stall—or choose one of the busy ones. In general, you're safer with starch (noodles, rice, potatoes) and vegetables (such as boiled corn) than with meat. Even though freshly deep-fried food is pretty well disinfected, you can't tell if every fragment of meat or fish has been cooked clear through. Watch your food being cooked to ensure it hasn't been sitting around in the sun for a while.

Keeping snacks such as fruit, bread, and nuts in your day pack helps you resist street-stall temptation.

Because your own hands can also transmit disease, wash them thoroughly before every meal. There may be no water, so this is a fine reason to carry antiseptic wipes. If silverware is wet when it reaches your table, dry it or pour some hot tea over it. In some situations, it makes sense to carry a camping-type set of metal or plastic utensils.

In Central America, cautious travelers seldom eat fresh green salads. Also avoid fruits and vegetables unless they have been peeled or cooked. They may have been fertilized with human or animal waste, irrigated with contaminated water, or sprayed with pesticides prohibited in the United States. Bacteria or pesticides that aggregate on the skin of the fruit or vegetable are no problem once the skin is removed. Thorough cooking kills bacteria, but merely rinsing vegetables with water does not. If the rinse water is contaminated, it adds to the problem. Adding sufficient chlorine or iodine to the rinse water helps make food safe.

Because they may have been made with unpasteurized milk or contaminated water, ice cream, cheese, and other dairy products are on the forbidden list in most less developed countries. This is less of a problem in Latin America because almost all milk is the Parmalat variety that is pasteurized and vacuum-sealed. (See comments in specific country sections of Chapter 3.) Watch out for mayonnaise and cream sauces as well.

Fruit will become an important part of your diet. Luscious fruits with earthy, lascivious tastes are abundant throughout Mexico and Central America. You will enjoy some so much that you will miss them at home. Bananas and pineapples can keep you going over some long stretches.

Bread is generally a safe, tasty way to fill up—unless it bounced off the truck onto a street before it got to your table. Yes, I saw that happen. Adding fresh lime or lemon juice to your food may overcome minor contamination.

Just when your health should be at its best to help compensate for the stress of travel, you may be unbalancing your diet. Respond by eating lots of peeled fruits and well-cooked veggies. Consider starting vitamin supplements before your departure and taking vitamins as you travel.

The Bottom Line

Remember that, as with the fruit of the poor lemon, not everything is as desirable as it looks. There's no reason to be obsessed or overly concerned; just know and follow the basic rules.

HOW TO DRINK AND STAY HEALTHY

The moment you enter many countries, you are sentenced to carry a two- to three-pound weight every day. You're on the honor system, but it would be wise to abide by the terms of your sentence. The weight I'm talking about is a bottle of potable water.

You see labels that say water has been "boiled" or "treated with ozone," and others that claim "natural water from mineral springs" (meaning nothing was done to purify it because it came from a supposedly safe source). A label in Guatemala proudly declared that the bottle contained "Mississippi Mountain Spring Water." If you've counted the mountains in Mississippi lately, you may not find that one too reassuring.

Even where tap water is technically potable, if you drink it, you may feel queasy simply because the bacteria cocktail is new to your system. If my trip is a short one, I stick with bottled water. If I'll be somewhere with genuinely potable water for a longer time, I drink the local water and let my stomach adjust.

In hot, humid weather, especially when you're exerting yourself, your body needs much more water than you normally drink. Yet not having ready access to clean water and having to pay for bottled water leads too many travelers to cut back on consumption. That's a mistake. Cutting back can result in exhaustion, urinary-tract problems, or even a kidney stone. Sound like fun? If you stop urinating for several days, or your urine attains a golden hue, gulp down a quick liter or two of clean water and increase your daily intake.

If troubled by minor diarrhea, replace the fluids you're losing. If safe water isn't available, drink other nonalcoholic fluids. Keep in mind that alcohol, as in the cold beer that tastes so good, is a diuretic. In other words, your output will ultimately be greater than your intake.

Illness at home is often a well-tended inconvenience, maybe even a respite from your job, but illness on the road is unpleasant and expensive in terms of risk and time. Your body needs water to function well, especially in hot climates. Pour it in, and daydream about free, plentiful, pure water at home.

Learn to drink healthy, and you can be a happy traveler.

Prevention

Some travelers say they drink water in restaurants, even tap water, with no ill effects. Maybe so, but that's like playing Russian roulette. Sooner or later, you will lose.

Keep well hydrated when traveling.

Don't assume that water served in restaurants, including expensive ones, is safe. Where water safety is doubtful, ask for bottled water, bring your own, or drink something else. I've never noticed any restaurant staff appearing offended by a guest drinking water he or she has brought in (bought in a store for one-third the restaurant price).

Bottled water is better than tap water only if it's not just tap water. Some unscrupulous merchants take used bottles and refill them with unpurified water from the local spigot. Ensure that what you buy has been firmly sealed at the factory. If you order bottled water in a restaurant, you should be the one to open it at the table. Check whether the bottle is filled to the customary level, with an air space at the top. If it's filled all the way to the top, suspect a backroom refill. It's safer to drink carbonated bottled water because it's hard to replace the little bubbles in the back room. Drink contaminated water, and you may spend a lot of time in one place.

Here's the cold truth: ice is water. When you order a drink, you must specify "without ice" (*sin hielo,* en Español). Otherwise, you'll have to figure out how to discreetly dispose of the ice cubes you've hastily hauled out of your glass. If some ice has already melted in the drink, give it a pass. The bugs that can harm you aren't much bothered by freezing temperatures, and the alcohol in your drink will affect you much more than it will them. Further, your ice cubes may be little chips off a large block that was carted or dragged through the streets to the restaurant.

Prudent travelers brush their teeth with bottled water and don't drink shower water. Many avoid tap water even aboard an airplane.

How to Disinfect Contaminated Water

When planning to filter, boil, or chemically treat water you've drawn from natural sources, draw from the safest sources possible. Look for wells, springs, water upstream from human habitation, swiftly running water, clear water, or water running over a rocky or sandy bed. Avoid water that's stagnant, smelly, scummy, or muddy; that contains decaying vegetation; or that's downstream from human, industrial, or animal contamination. Seems obvious, doesn't it?

Boiling

Suppose you're going to hike long enough that you can't carry all the bottled water you'll need. One solution is to purify what you need by boiling. Boiling requires a container, time, and fuel, but it works as long as the water is brought to a rolling boil. When the surface of heated water begins to be disturbed and vapors start to rise, the water still hasn't reached the temperature lethal to the bacteria, viruses, and parasites that concern you. Let it boil for several minutes.

Filtering

Water is commonly purified by distillation, exposure to ultraviolet light, microbial disinfection, reverse osmosis, or filtration. The last is by far the most common, especially in portable devices. Let's look at what we want to avoid in contaminated water. A fine filter can remove suspended solids, worms, larvae, and similar large organisms, plus protozoa (single-cell organisms that cause amoebic dysentery and giardiasis). Only very fine filters can remove bacteria that cause cholera, typhoid, bacillary dysentery, salmonella, and diarrhea. Chemical contaminants, which can make water unpleasant to taste and smell and are sometimes dangerous, can be removed by only some filters.

Manufacturers claim that portable filters, available from catalog companies and outfitters, remove bacteria and parasites, but filters do not stop viruses (including the type that causes hepatitis A) unless they add a chemical ingredient. They are, however, vulnerable to boiling and other purification treatments, including the addition of chemicals. Another limitation of filters is capacity. If a manufacturer states that its filter is effective for 100 gallons, how do you know when that limit has been reached? Select a filter that clogs and can no longer be used when it's reached capacity.

The brands I've used successfully, or have had good reports about, include Katadyn, MSR (Mountain Safety Research), General Ecology, Innova Pure Water, PuR, and Basic Designs. Some of the better filters are expensive (more than $200) and bulky, especially if you carry a spare cartridge, spare membrane, and maintenance kit.

Simpler and considerably less expensive is the Katadyn Micro Filter Water Bottle. It's a simple water bottle with a built-in filter that enables you to use whatever decent-looking water you find. It frees you from always having to find bottled water—then disposing of the plastic container.

If you take a filter, remember that weight and size matter, that you must follow instructions (including keeping the filter clean and not using it beyond its capacity), and that it can't protect you when you don't use it.

Iodine

Suppose it's late in the evening, and you've just checked into a hotel in Chichicastenango, Guatemala. There's a container of water on the nightstand, but you have no idea if it's been boiled or filtered. Even though you're very thirsty, it would be bad for international relations to build a fire in the middle of the floor to boil the stuff.

The EPA offers suggestions on the range of possibilities for what to do next (see **www.epa.gov/safewater/faq/emerg.html**). One option is a 2 percent tincture of iodine solution, available from any pharmacy, that will kill parasites, bacteria, and viruses. I don't use that because of the risk of spilling the iodine solution in my luggage. But iodine also comes in very inexpensive tablet form. The EPA asserts that when using iodine or chlorine (see next page), the water should first be filtered and allowed to settle. I've observed that, in the absence of filters, most people just drop the tab and cross their fingers. Give the tablets 20 to 30 minutes to do their job. Because the tablets deteriorate over time, toss them out after a year. There is also a crystalline iodine product. Both are available in camping-goods stores and through outdoor catalogs.

Potable Aqua (50 tablets; $9) iodine tablets are readily available in drug and sporting-goods stores, effective—and nasty-tasting. If anticipating the taste of iodine makes you shiver, you'll be pleased to know that the Potable Aqua

Traveller water bottle removes the yellow-brown color and singed-iron taste from iodine-treated water.

I consider iodine as backup purification. If you're thinking about using it as your primary disinfectant for an extended trip, consult your doctor.

Another approach to purification is a 2-ounce bottle of MSR's SweetWater Purifier Solution ($10), which will treat 80 gallons. A better option in terms of taste, and also available abroad, are Micropur tablets that use silver ions as the active ingredient (30 tablets for $14). I use the solution or the tablets in a pinch, but try to do some basic filtering first.

Chlorine

Chlorine also disinfects water. The strength of the solution determines how much to use, and you must carefully follow instructions on the label. One option is the Aquatab (see **www.aquatabs.com**), long used in Europe and Asia, but there are many.

SteriPEN

A final portable option is SteriPEN's Adventurer or Traveler, both of which use an ultraviolet-light wand to sterilize contaminated water. They're highly effective and compact (six inches long, about four ounces). Even at about $100, they can pay for themselves in convenience and by offsetting the cost of buying purified water.

Other Drinks

If you can't be certain that milk has been properly pasteurized, assume it hasn't been. Why risk tuberculosis or brucellosis? If milk is brought to a boil before being served in tea or coffee, it should be safe. Unfortunately, the misgivings about milk extend to milk products, including cheese and ice cream.

It's good that beer is okay to drink because you encounter an incredible variety of beers as you travel, often local brews in which people take great pride. Beer has a couple of drawbacks. It's a diuretic, and it's sometimes served warm (because there is no refrigeration and the ice melted two days ago). You are better off drinking from the bottle after wiping its mouth than pouring it into a glass. A straw is a good solution for some beverages, but it's hard to maintain your poise sitting in a bar drinking beer through a straw.

Wine is much less common than beer, more expensive, and seldom memorable. At the Alcove Restaurant in Dar es Salaam, Tanzania, a headwaiter in a rumpled tux offered me their featured wine: Thunderbird.

Soft drinks are fine from a clean-water standpoint—if you can handle being hit by a sugar meteorite.

Tea and coffee made from boiling water are safe. Highland nomads in western Nepal say, "Tea is the horse of the traveler." I agree and drink huge quantities of tea wherever I go. Loaded up with sugar, a few cups of tea will get you through the coldest morning. But remember, an otherwise safe liquid can be infected by a contaminated container or prolonged exposure to air. In practical terms, that means the tea is fine, but the teacup may get you. Take your own cup, clean what's available, take a chance, or go without.

If you ask local residents whether their water is safe to drink, they are likely to say it is, perhaps out of pride. They drink it because they're used to it and can't afford to buy bottled water or the fuel to boil local water. You, on the other hand, can't afford not to drink clean water.

Unfortunately, not all hotels and restaurants that advertise "filtered water" actually provide it. Some mean well and bought the equipment, but it broke down a couple of years ago and . . . well, you know. I make my decision based on the overall sanitation of the place.

To summarize: Use bottled water, and break the seal on the bottle yourself. Otherwise, boil water, filter it, or drop in those little tablets, and avoid containers that may be contaminated. It takes only a little thought to be a healthy traveler.

CHAPTER 17

Safety and Security

Toto, I've a feeling we're not
in Kansas anymore.
—Dorothy, in the movie
The Wizard of Oz (1939)

"You've got to be crazy!"

That's what I hear from friends when I say I'm heading for some distant place they perceive as dangerous. While it's normal to wonder how you'll be treated in Guatemala City, Johannesburg, Santiago, or any other place you don't know much about, I've been met with friendliness on every continent. People smile, call out greetings, offer to help, and want to talk. They welcome travelers to their country, proud of their culture and their kids.

It's true that traveling does present certain risks. However, it's important to know that risk abroad is very different from the drug-related crimes and armed robbery all too common in North America. In fact, the most frequent problems afflicting travelers abroad are stubbed or broken toes (apparently from stumbling around in dark hotel rooms), lost luggage, being bumped from an overbooked flight, and diarrhea acquired from contaminated water.

Although physical assault is rare, opportunistic, non-violent theft should be a concern. The traveler is an inviting target unless he or she knows what to expect and is prepared to avoid or respond to any problem. Many of the people you meet have seen the United States depicted

> Knowledge and preparation reduce risks.

on television as a land of unimaginable luxury. The fact that you're in their country tells them you have enough money to travel beyond horizons they'll never approach. As some associate you with what they've seen, you'll sense admiration—but perhaps a little envy, too. The possessions you carry may be worth more than the average annual income in their country, so to a few people you represent an opportunity for a little informal redistribution of wealth.

But hold on. Perhaps violent crime isn't a big worry, but that doesn't mean a traveler can safely stroll along in la-la land with eyes on the church steeples or nose in a guidebook. A *Condé Nast Traveler* poll revealed that 42 percent of the readers who responded had had money, clothing, or jewelry stolen while traveling (most of them in Europe). Almost half of the group who had lost something said it was taken from their hotel rooms; 26 percent experienced street theft (mostly by pickpockets); and almost 30 percent encountered some scam such as the basic taxi rip-off, a tricky currency exchange, or a slippery purchase.

Even though I believe that people who had experienced a theft were much more motivated to respond than those who hadn't, these percentages are appalling, showing either carelessness or lack of preparation. Because 33 percent of those who responded to the poll had been victims twice, that group must have included some slow learners or very unlucky folks. There's a clue in the fact that only 36 percent reported carrying their money in a money belt. Virtually all those losses could have been avoided with a little knowledge and preparation.

You'll find specific information about safety issues for Mexico and each country in Central America in Chapters 2 and 3.

To a lurking thief, a traveler wandering down the street looking lost or preoccupied appears the way a limping gazelle does to a hungry lion. Now, turn that image around. Picture a traveler walking with an air of self-assurance and purpose. I don't mean acting arrogant or tough, just confident and alert, aware of the surroundings. Because that person doesn't look like easy prey, especially if in the company of others, the thief will look elsewhere.

Remember that old joke about two guys suddenly confronted on the trail by a grizzly bear? The grizzly rears up and roars, about to charge. Ben cries, "What shall we do?" His friend Scott says, "I'm getting out of here!" "You're crazy," shouts Ben as the bear starts its rush. "You can't outrun that bear." "I don't have to," Scott calls back over his shoulder. "All I have to do is outrun you!" That's all each of us has to do as a traveler—simply make sure we're not the thief's first choice.

It's your job to know whether you need to be especially alert in the places you'll be visiting. Overseas, as at home, crime is most common in cities and anywhere else tourists congregate. High-risk areas include train and bus stations, streets around tourist hotels, and nightlife areas.

Some guidebooks offer good advice concerning security risks at your destinations, but it's worth taking advantage of other resources as well. Review Consular Information Sheets or Travel Warnings (see the following section), and talk with experienced travelers before you leave home.

Talk with other travelers as you approach a country. Seek guidance from the desk clerk at your hotel. Question local people. Adjust your alertness based on what you hear and see. If a situation requires caution, be cautious. No lapses.

We don't worry much about certain risks at home because we know how to avoid them. Abroad, however, risks are more real for anyone who doesn't know the territory. Unprepared tourists are right to worry—because they don't know how to protect themselves. Knowledge prevents problems. When a few simple routines become automatic, you can travel the world without fear.

Being apprehensive could ruin a trip. Being informed and keeping your wits about you is just plain smart.

WHICH COUNTRIES TO SKIP

Are there countries you should skip? There are, but neither Mexico nor any of the countries in Central America are among them. In Mexico, there are some occasional political disturbances, such as in Oaxaca, but they are typically short term and not directed at travelers. In recent decades, there has been violence in parts of Guatemala, Nicaragua, El Salvador, and, briefly, Panama. Those conflicts are now years behind us. (Please see the information about each country in Chapter 3.)

The terrorist threat discussed endlessly in the United States is not a matter of consequence in Mexico and Central America.

The fact is that disturbances in a distant country are frequently reported as being worse than they are.

Unfortunately, when talking with returning tourists, we tend to hear from the one person who had a problem, not from the dozens who had none. By analogy, when someone has a bad meal in a restaurant, he's likely to talk about it, and the meal gets worse with each telling. Almost anyone who has traveled has succumbed to the temptation of telling, and embellishing, some adventure. After all, stories about a coup or riot sound pretty exciting when repeated at home. Nevertheless, even taking sensationalism and exaggerations into account, there are always a few places, changing year to year, that a traveler should leave off the itinerary.

How do you identify which countries to skip? It's a matter of research and common sense. News reports, even if unnecessarily alarmist, signal places that deserve careful review before inclusion on your route.

The mission of the U.S. Department of State Bureau of Consular Affairs (**travel.state.gov**) is to protect U.S. citizens overseas. Consular Information Sheets describe crime and security conditions, political disturbances, areas of instability, health conditions, and much more in every country. They also include addresses and emergency telephone numbers for U.S. embassies and consulates. If conditions in a country are considered particularly dangerous or a major demonstration will occur on a specified date, the State Department also issues a Travel Warning recommending against travel to that place. Public Announcements alert travelers to specific short-term threats (for example, a coup or a terrorist warning). These publications tend to be extremely cautious because "hostage" is not a welcome word around the State Department. All can be found by clicking on "International Travel" near the top of the Web site's home page. If you contact the embassy of the country you intend to visit and ask about local safety, the response may not be candid. If there's an internal problem, the government may want to keep foreigners away to avoid bad publicity.

A recently returned traveler is a good source of information provided you can evaluate his frame of reference. Here's what I mean: A bunch of us were talking one evening in a Bangkok cafe as it bobbed gently on the Chao Phraya River. Those of us who had just arrived from South India saw Bangkok as intimidatingly modern and distressingly westernized. An Englishman, just arrived from vacationing in New Zealand, saw the same Bangkok as dirty, disorganized, and distressingly Asian. That's frame of reference: the eye of the beholder.

There are, however, real problems such as civil war or terrorist attacks. Terrorists sometimes pressure a government by attacking places that attract tourists. If bombs are being set off at an airport or scenic destination, even occasionally, go elsewhere. If hostage-taking is on an upswing, it's a good idea for travelers not to attract attention by looking affluent or dressing in pseudomilitary clothing.

Many places go through periods when they belong on no traveler's route. I'm thinking of *parts* of Angola, Colombia, India (Jammu and Kashmir), Sudan, Sri Lanka, the Kurdish section of Turkey, the Philippines (northern Luzon, Mindanao), and Zimbabwe. I'll skip Nigeria, Iraq, and Afghanistan for the foreseeable future.

Consider a few precautions when traveling in a genuinely high-risk area. Tell people at home what they should do in case you find yourself in an emergency situation. Check in with your embassy. Don't discuss your itinerary with strangers. Leave nothing controversial in your hotel room. Be cautious if someone seems to be following you. Keep a mental note of potential safe havens, and develop a plan of action should a dangerous situation arise. If shooting starts, take cover, and don't pick up a weapon. (Forget Rambo!) Stay out of sight, and try to remember why you came.

The bottom line: some places should be left for another day. Do the research. Find out whether a place is as forbidding as it initially sounds. If it's a close call, trust your instincts. If you decide to go, get updates from other travelers when you arrive. In making decisions, give the frequency of random violence, attacks directed toward tourists, and the attitude of the government considerable weight.

HOW TO PROTECT YOURSELF WITH A MAGIC CLOAK

In a crowded bus station in San José, Costa Rica, I heard a tourist complain loudly that someone had just snatched his passport from his shirt pocket. He kept it in his shirt pocket? Anyone who does something like that must be brain dead. There's no reason to be a victim when thievery can be avoided so easily. Knowledge and preparation form a magic cloak that, when followed without exception, makes a traveler almost invulnerable.

Perhaps the most important part of the routine is a mind-set you establish before you leave home: that you won't defend your dignity or property at risk of injury or life. Suppose you're walking along a street in Mexico City and some guy standing in a doorway with his buddies makes a nasty comment about you, your partner, or your country. Fortunately, you've already decided not to be provoked by a gratuitous insult. Does it make sense to play someone else's game on his home turf? So you walk on.

In the serenity of an easy chair, it's obvious that the possessions you carry aren't worth trading your life to protect. It's more difficult to embed that principle so deeply that you won't make a different decision in the heat of the moment or after several beers in some exotic port. That decision should become the first of your routines.

Money-belt Routines

Some of the most important routines concern your money belt:

- Keep all your valuables (passport, credit cards, driver's license, immunization record, airline tickets, and most of your cash and traveler's checks) in a money belt. Always. It's a small hassle to get them out when you need them, but it keeps them from disappearing unexpectedly. When I say "money belt," I mean all forms of concealment for valuables: a belt around your waist, a concealed pocket inside your belt, a pocket hanging inside your pants from your belt loop, a pouch dangling from your neck, a shoulder holster, and so on.
- Whatever the form of your money belt, it must be inside your clothing, riding comfortably without signaling its presence. Although its fabric may be water-resistant, it won't keep out rain or the perspiration generated during a long hike, so keep the contents inside a zip-top bag. Transporting valuables in a pouch outside your clothing, including the often-seen fanny pack, may be comfortable and convenient, but it puts them at great risk. Fanny packs can't be protected effectively and get clipped off every day.
- Lock your money belt in your luggage at night unless you feel you're in a high-risk area. If you are, keep the belt with you while you sleep.
- You can find lots of things on the beach—seashells, a volleyball game, maybe even a new friend—but you can lose things, too. When heading for the beach, leave your money belt in the hotel safe if you trust the safe. If you don't, lock it in your luggage in the hotel room. If you take it to the beach, ask a friend to wear it while you're swimming, or take it in with you in a waterproof pouch.

On many beaches, not all the sharks are in the water. Don't even think of hiding your money belt under your towel or digging a hole for it. As an acquaintance put his money belt under his towel, I noticed a teenage guy stroll by. He eyed us obliquely and kept going. Several minutes later, he eased down just behind us, only a few feet away. I watched in fascination as his foot slowly snaked across the sand until his toes could probe under my friend's towel. I yelled. He scrambled to his feet and tore off down the beach. My friend had underestimated the caliber of the competition.

- Keep a small amount of cash and traveler's checks in your luggage to avoid being cleaned out if a thief were somehow to get your money belt. For the same reason, it's prudent for partners to split cash, traveler's checks, and credit cards between them.

Making the small effort to follow these simple routines will make your trip a happier one. Convince yourself that the very first time you're careless with your money belt, it will disappear. Why learn the hard way?

Wallet Routines

- Put your wallet in a secure front pants pocket, a buttoned or Velcro-closed thigh pocket, or some other inaccessible place. Some travelers use a wallet attached by a loop to the belt. I grimace when I see a traveler stuff a wallet into a rear pants pocket, an inside jacket pocket, or a purse—all predictable places. When a thief knows where to look for your wallet, he's halfway to his goal.
- Make your wallet "sticky" by wrapping it with rubber bands.
- Act as if the thief can get your wallet wherever you put it. On that assumption, keep only business cards, a few dollars, and a couple of traveler's checks in it. Everything else belongs in your money belt. Sure, it's a little inconvenient, but it's a lot easier than canceling and replacing credit cards, wiring home for money, and suffering the anxiety of a major loss. Travel is supposed to be fun.

Luggage and Day-pack Routines

The objective is to prevent anyone from opening your luggage and removing what he wants—or walking off with the whole bag. These routines can foil his plans:

- Keep your luggage locked most of the time. If you have something valuable in your day pack, such as your camera, lock it while in crowded places or when checking it at a museum.
- Bus and train stations and, to a lesser degree, airports, attract people who admire your possessions. While waiting, keep your hand or foot through your luggage strap, lean against it, or otherwise keep in physical touch with it.

David, an Israeli as hirsute and bulky as a bear, asked if I would watch his pack one afternoon at a bus station. I agreed. When he locked his pack to my belt with a light chain, I knew he was an experienced traveler. That was his not-so-subtle way of saying he expected me to watch his pack as closely as he would watch it himself.

- When you check your luggage, ask the agent for the letter designation of your destination. Do not assume that the right tag is attached. Inadvertent errors happen, and I heard of a ticket agent who purposely mistagged bags, sending them to a city where a confederate waited to claim them. Clever, eh? Watch your luggage depart toward the plane, and watch as it's loaded on a bus.

- If your bag gets lost in transit, you have to prove it was in the custody of the carrier. That's much easier if you have a baggage claim check (try getting one at a Guatemalan bus stop).
- Your luggage can also go astray on arrival. Not all the folks watching the bags clunk around the carousel are passengers. Some are official porters who promote their services by snatching your bag and guarding it until you see it and come over. Then there is the unofficial porter who picks up your bag if it looks unattended. If you see it happen, he smiles and acts like a porter. If you don't, he's out the gate. I'm sure you've seen those warning signs that say, "Bags look alike." It must be true. To a thief, your bag looks like his.

Station yourself close to the point where bags enter the baggage-claim area. That way, you'll get first shot at your bag. If you're farther down the line, chatting with someone you met on the plane, your bag may leave the airport before you do.

At one airport, I was waiting for my backpack to roll into sight when a slightly built young man swooped down like a fish eagle on the day pack at my feet. His boldness probably meant he had confederates nearby to whom he planned to pitch my pack on the run. As always in a crowd, I was standing with my size 13 shoe firmly planted through the pack's strap. When the pack didn't come away in his hand as he expected, he slid sprawling across the floor. I'm sure he was back the next day.

- Vulnerability increases in crowded places such as a train station. After a long trip, you're tired and a little disoriented, thinking about the town, talking about lodging, or maybe looking for a friend, and you're not concentrating on the present. Zap! You've been stung. Theft may be nonviolent, but that doesn't mean it's polite. Even if you see the person who races by and grabs your day pack out of your hand, you have little chance of catching him. Be alert in crowded places, watch the people around you, and keep in touch with your gear. Force the thief to look for an easier target.
- If you have much walking to do or you'll be waiting for hours, consider storing your bag in a locker or the "left luggage" room.
- Suppose you're in a public place, can't store your bag, and can't stand taking it with you while you run errands. If you ask someone reputable-looking to watch it, set it clearly within his or her territory. Reduce the risk by locking it to something with your bicycle lock. Make sure you communicate with one another about how long the person will be there.
- If you sleep in a public place, lock your bag to something, or use it for a pillow. Even lacing the straps through a bench or around a stanchion will foil someone running by.

- If you have a compartment on a train, keep the door locked when you're out of the room, and lock your bag to the washstand or something else built in. If that won't work, lock two bags together. If you have an open berth on the aisle, use your bag as a cushion between yourself and the wall while you sleep, or lock it to something.
- Bus travel tests your vigilance. When your bag is traveling on the roof of a bus, secure it to a rail with a bicycle chain-lock. That keeps it from falling off on a curve or being pitched off into waiting hands.
- If you have your bag in the restroom, take it into the stall with you (yes, easier said than done).
- A hotel room is not always a safe zone. As you're leaving the room, take a moment to lock up things you'd rather not contribute to the local economy.
- The locks on your hotel room door and windows won't help unless you use them.
- Believing them easier targets for grab-and-run theft, thieves target women. A woman should wear her shoulder-bag strap diagonally across her chest rather than hanging off one shoulder. When a man is walking with a woman, he should walk between her and the street to guard against someone making a grab for her shoulder bag.
- If you have your day pack on your back in a crowded bus, beware of busy fingers trying to get inside. If you carry it over one shoulder, be alert against a grab-and-run. Each time you set it down, keep in touch with it; keep your hand on it or your foot through a strap. Keep it out of reach of passing hands. If you put a camera in your day pack, be especially alert.
- Carry a local-language newspaper prominently under your arm to help you pass as a local (if that's even remotely possible).
- Be alert when someone offers to help, especially when you didn't know you needed help. An offer needn't make you defensive, just alert. Similarly, don't be too quick to volunteer to help someone else. Don't suppress your friendly instincts, but take a moment to size up the situation.

The comments above and following are not meant to make travel seem daunting. It's just that knowing what to expect, following the simple routines I've described, and using the information in the rest of this chapter provide a magic cloak to guard your travels.

WHERE TROUBLE COMES FROM—AND HOW TO AVOID IT
We've reviewed protecting your money belt, wallet, luggage, and day pack from theft. Now we're ready to discuss other potential safety and security problems a traveler might encounter. You can learn to recognize and sidestep every one.

Political and Religious Discussions
As we all know, discussions of politics, sex, or religion can become very spirited. They are especially tempting topics on the road because a vigorous discussion can

generate cultural insights you might otherwise have missed. The problem arises when what seems like stimulating give-and-take to you may appear personal and confrontational to others. Tempers can flare even more when controversial subjects are combined with alcohol.

If you want to stir things up, try converting others to your way of thinking or insist that your country's political system is the only rational one. Voice your opinions about the merits and demerits of local persons of the opposite sex, and throw in a few complaints about the inconveniences you've encountered in their country. Then get ready for fireworks.

I'm not suggesting that you avoid discussions of politics, sex, or religion; I am suggesting that it's better to ask questions than to preach. Be open-minded and sensitive to the mood of the group. Keep it light.

We humans are not at our most tolerant these days, so should the mood sour, pay for a farewell drink for your new acquaintances, if appropriate, and bail out immediately. There's no upside to getting into an argument in a bar.

Alcohol, Drugs, and Firearms

Alcohol

Alcohol is as much related to problems of safety and security when you're abroad as it is at home. After a few drinks, you become a shade inattentive. You fail to recognize a problem developing, or you take a risk you'd otherwise have avoided. Suddenly, you're face-to-face with an unpleasant situation. If you gulp down a couple of beers after a hot afternoon of trudging or add a cool bottle of white wine to your dinner, stay a little more alert to your surroundings than you might at home.

Drugs

Latin America is not the Good Ship Lollipop, so, yes, there are drugs. I have one word of advice about drugs: DON'T! Don't buy them, don't sell them, don't use them, and don't transport them in or out. This isn't about morality. It's about safety and security. Using exposes you to impure drugs and can put your life on the line. Anyone who buys or sells drugs may be dealing with an informer or a cop. Sneaking illegal drugs through customs might work . . . except when it doesn't. More than one-third of all U.S. citizens incarcerated abroad for any crime are in on drug charges, many with

> Avoid drugs at all costs.

very long mandatory sentences. Anyone busted on drug charges learns quickly how very different the legal process is and how much more severe the penalties are in most foreign countries. Maybe you saw the movie *Midnight Express*?

Some drug sales are setups from the beginning. The seller has tipped off the cops or is a cop. The buyer is arrested during or immediately after the deal goes down, and the drugs are confiscated—probably for recycling. Naturally, the buyer's drug money disappears. Somewhere on the way to the police station, a large amount of money may be mentioned with the implication that its receipt might be related to the buyer's freedom. If not, the buyer may be held without trial for years. Under the legal systems of many countries, a person under arrest is considered guilty until innocence is proved. Perfunctory trials and harsh sentences are common. On bulletin boards in hotels, I've read pitiful notes posted on behalf of foreign prisoners begging for someone to contact a relative.

A traveler who expects the embassy to intervene, give him a good scolding, and put him on a plane for home should have a chat with the State Department ahead of time. Embassies have neither the ability nor the willingness to do much more than provide a list of lawyers and notify next of kin.

If a new acquaintance asks you to take a package home as a favor, agree or not as it suits you, but don't actually accept it without opening and inspecting the contents carefully. Whatever reasons are given for your not opening the package, they're not good enough. If the package contains drugs or other illegal goods, it is you who will answer to the law.

Sadly, illegal drugs require travelers to be thoughtful about accepting apparent hospitality. Whether you accept food or drink from someone should depend on the circumstances. If the offer is from someone you have reason to trust, no problem. If an offer comes from a new acquaintance or seems inappropriate in some way, be cautious. Bus and train stations are special-alert zones. If you have the slightest doubt about an offer, turn it down. You can decline on grounds of being a vegetarian, being a nondrinker, or having an upset stomach, or give no reason at all. Be polite, but put your own welfare first.

I recall a 22-year-old Japanese student who accepted an orange soda from a person he met in a bus station in Tanzania. He awakened 36 hours later in a hospital to which some kind passerby had taken him. After the drug wore off and his headache subsided, he asked about his backpack. The nurses shook their heads and shrugged their shoulders.

The State Department reports that no U.S. citizens have been arrested abroad in connection with prescription drugs they bought in the United States and took on trips for personal use in labeled containers. However, you can get into trouble by legally buying large amounts of certain drugs, such as tranquilizers and amphetamines, in one country and attempting to take them into other countries where they are illegal. The same goes for attempting to return with them to the United States if the quantity is such that customs might suspect commercial intent.

Firearms

Sentences for illegal possession of firearms abroad can be very harsh by U.S. standards. How does 30 years sound? Don't consider taking a weapon to another country without first obtaining a permit from its embassy. A little political instability can convince border guards, police, and other officials that your weapon indicates your intent to help the local insurgents. What could follow would not be pretty.

Prohibited Photographs

Because we'll discuss this subject more thoroughly in Chapter 26, I'll mention only briefly that a traveler can get into trouble by taking photographs of forbidden objects. What's forbidden? The list is pretty standard: bridges, airports, harbors, military personnel and installations, and some religious structures. I don't take photos of any police without first getting permission—and I never photograph demonstrations unless I'm certain I'm not being observed. From what I've seen, none of this is a problem in Central America.

Encounters with the Law

Few people arrive in a foreign country intending to break the law, but they may do so anyway, sometimes because of ignorance or carelessness. Buying, selling, using, or transporting drugs is by far the most effective strategy for winning a trip straight to jail. Being drunk or disorderly in public comes in second to drug issues. Other common problems involve visas, currency violations, fraud, theft, customs violations (bringing in or taking out something prohibited), traffic accidents, or violations of local statutes—for example, entering a restricted area. Carrying a weapon may or may not protect you, but it will get you stopped at the border of every country in the world.

When visiting a country, you are governed by its laws, and they may be based on principles of jurisprudence very different from those in your own country. The differences relate to whether an individual's rights or the government's rights have primacy. In most

> You are governed by the laws of the country you are in.

places, the government wins hands down. For example, detention for a week or more without formal charges or a showing of probable cause is common. There may not even be a right to immediately contact anyone outside jail. Bail may be denied, and right to trial by jury is far from universal. The best plan is to obey local laws.

When your path collides with officialdom, your behavior can make all the difference in how things turn out. Don't be disrespectful or show anger. That's hard to do, but it's essential. There is a saying in Ghana: "Once you have crossed the river, you can be rude to the crocodile." That wise counsel needs no explanation.

Suppose there's no question of guilt? You did what they say you did, and you both know it. No matter how silly the regulation seems that you're being charged with violating, don't criticize it. Express naive surprise. Apologize immediately. Promise that, now that you know the law, you'll never commit this offense again. However, if you did not commit any offense, don't say that you did.

If detention is prolonged or the interpersonal dynamics are deteriorating (for example, the guard is getting drunk or you're losing your cool), call for a superior officer. If it's appropriate, request a representative of your embassy or consulate. He or she probably won't get you out of jail, but someone from the consulate should visit you and put you in touch with a well-connected lawyer, preferably one who speaks your language (although maybe that won't matter if he's connected well enough). The embassy official will also notify your family or traveling partner, help get money transferred from home if you need it, and arrange for food and bedding (which usually doesn't come with the jail cell).

I've heard a couple of people say they responded to difficulty by offering a bribe. That's not a solution that comes naturally to me, and it entails some risks. We'll discuss bribes at greater length in Chapter 21, Etiquette.

It's fine to be persistent, but if you decide to employ assertiveness or anger, brace yourself to encounter the full weight of an infinite bureaucracy. At a remote border crossing, the odds that your display of temper or threats will intimidate a 19-year-old private holding a submachine gun are infinitesimally low—off the board, I'd say. At the same time, the chances that your show of anger will escalate the situation to your disadvantage approach 100 percent. The slightest hint that you deserve special treatment because you are a foreigner will provoke special treatment all right, but perhaps not in your best interests.

In Mexico and Central America, you can expect to cross borders without a hassle. If asked, I open my pack to be searched. I answer questions politely. Not wanting to say the wrong thing, I volunteer little information. When asked why I'm there, I say, "To see this beautiful country." If you're calm and patient, you can wait out most problems.

I am not advocating that you present yourself as a person who can be taken advantage of. That could be a mistake. Instead, try to establish some person-to-person contact with the official. Ask personal questions. Establish eye contact—difficult if the guy is wearing shades or one of those stiff army hats with a black visor. If you ask for his help or advice, he may transform himself into an individual human and show you how to solve the problem. Reasonable flattery works in every language.

As you travel, you will interact with more officials than you normally do at home. Most will be pleasant human beings. Only a very few will be tight-lipped, self-important creeps. If one starts to give you a problem, it's your job to keep the situation under control. It's not difficult when you're prepared.

Disturbances

What do you do about disturbances that spring up while you're on the scene? Fortunately, most aren't nearly as dangerous as they appear from a distance. Take the coup in which the commanding general of the army deposed the president of Bolivia. After firing a few machine-gun volleys into the air, the military imposed a curfew, shut down transportation for three days, and awarded the outgoing president a lifetime vacation in a remote village in the steamy lowland jungle. American newspaper reports made La Paz, the capital, sound like the last place in the world you'd want to be. For travelers, the situation was merely inconvenient, not dangerous.

On the other hand, I recall an event about 20 years ago that didn't seem threatening until it suddenly burst out of control. As I stood in a shop doorway in a Chilean town talking with the shop owner, a street intersection a few yards away filled with students. Before long, they were shouting angrily as fiery speakers demanded that the government reveal the whereabouts of students who had "disappeared." Squads of heavily armored policemen arrived, looking

menacing but not interfering. Without warning, someone threw a stone through a storefront window. As the glass shattered, so did détente. In an instant, clubs were swinging, and rocks were flying. I dove into the shop just as the owner hauled down his steel mesh security curtain with a clang.

Whether there's a student protest meeting, a police action breaking up a strike, or an all-out coup attempt, no traveler should let curiosity lead him into the middle of it. The rule is simple: stay away from trouble. If there's a flare-up when you're around, don't go to watch. If you go anyway, thinking you'll keep your head down, you may find yourself caught in a mob. Stay in your hotel. If there's action in the street below, stay away from the windows. Pull the curtains or blinds to stop flying glass. Store some food and water if you have time. Just in case water is cut off, fill the bathtub or whatever containers you can find. Keep your flashlight nearby in case the power goes off. Know where the fire escape is. If there's a curfew, obey it.

If it looks as if the situation may continue or deteriorate, ask the hotel manager to help you slip away. For a price, someone is ready to accommodate virtually any need.

Theft: Scams, Pickpockets, and Sneak Thieves

The vast majority of theft is so cunning it reminds me of the definition of true sarcasm: a blade so keen the victim doesn't know he's been struck until he turns to walk away, and his head falls to the ground. Victims don't know the thief has struck until they discover something missing. I have grudging admiration for the creativity that thieves put into separating people from their belongings, but not enough to reward it. Having learned what to watch for, I'm prepared.

The magic cloak of routines we discussed at the beginning of this chapter is excellent protection against standard brands of theft. However, an elite group of thieves has concocted some especially clever ways to take possession of your valuables. When you're in their neighborhoods, you can't afford even a short lapse of attention.

As you read the examples that follow, it may be hard to believe they could be real because they're so different from your daily experience. But they are real, every one of them. And there are dozens of variations in all languages. If you remember them, they'll remain nothing but amusing anecdotes to which you will add your own.

Scams

The variety of scams is as infinite as the imagination. A few scams have even achieved the status of classics, informally inducted into a Travelers' Hall of Fame. Fagin would be proud of his successors. As a neophyte traveler begins to tell the story of what just happened to him, his more experienced listeners exchange wry smiles and nod in recognition after the first few lines. It's like hearing a couple of bars of an old, familiar song. Here are some of the scams out there:

Doing something for you: A smiling, always smiling young man appears at your elbow offering to help load your luggage into a taxi, guide you to a hotel, find you a discount, get tickets for you, anything. If he's legitimate, he'll provide a helpful service and earn a tip. Nothing wrong with that, but if he's not legitimate, his offer may not be quite what it appears. A yellow caution light should go on when a stranger offers to help.

The first hustler you meet may be an "official" in an impressive-looking uniform at the airport or the train station. He takes you in hand, guides you through the baggage-collection process and steers you to a car waiting at the curb. If you get into that car, you're signing up for an expensive ride—and will wind up at an expensive hotel. It has to be expensive to cover his kickback. And, of course, he's no more an official than you are.

You're standing on a street corner, lost, looking for a restaurant you've heard about. Someone comes up and asks if you need help. "Oh, no problem, I'm going that way myself," she says. Somewhere along the way, it's your wallet that gets lost.

Then there's the taxi driver who offers to drive you to several tourist sites for a very low fare. What can you lose? After you see the first colonial church, he stops in front of a large jewelry store, which he begs you to enter "for few minutes only." If you go inside, the store gives him a coupon valid for five liters of petrol plus a commission on anything you buy (which, of course, raises its price to you). After you leave the store, he takes you to the next stop. When you come out, he's long gone, lining up somewhere else.

Selling you something that's misrepresented: If it were ivory, a rhino horn, an elephant hide (anyone trying to buy any of these first three deserves to be swindled), gold, or jade, it would be a great buy at the price—a steal, you might say. You would have done the impossible: outsmarted the local merchant. Of course, if it turns out to be plastic or cowhide, the price is outrageous. How many times have you heard someone say, "If it sounds too good to be true, it probably is"? Or, "There's no free lunch"? Clichés, yes, and so true.

You can definitely buy satisfying souvenirs in foreign countries at prices far below anything comparable at home—and often, there is nothing comparable at home. You can even buy authentically valuable items at bargain prices. However, if something is represented as handmade, antique, rare, or unique, and the price does not reflect that quality, *stop*! Think "no free lunch"! Make sure the claims are true before you buy. Otherwise, recognize the risk.

Suppose that a beautiful emerald catches your eye. The ever-so-soft-spoken salesperson whispers, "This small stone will be worth three times more in your country. Sell it there, and pay for your trip." You smile uncertainly and think, *oh, sure* . . . but you wonder if it just might be true. With practiced timing, the salesperson goes on, "If you can't sell this stone for at least 100 percent more than you pay here, you can take it to our embassy in your country, and they will give you a 50 percent profit. Just show them the sales slip." Well, now, you think, if that's true, I could really clean up with a more expensive stone. "How much is that one over there? The big one," you ask. To help set the hook, the salesperson produces a fancy Certificate of Guarantee. If your yellow caution light isn't glowing brightly by now, you're in big trouble—and not just in this gem store. Do I need to tell you that the embassy will greet you with a stone wall when you state your request for 50 percent profit, even though it has heard the same sad story many times and knows you're about to hit the roof? Of course, by the time you're talking to the embassy, you've already found out what the gem is really worth.

Keeping you from watching the ball all the way into the basket: After you've made a purchase, keep your eye on it until you leave the store. Let's say you've just bought a silver bracelet in Guanajuato, Mexico. Try not to let it be wrapped out of your sight. If it is, inspect the package before you leave the shop or at least the city. It's disheartening to discover a switch when you're thousands of miles away.

Giving you nothing at all for your money: Read the Letters to the Editor columns in a few travel magazines. They're full of laments about goods received that weren't what was ordered and purchases that never arrived. If you're having things made and shipped, it's reasonable for the merchant to ask you to pay in full at the time of purchase. It's also reasonable for you to decline. Compromise. Advance enough money to cover the merchant's costs. If that won't work, offer to leave part of the payment at a local bank with directions to release it on receipt of shipping papers. The best deal is to pay the shipper when you pick up the goods. The worst deal is to pay for something that never arrives—because it was never sent. Using a credit card may protect you if nothing arrives. See the credit-card section in Chapter 10. Every item I've taken to a post office myself and everything I've had a merchant ship via sea freight has made it home. Of course, two colorful rugs from the Tibetan Refugee Center in Darjeeling, India, didn't arrive until nine months after I did. If I'm fairly satisfied with a merchant's legitimacy and the purchase price seems small—and I really want an item—I take a risk.

Pretending to be students: You'll meet a lot of students as you travel. They're curious about you and want to practice speaking your language. They may dream of visiting your country and would love to have a contact. They can be engaging and interesting and introduce you to local life. The only thing wrong is that some of them aren't students at all.

They're hoping their "student" status engenders trust. After some conversational groundwork, they may ask for money to get them home to see their parents or to support some political-refugee project. Perhaps they are reluctantly willing to part with their family's cherished antiques. They assert student status to persuade you to drop your defenses, including your common sense. The bottom line: when approached by a self-proclaimed student, be as open as you usually are, but be alert.

Asking for help: A young man approaches you on the street and says, "Excuse me. Do you speak English? Will you do me a great favor? At our shop, we have an important document that we have translated into English. Would you be so kind as to tell us whether it is grammatically correct? It will take only a moment." Being a considerate traveler, you agree to help. You are taken to his uncle's store and wind up spending the next hour being shown jewelry, carvings, or whatever while waiting for the document that may or may not appear. The whole thing is a ruse to get you into the store. It's hardly the end of the world, just a little off-putting.

Another approach begins when a pleasant-looking, middle-aged man asks for help finding his way. He produces a map and asks you to take a look. Get deeply involved in his map, and something you own may be taking a trip without you.

Offering a morning price: You're offered a special "morning price" because you are someone's first potential sale of the day. In some place in the past, it was considered good luck for merchants to break the ice with an early sale, so they'd drop their prices to make it. The superstition may be gone, but the come-on lingers. No problem, as long as you don't really believe it's either a first sale or a special price just for you.

Charging times two: Somewhat less amusing is the "times two" hustle. The taxi driver agrees on a price to take you and your friend to the soccer match. When you arrive, he demands double the price you agreed to, insisting that the price quoted was for one person. In your generosity, you may think there was a misunderstanding. There wasn't. To keep discussions like these on an even footing, always remove your gear from the vehicle before commencing the payment ritual. Sometimes it helps to pull out paper and pen and ostentatiously take down the driver's license number. Mention the tourist police. Move the discussion off the street and into a store or hotel lobby. Whatever your style in handling matters like this, losing your temper could turn bystanders against you.

> Regardless of the circumstances, losing your temper is never a good idea.

Keep perspective: The small amount of money involved does not justify spoiling your day or risking escalation into a serious dispute. I'm not suggesting that you routinely give in, just that you acknowledge that taxi drivers are not representative of the rest of the population, live a pretty hard life, and still don't earn very much. About the best you can do is try to reach clear agreement before you get into the vehicle and then stay calm if a disagreement arises. If you want help, ask a shopkeeper to call a police officer.

Running the pigeon drop: This threadbare hustle is creaking along around the world. Someone "finds" some money, a watch, or something else of value on the street just as you pass by and calls it to your attention. Get ready: the curtain is going up. You are being invited to participate in a masterful performance. Before long, as a condition to sharing in some great benefit, you are asked to put up some "good faith" money. That may sound ridiculous as you read it, but for many people it somehow seems to make sense when the scam is under way. Go along for a while if you want some amusement and can stay in a public place, but be ready to fold the hand fast.

Asking you to take a picture: The teenager walks up with a smile, hands his camera to you, then retreats a dozen yards away to stand in front of a tourist attraction. Always a good neighbor, you snap his picture. He not only doesn't come back for his camera, but he also he sprints off into the distance. Puzzled, you turn around—to discover that his accomplice has slipped up behind you and disappeared with your day pack, camera, or whatever else you set down to do the favor. You were chosen precisely because you were carrying something you'd have to set down. His camera? It's defunct or a $10 cheapo.

I may write an entire book devoted to Street Scams around the World. Not only would it help travelers avoid problems, but it also would reveal the true creativity of the human mind.

Pickpockets

Pickpockets abound the world over. Some are five-thumbed fumblers, while others are such proficient artists they can score on anyone. Fortunately for travelers, Fagin's descendants tend to concentrate in predictable places and strike at predictable times. Like the bank robber Willie Sutton, pickpockets go where the money is. Knowing those places and times, you're better prepared to foil their quick hands. For example, travelers not alert for pickpockets in Rio de Janeiro, Tangier, and Saigon would do better to mail their money to a charity and stay at home.

Several cute young girls approach four elderly tourists. The smallest youngster shyly holds up a ragged piece of paper covered with drawings she says are hers. The tourists smile, cluck approvingly, and lean forward to admire her work. The other cute little girls, also very talented with their hands, busy themselves by picking the pockets and purses of the four art lovers. Those thefts are not discovered until the group gets back to the hotel. A variation involves a group of kids who run up and start jabbing you with rolled-up newspapers or sticks. It's a diversion to cover their sneak attack on your valuables.

Pickpockets seek easy marks. Favorite targets include obvious greenhorns, people wearing or carrying something expensive, and anyone whose attention can be distracted or who's had too much to drink. Here are some examples of their work and where they flourish.

- Walking through the colorful market, you stop in the midst of a jostling crowd to watch the camel auction. Later, you start to pay for a carved-bone necklace, and . . . guess what? In a crowd, especially when your attention is attracted to things around you, leave valuables behind or in your money belt. If you're carrying your day pack, keep it locked or in front of your body. Instead of carrying your camera or purse hanging off one shoulder, wear the strap diagonally across your chest. Keep your hand on it, not on the strap. If you're wearing a jacket, keep your purse under the jacket.

A fanny pack extends the same invitation as a dangling purse. Because it's almost impossible to protect, it should never contain your valuables. If you wear a fanny pack, a thief doesn't know what's in it, so it may serve as a lure anyway.

No experienced traveler carries a wallet in an insecure back pants pocket unless it's a decoy to send a pickpocket on his way. A front shirt or pants pocket that can be buttoned, snapped, safety-pinned, or zippered is more secure. A Velcro closure helps but will yield to a determined hand. When I carry my wallet in a front pants pocket, I stick my comb into it or put several rubber bands around it, either of which makes it more difficult to pull from the pocket. Whenever you take your wallet out of your pocket, it's vulnerable.

- Every time you pay for something, you show a pickpocket where you keep your money. That gives him a big edge—and gives you another reason to keep most of your cash separate from the money you need immediately. Keep telling yourself: if you put it where they can get it, they will get it.
- Some tourist destinations post a sign that warns tourists to be wary of pickpockets. The result is similar to what happened when Sherlock Holmes used a false fire alarm to trick a lady into revealing where she'd hidden a valuable photograph. When she heard the alarm, she promptly ran to save the photograph—and Sherlock had her. On reading the warning sign, most people touch their wallet to be sure it's still there. If it is, both they and the pickpocket now know it. Similarly, when someone shouts, "Purse snatcher!" almost everyone will touch his or her valuables. Then the thief's accomplice begins his harvest.
- Taking your belongings becomes child's play, sometimes literally, through skillful use of diversions. Someone "accidentally" bumps you fairly hard, but a bystander keeps you from falling. The hands of one or the other are about to lighten your load. A drunk lurches into you, maybe drops a bottle at your feet; a deformed beggar clutches your clothes; a loud noise or a fight attracts the attention of the crowd. In the jostling as the crowd presses forward to see what's happening, wallets find a new home.

As a group of colorfully dressed teenage girls runs up to several tourists, offering trinkets for sale, one drops her handful of coins to the cobblestones. Responding to her cry of alarm, the tourists obligingly start picking them up. As they help, they're stripped as quickly as if by piranhas.

A person stands behind a card table on the sidewalk, demonstrating sleight of hand. As the onlookers watch his hands, the other half of the team, the real expert, explores their pockets.

What should you do? Protect yourself from being a victim by accepting a very simple premise: a skilled pickpocket can get whatever you keep in your pockets or purse. Your response? Keep in your pockets only what you can afford to lose.

Sneak Thieves

In many restaurants and bars, you're vulnerable to sneak thieves. You set your camera and day pack on the chair next to you, and when you look again, they're gone. Instead, put your stuff on the table in front of you or on your lap. If you put your day pack and camera on the floor, put your foot through the straps. Use the chair next to you only if it's shielded by your body, out of reach of a snatch-and-run thief. If a couple of people sit near you and begin to argue loudly, watch your gear.

Many of us enter a semihypnotized state as we enter the fascinating experiences of the day in our journals or share experiences with our friends via postcards. In that stuporous condition, we're as defenseless as a deer on the road staring at oncoming headlights. You needn't abandon your literary efforts. Just tuck your goodies out of sight.

When you're exchanging a large amount of money, write down the amount you want and show it to the clerk rather than announcing it to listening ears behind you. Put your money securely away before leaving the bank. Cornelia, a German botanist friend, exchanged some money, which she stuffed into her breast pocket as she walked down the steps of the bank. Quick as a trout striking a lure, a guy reached over her shoulder from behind and left her poorer but wiser.

A particular trick has become fairly common in Latin America, and sophisticated variations of it are achieving classic status around the world. In Mexico City, as I was making a very early morning walk to catch a bus, a middle-aged woman approached and pointed to my day pack. I looked over my shoulder and saw a patch of nasty-looking yellow goo on the side. She produced some toilet paper and offered to help me clean it. Not wanting to miss the bus, I decided to wait and clean it at the station. I thanked her and kept going. A block or two farther, a stocky man caught up with me and pointed. He too offered toilet paper. This apparently coincidental profusion of toilet paper registered even in my sluggish early-morning mind. I stepped away from him just as two young men emerged from the shadows and converged on me. I bolted for a nearby church. They followed me inside but stopped short of the front pew, where I was surrounded by people attending Mass. After a few minutes, the two drifted away to play their tricks elsewhere.

I mention this experience as an example of diversion. The goo had been lathered on my pack by someone trying to get me to stop, take it off my back, and perhaps even hand it to the Good Samaritan to clean. Within seconds, the wolves would have swooped down, and that pack would have had a new owner.

At an airport security checkpoint, you put your carry-on luggage (maybe including your laptop) on the moving belt to be scanned by the X-ray machine. If you then get held up, keep an eye on your gear as it comes out the other side. It's vulnerable to being snatched by someone heading out of the airport.

You'll know you're a seasoned traveler if, when a distraction occurs to your right, you look first to your left. The list on page 417 may seem pretty complete—but it's not. As you travel, you'll come across variations or even something new. I hope you'll pass them on to other travelers.

Muggers

Theft encountered by tourists is almost always nonviolent. In only a few places is theft by force common. Even though none of them is in Mexico or Central America, it's worth taking a moment to consider what to do.

How to Avoid the Problem

As always, preparation and common sense are your greatest protection. If you're new in town, ask the manager of your hotel about areas to avoid or times of day when risk might increase. Know what not to wear—including brand-new shoes or clothes in bright colors, a fanny pack, short shorts, or a tote bag bearing the name of a tour group. Might as well wear a "come and get me" sign.

Don't make yourself a target by having too much to drink too far from your hotel, wearing an expensive watch or ring, flashing wads of cash, or hanging around where people make you feel creepy. Pay attention to your intuition. Don't walk down dark streets. Take a taxi if you feel uncomfortable.

Don't act bewildered or lost. In other words, don't behave like a first-day tourist. Any mugger is going to choose the easiest- and wealthiest-looking target, and that's not the person striding along with an air of confidence or the person drinking his nightcap at the hotel.

If you feel that someone walking toward you looks suspicious, walk in another direction. Walk in the center of the sidewalk, away from alleyways and parked vehicles.

If a male traveler decides to woo a local woman he's met in a bar, he'd be wise to keep an eye on his drinks (among other things). Otherwise, he may meet some new friends on the way home.

A recent study indicated that just walking with one other person reduces the chances of being mugged by 70 percent. Walking with two people reduces the chances by 90 percent. Makes sense to me.

How to React

If you're walking in a high-risk zone and someone approaches seeking something (the time or whatever), step away and casually go to "yellow alert." That's a sad commentary on human relations, but a good way to avoid a problem.

Decide in advance how you'll respond if confronted by someone who looks as if he's armed or willing to use force. Stay as calm as you can. Try to make the other person relax a little. Act self-possessed, but don't argue or show anger. Cooperate and disengage as quickly as possible. The idea is to escape without violence. Depending on the situation, it may be best to drop or throw your wallet or jewelry or whatever on the ground, then back away. If the thief stoops to pick it up, run.

I've heard a suggestion to carry a second wallet with just a few dollars in it to surrender to a mugger. Maybe, but it's more important to decide whether you want to risk your life to protect anything you have with you.

If an assailant demands that you come with him, it's only to give him greater advantage. Do not go with him. Pretend you don't understand. Act as if you think he's joking. If that doesn't work, yell, throw your wallet, and run in the opposite direction.

If you feel you must fight, use every weapon you have: keys spread between your knuckles, a pen, a bottle—even a day pack loaded with books swings a lot of weight. Fight all out! Yell for help as loudly as you can. Shout, "Fire!" Bite, pull, try to break a finger, go for the genitals (a grip is better than a knee). Act as if you've gone crazy.

In very few places will someone threaten a traveler's personal safety unless the traveler

- takes foolish risks,
- gets involved with people of a type he would avoid at home,
- uses drugs or alcohol to excess in public,
- doesn't do his basic research and puts himself in places he should have avoided,
- loses his temper and provokes a confrontation,
- values his possessions too highly, protecting them by risking his safety, or
- behaves in ways inappropriate to the culture.

Hotel Security

You can learn a lot about hotel security before you walk through the door. Guidebooks sometimes note hotels that have reputations for poor security. Ask other travelers about the hotel you're considering. Notice whether people you wouldn't want to pass after dark are hanging out in front. A shabby lobby may be a clue that the owners make their money less by pleasing guests than by ripping them off.

> Ask other travelers about a hotel's security.

While checking in, keep in touch with your gear. When you look at a room, take your bag unless you're confident there's no risk in leaving it untended.

Because the hotel staff and other guests will see the register after you sign in, a woman is well advised to use initials.

Don't let anyone see your valuables as you check in.

An ordinary door lock is almost worthless for security purposes. What television bad guys do to locked doors with a credit card also happens in real life. Even if it bars the general public, the lock on your door won't keep the hotel staff out. One security expert estimates that 85 percent of hotel-room theft is committed by dishonest hotel employees. Besides, who knows how many room keys are floating around in the hands of former staff, or former guests for that matter?

If someone knocks on the door claiming to be a hotel employee, call the desk to confirm the person's identity if you have the slightest reason to be concerned.

I assume that someone will be in my room while I'm out and that I can't outsmart anyone but a thief-in-training by hiding my valuables in some cranny. Therefore, I lock in my pack anything I'd rather not lose. When I have reason for concern, I lock the pack itself to something secure. Fortunately, most hotel staff members, baggage handlers, bus drivers, and the like don't have lock-picking skills. Even a tiny lock requires forcible entry, which you can spot immediately, and many

> Assume someone will be in your room while you are out, and prepare accordingly.

people won't steal when they think you'll notice right away. Locks also communicate that you're not a goose passively waiting to be plucked.

For effective security in a hotel room, you need a dead bolt or a chain-and-slide bolt. Even a hasp on which you can use a padlock will work.

Some travelers carry a battery-operated alarm about the size of a pager that combines a detachable flashlight and alarm clock with a smoke detector and vibration sensor. If the door moves while this unit is hanging on a doorknob, an ear-piercing alarm goes off.

Radio Shack (**www.radioshack.com**) sells a combination personal alarm and motion detector. Improvements (**www.safetyzone.com**) offers a wide variety of travel-safety items. If you prefer a low-tech solution, jam a simple plastic wedge under the door, or brace a chair under the handle. If there's no way of securing the door, change rooms or hotels unless the circumstances convince you there is no risk.

A thief doesn't always politely enter a room from the hallway, so don't build a Maginot Line at the door only to forget the windows and balcony door. Can the windows be locked? Do they have bars? Could anyone get into your room by climbing through the window? If an arm can reach through the bars, keep your gear well out of reach. Lock the windows when you leave. If the hotel rises higher than two stories, a room on the third through sixth floors at least puts you above outside-entry thieves with a fear of heights.

Hotel smoke detectors are not universal in many parts of the world. If you leave the key in the lock when you go to sleep, you won't have to search for it if there's a fire. If you hear a fire alarm, touch the doorknob. If it's hot, call the desk, or see if you can escape out the window. If trapped in your room, use a wet towel to block the space under the door, shut off fans or air conditioners, and try to signal from the window. If the knob is cool, take your money belt, lock the door behind you (if you recall the little boy who cried, "Wolf!" you know there's not always fire where there's an alarm), and head for the fire exit. Don't try to use an elevator to escape from a fire. If there's smoke, crawl under it. When choosing your room, avoid the ground floor if it's accessible to bad guys. But choose a low floor in case of fire. And glance around to find the fire escape.

If there's a DO NOT DISTURB sign, I may hang it on the doorknob when I go out to mislead anyone wandering the hallway. I usually don't leave my room key with the desk clerk when I leave for the day. That won't keep the staff out of my room, but it does keep the presence of my key in the box from advertising to others that I'm away. It also keeps passersby from reaching across the counter and snatching the key in the clerk's absence. Key control is often a joke.

Make sure the safe truly is.

What about leaving your valuables in the hotel safe as you take off for several days of scuba diving? Good idea, except that not everything called a safe is what you think of as a safe. Be sure the safe is someplace secure to which only the owner or manager has access. Otherwise, the "safe" might turn out to be a desk drawer or a space under the cash-register drawer.

An Englishwoman I met gave most of her money to the obliging desk clerk to put in the hotel safe. When the day came to catch her flight, she went to reclaim her money. The clerk denied having received anything from her. The manager shrugged his shoulders. That's when she realized she had no receipt.

Present your valuables in a sealed envelope with your name written across the flap. A reliable safe-keeping operation should have a printed receipt form. If your hotel doesn't, get a written receipt from the manager or owner. If they try to avoid giving you one, don't leave your valuables. Think twice about staying in the place at all.

Suppose you want to leave your bag behind while you take a trek through the rain forest or take a side trip to the beach. Leave it with the hotel manager if you can, with instructions to release it only to you. Ask for a receipt. Find out if it will be locked up, rather than left behind the front desk day and night. Even in a storage room, I lock my bag to something with my bike chain lock. Because your belongings will be stored with those of other travelers, someone else may pick up something of yours if it's not secured. When you return, check the contents. When the hotel staff sees that you are treating the security of your bag seriously, it will be more inclined to do so as well.

Being anxious about safety and security would be a waste of time and detract from the pleasure of your trip. Instead, don your magic cloak. The routines become automatic. I've never lost a single item to a thief as I've traveled, and I believe most knowledgeable travelers can say the same.

LOSING YOUR VALUABLES

Lost Airline Ticket

Treat an airline ticket as if it were cash. If it leaves your possession unexpectedly, call or go to the nearest office of the issuing airline and submit a lost-ticket application. This process will be much easier if you know the ticket number, flight numbers and dates, and amount of the fare. Because few of us memorize this stuff, it helps to have a copy of the ticket along. It will cost you time and money if you have to call your travel agent to get this information.

One U.S. airline states on its ticket that it will give no refund for a lost ticket. Others charge a fee to determine whether your ticket has been used. If it has, you get nothing. If it hasn't, the ticket may be reinstated, or you may get a credit for the price, minus the search fee, against the price of a ticket for some future flight. However, you may be asked to sign a form agreeing to pay for the replacement ticket if someone uses the lost original. The message here is to act fast before someone can use or exchange the stolen ticket. Airlines typically wait 90 days or more before issuing a refund.

If you lose your ticket while overseas, you'll probably have to buy a new ticket for the rest of your route. That would be very bad news because you would lose whatever discount you got on the original ticket.

To avoid the whole problem, keep that ticket safe in your money belt, and keep a copy stashed somewhere else.

There's another way to protect yourself from loss and theft, of course. In North America, the electronic ticket is common. This option is not available with every foreign airline that serves Mexico and Central America, but it is offered by all U.S. carriers to that region.

Lost Credit Card or ATM Card

If a credit card disappears, call immediately to cancel it. When a card is stolen, report it to the police, and get a copy of the report. If fraudulent charges show up on your bill later, you must notify the card issuer in writing within 60 days of receiving the bill to limit your loss.

If your ATM card disappears, notify the issuing bank, and get a new card.

Lost Passport

According to *Money* magazine, 3 of every 1,000 travelers have their passports stolen. That doesn't count the ones who lose them in other creative ways. How to prevent it? Keep your passport in your money belt when it's not in use. If you have to let it out of your possession, such as when turning it over to a hotel clerk to register with the police, get a receipt. Never leave town without checking that you've tucked it safely away.

Because having a copy of the first two pages of the lost passport greatly speeds replacement, make three copies of those pages before leaving home. Put one in your money belt, put one in your luggage, and leave one with someone who can fax it to you.

Make copies of your passport to facilitate replacing it.

If you lose your passport, get a police report, and take it, along with four two-by-two-inch photographs, to your embassy or consulate. The embassy will require a copy of your birth certificate. If you haven't brought it along but have left a copy with someone who can fax it you, you're in great shape. If you overlooked that detail, the embassy may accept an affidavit from someone vouching for your citizenship. The replacement passport will be good for only one year, but when you arrive home, you can trade it in for a new permanent passport.

Lost Luggage

A traveler can lose luggage anywhere, but we most often put it out of our sight and control at the airport, trusting that it will rejoin us thousands of miles away, consistent with our implied contract with the airlines. Now that planes are loaded to near-capacity, and less carry-on luggage is allowed, the rate of loss has increased considerably. Many travelers are almost surprised when their luggage shows up at the correct time and place.

Prevention is always best: don't schedule connections that are too tight, check in well ahead of departure time, make sure your bags are marked with the correct destination (which means knowing the code letters and seeing the tag go on the bag), and remove old destination tags. Take off the shoulder strap and zip away the backpack harness so the bags won't get hung up in baggage-moving mechanisms. Watch your bags as far as you can to ensure that they are put on the right vehicle.

If you take a bag aboard a plane and there's no room for it, don't just hand it over to an attendant. Take out any valuables, then get a claim check for it. Be ready to collect it promptly at your destination.

Put your name, address, and telephone number on the bag. Consider using a holder with a flap that conceals that information from prying eyes. Store the same information inside the bag, along with a copy of your itinerary and instructions concerning how the airline can contact you en route. Indicate clearly where you want the bag to be sent, which may not be your home address.

Now that more checked bags are being opened for security reasons, pack valuables (such as a camera, jewelry, medications, etc.) in carry-on luggage.

Get to the carousel before the bags do, and stand near where they first appear. That way, you'll pick it up before a thief can. If an airline can track your bag to the carousel, it may deny your claim that a thief snatched it

Suppose the bag is not there. First in frustration at the long wait and then with mounting alarm, you search for it as other passengers drift away. Check the lobby area and baggage-storage room in case your bag arrived before you did. If it's not there, do not leave the airport. Go to the missing-luggage office. Try to calm down. Force a smile. Then discuss the situation with the agent (who is probably not the person who made your luggage disappear). Fill in a claim form describing the bag and its contents. If you made a copy of what's in the luggage (and kept it in your carry-on), or maybe even have a picture of the bag, this is the time to use them. Put the form and a copy of your ticket and baggage-claim check in the hands of the most senior person you can find. Get that person's name, and keep a copy of the form. If you give up your claim check, get a receipt. Get the correct phone numbers to call to check on your luggage.

Tell the agent that your name and address are on a luggage tag and that your itinerary is inside. Let that person know where to reach you while you're waiting for the bag and where to deliver it when it's found. Motivate them to find that bag.

It's not much consolation at the moment, but airlines have a method of tracking luggage and claim that 98 percent of lost luggage is ultimately recovered. Some also claim to know the location of Atlantis.

If the delay is more than a few hours, the airline should reimburse you for reasonable expenses, such as basic clothing and toiletries. If the carrier's representative doesn't offer to do so, ask for authorization before making purchases, but do so in a courteous tone that takes it for granted. Keep receipts as a basis for reimbursement. If the lost bag delays your onward progress, ask the carrier to pay for a hotel. After you leave the terminal, call with regular inquiries.

It's reasonable to think that if a carrier lost your bag and couldn't find it, it would pay for it and its contents. Reasonable, yes; realistic, no. Under regulations that the airlines were active in drafting, their liability to you is limited. On domestic flights, the maximum reimbursement for checked bags is $3,000 per person (including any carry-on luggage stored by a flight attendant). On international flights, different rules apply, depending on which airline it is. If it has ratified the Montreal Convention, compensation is limited to about $1,500. If the airline has not ratified the Montreal Convention, it will cap compensation at an absurdly low $9.07 per pound ($400 for carry-ons stored by flight attendants). In practice, rather than record the weight of each bag, those airlines assume the maximum (30 kilograms) and cap liability at $600.

The airlines also have a list of items they exclude from coverage, which may include currency, cameras, camcorders, expensive jewelry, and medication.

If your luggage and contents are worth significantly more, ask the airline in advance about excess-valuation insurance. The cost is about $2 per $100 of coverage, up to $5,000. Note that this insurance may also exclude things you want to cover, such as breakables, antiques, musical instruments, art, and computers.

Your homeowners insurance, personal-effects policy, or credit card may cover whatever loss the airline's insurance doesn't. Furthermore, that reimbursement may be based on replacement value, which is in your favor. Please see the Travel Insurance section in Chapter 7, Going into Action.

Even when it's clear a bag has departed for luggage heaven, the airline may still take 3 to 12 weeks to reimburse you. Again, carry your valuables in your money belt, your camera in your day pack, and nothing irreplaceable in your checked luggage.

If you're not satisfied with what the airline offers, you can complain to the Consumer Protection Division of the Department of Transportation (call [202] 366-2220, or see **www.dot.gov**).

And if that's not depressing enough, go to **www.unclaimedbaggage.com,** where you can buy the contents of everyone else's lost bags.

CHAPTER 18

Woman on Her Own

> All travel is a quest, conscious or
> unconscious, searching for something
> that is lacking in our lives or ourselves.
> —Freya Stark

Some women won't travel on their own because they are concerned about harassment or assault. It's a fear with some basis, but, in the opinion of many female travelers, it needn't keep anyone at home. Mexico and Central America are not among the worst in the world in terms of being hassled but, unfortunately, women travelers are not free from risk there either.

Most women travel in groups of two or three, but many travel solo. Because knowledge routs fear and controls risk, this chapter discusses how a woman alone or with other women can minimize or eliminate potential safety problems.

The most common problem a woman may have is low-grade sexual harassment. The hassling may consist of a suggestive comment, a call, a whistle, a touch, or more aggressive intimidation—anything to test the woman's response.

There seems to be a relationship between offensive male behavior and generally unrealistic attitudes about relationships with women. In some cultures, men are raised with the idea that women are subordinate; women are expected to bend to the male will. Trash television has further shaped male attitudes about women, especially when they see foreign women act in ways that would result in ostracism in their own society. Soap operas don't do female travelers any favors. With this misinformation, some men feel it's their right to make advances, and they expect them to be welcomed. These attitudes are diminishing, but they're not gone.

And what about concerns about bodily harm? Statistics show that rape is far more common in industrialized nations, such as the United States, than in less developed countries. However, that's a little misleading. A female traveler is more visible than local women, on whom the statistics are based, and she's likely to be penalized by attitudes of local men toward women from developed countries. Furthermore, when a woman is in an unfamiliar culture, she may be unaware that certain behavior may be taken as provocative by local men. She's also likely to be less knowledgeable about dangerous areas she should avoid. So don't rely on statistics. So stay safe by educating yourself and trusting your instincts.

HOW TO TRAVEL SAFELY

A woman can do many things to deflect unwanted attention. Here are some suggestions, many from women who have traveled alone.

- Observe how local women dress, and imitate them. In cultures that retain old traditions, a local woman covers most of her body and tends to stay out of public view. In that context, a female traveler who wears tight shorts and a provocative T-shirt will quickly become conscious of the effect she's having, attracting some observers and offending others. Loose-fitting clothing that covers arms and legs is usually appropriate. It's easy to copy local customs, even without wearing local-style clothes.

- Consider not wearing brand-new tennies or shirts that feature a university or a team—they scream "tourist." And, naturally, wear little or no jewelry (not even clever fakes).

- Minimize eye contact with men. If a friendly smile can be misinterpreted, a wink can start a war. Dark sunglasses are good to have.

- If a man comes up to you on the street and asks a question, or asks you to make change, or whatever, shake your head, and keep walking.

- Common courtesies such as thanking a man for opening a door for you can lead to your being followed. An impassive nod may have to suffice.

- Pay your own way so the other person doesn't feel you are indebted.

- Drinking alcohol or smoking cigarettes in public may be considered provocative. It's not a question of right or wrong; it's a case of "when in Rome . . . ."

- Many women connect with other women travelers when passing through a zone of possible annoyance. Others ask a man to accompany them for a while, being up front about the reason. A show of a relationship discourages unwelcome attention, even more abroad than at home. An imaginary boyfriend or husband who is "on his way over" can help.

- Don't let a strange man touch you, except during a handshake or when giving help you've requested. An apparently neutral touch may be a way of testing your limits. A man may take advantage of a crowded place to press against a woman in an offensive way. The consensus is that she should raise hell, pushing him away with a shout. At the same time, be prepared to accept being squashed in a crowd as part of travel.

- If a man forces his attentions on you, don't just shake your head, smile, or say "No, thank you." Rather than behaving in an apologetic way, respond immediately and directly, saying "No!" or "Stop!" loudly and firmly, preferably in the local language. Frown fiercely and let bystanders know there's a problem, calling on them for help if necessary. Your plea should be addressed to one person (another woman is best) rather than to the crowd. Tears help engage bystanders. Blow a whistle. Being firm and determined is better than being rough or violent.

- When you arrive in a new town, ask the desk clerk, manager, or owner of your lodging to identify parts of town to avoid. Ask about restaurants where a woman traveler will feel comfortable. At the same time, be cautious not to let a male member of the hotel staff think you are flirting.
- A woman traveler I met in Malta had just left Barcelona following a nasty experience. After a few glasses of wine, she had left her waterfront hotel about midnight and had taken a solo walk along the beach in the moonlight. Faster than you can say, "She did what?" she'd been knocked roughly to the sand and robbed, losing passport, credit cards, and cash. That wouldn't have happened if she'd kept her valuables in the hotel safe, in a money belt, or at least locked in her luggage. Then there's the part about taking a solo walk on the beach at midnight.

A diner's friend waits his turn, Lake Atitlán, Guatemala

- In restaurants, reading a book or writing in a journal helps discourage men from approaching.
- Keep your hotel-room door locked. Otherwise, in some places, staff people with legitimate business walk right in. Don't admit anyone into your room until you're satisfied about who they are. Be alert when a male member of the hotel staff enters your room. Stand up. Let your body language show that you're on guard. Watch him. If a problem develops, call the front desk. If there's no phone, step into the hall and shout.
- Don't accept gifts from strangers. That sounds obvious, but some offers may be appealing, such as snorkeling, hiking, or surfing trips, or some other local adventure.

Luanna met an attractive young local man at a restaurant in a beach resort. Despite being a veteran traveler who had just completed two years in the Peace Corps, she accepted his offer to spend the day with him on his small sailboat. She was cautious enough to insist that they not go alone. "No problem," he said. "My mother lives in a village just down the coast. We'll sail there and pick her up." No village. No mother. Bad trip! If you feel a need for a chaperone, start the trip with one. Don't be lured beyond the range of help.

- On trains, try to find a compartment occupied by a family or several women.
- On buses, sit next to a woman rather than a man.
- Be aware that beaches tend to attract men who may become a problem.
- If something in the environment is making you feel uncomfortable, hire a taxi instead of walking.
- Some women travel with a fake wedding ring. If a conversation becomes overly personal, they refer to an imaginary husband, perhaps producing a photograph to back up the story. Note that an expensive-looking ring could present temptation of a different kind.
- If a situation is becoming uncomfortable, mention that you have a specific communicable venereal disease.
- I've yet to meet anyone who has used Mace, but it may offer a feeling of security in an extreme situation. Just don't try to take it onto an airplane.
- Don't be drawn into discussion of controversial topics, especially male–female relations.
- Be wary of any local lothario who prowls around tourist attractions. He's experienced in approaching foreign women and has had plenty of opportunities to develop his line. He may say he wants a chance to practice his English, or he may pretend to be a guide—anything to get you into a conversation. If you don't want his attention, don't answer even the first question.
- Study self-defense before leaving home. The self-confidence you project as a result of this training sends a signal.
- Please review Chapter 17, Safety and Security.

Resources

As a starting point for learning the extent to which women may be hassled in a specific country, consult a guidebook and ask other travelers. *Women Travel: Adventures, Advice, and Experience,* edited by Miranda Davies and Natania Jansz, discusses comparative levels of potential sexual harassment in 70 countries. One of Thalia Zepatos's objectives in writing *A Journey of One's Own: Uncommon Advice for the Independent Woman Traveler* was to help women feel more confident about traveling on their own.

Many excellent books have been written by and about woman travelers. Some are inspiring. Consider contemporary writers such as Marybeth Bond (*A Woman's Passion for Travel, Gutsy Women*) Jean Gould, Pam Houston, Frances Mayes, Sonia Melchett, Mary Morris (*Nothing to Declare: Memoirs of a Woman Traveling Alone* and others), Dervla Murphy (*Full Tilt: Ireland to India with a Bicycle* and others), and Jane Robinson (*Wayward Women*).

Other useful resources for women travelers include Journeywoman, a Web site for women travelers (**www.journeywoman.com**) and The Women's Travel Club (**www.womenstravelclub.com**).

Here are few other useful Web sites, some for advice, some for links:

- Her Own Way: A Woman's Guide to Safe and Successful Travel
  www.voyage.gc.ca/main/pubs/her_own_way-en.asp
- Top Tips for Women Travelers (Canadian, with many good links)
  studenttravel.about.com/od/womenstudenttravelers/a/womentips.htm
- Tips for women travellers (Australian)
  www.smartraveller.gov.au/tips/womtrav.html
- Travel Safety Tips for Women (by a detective)
  www.kevincoffee.com/women_safety/travel_safety_tips_for_women.htm
- Women Travellers (from the UK)
  www.fco.gov.uk/servlet/Front?pagename=OpenMarket/Xcelerate/Show Page&c=Page&cid=1098377409567
- Graffiti Wall: Women Travelers (practical tips from women travelers)
  www.ricksteves.com/graffiti/graffiti4.html

If a woman chooses not to be offended by stares, whistles, and comments, she can keep that kind of obnoxious behavior from spoiling a trip. A few women travelers I know recall exasperation and even anger at being made the center of attention when they wanted to be left alone. The majority, however, have felt safe and relaxed throughout their journeys.

Be informed. Be a little cautious. Keep perspective, and trust your judgment.

CHAPTER 19

Language

The treachery of the phrase book . . . is that you
cannot begin to follow the answer to the question
you've pronounced so beautifully.
—Pico Iyer,
"Excusez-Moi! Speakez-Vous Franglais?,"
Time (1990)

You may ask, "How can I travel in Latin America if I don't speak one word of Spanish?" Sure, it's helpful to speak Spanish, but if you can stumble through a few simple sentences and read some key words, you can manage fine. Still, some language homework will make your travels a lot easier.

On occasion I've been caught somewhere in the world with no vocabulary, no dictionary, no phrase book—nothing. Coming from the airport, a taxi dropped me off in front of a new shopping mall in Gaborone, the capital of Botswana. I looked around for the only hotel in town listed in the guidebook as charging less than 70 pula, about $40, per night. (I like the fact that the name of the currency in Botswana, which is 85 percent desert, is also the word for "water.") No hotel in sight. I didn't know how to say anything in the Setswana language, but it was time to ask for help.

Using gestures, I learned from a helpful soldier that the hotel had been torn down to make room for the shopping mall. The soldier pointed vigorously down the road. Always hopeful, I decided that he might be indicating another hotel. Of course, he was also pointing toward South Africa. There being no public transportation in sight and no other source of information, I swung my pack onto my back and started down the road.

Twenty minutes later, I arrived at a sleazy roadhouse. That the DISCO sign dwarfed the ROOMS 65 PULA sign communicated the management's priorities. After some spirited sign language to convey the thought that I was more interested in sleeping than dancing the night away, I was taken to a room modeled after a Devil's Island original. I figured the mosquito coils and the aerosol-bug-spray cans in the room would probably be needed since the cow standing outside the window had pushed her head into the room through the screen. Nevertheless, I had overcome a language barrier.

HOW TO OVERCOME A LANGUAGE BARRIER

Learning to pronounce 20 to 100 words will get you through anywhere. Even a dozen words, an expressive face, and two hands go a long way.

In vast reaches of the world, you'll encounter English, Spanish, French, or Arabic. Traveling in Mexico and Central America is a treat because Spanish, the most common language, is melodious and easy to learn.

Given the limited language skills of many American and Canadian travelers, it's fortunate for us that the English planted their flag as widely as they did a few centuries ago. Because English is spoken in varying degrees around the world, at least for a few meters on either side of the tourist trails, you can often get by without learning anything else. But there's no reason to do that. In return for a little linguistic effort, you can make more friends and fewer mistakes. The first step is to overcome the embarrassment of stumbling in a language strange to your ears.

> Into the face of the young man who sat on the terrace of the Hotel Magnifique at Cannes there had crept a look of furtive shame, the shifty, hangdog look which announces that an Englishman is about to talk French.
> —P. G. Wodehouse, *The Luck of the Bodkins* (1935)

People like to hear you speaking their language, and it helps make you feel a part of the country. There's a nice sense of accomplishment when you master some of the basics of the language. (Well, "master" may be overstating it a bit.)

How to Learn

The choice of strategies for learning depends on your objective. If it's to become fluent, then you follow one course of action. If it's to get by and learn as you travel, you take a very different path.

Let's start with learning enough of a language to meet a traveler's needs:

- Enroll in a high-school or college language lab, or hire a tutor.
- Ask the foreign-student office at a community college or university to connect you with someone willing to teach you language basics.
- Teach yourself from a good language book. Passport Books' *Just Enough* series is one of the best. Portable dictionaries are good. Take a look at the very useful BBC Phrase Books, with built-in dictionaries. *Easy Spanish Phrase Book* (Dover), inexpensive and compact, is very good for beginners. When you're ready, consider *501 Spanish Verbs*. In addition to bookstores and the Internet, your local library can be a good source.
- The better guidebooks include basic vocabulary and phrases.
- Laminated cards (from flash-card size up to four by eight inches) provide frequently used words and phrases in a handy, very lightweight form.
- In addition to being helpful, handheld electronic translators endlessly entertain bystanders.

- Check out language tapes, audio and video, from your library.
- An old favorite of mine, the *Traveler's Pictorial Communication Guide*, is packed with illustrations of clothing, menu items, lodging, transport, various services (for example, haircuts and medical help), and many other aspects of daily life. You point to the picture, and the idea gets across. *The Wordless Travel Book: Point at These Pictures to Communicate with Anyone* uses the same excellent concept.
- Use translation sites on the Web, such as **www.babelfish.altavista.com, www.freetranslation.com, www.google.com/translate, www.wordreference.com,** and **www.spanishdict.com.**
- If you're using Microsoft Word on a PC, you may have a built-in translation capacity. In Word 2007 or 2003, just right-click on a word or sentence, and "Translate" will be one of the menu options.

> People like to hear you speak their language.

Pronouncing words as you would in your own language may not be correct in another language. With respect to pronunciation, reading alone is not nearly enough. Listen to the language spoken on cassettes or videotapes. Let your computer search for audio-phrase-book CDs. The *Latin-American Spanish Phrase Book* in the Eyewitness Travel Pack series comes with a CD. Some swear by Rosetta Stone CDs (**www.rosettastone.com**), which permit you to listen to phrases accompanied by pictures and to speak into a microphone to hear how you're doing (but they're in the neighborhood of $200). As you progress through writing, listening, and speaking exercises, the clever program will grade you. Others prefer the Pimsleur Method (**www.pimsleurdirect.com**), which doesn't teach reading or writing. Instead, it's based on listening, comprehending, and responding, which are what you need most while traveling. Since it is audio only (on CDs or computer memory chips), it's handy to use while driving. And visit Foreign Languages for Travelers: **www.travlang.com/languages.**

Other possibilities:

- "Learn Spanish Now!" is a very good software program by Transparent Language (**www.transparent.com**) that allows you to adjust the speed of conversation. Other comprehensive foreign-language software programs are available, but they're expensive and, to my mind, overkill for a traveler's needs.
- Listening to radio stations in Spanish (or whatever language you want to learn) helps some people, but the hyperfast talk defeats most, including me. It's easier to learn from foreign-language music and movies from the library.
- The Spanish-language version of CNN is another resource (**www.cnnespanol.com**).
- Another Web site to check is **www.studyspanish.com.**
- Learn on the road. As soon as you enter a new country, make a list of

useful words—the words of courtesy and daily commerce. Point to things and ask questions. Practice that new vocabulary out loud. Don't let fear of mistakes slow you down, and don't worry about verb tenses.

Now let's consider the goal of fluency, say for purposes of education or employment. Certainly for people in international business, fluency in a second or third language is a requirement for communication and for understanding a culture.

- Check out international cultural-exchange programs through the American Institute for Foreign Study (**www.aifs.com**). Gather information from the National Registration Center for Study Abroad about schools abroad offering language classes (**www.nrcsa.com**), including many in Latin America.
- AmeriSpan Study Abroad (**www.amerispan.com**) can connect you with reasonably priced language programs in many countries. AmeriSpan offers Spanish courses at, for example, the highly regarded Instituto Cultural de Oaxaca. Also, the Centro Pan Americano de Idiomas in Monteverde, Costa Rica, and Casa de Lenguas in Antigua, Guatemala. The Central American Spanish School in La Ceiba, Honduras, has also been given high marks.
- Real fluency comes from immersion in a language and culture. Immersion can take the form, for example, of spending four months in the beautiful towns of San Miguel de Allende, Mexico, or Antigua, Guatemala, living with a local family and working with a personal tutor half of each day. Cost: perhaps $4,000 total. Many recommend the Instituto Cultural de Oaxaca (**www.icomexico.com**) in Oaxaca, Mexico (see above), for small-group classes. The same holds for the Centro Pan Americano de Idiomas (**www.cpi-edu.com**) in Costa Rica (homestays and very small classes) or programs arranged by the Adventure Education Center (**www.adventurespanishschool.com**), also in Costa Rica, and the Central American Spanish School in Honduras (**www.ca-spanish.com**), where students can stay with a host family.
- Enroll in a Mexico City university that offers courses taught in English and immerse yourself in the local lifestyle.
- Take a part-time job in a foreign country to practice your Spanish.
- Volunteer to teach one of your skills, maybe even English, in a foreign country.

What the Traveler Needs to Learn First

Here are some key words and phrases that every traveler needs to know. It helps to write them down or memorize them.

- Greetings and expressions of courtesy, such as "hello," "good day," "good-bye," "please," "thank you," "pardon me," "my name is . . . ," and "what is your name?"

- "Yes" and "no"
- Directions. Few phrases are as useful as "where is . . . ?"
- The word for *toilet*. If you ask for the washroom, bathroom, restroom, or little boy's or girl's room, you may mystify the listener.
- Food-related phrases (including "may I have the bill, please?")
- Lodging-related phrases (such as "Do you have a room with two beds?")
- Transport words, including *airport, bus station, train station, subway station,* and *gasoline*
- Phrases for bargaining in the marketplace, such as "How much is . . . ?" and "That's too much"
- Personal pronouns
- Numbers
- Words for the time of day
- The verbs *to be, to have,* and *to go,* combined with personal pronouns ("I am," "he is," etc.)
- Pleas for help, such as "I don't understand," "please speak more slowly," "stop," "help," "go away," and "I need a doctor"

There are some sure tests to show whether you've become operational in a language. If the bus to your destination is leaving a busy station in ten minutes, and you can buy a ticket and find the bus in time, you're a linguist. When you can make small jokes in a language, you're a linguist.

WHERE TO GET INFORMATION AND HELP

If your trusty phrase book fails you, it's a setback, nothing more. It merely means it's time to get some help. That's easy if you know where to look.

- Look for young people, on the theory they might be students studying English.
- Expensive or Western clothing suggests that a person may be well educated or in business, either of which may mean some training in English.
- Many countries have excellent tourist-information centers whose addresses are listed in good guidebooks. In most countries, someone on the staff speaks at least a little English.
- Talk with local travel agents to find out what's going on in the area and what the transportation options are. Let them know what you want, and ask for suggestions. It always seems that, for only a few dollars, someone's cousin's son is willing to give you a lift to where you want to go the next morning.
- Your embassy or consulate can help. A considerate staff person in the Citizens Service section may give you useful information on a person-to-person basis.

- The staff at your hotel can provide helpful information, especially if you develop a friendly relationship with them. They can direct you to banks, shops, doctors, tourist attractions, and restaurants, or find you a cab, opera tickets, a boat for your snorkeling trip, or even a mountain guide. They can tell you fair prices for local transport, popular types of clothing, and almost anything else. Of course, price information should be taken with a grain of salt because it may be biased toward the home team. If your own hotel can't help, try an upscale or chain hotel. Either the staff will be able to communicate in your language, or there will be a travel agent in-house who can.
- Draw on other travelers. When you meet someone who has recently visited a coming stop on your itinerary, ask about accommodations, restaurants, transport, exchange rates, everything.
- The corollary to seeking assistance from others is that you should take time to give information to others. It's one of the karmic laws of traveling.

WHEN SPEAKING ENGLISH

Speaking English in countries where it's not the primary language has made me more aware of its complex and confusing structure. If your local vocabulary isn't getting the job done, and you need to try English, tailor it to the situation.

- It's not condescending to use short words when speaking English to someone for whom it is a second or third language. Pronounce words clearly, and speak in short sentences. Make one point at a time. Gentle repetition is fine.
- Speak slowly but not so deliberately that it sounds patronizing.
- If phrasing a sentence one way doesn't work, try it a different way.
- Use expressions in your language that are similar to ones used in the local language.
- Use plenty of gestures.
- Contractions, slang, idioms, jargon, and abbreviations don't translate well.
- Watch the listener's eyes to see if he or she is following what you're saying. Ask whether you are being understood.
- Avoid raising your voice as if speaking to a child who is hard of hearing.
- Never mimic the accent of local people speaking English.
- Be polite and patient, and take responsibility for your own shortcomings in speaking the local language.

HOW TO ASK QUESTIONS

When language is an issue, a traveler must learn the art of asking questions in ways that elicit helpful answers. Otherwise, good-hearted people are likely to give you an answer intended to please you, even if they have to guess what that might be.

Approach with a smile. Hold your hands in sight, and let your body language convey a peaceful, friendly intent. Don't be aloof or demanding. If all this sounds obvious, remember that the other person may be smaller than you and uncertain of what to expect.

Begin a question by saying "good day" or "pardon me" rather than impolitely intruding with your desire to get an answer.

If you have no language in common, think of yourself as a preacher who has lost his tongue or a writer whose commandment is "show, don't tell." Use your hands, paper and pen, even the dust at your feet. Perform your question. Build a picture of what you want.

Avoid asking questions that imply the answer, especially when asking directions. Avoid questions that can be answered by "yes" or "no." Questions such as, "Is the train station down that street?" or, "Does the train leave at eight o'clock?" contain the seeds of disaster. The local person, only partially understanding, is likely to nod affirmatively or even say, "Yes," when there may not even be a train. Instead, say, "Where is the station?" and then, "What time does the train leave?"

If you lack confidence in an answer, follow up with a contradictory question. If a person has pointed to the left to indicate the direction of the train station, ask, "Is the train station that way (pointing some other direction)?" Whatever the next answer, it will tell you something.

A map does wonders to overcome pronunciation difficulties. If you have a guidebook or map with the name of your destination, show it to the other person.

Rob is confronted by a puzzling prohibition.

When Translation Isn't

As a reminder of the significance of nuance, here are a few of the many signs, apparently in English, that may make you smile as you travel:

- "The manager has personally passed all the water served here" (at an Acapulco hotel).
- "Because of the impropriety of entertaining guests of the opposite sex in the bedroom, it is suggested that the lobby be used for this purpose" (at a Zurich hotel).
- "Ladies are requested not to have children in the bar" (at a Norwegian cocktail lounge).
- "Please leave your values at the front desk" (at a Paris hotel).
- "Please take advantage of the chambermaid" (at a Japanese hotel).
- "Our wines leave you nothing to hope for" (at a Swiss restaurant).
- "If this is your first visit to the USSR, you are welcome to it."
- "Welcome! Don't enter!" (in Taiwan).
- "Specialist in women and other diseases" (at a Rome doctor's office).
- "Fur coats made for ladies from their own skin" (at a Swedish furrier).
- "Is forbidden to steal hotel towels please. If you are not a person to do such thing is easier not to read notis. Please do bathe inside the tub" (at a Tokyo hotel).
- "Drop your trousers here for the best results" (at a Bangkok laundry).
- "Ladies, leave your clothes here and spend the afternoon having a good time" (at a Rome laundry).
- "Order you summers suit. Because is big rush, we will execute customers in strict rotation" (at a tailor shop in Rhodes).
- "In face of dog, please walk back with slow. This dog are friendly with you. Only bark. Never harm before you" (on a Thai garden gate).
- A breakfast menu in India offered me "stress lemin, juices tin, tasty cult lates, choice omelet, con flakes, paper poasted, solid curmel custid." On top of all that, it promised to bring "bad tea" to my room.
- Then there's the sign in the lobby of the Jambo Inn in Dar es Salaam: "Women of immortal turpitude are strictly not allowed any room." It's true. I saw it every evening as I headed upstairs.

Always be patient. The person with whom you're talking doesn't exist merely to answer your questions. She wants to help, and she's doing you a favor. She's not ignorant and speaks her language well. It's your language she's having trouble with or your pronunciation of her language. Let her answer in her own way, and never imply that the difficulty is somehow her fault.

The bottom line: the language "barrier" is only a speed bump.

CHAPTER 20

Transportation

Going from point to point in other countries,
one follows a thin line of road, railway, or river,
leaving wide tracts unexplored on either side.
—Amelia B. Edwards
A Thousand Miles Up the Nile (1878)

There's the local joke that goes, "What's the maximum capacity of a Guatemalan bus?" The smiling answer: "One more."

The variety of transportation available in Mexico and Central America is not nearly as sedate as what you find from California to Maine. On the other hand, it's not nearly as challenging as what you find in, say, India. So, in this chapter we'll look at transportation in Mexico and Central America and at the wondrous variety in the rest of the world as well.

Transportation is such a neutral word. It suggests nothing of the amazing variety of methods we humans have devised to get ourselves from one place to another. The cautious traveler who restricts his movements to taxi or tour bus misses some of the richest experiences of travel. Picture yourself in Provence, France, drifting along a quiet river bordered by vineyards, or aboard a scraggly, spitting camel lurching along the dusty road to the airport in Varanasi, India, or swaying toward a Thai hill-tribe village while balanced on a crusty elephant back. Or imagine relaxing in a stately Austin Fairway taxi as you head for a gin and tonic in the faded luxury of Nairobi's Norfolk Hotel.

Fly into the heart of Africa's Okavango Delta in a five-passenger Cessna flown by a bush pilot with a beard so massive it obscures all but his eyes, then gingerly climb into a hollowed-out log canoe to glide along waterways lined with attentive crocodiles. Perch on bulging sacks of grain as a water-buffalo cart carries you down dusty Nepalese roads in sight of the Himalayas. Roll through the Indonesian hill town of Tomohon in a two-wheeled surrey called a *bendi,* soothed by the cloppity-clop of hooves on cobblestones. Settle back in a 25-foot outrigger canoe sailing from Manado, Indonesia, for a 10-mile voyage to some of the best snorkeling in the world.

Here's a fundamental truth: transport in the rest of the world is very different from what we're used to at home. It's far more than crossing space; it's part of the essence of travel.

Although transport in less developed countries is often picturesque, it's not always comfortable. Travelers love to tell stories about agonizing overnighters

> Your road is everything that a road ought to be . . . and yet you will not stay on it for half a mile, for the reason that little, mysterious roads are always branching out from it on either hand, and as these curve sharply also and hide what is beyond, you cannot resist the temptation to desert your chosen road and explore them. —Mark Twain, "Some Rambling Notes of an Idle Excursion" (1877)

on third-class, hard-seat trains. On some local buses, blaring music, lack of legroom, and animals pecking at your toes are pretty standard. If there's too much character and too little comfort, paying more will make any trip easier. There's always a veneer of upscale transport in which passengers are sheltered from the hurly-burly of the environment.

Taking local transport means talking with people, seeing the countryside close at hand, and discovering unexpected adventures. Even when things don't go quite right, it always works out if you remember that "the trip is the trip." Travel is more than destinations.

TRAVELING BY AIR

At home, we can choose among many airlines on the basis of ticket price, departure times, and destinations. Flying in Europe is similar, but in most of the rest of the world, it is quite different. Because there are fewer choices, you may have to take whatever flight you can get. In many countries, airlines have few planes, visit some destinations only infrequently, and customarily fly with all seats occupied. (For more on air travel, please also see Chapter 7, Going into Action—Airline Tickets, and Chapter 8, How to Save Money—Airfare).

How Safe Is It?

Most airlines keep their planes well maintained and provide great service; some do not. Flying on international airlines such as Thai Airways, Air New Zealand, and Singapore Airlines is a real treat. On an Air Madagascar flight from Antananarivo to Nairobi, the flight attendant appeared in the coach section bearing smoked kingfish, veal, Camembert with baguettes, a crisp white Bordeaux, and Taittinger Champagne.

In contrast, on my first flight on CAAC, the name of the Chinese national airline in the 1980s (now Air China), the pilot cranked the engines, and the passenger cabin immediately filled with dense, blue-gray smoke. When the attendants didn't even take notice, I realized it must be a common occurrence. In the early 1990s, the Chinese government licensed dozens of new airlines to serve newly mobile masses.

Aeroflot, the old Soviet carrier and once the largest airline in the world, never won a warm place in anyone's heart. Before 1994, its fatal-accident rate was among the worst of all major airlines. On flights that made it, service was atrocious. It's hard to believe, but the situation deteriorated after Aeroflot was split up among the former Soviet republics. Maintenance and air-traffic control systems are more stressed, planes are overloaded, and pilots are poorly trained.

So many of the old Aeroflot planes are being operated beyond their intended lifetimes that the U.S. State Department instructed its staff to avoid flying on domestic Russian airlines.

In Central America, some travelers avoid flights on local airlines in Belize, Honduras, and Nicaragua because they have from time to time been banned from landing in the United States. Some small airlines from El Salvador and Guatemala are allowed to land but are on probation.

To put flight risk into perspective, the Federal Aviation Administration reported the "death risk per flight" as 1 in 200,000 for Aeroflot, 1 in 1.5 million for Air Canada, 1 in 3 million for British Airways, 1 in 20 million for El Al, and zero for Singapore Airlines. Compare these odds with findings at the University of California, Berkeley, that odds of death from a coast-to-coast automobile trip are 1 in 14,000, from a bicycle accident 1 in 88,000, and from lightning 1 in 1.9 million. In the United States, roughly 95 people are killed each year in plane crashes. Compare that with 112 people killed each *day* in auto accidents. Overall, the odds of death from a commercial airline accident are put at 1 in 10 million.

Nevertheless, it's worth paying attention to those monotonous instructions the flight attendants recite at the beginning of each flight, at least when they point out where the nearest exits are. A smiling attendant for Southwest Airlines introduced himself and the other three attendants by name, and then recited the familiar information. As usual, he was ignored. At the end, he held up a $100 bill and said, "I'll give this to the first person who can tell me our first names." No one got that $100—but I'll bet every one of those passengers pays more attention to the instructions when they fly Southwest in the future.

> The sooner you are there, the sooner you find out how long you will be delayed.
> —Shelley Berman

Nuts and Bolts of International Air Travel

To make international air travel a happy experience (if that's still possible), a traveler should realize that the ground rules are different from those of domestic air travel. This is important because the inconvenience of a missed flight or lost luggage is much greater in a faraway place.

Buying Your Ticket

- Make reservations further ahead of departure than you may be used to.
- Check your ticket to see that it is correct. It's risky to take accuracy for granted when the ticket includes several flights, countries, and airlines.
- If an airline permits seat selection in advance of the flight, you're better off making an informed seat selection before arriving at the airport. For one thing, having an assigned seat reduces your vulnerability if the airline

overbooks the flight. Obviously, you also want a seat that suits your preferences. If two people traveling together select an aisle seat and a window seat, there's a chance that the middle seat will not be assigned. If it is, it's easy to arrange a switch. On the other hand, if you book seats next to one another, leaving an aisle or window seat vacant, it's likely to be assigned to someone else. Keeping that middle seat empty adds a lot of comfort to a long trip.

> No one seemed alarmed, so I practiced breathing evenly and holding up the airplane by the armrests.
> —Frances Mayes, *Under the Tuscan Sun* (1997)

If you crave a view, ask the agent to look at the seating configuration for the plane on which you'll be flying and assign you a window seat that is not over the wing. If the agent doesn't look at the configuration, he or she may be guessing, and you may wind up staring at shiny sheet metal for several hours.

On most planes, the best legroom comes with the front seats (just behind the bulkhead) and the exit-row seats. Sometimes bulkhead seats are held for unexpected handicapped passengers, families with children, or airline personnel. If one is empty when the cabin door closes, I leap for it, sometimes after checking with the flight attendant. The trade-off is reduced storage space and an oblique view of the movie screen (the latter is seldom much of a loss). Seats in the midcabin exit row also have extra legroom, and the seats in the row ahead may not recline, another blessing. These seats are almost always assigned only at the airport. My first stop at the airport is to try to reserve an exit-row seat.

To decide what seat number you want, check **www.frequentflyer.oag.com** or **www.seatguru.com,** both of which show seat configurations for various airlines (although not many foreign airlines). In addition, the Web sites of many airlines also show seat configurations.

- If your flight includes an actual meal (in contrast to the common faux meals), and you have a preference such as vegetarian, low-calorie, low-sodium, diabetic, religious, or children's, place your order when you buy the ticket.
- Being waitlisted on a flight overseas is definitely not the equivalent of having a reservation. If you're given a high number, forget it unless providence intervenes—but you may be able to give providence a jump start. If circumstances warrant, ask whether a small additional payment might help you move up the wait list. In Manila, I engaged a travel agent, for a small fee, who got me moved from number 37 on the wait list to a seat on the plane ten minutes before departure. He said he reminded the clerk that, as a foreigner, I would be paying in hard currency. There may even have been a more personal, microeconomic explanation for my good

fortune; who knows? Take it for granted that others on the wait list will also be invoking providence on their behalf.

- Do not accept a proposed itinerary that includes a change of plane along the way but does not allow enough time to connect. The time needed depends on several factors, all outside your control. If an online booking site will permit a 45-minute layover, I won't take it. Check with an airline agent, or allot yourself an hour and a half.

- Confirm and reconfirm flight reservations overseas. Fail to confirm, and your paid-for ticket may be canceled. You may get your money back someday, but in the meantime you'll be standing on the ground growling as you watch the once-a-week flight leave without you. If the ticket doesn't tell you when to confirm, do so at least three days (72 hours) before the flight. It's sometimes worth dropping by the ticket office on the day of the flight before going to the airport to ensure that departure time hasn't changed—or that the flight hasn't been canceled.

Arriving at the Airport

There's no longer a uniform way to know for sure how long ahead of the flight you need to present yourself to the airline's airport counter. The lead time differs from airport to airport, affected by peak traffic times, delays due to security inspections, and various "X" factors. Thus, you must ask each time. Call the airlines, and don't accept someone's guess.

Remember that the trip starts not at the airport, but at your home, hotel, or whatever your starting point. Do the checkout paperwork the night before if it's practical. If you're leaving from a large city, anticipate traffic accidents, breakdowns, and gridlock—expect the unpredictable. Allow twice as much time to get to the airport as you think you need.

I have a friend whose taxi was immobilized in downtown Bangkok traffic for so long that the driver fell asleep. In Gaborone, Botswana, the taxi driver who promised to pick me up at my hotel at 6:30 a.m. never showed. I barely made that flight by hitching a ride in the back of a pickup truck. In Calcutta, I walked out to the street at 7:30 a.m. with plenty of time to catch a taxi to Dum Dum Airport. That's when I discovered a general transportation strike had started at 7 a.m. I finally found a private "pirate car" willing to risk running a possible bus drivers' blockade, but his improvised fare schedule could have been drafted by the pirate Jean Lafitte.

Airline officials don't care when you arrived at the airport. They care only whether there is time for you to get through the process. Plan for lines at the ticket counter, the currency-exchange window, the tax-stamp window, and customs. In some airports, officials stop accepting passengers a half hour or more before flight time if it will take longer than that to clear security. If you arrive at one of those airports 25 minutes before departure, you're out of luck.

Suppose you're running late and there's a long line at the check-in counter. If you wait in line, you'll miss your flight. Go to the front of the line and, as calmly as possible, explain the situation to the agent. Try to enlist the sympathy of the person next in line. If your karma is good, he or she may make space for you. If everyone in line is also anxiously hoping to board the same flight, sprint for the gate. Baggage to check? Your karma isn't good enough.

Another motivation for early arrival is the strong correlation between luggage checked close to flight-departure time and luggage lost. If you check in late, your luggage may not make your flight, but it may go somewhere else. Rush the ticket agent, and you're asking for a luggage tag that says SLC (Salt Lake City) instead of SCL (Santiago, Chile).

> Airport officials don't care when you arrived, only if there is enough time to check you in.

There is also a relationship between the time you check in and your rights, if any, when you get bumped because the flight was overbooked.

Immediately after checking in, ensure that the agent pulled only the correct ticket coupon. If he or she has accidentally taken two coupons, you will have an untimely problem down the line.

Stay alert while waiting in the terminal for your flight to depart. The announcements that are so difficult to understand may be telling you that the departure gate has changed. Ask around. Watch other passengers. Bury your head in a book, and you may have more than enough time to finish it when you look up.

On Board

- Drink eight ounces of water hourly (coffee, alcohol, and carbonated drinks don't count) to compensate for the extremely low humidity in the cabin.
- Contact lenses, especially the thin, disposable kind, can adhere to the cornea in the low humidity. Have eyedrops available, or consider leaving your lenses in their case during a long flight.
- If you have a cold or an allergy, changes in cabin pressure may cause ear or sinus problems. Consider using a decongestant an hour or so before departure. If your ears bother you, try chewing gum, yawning, or pinching your nose shut, closing your mouth, and blowing gently.
- Get some exercise during a long trip. Roll your head and shoulders, twist your body, reach over your head, tighten the muscles in your buttocks, lift your thighs, and rotate your feet. Propping your feet up relieves pressure on the back of your thighs. Walk around the cabin, and get off the plane during layovers.
- Take a blanket and pillow from the overhead bin when you board. Otherwise, they may be claimed by the time you feel a need. Some airlines have become so unfriendly that they now require you to rent the blanket and pillow. That must build a lot of brand loyalty.

- If you're airborne when you discover you may miss a connection, see if the attendant can fix the problem before you arrive. If it will help, ask the attendant to arrange transport to another gate by electric cart or to try to delay departure of the other flight. If the attendant cannot help, move near the exit so you'll be one of the first at the ticket counter. Be creative and determined but always courteous with the customer-service person (who faces hours of hell dealing with angry people demanding attention).

If there's a long line at the ticket counter, don't get buried there. Minutes matter. Head for other airline counters to find alternatives, or for a telephone to call toll-free reservation numbers or your travel agent. The airline on which you were scheduled is more likely to help you than any other.

Even if it looks from the monitor as if it's too late to catch a flight, rush for the gate anyway. You never know. If no alternative can be found, ask the ticket agent for a hotel room and meals at airline expense—in a way that implies that both of you take this compensation for granted.

Overbooking, Delays, and Diversions

Airlines do not guarantee their schedules, and neither does the law. In the event of delay or cancellation, your remedies are mostly governed by airline policy, which means they're negotiable. If cancellation of a flight was not caused by a so-called act of God, an airline agent will offer to rebook you on another of the airline's flights. Some may offer a free coupon for a similar flight, but you may have to ask for it. If the airline diverts your flight to an alternate destination, it may offer you a hotel room.

When a flight is *delayed,* the airline's obligation to compensate you is very limited. If the delay was caused by bad weather, you'll even have to feed yourself. It the delay was caused by mechanical failure, the airline may provide meals and pay for telephone calls. It should also try to get you on another of its flights. When the starboard engine on our Madrid-to-Atlanta flight failed over the Atlantic, the pilot dumped fuel and returned to Madrid. The airline put us up in a five-star hotel, wined and dined us royally, and doubled our frequent-flier miles. The next morning, I requested an upgrade to business class from a friendly clerk—and got it.

In general, however, airlines will not reimburse ticket holders for inconvenience, financial losses, or broken romances related to a delayed arrival.

Your rights are different in the case of *overbooking,* which has become common practice and is quite legal. If you don't want to get bumped, check in early. Being somewhere in line when they fill the last seat does you no good, nor does holding a boarding pass mean you'll be allowed to board. You must receive a boarding assignment; that is, you must be checked in.

If a flight is oversold, the clerk will call for volunteers to be bumped. If you're willing to trade your time for money, tell the clerk ahead of time that you'll agree to be bumped, but only if there is an alternative flight acceptable to you and the airline pays for meal, hotel, and phone-call expenses. Before agreeing to be bumped, see whether the voucher has any restrictions, such as expiration or blackout dates, or advance-purchase requirements. In addition to a free flight, compensation may include some combination of an upgrade, a temporary pass to a first-class lounge, and a cash payment in the range of $200 to $500. It's all negotiable.

Suppose you don't volunteer, and the airline bumps you anyway. For flights in and originating from the United States, the policy of U.S. airlines is that if they can put you on another flight that arrives at your destination within an hour of when you were originally scheduled to arrive, you receive no compensation. If you arrive more than one hour late but less than two (four hours late for an international flight), you are entitled to a cash payment equal to the amount you paid for your one-way ticket or one-half the cost of your round-trip ticket, up to $200. If your arrival is later than those times, the airline doubles the payment, up to $400. Plus, of course, the airline must still get you to your destination. The airline may try to get you to accept free air travel sometime in the future in place of the cash payment. You don't have to accept. You can also make your own alternative reservations and request a full refund for the flight from which you were bumped.

When an airline cancels a flight, it will rebook you, but it may be much later or even on another day. If that happens, you can request a refund. You may get that—or less, depending on which airline it is. It's a rotten deal.

Here's the joker: if you checked in after the deadline shown on your ticket jacket, you may receive no compensation at all. And, of course, late arrivers head the list of bumpees. Even for a chronic late arriver, the lesson should be clear. Note that at most major airports it's possible to check in online and even print out a boarding pass. This overcomes the check-in hurdle and can also be a big time-saver if you have no bags to check. If you do, you'll still have to wait in that line. Too busy or forgetful to do it yourself? You can ask a service such as **CheckInSooner.com** to do it for you and e-mail you a boarding pass. However, this is not an inexpensive service.

The policies of foreign carriers with respect to overbooking are consistent with European Union (or other governmental) regulations, which are similar to U.S. regulations. The policies of U.S. carriers pertaining to flights originating outside the United States are inscrutable.

We travelers know that delays and cancellations have personal consequences, sometimes nasty ones. If you *miss a connection* because of mechanical problems, flight delays, or something else within the airline's control, or even bad weather, the airline is supposed to book you on its next flight. If that flight will strand you for a day or two, the airline may, but is not required to, pay for accommodations and meals. If you miss a connection because of something within your control, the airline may, but is not required to, try to rebook you. Your problem is greater if the onward flight was on another airline.

If you're about to miss a connection and your airline doesn't have a flight to bail you out, go into action yourself. Find help from another airline. And don't just hope your bags will make the transfer on their own (they probably won't). Get airline staff to help. Go to where the bags are if that will help get it done.

To summarize: reconfirm your ticket repeatedly, and get to the airport early. Avoid stress and disappointment, and take advantage of a little journal-writing time. If a problem comes up, being prepared will reduce its impact on your trip.

For information about lost luggage, please see Chapter 17, Safety and Security. You'll find additional information on air travel in Chapters 7 and 8.

How to Complain

Mechanical breakdown, schedule foul-ups, computer meltdown, missed connection, lost luggage: we all know how to complain about these increasingly common experiences, right? Maybe not.

- Only United and Continental permit you to file a complaint on the phone. The others require e-mail, fax, or snail mail.
- Let's discuss how to write an effective letter. Don't begin by telling the offending airline that you'll fly with it again only after hell freezes over. This and other threats simply take away the airline's incentive to treat you fairly and keep you as a customer.
- Instead, your complaint should be firm, calm, polite, and factual. Outline clearly what happened, where, when, and who did what. Include flight, reservation, and frequent-flier numbers.
- State specifically what you want in compensation in cash, credit, vouchers, or whatever for the airline's misdeeds. If you don't ask, it won't offer much. Rules govern what an airline must pay when it loses your luggage or bumps you from a flight. Beyond that it's up to you to get fair treatment. Make your request reasonably proportional to the problem. For example, if their plane didn't go for mechanical reasons and you had to stay over in a hotel and missed a meeting, asking for reimbursement of all out-of-pocket expenses plus a free ticket is reasonable.
- If the airline doesn't respond or tries to wear you down, be persistent. If you receive no satisfaction, you can also contact the U.S. Department of Transportation ([202] 366-2220; **airconsumer@ost.doc.gov**), or the FAA Consumer Hotline ([800] 322-7873; **www.faa.gov**).
- Still no help and increasingly outraged? Contact major travel magazines such as *International Travel News, Condé Nast Traveler,* and *National Geographic Traveler.* They may publicize your complaint and act as ombudsman. No airline likes to be in the hot glare of a critical spotlight.
- In the end, you can take your contract for service (the ticket) to small claims court, or hire a lawyer and go to war.

- What I've said here about how to complain is generally applicable to disputes with hotels, car-rental agencies, and other providers of goods and services.

Please see Chapter 8, How to Save Money, for full a discussion of how to save money on airfares.

TRAVELING BY BUS

SAVE Money It's been said that the elite fly, the middle classes take the train, and the people ride the bus. At home, buses come mostly in vanilla, but in the rest of the world, there's a rainbow of flavors. Even when the vehicle is sufficiently comfortable to pamper the most demanding traveler, traveling by bus is almost always an excellent way to save money while seeing the nitty-gritty of a country.

In Mexico and Central America, buses are a good way to travel and always provide opportunities to meet local people. But since few of those bus routes are world-class, and because you will travel to other countries as well, let's get an idea about some of the opportunities around the world.

Some trips combine spectacular scenery with luxury. The air-conditioned Scania superbus that cruises 1,200 miles from Santiago to Arica, Chile, has a bar, a bathroom, three movie screens, and a smiling hostess. As the sleek bus hums across the moonscape of the Atacama Desert, you spy huge boulders balanced on barren mountainsides. In most climates, rain and erosion would long ago have tumbled these hot-air-balloon-size rocks into dry canyons below. In the desert stillness, they hang suspended for centuries. As heat waves shimmer outside the window, cool air breezes across your face, and the hostess sets an ice-cold beer at your elbow. At night, your seat reclines to nearly horizontal, a leg rest pops out, and you're in bed. All that for about $50.

On the double-deck luxury bus from Windhoek, Namibia, to Cape Town, South Africa, the attendant serves near-gourmet meals and fine South African wines. When the splendid landscape fades into dusk, she appears at your side with soft pillows and warm blankets.

Another fine double-decker travels the Garden Route along the south coast of Africa from Cape Town to Port Elizabeth. For 800 kilometers, this bus passes through small towns and beneath branches heavily laden with blooming flowers. Your partner sits across a table from you, sharing tea and conversation.

For rugged beauty, it's hard to top the two-day cliff-hanger in the Himalayas from Kashmir to Leh in northern India, or the seven-hour trip west from Gangtok in the Indian state of Sikkim to the base of Mount Kangchenjunga, or the nine-hour trip from the humid lowlands of Ujung Pandang up to the cool plateau of exotic Torajaland in Sulawesi, Indonesia.

I should mention that the buses on these last three routes are rolling wrecks. In fact, many buses are rust-holed and threadbare, seats torn and metal surfaces shiny from the momentary grips of a million hands. Either the windows won't open or they won't close. Fans haven't worked in living memory, and overhead light fixtures are shadowy holes. Shock absorbers and springs don't. One thing that always works is the horn: shrill, penetrating, and sounding every few seconds. Another piece of equipment that works is the boom box, usually the size of a suitcase. If you're lucky, you'll get local music. If not, you'll discover what happened to the worst U.S. rap and disco tapes. Desperation hits when you find that your earplugs are tucked away in your luggage instead of nearby in your day pack.

It may not be fair to say that all bus drivers are aggressive, but I once saw a bus driver, reflexes programmed to blast away at any obstacle, honk furiously at a speed bump in the road.

When you ride one of these really battered buses, it's seldom to save money. It's because that's all there is to get to your destination. When you have a choice in Mexico and Central America, it's wise to pay more and take the best bus available. Third-class buses can be stressful, especially when the roads are in poor shape (not an uncommon situation in Central America).

Nuts and Bolts of Bus Travel

Unlike train stations, bus stations generally are not architectural marvels. This is true throughout Latin America. In fact, "yards" would be a more apt description. Picture dozens of buses parked helter-skelter in a dusty plaza. Travelers

mill around, loaded with everything from briefcases to small animals to heaping baskets of fruit. Vendors weave through the crowd as conductors shout and engines race. The word "cacophony" captures the essence of this scene but doesn't begin to describe how captivating it is.

There's probably a relationship between where a bus is parked and where it's going, but few travelers are likely to figure it out. Most buses display their ultimate destination on a tattered piece of cardboard in the front window. Of course, if you're not going to the end of the line or are transferring to some other bus along the way, your destination is not the one that's displayed. No problem. Stay calm and keep asking, and you'll soon be directed to the right bus. Then, to be certain, ask the driver. Because it's easy to confuse place names in a language strange to your ears, write the name on a piece of paper and show it to the driver. If you already have a ticket, show that to him. When you start wondering where to get off, enlist the aid of your fellow passengers. You'll get so much help, you'll feel like a member of the family by the time you wave good-bye.

When buying a ticket, try for an express bus. On a short trip, it doesn't matter much, but a long-distance local bus sometimes lurches forward only a few hundred meters at a time, stopping to pick up anyone who waves from the roadside. If you buy your ticket anywhere other than from the bus driver, find out exactly where the bus departs. It may be right outside the ticket office or somewhere across the bus yard or even blocks away. Make an assumption, and you may be making new plans.

When you give the ticket to the driver or conductor, he will tear or punch it or give you a receipt. Keep whatever you get. The ticket or receipt may be checked several times in the course of the trip and collected as you get out. Even though the driver may toss it out the window after you give it to him, he may not let you off without it.

> Keep your ticket; it may be checked several times throughout the trip.

The most pressing problem on a bus is lack of legroom. A tall person's knees are driven into the seat ahead, scrunched up to his chin, or forced into the aisle. That's when you find that your extended knee is a tempting place for someone to sit. For any trip longer than an hour, I try for a seat in the first row for the legroom—and view. If reservations aren't accepted, the driver may informally reserve a seat if you tell him about, or pantomime, the legroom problem. If you can't reserve a seat, get to the door of the bus early and, when it opens, take no prisoners.

If you think your comfort level may differ from that of a high-altitude llama herder, get a window seat so you get to choose whether the window is open or closed. Think about which side of the bus will be receiving the force of the sun and whether you want to be toasted.

The roof of a bus sometimes constitutes preferred seating in terms of space, fresh air, and electrifying views. Riding the roof also lets you keep an eye on your luggage and avoid watching the driver getting progressively drunk. To avoid being turned down, just climb to the roof without asking permission and snuggle out of sight amid packs and baskets. Speaking of electrifying, watch for wires hanging low over the road.

I know an experienced traveler who always talks to the driver—to test his sobriety. If he passes, she chooses a seat on the driver's side of the bus on the theory that in an emergency the driver will try to protect himself.

No matter what the schedule says, drivers sometimes will not depart until the bus is full. Of course, "full" has different meanings in different places. It may mean that the aisle is packed with produce, baggage, livestock, and farm equipment, and not one additional fare-paying life form can be leveraged into the vehicle.

People jammed together in the aisle edge toward you a millimeter at a time until they're almost on top of you. As you're settling in, the baby is handed to you by the woman perching on the back of your seat, and an unseen fowl pecks at your shoelaces. Try to defend what you consider your personal space, and your trip can be, shall we say, strenuous. If you see the humor and go with the flow, it will be memorable instead.

Because of all the practice they get, drivers can repair virtually any mechanical failure on the spot. On the mountain road to Rumtek Monastery in Sikkim, an explosion blew a ragged hole in the floorboard of our bus. An Israeli traveler in front of me turned calmly to his friend and said, "Car bomb." It turned out that a rear tire had detonated with such force that a large chunk of rubber had blown through the floor. The driver nonchalantly parked on a steep uphill curve, replaced the tire, and adjusted the clutch, all in 30 minutes. Of course, you still had to watch your step in the back of the bus, or you'd become axle grease.

Because a bus may come to an unplanned, extended halt far from any human habitation, experienced travelers carry a snack. Peanuts, fruit, bread, and water can help make a pit stop pleasant.

Security

Let's face it: travel abroad requires a little more caution than is necessary in the United States. It's up to you to make sure your luggage doesn't go astray.

Lock your bags when they're placed on a bus's roof.

Picture an agile young man dropping from a tree limb to the roof of a passing bus. After a furtive glance around, he grabs three of the many bags stored on the roof and tosses them off the back. As the bus slows for an uphill climb, he swings down to the back bumper, hops off, and sprints back to collect his loot.

Your job is to make sure yours isn't one of those bags. If joining your bag on the roof isn't your idea of fun, then lock it to a roof rail with a light, plastic-coated bicycle chain. This little chain also keeps the bag from sliding off as the bus rounds a curve. I met an American in Manuel Antonio National Park, Costa

Rica, whose backpack had bounced off the roof of a bus, taking with it his passport and traveler's checks. How many mistakes can you count in that picture?

If rain is a probability and your bag is on the roof, make sure it's covered by a tarp or inside a waterproof pack cover or garbage bag. Once you're rolling, the driver is unlikely to stop to do any waterproofing.

As fast as the helpful driver shoves tourists' bags into the underneath storage compartment that opens from both sides, someone may be pulling them out the other side. Now that's a bad way to start a trip. If someone is planning to snatch your pack, he's watching you—so you must be watchful, too.

When the bus lets someone off, see that your pack doesn't go along. Get off to stretch your legs—and watch. When the bus stops for lunch or a toilet break, don't leave anything valuable aboard even if the driver says he'll lock the doors.

If you're likely to sleep along the way, keep your day-pack strap looped around your foot, and keep everything else between you and the side of the bus. If your luggage is overhead, lock it to the rack. Of course, your real valuables are—where?—in your money belt. A friend puts her pack on her lap and rests her head on it to sleep (using it as an ersatz air bag). These precautions may seem a little excessive, but they quickly become part of a comfortable, even amusing routine.

Bus Passes

$AVE Money With a bus pass, you typically pay a fixed amount for unlimited travel on a bus network for the duration of the pass. In a large country, a pass can be a major way to save money. While some passes must be purchased outside the country, most can be bought on the spot. A pass usually puts you on a comfortable coach run by an established company. In fact, upscale bus services in many countries abroad use Mercedes or Scania coaches that are considerably more luxurious than buses in the United States.

In Mexico, consider the Bamba Experience (**www.backpackingmexico.com**), a hop-on, hop-off bus network that provides a great service for independent travelers.

With Green Tortoise (**www.greentortoise.com**) you choose from one of a series of "loop" routes that include Guatemala–Belize, Costa Rica–Nicaragua–Panama, and the west coast of Mexico. Operating as very informal tours, they're a cheap way to cover a lot of ground. Because passengers live aboard the bus, it's not for everyone.

Local buses are an excellent way to see the countryside, meet people, and learn about local culture. You immerse yourself in conversations with local people of all ages, trying to ignore the driver chatting with the conductor as the bus leans around yet another curve in the sky. You'll know it was a truly memorable trip if you swear, as you get off, never to ride a bus again.

TRAVELING BY TRAIN

In North America, trains—except for utilitarian commuter trains—have become an anachronism, remembered mostly by seamed-faced farmers who watched them puff across the prairies of their youth. In much of the rest of the world, trains are still woven into the fabric of daily life, aesthetically worn but still mechanically valiant.

On a train, you travel close to the land, slowly enough to absorb what's going on, with as much privacy or contact with people as you choose. You sleep wonderfully, rocking along to a soothing rhythm, waking to a new vista emerging with each dawn.

From a train window, the world is a visual banquet. I feel as if I'm stationary, watching a panorama of lives flowing past. I remember a young woman watching from her kitchen window, leaning on her elbows, holding my eye until the train rounded the bend.

A train passes through time as well as space. The train north from Singapore leaves the city's futuristic, mirrored-glass towers behind and within an hour is clacking through a Malaysian countryside little changed since man discovered he could plant and gather his food.

> Anything is possible on a train; a great meal, a binge, a visit from card players, an intrigue, a good night's sleep, and strangers' monologues framed like Russian short stories.
> —Paul Theroux, The Great Railway Bazaar: By Train through Asia (1977)

Throughout the world, trains transport travelers on thousands of routes in reasonable comfort. A dozen or more trains are worth a detour of many miles to ride. Writers in posh travel magazines rhapsodize about superluxury trains, but my favorites are old-fashioned trains that maintain the style of a half century past. I like trains that leave stations reeking of character (among other things) to pass first through inhabited areas that reveal how urban people live, then slowly through landscapes of mountains and forests, clear lakes, and curious faces.

Sadly, passenger trains are very limited in Mexico and Central America.

The first train tracks in Mexico were laid in 1857. Later, passenger trains with sleepers and observation cars connected all major Mexican cities. The government sold train systems to the private sector in the

> Most people have that fantasy of catching the train that whistles in the night.
> —Willie Nelson

1990s, and passenger service was eventually shut down. For what's left, see **www .mexlist.com/pass.htm.**

However, one passenger-train trip in Mexico deserves special attention, not for stylish furnishings or world-class food and service, but rather for spectacular landscapes.

In northwestern Mexico, board the Chihuahua al Pacifico Railroad for the comparatively short journey from Chihuahua through the Copper Canyon to

Los Mochis, a small fishing resort in northwest Mexico. This has been called the most dramatic train ride in North America, a claim based on canyons carved more than 6,000 feet into the earth's surface. Passengers may visit Cuauhtémoc, a community of German-speaking Mennonite ranchers, and get off at Divisadero or Bahuichivo to hike down into the canyon. If you have a few extra days, take the opportunity to experience the unusual culture of the Tarahumara people, renowned as long-distance runners.

> I always seem to have chosen the most eccentric and decrepit ways of getting to places.
> —Michael Wood, *Zambezi Express* (1981)

In addition, there are a couple of other interesting tourist trains. The first is the Tequila Express in Guadalajara, which puts much more emphasis on tequila than on the train (**www.tequilaexpress.com.mx**). The second is Expreso Maya, which runs between Cancún and Villahermosa with stops at excellent Maya ruins along the way (**www.expresomaya.com.mx**).

Costa Rica has no regular passenger trains, but there is an excursion train that runs from San José to Caldera on the west coast. It's a very pleasant daylong round-trip for $30 that passes through remarkable scenery (**www.ticotraintour.com**).

In Panama, there's a worthwhile one-hour, 48-mile train trip between Panama City and Colón (**www.panarail.com**). It travels along the Panama Canal to Colón on weekday mornings and returns to Panama City in the evenings.

Cost

Train travel is such a fine way to travel that, even though there are few opportunities in Mexico and Central America, it's worth knowing something about how much it costs in the rest of the world. In most countries, train travel is inexpensive, much cheaper than flying. A berth always costs more than a seat, but it's much more comfortable for overnight travel. Its cost depends on whether the berth is in a private compartment, in a shared compartment, or lengthwise along the aisle. However, remember that when you travel at night, the cost of transportation includes the cost of lodging.

It's seldom wise to buy the cheapest ticket available. Third-class, hard-seat trains are a rough way to travel in almost any country. Unless you're determined to see a country on $2 a day, are writing a book on ultimate hard-core travel, or are practicing extreme self-mortification in contemplation of reincarnation, skip third-class hard seats.

> Sometimes a bribe can help find a previously "filled" seat.

In a private compartment, you're comfortable and possibly free from cigarette smoke, and your luggage is relatively secure. You may even reach your destination fairly well rested. If you forgo a berth and sit up the whole way, you can save a few dollars, but that could be a foolish economy on a long trip. The downside is that if you travel in a two-person compartment, you miss fine opportunities for conversation. When I'm in the mood for company, I travel in large compartments or in open seating. When I need solitude, I try for a small compartment.

There are no rail passes in Mexico and Central America, but where they are offered (such as in Europe, which has several versions of the Eurail Pass) they can be an excellent buy.

LOCAL TRANSPORT

Just as music reveals the character of a country, so do its small vehicles. In the same way taxis and subways reflect the nature of Manhattan, *colectivos* in Mexico and motor scooters in Rarotonga capture the spirit of those places.

European public-transportation systems are extensive and efficient. Because they're familiar to us, we use them with little hesitation. However, modern transportation systems have few equivalents in the less developed world. Instead, small entrepreneurs have taken over—and their solutions are wondrous to behold. Local transport is inexpensive, usually uncomfortable, and almost always fun.

Because it's unfamiliar, local transport initially intimidates some travelers. With a little experience, though, they soon hop aboard all kinds of vehicles with confidence and a smile. They're at home in a VW van decorated with colorful murals, a pickup truck with a striped metal awning above bottom-polished wooden benches, or a horse-drawn cart with a fringed roof and a honey jar filled with fresh flowers.

Local transport includes *bemos, bendis,* bicycles, camels, canal boats, *colectivos,* elephants, jeepneys, *makoros, matatus,* minivans, motor scooters, *oplets,* outrigger canoes, oxcarts, *poda podas, pouse-pouses, taxi-brousses,* tongas, and many more vehicles. Because taxis, minivans, subways, and bicycles are so common around the world, we'll take a look at them. The others will come as a series of happy surprises.

Taxis

In a taxi, you travel in comfort and with a reasonable likelihood of reaching your planned destination, and you pay a premium for the convenience. Unfortunately, taxi drivers as a group seldom create a favorable impression. The problem is money. You have it, and they want as much of it as they can get. Hope for a working meter or, from an airport, a fixed fee. Otherwise, bargain with the driver regarding the fare.

In Latin America, especially in Mexico City, it's best not to ride in "outlaw" taxis. Company taxis have distinctive markings. Even private taxis will have some official markings. If you're approached by someone who is clearly using a personal car as an unlicensed taxi, take a pass. I'm not sure which is higher, the chance of skullduggery or of incompetence.

Because taxi drivers are experienced in dealing with travelers, you'll pay dearly unless you strike a bargain before the wheels roll. If you bargain in advance, you can ride for a reasonable price. If you don't bargain, the sky's the limit. Bargaining with taxi drivers as an art form is discussed in Chapter 14.

When it's time to pay, first get your luggage out of the taxi, then give the driver the exact fare agreed on. That way, in the event of a difference of opinion, your luggage can't be held hostage. If you have only a large bill, state the amount of the fare before handing it over. Otherwise, with your bill in his pocket, he may claim that the fare was higher than you agreed. Regardless, he may claim he has no change, hoping you'll be in too much of a hurry to wait. With a little forethought, you can avoid this scenario.

Before your hotel clerk calls for a taxi, ask whether the call will result in an additional charge by the driver. Sometimes the charge for being summoned can exceed the charge for driving all the way to the airport. You may prefer to walk to the curb and handle it yourself.

Because it's not unusual for a taxi driver to levy a supplemental charge based on how many bags he puts in the trunk, keep at least small pieces of luggage in the car with you.

In many cities, rates increase dramatically at night. Local law may permit charging double the fare on the meter. Spare your blood pressure a peak experience by asking in advance.

Minivans

You're standing on the curb in San José, Costa Rica, as a minivan skids to a brakes-locked stop in front of you. It has an end-of-the-line destination sign in its window, which is probably not the name of the place you want to go. You aren't sure what the fare is or what you're supposed to do next, and you have only seconds to decide whether to board. Confused, you step back and look for a taxi. After learning that taxi rides aren't exactly problem-free and cost 20 times more than the "people's transport," you try again.

When you board the minivan, you find all seats occupied, the roof too low to permit standing upright, and 15 people looking at you. Because you have no idea what the 12-year-old fare collector is saying, you're reduced to holding out several coins. He takes what he wants. Fortunately, it's usually less than ten cents.

You had a general idea of the direction in which you wanted to go when you got in, but after ten minutes of turning corners, you're not so sure. Seeing a street name that looks about right, you climb out—and realize you're lost. It really doesn't matter; it's part of your adventure. You can't go very wrong. When you've looked around, you catch another minivan, craning your neck to see out the window, thinking surely you'll see something familiar. Maybe you do, maybe not. Either way, you get home . . . or somewhere.

Before long, you realize how willing other passengers are to help. If your destination is some distance from the minivan route, someone may even jump off and show you the way. Because systems are so similar, your new knowledge will serve you everywhere in the world.

In most cities, local minivans race endlessly like slot cars around their circuits. You summon one with a wave as it approaches. For transportation from one town to another, minivans set out from established stations. If there's no schedule, minivans won't leave before their seats are full. Touts will try to steer you toward the van that employs them. They'll say that it is just about to leave, that theirs is the only van going where you want to go, or anything else they think might work. They'll try to get you to take a seat and to pay for the trip in advance.

Because the driver expects foreigners to be impatient, he may try to get you to convert his van into a private taxi by buying all unoccupied seats. If he asks if you would like to leave when the van is still only half full, find out what the deal is. There is no free lunch.

You might expect that the van with the most passengers would be the next to leave. Instead, it's common for a driver to get his buddies to sit in his van to pass the time, hoping that you'll see his van nearly full and choose it. After a while, you notice that every time a real passenger climbs in, someone else gets off—and the van goes nowhere. If the vans are filling up fast, take a seat. Otherwise, think of it as an opportunity to stroll around nearby, perhaps finding someone to talk with, until you see a van actually getting ready to go.

Intercity minivans charge set fees for local people, but the driver may ask you to pay whatever he thinks you're good for. If you've learned some vocabulary, ask another passenger what the fare is. Even better, watch what someone else pays, being aware that he or she may not be going to your destination. If you're carrying luggage, you may have to pay an extra fare, and you certainly will if it's taking a passenger's space. Don't pay until the vehicle is about to leave. That way, if another cranks up to leave first, you're free to switch if you want or need to. As you start to get out, the driver may offer a reduced fare. Let the drivers bid for your business.

> Hitching, among other virtues, forces you to converse with people you'd otherwise cross the street to avoid.
> —Tony Horwitz,
> One for the Road
> (1987)

Because drivers' incomes depend solely on fares, they let everyone aboard who can cram him- or herself in, and then they drive as fast as they can for as many hours as they can stay more or less awake. Driving without speedometers, they sometimes buy off official interference with bribes hurled out the window.

Minivans are ubiquitous, cheap, and almost always fun—and no traveler should fail to give them a try.

Subways

Many people travel to the great metropolitan areas of the world and still don't experience the metro, underground, or whatever the local subway system is called. Subway systems aren't common in Central America. However, Mexico City has more than 125 miles of subway track plus a surface light-rail system. The subway carries 4 million passengers a day. It also has the cheapest fare in the world—about 20 cents. The only other Mexican subways are in Monterrey and Guadalajara.

If you don't travel by subway at home, a foreign system can appear pretty intimidating. However, because subways are fast, convenient, and inexpensive, it's worth overcoming hesitation.

A route map, which you can get from a tourist office or the subway ticket seller, makes riding a lot easier. Although the map may look like a plate of spaghetti at first sight, you'll soon figure it out and feel confident on any subway system in the world.

On the subway, as on many other types of public transport, lots of folks are pressed together in a confined space, so it's wise to keep part of your mind on security. Keep your day pack in front of you. If you have a camera, keep it out of sight, or keep a hand on it. Carry nothing you care about in an insecure pocket.

Bicycles

Few means of local transportation provide the pleasure that comes from exploring on a bicycle. It's cheap and relatively safe, gives you great range, lets you see things at a gentle pace, and gets the kinks out of your legs. A few travelers sign up for a bike tour, and some plan a bike trip on their own, but too many forget that renting bikes locally is an option.

In Europe and a few other places, you can rent bicycles as multigeared and lightweight as you want. Elsewhere, expect a single gear and a handlebar bell. In most cities around the world, it's not hard to find places that rent bikes. Ask around. If there's nothing organized, it's not hard to find some local person delighted to earn a little money by renting his bike.

$AVE Money Riding local transport produces some of the finest and funniest memories from any trip. Seek it out—the more exotic the better. Ride a yak or a camel or an elephant; listen to the sounds of the creaking leather harness of the pony cart late at night. Using local transport is a great way to save money, but it does much more. It helps transform a tourist into a traveler.

CAR RENTAL

In the United States, Europe, and Oceania, we rent a car without a second thought (well, maybe we do think twice about driving on the "wrong" side of the road). But renting and driving a car abroad can be a challenging and sometimes perilous experience in much of the rest of the world.

In less developed regions, rental cars are often expensive, especially when you add in high-priced petrol, insurance, taxes, drop-off fees, the higher fees often charged at airport locations, and various mysterious surcharges. Reflecting irregular maintenance, mechanical problems are not infrequent, and breakdowns seldom occur at convenient places. Worse, driving may expose you to considerable liability, not to mention turn your nerves into banjo strings. Automobile accidents are one of the leading causes of injury or death for overseas travelers.

Why discuss car rental at all? First, the flexibility and freedom of having your own transportation is very appealing. Second, sometimes you need to rent a car to get where you want to go. Third, a rental car makes it easier to stay in hotels far removed from expensive downtown hotels. Because some travelers will rent a car in Mexico, Central America, or elsewhere abroad, this chapter will help make it a successful experience.

> The flexibility of having your own car can be very appealing.

Required Documents

Ask the rental agent, in advance, what documents you need to rent the car. In most places, that will be some combination of your own state driver's license, a credit card, and perhaps your passport. I bought an International Driver's License for an early trip and have never needed it. Your valid driver's license will be accepted in Mexico and Central America.

When to Rent

SAVE Money If you decide to rent from an international company, one way to save money (as much as 50 percent) is to reserve and pay for a car *before* you leave home. Talk with your travel agent. You may be able to get a deal on a car as part of a package with your airline ticket. If you walk up to an international car-rental counter overseas, expect to pay much more than if you'd made the arrangements at home. At that point, call home and make the deal there. You might get an even better rate from a small local company, but on your first trip to a distant destination, you may prefer the security and convenience of knowing there'll be a car waiting.

Several companies permit you to buy vouchers in the United States and choose your rental days after you arrive. Doing so adds flexibility while retaining the big savings compared with renting from the same companies locally.

When you reserve a car, the clerk will ask what time you'll pick it up. After you state a time, find out how long the company will hold the car if your arrival is delayed. Some companies flush your reservation after 30 minutes, others give you until closing time, and some will wait patiently for up to 24 hours. If a rental agency has your flight number, it should know if your flight is behind schedule. Nevertheless, if you'll arrive later than expected, let the company know.

If you won't be able to honor a reservation, cancel as early as possible. Not only does your courtesy free the car for another traveler, but it also may enable you to avoid a cancellation fee. Rental companies are beginning to charge no-shows. It's often $25, but it could be as much as the entire amount of the rental contract.

From Whom to Rent

SAVE Money Can you afford a rental car on a modest budget? It's difficult if you rent from one of the heavily promoted international companies. Nonetheless, out of habit, that's what most people do without realizing they're paying 30 percent to 100 percent more than they have to. If you still plan to rent from an international company, at least save money by comparison shopping because prices differ widely. You can do that on most of the major travel Web sites, such as Expedia, Orbitz, and the others listed in the discussion of airfares in Chapter 8, How to Save Money. You may get a wider choice of companies and better prices by entering the country name and "car rental" in a search engine and booking directly.

SAVE Money You almost always save money if you skip the car-rental counters at the airport, where rates reflect extra taxes and fees charged by the airport. If you don't see signs advertising away-from-the-airport rental agencies, try the Yellow Pages. Such agencies will usually come pick you up. If not, go into town, and rent from a local rental company.

SAVE Money You'll also save money by renting away from major tourist resorts.

SAVE Money In addition, here's a somewhat obscure way to save money. Ask a local agency if it has a car to be returned to another location. If you appear responsible, you may get the car without charge, paying only for the gas. I did this in New Zealand, and the agent even left a sack of freshly picked apples on the front seat for me. Believe it or not, when the Mamas and the Papas were still scrounging for gigs in small clubs for beer money, a national car-rental agency entrusted them with a new Cadillac to deliver from New York City to LA. So you clearly have a shot.

Certain companies may not rent to anyone with a blemished driving record, especially one reflecting a recent drunk-driving conviction or accident. Rather than learning about this restriction as you're trying to take delivery of the car, call ahead to find out what the policy is.

> Prices charged for car rentals vary, so shop around.

A company's age limits may also affect your choice. Some agencies require a renter to be at least 18 years old, some 21, and some 25. A few will not rent to a driver older than 70. In some places, such as the United Kingdom, there may be an extra fee. You should always be able to rent a car from some company, but check in advance so you won't be inconvenienced at a bad time.

The Terms of the Deal

Special rates: If you call because of a special rate you saw advertised, don't assume that the clerk at the reservation counter will offer it. Because you may have to ask for it, perhaps even insist on it, it's good to have the ad with you or to be able to cite the code number in it. Car-rental agents also have a pocketful of deals they can offer on their own, but they won't do so unless you prompt them. Instead, they'll try to sell you extras and upgrades (including various insurance options).

SAVE Money *Bargaining:* Save money by bargaining. Ask for a discount on the basis of your occupation, your membership in some organization (such as a corporation, automobile association, frequent-flier club, church group, or the Mickey Mouse Club), your age, your credit card, anything you can think of. Bring up competitors' prices. State how much you're willing to pay. Ask about weekend, by-the-week, and other discounted rates. You can sometimes get a better deal simply by walking from one counter to the next in full view of all the agents. When you get a quote from one, invite another to beat it. It's a very competitive business, so they'll often take what they can get.

Price: Determine exactly what is included in the quoted price and what isn't. Don't let yourself be surprised by "extras" such as an airport-pickup charge, a state or city surcharge, a late-return charge, an additional-driver fee, an underage-driver surcharge, VAT (value-added tax, which adds up to 18 percent in some European countries), an extra-equipment charge (for example, for a baby seat), a one-way drop-off charge (which can be astronomical), a collision or loss-damage waiver, theft protection (mandatory in some countries), charges for road service, and so on.

If asked for a deposit, use your credit card. If an agent demands a large cash deposit, you may return to discover it locked up or otherwise unavailable when you want it—and of course you'll be getting on a plane in a couple of hours.

SAVE Money Ask whether you get a price break when renting for a weekend or for five days or more. It can be less expensive to rent for six days than for four. Similarly, if you plan to use a car for more than 17 days, see whether the company has a lease option. If so, you'll save money over a straight rental.

Features: In many countries, air-conditioning and an automatic transmission are not standard. If you care, ask whether the car has any of the new high-tech features. For example, you might want a GPS navigational device with a video screen that shows the car as a moving dot on a map. After the driver chooses a destination, the system gives verbal prompts.

If the car has antilock brakes, be sure to know how to use them properly before leaving the parking lot.

Before leaving the airport, get a map or directions to your first destinations and find out where to drop the car on your return. Be sure you know what time the rental office closes at the return site.

Some companies offer automated checkout and check-in systems that resemble ATMs. The machine scans your driver's license and credit card and spits out a rental agreement for your signature. Is this getting a little spooky?

Size: If you reserve a small car and the agency is out of that size when you arrive, it should either upgrade you to another of its cars or obtain a similar car from another company without extra charge to you. If an agent offers you a car larger than you need, be wary. That large car may be available precisely because it's a gas-guzzler. On the other hand, be cautious about renting a microcompact in places with high-speed highways where it may be blown away by drivers doing 120 miles an hour. Ask how many passengers the car can transport in comfort.

Read the Contract

Reading this section and the one following on insurance may make you drowsy. Writing them almost did me in. But they're important, so stick with them. If there's a problem, it does no good to claim ignorance of a provision in the rental contract. Here are some things to look for:

- Does it define exactly what your responsibilities are?
- On the basis of the blank credit-card slip you signed, does the company tie up a big chunk of your credit line as security for damage to the car? It may not be just the rental amount; it could be all or part of the value of the car. You need to know whether your credit line is about to be tapped out.
- How does the company compute charges if you return the car before or after the end of the agreed-on rental period?
- Do you get unlimited free kilometers, or is the fee based on the number of kilometers driven? If you pay more every time the little odometer numbers click, you may not feel free to explore as many mysterious detours.
- Does the rental agreement contain instructions about what to do if the car breaks down? Is there a phone number to call in case of a problem? If you feel compelled to make repairs before receiving authorization, get receipts to support your request for reimbursement. Who is responsible for routine maintenance?
- Are you required to return the tank full of fuel? If so, and if you fail to do so, you'll be charged substantially above market price for the fuel needed to top off the tank. In some countries, rental companies deliver the car to

you with the tank full and instruct you to return it completely empty (the so-called fuel-purchase option). That's so they can charge you an inflated price for that first tank of petrol. Because it's a little perilous for most travelers rushing to catch a plane to skid into the parking lot on the last drop of fuel, the company gets the petrol left in the tank as a second bonus. Slick, eh?

- Are you permitted to drive the car into another country? I've several times been tempted to fudge on this one—most recently considering driving from South Africa into Mozambique—but I haven't done it. I think the risk of voiding the insurance is too great.

Insurance

The moment comes in every transaction when the clerk asks whether you want the collision insurance offered by the rental company, meaning an additional charge of $10 to $20 per day. (Car-rental companies insist that the collision-damage waiver is not insurance. They do so to avoid regulation by state insurance regulators, and they've managed to get courts to declare that it isn't insurance. But it does "quack like a duck.") This insurance covers only damage to the rental car, leaving you on your own regarding other liabilities. Furthermore, it is littered with exceptions to the coverage.

These policies are so overpriced and profitable to the rental company that the clerk has been trained to urge you to buy. His compensation may depend on how successfully he peddles this product. Therefore, he may even insist that whatever alternative insurance coverage you offer is invalid.

To respond rationally, you must know ahead of time whether you already have insurance that covers damage to the rental car and whether this rental-car company, despite what the clerk may say, accepts it. Because they don't know those answers, far too many travelers pay a high price for collision insurance they don't need.

Most domestic automobile-insurance policies offer an option providing collision coverage for cars rented in the United States, but they may not for rental cars driven abroad. Call your auto-insurance agent and specify where you expect to be driving. If there is coverage, ask whether the amount of coverage is limited to the value of your personal car (which might be less that the value of the rental car), additional drivers are covered, unusual vehicles such as RVs or trucks are covered, there is a limit on how long coverage is valid overseas (for example, 30 days), your regular deductible applies, and the policy provides liability coverage for injury to persons and property. If your domestic policy provides coverage, obtain acknowledgment from the car-rental company in advance, and carry evidence of the policy.

Ask your agent if coverage is available for rental cars abroad.

If you intend to use the insurance protection of your credit card (please see the section on credit cards in Chapter 10, How to Manage

Money Successfully), call the credit-card issuer to be certain its coverage is in effect where you'll be traveling. Then ask the car-rental reservations agent if the credit-card coverage will be accepted where you pick up the car. Because it is not universally accepted, insist that the reservations agent check with a local agent. If the local agent tells you on arrival that your credit-card coverage is not valid, verification in writing may come in handy. Should the agent still balk, call a regional office for confirmation. If you must pay for collision coverage to get the car, write on the contract that you are doing so at the clerk's insistence, and seek a refund when you return home. Be aware that the laws of some countries require renters to purchase local insurance regardless of credit-card coverage.

Defending their profit center, some car-rental agencies have started insisting that you show proof that your credit card does provide insurance. That proof is found in the Guide to Member Benefits you received. If you can't find it—and who can—the issuer will send you a copy. This proof is more likely to be demanded by smaller operations. Ask ahead of time.

Note that neither the car-rental company's collision insurance nor your credit-card collision coverage provides liability insurance covering damage you may do to people or property. If you have domestic automobile liability insurance, read your policy or ask your agent whether it's effective when driving a rental car abroad. In the United States, state law requires car-rental companies to carry various levels of liability insurance. Overseas, the situation varies.

If your own automobile liability insurance does not cover driving a rental car abroad or you have no automobile liability insurance, investigate buying "non-owner" liability coverage. Alternatively, consider buying $1 million in liability coverage from the car-rental company for the trip.

Some European border stations require that you present a "green card" proving you have third-party insurance coverage before they'll let you drive a rental car into their country. Look for it in the glove box. Without it, you'll be doing a U-turn at the border.

Insurance coverage may be invalidated when the driver was not listed on the rental contract, was intoxicated at the time of the accident, or violated a geographical limitation in the rental contract (such as taking the car across a border or on specified types of roads). The company will probably never know that you violated the limitation—unless you have a wreck in the forbidden zone. Then you'll get the bill for damages.

Don't take risks with insurance. Travel magazines are full of letters lamenting horrendous situations as a result of an accident for which the writers were not insured.

Inspect the Vehicle

My cardinal rule when renting a car from anywhere other than a big-city franchise: *see the vehicle* before handing over any money. Otherwise, the shiny car parked nearby as a lure may not be the car in which you depart the next morning amid grinding gears and acrid smoke. If the agent tells you that your car isn't available for inspection at the moment, it may be off hauling a load of swine and turnips. Ask that it be brought to your hotel before you sign up. If the car promised isn't the one that shows up the next day, be insistent. The company may discover something more suitable or drop the price as you drop your standards.

Inspect the car for damage before you leave the lot. In some countries, it may already look like the loser in a destruction derby. On the other hand, some rental agencies are very picky, and returning with a tiny dent or scratch could result in demand for payment on the spot. If there are dings, have the agent note them on the contract. When you return, look at the car yourself. If a rental company doesn't inspect at the moment you return, you may want to have the clerk note on the contract that there is no damage. Damage "discovered" after you've left may be charged to your credit card, and you will not have much of a defense.

It's amazing how many people just get in the car and drive away, putting many miles between themselves and help before they discover a problem. Check the lights, air-conditioning or heater, horn, windshield wipers, seat belt, and brakes. Make sure there is a spare tire and jack. If the tires aren't safe, change tires, change cars, or change companies. While you're inspecting, make a note of the license number, make, model, and color of the car. If the car is stolen while in your custody or you misplace it in a crowded parking lot, you'll feel foolish if you can't identify it. If you'll be driving the car for an extended period, ask for an extra key. If one isn't forthcoming, consider having one made. Solving a lost-key problem is much more time-consuming in Belize than in Baltimore.

Before you roll away, be sure you understand how to operate all switches, knobs, gears, and repair equipment. Ask whether the car has an electronic anti-theft device. If so, have it demonstrated. Otherwise, you may wind up with a car that won't start or has a shrieking alarm that won't stop.

If the tank is supposed to be full, see that it is.

Safety and Scams

For safety reasons, it's better not to stop if anyone other than a police officer tries to flag you down. The "Good Samaritan" scam involves someone waving at you, apparently to alert you to a problem with your car. Perhaps another car pulls alongside, and a passenger points at one of your tires with an expression of alarm. While you and the Samaritan check out the imaginary problem, his confederate raids your car.

If you are rear-ended in a remote area, the "accident" may have been intentional. Don't get out of your car if you have the slightest doubt about the situation. If you can, drive to a service station or some other well-lighted, public place. Otherwise, stay in your locked car, and wait for the police.

Someone who has access to your car, for example in a service station, may start a slow leak in a tire. I've seen a handcrafted blade that attaches to the toe of a shoe for exactly that purpose. When the tire goes flat later, someone will be there to help you out—and help himself. It's sad to say this, but anytime you accept help, you or your partner should keep an eye on the helpers.

Be alert for thieves who may try to snatch something from your car when you stop at a traffic light. In Buenos Aires, this has gotten to be such a problem that many drivers slow a bit, combine a quick sideways glance with a prayer, and cruise right through red lights. Keep doors locked, and, if circumstances warrant, windows up. In some places, it's better to keep your gear on the floor than on the front seat. Don't leave a tempting target for a quick hand slipping inside a window.

Be alert when driving in an area that seems risky. If someone approaches your car, perhaps indicating he wants to ask directions, be prepared to drive away immediately. If caught off-guard by someone who demands your keys, consider tossing them to him—but missing. Escape as he retrieves the keys.

If an unmarked car with a flashing light signals you to stop, drive to a well-lighted place to do so. Unless you are certain it's the police, keep the car doors locked, and roll the window down just far enough to show your license. Ask for identification. If you're not satisfied, refuse to get out of the car, and ask to be escorted to a police station.

If you believe you are being followed, make a series of turns. If the other vehicle is still with you, look for a police station or a busy petrol station.

A rental-car company sticker is an invitation to thieves, so ask for a car without one. If there is one on the car, remove it. Remember the glee you felt as a child when you saw Christmas presents under the tree? That's how a thief feels when he spots a rental car. It's a giant stocking stuffed with cameras and luggage.

Park in well-lighted areas, and don't leave any belongings visible. Assume that a rental car will be broken into, and never leave anything expensive in the car overnight. Think of it as wheels, not as a secure place to leave your gear. Locking something in the trunk is better than leaving it on the seat, but even that provides little real protection.

You may have an opportunity to make the car temporarily secure by engaging the services of a car guardian. In places such as Mexico City, the offer from scruffy adolescents to guard your car is straightforward blackmail. They're offering to guard it from themselves, and, frankly, it's a good investment of a few pesos.

Driving conservatively is good practice because traffic can be quite chaotic, and foreign rules of the road, both official and informal, may be unfamiliar to you. Reading signs in a foreign language takes your attention off the road for a few extra seconds. Discuss rules of the road with the car-rental agent, and get general advice as well. Besides avoiding an accident, you will also avoid a traffic ticket by driving conservatively. If you get a ticket in some parts of the world, when and how much you pay is likely to be a matter of negotiation—on a very uneven playing field. If the police photograph your car committing a violation, they will bill the car-rental firm, which will add the sum to your credit-card bill.

Besides slowing reflexes when they're needed the most, being intoxicated while driving can lead to jail. In Europe, penalties for driving under the influence are severe. Further, "influence" is defined as a blood alcohol level only one-half to one-quarter what it is in the United States. Roadblocks with Breathalyzer tests are not uncommon.

In almost a dozen countries—not including Mexico or Central American countries—cars drive on the left side of the road. You can learn to do it, but it will take a few hours before your reflexes adjust. So how do you avoid trashing the car during that time?

- Consider renting a car with an automatic transmission.
- Locate all the gadgets (horn, lights, wipers, signals) before leaving the rental lot. You'll wish you had if you need one of them halfway through a roundabout!
- Take a practice spin in the rental lot or on some nearby bunny slope.
- Avoid starting off during rush hour.
- Take advantage of a partner who can handle the map, read street signs, and such. Ask about signage and driving customs before you leave the lot.

In the end, driving on the "wrong" side of the road isn't the hard part. The hard part is the constant embarrassment of walking up to the wrong side of the car, then trying to pretend you're just there to check the tire pressure.

Stress

The monetary costs of car rental seem modest compared to the mental havoc some people experience when driving a car in less developed countries. Ill-maintained roads are crowded, and the horn takes the place of the brake. If you aren't used to sharing a narrow road with massive trucks and rattletrap cars lurching along without benefit of headlights, and if you don't find pleasure in weaving through throngs of bicycles, horse-drawn farm carts, and basket-laden pedestrians, think twice!

Bending or breaking traffic laws, including speeding, is a very bad idea. You want absolutely no interaction with the local police.

In Guatemala, Costa Rica, Rwanda, India, and Sri Lanka, I rented cars that came with a driver. That is no extravagance. In each case, the cost for the driver was, at least after the expected bargaining, negligible when balanced against the guidance and tranquility he provided. At the end of each day, the driver found suitable lodging for me (he usually curled up in a back room of the hotel). It's not unusual to hire a car and driver from a nontraditional source, such as a travel agent or desk clerk, for considerably less than you'd pay for the vehicle alone from a heavily promoted car-rental company.

Even though I regret the isolation of traveling in a private car and miss the camaraderie of public transportation, I love the freedom and spontaneity it allows. While I've often felt relieved, from a liability standpoint, when I've returned a car safe and sound, I've never once regretted renting one.

TRAVELING BY WATER

Cruises

The purpose of taking a cruise is not simply to be transported from one place to another, so the topic doesn't fit easily in this chapter. Still, because cruises are a common way to travel, I'll provide some information about them.

Cruises throughout the Caribbean and the Gulf of Mexico are wildly popular, often calling at ports on Mexico's east coast. Central American cruises visit Panama, Belize, Honduras, or Nicaragua, with some continuing to destinations such as Ecuador and Peru. Adventure Life is a well-regarded specialist in South and Central American cruises and tours; see **www.adventure-life .com.** For unbiased information about cruises, read *The Unofficial Guide to Cruises* (**www.wiley.com**). For telephone numbers of American-flag cruise lines: **www. cruiselinenumbers.com.**

Many other popular cruises depart San Francisco, Los Angeles, and San Diego to visit Mexico (Acapulco, Puerto Vallarta, and so on) and various Central American ports.

Also, **www.smallshipcruises.com** lists a number of Central American cruises.

Because the cruise industry advertises in every medium and travel agents love to book cruises, you'll have no difficulty obtaining information about cruise opportunities anywhere in the world. But while many brochures and Web sites feature couples looking romantically into one another's Champagne-glazed eyes, they're sometimes a little short on the kind of details you need to know. When you find a cruise that seems to fit your objectives, ask for a copy of the contract and read it.

Be sure you receive answers to the following questions:

- **SAVE Money** *Price:* First, determine the published price (usually easy to do on the Internet). Then ask precisely what it includes and excludes. Published fares for cruises are similar to hotel rack rates in that there's no need to pay them. To save money, ask for a discount for signing up early, or late, or because you can't afford the listed price, or for any other reason you think of. Like an airline seat, a cabin is a dead loss if it's empty when the ship sails. If the cruise operator can't fill it, you'll probably get a discount, but only if you ask. Give the operator a price to beat. Invite it to find a basis on which you qualify for a discount. If the price is inflexible and you're willing to pay it, ask for an upgrade to a better cabin at that price. If there's a single-supplement charge, will the company waive it? Is cancellation insurance included in the price? If it's not, you may want to consider buying it if there's a reasonable possibility you might miss the sailing.

Bear in mind that tips (including to people you never saw) add substantially to the cost. Ask about the recommended amounts. Other common add-ons—such as port fees, taxes, and "miscellaneous" charges—also increase the cost. Probably the largest hit, often not expected, is the cost of onshore excursions. In my limited cruise experience, these excursions are almost always worthwhile and way overpriced. A growing number of passengers now arrange these excursions directly with local companies at much lower cost. For guidance, take a look at **www.cruisescritic.com, www.cruisemates.com, www.cruisepromotions,** and **www.shoretrips.com.** These excursions are especially easy to arrange in ports in the Caribbean and Mexico. Look at the cruise lines brochure or Web site to see what it considers to be worthwhile excursions. Check the Web site for the port city itself. Or just walk down the gangway and hire a local car and driver—gain freedom, save a bundle.

Of course, at the end of the trip, the purser will amaze you with the cost of all those late-night exotic drinks you consumed.

- *Cabin:* What is the size of the cabin, and what does it include (for example, type of bathroom, size and number of beds, desk, window or porthole, view, balcony)? Because you pay for space, consider how much time you plan to spend in the cabin. Be aware that a cabin with a porthole or window may cost twice as much as an interior cabin—but I recommend taking an inside cabin only if you happen to be a vampire and like coffins. Make sure it's not within earshot of a bar, a restaurant, or the engine room.

- *Shipmates:* What will be the ages and nationalities of your shipmates, and how many will there be? If the group is too large, time ashore may be reduced, and meal service may be slow. See whether the cruise tends to cater to a particular age group and, if so, whether it's one you'd be comfortable with. Ask whether any large groups or organizations will be on the cruise. If so, might they set a tone for the trip that could make you unhappy? As a rule, the fewer the passengers, the better.

- *Dress:* If you'll be expected to resemble an emperor penguin at the dinner table, is that what you want?

- *Scheduled activities:* Are there any? Are there lectures? If so, are they in a language you understand? How long will you actually be ashore in each port?

- *Size of the ship:* This matters a lot. In terms of stability and variety of activities, a large ship may have more to offer—but do you really want a putting green? In contrast, a smaller ship is more intimate and has access to small bays, islands, and ports that cannot accommodate a superliner.

- *Philosophy of the ship's operator:* If it is to provide endless banquets and 24-hour cocktail parties, that's fine if that's what you want. If you prefer more activities, such as snorkeling, sea kayaking, nature hikes, visits to villages ashore, and so on, make sure that's what you'll get.

Discounted Cruises

SAVE Money If you're interested in a cruise, save money by contacting a discount-cruise specialist. The following are a few of the many companies that sell cruises at a discount:

- Cruises Only, (800) 278-4737 or **www.cruisesonly.com**
- The Cruise Marketplace, (800) 826-4333 or **www.cruisemarketplace.com**
- Cruise Shoppe Operations, (800) 338-9051 or **www.miamicruiseshoppe.com**
- Cruises of Distinction, (800) 634-3445
- CruiseWorld, (800) 228-1153 or **www.cruiseworld.com**
- AAA (members only), **www.aaa.com**
- White Travel Service, (800) 547-4790 or **www.cruisewizard.com**
- World Wide Cruises, (800) 882-9000 or **www.wwcruises.com**
- CruiseCompete (which allows you to pick a cruise and have travel agents compete to book it), (800) 237-8278 or **www.cruisecompete.com**

Sailing

Serving as a crew member on a sailboat cruising the Caribbean sounds pretty romantic. After all, it's a free ride to exotic ports, isn't it? Yes and no. Volunteer crew members may pay no money, but they contribute plenty of work. Still, it can be a fine trade-off. Ship captains are looking for experienced sailors, but you may be accepted if you can cook, provide medical services, or record the trip on film or in writing.

One way to find a ride is to visit marinas that cater to oceangoing yachts. Introduce yourself to owners and captains and mention your availability. Present yourself as a person who will be a pleasure to be with for several weeks in a very confined space. Put a notice on yacht club and marina bulletin boards, and give your phone number to marina personnel. Watch ads in local newspapers and boating magazines.

Whitewater Rafting

Whitewater adventure trips are not strictly considered transport, but there are fine opportunities for rafting in Mexico, Costa Rica, Nicaragua, and elsewhere. Unfortunately, just because an outfitter is in business doesn't mean its staff knows what it's doing. Ask how much experience the guides have on the river you have in mind. Ask about safety equipment in good condition (life jackets, helmets, throw rings, etc.)? Will safety kayakers accompany the trip? Will the river be at a safe level? Are the rafts self-bailing? Do the rafts have foot cups? If wet suits are needed, will they be provided? A good outfitter should ask you some questions about your experience and physical condition.

The importance of the answers to these questions varies depending on how challenging the particular river is. If a river is ranked I, II, or III, there's little to worry about. If there are Class IV or V rapids, you should listen closely to the answers.

If whitewater trips were completely safe, they wouldn't be any fun. After all, you're in it for the thrill and the challenge. Still, you're relying on the skill and equipment of an outfitter and its guides, so don't take anything for granted.

Freighter Travel

Opportunities for freighter travel in the traditional sense have diminished substantially over the past several decades. That is due, in part, to regulations that require a doctor on board if there are more than 12 passengers. However, after hitting a low in the mid-1980s, the capacity for passengers on freighters is again on the upswing. Increased mechanization has freed more officers' staterooms for passengers. Freighter travel isn't as cheap as it was in the past, but it's still possible to travel in a first-class freighter cabin for about $90 a day, considerably less than many cruise ships (and there are discounts for off-season travel). Cabins are likely to be more spacious than those on cruise ships, and there are often accommodations for singles with no surcharge. Most are outside cabins with large windows, comfortable sitting areas, and private bathroom facilities. Because the best cabins go to those who reserve first, some travelers plan a year or more in advance.

Wholesome meals, included in the price, are usually served in the officers' dining room. Depending on the carrier, these meals may be very ethnic, so make sure you know what to expect. There won't be a dance band or over-the-hill entertainers in shiny tuxedos, but there will probably be a sundeck, a VCR, a library, and, perhaps, a saltwater pool. The crew is there to work, so you'll have plenty of time to write the novel that's been waiting to spring to life.

Freighters travel slowly, providing more time at sea than you'd have on a cruise ship—and that's exactly what most freighter travelers are after. Because freighters are working ships, they may not adhere to their planned schedules. If you're kept at sea extra days because the ship detours to an unexpected port to capture a cargo, there's no extra charge.

> You will spend more time at sea on freighters than on cruise ships.

I don't know how Joseph Conrad would feel about modern freighters, but they can be a fine way to travel if you're flexible and seek the ultimate in relaxation. There's more to be said about travel by freighter, but because there are virtually no passenger-carrying freighter trips in the Central American region, this is not the place.

HITCHHIKING

So much public transport is available around the world, and it's so much fun and so cheap, that hitchhiking should be avoided unless absolutely necessary. Where there's no public transport, there is often almost no private transport either, and hitchhiking may become a necessity. If you don't accept rides with drivers who are drinking, hitchhiking may not be very risky—but who ever knows for sure?

Sixteen road-tested tips for successful hitchhiking:

- Early in the morning, when trucks start their journeys, is usually the best time to hitchhike. Stroll out after a leisurely breakfast, and you may have missed the wave. Ask local people. Be hesitant about hitchhiking after the sun falls below the yardarm and alcohol flows more freely. Besides, you may not want to fall asleep with some stranger driving.
- Stores, petrol stations, border posts, restaurants, and other places at which drivers stop are ideal for picking up a ride. Local people can tell you whether there's an informal depot for hitchhikers in town or whether it's better to walk to an out-of-town intersection.
- As you stroll to the roadside to find a ride, repeat to yourself: *pedestrians do not have the right of way.* Soft-shell humans must yield to trucks, buses, cars, oxcarts, camels, bicycles—everything. Not only will vehicles not stop, but most won't even swerve.
- If several people are waiting for a ride, it's the universal custom for the most recent arrival to take the position farthest down the road from approaching traffic. In other words, the early bird gets the Mercedes. A couple of times, I've been standing in the middle of an ad hoc line of local people waiting to catch a ride when a driver has stopped and beckoned to me to get in. He may have wanted English conversation or believed that he could charge me a higher fare, but I won't cut in front of local people who've been waiting longer.
- If not waiting in a line, give the impression that you're walking, not just standing by the roadside. Drivers like to think you're making an effort to get somewhere on your own.
- In choosing a spot, make sure oncoming drivers can see you clearly and have a safe place to pull over. Stand far enough off the road that you can't be clipped by a load hanging off the side of a truck.
- As a car approaches, make eye contact with the driver (which means no dark glasses). Smile and look like someone a driver would like to talk with. Make your gear look clean and compact.

- There is no universal hitchhiking signal. The traditional closed fist with upraised thumb, so natural in most of the Western world, is an obscene gesture in some places. In Indonesia, you raise and lower your open palm, holding it facing down and parallel to the road. In other places, you point your index finger and shake it up and down at the place where you'd like the vehicle to stop. Some hitchhikers hold up a sign with their destination written on it (as spelled in the local language, which is not necessarily how the name is spelled on your map). Some prefer not to use a sign because it somewhat commits them to ride with a driver whose company they would rather do without.
- Some hitchhikers make obscene gestures toward drivers who don't pick them up. Not only is that offensive behavior by a guest, especially one seeking a favor, but it's also a disservice to other hitchhikers. Giving a smile or a wave will work out better for you and for other travelers.
- I recommend against a single woman hitchhiking alone. She's likely to get picked up quickly, but then what? It's much safer to hitchhike with a companion. A man and woman together will have good luck.
- Be cautious about accepting a ride in a vehicle with more than two men. I'm not saying not to do it, just to be careful.
- Some people won't accept a lift from anyone who speeds by and then turns around to offer a ride. That eagerness may indicate a motive other than hospitality.
- Before getting in, ask the driver's destination before mentioning yours. If you have any reason for concern, courteously decline the ride. The world is not as gentle as it once was.
- If it's practical, keep your belongings next to you in the car. You're vulnerable with your backpack in the trunk.
- The driver who picks you up may expect some pay, which is reasonable given relative economic circumstances. You might bring up the subject before you climb in, or at least early on, to make sure there's no disagreement later. If local people pay, there may be fairly standard fares for certain distances, but a traveler will probably be asked to pay a small premium. I sometimes buy the driver a snack.
- Don't buy alcohol while under way. It's common for drivers to drink, and it causes a lot of fatal crashes. If you feel you should depart, say you're sick or have to relieve yourself. Staying alive is more important than courtesy.

CHAPTER 21

Etiquette

> Wherever you go, you will receive impressions
> of the places you see and the people you meet.
> Do not forget that those people will
> receive impressions of you.
> —Broughton Waddy and
> Ralph Townley
> *A Word or Two Before You Go* (1990)

Etiquette, custom, and tradition exist because they help make us comfortable in our relationships with other people. Most travelers know intuitively that to be welcomed as guests we have to know and observe local ground rules. Given the subtleties of the thousands of different ceremonies and rituals on this planet, can any traveler get up to speed? Actually, it's less of a problem than it seems.

Before starting your trip, read up on customs at your destinations. When you arrive, be alert to how local people behave in the key areas of eating, personal space, sanitation, gestures, and relationships between genders. In Mexico and Central America, you can expect a slower pace than in North America. Attitudes toward time are much more relaxed. And the nature of relationships helps determine whether things go smoothly.

Cultural intrusion from Western societies has already become incredibly far-reaching. Gezing is a small town in the Sikkimese foothills of the Himalayas, just down the mountain from the venerated Pemayangtse Monastery. Strolling through town late at night, when fires had been banked and lanterns shuttered, I passed a lopsided shack. Inside, a dozen kids were enthralled by a row of battery-run video games. Unlike Johnny Appleseed, we should avoid sowing seeds of our culture as we travel.

Unfortunately, travelers of a few nationalities are held in "minimum high regard" (as they say in the U.S. Senate) around the world. They've earned criticism for self-centered, jingoistic behavior and unwillingness to respect local culture.

CUSTOMS

The language of courtesy: As a nonlinguist, I'm proof that anyone can quickly command the few words necessary for basic courtesy. Learn and use the local words for "hello," "please," "thank you," and "excuse me." Travelers too often begin an encounter by bluntly asking a question, such as, "Where is the post office?" It's far better to speak first in the other person's language even if all you can say is, "Good morning." It shows respect and has a positive effect on what happens next.

Body language: In parts of Southeast Asia, standing with your hands on your hips as you address someone projects hostility. This is a good posture to avoid when dealing with an official.

Business cards: They're taken more seriously in other countries than in the United States and are offered at even a superficial meeting. You can get along without them, but you'll gain status if you bring some with you. They also help avoid errors in pronunciation and help new friends keep in touch with you.

Curiosity: You're likely to be the object of considerable curiosity, often undisguised. I have a photo that shows me walking down a narrow lane in Darjeeling, India, in the midst of a group of striking tea workers carrying placards. The cause of the strike appears momentarily forgotten as every marcher stares at my six-foot-four-inch frame. Unusual height, blond hair, or anything else that's different from local appearances may attract considerable curiosity. Learn to accept it graciously.

Discretion when speaking to other travelers: Don't offend someone or embarrass yourself by saying something inappropriate on the assumption that people around you don't understand English, or whatever language you're using.

Dress in accordance with local custom: Assuming that you won't be dressing exactly as local people do, at least modify your normal dress to fit local standards. Not surprisingly, restrictions on dress affect women more than men. (See Chapter 18, Woman on Her Own.) For women, local custom often means dressing in loose clothing and covering shoulders and legs. Watch local people. In many temples, head and legs must be covered, and feet must be free of shoes. Even though toplessness and sometimes total nudity are acceptable on quite a few European beaches and in various isolated spots around the world, wearing a skimpy bathing suit is a poor idea unless you're certain it won't offend local sensibilities.

If you're unsure about a particular custom, ask.

It's unusual to see local men or women wearing shorts in Latin America, but male travelers can wear shorts without giving offense. However, female travelers in shorts may attract unwanted attention anywhere. And you'll very seldom see local women wearing skirts that stop above the knee.

Eating: In some countries, the custom is to finish everything on your plate. In others, you're expected to leave a bit, indicating that the host was so generous you couldn't finish. You please any host by sampling some of everything. If something doesn't look palatable, it is better not to ask what it is because the reply is unlikely to improve the situation. Beyond all else, don't eat anything that might jeopardize your health, not even to be courteous. "I'm a vegetarian" goes a long way.

Elderly: Old people are treated with special respect in non-Western countries. Treat the eldest person as spokesperson for the group.

Face: Publicly embarrassing a person can give grave offense. "Face" is taken seriously, and offenses are not lightly forgiven. Public displays of temper should be avoided altogether.

Feet: In some places, such as Thailand, it is offensive for the soles of your feet, with or without shoes, to face toward another person. You may need to concentrate on this one for a while to avoid doing it without thinking. Speaking of your feet, step over the low sill at temple doorways because good spirits live under the sill.

Gestures: Familiar gestures may not travel well. For example, the thumb-and-forefinger "okay" sign you flash in a friendly way in Chicago refers to an intimate part of the anatomy in Brazil. In Britain, giving someone a "V" sign with your palm facing inward is the equivalent of the middle-finger sign in the United States. In Peru, as in Europe, pointing to the corner of an eye means: "Be alert; keep your eyes open."

If you thumb your nose at someone in Europe, be ready to step back. Beckoning someone by crooking your finger is an insult in Asia and the Middle East. In parts of South America and Europe, slapping the back of one fist with the other hand conveys your wish that the other person undertake an improbable activity. In Greece, an upward nod of the head means "no," whereas tilting the head to one side means "yes." If you raise an open hand to refuse something offered to you in Greece, your gesture may be understood as, "Go to hell." In that connection, be warned that a Greek may smile when angry. In India, emphatic wagging of the head side to side doesn't mean "no." It might mean "yes" or any number of other things.

Greetings: In many countries, greetings are exchanged frequently. It's fun to call out a greeting in the local language. Throughout Mexico and Central America (okay, except in Belize), you smile and say, "Buenos días," in the morning. On the tiny island of Gili Trawangan in Indonesia, "good morning" is "selamat pagi." (It's "pagi-pagi" if the hour is very early, but I never had the opportunity to use that one.) Everyone walking along Himalayan trails in Nepal smiles, makes eye contact, and sings out "namaste," meaning, more or less, "I salute the spirit within you." Throughout the Arab world, you'll be greeted with "salaam aleikum." In Israel, "shalom" is said both on arriving and departing.

In much of Asia, it's traditional to greet a person by bringing the palms together, fingertips anywhere from chest to eye level depending on the level of respect being conveyed, and inclining the head forward a little. In Thailand, this gesture is known as the *wai* and is still common in small towns and the countryside.

The handshake, ubiquitous in the West, is less common in the rest of the world. Follow the local person's lead. As a rule, a man shouldn't extend his hand to a woman unless she initiates the gesture. Zambia and several other African countries add a nice touch: your left hand grips your own right wrist as you extend your hand.

In Latin America and many other areas, be prepared to receive a hug and one or more kisses on the cheek, regardless of the gender of the other person.

Remember that personal space is cultural, and try not to feel invaded if the person you're talking with stands closer than you are used to.

Because people in other countries are more formal when meeting than are people in the United States, be hesitant to address new acquaintances by their first names unless requested to do so. In fact, you may be expected to use an academic or honorary title with the last name. Unfortunately, it's not always easy to know what the last name is. In Latin America (except in Brazil), many names are a combination of the father's and mother's surnames. Thus, you would address Señor Fidel Romero Santamaría as Señor Romero, using his father's surname. When you see a written name in China, the surname is first and the given name last. If uncertain, rather than give unintentional offense simply ask the other person how he or she would like to be addressed. Similarly, when a person says his or her name, ask that it be repeated until you have it right. You'll be respected for knowing, or wanting to learn, the custom.

> If an ass goes traveling, he'll not come home a horse.
> —Thomas Fuller, English clergyman

Head: In some places, the head is considered the seat of God in a person. Therefore, avoid touching anyone's head, and that includes not patting a child's head. If you do so accidentally, offer an immediate apology. In various places, including in temples and at religious ceremonies, a woman is expected to cover her head.

Hospitality: In many cultures—and Arabic cultures are good examples—hospitality is taken very seriously. You risk giving offense if you don't accept a sincere offer of food, shelter, or assistance. Nevertheless, be very circumspect in the Arab world when talking to or about someone else's wife or daughter. Hospitality does not extend that far, and your comment could be taken more personally than you intend. Remind yourself of the penalty for thieves, and extrapolate.

Also be cautious about expressing excessive admiration for someone's property, say, a gold watch. He may insist that you accept it as a gift. If you refuse, you risk giving offense—but you might be expected to reciprocate.

Humor: Few local people are amused by a traveler's jokes about local cuisine, government, and so on. What they might say among themselves they resent hearing from an outsider, no matter how humorous the intent.

Left hand: Because toilet paper is sometimes not readily available in non-Western countries, some local people use the left hand as a substitute (in conjunction with a bucket of water when it's available). Even assuming that you carry TP with you, make it a practice not to eat with your left hand. If you forget, your dining neighbors will consider you uncivilized, not to mention unclean.

Littering: Tossing litter, even a cigarette butt in a country that doesn't regard itself as an ashtray, can result in arrest and a fine.

National honor and other hot topics: Citizens of most countries are very sensitive about their national honor. This feeling is intense in Latin America, as well as in countries governed by any form of monarchy. (Some African quasimonarchies are more than a little touchy as well.) Don't show disrespect for a national flag, criticize a national leader, or comment publicly about controversial aspects of the society. Avoid discussing religion, politics, and border conflicts. And I assure you that no one wants to be reminded that his or her country receives foreign aid from your country. As a guest, err on the side of discretion.

Nuance: When people for whom English is not the first language speak to you in English, they may not understand the nuances of what they're saying. For example, if someone calls out, "Hey, you!" or, "Hey, mama!" there is probably no intention to be rude. They are seeking your attention but have a limited vocabulary from which to draw. Keep this in mind, and you're unlikely to be offended.

Personal habits: Some habits that are accepted in the United States—such as chewing gum in public, interrupting when another is speaking, and slapping someone on the back—may give offense elsewhere.

Plumbing: It's a little fragile in lots of places. In practical terms, that means don't automatically flush TP down the toilet. The practice may be to put it in a bucket nearby that will be emptied . . . periodically.

Public affection: There is little public display of affection in many countries. With the modern tide inundating the world, this inhibition is diminishing, but travelers should respect the local custom. Holding hands is fine, whether as a sign of affection or as a self-defense strategy, but holding more than that may not be.

Punctuality: Because punctuality is not always prized in Latin America, here are two tips: First, if you arrive at the scheduled time, you're unlikely to give offense. Second, if the other person arrives significantly later than you did, hold your tongue and temper because his arrival may be consistent with local protocol.

Religion: Even if it is just impressive architecture to you, it may be a holy place to someone else. If in doubt about the appropriateness of taking pictures, obtain permission or don't do it. Don't let your conversation interfere with someone else's worship. Activity in Islamic countries will stop for prayers five times a day. Although you're not expected to participate, you must not interrupt or show impatience.

Servers: We all know that being demanding of a serving person in a restaurant is impolite at any time. Furthermore, what seems like poor service may be consistent with a custom unfamiliar to you. For example, it may be customary to serve dishes in what seems an odd sequence. If you're polite, perhaps the server will point out the things on your plate that are garnishes, not intended for consumption. Otherwise, she'll watch happily as you gulp them down with a grimace (yours, not hers).

Shoes: In much of the non-Western world, it's the custom to remove one's shoes before entering certain spaces, including homes and temples. Watch others. If in doubt, slip your shoes off at the door.

Thank you: In many countries, you should arrive with candy or flowers or some other small gift if invited to dinner in someone's home. However, a gift of flowers demonstrates the complexity of local customs. In various places, you should not give an odd number of flowers, or chrysanthemums or purple flowers (both of which may be suitable only for funerals), or roses (which may have an overly personal, romantic connotation). How to know? Ask. When someone does you a favor, send a thank-you note. Give such people something tangible to let them know they didn't drop out of your thoughts the moment you left.

Observing the customs I've described will ease your way a great deal, but I can also suggest two books that provide more comprehensive guidance. They are *Do's and Taboos around the World* and *The Do's and Taboos of International Trade,* both available from the publisher at **www.wiley.com**, Amazon (**www .amazon.com**), and other sources.

In addition, I recommend CultureGrams, produced by ProQuest (**www .culturegrams.com**). Annually updated CultureGrams cover more than 200 countries, including Mexico and Central America. Each four-page CultureGram provides a comprehensive background on that country. It describes what to expect in terms of language, religions, attitudes, local food, tipping, holidays, customs and courtesies, and visa and inoculation requirements. You can download CultureGrams singly for $4 each or buy the whole set in the $160 World Edition. CultureGrams are a real asset and a bargain.

BEGGING

Beyond the borders of developed countries, travelers are often shocked and saddened by the number of excruciatingly poor people. Few are beggars by choice, just people struggling to survive. Children are sometimes forced to beg because their parents have learned that children arouse tourists' compassion. Stories persist of parents or master panhandlers who cripple children horribly to make them more pathetic and therefore more successful as beggars.

Naturally, beggars congregate where there are tourists with money. Therefore, you must come to terms emotionally with beggars and develop a mind-set that permits you to be neither constantly depressed by their condition nor constantly annoyed by their appeals. At the same time, their existence should never come to seem acceptable. There is no easy answer.

Because tourists like to give candy to children, small shops near scenic attractions sell candy for just that purpose. Some tourists who know better than to dispense candy feel okay about handing out pens, maybe on the idealistic theory that a pen will permit a poetic genius to emerge. Catching on quickly, kids ask for pens and then sell them.

Shy schoolgirl and protective brother, Lake Atitlán, Guatemala

It's probably impossible to assess the authenticity of a beggar's true condition. A woman with a child on her hip came up to me on a Calcutta street. Asking not for money but for milk, she guided me a block or so to a small shop, where I bought her a carton of milk. I left feeling that I'd made a good choice. Did she sell the milk back for cash as I turned the corner? I don't know. Should I care, or is it her right to use the best device she can to secure money for whatever she determines are her most pressing needs?

Some tourists use skepticism to mask inherent stinginess. Others give something to every supplicant for a while, then nothing to anyone. I have a friend who, each time she visits India, selects a reputable charity and makes a contribution, but doesn't give to individual beggars.

If you are moved to respond to the ubiquitous "hey, mister" from a child tagging along behind you, one choice is to personalize the experience by giving a postcard that features your hometown. You might show photographs of your house or your significant other. I know a guy who carries an inflatable globe. He puffs it up and shows kids the world and their place on it. Another traveler plays tunes on his harmonica and lets kids experience the magic of his zoom lens and a magnifying glass he carries. Balloons, tops, and sleight-of-hand tricks draw a crowd in seconds. These things solve no fundamental problems, but they let kids be kids for a while in a hard world.

If you give to even one person in public view, you are marked, and memories are long. A generous person could probably return to Bombay after an absence of ten years and be remembered for her generosity.

Before you leave home, consult your feelings about responding to beggars. A traveler wants to be liked, but leaving a trail of trinkets behind scarcely enhances a person's image in the eyes of local people. We should face the reality that begging often changes values and lowers self-esteem. Of course, it may also keep a family alive. Whatever you decide, the reality of deformed, emaciated children will strike you like a stinging slap in the face.

TIPPING

Tipping protocol in Latin America is similar to that in the United States. Travelers commonly tip airport baggage handlers, porters, room-service providers, waiters, tour guides, taxi drivers, and almost everyone associated with a cruise. The total of these tips can be substantial enough that you should include them in your budget. If you arrive in a country with none of its currency, don't worry. A $1 bill is readily accepted as a tip almost everywhere.

Watch to see if a service charge has been added to your bill in a restaurant or hotel. If so, the establishment expects you to tip no further. Of course, the waiter may still try for a tip from anyone whose travel clothes look fresh off the rack. Waiters used to tourists are likely to work them for a tip regardless of local custom and pressure them by showing displeasure if they don't get one.

The chance of your tip reaching the intended recipient is much greater if it comes directly from your hand rather than being left on the table.

Extremely low wages in most underdeveloped countries are a motivation to be generous in tipping, certainly by local standards. Along with giving a tip, I look the person in the eye and say, "Thank you for helping me."

In many countries, tipping is genuinely discouraged except at upscale establishments that cater primarily to tourists. If you're unsure, check your guidebook, and ask several people outside the tourist industry.

Again, tipping is firmly established in Latin America, but anywhere it's not the local custom to tip, don't impose a foreign custom.

BRIBES

Despite euphemisms such as *mordida* ("little bite" in Spanish), *baksheesh, dash,* and *wairo,* what we're going to talk about is, if I may be so indelicate as to call it by its true name, a bribe. Because bribery is not a custom most of us grew up with, it makes us nervous.

In many countries, a bribe is not always considered improper, let alone illegal. It's often looked at as a just reward for having wiggled oneself into some minor, underpaid, bureaucratic job from which a little leverage can occasionally be exerted. The problem is that once an official has learned that a few travelers will pay extra for his services, he makes demands on all who follow. However, in some other circumstance, offering a bribe could offend someone or lead to legal trouble.

I've probably missed a few subtle signals from time to time, but a guard at the U.S.–Mexico border left no doubt. I needed permission to take my car into Mexico. He was willing, all right, and named his price. Because I had the proper documents and there was little risk to my safety, I ignored his demand. He backed off, and nothing happened.

> In many countries, a bribe is considered proper.

A couple of times, a customs official has asked me to give him something from my backpack. The first asked for several film canisters, which he probably intended to sell. The other boldly asked for my camera. The first I pretended not to understand; the other I refused with a laugh as if we both knew he was joking. Nothing happened.

When I tried to buy a train ticket on the midnight special out of New Delhi, three clerks told me the tickets were "finished." Not willing to give up, I casually laid a few dollars on the desk of the senior ticket master. Giving my offering the briefest glance, he repeated that there was nothing he could do for me. As I was leaving, he called to my attention that I had left something on his desk, indicating the bills with a one-eyebrow-raised nod. Sheepishly, I picked them up, feeling as if I'd been caught with my hand in the cookie jar. Twenty minutes later, a Sikh acquaintance straightforwardly bribed a porter to let us board the train. A second bribe gained us icy-cold metal berths. I spent most of the night reading Shakespeare and drinking Indian Army rum to keep warm. We got to Udaipur in time to hear an Elvis Presley imitator perform at a New Year's Eve party at the famous Lake Palace Hotel. That was *baksheesh* well spent.

If an impasse develops between you and an official who won't do what you need unless you pay him, ask to see a superior official. If the first guy is trying shakedowns on his own, you may get help. If everyone is in on it, you may be stuck.

Obviously, there's no formula for calculating the amount required to make something happen. It seems to be related to the service you need, the grandeur of the official, and the assessment of the bribe seeker as to how impatient or wealthy you are. In one situation, you might offer a small amount to a low-ranking official right away. Another time, you might be better off going to the person in charge. If time permits, start with a small amount and then pull incremental amounts from different pockets as needed. The ultimate amount will reflect the relative value of money in the official's life and the urgency of your desire.

When offering a bribe, be discreet. Use ambiguous words when making an offer. Ask if there isn't "some other way" to handle the problem. For example, perhaps you could pay a small "fine" to the official on the spot or buy an unspecified "permit." If you do the deal in silence, you can, as politicians put it, maintain deniability. Don't let other officials see money change hands, and never let anyone see how much money you have.

DOING FAVORS

Someone may ask you to have an application form sent to him from a university in your country. Another may ask you to make a telephone call to her relative in the States or to send back a copy of the photograph you took of her family at the dinner table. Because a traveler receives so much help while on the road, doing favors is essential to balance the scales. Further, the favor one traveler does for someone may motivate a kindness to some other traveler. Or it may just be the right thing to do. You don't have to agree to do everything anyone asks, but when you promise to do a favor, do at least what you promised and more if possible. By extension, when you meet a foreign traveler in need of assistance in your home country, you are honor-bound to help. It's part of the traveler's code of ethics.

CHAPTER 22

Meeting People

> Travelers are often advised to take a long book
> on their journeys, but who would devote his attention
> to a book when he can turn the dog-eared pages of a
> total stranger whom he may never meet again?
> —Quentin Crisp
> "Riding with a Stiff Upper Lip"
> The *New York Times* (1983)

MEETING LOCAL FOLKS

Long after the scenic wonders have merged in your mind, you remember the guide you talked to while walking through the Costa Rican rain forest, the family you stayed with in Oslo, and endless conversations on Indian trains. You remember the people, and they remember you. They remember whether you liked their country, whether you were polite, and whether you were sincere. Meeting local people is the essence of independent travel.

Travelers too often base their opinions of local people on the few who make their living working the tourist trail, selling food, products, and services (including, unhappily, taxi drivers)—relationships that are commercial, superficial, and sometimes adversarial. That's why it's worth the effort to meet normal people outside the areas frequented by tourists. Even if you feel inhibited by language or fear of rejection, it's worth doing. You learn about family life, politics, religion, local food specialties, symbolism in arts and crafts, their view of your country, and who knows what else. You may be permitted to witness special rituals or be taken to places you wouldn't otherwise have found. And you make genuine friends.

One easy way to meet local people is via an introduction from a friend, including the ever-helpful "friend of a friend." Another way is to ask your alumni office whether any graduates of your high school or university live where you're going. Ask for a letter of introduction from your place of worship to counterparts abroad with which it has relationships. Get names from professional associations (lawyers, florists, anyone).

If your city has a sister city abroad, the sister-city organization will have names and addresses of contacts. Overseas members of your local social and business clubs will be delighted when you look them up. I've seen Rotary, Kiwanis, and Lions signs in some pretty far-out places. Your branch of the Friendship Force, National Council for International Visitors, Girl Scouts, or Boy Scouts can give you addresses of international visitors who have been in your hometown.

On the road, make contact by joining an athletic contest. Volleyball, soccer, table tennis, and badminton are played worldwide. Get out your Frisbee, and invite someone to toss it with you. Attend local sporting events. Ride local transportation. Walk through residential neighborhoods. See if the local tourist office introduces travelers to local people.

It's not enough to return home and report about how hospitable "they"—the locals—were. You'll almost always have more money and time than they, so put both to good use. While still with them, leave favorable memories behind.

MEETING OTHER TRAVELERS

When I started traveling, it felt great to occasionally meet travelers who spoke English as their first language. I felt comfortable with them, perhaps because we had so much in common. Over the years, having become more at home away from my hearth, I've discovered the immense rewards of meeting travelers from distant lands, people to share with and learn from. It's more than worth the struggle to communicate.

> Knowledge of another culture should sharpen our ability to scrutinize more steadily. To appreciate more lovingly, our own.
> —Margaret Mead, Coming of Age in Samoa (1928)

Although I understand the impulse, it saddens me now to see some travelers from certain countries relentlessly seek out countrymen, forming a clique, creating an artificial home away from home. They miss so much.

Travel is an opportunity to be more extroverted by taking the initiative to meet other travelers. The potential for learning, a good conversation, or a long-term friendship makes the effort worthwhile. Here are just a few of the benefits you can expect from making friends with other travelers:

- You collect information that improves your trip. Travelers are like reliable, interactive, up-to-date guidebooks, talking about trustworthy places to buy cheap airline tickets and the location of the best scuba dive boat. If a guidebook lists three places to stay in Antigua, Guatemala, they'll be filled with people who've read that book. But from other travelers you'll get opinions about another dozen places to stay. The best information is on the traveler's grapevine.
- You may feel a sense of security from traveling with others.
- A small group can negotiate better rates for rooms, a vehicle, or a guide than one person can on her own.
- You enjoy the refreshing equality of friendships formed on the road. Personal details about job, possessions, and education are unknown and irrelevant—and no longer suggest status. In order to base my feelings about other travelers on how I experience them in the present, I avoid asking personal "background" questions that could lead me to make generalizations.

- You're likely to have many shared values. After all, you all made the effort to bring yourself to the distant place at which you've met. Having experienced similar obstacles and marvels along the way, you feel a special camaraderie and bond, a good foundation for friendship.
- You have someone with whom to share tales of the open road.
- Traveling on your own can get lonely, and there are times when companionship provides an emotional lift.

That leads to the issue of how to meet other travelers. In many cities, there are areas notable for the density of accommodations for budget travelers. The Thamel section of Kathmandu is an example, as are Khao San Road in Bangkok and Sudder Street in Calcutta. There are many examples in Central America, such as Calle Santander (and nearby blocks) in Panajachel and the village of San Pedro la Laguna across Lake Atitlán, both in Guatemala, as well as the town of Fortuna near Arenal Volcano in Costa Rica. Walk around the Boul'Mich (Boulevard Saint-Michel) in Paris, the Piazza San Marco in Venice, Jalan Sosrowijayan in Yogyakarta (Indonesia), and similar crossroads all over the world, and you'll find plenty of travelers.

Sometimes there are specific hangouts. For example, in Nairobi, those places were the Thorn Tree Café and the Iqbal Hotel. When the hotel's neighborhood declined, travelers shifted to the Terminal Hotel. Some gathering spots are mentioned in guidebooks; others you find on your own. Travelers congregate at train and bus stations, airports, restaurants, and scenic attractions. All you need is a smile, a friendly greeting, and a ready question.

When traveling as a couple, you have to initiate conversations with other people. Otherwise, they'll tend to keep their distance. Older travelers may need to take the initiative as well. Why remain separate just because you're 25 years older than travelers around you when you can close the gap so easily?

> Travel is an opportunity to be more extroverted.

Somewhere along the way, you may meet expatriates. Although the word "expatriate" literally connotes banishment and exile, most expats live voluntarily in a country other than their own. Some are military personnel who ended their careers while stationed overseas. They've become accustomed to a pleasant lifestyle and may no longer have intimate ties at home. Ex–Peace Corps volunteers are known for developing attachments to "their" countries and remaining for years after their formal service ends. Many North American oil-company workers retire in northern South America. Thousands of people who have long-term jobs with multinational corporations move from country to country like lonely satellites. Some people who work for humanitarian organizations become stateless, circling the globe for life. From Ecuador to Honduras to Malawi to Laos, missionaries remain away from home for decades, some of them helping local people obtain justice. Places such as

Mexico, Panama, Nicaragua, and Costa Rica have become retirement homes for hundreds of thousands of Americans.

Almost all expats know their way around the place where you meet them, share a language with you, and can supply excellent information. A traveler who accepts their hospitality should bring something to the table besides conversation. Buy the beer, help with the cooking, or fulfill a request to send something from home.

Two final thoughts about meeting other travelers: First, you'll inevitably meet people who have traveled longer and farther than you have. Learn what you can from them, but never let their exploits diminish your trip. Second, when sharing travel anecdotes, it's important to share air time as well. The other person has at least as much interest in sharing his or her experiences as you do in listening to yourself talk.

ROMANCE ON THE ROAD

Let's face it: travel can be an aphrodisiac. Not only is the trip a terrific high, but you're also meeting other travelers with whom you share some important values. And you have time. In addition, there are all those exotic, attractive local people. Ah, if only life were so simple. The fact is that the idea of engaging in a relationship (okay, sex) on the road deserves some serious thought beforehand.

Cybercafe and video-rental shop, Condega, Nicaragua

Your Travel Partner's Feelings

If you're traveling with a partner, would your involvement with another person cause your partner a problem? How would you feel if your partner became involved with someone else? Could a third person join your partnership comfortably? A good traveling partner is not to be offended thoughtlessly. If there could be a problem, talk it over honestly early on, before you have to split up the partnership's assets.

Other Travelers

Given all the time spent in sensual settings, romances on the road are hardly unknown. It's easy for travelers to get to know one another quickly through the candor and vulnerability that emerge in remote places. A relationship may develop that will bridge oceans and international time zones—or last at least until paths diverge.

In no case, however, does the magic of an exciting new relationship confer immunity to sexually transmitted diseases. Some of these afflictions are annoying, some are serious, and some are fatal. You can't know your new friend's sexual history. Each of us must make his or her own decision about abstinence, but the imperatives of safe sex are worldwide. If you don't drink the water, does it make sense to carelessly take a risk of a much greater magnitude?

Local Contact

You may find yourself emotionally and physically attracted to a local person. That's the good part. The bad part is that in many countries, sexually transmitted diseases are widespread. That's particularly true with respect to local people associated in some way with the tourist trail. At the very least, condoms and hygienic caution are a must.

If you develop a loving relationship with a local person, don't unintentionally create expectations that won't be met. For example, if the relationship is to continue, one of you will have to learn to live in a new culture. The ramifications deserve serious consideration.

There can be a darker side to a relationship with a local person. Travelers have been seduced for reasons that are more mercenary than romantic, and something other than a heart may be stolen.

CHAPTER 23

How to Get the Most Out of Your Trip

The journey not the arrival matters.
—T. S. Eliot

Sometimes on a trip, I feel like the leaf Theodore Dreiser imagined floating along on the surface of a stream, completely at the mercy of outside forces. At other times, I have the illusion of being in control. In either case, there's one vital variable that can make or break my trip. That's my state of mind.

State of Mind

Days and nights are filled with new experiences: art, architecture, exotic and perhaps erotic dance, theater and music, magnificent landscapes, physical challenges, and new friends. What a great way to live!

At the same time, everything is different. Language and food may be difficult to digest. Everything has to be bargained for. Something set down unattended can disappear in the blink of an eye. Decisions must be made all day long. Travel is an excellent investment, but like most investments, it's not completely free from stress.

Any traveler who expects for plans to work out as smoothly as they do at home, or who is determined to force those plans through despite changes in circumstances, will be unhappy. To enjoy the trip, give yourself permission to change course, to go with a better idea when one comes along. When it starts raining and the trail turns to mud, you have to be ready to find the humor. Feeling that the rain god has a personal grudge against you will definitely make the mud deeper.

You chose your destinations for the very reason that they are different from your own country. Take pleasure in the differences. Leave generalizations, preconceptions, and stereotypes at home.

I watched a traveler radiate exasperation as he turned from the clerk in a small Guatemalan hotel and snapped to his partner, "He doesn't even understand plain English." Sure, the traveler was hot and tired, but that didn't excuse his behavior. If he'd seen the clerk as a person, he would have acknowledged that the young man was trying to help. It was the traveler who was falling short.

He hadn't learned basic, utilitarian Spanish phrases and didn't have a phrase book handy. To restore calm, his partner responded, "Be or be one." What she meant, as they both knew, was be patient or you'll soon be a patient.

Officialdom

If officialdom in Latin America had a family crest, it would feature a hand stamp. When you need something from an official, whether you get it may depend on your state of mind. For example, if you convince yourself that a bureaucrat has intentionally singled you out to ignore, you may feel justified in becoming angry. On the other hand, if you understand that time is treated differently than in your country and that waiting is part of life for everyone, it's easier to remain a little detached. Visualize yourself as bamboo swaying in the wind. If there's something you can't change, go with the flow. Learning to accept things calmly conserves vast amounts of energy.

When I see a traveler leaning angrily over an official's desk, demanding some privilege on the grounds of being a foreigner, I assume he must value self-indulgence over peace of mind or success.

When you can pass by an official anonymously, do so. If he's an obstacle or you need assistance, try to make him want to bend a regulation. Look him in the eye, smile, make personal comments, and compliment his country, the weather, anything. If you can't persuade him to do what you want, ask him to suggest a solution himself.

People Who Want to Sell You Something

State of mind makes a big difference when interacting with people selling things. Persistent peddlers can test your sanity unless you settle on a way of dealing with them. I was blissfully strolling across the sunny Plaza de Armas in Veracruz when a woman started following me, pestering me to buy one of her hand-woven belts. Snapping at or ignoring her would have been unfair, not to mention abrasive. I tried to connect with her urgency by imagining that she was supporting a large family and remembering that for eight months of the year, there are no tourists to whom she can sell anything. I still didn't want to buy another belt, so I looked at her and said, pleasantly but firmly, "No, *gracias.*" She wouldn't go away. I stopped walking and said, "*No tengo dinero* (I have no money)." That discouraged without offending her. If a merchant just won't stop, I go about my business without getting annoyed.

Expectations about Time

Expectations about time will make a big difference in the serenity of your travels. Think of travel as a marathon rather than a sprint. You have to pace yourself, even losing a little time here and there. Traveling too fast is a prescription for burnout.

Most of the world's population takes the longer view of life, not being too concerned when things don't happen precisely as scheduled. This attitude may be related to feelings of powerlessness. At home, you believe you can affect your environment, and so you attempt to do so. In much of the world, people view themselves as objects on which the system acts as it will. If you're obsessive about punctuality, independent travel will either be a liberating experience or leave you a quivering heap. Your choice. Think of getting stressed as similar to getting sunburned. It can spoil your trip, so why not avoid it?

Persistence

I wanted to see the interior of an elegant theater in Oaxaca, but the massive front doors were locked. I tried the side door, then the rear—both locked. It was a rainy, dreary day, and I was about to give up and head for cover. Then I thought, I'll just take a look around that last corner. Sure enough, there was an open door, and a man with a peg leg, probably in his 80s, emerged to show me around. As he thumped along, he reminisced about the past glories of the theater and then lapsed into whispery tales of the Aztecs, breathing life into the past. Since then, I've characterized persistence in terms of always turning one more corner. That means asking one more question, walking a little farther, seeing if there isn't some way to make something happen. I'm not talking about being obsessed or

Rob working on his journal

bullheaded. I mean that with just a little more effort, turning one more corner, you're likely to get more of what you want.

Context

Travel has helped me understand people's behavior in its own context, rather than in mine. Seeing hundreds of Chinese crouched roadside using hand tools to break boulders into piles of pebbles, I felt critical of the government for not having provided a more mechanized way of doing the job. Miles farther down the road, someone pointed out to me that machines would throw those hundreds of people, and perhaps millions more, into unemployment. That's what I mean by seeing things in context.

I've also learned not to generalize about an entire country because of an unfortunate experience with one person. That taxi driver was just a taxi driver, not a national symbol.

Attitude

I traveled with a partner who was so relentlessly positive she was almost other-worldly. She'd find the single ray of light in the gloomiest sky. When I asked how she was feeling after an incredibly hot, jolting, all-day bus trip, she responded with admiration for some beautifully shaped trees she'd noticed along the way. She knows that happiness is not a destination; it's an attitude.

> If you can keep your head when all about you / Are losing theirs . . . wait and not be tired by waiting . . . fill the unforgiving minute / With sixty seconds worth of distance run, / Yours is the Earth and everything that's in it . . .
> —Rudyard Kipling, *If* (1895)

In many countries, it's a serious loss of face to display anger. It follows that the hot temper of a traveler will be met with glacial resistance. Ralph Waldo Emerson advised us that a man should behave "so that, on what point soever of his doing your eye falls, it shall report truly of his character."

It's no myth that there are obstacles in the road over which a traveler may stumble. A train you planned to catch has been discontinued, your bus misses a connection, or a border post closes early. You're grounded when transportation workers strike. The power blackout snuffs out the air-conditioning for which you paid double room rent. Your snorkel snoozes in its stuff sack while a mystery bug scrambles your intestines. Things happen. Stifle that temptation to whine. Often, if you're unhappy, people around you are, too—and they certainly don't want to hear about your problems.

I prepare myself to accept, genuinely accept, discomforts as I travel. Temporary discomfort is part of the price of admission to the rest of the world. You can control how unhappy you want to be. The hard bed is softer to a relaxed body.

When there's a situation you just can't influence, take it in stride. Be open, not defensive. Follow your own path, not one intended to meet someone else's approval. Act with intensity when you must, but let your trip be characterized by calm.

Give Yourself a Treat

In their efforts to stay within a budget, some travelers live at a scruffier level than makes sense. Even though you've prepared yourself for a standard of living lower than at home, excessive frugality is not a virtue. If carried to an extreme, it may make you forget the reasons you decided to travel in the first place.

On the island of Lamu, I met a young couple from Australia. They'd rented a single-room hut in the middle of the island, reached by a long walk across rock-strewn fields. Their paradise had one lantern, a concrete-like mattress, an outdoor toilet and shower, and no protection from mosquitoes, and they had to fight off snapping dogs every time they put a foot out the door. They'd chosen that lovely cottage solely because it cost only $5 a night. On the other hand, I had a large room with an attached bathroom, an overhead fan, and a balcony overlooking the sea and the social life of the village, for which I paid $9. I believe that couple had lost perspective.

There is usually some correlation between cost and sanitation. If paying $2 less rents you a crop of bedbugs or a mosquito net full of holes, it's time to remember why you're traveling.

SAVE Money Throughout this book, I've made suggestions on how to save money. The concept of giving yourself a treat does not contradict those suggestions. My point is to avoid false economies, to avoid being penny wise, pound foolish. Ask yourself which is the better choice: renting a cheap room directly across from the bus station and staying awake all night, or finding a quieter place for a few more dollars? Would it be wiser to book a berth than to sit up all night on a long train trip? Don't you deserve an air-conditioned room after a trek through the steamy jungle? Every once in a while, check to see if you're treating yourself well enough.

The Regent Hotel in Kowloon, Hong Kong, is a masterpiece of satiny black marble and gleaming brass. Beyond the soaring glass wall of the bar, a zillion lights twinkle from Victoria Peak, and yellow lanterns swing from the bowsprits of hundreds of junks in the harbor. Standing at that bar, I imagined standing on the bridge of the Starship *Enterprise* looking into the galaxy. You owe yourself an evening in that bar even though a mai tai costs five times what it would a few blocks inland.

The old-fashioned Oriental Hotel on the bank of the Chao Phraya River in Bangkok ranks among the very best in the world. Treat yourself to afternoon tea at Noel Coward's favorite table. Listen for echoes of conversations between Somerset Maugham and an Oxford-educated Thai prince; imagine Joseph Conrad grumbling about the waiter being too slow returning with a mug of rum.

In Nairobi, the venerable Norfolk Hotel was the scene of some of the wild social excesses of colonial Kenya. If you happen to see a party going on, watch for an evanescent Karen Blixen or Beryl Markham across the room. Perhaps the grizzled old man wearing the bush hat and pulling on an icy Tusker beer can tell you stories of guiding Scott Fitzgerald or Teddy Roosevelt on safari. When you hear Winston Churchill's booming laugh behind you, you may have had one whiskey and soda too many.

Feast at the all-you-can-eat *braai* (barbecue) under the stars at the Victoria Falls Hotel in Zimbabwe. The thunder of falling water plays a million-year-old bass behind the string dance band. It's a fine splurge after you've been minding your budget.

As a kid, I tried out for a Little League baseball team. Incredibly nervous my first time at bat, I was relieved when the umpire called the first three pitches balls. The next two were strikes. Hoping I'd get on base with a walk, I let the last pitch go by without swinging. The umpire called it a strike, and I walked away dragging my bat in the dust. I've never forgotten that experience and never let it happen again. I decided not to let life whiz by without taking a swing, a full swing. That includes involving myself wholeheartedly in whatever appeals to me as I travel.

When it's time, bust that budget. After all, when planning your trip you built in a little surplus for that very purpose. Think about what turns you on. A white-water raft trip? Scuba diving with dolphins and whales? Front-row seats for an outdoor performance of the *Ramayana* in the full-moon shadow of an ancient Hindu temple? Because you can experience some things only when you're there, is the price really so high? How would you value the same amount of money at home? It may seem expensive at the moment, but don't let being on the road rob you of perspective. Treating yourself well creates lifelong memories.

Que Sera, Sera

Consider letting go of a need for consistency and efficiency when traveling. The airline insisted that passengers turn up three hours ahead of flight time and then didn't allow us on board until 45 minutes after the scheduled departure time. After baking on the sun-scorched runway for 30 minutes, we were told to climb back off the plane. Milling around under the blazing sun, we discovered that this was happening because someone forgot to load the lifejackets required for the flight. I felt a little exasperated, but I've learned to look automatically for the humor in situations. Lifejackets? For a flight across Saudi Arabia?

Mechanical malfunctions are so commonplace that people learn patience without anxiety. The one o' clock bus will leave when it leaves. If it breaks down, it will be fixed when it's fixed. *Inshallah*, or, "as God wills," expresses the view in Muslim countries that not all is subject to human control. The flow of life is a deep current, one against which travelers are well advised not to struggle. Instead of grumbling, say, "Que sera, sera," with a rueful smile.

CHAPTER 24

Communications

Travel sharpens the senses. Abroad, one feels,
sees, and hears things in an abnormal way.
—Paul Fussell
The Norton Book of Travel (1987)

Each of us is either "on the bus," writer Ken Kesey said, or "off the bus." He meant that we either make a commitment to something or we don't; we can't have it both ways. We have to make choices, and one of mine is to be completely where I am, not halfway somewhere else. I've found that having much contact with home during a trip pulls me back down the steps of the bus. However, if you want to or need to be in touch with home, it's easier if you understand how the systems work.

E-MAIL ON THE ROAD

Electronic mail has made it easy and inexpensive for travelers to stay in touch while on the road. Most pleasure travelers wouldn't consider carrying a laptop computer for purposes of communication. They don't want the extra weight or the task of defending it against thieves. Still, some laptops have become even lighter (under three pounds) and more compact, making transporting them much easier. Many hotels, certainly all upscale ones, provide Internet access for guests. In addition, points for wireless access are increasingly common.

There's an easy alternative—the cybercafe or Internet cafe. It's amazing that the whole concept was originated as recently as 1994 in London and has spread around the globe faster than Starbucks. The first Internet cafe in the United States appeared in Manhattan's East Village in 1995. The term *cafe* was chosen because cafes have historically been places where information is exchanged. Some are homey, quirky cafes that may actually serve food and beverages, but many are chain operations started by trend-spotting entrepreneurs. Even many public spaces, such as airports and libraries, have Internet kiosks.

Oddly, the rate of growth seems to have slowed, perhaps even reversed in wealthier countries. That's because these cafes were initially established to serve local residents who, now that computer ownership has greatly expanded, need them less. As a result, travelers may find it necessary to ask around a bit more. Ask the desk clerk, or ask at a store or restaurant. Before you leave home, consult **www.world66.com/netcafeguide** or **www.cybercaptive.com** for locations of

Internet cafes around the world. Just enter the country or city, and you'll receive full details about local Internet cafes.

Happily, Internet cafes are plentiful in Mexico and Central America.

The fee is usually charged per minute or per hour, so make sure you understand the costs before you log on. Some are reasonable, costing less than a bottle of Bohemia beer for an hour, while others can be more expensive ($4.50 for 90 minutes in Oslo). You use the rented computer for two tasks. The first is to send messages. That's pretty straightforward unless the keyboard is not the one you're used to. If it's not, the symbols and instructions may also be very different, perhaps indecipherable. That's less of a problem in Latin America than in, say, Turkey.

At a typical international chain hotel, you'll pay a pretty penny to use the business center (often four or five times what computer time costs in a cafe across the street). Paradoxically, budget and midrange hotels often have a public computer or two you can use for free or for the going local rate.

The other task is reading e-mail that's been sent to you. To do that, you need to have created an account with one of the numerous free e-mail services. Hotmail, Yahoo! Mail, and Google's Gmail are some of the most popular. Once registered, you can go to the service's Web site, log on, and check your mail.

TELEPHONES

In the past, few travelers called home with any frequency because either they couldn't find a phone or the cost was outrageous. In parts of the world, including parts of Latin America, the former is still a challenge. On the other hand, in tiny San Pedro la Laguna on the north shore of Lake Atitlán in Guatemala, an operator in a two-room adobe office connected a traveler with San Francisco in seconds. From a pay telephone in Te Anau, New Zealand, another traveler heard his friend's voice in Memphis as clearly as if she were next to him. Overall, improvements in communications technology have made international calling much simpler than it used to be.

There's no need to be intimidated by a foreign telephone system. Even though it's different from the one at home, you can figure out how it works. If the booth has no instructions in one of your languages, the illustrations should get you through. If there are neither instructions nor illustrations, look closely at the instrument. Are there buttons that invite you to push them? If necessary, ask a passerby to show you how it works.

The sound of the dial tone is not universal. It may be the sound you're used to, or it may be a sound you associate with a busy signal. Don't hang up; they're all dial tones.

Before calling home from overseas, consider a few basic principles. Calling collect is usually very expensive. That's also true for calling through a hotel switchboard. Using a major company's phone calling card from home can also be expensive. In other words, you need a special strategy.

Calling Cards

Many agree that the best solution is a low-cost, prepaid (or debit) calling card. These cards are widely available in the United States, and there are some good deals on the Internet. Friends recommend the Enjoy Prepaid EZ Plan calling card (**www.enjoyprepaid.com**). The cards are inexpensive, and you can opt to have them automatically reloaded (meaning they won't suddenly cut off when the prepaid amount runs out). Another good one is called Pingo (**www.pingo.com**). A call to the States from Mexico, for example, might cost about 10 cents a minute. You can even use the cards with a mobile phone to be charged local minutes only on the plan.

Here are a few caveats: First, these cards vary widely in per-minute charges, so always check before buying (including cards issued by the big guys such as AT&T, Verizon, and Sprint). Divide minutes into the price. Second, ensure that whatever card(s) you buy will work in the countries you will be visiting. They don't work everywhere. Third, take more than one card. A good backup might be the Verizon prepaid card available at Costco.

The lowest rates—and the ones with the least hassle—may be found by buying cards in foreign countries as you go. You'll find them in post offices, hotels, gift shops, pharmacies, bus stations, and similar places. There are a couple of drawbacks: you have to take time to find a card on the road, and you're likely to wind up with unused minutes when you depart. But you can always give the card to another traveler or a local person.

Here are several tips for using telephones overseas:

- **$AVE Money** To save money, avoid having a hotel operator place your call. If you want to call from a hotel anyway, find out in advance how much the surcharge will be. The hotel surcharge often adds 40 percent to the cost of the call, and many international chain hotels routinely charge guests five times the actual cost of the call. Also watch out for substantial hotel charges for local calls and even for access to calling-card and 800 numbers. You're paying a high price for convenience, so unless you really have to lie in bed to make the call, head downstairs to the lobby pay phone.
- Find a public telephone booth. To place an international call, you need the international access code and the country code for the country you're calling. To that, add the area code and local number you want. Most booths now use some type of local phone card. Beware: some pay phones are privately owned. One friend in Mexico placed a collect call to the

United States on one of these landmines. The recipient was billed $50 for a one-minute conversation.

Find a local telephone storefront. All over Latin America, you find places where you walk in, make your phone call, and pay for whatever minutes you use. Sometimes you dial the number yourself, but more often you hand the number to an attendant who makes the call and directs you to a numbered booth (handy if you can't figure out how to dial home!). Sometimes these places are dedicated only to phones, but they may be combined with a convenience store, laundry service, or Internet cafe.

In many cities, Internet cafes provide the ultimate cheap phone call—free. If Skype is installed on the computer, and there's a headset with microphone, you can call another Skype user for nothing more than the basic charge for using the computer. If the person you're calling doesn't have Skype or you don't want to worry about catching the other person at the computer, deposit money ahead of time in a SkypeOut account, and just pay a few cents a minute to call that person's regular phone. From anywhere in Latin America, you can call the United States or Canada on SkypeOut and talk 20 minutes for less than a dollar. The catch? The call goes over the Internet, not through a regular phone line, so there may be an echo or delay. Still, most people find this a worthwhile trade-off, considering the price. See **www.skype.com.** An ideal accessory is the IPEVO handset (**www.ipevo.com**). After you download a free driver, you simply plug this handset into your USB port, and you can call anywhere in the world for almost nothing.

- **SAVE Money** Calling cards for customers of major carriers, such as AT&T's USADirect, let you call the United States from more than 150 countries. Go to **usa.att.com/traveler,** where you enter all countries on your itinerary and get a list of toll-free access codes. Then dial (not through the hotel operator) the access number assigned to the country from which you are calling. Once you connect with that number, you dial the U.S. number you want, along with your personal billing number. To phone someone in another country while abroad, use the same access number to call back to the United States. Your call is then rerouted. As you might guess, the latter is an expensive service. Other carriers, such as Verizon, have similar cards, which cover Latin American countries. Such telephone-company calling cards do save money compared with in-room hotel rates, but they are not the least expensive option by far.

- Some travelers in Latin America call from government international telephone offices because there are no surcharges. Such offices are often near or within the central post office (often referred to as the PTT, for Postal, Telephone, and Telegraph). Your hotel clerk will know where it is.

If you're out for a stroll when the urge to phone hits, look for a microwave tower on top of a building that doesn't have a lot of people in military uniforms standing around it.

- **SAVE Money** Save money by placing your call during hours when rates are lowest. In some countries, such as Mexico, prices are the same at all times. Other markets may have cheaper rates at night.
- **SAVE Money** If calling collect is your only option, save money by making a one-minute call and then having the other person call you back.
- In countries where the government operates with a heavy hand, your call may be monitored. That should definitely affect how vigorously you criticize the country or its leader. Fortunately, this isn't an issue in Mexico and Central America.
- If there's an emergency at home, your friend or relative can contact the Office of Overseas Citizen Services at the State Department (call [800] 407-4747 or [202] 501-4444), which will relay a message to the appropriate U.S. embassy on your itinerary. Embassy personnel will attempt to locate you. You can make this process easier by registering with the State Department online (**travel.state.gov**) before you leave on your trip.

Cell Phones

Many travelers feel that using e-mail or a local telephone to contact home when necessary is preferable to carrying a cell phone during an adventure in a foreign country. Because the former are not under your control and require at least a small effort to use, communications are not continuous. In contrast, the cell phone in your pocket is a constant temptation, a potential distraction, to take you away from being 100 percent present where you are.

Use a cell phone at home? Fine. Bring one with you when there's a solid reason such as a pending crisis or decision—even unavoidable business? Of course. Need it to make reservations along the way, stay in touch with travel companions, or even for safety? By all means. But, let's be honest, some folks are addicted to their cell phone. They place calls endlessly simply because they can. Their adventure is interrupted by folks at home calling to chat.

In reality, most travelers are not indispensable at home, nor is there a crisis looming. Taking this auditory tether on an international trip out of habit has consequences in terms of the nature of the trip. So ask whether you really require the extra baggage (literally and figuratively). Do you need to stay connected to home 24/7, or would it free your spirit to leave home at home and bask in the vast silences of far away places?

Some travelers expect to disembark from the plane, whip out a cell phone, and be able to start talking at local rates, billed to their carrier back home. Reality is far different. Mobile-phone companies are like individual fiefdoms, cooperating with one another only when it's financially advantageous for them, so there's no overarching reliable grid. Once outside major cities, coverage is similar to that in the rural United States: very spotty. On top of that, incompatible technological standards keep some U.S. phones from operating at all in other countries.

And if you step off that plane without having made arrangements in advance, that cell phone might as well be a hockey puck. Sprint, AT&T, Verizon, and others have a patchwork of roaming alliances around the world, so first you have to see if you can receive calls where you are going. If you can, the carrier has to switch on that service for you (sometimes with an additional monthly charge, so you should cancel later). If you use your cell phone, be ready to pay big bucks for every call. You may pay from 50 cents to $1.50 per minute (even $3 in Costa Rica on Sprint) for every incoming and outgoing call. Text messaging is usually far cheaper—but that still keeps one foot at home.

Consider two ways to cut costs. First, if you have an "unlocked" cell phone, you can (in fact, you have to) buy a SIM (subscriber-identity module) card in your destination country that will let you call at local rates on a prepaid plan. The other option is to leave your own phone at home, rent one locally, and use a prepaid plan for calls. Neither option will save you much on international calls unless you use it in conjunction with a phone card. You're still far better off using public phones unless you have a lot of local calls to make.

For those who feel they can't live without their BlackBerry, or something like a T-Mobile Dash or Motorola SLVR mobile phone, those devices should work in at least the main cities of Mexico and Central America. Again, the best way to relax and forget about home is to not bring home with you.

Titans of industry traveled the world in the past and their trains and steel mills kept running despite the boss's being unreachable. Just because the communications technology now exists doesn't mean you should use it as you explore the world. Carry a cell phone if you must be reachable on the road. Otherwise, ask people to send you an e-mail or wait until you return home.

MAIL

The challenge is to enjoy the pleasure of sending and receiving mail without letting the process disrupt your trip. Some travelers write home in bursts, days or weeks apart. If you keep an informal log listing the date of the most recent burst, you'll know where to pick up geographic descriptions when you write next.

American Express

American Express offices abroad used to be like Pony Express outposts for independent travelers on extended wanderings, a communications lifeline. The AMEX client-letter service was a reliable way to receive regular mail. Over time, though, the old reliable "express" has become almost an anachronism, far less needed for keeping in touch. American Express doesn't even publicize the service anymore as a card benefit, but it is still available at nearly all its offices. Call the office directly to verify policies and availability.

To pick up mail, you're supposed to have an AMEX card or AMEX traveler's checks, and some identification. However, many offices will allow a traveler to pick up mail merely by paying a small fee.

When giving your itinerary to pen pals at home, include addresses of appropriate AMEX mail drops. A complete list of foreign offices is available from AMEX, but choose only those offices that you can confirm are mail drops. Because most of the offices also have fax machines, include fax numbers, too. A fax via AMEX is a fast, reliable way to reach a traveler.

Remind your correspondents that it takes two or three weeks for a letter to make its journey. Note on your itinerary the date by which a letter should be mailed to reach an AMEX office before you do. On the itinerary, type a reminder to CAPITALIZE and underline your last name. To reduce the chance of misfiling, ask the writer not to include your middle name or initial.

When you stop in for mail, ask the clerk to check under the first letter of your last name and under the first letter of your first name. If you're not sure you

Health warnings raise public consciousness.

are communicating, write out your name. Because your eye is more likely than hers to recognize your name, lean over the clerk's shoulder if you can to see for yourself.

Rather than wasting a day or more or detouring for miles to check in with a mail pickup point, ask friends to send a copy of each letter to the next mail stop down the line on your itinerary. That will prevent regrets about a wonderful letter left behind.

If you arrive at a mail pickup point ahead of schedule, ask that mail for you arriving there later be forwarded to an office farther along your itinerary. The office will do it for a small fee. When you depart from the itinerary you left with friends at home, tell the AMEX office where to forward mail that might arrive in your wake. An office will usually hold your mail for 30 days.

Most people prefer AMEX over receiving mail via local general delivery. If you decide to use general delivery, advise your correspondents to address letters to your name, "c/o Poste Restante, General Post Office" in a specific city and country. No further address is needed.

Give your own cards and letters a fighting chance of getting home by taking them to the post office rather than leaving them with a hotel clerk to be mailed.

Fax Machines

Before e-mail, the fax machine was the most reliable way to get a quick message or document to or from someone in a hurry. You can send a fax from Guatemala City to San Francisco even when local residents can't reach one another across town by telephone, and it's still a good backup when you get stuck without an Internet connection. Don't leave home without a list of fax numbers for people you may want to reach. For people who don't have a fax machine at home, a variety of services send a fax into the person's e-mail inbox. He or she can print it out from there. Services such as jConnect (**www.j2.com**) provide a free "receive only" account for the bare-bones option.

In cities of any size, signs advertise fax services on many downtown blocks. The fax machine itself may be located in an upscale travel agency or in the back of a bakery next to a grandmother dozing with a lap full of knitting.

The charge for sending a fax is usually less than you'd spend on a long-distance call. There's also a minimal fee when you receive a fax. Include the fax number from which you are sending so the person you are contacting can reach you later.

To reach you in an emergency, home folks can send a fax to your hotel, to an AMEX mail-service office, or through one of the fax services.

CHAPTER 25

Shopping and Shipping

> But there is one priceless thing that I brought back from
> my trip around the world, one that cost no money and
> on which I paid no customs duty: humility, a humility
> born from watching other peoples, other races, struggling
> bravely and hoping humbly for the simplest things in life.
> —Félix Martí-Ibáñez
> *Journey around Myself* (1966)

As I write this, I look around the room and see a bag made from hand-woven Guatemalan fabric, a Mexican silver sculpture, a yak-wool hat from Kashmir, a Masai gourd (to hold blood and milk), a Peruvian flute, and more. I'm no big shopper, but who can resist magnificent craftsmanship or quirky things you've never seen before? And no one should miss the colors, sounds, and aromas of local market days.

I flinch when casual acquaintances ask me to bring "something wonderful" home for them. I resist the pressure of having to shop because I don't want to be concerned about theft or breakage, and I don't want to tote that extra weight. Yet I sometimes still arrive home laden like a trans-Saharan camel.

Note that I don't consider cost an inhibition to buying. Except in Europe, prices usually are so reasonable in relation to the quality of products that most of what you see seems very affordable. Of course, the original cost may not be the final cost. Consider how much you'll have to spend on your purchase after you get home. For example, I bought a fine piece of batik fabric art in Yogyakarta, Indonesia, for about $15 but spent more than $100 at home to have it properly mounted.

To keep buying under control, I remind myself of two things. First, it's possible and sometimes preferable to enjoy things for themselves rather than having to possess them. Second, many things look terrific in their own context but lose all appeal when transported to a domestic coffee table. Funky ethnic hats become moth-eaten relics at home, and the lederhosen bought in Munich mildew at the bottom of a drawer.

Two kinds of travelers won't consider their trips successful if they don't shop. One is the knowledgeable collector who's studied the market and knows exactly what he or she wants to buy. The other is the compulsive shopper, a condition that, unlike diarrhea, is not self-limiting.

The temptation to buy peaks when one first rolls into a country. For small souvenirs, go ahead. Waiting to save pennies "somewhere else" may mean missing out. For more-expensive purchases, shop around, comparing quality and price. After a few hours, you'll notice substantial differences in workmanship that weren't evident at first. Buying during the last few days of a trip also minimizes problems of breakage, theft, and weight.

HOW TO PREPARE YOURSELF BEFORE BUYING

SAVE Money Save money by beginning the process before you leave home. Make a list of clothing sizes of people for whom you may buy gifts. It helps to know sizes in inches or centimeters because size codes at home have little in common with those abroad. Decide how much you feel comfortable spending, and build that amount into your budget.

If a country is renowned for certain items, do the research needed to evaluate quality and prices. Take a list of what you're interested in and what those items sell for at home. This research is particularly important if you're considering buying jewels or electronic or photographic equipment. Travelers who neglect advance research often buy something that isn't quite what they wanted and pay more than they would have at home. Plus, they get to lug it around the world, then pay duty on it.

Bargaining should be in the forefront of your mind, especially if you intend to visit on local market days, when a cornucopia of handcrafts from the countryside flows into town. The initial price quoted may be twice or even ten times the price at which the merchant will eventually sell. It's up to you to get the price down.

HOW TO TELL IF IT'S THE REAL THING

There are bargains, and there are rip-offs. High quality cannot be assumed. If you're thinking of buying something, inspect it more closely than you would at home because you won't be able to return it for a refund. In clothing, cheap thread and careless stitching can result in unexpected vents at an inconvenient moment.

Authenticity is always a question. Is it batik or print? Elephant hair or black plastic? Leading the list are phony designer labels. Of course, when you see foreign track shoes labeled "Niko," you might wonder about the quality. If an item is offered as an antique, be cautious. If you like it for what it is, fine; just don't pay an inflated price for an antique that isn't.

> Inspect all purchases closely; you won't be able to return them for a refund.

Jewels are difficult purchases. Unless you can tell whether a gem is genuine and know what it would cost at home, you're just off the turnip truck in the showroom of the gem dealer. If a dealer offers to authenticate a jewel or some precious metal, take it for granted that he'll provide test results that will appear to prove his representation. If the price is substantial, get an outside expert. For high-ticket items, try to buy from a merchant for whom you have a positive reference—perhaps a reference from someone at home. "Caveat emptor" was never more true than at your friendly jeweler.

According to *Condé Nast Traveler,* most complaints from readers about foreign purchases involve electronic equipment in Hong Kong, artwork in Italy, glassware in Venice, jewelry in Bangkok, and rugs in Turkey, Morocco, and India. That's good information to remember.

HOW TO GET WHAT YOU BOUGHT

When you make a purchase, guard against a switch while it's being wrapped in the back room. Yucatán hammocks are famous for their excellent quality, but the one you examine in the front of the shop may be of higher quality than the one later handed to you in a plastic bag. Either stick with your purchase as it's wrapped or examine it before you leave the shop. If you don't do either, check it as soon as you're back in your hotel.

Before you pay for something, figure out how much change to expect, and then count what you receive. If a merchant intends to pull a scam, he'll also be doing something to divert your attention so you won't notice. Be alert.

When possible, pay with a major credit card. If a problem arises, such as a switch, damage during shipping, or no shipping at all, you can challenge the charge.

HOW TO GET IT HOME

The best way to get it home is to take it home with you. That's especially true if it's fragile—or a rug. It's amazing how a silk rug can turn to cotton if shipped by the vendor. But if you're not ready to wrestle purchases all the way home, you have to figure out how to ship them. You, the merchant, your concierge, or a freight forwarder can send them by courier, air express, sea freight, or the post office. You may even find a homebound traveler to carry them. If you've paid in full, consider insurance.

The local post office, the most common choice, is much less expensive than courier and air-express services. In some countries, however, you must prepare your purchases for shipping. In India, I had to hire a tailor to wrap my purchases in burlap until they resembled mummies before the New Delhi post office would anoint them with its elegant red-wax seals.

Federal Express, DHL, and UPS offer fast, reliable service—at high prices. Another alternative is a local freight forwarder. Its representative will pick up your purchase from the vendor and pack and ship it. Its counterpart at the port of entry will handle customs and forward the item to your home. This, too, can be an expensive service. Ask about undisclosed "related charges" for a forklift operator, temporary storage, or whatever.

The charge for shipping by sea, usually based on size rather than weight, is reasonable, but delivery may take months.

A knowledgeable concierge can handle shipping for you, but a $15 room usually doesn't come with a concierge.

CUSTOMS

In the past, clearing customs meant only a minor hassle and a slight delay. The process used to be about collecting money and diminishing the flow of firearms, Illegal drugs, and prohibited items (cultural artifacts, antiquities, body parts of endangered species, and so on). Welcome to the new era of antiterrorism. Borders are becoming fortress walls.

Technically, customs has a role different from security—but the two now seem intertwined. You need to know the *exact* rules applicable at the time of your trip. Because they change erratically, the only way to be certain is to consult the Web site of the Department of Homeland Security (**www.dhs.com**).

Searches

Searches are not nearly as random as one might believe. The agent sizes up people as they wait in line. Sometimes, informers mingle with passengers, hoping to pick up suspicious behavior. Anyone fitting a certain profile or behaving in an unusual way is in for a search. If an agent is getting an assist from a drug-sniffing dog, do not attempt to pat him (dog or agent). Of course, anything suspicious on an X-ray will lead to a search.

If you're stopped by an agent, remain calm. Even if you think you may have committed a minor violation, don't hesitate to open any bag when asked. Volunteer no information, and don't try to bluff your way through by blustering or threatening. Every agent has been through this drill many times and won't be intimidated, but you can make one angry if you try. If a problem develops, ask what your rights are. Call a lawyer if necessary.

> Don't clear a stranger's bag through customs.

In some countries, customs agents have been known to steal from bags as they search them, so don't let your attention wander during the search.

Favors

If someone you don't know asks you to clear a bag through customs while he does some other chore, don't do it. The problem used to be illegal drugs that could put you in the slammer for a long time. Now, in this age of terrorism, it's the B-word.

Duty

Customs officials want to see what you're bringing in—and sometimes what you're taking out. They look for items acquired abroad on which you must pay duty, and for items not allowed into their country at all.

When returning home, you'll be asked to fill out a customs declaration listing your purchases. Misrepresentation or failure to declare something can result in penalties, seizure and forfeiture, and even prison. That would be a heck of a way to end a trip; who would give your slide show?

Outbound from your country, you can obtain a Certificate of Registration from customs (CBP Form 4457) confirming that your camera, jewelry, and other named expensive items are leaving the country with you. This certificate ensures that you won't have to pay duty on these items on your return.

Customs agents have a pretty good idea of the market value of what they see. If one challenges your valuation, it's very important to have a receipt. Of course, the concept of a receipt would make vendors in local markets smile. If an inspector discovers an item not listed on your declaration, you may be given a chance to amend the declaration. If you decline, he can impose a fine and increase the duty. If an agent catches a traveler concealing something or using a falsified receipt, he can confiscate the item or increase the duty greatly.

Duty rates are set by Congress with considerable, shall we say, input from big-business lobbyists. The rates are published by the International Trade

Marketplace in Chichicastenango, Guatemala

> I had once spread my wings, and now that I had returned to my nest again I was dissatisfied.
> —Richard Halliburton, *The Glorious Adventure* (1927)

Commission; see **www.cbp.gov** ("CBP" stands for "Customs and Border Protection").

Certain exemptions from duty are available for goods in your possession and for personal use. They depend on where you're coming from, how long you've been there, what you purchased, where the goods were made, and what you paid for the goods. In other words, figuring it out *is* like brain surgery. Just as a ballpark example, you might expect an exemption of $800, then duty of 3 percent on the next $1,000. Above that, applicable duty rates would apply (mostly up to 10 percent; in some cases, up to 25 percent).

The largest exemption, the Generalized System of Preferences (GSP), is granted for purchases made in less developed countries. To help them export their goods, the United States permits many purchases made in about 125 countries to enter free of duty. Goods from North American Free Trade Agreement (NAFTA) and Central American Free Trade Agreement (CAFTA) countries also receive reduced duty rates.

Recipients of gifts shipped from abroad will owe duty on them (which the giver cannot prepay).

You owe no duty on a gift you mail home if the value is less than $200 and you send it to someone other than yourself. Write "unsolicited gift; value less than $200" on the package. A customs inspector may open these packages. Gifts that you carry back with you are subject to duty unless they fit within your exemption.

Unique works created by professional artists are admitted free of duty. However, mass-produced items and the work of craftsmen are subject to duty.

An item must be at least 100 years old to be considered an antique. If so, the good news is that it may be admitted free of duty. The bad news is that you may have violated the laws of a foreign country if you removed it without an export permit. If you purchase an authentic-looking reproduction, obtain a written statement from the vendor confirming that it's a reproduction. That will help you get it out of the country but makes it subject to duty at home.

Prohibited Items

Items not permitted into the United States include plants, fresh fruit, vegetables, meat, illegal narcotics, switchblades, poisonous items, and hazardous articles such as fireworks. Drugs and medical devices sold overseas but not approved by the Food and Drug Administration are not permitted even if purchased legally. Imported firearms will be confiscated.

Items made from ivory, tortoise shell, coral, leopard fur, hides, shells, and feathers or teeth of an endangered species are also prohibited. You may be fined for attempting to bring them in. Don't think that just because the vendor assured you there would be no problem, customs will permit you to keep them. In fact, a traveler discovered with an unapproved antiquity may be considered a thief.

Copies (knockoffs) of brand-name merchandise probably violate someone's patents or trademarks. If the customs agent spots a fake Rolex or a stack of pirated CDs or computer programs, he's likely to confiscate and destroy them. All you can do is grin and bear it. After all, you paid that guy on the beach only $20 for the "Rolex."

For more information on customs regulations, including current duty rates, contact a customs official at one of the more than 40 district offices in the United States. Also obtain a copy of *Know before You Go: U.S. Customs and Border Protection Regulations for U.S. Residents.*

Duty-free

"Duty-free" means only that goods are being sold without addition of a local sales tax or import duty. That means low prices, right? Very seldom. In fact, duty-free shops often sell imported luxury goods at inflated prices. The absence of local tax is almost immaterial. These shops are often traps for wealthy or inexperienced tourists. A duty-free purchase may make sense if you have foreign currency left that you can't exchange before leaving the country. The fact that you bought something in a duty-free shop overseas has no effect at all on whether you owe duty on it when you return home.

CHAPTER 26

Remembering

Like all great travellers, I have seen more than I
remember, and remember more than I have seen.
—Benjamin Disraeli

Memories can become faint glimmers or remain vivid and rich over the years.
It's up to you.

By far the best way to gather memories is to be completely present where
you are, immersing yourself in the experience, imprinting conversations, colors,
sounds, and breathtaking views into your cells. Maps, handicrafts, coins, receipts,
literature, and souvenirs all contribute to memories, but being 100 percent present
should be the highest priority. That may mean not reading international editions
of magazines or newspapers as you travel. "News" usually isn't, and when you
return, little of substance will have changed.

Being fully present means stopping often to appreciate where you are—seeing
more by seeing less. It also means taking risks, making an effort, and reaching
out to people.

KEEPING A JOURNAL

Because memory is so fallible, mental images benefit from backup systems. One
backup is a good journal. A journal also helps you share your experiences with
friends, including those you won't meet until 20 years after the trip. A journal
packed with reports of people, emotions, events, and
ideas provides information and insights for years.

> A journey is best
> measured in friends
> rather than miles
> —Tim Cahill,
> Road Fever (1991)

Accuracy and truth are requisites of a worthwhile
journal. Accuracy is a matter of practice and paying
attention. The truth is sometimes hard to write when
dealing with issues close to the bone, such as when you
didn't meet a challenge as well as you wanted to. Still,
those are the very truths to record. It may be easier to explore emotions on paper
if you intend no one else to read your words. When traveling with a partner,
journals should be explicitly confidential.

I keep track of observations by scribbling occasional notes on a piece of paper
during the day. Otherwise, with so much sensory input, I'd lose a lot before I had
time to record it all in my journal. When I miss a day or two of journal writing,
daily notes help me catch up.

Drawings capture details that might otherwise be missed. A trek across western Nepal became even more interesting after I sketched the subtle ways in which the construction and design of buildings in each mountain village differed from those in neighboring villages separated by less than a mile.

Make observations about people you see or meet, record feelings about what you did, and include changes in your perspective and plans. Explore similarities and differences among cultures in terms of religion, architecture, art, agriculture, and language. Attempt to capture the spirit, as well as the form, of a temple, landscape, or person.

Someone said, "Ixion breakfasted with the gods and remembered only the pattern of the tablecloth." That's how I feel when I record only facts. Dry reporting doesn't retain the flavors. Try to make that journal sing with impressions, reactions, and reflections.

> To lose a passport was the least of one's worries: to lose a notebook was a catastrophe.
> —Bruce Chatwin, The Songlines (1987)

I walked for a while with an older man I overtook on a hike in Costa Rica. Each time the trail turned a bend and a new panorama unfolded, he'd lift a small tape recorder to his lips and whisper, "Beautiful, beautiful," or "Spectacular," or something similar. Not once did he draw a verbal picture of what he saw. He gave himself nothing from which to re-create the "beautiful" sights he'd experienced.

For some, blogging is an adjunct or alternative to the handwritten journal. In theory, you can post from any Internet connection though formatting and uploading photos is time-consuming without your own laptop. If you have the tech chops, you can write text and upload it to a blog with a BlackBerry or smart phone like a Treo. Better for short posts than long missives.

One huge advantage of blogging is that placing your thoughts on a secure server protects against the disaster of losing a journal while on the road. For some, blogging is an online version of a journal, meant for themselves. For others, it's the techie equivalent of calling home to keep people posted and, thereby, keep them from worrying about the traveler's health or safety.

But here's the rub. If the blog you create is immediately shared with others, maybe even inviting feedback, will it be as honest as it needs to be to have value? A "gee whiz" travelogue falls far short. But for people accustomed to baring their souls on MySpace and Facebook, maybe that's not a problem.

Are you interested in publishing articles related to your experiences? If so, read a book on travel writing before you leave to learn the type of information to collect. If you fail to collect what you need, you may regret a missed opportunity.

SAVE Money Here's another way to save money. If you meet Internal Revenue Service criteria applicable to writing for publication, which are too complex and subtle to describe here, you may be able to deduct some or all of your travel expenses on your income-tax return. If publishing is a possibility, keep track of expenses to support the deductions you claim. Ask a lawyer, an accountant, or the IRS about guidelines for deductibility.

> You perceive I generalize with intrepidity from single instances. It is the tourist's custom.
> —Mark Twain (1890)

TAKING FINE PHOTOGRAPHS

In the past, the right photographic gear took time to collect, added weight, and took up precious space in your luggage. Equipment, film, and developing added significantly to the cost of the trip. On top of that, we had to guard the equipment and care for the film. Now, compact digital cameras have almost eliminated these problems.

Even though the process of collecting images, whether on film or electronically, may intrude between observer and experience, most travelers—and I'm one—brush this objection aside because they're determined to return home with photo-memories. That being the case, here are a few tips that can help ensure high-quality photographs.

Why Am I Taking These Photographs?

- Be clear on the purpose of your photos. Will they join a series of images gracing your walls? Reside in an album, computer file, or DVD, waiting to be called on to stimulate your memory years in the future? Prove to your friends that you stood your ground within the leap of that black leopard? Accompany an article you plan to sell? Having a clear purpose, or purposes, helps your photos tell a coherent story.
- A photographer who simply snaps away each day is likely to discover, when he reviews the images, that he's failed to capture the essence of a country or culture. Before you leave a place, consider what characteristics best represent it, and see whether you have captured them.
- If your objective is to tell a story, think about the type of photographs required, and keep your objective in mind all day. If you simply want fine individual photographs, your task is much easier because one shot need not be linked to another.
- If you hope to sell your photographs, contact newspapers, travel magazines, and special-interest publications to find out whether they prefer or require. Even if your photographs will be published in black and white, most publishers will accept color images. In other words, shoot with your market in mind. Keeping good notes prevents you from losing a sale because you can't identify the subject and location of a photo. Notes also keep you from stumbling through a public presentation and joining the crowd in guessing what you're seeing.
- Imagine yourself at the Maya ruins at Chichén Itzá. One photographer after another stands in the footprints of those who have come before, each

snapping the obvious shot. If you want to record something pleasing for the bedroom wall, standing where everyone else does is fine. Similarly, if you're taking the shot to accompany a story, the editor probably wants a familiar image that readers can identify. If, however, your goal is personal interpretation, try to stand where others have not, or capture the image under unusual conditions. See the subject with imagination unique to yourself.

Tips for Taking Fine Photographs

A great photograph sometimes just happens, but that's rare. Even given good equipment and fine subjects, the photographer needs to contribute skill and thought to get superior results. In this section, we'll discuss ways to improve the quality of the shots you bring home.

- Sometimes the shot of the year requires incredible patience as you wait for perfect light or the ideal cloud formation. It can also be captured by a photographer who recognizes opportunity and knows the equipment well enough to take a well-composed shot on three seconds' notice. It rarely emerges from ignorance or luck. If you're not already experienced, consider a course on outdoor or existing-light photography. Check out a good book on photography, and practice.
- See the subject of your photograph for itself. Take time to look at it, to enjoy it. When you snap a hurried picture without really seeing the subject, that emotional distance shows in the result.
- When you know the subject matter is wonderful, consider bracketing. That is, take the first picture at the exposure and shutter speed you or your camera thinks is correct. Then take a photograph at the next smaller f-stop and one at the next larger (or you can bracket by changing shutter speed instead). Of course, if your camera is fully automatic, it will neutralize your aperture change by changing the shutter speed. If you can, switch to manual.
- Look at the subject through the viewfinder with your camera horizontal, then with it vertical. The difference can substantially change the mood of a picture, as well as avoid clutter. The ability to edit so easily is another huge advantage of digital photography. You can crop, zoom in, and so on to remedy carelessness in the original shot.
- The lens loves clouds, shadows, and the gentle light of early morning and late afternoon. At noon on a clear day, the light will be flat, and results will lack drama. Having said that, not every image must be ideal. Sometimes you simply have to work with the light you have to get the shots you need to tell the story.
- To avoid shooting cliché photographs, experiment by shooting from unusual angles. If you're about to take a picture that would look good on a postcard, change your angle (or forget it and buy the postcard). The most important photographic equipment is your legs: Get out of the vehicle.

Climb up the hillside. Scout alternative points of view. See what the shot would look like from one knee or with your elbows on the ground. Avoid the common standing-at-eye-level shot, but don't let the quest for an unusual angle lead you into taking foolish risks.

- The closer you are to the subject, the better your photograph. In Darjeeling, India, a zoo guard (for a little *baksheesh*) let me inside the cages to photograph the wild animals. That was a little too close.

> The closer you are to the subject, the better your photograph.

At the other extreme, I reached Bharatpur Bird Sanctuary in Bharatpur, India, just as rare Siberian white cranes arrived at the end of their long migration. Excited, I fired off most of a roll as they glided onto the far bank of the marsh, soft late-afternoon light illuminating their snowy backs. On another occasion, trudging in a steady downpour through Perinet forest in Madagascar, my guide pointed up at several catlike Indri lemurs high in the treetop canopy. Snapping quickly to minimize raindrops on the lens, I got a half-dozen shots before being driven undercover. Can you guess what those two sets of photographs had in common? Both featured bland scenery against which you could see, if you looked closely, several white dots in one set and several brown dots in the other. Only the photographer would have the slightest idea why anyone had bothered to snap the shutter. The image you see in your mind's eye is not always what shows up on film. Move closer or zoom in.

- Photographing wildlife is harder than it seems. If the subjects don't almost fill the frame, the photo may be disappointing. Timing is critical. When animals see you, they get nervous and start to move away. If you're slow, you wind up with discarded photos of hind ends. Approach as near as you safely can, preferably downwind from the animals, and settle in. Stay still, not looking directly at them. In a short time, they'll return to grazing or playing, and you'll have your shot.
- Most beginning photographers center the subject in the viewfinder. It's called bull's-eye vision. There's another method, sometimes called the "rule of thirds." Imagine drawing a tic-tac-toe grid on your viewfinder, creating nine squares. Placing your subject at one of the four intersections on that grid may create a more interesting photograph.
- Placing the horizon in the middle of the frame produces a predictable picture. If the sky is your reason for taking the picture, place the horizon in the lower third of the frame.
- When composing a shot, try to do three things every time: 1. Look beyond your subject to examine the background for anything that would detract from the shot, such as electric wires, advertising signs, tourists, or anything else that conveys a mood different from the one you're after. Because the background can make or break the picture, keep it as uncluttered as

you can. 2. Look at the subject directly, not through the viewfinder, with one eye closed to see if your composition changes. 3. Just before you shoot, take your eye away from the viewfinder to see whether something is about to move into the picture. This small precaution helps reduce the number of photos that include the front bumper of a bus or half of some pedestrian's face.

- Try framing a distant subject by using something in the foreground. Shoot through an arch, or use a tree trunk and branch or anything else that's handy. The idea is to add a sense of scale and dimension to the shot.

- Choose action shots over posed shots. Catch people doing something. Capture excitement.

- Turn around. I captured several very good images of a vacant barn that burst into flame just after dawn in an Andean village. Then I turned around and took pictures of the faces of villagers watching the blaze. Their expressions and the firelight on their faces told an incredibly powerful story. Since then, I often look back over my shoulder to see human reactions to whatever's happening.

- There's no reason you can't take a good photograph while you're moving, such as when aboard a train. Choose a fast enough shutter speed to freeze the subject. For most situations, 1/500 of a second is fine. The odds against a blurred photo are better if you shoot while the subject is coming toward you or receding into the distance.

- Using a reflection can produce a superior photograph. On the other hand, reflections can be an obstacle. When shooting through glass, such as a car window, try to get the sun behind you. Hold the camera close to the window, but don't allow it to touch. If it does, vibrations from the vehicle may blur the picture. A polarizing filter can help eliminate reflections off glass.

- It's easy to be mesmerized by the grandeur of monuments and landscapes, but don't miss the smaller world. Use a macro lens from time to time. Try shooting unusual architecture from odd angles and extremely close-up.

- Many captivating images are of people, the closer the better. Monuments help you recall where you were, but they can quickly become boring in your living room. Photographs of local people keep a trip alive. Next best are slices of everyday life, the shots that capture the essence of what a place felt like as you walked along.

- Recording the subject and the camera setting of each shot as I take it would drive me crazy. Still, if you're shooting dozens of Spanish colonial cathedrals or monasteries, they tend to blend together. If using film, you can number each film container. As you use one, enter that number in your journal, indicating locations where you started and finished the roll. Another solution is to photograph something easily identifiable, such as a historical marker, to serve as a fingerprint of the location.

This Guatemalan man's clothing identifies his home village.

> Traveling is not just seeing the new; it's also leaving behind. Not just opening doors; also closing them behind you, never to return. But the place you have left forever is always there for you to see whenever you shut your eyes.
> —Jan Myrdal, *The Silk Road* (1980)

- Try not to shoot carelessly, but capture lots of images. When your subject is hot, keep shooting.
- Good equipment and good technique are helpful, but developing an eye for what constitutes a memorable photograph is essential. We learn from feedback, so study your own photographs and those in good travel books until you have a feel for what works. Develop your own style. Take photographs that capture your point of view or that contain a message. The more you study the art of photography, the better you'll do.

When to Shoot and When Not To

How would you feel if an odd-looking person speaking a strange tongue suddenly pointed a camera at you? Some people are fearful of, or offended by, being photographed. For some, it's because of modesty; for others, it violates spiritual beliefs. Some may be embarrassed by their poverty, aware of the contrast between their society and yours. Almost everyone responds in one way or another to being photographed, and that reaction appears in the picture. If someone objects, your image will show a person holding up a hand or half-turning from the camera with a displeased expression. People want to be treated with respect and friendliness rather than as a trophy. It's better to ask permission.

If you see a person you'd like to photograph, try taking a photo or two of something else nearby before approaching her directly. If she notices you, lower the camera, wave, and walk closer. Make eye contact, nod, smile, and take an interest in the work she's doing; try to indicate that you see her as an individual, not a curiosity. Then ask permission. If she agrees to be photographed, you have time to get a good result. If she says no, that's the end of it. If tempted to take a picture notwithstanding protestations, imagine how you'd feel if you were that subject.

In Mexico and Central America, the only reluctance I encountered came from some policemen. They generally consented once I made personal contact and exchanged a few words. When they didn't, I smiled and walked on.

On the other hand, some people enjoy being photographed because it makes them feel special. They pose, smile, and shake your hand. There are also people who enjoy it because they expect to be paid. If you don't mind paying, go ahead. The amount is almost always negotiable, at least before you take the picture. If you don't want to pay in that situation, don't take the picture.

I was sitting on a small hill in the Masai Mara Game Preserve in Kenya watching some elephant families at play when a white Toyota minivan stuffed with tourists stopped nearby. The tourists were pointing excitedly toward a half-dozen

Masai shepherds. Each of the elegantly tall Masai, resplendent in bead necklaces and animal skins, stood balanced on one leg, gripping an iron-tipped spear. As the tourists slung their expensive equipment into position for a photographic orgy, the Masai clearly indicated they wanted to be paid. The tourists snapped away, ignoring increasingly vocal demands. Then the van started to move, photo-satiated tourists now indifferent to the Masai. In seconds, the Masai raced forward, surrounded the van, and repeatedly thrust their nine-foot spears into its body. The driver spun off down the dirt path, panicked tourists screaming. Those tourists have a story to tell—but did they understand the lesson?

There are also things you should not photograph. General prohibitions include airports, bridges, harbors, and military installations, but you must watch for specific situations. If you take a picture of that 60-year-old warship in the decrepit harbor of Dar es Salaam, or record on film that old bridge spanning the Moscow River, just hope you weren't being watched by some official. Current relations between the country you're in and your own may determine whether you'll go straight to jail—or merely have your camera confiscated. That choice won't be yours. The "No Photographs" signs outside certain temples in the Royal Palace enclosure in Bangkok are draped with rolls of exposed film. Subtle, eh?

For local guidance, check your guidebook. Read local handouts. Watch for signs. Ask someone. If you're not being watched, you may get away with it. Of course, you may be betting your camera or your freedom. If in doubt, ask. If there is no one to ask, let your sense of appropriateness prevail.

CAMERAS

Deciding *why* you're taking photographs and understanding *how* to make them superior has always been more important than which hardware you use. The availability of affordable, compact, highly automated digital cameras—which come with the ability to self-edit—further simplifies hardware issues. Because of factors such as lighter weight, smaller size, much greater capacity, and ability to edit easily, I've made the transition to digital. Still, because tens of millions of film cameras are being taken on trips, we'll consider both types.

If you're going to buy a camera for the trip, get decent equipment, learn how it works, and use it before leaving. It's all too common for someone to buy a new camera, toss it in the bag, and jump on the plane. Unless you're a masochist-in-training, read the manual, then shoot and critique before you leave. Solve problems at home, where you can get advice easily.

If you plan to take an older camera that you haven't used for several months, give it a trial run before leaving to make sure it works.

For easygoing photographers, an ultralight, fully automatic camera—film or digital—with a built-in flash, basic zoom lens, and autofocus is quite adequate. Although lack of manual control of lens speed and aperture and, therefore, of depth of field limits the effects that can be achieved, striking images are still possible. On the other hand, these cameras can be fooled by light conditions and may not be appropriate for travelers seeking images of publishable quality.

Some who travel with a 35-millimeter SLR (single-lens reflex) camera body and several lenses also take a backup camera body to be ready with both color and black-and-white film or film of different speeds. Of course, a backup is not necessary with a digital camera.

There are so many fine camera manufacturers that you can hardly go wrong; just keep weight, size, and durability in mind. Check the Internet, consumer magazines, and photography trade publications for help in evaluating the alternatives.

If you want to take photographs under water, your choices include an expensive camera, a midrange camera, a cheap throwaway (which will work fine for shallow snapshots), or a waterproof housing that protects most cameras and camcorders.

Zoom Lens

When I see someone with a gigantic telephoto taking a close-up of the left eye of a rhino 200 yards away across the savannah, I assume he or she is on a tour, has three bearers to cart the camera gear, and is only seeing the world through a camera lens—and I'm still envious. For my SLR, I use a 70-to-300-millimeter zoom lens and a telextender. My digital has a 12x optical zoom built in.

Filters

I take two filters. The first is an ultraviolet filter, the principal purpose of which is to protect the lens from being scratched. The second is a polarizing filter, needed only occasionally to cut glare and reflections and intensify colors. A polarizing filter consumes about two f-stops worth of light, requiring a slower shutter speed to avoid losing depth of field. Furthermore, if you don't align a polarizing filter properly with each shot, it makes the picture worse. Don't leave it on the lens when there's not a specific reason to use it.

Lens Cover

Because a lens cover is an escape artist and difficult to replace on the road, attach it to the barrel of the lens with a "keeper," an elastic band designed for that purpose. I carry a spare keeper just in case.

Lens Hood

A collapsible rubber lens hood, or a screw-on metal or plastic hood, shields the lens from glaring sun, thus preventing reflections and flare. But then so does a well-placed hat or hand.

Tripod

The steadiness with which you hold your camera, especially in dim light, affects the sharpness of your photographs. When a full-scale tripod would be awkward and too heavy to carry, consider a tripod about five inches tall with a C-clamp on one end or a monopod with a ball head.

Cleaning Stuff

A simple brush, lens-cleaning solution, and soft lens tissues help keep the lens spotless. Microfiber cloths sold in camera shops are excellent. Q-tips are good for cleaning the viewfinder and the perimeter of the lens. Your handkerchief is not for cleaning a lens.

Camera Bag

An SLR camera bag is bulky and a target for sticky fingers when abroad. A stuff sack or army-surplus shoulder bag keeps the camera out of sight and shielded from dust. Even a zip-top plastic bag provides temporary protection. Another plus for digital cameras is that their small size lets most slip easily into a pocket. Protect camera equipment from heat, cold, rapid changes in temperature, grit, and moisture (especially salt spray).

Batteries

Superautomatic multigizmo cameras suck energy from batteries like starving leeches. The biggest guzzlers are the autowinder, autofocus, and playback (for digitals) features. Batteries are especially vulnerable when it's really cold, so keep your camera inside your jacket when practical, and keep spare batteries warm.

If your SLR goes into an electronic coma in Europe, you can find a replacement battery within an hour. In much of the rest of the world, your camera might be disabled for quite a while. Furthermore, a battery may cost five times as much in remote places. The lesson is clear: carry spare batteries.

Since digital cameras also depend on batteries, I consider a battery charger indispensable on the road. That may also require a converter and/or adapter.

Film

Slide or Print

Slides (transparencies) are noted for excellent color and sharpness, and it's exciting to see a life-size lion yawning on the wall of your living room. On the other hand, slide film is less forgiving of incorrect exposure settings, so shooting slides requires more skill than shooting prints does. In addition, less can be done in the lab to improve incorrectly exposed slide film. If you shoot slides but want something to hang on the wall, you can have prints made from your slides (although the process is relatively expensive).

> Many beautiful sights are impossible to transfer onto film; rather than intrude my camera into an experience for no purpose, I simply enjoy them.
> —Galen Rowell,
> *High and Wild* (1983)

Digital

Digital photography requires no film to buy, protect, and develop. But there is a memory card. The one that comes with the camera is usually hopelessly inadequate in terms of the number of images it will hold. It's common to replace it with a one-gigabyte card that will hold about 1,000 images. That's seems like plenty, right? Not when you get rolling with a digital (as you should). I always carry a backup memory card (at least one additional gig of memory).

To safeguard images in the camera, you can periodically copy them to your backup card. The originals can be left on the card in the camera or, if you need space, deleted. While on the road, you can also take either card to a photo shop and have the images transferred to a CD-ROM. Both the backup card and the CD are easily transportable and much less vulnerable to a camera thief. Another option is to use a cybercafe to upload images to a Web site—but that can be very slow.

Where to Buy

SAVE Money High-volume outlets sell film and cameras at prices local retail stores can't match. Check the back pages of *Popular Photography* or other photography magazines for advertisements. When ordering film from one of these outlets, ask about the expiration dates of the film. As film draws

Ethical Travel (**www.ethicaltravel.org**) focuses on the positive impact international travelers can have. Toward that end, it published a list of suggestions that include (paraphrased):

- Patronize locally owned businesses.
- Avoid giving gifts directly to children. Find out what is needed and who can best distribute your contribution.
- Don't be upset if you're expected to pay a little more for things than local people are.
- Learn and respect the traditions of your host country.
- Interact with humor. Anger is not respected and will not defuse a difficult situation.
- Learn to listen.
- Learn not to speak with absolute certainty.
- Be open to reality. Leave preconceptions at home.
- Go with the flow.

close to its expiration date, outlets sometimes cut the price in half. That's a great way to save money because you'll expose it within the next few weeks anyway.

> Too often travel, instead of broadening the mind, merely lengthens the conversations.
> —Elizabeth Drew

The Web is wonderful for doing research on brands, features, and prices. You'll also find many qualitative comments from users, although there's no way to know how impartial they are. On the other hand, the pro hanging out behind the counter of a local camera store is an extremely valuable resource, both for choosing the right camera for your needs and for showing you how to operate it. That's often worth paying a bit more.

If you are thinking of buying photographic equipment overseas, research the item you want, including domestic prices, before you leave. Some overseas "bargain" prices aren't bargains. When buying photographic equipment abroad, be sure you get authentic, new equipment. Watch out for warranties that require the equipment to be returned to Mexico City, Panama City, or some other faraway place for repair. If you wait to buy your trip camera abroad, you'll be depending on a camera with which you haven't practiced, and one that may turn out to be defective.

Film Care

Don't leave either camera or film sitting in direct sunlight or in a space likely to become very hot. When there's film in your luggage, follow the same rules. Wrap film to shelter it from extreme cold. When film is very cold, prevent condensation by warming it gradually before loading it into the camera.

Do airport X-ray machines damage film? First, let's discuss carry-on luggage. The National Association of Photographic Manufacturers evaluated the effects on various types and speeds of film of up to 100 passes through carry-on X-ray machines and concluded there was no problem. However, it still said to avoid putting film faster than ISO 400 through the machines. That may be reassuring in the United States, but when I go through an airport X-ray security station abroad, I pass my camera and film around the X-ray tunnel. Even if the attendant insists there's no danger, it makes me feel better. Given increasing security precautions, that may mean that the official examines each roll of film separately. Or he or she may simply insist that it be X-rayed or left behind. X-rays have no effect on digital or video cameras.

Film in checked baggage is a different matter. Because luggage may be zapped by high-powered X-ray machines on the way to the belly of the plane, film can be damaged. Most sources warn against leaving film in checked luggage.

My last comment may be one of the most important for users of nondigital cameras. Anytime you'll be away from where you store your film, check to see that you have plenty of *unexposed* film in your pocket or pack. Don't wait until you're face-to-face with a silverback gorilla before discovering you're out of film.

REMEMBERING PEOPLE AND PLACES

You meet a lot of people as you travel. Some are casual acquaintances; some you come to know well. Most travelers keep a list of names and addresses, but as time passes, a list alone may not be enough. To help keep each person fresh in mind, I add the date, location, something about the circumstances, and sometimes a brief physical description.

Near the end of a trip, I list places that turned out to be special. Not long after I'm home, I reflect on how I feel about the trip, what I learned, what I'd do differently. This is actually the first step in planning my next adventure.

Each of us has his or her own ways of keeping images vivid for years. But even if I were to travel with neither camera nor journal, the images would stay alive so long as I'd been 100 percent present each day on the road.

PART FIVE: The Finish Line

CHAPTER 27

Home Again, Home Again

A boat was leaving in about ten days and the
knowledge that I would be on that boat had
already brought the journey to an end.
—Henry Miller
The Colossus of Maroussi (1958)

It feels strange to come home, and I'm never ready to try to sum up for someone else the feelings and experiences of weeks or months on the road.

Home from the airport, I hang my weary khakis and well-worn canvas shirt on a corner of the door and pull a collar-to-ankle *djellaba* over my head. As I set my money belt on the bureau, the routine kicks in, and I drop it out of sight in a drawer. I pause, realizing I won't wear it again for . . . who knows how long? I'll miss it in the morning; it's been next to me every day of the trip.

I turn on the water heater, build a fire in the fireplace, put on some Mexican classical guitar music, open a bottle of wine, and start thumbing through the mail my neighbor has piled on the piano bench. My eyes wander to mementos of earlier adventures: framed photographs covering the walls, a hand-braided belt from Guatemala, a midnight-blue-and-scarlet rug from the Tibetan Refugee Center, ceremonial masks from Mexico.

> "Here I am, safely returned over those peaks from a journey far more beautiful and strange than anything I had hoped for or imagined—how is it that this safe return brings such regret?"
> —Peter Matthiessen,
> *The Snow Leopard* (1978)

I don't call anyone, sometimes for days, because I'm not ready to be back, let alone to begin telling trip tales. I want to ease back into my old world at my own pace, extending my time to think about new commitments and changes in priorities.

I feel stressed for a while after a long trip. There's so much to catch up on, and the pace of life is always faster than I remembered. I feel a reverse homesickness, missing being on the road, missing people I met along the way.

On the road I was unique, a foreigner, a person who stood out in a crowd, whose opinions were sought, who was from the wealthiest nation on Earth. At home, I'm just one of more than 300 million people. It's hard not to notice the difference.

Having accepted the risks of the high seas and navigated safely back to home port, I return with new perspectives and knowledge. Physically, I'm fit, and my spirit is revitalized. Yet before me is the daunting challenge of bringing to my everyday life the energy and spirit of adventure I felt during my travels.

I must continue to seek the unknown, to take chances, to stretch my mind and body. Above all, I must reject ruts and the trap of the comfort zone. That is every traveler's challenge.

Although I'm different from the person who left colleagues and friends behind, they don't see it. One may ask, "Where was it you went?" but, as he hears unfamiliar, almost alien, names, his eyes soon begin to glaze. Where I've been is not quite real to him. If you understand that, you protect yourself from disappointment.

Seldom does anyone ask a serious question about what ordinary people are like in country A or B. There's little chance of substantive discussion about life on distant shores. You may return bursting with thoughts and feelings about the things and places you have seen, but you may not have many chances to share them.

After you've been back a few months, the trip is still resonating in your mind, but your colleagues may have forgotten you were ever away. Remain too enthusiastic about your just-completed odyssey, and you risk becoming a conversational black hole, the bane of hostesses. It's a reminder of how important it is to travel to satisfy your own goals, not the opinions of others.

When I feel a compelling need to share what I've experienced, I seek out other travelers. Like me, they're willing to watch anyone's slide shows from anywhere; they're eager to discuss politics and whitewater rivers, mountain treks and hanging out on remote beaches. Beyond that, I write, using word pictures to re-create favorite places.

When I've been home about a month, I find myself reading articles and collecting stories. Without realizing it, I've begun planning my next adventure.

The Roman poet Martial said, "So, Posthumous, you'll live tomorrow, you say; too late, the wise lived yesterday."

May the wind be always at your back.

Rob on a very hot afternoon in Chichén Itzá, Mexico

The best adventures come full circle, depositing intrepid explorers back into their cozy armchairs to dream of the next challenge. From the disappearance in Utah of cowboy roamer Everett Ruess to the loss of billionaire explorer Michael Rockefeller in the wilds of New Guinea, the tales of those forfeited to the call of wild adventure ring with mystery, intrigue, and excitement to this day. Murdered, drowned, or eaten alive—these are mysteries of disappearance likely to remain unsolved but never forgotten.

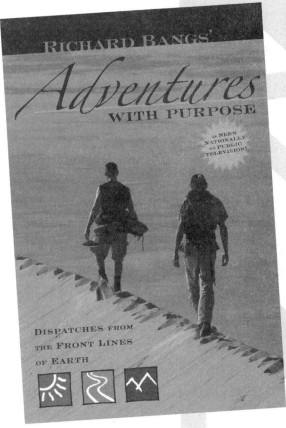

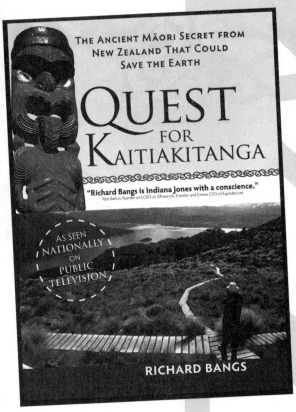

RICHARD BANGS'
QUEST FOR KAITIAKITANGA

The Ancient Maori Secret from New Zealand that Could Save the World

by Richard Bangs
ISBN 10: 0-89732-658-X
ISBN 13: 978-0-89732-658-2
$16.95
150 pages

A companion to the second in the series of PBS specials on Adventures with Purpose, *The Quest for Kaitakitanga* is a grand adventure that traces a trail from the bottom of the earth, the southern-most tip of the South Island of New Zealand, up through the heart of this country, ending at the tree of the Maori spirit myth at the north end of the North Island.

DEAR CUSTOMERS AND FRIENDS,

SUPPORTING YOUR INTEREST IN OUTDOOR ADVENTURE, travel, and an active lifestyle is central to our operations, from the authors we choose to the locations we detail to the way we design our books. Menasha Ridge Press was incorporated in 1982 by a group of veteran outdoorsmen and professional outfitters. For 25 years now, we've specialized in creating books that benefit the outdoors enthusiast.

Almost immediately, Menasha Ridge Press earned a reputation for revolutionizing outdoors- and travel-guidebook publishing. For such activities as canoeing, kayaking, hiking, backpacking, and mountain biking, we established new standards of quality that transformed the whole genre, resulting in outdoor-recreation guides of great sophistication and solid content. Menasha Ridge continues to be outdoor publishing's greatest innovator.

The folks at Menasha Ridge Press are as at home on a white-water river or mountain trail as they are editing a manuscript. The books we build for you are the best they can be, because we're responding to your needs. Plus, we use and depend on them ourselves.

We look forward to seeing you on the river or the trail. If you'd like to contact us directly, join in at www.trekalong.com or visit us at www.menasharidge.com. We thank you for your interest in our books and the natural world around us all.

SAFE TRAVELS,

Bob Sehlinger

BOB SEHLINGER
PUBLISHER